The Blackwell Handbook of Global Management

Handbooks in Management

Donald L. Sexton and Hans Landström
The Blackwell Handbook of Entrepreneurship

Edwin A. Locke
The Blackwell Handbook of Principles of Organizational Behavior

Martin J. Gannon and Karen L. Newman
The Blackwell Handbook of Cross-Cultural Management

Michael A. Hitt, R. Edward Freeman, and Jeffrey S. Harrison
The Blackwell Handbook of Strategic Management

Mark Easterby-Smith and Marjorie A. Lyles
The Blackwell Handbook of Organizational Learning and Knowledge Management

Henry W. Lane, Martha L. Maznevski, Mark E. Mendenhall,
and Jeanne McNett
The Blackwell Handbook of Global Management

THE BLACKWELL HANDBOOK OF GLOBAL MANAGEMENT
A GUIDE TO MANAGING COMPLEXITY

Edited by

HENRY W. LANE, MARTHA L. MAZNEVSKI,
MARK E. MENDENHALL, AND JEANNE McNETT

Thank you.
Harry Lane

love, Jeanne McNett
Martha Maznevski

Blackwell
Publishing

350 Main Street, Malden, MA 02148-5020, USA
108 Cowley Road, Oxford OX4 1JF, UK
550 Swanston Street, Carlton, Victoria 3053, Australia

First published 2004 by Blackwell Publishing Ltd

Library of Congress Cataloging-in-Publication Data has been applied for.

ISBN 0-631-23193-5 (hardback)

A catalogue record for this title is available from the British Library.

Set in 10/12pt Baskerville
by Graphicraft Limited, Hong Kong
Printed and bound in the United Kingdom
by MPG Books, Ltd, Bodmin, Cornwall

For further information on
Blackwell Publishing, visit our website:
http://www.blackwellpublishing.com

Contents

List of Figures

Notes on the Contributors

Nicholas Athanassiou (University of South Carolina) is an Associate Professor at Northeastern University, which he joined in 1995 after a 16-year corporate career during which he held a number of senior executive positions in Europe, Japan, East Asia, the Middle East, and the United States. His major research interests are in international business, with a focus on top management teams, global innovation management processes, and global teams. His research has been published in the *Journal of International Business Studies*, the *Strategic Management Journal*, *Management International Review*, the *Journal of World Business*, *Entrepreneurship: Theory and Practice*, the *Journal of Business Research*, and the *Journal of Management Education*.

Zeynep Aycan is an Associate Professor of Industrial and Organizational Psychology at Koç University, Istanbul, Turkey. Having trained as a cross-cultural psychologist, Zeynep examines the impact of culture on various aspects of business life, including leadership, work–family conflict, and international human resource management. She has published three books: *Expatriate Management: Theory and Research, Leadership, Management, Human Resource Practices in Turkey*, and *Culture and Organizational Behavior*, and some thirty-five research articles in journals including *Human Relations*, *Applied Psychology: An International Journal*, the *Journal of Cross-Cultural Psychology*, and book chapters. She is the founder and the co-editor of the *International Journal of Cross-Cultural Management*. Zeynep also has served as a consultant and trainer to companies including Bechtel-Enka (JV in Kazakhstan), Phillip–Morris, Migros, and Alcatel. She is the recipient of two prestigious awards (2001, 2003) from the Turkish Academy of Sciences for her contributions to the national and international development of social sciences and practices in the area of management.

Schon Beechler, Director of the Columbia Senior Executive Program and Professor, is a specialist in the management of multinational corporations and in Japanese management. In her teaching and consulting work she specializes in leading and managing change, global leadership development, and cross-cultural team effectiveness. Her major research interests include a study to measure the impact of executive education training on the global strategic leadership and management competencies of global senior executives and a project entitled "Organizational Competitiveness: Exploring the Roles of Human Resource Management and Organization Culture in Multinational Corporations," funded by the National Science Foundation. Her recent research publications have appeared in *Human Resource Management* and the *Academy of Management Review*. She has also contributed to books and practitioner-oriented journals and has edited two books on Japanese management, *Japanese Business Enterprise* (with Kristin Stucker) and *Japanese Management Overseas: Organizational and Individual Learning* (with Allen Bird). She has lived, studied, and worked in Japan for over six years, including a Fulbright Scholar appointment.

Iris Berdrow is Associate Professor of Management and Coordinator of the World of Business at Bentley College, Waltham, MA. Her research interests are in global alliances, learning partnerships, and competency based education. She has recently published in the *Strategic Management Journal, Long Range Planning*, and the *Journal of World Business*, and is co-author of *The Bases of Competence: Skills for Lifelong Learning and Employability*.

Allan Bird is Eiichi Shibusawa-Seigo Arai Professor of Japanese Studies at the University of Missouri-St. Louis. He co-edited *Japanese Multinationals Abroad: Individual and Organizational Learning*, and edited the *Encyclopedia of Japanese Business and Management*. His research has been published in various journals, including *M@n@gement*, the *Academy of Management Executive*, and the *Journal of Management Inquiry*. He has lived and worked in Japan for eight years and has also worked in South Korea, Taiwan, Thailand, and Finland.

Julian Birkinshaw is Associate Professor of Strategic and International Management at the London Business School. His research focuses on entrepreneurship, innovation, and change in large multinational corporations. He is the author of seven books, including *Entrepreneurship in the Global Firm, Inventuring: Why Big Companies Must Think Small*, and *Transnational Management* (4th edition).

Nakiye Boyacigiller is Dean of the Graduate School of Management at Sabanci University in Istanbul, Turkey. Well known in cross-cultural management circles, Boyacigiller is currently Vice-President of Programs for the Academy of International Business, and is a past chair of the International Management Division of the Academy of Management. She is currently researching competitiveness in MNCs with funding from the National Science Foundation. She is a member of six editorial boards, and her edited volume, *Crossing Cultures: Insights from Master Teachers*, is forthcoming.

Mary Yoko Brannen is Professor of International Business at San José State University and Associate Professor of executive education at the University of Michigan Business School. She was born and raised in Japan, studied in France, Spain, and the United States, and has consulted in cross-cultural issues for over fifteen years to various Fortune 500 companies. Her research focuses on ethnographic approaches to understanding the effects of changing cultural contexts on technology transfer, work organization, and individuals' assumptions regarding work. Her book, *Global Meeting Grounds: Negotiating Complex Cultural Contexts Across Organizations*, is forthcoming. Her work has been published in the *Academy of Management Journal*, the *Academy of Management Review, Human Relations*, the *Journal of Management Inquiry*, the *CEMS Business Review*, the *Handbook of International Management Research*, and *Advances in International and Comparative Management*, among others.

Sue Canney Davison is Director of Pipal Ltd., Nairobi, Kenya. Her books include *Leading International Teams*, and she has written numerous chapters for edited books. Her journal articles include publications in the *Journal of Management Development and Organization Studies*. Her main conceptual and consulting interests are international and virtual team start-up, ongoing dynamics and performance; effective facilitation processes; and individual/ group and cross-cultural interchange. Her practical interests include understanding different cultures, sustainable development, environmental and personal regeneration, and community leadership, particularly in Africa.

Deanne Den Hartog holds an M.Sc. and Ph.D. in organizational psychology from the Free University in Amsterdam, the Netherlands. She is currently full professor of organizational psychology at the School of Economics and Business of the Erasmus University in Rotterdam, the Netherlands. Her research has focused mainly on cross-cultural and transformational leadership processes. Other research interests include HRM and team effectiveness. She has published her work on these topics in a variety of journals (including *Leadership Quarterly* and *Journal of Organizational Behavior*) as well as in chapters in international volumes and two Dutch books.

Joseph J. DiStefano is Professor of International Business and Organizational Behavior at International Institute for Management Development (IMD). His research interests focus on cross-cultural management. Professor DiStefano has authored and co-authored several books (including *International Management Behavior: From Policy to Practice*, Blackwell) and articles and over one hundred case studies. Prior to joining IMD, he was the founding Executive Director of the Richard Ivey Business School's Asian campus in Hong Kong, where he was the Shirley Chan Memorial Professor of International Business. He is Professor Emeritus of the Ivey Business School, University of Western Ontario.

Bjørn Z. Ekelund is a Norwegian business consultant and psychologist. He has been managing director of small consultant organizations since 1987, at the same time doing extensive consultative work around team analysis and team development. He works closely with academic and professional institutions in order to leverage the quality of his consultancy and increase the practical relevance of academic knowledge. Since 1993, he has been managing director of Human Factors AS, Norway.

Cristina B. Gibson is currently Assistant Professor at the Graduate School of Management, University of California, Irvine. Her research interests include social cognition, communication, interaction, and effectiveness in teams; the impact of culture and gender on work behavior; and international management. Her research has appeared in journals such as the *Administrative Science Quarterly*, the *Academy of Management Journal*, the *Academy of Management Review*, the *Journal of Management*, the *Journal of International Business Studies*, and the *Journal of Cross-Cultural Psychology*. She is co-author, with P. Christopher Earley, of *New Perspectives on Multinational Teams*, and co-editor of *Virtual Teams That Work: Creating Conditions For Virtual Team Effectiveness*.

Julia C. Gluesing is Associate Director of the Institute for Information Technology and Culture at Wayne State University, Detroit, MI. She is experienced in the practical application of the theory and methods of anthropology, cross-cultural communication,

and organizational culture to the understanding of business issues, and in the development and implementation of solutions to strategic business problems. Her particular
specialization is global virtual teams in product development. Julia received her Ph.D. in
Business and Industrial Anthropology from Wayne State University, Detroit, and her MA
in Organizational and Intercultural Communication and Research from Michigan State
University. She is a contributing author in *Virtual Teams that Work: Creating Conditions
for Effective Virtual Teams*, and has published about global teaming in scholarly journals,
including *The Anthropology of Work* and the *Journal of Organizational Behavior*. She has just
completed a grant from the National Science Foundation to study the co-evolution of
global teaming and virtual technology.

Carolina Gómez, an Assistant Professor at Florida International University, has work
experience with Northern Telecom in both marketing and business planning, and with
General Electric, where she was part of a leadership development program that enabled
her to work in the different functional areas. Dr. Gómez has also consulted for GE in the
areas of cross-cultural values and self-managed work teams, and has provided training in
creative problem-solving for teams. Her research focuses on the influence of culture on
management in the areas of testing the cross-cultural generalizability of organizational
theories, such as organizational justice (with a specific interest in Latin America), the
management of multinational subsidiaries abroad, and international entrepreneurship.
Carolina has presented and published papers in forums such as the *Academy of Management
Conference*, the *Academy of International Business*, the *International Association of Business and
Society*, the *Academy of Management Journal*, *Group and Organization Management*, the *Journal of
Experimental Social Psychology*, and the *Journal of Business Research*.

Danna Greenberg is an Assistant Professor of Management at Babson College, where
she teaches undergraduate, graduate, and executive courses in Organizational Behavior,
Negotiation, and Mergers & Acquisitions. Her research focuses on the relationship between
the individual and the organization in times of change. Most recently, she has studied this
relationship in the context of mergers and acquisitions, organizational responses to crises,
and growth in multinational organizations. She has written many articles for such journals
as the *Administrative Science Quarterly*, *Academy of Management Learning and Education*, and the
Journal of Applied Behavioral Science. Her work has also appeared in *The Portable MBA in
Management* and the forthcoming book, *Mergers and Acquisitions: Creating Integrative Knowledge*.

Terence Jackson holds a bachelor's degree in Social Anthropology (University of Wales,
Swansea), a master's in Education (University of Keele, UK), and a Ph.D. in Manage-
ment Psychology (Henley Management College, UK). He is Professor and Director of the
Centre for Cross Cultural Management Research at ESCP – EAP European School of
Management (Oxford – Paris – Berlin Madrid). He edits the *International Journal of Cross
Cultural Management* and has just published his sixth book, *International HRM: A Cross Cultural
Approach*. He has published numerous articles on cross-cultural management ethics, man-
agement learning, and management in developing countries in such journals as *Human
Relations*, the *Journal of Management Studies*, and the *Asian Pacific Journal of Management*. He is
currently directing a major research project on management and change in sub-Saharan
Africa, and his book *Management and Change in Africa: A Cross-Cultural Perspective* will be
published in 2004.

Bradley L. Kirkman is Associate Professor of Management at the DuPree College of Management at the Georgia Institute of Technology. He specializes in using work teams across cultures and has conducted research and presented papers in Argentina, Australia, Belgium, Canada, England, Finland, France, Mexico, China, the Philippines, Turkey, and the United States. His articles have appeared in such journals as the *Journal of Cross-Cultural Psychology*, the *Academy of Management Journal*, the *Academy of Management Review*, the *Academy of Management Executive*, *Personnel Psychology*, and *Organizational Dynamics*.

Tatiana Kostova is an Associate Professor in International Business at the Moore School of Business, University of South Carolina. Her research focuses on the management of multinational corporations, more specifically, the relationships between headquarters and subsidiaries and the transfer of management practices and knowledge. Her research has been published most recently in the *Academy of Management Review* and the *Academy of Management Journal*.

Henry (Harry) W. Lane is the Darla and Frederick Brodsky Trustee Professor in International Business at Northeastern University. He has been the Associate Editor of the *Journal of International Business Studies* and a Visiting Professor at business schools in Europe and Latin America. Professor Lane also is active as a consultant and faculty member for university and corporate courses around the world. His research interests are intercultural management, the management of global innovation, and organizational learning and strategic renewal. He has authored or co-authored numerous books and articles and has written over seventy case studies. His articles have appeared in the *Journal of International Business Studies*, the *Academy of Management Review*, the *Academy of Management Executive*, the *Journal of World Business*, *Management International Review*, *Organizational Dynamics*, the *Journal of Business Ethics*, *International Studies of Management and Organization*, the *Journal of Business Administration*, the *Journal of Management Development*, *R & D Management*, and the *International Journal of Organizational Analysis*.

Orly Levy is an independent consultant based in Tel Aviv, Israel. Her research and consulting practice currently focus on cognitive and cultural challenges of cross-border management, with particular attention to high-reliability performance. Her work on the relationship between managerial global mindset and global strategy was selected by the Academy of Management as one of the best six dissertations for the 2001 Newman Award. She received her Ph.D. in Sociology from the University of Wisconsin-Madison.

Donald A. Marchand is Professor of Strategy and Information Management at the International Institute for Management Development (IMD) in Lausanne, Switzerland. He is the co-author of *Making The Invisible Visible: How Companies Win with the Right Information, People and IT* (John Wiley and Sons) and *Information Orientation: The Link to Business Performance* (Oxford University Press). Professor Marchand is an acclaimed speaker and advisor to senior executives of leading companies in Europe, North America and the Asia Pacific. He is founder, chairman and president of enterprise IQ the first company offering proven metrics linking business performance to how effectively a company uses information, knowledge, people, and IT.

Martha L. Maznevski is Professor of Organizational Behavior and International Management at the International Institute for Management Development (IMD) in Lausanne,

Switzerland, where she researches, teaches, and consults in the areas of multicultural and virtual team performance, international management, and global leadership. She has published a textbook and articles in scholarly and management journals, and has experience in North America, Europe, and Asia. Her current research focuses on high-performing virtual teams and networks in global organizations.

Daniel J. McCarthy is the Patrick and Helen Walsh Research Professor and Co-director of the High-Technology MBA Program at the College of Business Administration at Northeastern University. He has taught, consulted, and conducted research internationally for over two decades, and has been recognized as one of the top two scholars internationally in business and management in Russia and Central and Eastern Europe. His recent books include *The Russian Capitalist Experiment* and the forthcoming *Corporate Governance in Russia*, as well as the co-edited special issue of the *Journal of World Business* on corporate governance in transitioning economies, and articles on Russian corporate governance in *Organizational Dynamics*, the *European Management Journal*, and the *Journal of World Business*.

Edward F. McDonough III is Professor of Organization Behavior at Northeastern University. His research focuses on managing global new product development, and his articles have appeared in the *Harvard Business Review*, the *Academy of Management Journal*, the *International Journal of Project Management*, the *Journal of Product Innovation Management*, the *Journal of International Marketing*, *Research-Technology Management*, the *R&D Management Journal*, and the *IEEE Transactions on Engineering Management*. He was the Vice-President of Research for the Product Development & Management Association and President of the College of Technology and Engineering Management in the Institute of Management Sciences.

Jeanne McNett is an Associate Professor of Management at Assumption College in Worcester, MA. Her research interests are in the areas of education and training for cross-cultural effectiveness, corporate ethics in the international setting, and application of the liberal arts in the business environment. Her career includes long-term assignments in Japan, Saudi Arabia, Germany, Britain, and Algeria. Her research includes publications in the *Journal of Management Education* and *Insights*, and *Virginia Woolf: Turning the Centuries*. She is also an active case researcher and writer.

Mark E. Mendenhall holds the J. Burton Frierson Chair of Excellence in Business Leadership at the University of Tennessee, Chattanooga. His areas of scholarly and consulting expertise are the development of global leaders and the cross-cultural adjustment of expatriate managers. His other research and consulting interests are in the areas of leadership and organizational change and the nonlinear dynamics of organizational systems. He has published widely in the area of international management in such journals as the *Academy of Management Review*, the *Journal of International Business Studies*, and the *Sloan Management Review*. His most recent book is *Developing Global Business Leaders: Policies, Processes, and Innovations*.

Edwin L. Miller is Professor Emeritus at the University of Michigan Business School and a Fellow of the Academy of Management. He has published extensively in the area of international human resource management with a specialization in expatriate staffing and international management training and development. His publications have appeared in such journals as the *Academy of Management Journal*, the *Academy of Management Executive*, the *Journal of International Business Studies*, the *California Management Review*, and the *International Management Review*. He has recently published in the *Journal of World Business*, and his articles have appeared in such books as *Developing Global Business Leaders: Policies, Processes and Innovations* and *The Handbook of International Business* (1st and 2nd editions).

Joyce S. Osland is Professor of Organizational Behavior at San José State University in San José, California. She lived and worked overseas in seven countries for fourteen years, primarily in West Africa and Latin America, as a manager, researcher, consultant, and professor. Her current research interests include expatriates, cultural sensemaking, Latin American management, and global leadership. Her recent publications include *Broadening the Debate: Pros and Cons of Globalization* and *The Journey Inward: Expatriate Hero Tales and Paradoxes*, as well as the seventh edition of *Organizational Behavior: An Experiential Approach*, and *The Organizational Behavior Reader*.

Mark F. Peterson is the Internet Coast Professor of Management at Florida Atlantic University. He has published over eighty chapters and articles in journals including the *Administrative Science Quarterly*, the *Academy of Management Journal*, the *Journal of Organizational Behavior*, *Group and Organization Management*, *Organization Science*, *Organization Studies*, *Human Relations*, and the *Annual Review of Psychology*. His recent publications have been about methods issues that researchers face in international collaboration, and about the sources that managers in different parts of the world rely on to handle the work situations they face. He serves as Associate Editor for *Group and Organization Management* and Consulting Editor for *the Journal of Organizational Behavior*.

Sheila M. Puffer is Professor of International Business at the College of Business Administration at Northeastern University. She is a recent editor of *The Academy of Management Executive* and has also been recognized as the foremost scholar internationally in business and management in Russia and Central and Eastern Europe. Her recent books include *The Russian Capitalist Experiment* and the forthcoming volumes *Corporate Governance in Russia* and *International Management: Insights From Fiction and Practice*. She is also co-editor of the special issue of the *Journal of World Business* on corporate governance in transitioning economies, and articles on Russian corporate governance in *Organizational Dynamics*, the *European Management Journal*, and the *Journal of World Business*.

Betty Jane Punnett, a native of St. Vincent and the Grenadines, has lived and worked in the Caribbean, Canada, Europe, Asia, and the United States. She joined the University of the West Indies in 1997, after teaching at the University of Windsor in Canada for 12 years. She is currently Professor of International Business and Management and head of the department at Cave Hill. Her major research interest is culture and management and she is currently working on several projects in the English Caribbean, including a project focusing on effective management, funded by the Ford Foundation. She has published widely in the international business management field, including four texts, over fifty journal articles, and many contributions to edited books. In addition to her academic experience, Professor Punnett works as a consultant for a variety of private- and public-sector organizations and offers seminars and workshops for practicing managers. Her current writing includes *International Business – A Caribbean and Latin American Perspective*, forthcoming. *International Dimensions of Organizational Behavior and Human Resource Management*, and the new edition of *The Handbook for International Management Research*, of which she is co-editor, also are forthcoming.

Laurence Romani is research associate at the Institute of International Business (IIB) of the Stockholm School of Economics, Sweden. Her research interests are in the field of cross-cultural management with a focus on culture theory. She contributed to the second edition of *International Human Resource Management and Reflecting Diversity: Viewpoints from Scandinavia.*

Lilach Sagiv is a lecturer in the School of Business Administration at the Hebrew University. She has studied the role of values at the micro, meso, and macro levels. Her current research focuses on the impact of cultural dimensions of values on organizational behavior and processes. She is also investigating the mechanisms that link personal values to actual behavior.

Mikael Søndergaard is Associate Professor at the University of Aarhus, Department of Management, School of Economics and Management, Denmark. His research interests include cross-cultural issues and international issues from an organizational behavior perspective. He has contributed to numerous edited books and has contributed articles to journals including the *International Journal of Cross-Cultural Management, European Business Forum*, the *Academy of Management Executive*, and *Organization Studies.*

Francis C. Spital is Associate Professor at Northeastern University and Coordinator of the Human Resources Group. He has published in the *Harvard Business Review*, the *Academy of Management Executive*, the *Journal of Engineering and Technology Management*, and *Research Technology Management*. His research interests include the dynamics of strategic and technological change.

Günter K. Stahl is Assistant Professor of Asian Business and Comparative Management at INSEAD. He has authored or co-authored several books and numerous journal articles in the areas of leadership and leadership development, cross-cultural management, and international human resource management. His current research interests also include international careers, trust within and between organizations, and the management of mergers and acquisitions. At INSEAD, Günter has taught MBA students and executives on various topics, including value-based leadership; strategic human resource management; business ethics; cross-cultural management; and management of alliances, mergers, and acquisitions. He has also acted as a consultant for a number of corporate clients, and was involved in the design of innovative leadership development systems that are used by leading multinational corporations.

Sully Taylor is Professor of International Management and Director of the Master of International Management program at Portland State University. Her research focuses on the role of the human organization in creating global competitiveness, and also on women expatriates. She is co-author of *Western Women Working in Japan: Breaking Corporate Barriers, Does It Really Matter if Japanese MNCs Think Globally? The Impact of Employees' Perceptions on their Attitudes*, and *Toward an Integrated Theory of International Human Resource Management.*

David C. Thomas is Professor of International Management in the Faculty of Business Administration, Simon Fraser University, Canada. He is the author of four books, including *Essentials of International Management: A Cross-Cultural Perspective*. In addition, his research has appeared in such journals as the *Journal of Applied Psychology*, the *Journal of International Business Studies*, the *Journal of Cross-Cultural Psychology*, the *Journal of Organizational Behavior*, *Advances in International Management*, the *Leadership Quarterly*, and *Organizational Dynamics*. He is currently the International Business Area Editor for the *Canadian Journal of Administrative Sciences* and serves on the editorial boards of the *Journal of World Business*, *Advances in International Management*, the *International Journal of Organizational Analysis*, and the *International Journal of Cross-Cultural Management*.

Ellen Whitener specializes in organizational behavior and human resource management. Her current research focuses on building trusting relationships within organizations and evaluating the impact of human resource practices on employee attitudes and performance. She also serves as senior associate dean at the McIntyre School of Commerce, University of Virginia.

Pei-Chuan Wu is Assistant Professor in the Department of Management & Organisation, NUS Business School, National University of Singapore. Her core interests include strategic human resource management and firm performance; comparative studies of HRM and IHRM; and culture, HRM, and the psychological contract. Recently her research article was published in the *International Journal of Cross-Cultural Management*.

Preface

Introducing the International Organizations Network (ION)[1]

Ten years ago, leading researchers called loudly and clearly for well-coordinated multi-researcher multinational projects.[2] The calls cited two important benefits of such studies. They would allow us to explore the answers to international management questions, which require conducting research in multiple contexts at more or less the same time. They would also counter the cultural biases we all bring to our thinking and turn those biases into synergies. Since the 1990s several well-coordinated multi-researcher projects have been or are being conducted, and we are seeing the fruits of their labors. Some early examples include the GLOBE study on leadership[3] and the event management study on decision-making.[4]

Another group of researchers have been experimenting for the last few years with an alternative model of coordinated research – a loosely-coupled research network. ION (International Organizations Network) was formed with a mission to increase the quality and impact of research on people and their effectiveness in international organizations. The network's vision is to be a catalyst for the creation and application of knowledge and understanding that powerfully impacts how international organizations are managed. ION strives to initiate and facilitate high-quality research addressing management-related challenges of importance to global enterprises, such as motivation, leadership, teams, organizational structure, and human resource systems. ION also works to facilitate the translation of research findings into practical implications for organizations and educational material for innovative and effective teaching. In essence, we are scholars who care deeply about managers and executives who find themselves working in the global business environment.

Structurally, ION is a loosely-coupled, global network of scholars and professionals with a broad range of disciplinary backgrounds and specific topics of interest. The members are highly active at the leading edge of the field, publishing academic and management-oriented articles and books, editing journals, presenting research at conferences, developing and sharing innovative teaching methods, and consulting frequently to companies on issues related to international management. To advance the goals of the field, ION's members are strongly committed to active collaboration on a worldwide scale. Like the most effective multinational enterprises, ION leverages the different perspectives associated with multiple disciplines and geographic regions to achieve innovation and synergy. Since its founding in 1999, the ION network affiliation has grown to include over seventy scholars located in more than twenty countries.

As a loosely coupled network, ION's purpose is not to conduct specific research projects. Instead, it supports the research community itself. No primary research project has been initiated by ION as a group. ION has, however, helped match up researchers conducting similar studies, facilitating them as they work together to create a more powerful single study. Through the ION network, scholars have helped each other find appropriate literature in other cultures, tackle methodological issues, and explore implications of unpredicted results. Some ION members work closely with others in the network, while some work almost exclusively with people outside the network.

How ION Works

The core of the ION network consists of about forty international management scholars who study various aspects of how people work in international settings. In terms of traditional disciplines, most members of the core are trained in and teach organizational behavior/occupational psychology or organizational theory. Some are in the strategy field, and emphasize execution and implementation as much as the theory of the firm. Interestingly, almost all members cross traditional discipline boundaries regularly both in their research and in their teaching, and in fact this "lack of academic home" was one characteristic that brought the network together.

The ION core meets annually at its own three-day meeting. The first two meetings were sponsored by the University of Virginia in 1999 and 2000. The meetings are conducted as a workshop, and research in progress is shared. Research in its earliest stages benefits from brainstorming, implications of preliminary results are shared and discussed, and paper drafts are critiqued before submission for publication. Members of the network also get together whenever possible at academic meetings around the world, "drop in" on each other when traveling, and submit joint symposia or conduct professional workshops on topics of importance to international management. Core members initiate professional and social events – which are attended by an ever-broadening group of colleagues – at various academic conferences.

A key to developing an effective, loosely coupled coordinated research network seems to have been creating a tightly-coupled social system. New, important knowledge about social systems is best created with the help of a deep, close social system. When people in such networks connect in multiple ways, beyond narrow definitions of work, they understand each others' backgrounds and contexts and create shared experiences from which the knowledge is generated. ION annual workshops, no matter what the topic or setting, are always structured to facilitate deep conversation and dialogue around the thorniest issues of the field. Parts of the workshop take place in settings that help members learn together about the local history and perspectives, linking together to create insights about the field of international management.

Many of ION's accomplishments are intangible, or are indirectly related to tangible outcomes. For example, through dialogue members develop a better perspective on how their research fits into the field, and then articulate its contribution more clearly to reviewers and students. In workshops, members question the received wisdom of the field and share tacit insights about the messiness of data analysis, developing a platform for more solid theory development and empirical rigor. Since all members cross traditional academic disciplines, a wide scope of knowledge is shared.

But some accomplishments are tangible. ION was a key player in the launching of the International Journal of Cross-Cultural Management. It has supported candidates for positions in various academic associations. It has provided a strong network for appointment, promotion, and tenure recommendations and reviews. It has generated several joint research projects and co-authorships, and presented joint papers and symposia. At the recent conference "Identifying Culture," sponsored by the Institute of International Business of the Stockholm School of Economics, ION was cited as a highly effective effort to influence a field systematically in management academics.

THE BLACKWELL HANDBOOK OF GLOBAL MANAGEMENT: A GUIDE TO MANAGING GLOBAL COMPLEXITY: THE PROCESS

While our experiment with a loosely-coupled research network has so far generated positive and interesting results, there remain some particularly difficult challenges.

One challenge is related to group-generated projects. We have found that in order to maintain and strengthen the social system around the advancement of the field, the group must create something meaningful together. However, the "something" cannot be a single research project, since that would run counter to the network's objectives.

The response to the challenge was this Handbook project. In August of 2000, the editors of this book were approached by Blackwell Publishing to write a handbook for global managers. After discussing the project with Blackwell, we realized that a greater opportunity existed than simply writing another book: utilizing the combined talent, knowledge, experience, and wisdom of the members of ION to bring the most current knowledge based on research and experience to global managers.

In Boston, during a frigid three days in late February 2001, 37 scholars of the ION membership met at Northeastern University in Boston to strategize how to go about tackling this project. How can a group of scholars who use different research methodologies, focus on different competencies of global management in their work, have a wide variety of experiences in consulting, and bring different theories to the understanding of global management, combine their efforts to write "the best book that has ever been written" for executives on global management?

This volume is a product of collaborative efforts of the members of ION. The network members agreed to write it jointly, and took on the ambitious goal of producing a coherent book that translates the very leading edge of international management thought and practice into a single statement on managing global complexity. The Handbook certainly articulates the most important findings from our field together with their implications, in a relatively seamless way, with contributions from 41 authors.

The problem with most books that have as their goal to educate global executives is that they are written by only one or two people. Even if the author is a genius, he/she is a genius within a limited area of global management. A single author – or double or triple author partnerships – simply cannot have a broad enough perspective, range of experience, and specific expertise to cover the wide complexity of issues and competencies needed to effectively manage in the global business environment. With ION, we had an international group of experts that could provide the needed scope of expertise to cover the topic.

The most common way to organize a book such as this would be to simply have each expert write a chapter on his/her area of expertise, combine them together, and publish the book; however, our experience with such edited books is that each author tends to write in isolation of the others, and in the end the book does not "connect the dots" between the various skills and issues of global management. None of the skills and issues are independent of each other – our goal was to not only specify the skills and issues of global management, but to show in a clear way how they are linked, how they depend on each other, and how they fit together.

Also, the ION writers wanted to portray the complexity of managing globally not in a "silo-based, step 1-then-step 2" format but rather to bring clarity to the actual dynamics of global management, which are usually nonlinear and systemic in nature. We wanted to wrestle with the reality of the milieu of the global manager (which is chaotic, paradoxical, confusing, and systemic) and clarify it, and then to provide approaches (based on the best research in the field) that can assist the manager to manage productively within the complexity of his or her job.

The theme and flow of the book were "negotiated" through several iterations of small-group and large-group interactions at that ION workshop at Northeastern University in 2001. Two and a half intense days were spent in mapping out a dynamic framework for the book. This constituted fleshing out what globalization actually is (versus what most people say or think it is) and targeting processes of globalization that, if managed well, raise the potential for productivity in any global organization. ION members were then formed into teams around these process management areas, where they developed plans for how they would write their respective sections.

The next year was spent in more thinking, discussion, and writing. The project team reassembled in Lausanne, Switzerland at the International Institute of Management Development (IMD) in February of 2002 to provide feedback of section drafts, coordinate each section with concepts from the other sections, and to ensure that no critical idea or issue had been overlooked. Another meeting of writers was held in Charleston, South Carolina, in October of 2002 and further refinements to each chapter in each section were made.

In 2003 it was time to pilot test the ideas. In February, during the annual meeting held this time at the University of Missouri St. Louis, we hosted an ION Executive Dialogue. For two days we brought together senior executives, the authors of this Handbook and other members of ION to engage in a dialogue based on the material in the book and to provide feedback to the authors. Further refinements to the manuscript were made based on these discussions before final publication.

We offer you, now, this book as a culmination of our efforts.

The book has been written in such a way that it is not necessary to read it from beginning to end, though this would be a beneficial way to begin to approach the book.

Each section is linked to all the other sections conceptually. By starting with a topic that you are currently struggling with or that you need more information about, you will find yourself being subsequently led to other sections of the book in a natural progression. That said, we do suggest beginning with the Introduction, as it sets the conceptual foundation upon which all the sections and their chapters build.

The writers of this book, and its editors, wish to thank Rosemary Nixon from Blackwell Publishing for the indefatigable patience and trust she has shown us throughout this process. From the start she sensed strongly the value-added this project would have for managers and executives, and for the entire field of international management. She is a visionary editor, the type that one rarely sees in the publishing industry. Our special thanks also go to the McIntire School of the University of Virginia, the College of Business Administration at Northeastern University, IMD, the CIBER Center of the University of South Carolina, the University of Missouri, St. Louis, and the Frierson Leadership Institute of the University of Tennessee, Chattanooga for financial and other support for this project. Finally, we would like to thank the executives who participated in the ION Executive Dialogue: Rocky Felice, Limitedbrands; Norihito Furuya, JAL Academy Co. Ltd.; Valerie Harley, Ablestik Laboratories; Alan Jarvis, GMAC; Jim Rush, Marsh, Inc., and George Schenk, Monsanto Company.

NOTES

1 The "Introduction to ION" first appeared as an article in *Insights*, the research news publication of the Academy of International Business. Maznevski, M. L. (2002), Learning from loosely-coupled research coordination: The ION network, *Academy of International Business Insights*, 2(4), 5–7.

2 Boyacigiller, N. A., & Adler, N. J. (1991), The parochial dinosaur: Organization science in a global context, *Academy of Management Review*, 16(2), 262–90.

3 House, R., Javidan, M., Hanges, P., & Dorfman, P. (2002), Understanding cultures and implicit leadership theories across the globe: An introduction to project GLOBE, *Journal of World Business*, 37(1), 3–10.

4 Smith, P. B., Peterson, M. F., & Schwartz, S. (2002), Cultural values, sources of guidance and their relevance to managerial behavior: A 47 nation study, *Journal of Cross Cultural Psychology*, 33, 188–208.

H. W. L.
M. L. M.
M. M.
J. M.

Part I

INTRODUCTION: UNDERSTANDING PEOPLE AND CONTEXT

1

Globalization: Hercules Meets Buddha

Henry W. Lane, Martha L. Maznevski, and Mark E. Mendenhall

Globalization of business seems to be a *fait accompli*, a truism no longer questioned: *corporations have to be global in their business*. This claim reflects the era in which it was written as the opening sentence in this Introduction. We think it critical to ask, though, is it still true, or has globalization reached its zenith and is now set to contract?

The planning for this book and the development of its structure started in February 2001. At that time, even though the dot.com bubble had burst and the economies of the United States and other countries had slowed considerably, there was still a belief in the inevitability of globalization. The manuscript was finished in April 2003. Two historic events took place between those dates that could affect the course of globalization: the September 11 attack on the World Trade Center and the war in Iraq. Many observers had started asking how these events would affect the conduct of business. Would the juggernaut of globalization continue or would companies pull back into "safe" countries or possibly retrench within their own borders?[1] Worst-case scenarios included a reduction in immigration into the United States, resulting in fewer students and potential employees, thus reducing innovation; tensions between the United States and Europe and within Europe making trade liberalization more difficult; product boycotts; and terrorism and increased security complicating outsourcing and increasing uncertainty.[2]

On top of the threat of terrorism and the unknown aftermath of the war was an outbreak of a new "global disease," Severe Acute Respiratory Syndrome (SARS), that was affecting travel particularly to China and Hong Kong. Continental Airlines suspended all flights to Hong Kong and other carriers sharply reduced their schedules. Some companies restricted or banned travel to East Asia and supply-chain disruptions were feared.[3] Conducting business globally was becoming more uncertain and more difficult.

Are multilateralism in foreign affairs and globalization in business, which depends on multilateral relations, finished? Multilateralism and globalization have brought benefits to many countries and peoples of the world. Will they retain the same format in the future as they had prior to the war in Iraq or keep to the same trajectories they were following? Undoubtedly, the global political and economic systems will change. As this book nears its completion, the nature and impact of future changes can only be speculated about, not predicted with any certainty.

Our crystal ball is no clearer than those of others, and trying to make specific predictions about governments' or companies' actions is a risky business. The prospect of terrorism, the aftermath of the war, and "global diseases" are factors that will contribute to increasing uncertainty in the environment facing executives in global companies. If anything, their job is going to become harder. The world is not becoming simpler and easier; it seems to be becoming more complex and difficult, or, perhaps, we are being forced to recognize its complexity. Larry Ellison, CEO of Oracle Corp., was quoted as saying "It's a dangerous world. We had this amazing 10-year period [the 1990s] when we pretended it wasn't."[4]

Managing in a complex international arena that is rapidly changing is the theme of this book. We believe that the events since September 11, 2001 reaffirm our perspective of globalization as complexity – a characteristic that is likely to endure. As British Prime Minister Tony Blair said, "We are all internationalists now, whether we like it or not."[5] Executives need to embrace this perspective more than ever, understand more fully the complexity with which they are dealing, and learn to cope more effectively with it.

The banality of the term "globalization" masks the reality of what it means, obscuring the important issues of doing business globally with success. Things are not going smoothly in corporate globalization, and many efforts fail to meet expectations. Globalizing a company is more complicated than we anticipated. It is easy to talk about and aspire to, but difficult to achieve. This book responds to the challenge that today's managers face. It offers a different look at what globalization means and how to respond to it. We draw on the latest research on managing global organizations, extensive experiences with a broad spectrum of international companies, and integrative dialogue with academics and executives about effective management. Our goal is to understand the globalization process more completely – to explain it or "unpack" it to see what is really there and how it affects managing.

Rather than define globalization as the proportion of trade conducted across national borders, or by some other economic or social measure, we argue that, as we talk about it in business, globalization is a manifestation of complexity. Understand its complexity, and you will understand globalization. Understand the processes necessary to deal with complexity, and you will understand what is necessary to globalize an organization.

The complexity of globalization flows from conditions of multiplicity, interdependence, and ambiguity, all of which are interrelated. These conditions in turn are in a state of constant change or flux. In complex environments, predicting the future is impossible and trying to rigidly control global organizational outcomes may be dysfunctional. Complexity of this type cannot be controlled. But it can be managed – or at least channeled – to create functional and even valuable organizational outcomes.

Managing complexity requires a new way of thinking. In addition to focusing on factors such as the organization's design, detailed lists of assets and financial projections, today's global executives must learn to manage their organizational processes. The key processes in a global organization are collaborating, discovering, architecting, and systems thinking. And the key element to channeling or managing complexity lies in the connective glue that binds the processes to complexity: people. Our model for managing these processes in organizations is shown in figure 1.1.

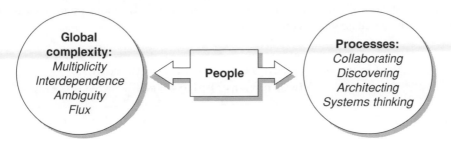

FIGURE 1.1 Managing global complexity[6]

We think about executives in the modern global corporation as being like Hercules, the Greek hero. The stories of his exploits, The Twelve Labors of Hercules, are accounts of his use of strength and power to overcome obstacles on his path to atonement and fame.[7] Hercules is the embodiment of what the Greeks call *pathos*, virtuous struggle and suffering that leads to fame.[8] The heroic Hercules model originates in the home of Western civilization, Greece. Greece is the cradle of Western rational thought, a cognitive model that encourages our use of comparison, measurement, categorization, and analysis in understanding the world around us.[9] We argue that such an analytic, strength-based mode of thinking and doing may not be sufficient in the complex environment we call globalization and should be augmented with other ways of comprehending the phenomena we find in our environment and with new techniques for meeting its challenges.

Western rational thought is not the only mode of understanding the world and our place in it.[10] The Eastern way of "seeing and understanding" as presented in Buddhism and Taoism seeks to go beyond the world of categories, opposites, and analysis to achieve true understanding of a world of infinite complexity and variety. Two of the basic tenets of the Eastern way are that all things and events are interrelated and that change is constant and natural. The latter was an adaptation of Buddhism as it was absorbed and modified in China to become Taoism. The Tao is the "The Path" or "The Way." It is the way or process of the universe. Hui Nan Tzu, a Chinese philosopher, described these relationships when he observed: "He who conforms to the course of the Tao, following the natural processes of Heaven and Earth, finds it easy to manage the whole world."[11]

Hercules should meet Buddha. The skillful use of management processes will help manage the "whole world's" complexity. We do not propose managers eliminate rational analytic approaches to management and globalization or perseverance over obstacles in the path in favor of the intuitive wisdom of Eastern mysticism. We do suggest that to globalize successfully, managers' toolkits and worldviews need to be updated. We must remember that tools such as analytic spreadsheets are not reality, but rather, representations of reality based on an assumed understanding of the characteristics of countries, peoples, and anticipated markets. As Alfred Korzybski said, "the map is not the territory,"[12] and managers must not confuse the two. They must look beyond the tools to see the reality of their environment, to select and combine from the approaches symbolized by Hercules and Buddha. This book is about the importance of understanding more completely and from a different vantage point the global context in which executives find themselves; about how they can enact processes that fruitfully channel and manage the complexity in globalization to create value.

Globalization: Defined by Structures, Managed by Processes

Globalization – in terms of international economic integration – has been enabled and characterized by the erosion of boundaries.[13] Trade liberalization has opened borders across which capital moves easily. One of the most notable features of the new world economy has been the closer interconnection among countries of the developed and developing world: "The great novelty of the current era is the extent to which the poorer nations of the world have been incorporated in the global system of trade, finance and production as partners and market participants rather than colonial dependencies."[14]

A second feature of globalization as boundary erosion has been the relaxation of foreign direct investment (FDI) restrictions. During the 1990s there were over a thousand changes around the world to national laws governing FDI; almost all of them had the effect of creating a climate more favorable to it.[15] These changes were complemented by an increase in bilateral investment treaties: in 1980 there were fewer than two hundred bilateral treaties in existence, while at the end of 1999 there were almost two thousand.[16]

Airline travel and reliable, inexpensive communications have shrunk the globe so effectively – diminishing physical boundaries – that corporations are now able to manage far-flung operations. The UN estimates that there are 63,000 transnational corporations, and that these companies have 690,000 foreign affiliates spanning "virtually all countries and economic activities." The foreign affiliates of the top 100 of these firms employ over six million people around the world.[17] In addition, more recently the emergence of information services and the addition of new technologies such as the Internet have dramatically accelerated the globalization process. It is possible to do business in Asia through a website without leaving Paris.

Both responding to and feeding the trend of boundary erosion, companies are rapidly trying to globalize. Why? Because growth is coming from international markets and new ideas and innovations are springing up in companies around the world. In the increasingly competitive market, this search for growth must be increasingly far-flung. For years, companies restructured and systematically wrung costs out of operations to improve profitability, to capture market share, or to stay in business. As these efforts achieved their ends, new areas of opportunity for increasing profits had to be found. They began to work across boundaries – internal product/service boundaries and national borders. Internally they developed new products and services and began selling "solutions." Many companies moved from a strategy of "best product" to "total customer solutions."[18] International markets also provided growth. As foreign firms entered a market, local companies had to adapt and they began expanding internationally to remain competitive in an increasingly complex global marketplace. The quest for growth has become continual, demanded by financial markets and shareholders. And international markets are where opportunities for growth are. Some companies continue to search for growth by expanding into new international markets and some are searching for it from innovations to be achieved by integrating and expanding their current global operations.

In many industries these efforts mean that more capital and greater size are necessary to operate in the global marketplace. To obtain this capital and size, companies engage in more alliances, mergers, and acquisitions, leading to a consolidation of industries. Even large, established companies – that traditionally acquired smaller companies but only competed against others their own size – are now increasingly seeking alliances and mergers with other large companies to gain complementary assets and competencies. The total number of mergers and acquisitions worldwide grew at 42 percent annually between 1980 and 1999.[19]

Consolidation is taking place across borders as well as within countries. Of the 42 percent growth rate in M&As, 25 percent (in number and value) were cross-border deals. Some examples that have commanded attention include Pharmacia-Upjohn and Pharmacia-Monsanto,[20] DaimlerChrysler, Ford's purchase of Jaguar and Volvo, GM's acquisition of Saab, Terra Networks' (Spain) acquisition of US-based Lycos, and the French Vivendi's purchase of numerous companies in North America, including Universal Studios, which was owned by the Canadian company, Seagram's. Vivendi bought Seagram's in order to acquire Universal.

Clearly, the forces of deregulation, consolidation, and technology are reshaping corporate and social landscapes. The UN states:

> And just as the earlier boom in the United States contributed to the emergence of a national market for goods and services and a national production system, complemented by a national market for firms, so is the current international boom reinforcing the emergence of a global market for goods and services and the emergence of an international production system.[21]

This is the phenomenon that Levitt, a pioneering observer of globalization, wrote about in the early 1980s. He defined globalization as a "shift toward a more integrated and interdependent world economy . . . having two main components: the globalization of markets and the globalization of production."[22] Many academics and executives have taken their cue about the nature and course of globalization from Levitt by, for example, defining globalization as simply "the production and distribution of products and services of a homogeneous type and quality on a worldwide basis."[23] The globalization of markets usually "refers to the merging of historically distinct and separate markets into one huge global marketplace" and the globalization of production is explained as the sourcing of "goods and services from locations around the globe to take advantage of national differences in the cost and quality of factors of production."[24] Many managers discredited Levitt's ideas, interpreting his prescriptive statements in simple ways. In fact, Levitt's thoughts may have preceded managerial capabilities. These managers applied simple solutions to their firm's globalization efforts, often with disastrous results.

The statistics about globalization are impressive, as is the image of large, cost-efficient firms developing standard products and selling them throughout the world, which has become common.[25] Similarly, the image of a world converging to sameness and firms becoming more important than governments often is also communicated, intentionally or unintentionally, with this perspective.

But is globalization a reality? Or has the reality been misperceived, the numbers misinterpreted, and a myth created? Not everyone agrees with the standard globalization picture described above. Rugman and Moore, for example, argue that "globalization is a myth." They show that large firms' business activities and their trade in goods and services take place not globally but in clusters (for example, Silicon Valley, Hollywood, Grenoble), regional blocks (for example, the European Union, NAFTA, Japan), and within nations. Their advice is to "think regional, act local and forget global."[26] We note that if globalization is defined by standard terms, then in reality there are few, if any, truly global companies operating in all markets.

Descriptions of globalization are like the descriptions of the proverbial elephant made by the blind men who each touched different parts of the animal: the descriptions are accurate as far as they go. Yet they do not describe the elephant, only some of its parts. Most of the globalization descriptions include an increasingly global reach from very narrow perspectives. This may mean entering new markets, following customers to new countries, establishing new sources of cheaper supplies and/or labor, finding new locations in which to place parts of the value chain, exploiting new sources of intellectual capital (knowledge), and reaching into new locations electronically through the Internet. However, such perspectives are firm-centric views. They suggest that companies and executives simply are doing more of what they have always done, just in more places and with more technological sophistication. These perspectives are economic, market-oriented and technology-oriented ones that, although not incorrect, describe only a part of the reality.

We suggest that we need to focus on the *processes* of globaliz*ing* in order to fully grasp the elephant. When we examine the processes companies undertake as they globalize, we lose the sterile statistics and see the people who create and manage the trends. This picture at the doing/implementation level is often much less rosy than the ones given by macro-level descriptions. The sailing is not smooth and many efforts fail. The road to globalization is strewn with the debris of ill-considered mergers, acquisitions, and new market entry attempts. At the same time, it is also strewn with exceptional learning, innovation, and opportunities.

Globalization is about complexity. It is first about accepting and characterizing the complexity, and also about managing – or at least channeling – the complexity by using fluid processes.

THE CONDITIONS OF COMPLEXITY

As companies expand their global reach, increasingly they encounter organizations and governments that influence their operations or claim jurisdiction over their corporate activities. The current corporate environment is a *mélange* of global competitors, multiple countries, and governments with differing social, legal, regulatory and political constraints and physical infrastructures; numerous cultures and languages; all facilitated by technology and more tightly linked than ever in the past. This situation makes management – in terms of control over defining paths to desired outcomes – more complicated and less predictable than in the past.

We have identified three characteristics which together function as a foundation for the increasing complexity of globalization: multiplicity, interdependence, and ambiguity. Each of these characteristics is difficult to manage by itself, and combining them presents even more challenges. As if that were not enough, each of them is always shifting. The entire network of complexity is in a state of constant flux. No wonder global managers are bewildered! Unpacking complexity's components is the first step to linking complexity with the processes to manage it.

Condition 1: Multiplicity – many voices, viewpoints and constraints

Multiplicity is our shorthand concept for recognizing that corporations face many different models for organizing and conducting business, and in fact for functioning globally in general. With globalization, executives deal with more organizations, governments, and people. Importantly, though, many of these entities are also different from the executive's own organization, government, and people, and from each other as well. Globalization is not just about "more"; it's about "more *and* different." This is the multiplicity aspect of complexity.

Multiplicity of competitors

Some companies notice globalization first when they experience multiplicity in their competitive environment. Grocery shopping, for example, has traditionally been dominated by local players who know the market well. Domestic grocery stores in most countries around the world, though, have recently begun to face competitors from abroad who play the game quite differently. In the Boston area, two of the three largest supermarket chains are owned by J. Sainsbury plc of the United Kingdom, which has established a major presence in the Northeast United States. The third is owned by Royal Ahold of the Netherlands. With worldwide sales of 67 billion euros in 2001, Royal Ahold has 450,000 employees in 9,000 stores serving 40 million customers every week in 28 countries on four continents.[27] Local Boston grocery stores, even without "globalizing" themselves, are now competing with the multiplicity associated with globalization of their industry.

Multiplicity of customers

Royal Ahold and J. Sainsbury plc, as multinationals operating in many environments around the world, also face multiplicity in their customers. Customers in different countries, regions, or demographic groups have different priorities and preferences, and customers in developing markets differ significantly in their needs and desires from those in developed markets.[28]

Very few consumer products are global – even Coca Cola and McDonald's change their formula and menu for different parts of the world, and Nokia and Sony put different features in their products for different markets. Business-to-business firms, too, face different customers in different parts of the world. When BASF, the chemical company, sells products to DaimlerChrysler, a large automobile manufacturer, it usually negotiates a global contract with headquarters, then provides delivery and after-sales service locally to local production units. BASF therefore deals with many types of customers even within the same buyer firm. Because of multiplicity in customers – their culture, environmental context, traditions, and so on – many organizations begin to globalize with local distribution or sales units, and perhaps local production. Even those organizations with more integration across global units, though, must manage their broad scope of customers.

Multiplicity along the value chain

Two fundamental forces influence companies operating in multiple, national markets: those pushing toward *global integration* and those pulling toward *local responsiveness*.[29] Forces for global integration push companies to minimize duplication of efforts and increase efficiencies by placing specific value-chain activities in appropriate locations around the world. This allows them to capitalize on the interaction between the company's competitive advantage in the particular activity and the country's locational comparative advantage for such an activity.[30] Easier movement of capital and reduced transportation and communication costs facilitate splitting up a corporation's value chain, and today's firms find that strategic placement of the value-chain activities is necessary for survival.[31]

For example, consider EMC, a leader in data storage networks. Its head office is in Massachusetts; it conducts R&D in the United States, Israel, and France; it manufactures systems in Ireland and the United States; and has over 5000 direct service personnel located in the United States, France, Brazil, Ireland, Germany, Japan, and Australia. If EMC is not complicated enough, consider Schneider Electric. Headquartered in France, it has organized to be close to its customers. The result is that it has more than 7,400 sales outlets, 620 marketing facilities and 150 manufacturing facilities in 130 countries. The 3,000 members of its R&D departments operate in 15 countries.[32] In managing their value chains, both EMC and Schneider Electric operate in multiple environments, each one with a different infrastructure. To be effective they must take these multiple contexts into account.

Multiplicity of governments

In July 2001, the European Union rejected General Electric's proposed $42 billion acquisition of Honeywell. The two companies officially called off the proposed merger in October 2001. Commenting on the ability of the European Union to halt a merger of two US companies, *TIME* World Editor Michael Elliott commented: "Welcome to globalization. The collapse of the GE–Honeywell merger shows that companies that benefit from a global market can now be governed in all they do by any of the countries or regions in which they do business. . . . We'd all better get used to it."[33] Jack Welch, former CEO of General Electric, when asked why Europeans can influence a merger between American companies, said, "That's the law. That really is just the way the world works."[34]

In fact, the EU and US authorities can block any merger or acquisition regardless of the nationalities involved, as long as the result is significant for its own market. Significance is usually defined in terms of open market access and impact on the customer or consumer, rather than using market share statistics per se.[35] Although this was the first time that a proposed merger between two US companies had been blocked solely by European regulators, a year earlier the US authorities blocked the Air Liquide (French) acquisition of British Oxygen.[36] Regarding the GE–Honeywell merger, the EU felt considerable political pressure when the US authorities waved the merger through with hardly any analysis and GE executives clearly – and publicly – expected the EU to follow suit. GE employed 85,000 people in Europe and had $25 billion in European revenue in 2001; furthermore, the EU was concerned about further consolidation in the aerospace industry. The EU believed the merger was unwise, and blocked it.

This exposure to foreign laws and intervention is a reality in cyberspace as well. Yahoo is the second leading Internet portal in the world and the leader in establishing overseas operations. In 2001, Yahoo had 24 international sites in 13 languages and approximately 40 per cent of its users were located outside the United States. Many governments, especially European ones, were becoming increasingly annoyed with the Internet's free-for-all content, much of which violated local laws. Yahoo, the most visible Internet company in France, soon found itself embroiled in a test case over Internet jurisdiction. In April 2000, *La Ligue Contre le Racisme et l'Antisémitisme* (LICRA), together with the Union of French Jewish Students, filed suit against the US company for allowing users to post-Nazi era memorabilia items for sale on the Yahoo American auction site. Although the site was primarily directed toward American users, the fact that the site could be viewed in France was considered a violation of a French law prohibiting the display of Nazi symbols.

On September 1, 2002, China blocked the search engines Google and Alta Vista with what has been dubbed the "Great Firewall of China," in its attempt to stop access to pornographic and "subversive" material.[37] Less than two weeks later, Google was back on line with no explanation.

These examples suggest that even cyberspace is not outside the reach of regulators.

Multiplicity of stakeholders: The power of NGOs

Thousands of non-governmental organizations (NGOs) are monitoring corporate activity around the globe. They include large, well-established groups like Greenpeace, the World Wildlife Fund, Oilwatch, Amnesty International, and Human Rights Watch, as well as numerous smaller groups. NGOs are not new players in the business environment, but they have exploited the Internet more quickly than have some corporations, and their influence is being felt strongly. They have leveraged this technology to bring to light and publicize corporate activity that in the past would have largely gone unnoticed.

NGOs traditionally watch and criticize human rights and environmental issues, and are moving publicly into other areas. The Positive Futures Network and many others speak out against globalization. Opponents of the World Trade Organization (WTO) have disrupted the meetings, protesting against what they see as the non-democratic imposition of globalization. These NGOs are a fixture in corporations' new global reality; they are not going away.

As companies grow globally, they not only face *more* competitors, customers, value-chain locations, governments, and other stakeholders; they face entities that differ from each other in terms of their structure, motivations, and traditions. Managing such multiplicity effectively is part of globalizing.

Condition 2: Interdependence – it's all connected

The second aspect of the complexity we call globalization is interdependence. With fast and easy movement of capital, information, and people, distributed units are no longer isolated. Such interdependence can be simple or complex.[38] With simple interdependence, activities may be discrete or, perhaps, move sequentially through a system, such as in a manufacturing assembly line and in routine processing of orders or insurance claims.

When an outcome relies on close interaction and coordination, such as when a process must go back and forth among many units, each making changes that rely on and influence others, interdependence is much more complex. Account teams in advertising and medical teams working on complex surgeries are examples of outcomes that require complex interdependence among various people and units.

In automobile firms, product design was traditionally done sequentially, with one set of engineers handing the work over to the next set until the project was finished. In trying to reduce time-to-market and to improve the designs themselves, the firms moved to more complex designs, beginning the process with a multifunctional team of engineers, marketers, and other professionals (more multiplicity!). Ideally, the team works together incorporating all disciplines all along the design process.

Globalization has created a world of complex interdependence. With fast and easy movement of capital, information, and people, distributed units – organizations or people – cannot be isolated, nor can they assume a simple relationship in a sequential sequence. Furthermore, companies are finding that they *must* enter into interdependent arrangements through outsourcing, alliances, and network arrangements related to their value chains in order to stay price-competitive or continue to create value. Interdependence is not only a feature of the external environment; it also is something companies create themselves to cope with the challenges of the external environment.

Economic interdependence

The currency crises of the 1990s in Asia and Latin America influenced businesses and consumers around the globe through their effects on the financial institutions in North America and Europe. A dramatic example of economic interdependence was the September 11, 2001 attack on the World Trade Center in the United States. Prior to this most people in the West saw little linkage between the United States and Afghanistan. However, on that day the United States and the rest of the developed world realized how interconnected countries in the developing and developed world have become. The attackers, in fact, used this interdependence to create a disturbance, the goal of which was to reduce the interdependence.

The attack had an obvious and immediate impact on the airline and travel industries. But it was not just these frontline businesses that were affected. In fact, the insurance industry was the most affected.[39] Take, for example, Chubb Corporation, which writes both property and casualty insurance. It took a $420 million charge in after-tax income to offset losses due to the September 11 attack. MetLife took a $208 million charge. Lloyd's of London had substantial insurance coverage of United Airlines, American Airlines, and the World Trade Center. MunichRe and SwissRe, the world's two largest reinsurers, were hit badly as they made payments to the direct insurers. Claims from the World Trade Center attack included property losses, business interruption, workers' compensation, health insurance for non-work-related injuries, life insurance, and automobile insurance for vehicles damaged or destroyed. Other insurance companies, such as Zürich and Aegon, which invest heavily in "safe" equities, saw their stocks plunge as their investment portfolios were affected by post-September 11 market dives. This one event on September 11, 2001 surfaced intricate webs of economic interdependence around the world.

There is a positive side to interdependence. Companies can leverage the interdependence by obtaining capital in one part of the world to finance activities in another. However, they must be aware of the economic interdependence and the extended web of relationships in which they function. The interdependence can have an enormous impact on costs and sales. Companies that ignore their interdependencies may be caught by surprise when events in one part of the world affect their business in another part.

Interdependence along the value chain

As with the automobile design teams, firms have found that it is *possible* to get things done faster and better with cooperation (interdependence), even if it is more difficult. At the extreme, a firm may locate each value-chain activity in the part of the world from which the firm can best serve the rest of its global activities. This creates complex interdependencies among the company's different geographic locations. Such interdependencies usually are among activities that are likely to be situated in culturally different locations and time zones, thus, creating greater managerial challenges to managers than do traditional sequential value-chain arrangements. This also creates a different set of risks, as was shown by the 2002 port strikes on the West Coast of the United States. A ten-day shutdown of product flows caused months of havoc. Finished goods, components for final assembly, and new materials flows were interrupted.

Interdependence in alliances

Companies also contribute to the trend of increased interdependence when they enter deliberately into formal and committed relationships with each other. Corporations that operate globally want partnerships with their suppliers, and they want integrated solutions from these suppliers, not just products. The result is usually closer relationships and greater interconnectedness of operations between firms. Suppliers cope with significant shifts in their customer relationships by changing operating structures and systems. The appearance of networked organizations and global account management structures are indications of this trend.

Xerox and Schneider Electric, one of Xerox's component suppliers for its equipment and manufacturing technologies, created such a relationship.[40] The two organizations had numerous sets of senior executive meetings that led to a formalized agreement for Schneider to be the preferred supplier for the entire Xerox product line, worldwide. This arrangement had the potential for increasing Schneider Electric's worldwide sales to Xerox; Xerox had the potential for significant cost savings. The organizations provided each other with significant proprietary information, and R&D streams were disclosed so that Schneider could realign product development efforts to fit the future needs of Xerox. Responsibilities at both global and local levels were matched against local and centralized operational bases. France-based Schneider Electric then identified 25 global account managers, including those from its Schneider Electric North America subsidiary, and started training them to function in this new operational mode. This alliance performed very well for both companies for a number of years and illustrates well how companies can benefit from accepting and channeling the complexity associated with interdependence.

Both technology and international trade law have contributed to greater interdependence in global business, and at the same time have allowed companies to use interdependence to create more value for their firms. Computers and communications technology allow for fast and effective communication of data and dialogue, and trade laws allow for movement of capital and goods. Interdependence contributes to complexity that managers cannot ignore – and in fact must manage – in the process of globalizing.

Condition 3: Ambiguity – what does it mean?

With ambiguity, although there may be plenty of information, the meaning or implications of the information are not clear. It is a condition rife with multiple meanings, incorrect attributions, erroneous interpretations, and conflicting interests. Situations, intentions, corporate actions, and individual behaviors can be interpreted in many different ways, and implications for action are confusing. The problem here is not the need to obtain more information and apply probabilities to the outcomes; that is uncertainty. Ambiguity involves not being able to understand and interpret the data in a way that guides action effectively. Ambiguity goes beyond uncertainty. Three aspects of ambiguity contribute to the complexity of globalization: lack of information clarity, cause–effect relationships, and equivocality.

Lack of information clarity

Information itself can be simply unclear – sometimes we cannot even know "the facts." For example, reports or statistics from different sources may use different indicators to analyze the same subject, coming to different conclusions. The economic situation often is characterized by this lack of clarity: is the world economy growing, stagnating, or shrinking, and by how much? We may not "know" until June of a given year the economic growth figures for the previous year, and even then, these data are debated by experts. Companies cannot know clearly what their market share is at a given moment: market share depends on how one defines the market. Companies in the distribution system may report sales in different ways (e.g., sales to a wholesaler or to a final customer); and there is almost always a lag (different in different firms) in the time between sales and information gathering. Most people have long thought that financial figures derived by accountants were "correct" and could be interpreted as the clear, true picture of a given company's situation. The 2001–2 scandals at companies such as Enron, WorldCom, Tyco, and Vivendi have shaken the general public's faith in these statements. Senior managers have always known, though, that even audited financial statements can be ambiguous. The complexity of today's financial markets (in both multiplicity and interdependence) has increased the ambiguity in terms of information clarity.

We all prefer to make decisions about future actions based on clear information. This is the approach that Hercules would take. In business, limited resources must be invested in a limited number of projects, changes, and visions. Companies have a very strong need to base these decisions on clear information, or "the facts." When the facts are unclear, decision-making is very difficult indeed. The most common response to lack of information clarity is to grasp at the facts that do seem to be clear, such as accounting figures, and rely on those. Today's companies are discovering that this can be a dangerous response, though, and new approaches to managing this type of complexity are needed.

Cause–effect relationships

Another aspect of ambiguity comes from confusion around the relationship between means and ends, inputs and outputs, actions and outcomes. Does one action actually cause what we see as the outcome? Are both caused by something else? A 3M manager commented on three bullet points in a strategic plan: increase market share, increase profits, and increase new product introductions. He identified three possible cause–effect relationships between these objectives: market share leads to profits which provide funds for new product development; new product development leads to both market share and profits; and profits allow new product development which gives higher market share.[41] There are, of course, many other ways in which the three objectives can be related. Each of these different explanations, though, is associated with a different set of priorities and actions.

Consider European mobile telecommunications companies in the 1990–2002 period. According to common industry knowledge, a critical mass of infrastructure and subscriber base causes profitability. Vodafone, BT, and Orange, among others, have acquired smaller players throughout Europe in a race to achieve such "critical mass." Some have also acquired companies in Asia and the Americas to increase their critical mass even further, as well as to establish a foothold in other markets. The telecoms then discovered that pan-European (or broader international) coverage does not necessarily bring critical mass. Even within Europe, the markets are regulated differently and consumers look for different product benefits. Other international markets are even more different (multiplicity!). Because of this multiplicity, the different parts of the company cannot simply be added together to create critical mass. In fact, the acquisitions disperse management effort so much that the company cannot concentrate on its most important markets. These European telecoms have begun to sell some of their acquisitions. Moreover, given the difficulties of achieving results in smaller markets that they previously thought would flow from critical mass, they are examining other assumed cause–effect relationships in the industry.

Equivocality

Equivocality is a condition in which multiple interpretations of the same facts are possible. With this condition, we have the facts and we can identify two or more things they could possibly mean, but to identify the "right" interpretation is difficult. If the same customers keep purchasing the same brand – a fact which we can establish – does this mean they are loyal to the brand or simply shortcutting cognitive processes and making automatic decisions? The implications for marketing campaigns are important. In the former case we might run a campaign that increases their loyalty, giving them points or discounts, with advertisement that creates links between our product and loyal emotions. In the latter case we might work through the distribution system to ensure that our product is always the easiest to purchase, and not focus at all on loyalty programs.[42]

Royal Dutch Shell faced a serious equivocality issue with its Brent Spar misadventure. After examining many alternatives for the disposal of its Brent Spar oil platform in the North Sea when it was no longer functioning, the company planned to destroy and sink it. The executives chose this alternative because it was the most environmentally sound and maximized financial and social responsibilities as much as possible. Shell knew that environmentalists were concerned with the company's activities (fact), and therefore assessed that this alternative would be acceptable (interpretation based on fact). However, Shell executives did not understand the equivocality in the minds of the general public, nor did they completely understand the goals of Greenpeace. Shell managers simply made their decision and proceeded to begin the destruction.

Greenpeace's goal was not only environmental protection in specific incidents, but also the destruction of companies and industries it perceived as harmful to the environment in general. Greenpeace understood the equivocality of the facts in the minds of the general public and used this ambiguity to attack Shell. They saw the counter-intuitive decision about Brent Spar as a perfect opportunity to impose their own clarity upon the ambiguity and strike a blow against Shell. Once the situation was presented in the media by Greenpeace, the general public could not conceive how the sinking of the oil platform could possibly be environmentally sound, no matter how many rational responses Shell made. Environmentalists around the world rose to action with a powerful boycott and Shell eventually canceled the plan.[43]

One observer commented:

> Shell is not going to forget lightly its misadventures with the Brent Spar. The Oil Major was taken by complete surprise when the Greenpeace campaign against sinking that former drill platform achieved its goals. What happened to Shell can in fact happen to any corporation. Losing control of the situation as result of the activities of a pressure group has become a nightmare scenario for the modern multinational enterprise.[44]

We would conclude, more broadly, that with increased multiplicity, especially when such multiplicity represents increased interdependence – which itself creates opportunities for a greater variation in goals, motives, and values – ambiguity is also greater. It is up to managers to address the ambiguity; controlling it is futile. Shell now assigns significant resources to public relations and has implemented a triple bottom line (financial, environmental, and social). The company may find itself in another sticky situation, but it is much better prepared now to manage the ambiguity with processes.

THE MULTIPLIER EFFECT: MULTIPLICITY × INTERDEPENDENCE × AMBIGUITY = DYNAMIC COMPLEXITY

Tightly coupled, complex global organizations operating in tightly coupled, global environments become more vulnerable as their potential for interdependence increases.[45] The increase in complexity leads to a decrease in buffers, slack resources, and autonomy of units. There also is less time to contemplate corrective action. Ambiguity makes problem diagnosis and action planning difficult, and managerial control is decreased. Problems appear and must be resolved. "Now" has become the primary unit of time in the world of global managers.

If customers, governments, interest groups, competitors, and the physical environment were passive, a corporation could manage the complexity by simply adding more managers, computers, and operations. That would be an increase in detail complexity.[46] However, globalization is characterized by *dynamic complexity*.[47] There is simultaneously an increase in scale of operations and an increase in the interconnectedness among the players who have differing agendas, motives, and goals. Subsystems are interconnected in such a way that cause and effect are no longer easy to determine. The effect of multiplicity is a greater issue because it is accompanied by an increase in interdependence. The increase in interdependence and multiplicity leads to more ambiguity. Ambiguity makes understanding multiplicity difficult. And so on. Such a scenario can create messy situations for executives, but global managers must deal with such situations.

Monsanto, for example, is a company that experienced an increase in complexity when it changed its strategy. It operates in at least two very different markets. The mature market for herbicides is based on chemistry. The new market for genetically engineered crops is based on agricultural biotechnology. With advances in biotechnology, companies like Monsanto[48] can provide potential solutions to a number of problems faced by farmers. Genetic engineering can make crops resistant to weeds, insects, and disease; increase the nutritional content; produce crops capable of growing in less hospitable environments such as deserts; and increase the shelf life of fruits and vegetables. Theoretically, the increased yields offered by such technologies could help alleviate hunger in developing countries.

There are many different reactions to genetic engineering around the world, ranging from unquestioning support to open hostility (multiplicity). The application of these new technologies will depend on and will influence many social, environmental, and economic factors (interdependence). The long-term impact of genetically modified organisms on humans and on the environment is unclear (ambiguity). Any one of these conditions would make managing for the future in the agricultural industry difficult; their combination makes predictability and control impossible. Monsanto must develop leaders who can handle not only the science but also manage the complexity of multiplicity, interdependence, and ambiguity throughout the world – a real challenge.

FLUX: THE LAST STRAW

As if multiplicity, interdependence, and ambiguity were not enough on their own, the whole system is always in motion, always changing. And it seems to be changing at a faster rate all the time.

In the agriculture example above, long-term climate changes may influence how people think about genetic modification, but may also influence the effectiveness of the modifications themselves. In the shorter term, even seemingly unrelated crises like "mad cow" disease (BSE) and foot and mouth disease can influence how people think about the genetic modification of plants. In the petrochemical sectors, Shell and other companies must manage continual changes in governments and the relationships among countries (ranging from cartels to wars), scientific developments, consumer and industrial usage patterns, and even climate change. Telecoms companies were jostling for position with third-generation technology until market conditions and difficulties with technology made it clear that the launch of 3G was further away than they had anticipated. This realization required major restructuring and rethinking of current operations, especially after the bursting of the dot.com bubble left telecoms undercapitalized. With mergers, acquisitions, alliances, and divestments, former competitors can become partners, and former partners can become competitors. Predicting the future with any certainty is impossible, and explanations of the past are not always reliable.

How can managers find the path to effectiveness in the midst of this complexity? If the world facing managers has become more diverse, more interdependent, more ambiguous, and is constantly changing, how do they cope? Executives told us that their companies had to be innovative, fast, and agile to compete globally. Borealis, a Danish specialty chemicals company, has even trademarked a description of the goal: Nimblicity™.[49] How is this achieved?

RESPONDING TO COMPLEXITY THROUGH PEOPLE AND PROCESSES[50]

There would seem to be two straightforward alternatives for dealing with increased complexity: *amplification*, or the *elimination of input variety*. Elimination of variety is the reduction of input variety[51] achieved by not being able or willing to see and understand the complexity in the environment impinging on the company, or by seeking or creating situations of certainty that executives think can be controlled, and thereby ignoring potentially high-impact external conditions, situations, and behaviors. Such ostrich-like behavior is not likely to bring success.

Amplification[52] means increasing the number of decision-makers. Generally speaking, more decision-makers or team members lead to more variety. Yet mere amplification will not necessarily work. If, for example, executives operating out of a corporate headquarters in Norwich, Connecticut cannot generate the requisite variety in their decisions to match the variety existing in a global marketplace, simply increasing the size of the team may not work. If multiple decision-makers are highly homogeneous, with similar outlooks, a similar vested interest in the outcome, and reliance on the same selected sources for their information, their "sensory input" will be fooled. That is, they will think they are facing less variety than they actually are.[53]

In organizations, the response to complexity generally has been a combination of amplification and elimination, through the use of structures and policies. Organizational structures have become more and more complex, with more managers, more multi-dimensional matrices and other organizational logics. British Petroleum was originally organized by country units, then by businesses first and geography second. With the acquisition of Amoco, it has since become organized using a complex set of principles, with some units geographic, some business-focused, and others customer- or function-focused. The more complex structures become, the more unwieldy they are. Moreover, they cannot always adapt quickly to new circumstances, since they are designed to fit a particular set of contingencies.

Companies may also develop complex sets of policies – either formally or informally – for managing different situations. Policies may cover marketing objectives, return on investment requirements, global compensation plans, and so on. However, the more the organization faces multiplicity, interdependence, and ambiguity, the more policies it needs and the more complex these policies need to be to cover all the important situations. And with flux, the policies must be changed continually.

This book presents the view that the appropriate response to complexity is through the deliberate development of *requisite variety*.[54] Simply, this means that the variety or multiplicity found in the environment can only be recognized, understood, and interpreted correctly by a matching condition of variety or multiplicity in the organization or, as Ashby said, "only variety can destroy variety."[55] In human information-processing terms, development of requisite variety means that when there are complex, ambiguous inputs coming from the environment, organizational decision-makers must have the cognitive complexity, and firms need the organizational capacity, to notice these inputs and to process them.

To respond to today's global complexity, organizations must shift the focus of response. Instead of structures and policies, the appropriate response to complexity today focuses on *processes* and *people*: the right people to decipher the informational content in the environment and appropriate organizational processes for managing the complexity and executing action plans. As Weick and Van Orden state: "globalization requires people to make sense of turbulence in order to create processes that keep resources moving to locations of competitive advantage."[56] This suggests that the Buddha of people and process may need to receive greater emphasis, while the Hercules of amplification is rethought and perhaps receives less emphasis.

People: The World on Their Shoulders

There is no doubt that managing complexity places new requirements on the people who work in organizations affected by globalization. Talent acquisition and retention therefore become critical in developing the capacity to operate globally. Future global managers must be groomed and their competencies developed early in their careers. Executives told us that there was no time for training after discovering a certain competency was needed. They were moving too fast.

Managers must develop a global mindset. This means having the ability to develop and interpret criteria for personal and business performance that are not dependent on the assumptions of a single country, culture, or context; and to apply these criteria appropriately in different countries, cultures and contexts. Jack Welch called this the globalization of intellect: "The real challenge is to globalize the mind of the organization. . . . I think until you globalize intellect, you haven't really globalized the company."[57]

Consider Lincoln Electric's history of international growth. The company's corporate culture of rugged individualism – with its origins in the Midwestern United States – shaped its early strategy for international development. When Lincoln transferred abroad, unchanged, its US manufacturing labor selection, compensation and incentive systems, it experienced limited success in markets that were similar to the United States, such as the UK, and Australia, and outright failure in others that were less similar, such as Indonesia and France. A new generation of internationally experienced (complex) top managers eventually emerged. These managers understood the extent to which the Lincoln Electric approach was dependent on its American context, and began to modify the company's strategy, organization structure, and systems to allow for cultural and institutional differences. Then, Lincoln's international business began to recover.[58]

PROCESSES FOR RESPONDING DYNAMICALLY

High performance in a global environment requires conceptual and behavioral skills that result in action based on an accurate assessment of the context in which a firm finds itself. Effective global managers take into account not only the economic dimensions of globalization, but also contingencies including context and task as well as personal global competencies, effective teaming and leading, and the management of specific strategic initiatives. These are integrated to provide a more comprehensive view of globalization as a platform for sophisticated execution. Four types of processes are particularly critical to managing global complexity: collaborating, discovering, architecting, and systems thinking.

Collaborating is the establishment of relationships characterized by community, flexibility, respect, trust, and mutual accountability. When people and units collaborate effectively, they are more likely to see the reality and implications of multiplicity, manage interdependence for synergy, and explore different aspects of ambiguity. The relationships provide a continuing strength to confront dynamic complexity and provide a foundation for action.

New product development teams at Roche Pharmaceuticals often partner with people in other organizations to engage in basic science, conduct clinical trials, and develop and execute product launch strategies. The most effective of these teams collaborate to share and create knowledge and approaches that adapt to the environment as it changes.

Discovering is about learning and creating. It encompasses a set of transformation processes that lead to new ways of seeing and acting, which lead in turn to the creation of new knowledge, actions, and things. When organizational processes support and incorporate discovering, people explore multiplicity, experiment with interdependence, and articulate ambiguity. Continual discovering helps adapt to the constant flux found in the global marketplace.

Managers throughout the Dow Chemical Company, one of the world's largest chemical companies, are encouraged to engage in ongoing discovering. They learn about and create not just new chemical compounds and their uses, but also new ways of managing and working together. This discovering has led to a company-wide shift in strategy toward science solutions rather than their earlier focus on chemical solutions.

Architecting is the process of aligning and balancing. The mindful design of processes that align, balance, and synchronize the different parts of the organization provides a platform for coordinated responses to global complexity.

Most global financial services firms have grown through acquisition, leaving a structure of sometimes hundreds of locally autonomous units. In retail banking and insurance, decentralization allows for the local responsiveness that is critical. However, it does not encourage global integration and the accompanying learning effects and other synergies. As a result of decentralization, the firm as a whole may act as a holding company and may also risk missing local opportunities. Some firms are now experimenting with the systematic development of networks that cross the local units. These networks create webs of information sharing, informal policy alignment, learning, and adaptability, without adding complexity to the formal structure. Such networks do not arise spontaneously; they must be developed carefully, for example with joint projects on corporate issues, executive education seminars, and new product or service initiatives for global clients. The networks must also be maintained consciously, not just with a website but also with ongoing, meaningful activities. The companies that have engaged in carefully architecting such networks are finding them a valuable tool for achieving global integration in an industry dominated by local responsiveness.

Systems thinking is the ability to see the interrelationships among components and levels in a complex system and to anticipate the consequences of changes in and to the system. In the terms we have been using, it is the ability to understand the external context of the firm and the interdependencies that exist with it, to understand the capabilities and weaknesses of the firm, and to constantly match and adjust the firm's capabilities and direction with the demands of the environment.

The processes of *collaborating*, *discovering*, *architecting*, and *systems thinking* are interrelated, and all are important for addressing complexity. None of these processes will address complexity effectively by itself.

Over a decade ago, C. K. Prahalad characterized the world of global business:

> a world where variety; complex interaction patterns among various subunits, host governments, and customers; pressures for change and stability; and the need to reassert individual identity in a complex web of organizational relationships are the norm. This world is one beset with ambiguity and stress. Facts, emotions, anxieties, power, and dependence, competition and collaboration, individual and team efforts are all present. . . . Managers have to deal with these often conflicting demands simultaneously.[59]

Prahalad saw the outline of globalization and described it accurately. In this book we intend to paint the picture in more detail with the broad strokes and bold colors required to bring it to life, and to understand its implications for global executives and their companies.

Managing Globally – Overview of the Book

This book articulates the repertoire of organizational processes and individual skills needed for managing complexity. There is no one best solution (structure, strategy, set of practices, etc.) for any one company, let alone for an industry or for all companies. Anyone who claims the opposite – who offers "the best way" – is eliminating input variety, thereby simplifying reality dangerously. But there is a set of organizational processes and personal characteristics that a company can use as a guide to find its own success as managers develop a good set of alternative paths, decide on an appropriate path, and move together along that path, changing paths as necessary, adjusting to the journey as they go. We think this focus on the process of the journey rather than the specific results brings Hercules toward Buddha.

The four remaining parts of this book articulate these processes, as well as the concepts that managers need to know in order to engage in them. The parts build on each other sequentially, creating a coherent statement of the system of effective global managing. As with any interdependent system, though, readers can enter the book at any chapter and move through it in any order, building their own pictures of how to respond to global complexity. A reader who begins with a chapter on a particular strategic initiative may be referred to a part of the global competency or

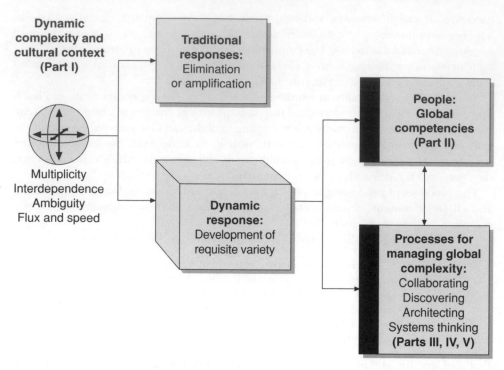

FIGURE 1.2 "Map" of the *Handbook*

context part of the book for more information, and a reader who begins with a chapter on building teams may be referred to other parts for depth on particular building blocks or applications. A "map" of the book is shown in figure 1.2.

This first part focuses on the context of global operations, recasting globalization as complexity to be managed with processes through the glue of people. In addition to this chapter on globalization, this part on context also has a background chapter examining culture. People and human processes are central to our approach to globalization, and culture is associated with multiplicity in social relationships and people's expectations about interdependence, approaches to managing ambiguity, and responses to flux. The next chapter relates what we know about culture and its relationship to people in the context of globalization.

The second part examines the set of essential traits, attitudes, orientations, and skills required of all effective global managers, which we call "global competencies."

The third part focuses on interaction processes among individuals in leading and teaming.

In the fourth part, we present approaches to a set of relevant strategic initiatives, and illustrate how to bring together context, individual competencies, and leading and teaming to execute strategy effectively.

The final part focuses on the particular challenge of emerging and developing economies. Although ideally this shouldn't be a part all to itself, and one day it won't be, these markets are still considered to be sufficiently different from what most business executives are used to, so we think it helpful to address issues related to emerging and developing markets in a separate part.

The book concludes with a statement on creating knowledge about how to manage globally. It identifies the roles of managers and business academics in this process and provides suggestions for future collaboration.

As we conclude our introduction, we are reminded of the American journalist H. L. Menken's observation that "for every complex problem there is a simple solution. And it is always wrong." Our work suggests that as managers globalize their companies, they face an increasing complexity whose challenges require more than the simple solutions we have used until now. In order to address these challenges, challenges which this book explores, managers need to focus less on the specific solutions and think more about the managerial processes that address complexity. In fact, understanding globalization as a *manifestation* of complexity allows us to look at its causes, to move beyond the specific results on which we until now have been focused. Our approach suggests that Hercules and Buddha form an alliance.

NOTES

1 See, for example, How war will reshape the economy, *BusinessWeek*, April 14, 2003, pp. 29–31.
2 The postwar stakes for business, *BusinessWeek*, April 21, 2003, pp. 38–39.
3 Damage in the delta, *BusinessWeek*, April 21, 2003, pp. 56–57.
4 How war will reshape the economy, p. 30.
5 Nussbaum, B. (2003), Building a new multilateral world, *BusinessWeek*, April 21, p. 43.
6 The editors would like to thank Todd Weber for the figures in this Introduction.
7 http://www.perseus.tufts.edu/Hercules/bio.html
8 http://www.perseus.tufts.edu/Hercules/labors.html
9 Capra, F. (1984), *The Tao of Physics*. New York: Bantam Books.
10 This discussion of Buddhism and Taoism is based on Capra (1984).
11 Capra (1984), p. 95.
12 Korzybski, A. (1995), *Science and Sanity: An Introduction to Non-Aristotelian Systems and General Semantics*. 5th edn., New York: Institute of General Semantics.
13 Porter, O., & Steger, U. (eds.) (1998), *Discovering the New Pattern of Globalization*. Ladenburg: Ladenburg Kolleg, Daimler Benz Foundation.
14 Sachs, J. (2000), International economics: Unlocking the mysteries of globalization, in P. O'Meara, H. D. Mehlinger, & M. Krain (eds.), *Globalization and the Challenges of a New Century: A Reader*. Bloomington and Indianapolis: Indiana University Press, p. 217.
15 *World Investment Report 2000: Cross-border Mergers and Acquisitions and Development*. United Nations, New York and Geneva, p. xv.
16 *Ibid.*
17 *Ibid.*
18 See Hax, A. C., & Wilde, D. L. II (2001), *The Delta Project*. Basingstoke: Palgrave, for a discussion of these strategic options.
19 *Ibid.*
20 On July 15, 2002, Pfizer announced the purchase of Pharmacia; http://apnews.excite.com/article/20020715/D7KPEVB80.html
21 *World Investment Report 2000*, p. xx.

22 Hill, C. (2000), *International Business: Competing in the Global Marketplace*. 3rd edn., New York: Irwin McGraw-Hill, p. 5.

23 Rugman, A. M., & Hodgetts, R. M. (2000), *International Business: A Strategic Management Approach*. 2nd edn., Harlow: Financial Times Prentice Hall, p. 438.

24 Hill (2000), pp. 5, 7.

25 See Rugman, A., & Moore, K. (2001), The myths of globalization. *Ivey Business Journal*, September/October, 64–68 and Rugman, A. (2001), The myth of global strategy, *Insights* (Academy of International Business), 1(1), 11–14.

26 Rugman & Moore (2001).

27 These countries include the Netherlands, Belgium, Sweden, Norway, Denmark, Latvia, Lithuania, Estonia. Spain, Portugal, Poland, the Czech Republic, Slovakia, Brazil, Argentina, Chile, Peru, Paraguay, Guatemala, El Salvador, Honduras, Costa Rica, Nicaragua, Thailand, Malaysia, Indonesia and the United States; www.ahold.com

28 Prahalad, C. K., & Lieberthal, K. (1999), The end of corporate imperialism. *Harvard Business Review*, July–August, 69–79.

29 Bartlett, C. A., & Ghoshal, S. (1998), *Managing across Borders: The Transnational Solution*. 2nd edn., Boston: Harvard Business School Press, and Prahalad, C. K., & Doz, Y. L. (1987), *The Multinational Mission: Balancing Local Demands and Global Vision*. New York: The Free Press.

30 Kogut, B. (1985), Designing global strategies: Comparative and competitive value-added chains. *Sloan Management Review*, 26(4), 15–28.

31 Sachs (2000).

32 http://www.schneider-electric.com

33 Elliott, M. (2002), The anatomy of the GE–Honeywell disaster. *Time.com*, February 25; http://www.time.com/time/business/article/0%2C8599%2C166732%2C00.html

34 *Ibid.*

35 Steger, U. (2003), *Corporate Diplomacy*. New York: John Wiley, p. 51.

36 EU kills GE–Honeywell, *CNNMoney*, July 3, 2001; Steger (2003).

37 Einhorn, B., & Keenan, F. (2002), The great firewall of China. *Business Week*, September 23, and Fackler, M., China ends Google search block; http://apnews.excite.com/article/20020912/D7M08TS00.html

38 Thompson, J. D. (1967), *Organizations in Action*. New York: McGraw-Hill.

39 WTC claims could hit $30B, *CNNMoney*, September 13, 2001; http://money.cnn.com/2001/09/13/news/insurance_wtc/index.htm

40 Lane, H. W., DiStefano, J. J., & Maznevski, M. L. (2000), *International Management Behavior*. 4th edn., Oxford: Blackwell.

41 Shaw, G., Brown, R., & Bromiley, P. (1998), Strategic stories: How 3M is rewriting business planning. *Harvard Business Review*, May–June, 41–50.

42 Sean Meehan, 2002, personal communication.

43 Wilson, M., & Lombard, R. (2001), Globalization and its discontents. *Ivey Business Journal*, September/October, 69–72.

44 Lubbers, E. (1998), The Brent Spar syndrome. *Telepolis*, September 22.

45 Weick, K. E., & Van Orden, P. (1990), Organizing on a global scale: A research and teaching agenda. *Human Resource Management*, 29(1), 49–61.

46 Senge, P. (1990), *The Fifth Discipline*. New York: Doubleday.

47 *Ibid.*

48 Genetic markets tempt more firms, *Industry Week*, July 7, 1980.

49 http://www.borealisgroup.com/public/about/hr/borealis_values.html

50 We would like to thank Professor Bert Spector of Northeastern University for his contribution to this part.

51 Harnden, R., & Allenna, L. (eds.) (1994), *How Many Grapes Went into the Wine: Stafford Beer on the Art and Science of Holistic Management*, Chichester and New York: John Wiley, p. 135.

52 *Ibid.*, p. 16.

53 Beer, S. (1981), *Brain of the Firm: The Managerial Cybernetics of Organization*, Chichester and New York: John Wiley, p. 356.

54 Ashby, W. R. (1972), *Design for a Brain*, London: Chapman & Hall, and (1973) *Introduction to Cybernetics*, London: Chapman & Hall.

55 Ashby (1972), p. 207.

56 Weick & Van Orden (1990).

57 Rohwer, J., & Windham, L. (2000), GE digs into Asia. *Fortune*, October 2.

58 Hastings, D. F. (1999), Lincoln Electric's harsh lessons from international expansion. *Harvard Business Review*, 77(3), 162–178.

59 Prahalad, C. K. (1990), Globalization: The intellectual and managerial challenges. *Human Resource Management*, 29(1), 30.

2

People in Global Organizations: Culture, Personality, and Social Dynamics

Mary Yoko Brannen, Carolina Gómez,
Mark F. Peterson, Laurence Romani,
Lilach Sagiv, and Pei-Chuan Wu

Managing the complex global forces that affect all businesses requires managing organizational processes effectively. Managing processes effectively requires influencing and accepting influence from people. Beginning from the first greeting on the first day of one's first job and continuing until the final goodbyes are spoken at a retirement ceremony, we are all surrounded by people when doing our work. This interdependence with other people that is an integral part of any job requires anticipating what people want while trying to accomplish goals for one's personal work, department, or organization, fulfill one's own needs, and follow one's own preferences. Senior multinational corporate executives who strive to accomplish the Herculean tasks of pursuing a corporate strategy are forced to depend on sometimes cooperative and sometimes recalcitrant board members, colleagues, and subordinates. At times, the personal characteristics of some key organization members can shape an organization's culture, while an existing organizational culture can encourage individuals to change or adapt their personal attitudes and behavior. At every organizational level, accomplishing anything requires understanding one's self and one's associates.[1]

How does one develop an understanding of people? Most of our understanding of people comes from intuition developed from a lifetime of relationships. This intuition is invaluable, yet we all find that it can fail. We all have misread a colleague and sometimes even fail to recognize something about our own motives and beliefs. The potential to misread is heightened when the life experiences that have shaped our own intuition differ from those that have shaped the thinking of a colleague or negotiation partner having another cultural background. We can become disconcertingly disoriented when we find ourselves among people in the unfamiliar milieu of a culture that is new to us. The potential to misread a culturally different person is one of the personal, human aspects of global complexity. When facing challenging intercultural situations, careful reflection about culture and people takes on more than usual importance for pondering questions like "Why is my colleague behaving in such an unexpected way?" or "How will others react if I . . . ?"

In this chapter, we seek to promote constructive reflection about this intuition by summarizing prominent ways of thinking about culture and psychology. The previous chapter argued that people are the glue between complexity and the processes of managing it. Managers embroiled in the complexity of globalization must understand people – themselves and those with whom they work – in order to link complexity with processes. The chapter focuses on the elements of social science that most help us to understand how people react to and manage global complexity. Most of the chapter discusses culture and its relationship to differences in values, attitudes, and behavior. Cultural differences are strongly associated with different ways of managing and approaching situations in different parts of the world, and any manager addressing global complexity must have an understanding of these patterns and their dynamics. On the other hand, there are some universals of personality that are found in all parts of the world. An understanding of these basic universals is also helpful and we provide an outline of them in this chapter. The rest of the *Handbook* will apply this view of culture and individuals to a broad range of management problems.

The chapter has six parts. It provides a basic idea of culture and culture themes, presents some ways of mapping cultures, considers how culture affects social processes in organizations, outlines the dynamics of cultural mixing and changing, provides a way of thinking about how individuals differ within any given culture, and concludes with some limitations, qualifications, caveats, and controversies in the perspective we take.

Toward a Working Understanding of Culture

The word "culture" is used very loosely to mean anything from patterns in eating norms to visual and performing arts. Anyone who has traveled from one part of the world to another knows that "they do things differently there," but articulating what is "different" – what culture is really about – becomes messy and confusing. When people who have had multi-country careers get together for dinner, a large part of the conversation is usually devoted to stories of surprises and delights in differences in other parts of the world: "When I was living in Egypt one of the customers took me out for dinner and you wouldn't believe. . . ." "Really? Amazing! That reminds me of when I was living in Hong Kong and. . . ." Interestingly, though, the conversation almost always turns to stories of universals: "It turned out he was just trying to impress his boss, and she was trying to get a better deal from the supplier. I guess we really are all the same, aren't we?" What is culture, and what does it affect? Although the answer is by no means free of controversy, research in the social sciences (especially anthropology, sociology, and psychology) does provide some good answers and guidelines.

Culture is *a combination of interdependent, gradually changing elements – including assumptions, beliefs, values, practices, and institutions – that is distinctive to a particular society. Assumptions* are aspects of culture that are taken for granted. When the results of the United States presidential election between Gore and Bush were contested, people in that country generally took for granted that letting the Supreme Court decide was appropriate. *Beliefs* are understandings about cause and effect relationships. A nineteenth-century British novel, *Erewhon*,[2] subtly questioned the belief that people are responsible for their own criminal behavior by contrasting it with the belief that people are not responsible for their own illnesses. An alternative belief system would be that people's criminal behavior is caused by personal experiences of poverty or victimization over which they have little control, while illness is largely a consequence of the lifestyle a person chooses. *Values* are preferences for certain states of affairs either in one's own life, in one's society, or in the world in general. For example, the value of individual freedom and equality is evident in many Western countries, while the value of family dependence and respect for seniors is evident in much of Asia. *Practices* are patterns of behavior typical of a society. For example, some organizations tend to make decisions in a relatively participative way, while others rely more heavily on the chain of command. *Institutions* include both emergent and explicitly created social structures. For example, national governments are institutions that are explicitly created by treaty and constitution, while professions are emergent institutions that exist due to complex interconnections among universities that train professionals, international professional associations, and informal contacts that occur among professionals in different societies. Cultures are loosely bounded by a *society*. A society consists of a set of people who interact more with one another than they do with others, and who share some sort of identity. Culturally relevant groups can include a nation, a religion, a region within a nation, an occupation, an organization, a gender, or a number of other social institutions.

The idea of culture, however, is more than just a set of elements taken separately. It also includes links between these elements. For example, while individual freedom and equality may be a common value, assumptions linked to the historical challenges to individual freedom or equality in particular countries affect the nuances of what these ideas mean.[3] The meaning of these values is also linked to the societal institutions that maintain them through, for example, various mechanisms for selecting governing bodies and various means of promoting and enforcing them.

Cultures do change. However, their significance to many parties, together with the interconnectedness of various aspects of culture, impede change and make it very difficult for even the most powerful members of a culture to predict or manage change.

Culture has a number of characteristics with important implications for international management.

Culture is learned. In the late nineteenth century, the notion that "culture" is distinct from "nature" was shared across countries in the Western world. Today most researchers agree that culture is learned. It is a group's response to basic societal problems. Whether these problems are at the societal level (societies deciding, for example, how they view nature) or that of a work group (deciding how to deal with a specific type of problem), it is the assumption and subsequent norms used that then get transmitted to the "younger" or newer generation. The learning comes both through explicit teaching and through observation.

Culture is shared. The assumptions, values, and often norms held by a "culture" must be shared by a group of people. Cultures vary in their strength. Some cultures are strong in the sense that values are broadly shared and strongly held by individuals, while others are weak and less shared.[4] Cultures can be shared within a country, a region, an organization, and a profession. Elements are cultural if they belong to the social realm (interaction among people in a loose or tight group), if they are socially transmitted, and transmitted through generations.

Culture links individuals to groups, but allows for individual variability. Culture is learned and defines membership in a group, but since culture translates to individual values and goals we often attempt to understand the impact culture has on the individual. Still, culture is different from personality in that the cultural values must be shared by a group of people. Despite the fact that culture represents a set of probable behaviors, we can and should expect individual variations within a cultural group. Within the United States, a culture oriented towards the individual, we find people that value the group, whether it is a work group or other group. This may be a result of an individual's personal experience or their membership in different cultural groups apart from their status as a US citizen.

Cultures have many boundaries. National culture, the form of culture most typically considered in international management, is but one type of culture. Within a country's national boundaries we may find regional, ethnic, religious, generational, industry, occupational, and corporate cultures. Therefore within Brazil, we see differences in the cultural values that managers or retail business express, as we may see differences in industries and in organizations.[5] Within a country as diverse in its population as the United States we see a variety in regional, ethnic, religious, industry, and organizational cultures. In cultures such as India and much of Latin America, where the population is clearly divided into different social classes, such social classes often show cultural differences.

To global managers, the benefit of identifying something – a behavior, an attitude, an interpretation – as "cultural" is that it becomes more predictable and manageable. Culture is patterned. The pattern overlays individual and environmental elements in a complex way, but identifying the patterns helps managers use it to address and learn from complexity.

MAPPING THE CONTENT OF CULTURE: WHAT IS CULTURE *ABOUT*?

Describing cultures is a kind of map-making. A map is a simplified picture of the reality of a particular space. Just as geographic cartographers have developed expertise in many kinds of map-making, international management researchers have spent considerable effort in developing ways to map culture.

A good map (geographically speaking) is one that highlights the right features, depending, of course, on what information the map-reader needs to know. It also tells the map reader the distance between two points and provides some information about how to get from A to B. Hikers in the Bernese Oberland in Switzerland want a small-scale map with footpaths and contour lines marked for altitude; estimated walking time between points is also helpful. When the same people are driving to Zurich they don't need contour lines but may need a map that shows where gas stations are located along the highway. When they get on the flight home to Bangkok, they may look at the airline's flight paths on a large-scale map of the world. Each of these maps is drawn from research about the features relevant to the map-reader. Increased accuracy of the research leads to better maps (think about the first maps of the "New World").

It is always important to remember that the map is not the territory; it is simply a picture of the territory. A map may miss features that are important to the map-reader, or the geography may change between the time the research was done and the time the map reader uses the map. However, even with out-of-date or missing information, maps can be useful. If someone does not know the territory at all, some kind of map is usually better than no map. Once people understand a territory well – once their knowledge becomes more detailed than the map – the map is no longer necessary.

Cross-cultural social scientists have been mapping culture for many decades. They have developed ways to research and measure the features of culture that most influence important international practices, and can give some estimates about the social distance between two cultures. Used together with effective communication (see Part II: Global Competencies), these maps serve as a strong foundation for connecting people across cultures.

Global managers will manage people better in the environment of complexity if they become cultural map-makers and map-readers, developing and reading maps of cultural differences. Culture maps will never cover all information a manager needs to know about people in different contexts, and some maps may contain information that is out of date or inaccurate in some detail. However, in a complex global situation some map of people is better than no map, and international management research provides a library of good maps. Good managers will update the maps themselves, and eventually rely on their own knowledge.

There are three major approaches to mapping the content of culture in international management, each of which continues to influence management training and consulting. The first two provide map-making tools, as they detail how to compare cultures on particular features. One approach to culture is that all societies face a *common set of problems* that are associated with inevitable physical and psychological characteristics of human beings: the physical world, and the social world. For example, all societies need to deal with the problem that some people will have more resources than others. Different societies reach different solutions to basic problems like those due to idiosyncrasies in their physical situation and their history. For example, some societies will accept the uneven distribution of resources, while others will try to redress such imbalances. Each culture's solution to this set of problems will show up in its approach to management.

A second approach, often linked to the first, is that cultures vary in the *values* that their members tend to express. For example, the value accorded to wealth and resources differs from one culture to another. Traditional Melanesian societies of the Pacific considered it appropriate to place those people who had the most resources in leadership roles.[6] However, Catholic societies of medieval Europe considered it appropriate to place wealthy Jewish merchants in a quasi-outcast role, and the twentieth-century communist societies of central Europe considered it appropriate to take property away from wealthy people.

A third approach to culture provides detail to fill in the color on maps, providing details that are not comparable across maps. This approach highlights the fact that each society has at least some *qualitatively distinctive problems or values* that are at most only vaguely comparable to problems or values that other societies face. For example, the preceding examples of Melanesian "big man" leaders, Jewish merchants in medieval Europe, and wealthy people living under communism can be compared on the basis of how people with resources are viewed. Yet each also has historically unique characteristics that limit comparison.

International management scholarship has most fully addressed the first two approaches that appeal to basic problems and societal values, and their value in providing useful maps is clear. But the research also recognizes and sometimes provides examples of the third approach, emphasizing unique qualities of societies.

Culture as a response to societal problems: Kluckhohn and Strodtbeck. The view that societies face a common set of problems has been a theme in cultural anthropology throughout the twentieth century and beyond. Kluckhohn and Strodtbeck were anthropologists who identified a set of common human problems that all societies inevitably face. Societies differ, however, in the beliefs and assumptions they develop to respond to those challenges.[7] These problems are: How do we view people? How do we see the world? How do we relate to one another? How do we use time? The set of problems they proposed has been among the more influential in cross-cultural management thinking.

The first question is about the *nature of the individual*: What are human beings like? Are they good, evil, or neutral? If a society views people as evil, the society assumes that its members are tempted to engage in acts that are evil and may well take it for granted that elaborate mechanisms are needed to control people. Organizations in such societies may tend to closely monitor and supervise employees. In societies where people are assumed to be good, there are likely to be fewer locks on doors and less supervision of employees. Another aspect of this orientation is whether a culture views people who behave inappropriately as being changeable or not. In cultures where people are viewed as good and changeable, organizations may be inclined to invest in training their employees. In cultures where people are considered to be a mixture of good and evil and hard to change, the emphasis may well be to choose the correct person for the job.

The second problem has to do with a society's view of their *relationship to nature*: Are we subjugated to nature, in harmony with nature, or do we have mastery over nature? In some cultures it is believed to be natural for humans to try and control the world (mastery over nature or a free-will orientation), while in others it is believed that people's lives are controlled by forces such as nature and the supernatural (subjugation to nature or a deterministic orientation). Finally, in other cultures, people believe they should work in harmony with nature to maintain a balance. For example, people from the United States on average have a belief that they control the environment. This belief is evident in the massive engineering projects that are undertaken to build dams, roads, and other such mechanisms to "overcome" obstacles imposed by the environment. In business, people from the United States translate this value to a belief that one can control what happens and, as such, plans are helpful in guiding our actions. People from the United States often clash with other cultures, for example those of the Middle East or Latin America, where, often because of religion, people believe that what happens to us is somewhat out of our control. For example, when dealing with an Arab, an American may find that the Arab may respond to a plan by saying "If God is willing."[8] If people believe that you can't control everything, then planning has less of an instrumental value. Similarly, in many Asian countries such as China, great emphasis is placed on the layout and placement of objects and space so as to allow the earth's forces to work for you, as is reflected in the art of feng shui.

Another third important question a society has to answer with regard to their view of the world related to their *relationships with other human beings*: Is it collateral (primacy given to goals and welfare of groups), individualistic (primacy given to the individual), or lineal (ordered position within groups)? In societies known as collective societies, people are distributed into groups, such as families. In individualist societies, the individual and his/

her achievements serve as the main focus in defining the person. This dimension also surfaced in Hofstede's monumental study. Hofstede surveyed managers and employees of an American corporation, IBM, in more than forty countries. He analyzed this data and found four cultural-level dimensions, two of which he interpreted as reflecting individualism versus collectivism. Individualism exists in cultures where ties among individuals are loose, and people are expected to look after their own interests or those of their close families. In collectivist cultures, in contrast, people are integrated into strong, cohesive groups (ingroups) to which they are expected to be loyal and which will take care of them throughout life.[9]

Another important orientation in a society refers to our *primary mode of activity*: Is our basic orientation one of being, doing, or reflecting? In some societies, people focus on "being" and living life spontaneously.[10] In other societies, people focus on "doing" or achieving. Finally, in other societies, people take a thoughtful, reflective, and rational approach; things are done only after some reflection and analysis. In doing cultures, individuals focus on achievement and, therefore, one can reward individuals according to their achievements.[11] Nevertheless, in being cultures, such rewards may have a different effect as individuals are more focused on experiencing the moment. Hence, at work, being-oriented individuals believe their co-workers and the environment created are as important as the rewards provided.

Finally, the fifth orientation asks *how do we view time*: Do we focus on the past, present or future? Some cultures emphasize the past and, therefore, people in these cultures judge actions based on the adherence to traditions and the way things have been done. In these societies, change is often seen to be for the worse. In other cultures, people focus on the present actions and their consequences. Finally, in still other cultures, people are oriented toward the future and, therefore, welcome change and progress. Future-oriented cultures are able and willing to look forward and make sacrifices today for benefits that may come years ahead.

Other approaches to societal problems. Other prominent approaches to culture analysis use societal problem perspectives. Hofstede appeals to three societal problems that others had used to give order to the extensive literature about culture that had developed through the first half of the twentieth century. These problems are relation to authority, conception of self, and primary dilemmas or conflicts and ways of dealing with them.[12] Schwartz builds his framework around the problems of relations between the individual and the group, how to guarantee responsible behavior, and relations between humankind and the natural world. Trompenaars and Hampden-Turner draw from Parsons and Shils to identify a set of societal problems. These problems are relationships among people, relationship to nature, and time. Inglehart organizes his analysis around three basic ways in which societies handle a host of specific problems by distinguishing among traditional, modern, and postmaterialist societies.[13]

Advantages and limitations of culture as societal problems. Theories that describe the basic problems that societies face have some advantages. One is that they direct attention to characteristics of cultures that affect the thoughts and actions of people in a society, but of which a society's members may not be consciously aware. This helps us create maps of assumptions that guide thinking and action in management. Another advantage is that there is a certain intuitively appealing logic to them. When pointed out, it seems obvious that, in fact, all societies do face the sorts of problems that Kluckhohn and Strodtbeck and others specify. The map is easy to understand. A third is that they are comprehensive, but not overly specified. That is, there may be many specific attitudes, values, beliefs, and assumptions that can be linked to these basic problems. Given that the problems are common to all societies, perhaps some of these attitudes, values, beliefs, and assumptions will have enough in common to all societies to be compared. Yet given that all societies have unique histories and face unique physical conditions, the intuition that each has something qualitatively unique is not challenged by problem-based theories. The map this approach creates is flexible and applies to many situations.

Perhaps the major limitation of problem-based theories is that their flexibility in application makes it quite difficult to specify which society shows a particular sort of response to a given problem. In other words, the measurement tools are not well developed enough to provide the accuracy needed for reliable maps. For example, do we infer that a society thinks that people are good based on what the society's members say, or based on how many members of the society are in prison?

The solution that international management scholars and consultants have tended to use most heavily is to *keep in mind* the basis of culture in assumptions and beliefs that reflect responses to basic problems, but to *classify particular societies* using the values that members of the societies express. It is to these taxonomies of values that we will now turn.

Culture as values. Several systems for mapping cultural values have been extensively used to compare cultures and anticipate the implications that cultural differences have for the way people are likely to respond to particular management practices and ways of organizing. The maps developed from this research have been well established.

Cultural values are shared, abstract ideas about what is good, right, and desirable in a society.[14] They represent the goals that members of the society are encouraged to have and they serve to justify actions taken in the pursuit of these goals.[15] As a result, cultural values are reflected in widely shared norms, symbols, rituals, practices, and ways of thinking.[16] They are expressed in both the *personal values and goals* that members of the culture emphasize and in the way *social institutions* like families, schools, organizations, and political systems operate and function.[17]

Cultural studies of values have their origins in surveys of the values that individuals express. One of the major values surveys, the Rokeach Value Survey, was developed to cover a very broad range of values held by people in the United States that could be applied to everything from predicting voter behavior to diagnosing people with psychological problems.[18] Another approach to values that influences cultural research is an organizational value-survey tradition. This tradition is based on questions that ask people about the importance of various work goals, such as the relative importance they place upon good pay, job security, and comfortable working conditions. Their answers are then used for such applications as designing reward systems and anticipating how people will respond to work condition changes. A third tradition is to ask people how they would respond to various specific situations described in short scenarios or vignettes.

Studies of cultural values typically are based on these three sorts of surveys. Since they are based on surveys, they start from responses by individuals and on what individuals think. When these surveys are analyzed, statistics are sometimes used to find *collective patterns* that are implicit in what *individuals* say, or to use *the patterns in what people consciously express* to infer *unconscious* aspects of their values. Since the way people think is only indirectly affected by the sorts of societal problems that Kluckhohn and Strodtbeck or others have proposed, taxonomies based on value dimensions are only loosely related to categories based on societal problems. Maps based on values and maps based on social problems show different kinds of information.

A major contribution of cultural values research has been to provide specific information about the values that characterize particular nations and, sometimes, ethnic or linguistic subgroups within nations. There are several frequently encountered studies that provide this sort of information. The most widely used is Hofstede's analysis of 53 nations and regions based on a survey done with IBM. The survey relies on questions about work goals and preferences for how work should be organized. Hofstede provides data for each nation that he and his colleagues studied on four value dimensions: individual versus collectivism, power distance, uncertainty avoidance, and masculinity/feminity.[19] Trompenaars and Hampden-Turner describe a cultural values model that is encountered often in international management consulting. The survey is based on responses to short vignettes. They provide information for several dozen nations about the value dimensions of universalism/particularism, individualism/communitarianism, achievement/ascription, neutral/emotional, and specific/diffuse.[20] Inglehart and his colleagues developed a World Values Survey based on household samples that is especially designed for political science and public policy applications, but also includes a number of questions about work goals and values. Data are readily available for 43 nations on a number of work goals, on composite measures of traditional authority versus secular rational authority values, and for survival values versus well-being values.[21]

We will organize our discussion of cultural values around yet another taxonomy developed by Schwartz. It is based on a taxonomy that draws heavily on the Rokeach Value Survey. However, Schwartz substantially adapted the Rokeach Value Survey to change its emphasis from US values to values that are globally relevant, and to analyze it in ways that represent societal values rather than individual values. Schwartz's taxonomy has the advantage of paralleling the Kluckhohn and Strodtbeck problems of societies somewhat more closely than the others, and is also among the more comprehensive. As we describe Schwartz's taxonomy, we will also note its links to the other well-known cross-cultural views of values. These different systems for classifying cultural values provide data for overlapping sets of nations. Comparing these taxonomies for those nations where their data overlap supports the utility of culture-value models by showing that there is considerable consistency among them.[22]

Schwartz's value survey. Schwartz and his collaborators derived seven cultural value dimensions that can be conceptually organized around three problems that all societies face.[23] These problems are reminiscent of those that Kluckhohn and Strodtbeck propose. Each value dimension is positioned as representing one way of handling one of the three problems. The dimensions have been validated using data from teachers in the belief that teachers are key socializing agents in society and that they have a distinctive and unique role in influencing large numbers of people throughout a society. Schwartz has provided scores for these dimensions in 24 nations. He and his colleagues have proposed a number of implications that the dimensions he has identified are likely to have for businesses.

One problem is how a society regulates the relations between humankind and the surrounding natural world. Schwartz labels one pole of this dimension *mastery*. In mastery cultures, people are encouraged to master, change, and exploit the environment in order to attain personal and group goals. He proposes that organizations in such cultures are likely to be dynamic, competitive, and strongly oriented toward achievement and success. They also are likely to develop and use advanced technology to manipulate the environment and promote goal attainment. The opposing pole to mastery is labeled *harmony*. In harmony cultures, people are encouraged to deeply understand the natural environment and try and integrate into it, rather than change or exploit it. Managers in such cultures are likely to view the organization holistically and to focus on the complex relations among its parts. Leaders are likely to try to understand the social and environmental implications of organizational actions and to seek non-exploitative ways to work toward organizational goals. The mastery–harmony value dimension is conceptually similar to Kluckhohn and Strodtbeck's idea of relation to nature, although Schwartz's constructs place more emphasis on the control people seek to exert over one another as well as over the physical environment. Hofstede finds that nations oriented toward mastery also tend to place greater value on what he calls achievement and material gain (cultural masculinity) than on social support and quality of life (cultural femininity). He also finds that nations oriented toward harmony tend to place greater value on avoiding uncertainty than do other nations.[24]

Schwartz suggests that the nature of relations between the individual and the group is the one societal issue that any group of people needs to resolve. Schwartz notes that a society has to decide to what extent people are autonomous rather than being embedded in the group. In *embeddedness* cultures people are perceived as entities that are bounded by the collectivity, that they find meaning in life through participating in the group, and that they identify with its goals. Organizations in such cultures are likely to function as extended families that take responsibility for their members in all domains of life. In return, organizations expect their members to identify with and work dutifully toward shared organizational goals. In *autonomy* cultures, by contrast, individuals are perceived as autonomous, separately bounded entities that find meaning in life through their uniqueness. Schwarz distinguished between two types of autonomy that are distinguishable in his data set. *Intellectual autonomy* means that individuals are encouraged to follow their own ideas and intellectual directions independently. *Affective autonomy* means that people are encouraged to find positive experiences for themselves. In cultures that emphasize autonomy, organizations are likely to treat their members as independent actors with their own interests, preferences, abilities, and allegiances. Organizational members are likely to be granted some autonomy and may be encouraged to generate their own ideas and act upon them. The embeddedness–autonomy distinction is similar to the various collectivist–individualist dimensions that are the most frequently studied dimension in international culture analysis.[25]

Schwartz notes that another societal issue that confronts all societies is how to guarantee responsible behavior among cultural members, since such responsible behavior is necessary to preserve the delicate social fabric. One solution to this challenge is found in hierarchical cultures, which rely on hierarchical systems of ascribed roles and perceive the unequal distribution of power as legitimate. Individuals are socialized to comply with the roles and obligations attached to their position in society. Organizations in such cultures emphasize the chain of authority, assign well-defined roles in a hierarchical structure, and demand compliance in the service of goals set from the top. Organizational members are expected to put the interests of the organization before their own interests.

An opposing solution to this challenge of how to preserve the social fabric is found in egalitarian cultures; cultures that encourage people to view each other as moral equals who share some basic interests as human beings. Individuals are socialized to internalize a voluntary commitment toward others. Organizations in those cultures may be built upon cooperative negotiation among members who flexibly enact their roles as they try to affect organizational goals. Leaders are likely to motivate others by enabling them to share in goal-setting and by appealing to the joint welfare of all.

The hierarchical emphasis (the third orientation within this value orientation) was also identified by Hofstede and Schwartz in their work. Hofstede labeled this societal value as power distance, or the extent to which people accept or reject the uneven distribution of power among society members.[26] The implications of power distance on work behavior are obvious. In cultures that accept large differences in power between individuals, the organizations will have more layers and the chain of command becomes important. Individuals will respect those who have a title or position above theirs. These individuals will seldom question decisions made by people above them, assuming that their power/ title gives them the right to make such decisions and that, given their power/title, their decisions must be correct.

Hofstede and Bond.[27] We have noted above points at which research by Hofstede parallels the dimensions that Schwartz proposes. Hofstede provides an extensive database representing 53 nations based on data collected through IBM in the late 1960s and early 1970s. He also provides somewhat more speculative data for 16 other nations based on other data sources. He breaks down the IBM data into ethnic subgroups for five nations.

One of these dimensions is named uncertainty avoidance, which refers to the degree to which members in a society feel uncomfortable with ambiguous and uncertain situations. In societies that rank high on uncertainty avoidance, people prefer career stability and more formal rules. In contrast, individuals from low uncertainty avoidance cultures may prefer some flexibility in their roles and jobs and are more mobile when it comes to jobs. Finally, the last dimension is referred to as masculinity versus femininity, which refers to the extent to which cultures underscore values and behaviors that have stereotypical "masculine" versus "feminine" traits. Cultures that emphasize masculinity encourage people to endorse challenge, advancement, recognition, and the opportunity for high earnings. Cultures that emphasize femininity encourage people to endorse good relationships with others, cooperation, and security.

Research conducted by Bond drawing from cultural values that are distinctively Confucian found evidence for another cultural value, *long-term versus short-term orientation*, that also has come to be incorporated into Hofstede's framework. On the long-term orientation side, the focus is on values oriented toward the future such as being thrifty and persistent. On the short-term side, the values focus on the past and present, with values such as respect for tradition. Interestingly, recent research has shown that cultures with a present to long orientation, such as US and European firms, tend to define winning in terms of performance measures that focus on the company's achievement today. In contrast, Japanese firms tend to measure winning in terms of market share that reflects an even more long-term perspective.[28]

From Parsons and Shils to Trompenaars and Hampden-Turner. Trompenaars and colleagues have developed a taxonomy of cultural values that has been used extensively in management consulting and training. Trompenaars and Hampden-Turner discuss a series of dimensions for which they found cross-country differences based on a survey distributed to 15,000 employees from a variety of industries in over fifty countries.[29] They group the value distinctions in three broad categories: those that deal with relationships with others, those that deal with time, and those that deal with people's relationship to the environment. Trompenaars and Hampden-Turner describe five dimensions about relationships with people: universalism/particularism, individualism/communitarianism, achievement/ascription, neutral/emotional, and specific/diffuse. Most of these dimensions highlight some distinctive aspects of individualism and collectivism. The first three are based on a theory developed by Parsons and Shils.[30]

Trompenaars's "relationship with others" dimensions. One cultural dimension contrasts universalism versus particularism in relations with other people. Universalism means using the same standards of ethical behavior for everyone rather than using different standards for your friends, family, or other in-group than for other people. For example, the common US value that everyone is equal before the law is a universalist value. This value tends to affect both the judicial institutions in the United States and the response of people in the United States when powerful people are viewed as receiving special treatment. In contrast, a culture with a particularistic orientation bases treatment on the specific or particular relationship between individuals. A particularistic society might take it as normal that powerful individuals are not punished for violating social norms.

The individualism versus communitarianism that Trompenaars and Hampden-Turner borrow from Parsons is quite similar to Schwartz's distinction between autonomy and embeddedness or Hofstede's distinction between individualism and collectivism. For example, societies that believe that work should be organized collectively around work teams rather than individuals are also likely to believe that responsibility for one team member's mistake should be shared by the entire team.

Trompenaars and Hampden-Turner also draw from Parsons and Shils's suggestion that whether a society adopts the value that one's status should be ascribed or achieved affects relationships between individuals. Ascribed status is based on sources the individual is born with, like gender or ethnic or social group. In cultures that rely on ascribed sources of status, people are born to their position in society, and can do little to change it. Conversely, societies that value achieved sources of status, like education or other personal achievement, are more mobile and allow people to change their position in society. Gaining the social status of becoming a manager can be based either on achievement – such as what the person has accomplished before being assigned to that position – or ascription – such as whether the person is the former manager's nephew. In a work environment oriented toward achievement, employees tend to be judged on their performance. Effective managers may rise to top positions more quickly, but they are expected to keep on performing well in order to maintain their position.

The neutral/emotional distinction refers to the degree to which expressing emotions is accepted. In a neutral culture, people tend to be detached and objective, viewing relationships as instrumental and focusing on the achievement of objectives. In contrast, in emotional cultures, where business is seen as a "human affair," displaying a range of emotions is seen as appropriate. People may exhibit anger and happiness easily. The strength and degree of expression of emotions that is considered appropriate varies by culture.

The distinction between specific versus diffuse relates to the degree to which people separate different parts of their lives. In specific cultures business is separated from other parts of an individual's life; therefore business relationships tend to be limited and focused on specific objectives. In contrast, in diffuse cultures, there is no such clear delineation between business and the rest of an individual's life. In diffuse cultures, individuals truly come to know each other as part of business. An example is the use of titles in Germany compared with the United States. In Germany, "Herr Doktor Muller is Herr Doktor Muller at his university, at the butcher's and at the garage,"[31] whereas in the United States a professor may be "Dr. Jones" in the classroom but may be referred to by her first name, or as "Ms. Jones," in other social situations.

Trompenaars and his colleagues have also analyzed their data set to determine whether each of these five original dimensions about relationships with people is distinct, or whether they group together in a meaningful way.[32] The results identified one dimension combining achievement–ascription and universalism–particularism and another dimension reflecting collectivism–individualism. Both measures were found to be highly correlated with Hofstede's measure of individualism–collectivism, suggesting that much of the Trompenaars project reflects some interesting nuances of that basic idea.

Trompenaars's time and relationship with the environment dimensions. Trompenaars distinguishes between *sequential and synchronic* perceptions of time.[33] A sequential or monochronic perception treats time as linear such that there is a succession of events with a clear start and end point. A synchronic or polychronic perception treats time as multiple and extensive such that several events happen simultaneously. In societies that take a synchronic approach to time, people will tend to do several things at once. In societies that take a monochronic approach, people will tend to differentiate activities into sequences. Trompenaars develops implications for a number of business practices. For example, simultaneously engaging in multiple project management is likely to be appropriate in synchronic societies, while focusing on one project for a given period is likely to be more appropriate in sequential societies.

Trompenaars and Hampden-Turner propose another cultural dimension, *inner versus outer directedness*, based on Rotter's measure of the internal versus external *locus of control* expressed by individuals.[34] Locus of control is a measure developed in the United States to represent various aspects of the extent to which people believe that they control their own destiny rather than having their lives shaped by uncontrollable forces. As a culture measure, Trompenaars uses it to represent the extent to which people in a given nation tend to believe that they can control and influence their environment. In inner-directed countries, where people show a strong belief that individuals can control their environment, managers are likely to engage in analysis and planning, exert effort to achieve plans in the belief that doing so will really matter, and believe that luck has little to do with success. In outer-directed countries, people tend to believe that personal relationships, networks, political conditions, and luck determine success. Consequences for business life might be seen in employees' strategies for success.

One set of analyses identified two main elements in the relation to nature measure. One had to do with whether personal planning as compared to the actions of other people determines an individual's success. The other had to do with whether a person's effort or broader societal circumstances determined success. The first of these is strongly correlated with Hofstede's measure of individualism and collectivism, while the second is relatively unique.

Hall and Hall: High- and low-context societies. Hall and Hall noted the difference between the way people communicate in high- and low-context cultures.[35] Context has both long-term elements, such as the history of the relationships among a set of people, and short-term elements, such as characteristics of a particular setting in which the people are interacting and the non-verbal signals that affect the meaning of spoken words. In low-context cultures, context has very little importance and words themselves are used to transmit the meaning. In the Netherlands, for example, if a person wants to indicate disagreement s/he says "No." In high-context cultures, people who are communicating must use their understanding of their relationship and non-verbal signals to read between the lines to ensure proper understanding. Thus, in Japan, when someone says "Maybe" often the true meaning is no. "Maybe" is used to save face. The word "maybe" then takes on different meanings depending on the situation. No data are available to classify specific nations according to the high-context versus low-context distinction, but high-context communication seems to be typical of most collective cultures.

Organizing the theories of societal problems and the taxonomies of cultural values. The similarities in the theory-based analyses of societal problems and the survey-based taxonomies of cultural values encourage attempts to integrate them. We have noted a number of links in the preceding discussion. Table 2.1 summarizes links among the analyses of societal problems. Table 2.2 draws from Hofstede's[36] statistical analyses to summarize empirical relationships among the taxonomies of cultural values. These tables provide a summary of the tools cultural map-makers can draw from to develop the maps that are important and relevant to them.

Country clusters based on cultural values. The cultural values projects have the benefit of providing managers with scores on specific value dimensions for a large number of nations. These scores can be used for preliminary business planning, just as can country risk ratings. They can also help individual managers anticipate what to expect when visiting a particular country. However, for daily business use, there are limitations on how many scores for how many countries people can ordinarily remember without looking them up. Moreover, because there are individual differences within cultures, managers cannot draw an automatic line from a country score to the individuals within the country. Instead, daily business interactions require an intuition for what to expect when doing business in major categories of countries until one has developed extensive personal experience with specific countries, or even subcultures within countries. The question then becomes, how should countries be clustered into categories? Should we treat the nations of Africa as one set and Latin America as another? Or should we think of former French colonies, former Portuguese colonies, former British colonies, and former colonies of other nations as similar throughout the world?

The most recent project to address this question is Project GLOBE.[37] This project, based on a value survey of over sixty nations, provides good evidence for ten clusters of countries. These are: Anglo (e.g., England, the United States, white South Africa), Latin Europe (e.g., Israel, Italy, French Switzerland), Nordic Europe (e.g., Finland), Germanic Europe (e.g., Austria, the Netherlands), Eastern Europe (e.g., Hungary, Kazakhstan), Latin America (e.g., Brazil, Mexico), Sub-Saharan Africa (e.g., Zambia, black South Africa), Arab (e.g., Turkey, Morocco), Southern Asia (e.g., India, Malaysia, Iran), and Confucian Asia (e.g., Taiwan, Japan). If a manager has extensive experience in one

TABLE 2.1 Theories of societal problems

	Nature of the individual	Relationships with other human beings	Relationship to nature	Time perception	Primary mode of activity
Kluckhohn & Strodtbeck					
Inkeles & Levinson (used by Hofstede)	Conception of self	Relation to authority	Primary dilemmas or conflicts and ways of dealing with them		
Schwartz (from Kluckhohn & Strodtbeck and others)		Relations between the individual and the group How to guarantee responsible behavior	Relations between humankind and the natural world		
Trompenaars (from Parsons & Shils and others)		Ascribed status/ Achieved status Communitarianism/ Individualism/ Particularism/ Universalism	Relationship to nature	Time	

TABLE 2.2 Taxonomies of cultural values

Hofstede	Collectivism/Individualism Masculinity/Femininity	Power distance	Uncertainty avoidance	Long term/Short term
Schwartz	Embeddedness/Autonomy	Hierarchy/ Egalitarianism	Mastery/Harmony	
Inglehart	Modernism/Postmaterialism		Modernism/ Traditionalism	
Trompenaars & Hampden-Turner	Universalism/Particularism Individualism/ Communitarianism Neutral/Emotional Specific/Diffuse Achievement/Ascription		Control over environment/control by environment	Past/present/future Sequential time/ synchronic time

country and a strong intuition about how to manage there, this experience and intuition is more likely to transfer easily to other nations in the same cluster than it is to nations in other clusters. A Japanese manager who has worked in the United States may then be assigned to Australia. In that case, the manager is more likely to benefit from his or her intuition of United States culture to begin learning about Australia than from his or her intuition about Japanese culture. A clear limitation, of course, is that the United States and Australia are not the same. While nations in different clusters tend to differ more from one another than do nations within a cluster, they are by no means culturally identical.

Preferences for process: Sources of guidance. A final approach to mapping cultural dimensions is the process by which culture affects work activities. We defined values as preferred states of affairs. Values can be about outcomes in the sense that a preference for harmony is sometimes described as a preference for a world of peace and beauty. Values can also be about preferred processes in the sense of preferred ways of interaction, making sense of what is happening, and making decisions. For example, Hofstede's idea of uncertainty avoidance includes as one element a preference to make decisions by following rules. Much of the preceding discussion about the organizational implications of the Schwartz Value Survey are propositions about probable implications that the value dimensions have for the process that managers should follow to make decisions. In organizations, relative preferences for outcomes like making money over having free time for family have implications for compensation systems. Relative preferences for processes, like following rules to make decisions rather than following a supervisor's guidance, making decisions autonomously, or discussing work problems with colleagues, have similar implications for many aspects of the way an organization operates.

Smith, Peterson, and colleagues have studied managers' preferences about the process by which work events should be understood and how decisions should be made about the best way to handle them.[38] They provide data for 47 nations about how much managers say that they rely on each of eight *sources of guidance* to handle various every day work events. Four of these sources were summarized into an index of *verticality* that combines high reliance on formal rules and on one's superior with low reliance on one's own experience and one's subordinates. Separate results are provided for preferences to rely on *unwritten organizational rules* about what to do, *staff specialists, colleagues in other departments,* and *beliefs typical of the respondent's country* as to what is right.

The application of this research is straightforward. For example, some management practices such as participative decision-making assume a low level of verticality, while some human resources programs such as organizational culture interventions assume that unwritten organizational rules are especially important. Whenever a management practice or human resource program is being transferred from one location to another, managers would be advised to consider what sources that practice or program assumes are used and assess whether these are in fact typical in the setting to which the transfer is made. For example, an issue in airline safety is whether a pilot in a crisis situation will follow personal judgment, explicit procedures, or the directions provided by air traffic controllers. Organizations seeking to promote airline safety need to know the answer to this question in order to appropriately train pilots. In general, managers have a choice of using practices that depend on the decision-process preferences of people in the society where they are operating, be prepared to adapt their usual practices, or plan an effective program of intervention to introduce practices that are less consistent with the sources typically used in the receiving country.

Culture as qualitatively unique problems and values. Proponents of each set of cultural value dimensions that we have summarized show a healthy awareness of the limitations of any set of dimensions for describing cultures, including their own. While dimensions provide a degree of structure to what otherwise can be overwhelming complexity, our definition implies that culture consists of a great deal more than what these dimensions cover. Over-applying these sorts of dimensions can result in what has been called *sophisticated stereotyping*. This occurs when one ignores the nuances of a culture or the specifics of the context in which cultural values occur.[39] For example, a manager who believes that a culture with large power distance and uncertainty avoidance requires authoritarian management may use this sophisticated stereotype to conclude that there is no way to implement employee involvement strategies. One would expect that practices such as self-managed work teams and ongoing innovation would be difficult in Mexico, given its large power distance and high uncertainty avoidance. Yet a recent case study describes a Canadian company that implemented many progressive learning-oriented management techniques in its subsidiary in Mexico.[40] The company was able to implement them in part because of the higher than average level of education among their employees as compared to the society in general, as well as the training given and a strong corporate culture. The Mexican managers in the subsidiary also adapted the practices to fit the culture. For example, realizing that Mexicans tend to include family members in their work lives, they took the traditional approach to implementing self-managed work teams a step further. They involved the families in many company activities so that the work groups – by virtue of knowing each others' families – could become part of the employees' in-group. The lesson of experiences like this is that the combination of high power distance and uncertainty avoidance should encourage further analysis of both exactly how these values are expressed in that society and of exactly what employee involvement requires. The same lesson applies to any combination of cultural values and management practices. A full understanding of a culture requires time and observation of its intricacies and collaboration with those people who have in fact spent their lives in that culture.

A number of culture analyses can help a manager with particular interest in developing an in-depth knowledge of a small number of personally significant cultures. These analyses complement the views of societal problems and cultural values by using anthropological tools rather than the value surveys. For example, one study combines historical, psychological, and anthropological methods to provide accounts of national differences in psychological contracts.

Psychological contracts.[41] An international group of scholars collaborated to provide descriptions of the distinctive ways in which psychological contracts tended to be formulated in each of their countries. Psychological contracts cover a range of phenomena that have to do with the reciprocal responsibilities and obligations between an employer and an employee. Psychological contracts have *relational* elements and *contractual* elements. Relational elements are those largely non-articulated understandings between people. Contractual elements are those that specify what each party is to contribute and what each will receive in exchange. The analyses of 14 nations indicate that much of the world has seen a cultural shift toward transactional contracts in recent years. Nonetheless, the project coordinators illustrate the sorts of differences in psychological contracts found among the nations studied by noting:

- psychological contracts based on conflict, rather than agreement, in French employment relations;
- the sense of belonging at the heart of the Japanese experience of organizational membership and how economic changes affect it;
- workers' perceptions of whom their employment relationship is *really* with (whether the employer, as is typical in the United States; co-workers, as in Australia; or the state itself, as in France);
- the meaning of "high performance" for workers in societies where many workers are reluctant to be singled out as high performers, such as Australia and the Netherlands;
- societal forces that create highly similar psychological contracts across workers and firms, as in Belgium;
- the highly idiosyncratic employment deals of many American workers and the institutional factors that promote such differences.[42]

Each of the country analyses includes a description of the current state of psychological contracts, as well as an analysis of the societal process by which the current state has developed.

Mapping cultural space is more complex than mapping geographic space. Human systems are not as amenable to measurement, and we do not have nearly as much experience in drawing the maps. With the help of the discussion and resources above, global managers should be able to begin drawing and reading the cultural maps that are most relevant to their own context of global complexity, whether it is about common problems, values, or specific management practices.

Culture Process Theories

The models of societal problems and cultural values provide a sense of what a culture is like. Some of them, like the analyses of psychological contracts in different nations, and Hofstede's analysis of why certain societies have come to develop particular ways of handling universal problems, consider the process by which a society's culture has come to be the way it is today. These models also provide explanations for how people in a culture are likely to respond to management practices and human resources programs. Still, their explanations of how people in a culture behave are restricted to too small a range of culture dimensions to capture all about the process of how culture affects daily behavior. Another sort of analysis, that which traces how culture affects social processes over time, provides additional depth for understanding culture's effects.

Corporate culture is unique and dynamic, as shown by both Schein and Hatch.[43] Schein defines the organizational culture as a pattern of underlying assumptions resulting from functional knowledge that was used in solving the company's needs of external adaptation and internal integration. He presents organizational culture as something that has been progressively created as a function of the company's needs. Schein tells us that the culture-creation process starts when the group (employees of a company) faces a problem. A person believes in one solution and convinces the group to adopt her belief. If the idea happens to work repeatedly, and the group has a shared perception of that success, the idea originally in the form of a belief is adopted as a correct way to do. The idea evolves from someone's original belief to a shared value in the group and, finally, as a shared basic assumption. Culture is consequently presented as a constructed pattern of knowledge engraved at the level of basic assumptions. Schein presents a cognitivist understanding of the culture (culture as systems of knowledge), develops its semantic aspect (shared meanings of a success), and applies it as a functionalist instrument of task accomplishment. In Schein's view, culture is not something static and imposed by the leader but a specific knowledge, which is progressively established. This is a first aspect of the dynamism of culture: it results from a never-ending process initiated by the company's needs of external adaptation and internal integration.

Another stream of research has focused on negotiated culture, or what happens when two or more cultures "get together" through a merger or other cross-cultural interaction.[44] Negotiated culture is an ongoing, emergent, working arrangement of imperfectly shared rules and routines. Imperfect because, in the post-"Cold War" era when interactions between cultures are less hegemonic, existing arrangements are frequently changing, conditions are less certain, and actors have more influence over transnational outcomes. As a result, cooperative arrangements do not evolve according to predetermined formulae. Emergent working cultures do not simply reflect one or the other culture. Neither are they a blend or hybrid of the constituents' best practices, nor a representative of some global universal work culture. Rather, cross-cultural actors are frequently faced with situations where no repertoires exist, and so they create ones that are particularistic to the cross-cultural context at hand. In other words, given culture A and B, the negotiated cultural outcome will neither be simply A or B nor even AB. Some other outcome, more like a mutation containing parts of both cultures as well as some aspects of its own making, idiosyncratic to its own context, will be the result.

Even though negotiated cultural outcomes may not be determinable, the processes by which shared working cultures evolve have common elements. The process involves a construction of new understandings, as actors make sense of an interactive organizational terrain. There are individual, structural, and contextual influences on the trajectory of negotiated outcomes, and the negotiation is a continuously changing combination of information and action influenced by these elements.

Individual influences include the actors' cultures of origin and other individual characteristics. These are starting points providing a set of meanings and behaviors that become a tacit basis from which the new transnational culture evolves. Important structural influences on the negotiated culture are the organizational structure (joint venture, new acquisition, wholly-owned subsidiary, etc.), strategy toward internationalization, and the location. These structural conditions influence the extent to which different aspects of the culture need to be negotiated, and how. Contextual elements that influence negotiated culture are historical, institutional, and organizational.

During the culture negotiation process, events and actions are interpreted and re-interpreted in various ways, depending on the influences described above. In this "recontextualization" of events and actions they are given new meaning, and the new meanings come to life on their own. In this way, a new culture is created.

Research on the process of cultural dynamics in multinational firms is in its infancy, and we can expect more guidance in the future as lessons from corporate culture and anthropology research are incorporated. In the meantime, the most important advice to managers is to pay attention to the processes of culture change and not assume that cultures are static or additive.

INDIVIDUALS

Cultural views of people emphasize the socializing influence that a society of some sort has on promoting some level of conformity in the ways of thinking and acting of people who are part of a society. Yet people are also individuals and react to socialization attempts in idiosyncratic ways.

We will begin by using the language of *personality traits* to talk about relatively stable, unique characteristics of individuals. Personality differences among individuals take a variety of forms and can be linked to a variety of biographical, physical, psychological, and emotional sources. We will emphasize those traits that research suggests to appear everywhere in the world. Next, we will also briefly recognize variability in individuals' *skills and abilities*. We will then consider another form of diversity by talking about the groups with which different people share an *identity*, for example, gender, race, and ethnicity.

Personality traits: The "Big Five" and others

Psychologists have long used the idea of personality to talk about the more stable internal characteristics and patterns that uniquely distinguish one individual from another.[45] The idea of personality fits the common human intuition that each person shows at least a somewhat consistent tendency to think, feel, and act in certain ways.[46] For example, some people are quiet and reserved, while others are outgoing. To the extent that personality really does explain behavior across a broad range of situations, personality theory has the potential to be applied to both human resources decision-making and to the way one behaves toward particular other people. For example, are reserved people better than outgoing people for managerial positions or overseas assignments? Are some personality types better suited than others to analytic as compared to sales jobs? Even when there is no better or worse personality for a particular job, personality can still be important for understanding the distinctive ways in which a particular person will fulfill a particular job. Given the difficulty in accurately diagnosing personality, managers need to be cautious about using personality trait labels too rigidly. Nevertheless, recognizing that people have stable characteristics of the sort reflected in personality traits can help managers keep in mind that some patterns in their own behavior and those of the people with whom they work may be easier to accept and accommodate than to change.

Psychologists have identified hundreds of personality traits. In order to introduce some order, researchers have recently sorted through this complexity and identified five major personality factors. These "Big Five" personality traits have come to be well known and recognized. They are: extroversion, agreeableness, conscientiousness, neuroticism, and openness to experience.[47]

Extroversion reflects an individual's comfort level with new relationships; how that individual interacts with other people. Extroverts tend to be sociable, talkative, assertive, aggressive, excitable, and active. In contrast, introverts are retiring, reserved, and cautious in new relationships. Introverts are more shy and reserved, and prefer to work alone. Who in a group is more or less extroverted and how many group members are extroverted are likely to affect interpersonal relationships and a group's dynamics.

Agreeableness refers to an individual's ability to deal with others. High agreeableness refers to the degree to which someone is trusting, good-natured, compliant, modest, gentle, and cooperative. People with low levels of agreeableness tend to be irritable, ruthless, suspicious, and inflexible toward others. Members with low levels of agreeableness tend to act aggressively and competitively, not only toward the organization's suppliers and competitors, but also toward their fellow organizational members.

Conscientiousness refers to the series of goals a person aims at. Individuals high in conscientiousness focus on a small numbers of goals at one time. They tend to be careful, thorough, responsible, organized, and scrupulous. Those low in this dimension are more likely to pursue a wide range of goals, and tend to be irresponsible, disorganized, and unscrupulous.

Neuroticism refers to a person's level of emotional stability. Individuals with high levels of neuroticism tend to be anxious, depressed, angry, and insecure, while those low in neuroticism (that is, those who have high "emotional stability") tend to be calm, poised, secure, and emotionally stable.

Openness to experience reflects a person's degree of rigidity in beliefs and interests. Individuals with high levels of this tend to be intellectual, imaginative, creative, artistic, curious, sensitive, and open-minded. They are likely to be interested in learning and gaining professional knowledge and tend to adjust well to new tasks and requirements. On the other hand, those with low levels of openness tend to be down-to-earth, insensitive, and conventional, less willing to try new things and prone to avoid unstable, changing roles. Openness to experience is likely to be related to openness to new cultures.

Do these traits apply to people throughout the world?

There are two kinds of international issues in applying the Big Five or any other set of personality traits. One is whether these traits can be used equally well to understand people throughout the world. The second is whether a particular trait is characteristic of people throughout a given nation.

Throughout this book, we will be concerned with the extent to which management practices found effective in one nation or research done in one nation applies elsewhere. Like many social science ideas, the Big Five personality traits were identified based on research done within the United States. The first four, all except openness to experience, seem to travel well and are useful for understanding people in most nations that have been studied to date.[48] Some personality traits, however, seem to be particularly important in distinguishing among people in particular societies and not in others. That is, a manager working outside his home nation should not be surprised to find that other aspects of personality may be particularly important for understanding colleagues in that nation besides those represented in the Big Five.

There is also a long tradition of trying to understand nations based on typical levels in their populations of various personality traits. The evidence that typical or average personalities differ between nations is mixed. The aspects of personality that have been compared most frequently do not always clearly parallel the Big Five personality traits. For example, some early evidence in the 1960s appeared to show that nations differ in the typical need for achievement of individuals, and that this difference in need for achievement might help explain economic development.[49] More recently, nations have been shown to vary in "locus of control" – the propensity of citizens to believe that they themselves have control over what happens to them. Explanations of economic development or policies of nations that came to be called "national character" were helpful both for identifying some aspects of personality and for drawing attention to links of economics and politics to other aspects of national culture. However, they have been generally replaced by the ways of describing national culture based on values and assumptions that are discussed elsewhere in this chapter.

Skills and abilities

Another relatively stable characteristic of people is individual differences in skills and abilities, which, like personality, is affected by inheritance and varying periods of learning. Skills refer to techniques that people need to perform to carry out work functions and roles, and are ordinarily more amenable to training than are abilities. Ability refers to a person's capacity to quickly learn the skills needed to accomplish a particular job.

Intellectual ability, or general intelligence, is an important indicator for tasks involving mental activities. IQ tests can be used by companies to assess individuals' intellectual abilities. Important dimensions include number aptitude, verbal comprehension, perceptual speed, and inductive reasoning. Generally speaking, a high IQ is not a basic requirement across all job categories. Some jobs require one or two facets of intellectual ability, while others with a highly complex nature may require most of them.

Physical ability includes a number of specific aspects of strength and dexterity. Nine basic physical abilities have been identified based on analyses of hundreds of jobs.[50] They are: dynamic strength, trunk strength, static strength, explosive strength, extent flexibility, dynamic flexibility, body coordination, balance, and stamina.

Emotional Intelligence (EQ)[51] comprises four fundamental "people skills" that can be differentiated from general intelligence. These four abilities are critical to success and can be described as the abilities to delay gratification, control emotions, deal constructively with anger, and read other people's feelings.

The availability of potential employees with various skills and abilities is internationally variable. Multinational organizations and national governments increasingly show a preference for hiring local employees rather than sending expatriates. However, this preference is often conditioned by the availability of local people having the extensive experience and education needed to develop particular skills and abilities. Such practicalities often underlie the need for intercultural contacts between expatriates who are involved in short-term or ongoing training and technology transfer from headquarters to local operations. When the skills needed in an overseas location are not locally available and are rare at headquarters, people are often given international assignments for reasons of skills, regardless of personality or other considerations.

Identity

People involved in international business also deal with the relatively stable social identities of themselves, their family, and their business contacts. Individual identity starts from the very simple question: "Who am I?" A person may have many different identities with a variety of social categories or groups.[52] The same person may or may not have a strong identity with a particular family, a religious group, an employer, an industry, a nation, a political party, a gender group, a nation, or a national subculture. These various groups each have norms about appropriate ways of thinking and behaving that shape the thoughts and actions of those who identify with that group.

One's identity also influences with whom one will want to associate.[53] IBM in Tokyo has long had the experience that expatriates from the United States tend to cluster together. That large numbers of IBMers and US expatriates from other companies attend the same Baptist church in suburban Tokyo when they would show more varied religious identities at home reflects the strong influence of national identity.

Recent events can influence the strength of various identities in shaping a person's behavior. People who grew up speaking two languages where one reflects their parents' culture and the other the culture of the society where they lived as children often report behaving differently when they are speaking or thinking in one of their native languages than when they are using the other. The switch from one language to another is a temporary switch in the strength of one's identity. The tendency of national identity to be heightened when one's nation is threatened is also a common experience of people when national safety is threatened. For managers working in international situations, the idea of identity draws attention to the possibility that their own thoughts and behavior may shift when an intercultural interaction changes the aspects of their own identity that are most meaningful while the interaction is occurring. Working with a foreign colleague can either increase the salience of one's own nationality if nationality is somehow being threatened, or can increase the salience of norms typical in a common occupation, organization, or industry identity that is shared with the colleague.

Other characteristics of people: Values, perceptions, attitudes, choices, and behavior. The field of psychology is quite complex and there are a number of sometimes competing and sometimes complementary ways of thinking about people. We have chosen here to focus on the more significant, relatively stable characteristics of people that have broad influence on their way of thinking and behaving, to illustrate how they relate to culture in approaching the management of global complexity. Another way of understanding individuals is to consider their values and assumptions. Values and assumptions were considered in our discussion of culture, where we emphasized the links of values held by one individual to cultural values held by others in their same society. But individuals within cultures differ in their values, as well. Other ways of thinking about people are by using ideas like perceptions, attitudes, choices, and behaviors. These are all shaped by more basic aspects of psychology that influence how people react to particular situations.

The cultural imperative and business conditions

Much of the present *Handbook* extends and applies the preceding discussion of culture to a broad range of business problems. There is a sense in which one needs to live a culture to understand it. Unfortunately, managers rarely have the luxury to fully experience the cultures of all societies in which they will need to have business dealings. No one can have the full insider experience of growing up in more than one or a very small number of societies. Even the more discursive accounts of psychological contracts and the dynamics of cultural processes only help managers begin the process of learning about the cultures with which they will interact. Completing the process requires more than reading about culture. Knowing the territory goes beyond reading the map.

A healthy focus on culture can have the side effect of neglecting other aspects of business conditions. Different countries have widely different business conditions of various sorts. *Political conditions* include the nature of the regime of the country, the role of minority parties, and the issues most prominent in social debate. The *jurisprudence* of a nation covers various legal constraints on organizations, including requirements and restrictions on expatriates and constraints on foreign business owners. The *economic* development level and economic system affect both sales markets and labor markets. The *educational system* affects the availability of potential employees for various levels of management as well as skilled and unskilled labor. The type of *industry* in which a company is active affects its organization and management. An organization's *technology* places some constraints on its ability to readily adapt to local culture. Some technologies require engineers or people having other sophisticated skills, some are amenable to relatively unskilled equipment operators, while some largely replace employees with automation.

While this book is not intended to have the scope to go into all of these business conditions in depth, they are important elements in the complex set of international phenomena of which culture is a part. Several writers have explained the links between culture and other business conditions. Hofstede (2001)[54] shows that many social and economic indicators are linked to cultural dimensions. Among the more substantial is a consistent relationship between a nation's GNP and its level of individualism. Some experienced diplomats and economic development experts have argued that even in the developing world, the differences between the more and the less economically successful nations in Africa, Latin America, Asia, and the Caribbean are due to culture.[55] Inglehart and his colleagues provide two ways of thinking about the relationship between culture and business conditions.[56] One is by carefully valuating the classic Marxian position that a nation's economics determines its culture as compared to the Weberian position that culture drives economics. They also propose a progression from traditional societies to modern societies to postmaterialist societies, each of which has cultural, economic, and political elements. Our sense is that there is a complex reciprocal relationship between various aspects of politics, economics, and culture.

In past years managers have placed excessive emphasis on business and economic conditions at the expense of culture, partly owing to a lack of good information about culture. This *Handbook* – and in particular this chapter – is designed to help redress that imbalance by providing information managers need to understand culture and its relevance for management.

NOTES

1 Schneider, B. (1987), The people make the place, *Personnel Psychology*, 40, 437–453.

2 Butler, S. (1871/1970), *Erewhon*, Peabody, MA: Viking Press.

3 Maznevski, M. L., Gibson, C., & Kirkman, B. (1998), When does culture matter?, paper presented at the Academy of Management Annual Meeting, San Diego, August. Meyer, A. D., Tsui, A. S., & Hinings, C. R. (1993), Configurational approaches to organizational analysis, *Academy of Management Journal*, 36(6), 1175–1195.

4 Trompenaars, A., & Hampden-Turner, C. (1998), *Riding the Waves of Culture: Understanding Cultural Diversity in Global Business*, 2nd edn., New York: McGraw-Hill.

5 Lenartowicz, T., & Roth, K. (2001), Does subculture within a country matter? A cross-cultural study of motivational domains and business performance in Brazil, *Journal of International Business Studies*, 32, 305–325; Meyer, J. W., & Rowan, B. (1977), Institutionalized organizations: Formal structure as myth and ceremony, *American Journal of Sociology*, 83, 340–363; Cooke, R. A., & Szumal, J. L. (2000), Using the organizational culture inventory to understand the operating cultures of organizations, in N. M. Ashkanasy, C. P. M. Wilderom, & M. F. Peterson (eds.), *Handbook of Organizational Culture and Climate*, Thousand Oaks, CA: Sage, pp. 147–162.

6 Stewart, A. (1990), The bigman metaphor for entrepreneurship: A "library tale" with morals on alternatives for further research, *Organization Science*, 1, 143–159.

7 Kluckhohn, F., & Strodtbeck, F. (1961), *Variations in Value Orientations*, Evanston, IL: Row, Peterson. Adler, N. J. (1997), *International Dimensions of Organizational Behavior*, 3rd edn., Cincinnati, OH: South-Western College Publishing. Hofstede, G. (1980), *Culture's Consequences: International Differences in Work-Related Values*, Newbury Park, CA: Sage.
Inkele, A., & Levinson, D. J. (1969), National character: The study of modal personality and sociocultural systems, in G. Lindzey & E. Aronson (eds.), *Handbook of Social Psychology*, Reading, MA: Addison-Wesley, Vol. 4, pp. 418–506. Lane, H. A., DiStefano, J. J., & Maznevski, M. L. (2000), *International Management Behavior*, 4th edn., Oxford: Blackwell. Parsons, T., & Shils, E. (eds.) (1951), *Toward a General Theory of Action*, Cambridge, MA: Harvard University Press. Schwartz, S. H. (1999), A theory of cultural values and some implications for work, *Applied Psychology – An International Review – Psychologie Appliquée – Revue Internationale*, 48(1), 23–47. See Lane et al. 2000 for detailed examples of each of these dimensions.

8 Adler (1997).

9 Hofstede, G. H. (1997), *Cultures and Organizations: Software of the Mind*, rev. edn., New York: McGraw-Hill.

10 Kluckhohn & Strodtbeck (1961).

11 Adler (1997).

12 Hofstede, G. H. (2001), *Culture's Consequences: Comparing Values, Behaviors, Institutions, and Organizations across Nations*, 2nd edn., Thousand Oaks, CA: Sage, p. 31.

13 Schwartz (1999); Trompenaars and Hampden-Turner (1998); Parsons & Shils (1951); Inglehart, R. (1995), Changing values, economic development and political change, *International Social Science Journal*, 47, 379–404.

14 Williams, R. M. (1970), *American Society: A Sociological Interpretation*, 3rd edn., New York: Knopf.

15 Bardi, A., & Sagiv, L. (2003), The European Union and Israel: Comparison of cultures and implications, in K. Boehnke (ed.), *Europe and Israel*, Wiesbaden: Deutscher Universitätsverlag.

16 Sagiv, L., & Schwartz, S. H. (2000), A new look at national culture: Illustrative applications to role stress and managerial behavior conference presentations, in: N. M. Ashkenasy, C. P. M. Wilderom, & M. F. Peterson (eds.), *The Handbook of Organizational Culture and Climate*, Newbury Park, CA: Sage, pp. 417–435.

17 Schwartz (1999).

18 Rokeach, J. (1973), *The Nature of Human Values*, New York: The Free Press.

19 Hofstede (2001).

20 Trompenaars & Hampden-Turner (1998).

21 Inglehart, R., Basanez, M., & Moreno, A. (1998), *Human Values and Beliefs: A Cross-Cultural Sourcebook*, Ann Arbor: University of Michigan Press.

22 Hofstede (2001).

23 This discussion synthesizes Schwartz's work, drawing particularly on the following references: Schwartz, S. H. (1994), Beyond individualism/collectivism: New cultural dimensions of values, in U. Kim, H. C. Triandis, C. Kagitcibasi, S. Choi, & G. Yoon (eds.), *Individualism and Collectivism: Theory, Method, and Applications*, Thousand Oaks, CA: Sage, pp. 85–119; Schwartz (1999); Sagiv & Schwartz (2000). The data for the 24 countries are published in the 1994 reference.

24 Hofstede (2001).

25 Oyserman, D., Coon, H. M., & Kemmelmeier, M. (2002), Rethinking individualism and collectivism: Evaluation of theoretical assumptions and meta-analyses, *Psychological Bulletin*, 128, 3–72; Triandis, H. C. (1995). *Individualism & Collectivism*, Boulder, CO: Westview Press.

26 Hofstede (1980).

27 This discussion is synthesized from the following sources: Hofstede (1980, 1997, 2001); Chinese Culture Connection (1987), Chinese values and the search for culture-free dimensions of culture, *Journal of Cross-Cultural Psychology*, 18(2), 143–164. The most comprehensive report of scores using Hofstede's survey is reported in his 2001 work.

28 Katz, J. P., Werner, S., & Brouthers, L. (1999). Does winning mean the same thing around the world? National ideology and the performance of global competitors, *Journal of Business Research*, 44, 117–126.

29 Trompenaars & Hampden-Turner (1998).

30 Parsons & Shils (1951).

31 Trompenaars & Hampden-Turner (1998), p. 84.

32 Smith, P. B., Dugan, S., & Trompenaars, F. (1996), National culture and the values of organizational employees: A dimensional analysis across 43 nations, *Journal of Cross-Cultural Psychology*, 27, 231–264.

33 See also Hall, E. T. (1976), *Beyond Culture*, New York: Anchor Press/Doubleday.

34 Hampden-Turner, C., & and Trompenaars, A. (2000). *Building Cross-Cultural Competence: How to Create Wealth from Conflicting Values*, Chichester: John Wiley; Smith, P. B., Trompenaars, A., & Dugan, S. (1995), The Rotter Locus of Control scale in 43 countries: A test of cultural relativity, *International Journal of Psychology*, 30, 377–400. Rotter, J. B. (1966), Generalized expectancies for Internal vs. External control of reinforcement, *Psychological Monographs*, 80, 1–28.

35 Hall, E. T., & Hall, M. (1988), *Hidden Differences: Doing Business with the Japanese*, New York: Prentice Hall.

36 Hofstede (2001).

37 Gupta, V., Hanges, P. J., & Dorfman, P. (2002), Cultural clusters: Methodology and findings, *Journal of World Business*, 37, 11–15.

38 Peterson, M. F., & Smith, P. B. (2000), Meanings, organizations and culture: Using sources of meaning to make sense of organizational events, in N. M. Ashkenasy, C. P. M. Wilderom, & M. F. Peterson (eds.), *Handbook of Organizational Culture and Climate*, Thousand Oaks, CA: Sage, pp. 101–115. Smith, P. B., & Peterson, M. F. (1988), *Leadership, Organizations and Culture: An Event Management Perspective*, London: Sage. Smith, P. B., Peterson, M. F., & Schwartz, S. (2002), Cultural values, sources of guidance and their relevance to managerial behavior: A 47 nation study, *Journal of Cross Cultural Psychology*, 33, 188–208.

39 Osland, J. S., & Bird, A. (2000), Beyond sophisticated stereotyping: Cultural sensemaking in context, *Academy of Management Executive*, 14, 65–77.

40 Gomez, C. (in press), The influence of environmental, organizational, and HRM factors on employee behaviors in subsidiaries: A Mexican case study of organizational learning, *Journal of World Business*.

41 Rousseau, D. M., & Schalk, R. (eds.) (2000), *Psychological Contracts in Employment*, Thousand Oaks, CA: Sage.

42 Rousseau & Schalk (2000), p. 3.

43 Schein, E. H. (1984), Coming to a new awareness of organizational culture, *Sloan Management Review*, 25(2), 3–16. Hatch, M. J. (1993), The dynamics of organizational culture, *Academy of Management Review*, 18(4): 657–693.

44 Brannen, M. Y. (1994), Your next boss is Japanese: Negotiating cultural change at a western Massachusetts paper plant, Ph.D. dissertation, University of Massachusetts, Amherst. Brannen, M. Y. (1998), Negotiated culture in binational contexts: A model of culture change, *Anthropology of Work Review*, 18(2), 2–9. Brannen, M. Y. (2004), *Global Meeting Grounds: Negotiating Complex Cultural Contexts Across Organizations*, New York: Oxford University Press. Brannen, M. Y., Liker, J., & Fruin, M. (1999), Recontextualization and factory-to-factory knowledge transfer from Japan to the U.S.: The case of NSK, in J. Liker, M. Fruin, & P. Adler (eds.), *Remade in America: Transplanting and Transforming Japanese Production Systems*, New York: Oxford University Press. Brannen, M. Y., & Salk, J. (1999), Partnering across borders: Negotiating organizational culture in a German–Japanese joint-venture, *Human Relations*, 53(4), 451–487. Gluesing, J. (1995), Fragile alliances – Negotiating global teaming in a turbulent environment, Ph.D. Dissertation, Wayne State University. Kidahashi, M. (1987), Dual organization: A study of a Japanese-owned firms in the United States, Ph.D. Dissertation, Columbia University. Kleinberg, J. (1998), An ethnographic perspective on cross-cultural negotiation and cultural production, *Advances in Qualitative Organization Research*, 1, 201–249. Salk, J. E. (1992), International shared management joint venture teams: Their developmental patterns, challenges and possibilities, Ph.D. Dissertation, Sloan School of Management, Massachusetts Institute of Technology. Salk, J. E., & Brannen, M. Y. (2000), National culture, networks and individual influence in a multinational management team, *Academy of Management Journal*, 43(2), 191–212. Sumihara, N. (1992), A case study of structuration in a bicultural work organization: A study of a Japanese- owned and managed corporation in the U.S.A., Ann Arbor, MI: University of Michigan Dissertation Services.

45 Allport, G. W. (1937), *Personality: A Psychological Interpretation*, New York: Holt, Rinehart & Winston, p. 48.

46 McCrae, R. R., & Costa, P. T. Jr. (1997), Personality trait structure as a human universal, *American Psychologist*, 52, 509–516.

47 On the five factor model, see McCrae & Costa (1997) and Hogan, R. T. (1991), Personality and personality measurement, in M. D. Dunnette & L. M. Hough (eds.), *Handbook of Industrial and Organizational Psychology*, 2nd ed., Palo Alto, CA: Consulting Psychologists Press, vol. 2, pp. 873–919.

48 Triandis, H. C., & Suh, E. M. (2002), Cultural influences on personality, *Annual Review of Psychology*, 53, 133–160.

49 McClelland, D. C. (1961), *The Achieving Society*, New York: Van Nostrand Reinhold.

50 Fleishman, E. A. (1979), Evaluating physical abilities required by jobs, *Personnel Administrator*, June, 82–92.

51 Goleman, D. (1995), *Emotional Intelligence*, New York: Bantam Books.

52 Tajfel, H., & Turner, J. C. (1986), The social identity theory of intergroup behavior, in S. Worchel & W. G. Austin (eds.), *Psychology of Intergroup Relations*, Chicago: Nelson-Hall, pp. 7–24.

53 Nkomo, S. M., & Cox, T. Jr. (1996), Diverse identities in organizations, in S. R. Clegg, C. Hardy, & W. R. Nord (eds.), *Handbook of Organization Studies*, Thousand Oaks, CA: Sage, pp. 338–356.

54 Hofstede (2001).

55 Harrison, L. E. (1985), *Underdevelopment Is a State of Mind*, New York: Madison.

56 Inglehart (1995); Inglehart et al. (1998).

Part II

GLOBAL COMPETENCIES

3

Global Competencies: An Introduction

ALLAN BIRD AND JOYCE S. OSLAND

> *A few years back French and German managers met on a sunny day to discuss a possible joint venture between their two companies. After a productive morning spent identifying possible synergies as well as delineating key issues and concerns, they developed an agenda to guide further discussions and adjourned for lunch. Over lunch, one of the French managers commented on the beautiful weather and suggested that the group take the rest of the afternoon off and head out to a local soccer match. The Germans politely declined, and so the group returned to the office to continue discussions. But the progress of the morning soon disappeared as the French managers raised one concern after another. By the end of the day little progress had been made and both groups left with serious doubts about the possibility of a joint venture. What had started out on such a positive note now seemed headed for failure.*
>
> *In subsequent interviews, the German managers expressed confusion and frustration with the slow rate of progress in negotiations. They could not understand why the French were being so difficult. For their part, the French said they just couldn't seem to develop a good rapport with the Germans and were reluctant to move things forward until they did. Both sides knew there was a problem, but neither could point to anything specific.*

Our French and German managers find themselves bumping up against the reality of working in the "brave new world" of globalization. Despite all the ballyhoo and commotion about new business models, networked organizations, virtual teams, technological advance, and the like, the real work still has to be done in the trenches by managers who must rely on their knowledge and skill to get the job done. Getting the job done seems more difficult now, though, than it did before. We'll return to their plight later in this chapter and see if we can help them out. First, let's sort out effective global managing, what it means and what it takes.

The Search for Global Competencies

Current books on international management begin by describing the global business environment and its imperatives, explaining the importance of effective global management, and calling for global leadership. This clamor for global leaders and their development is often followed by a laundry list of "must have" characteristics for present or future global managers.[1] Absent from this discussion is an underlying model that explains how this list of managerial characteristics leads to effective management and how these attributes apply in given situations, in isolation or combination. Without a contextual understanding, the practical value of such lists is limited.

In Part II, "Global Competencies," we take a different approach. We begin with the distinction that, while many managers may work in a global context, not all are global managers. To get a better handle on how to tell the difference between the two, we go back to basics to get a sense of what it is that managers do. With this foundation laid, we then search for the set of *essential* traits, attitudes, orientations, and skills required of all effective global managers. This chapter sets the frame for our discussion in subsequent chapters in this part of the book by:

1 distinguishing between expert and novice global managers;
2 describing a dynamic process model that reflects how managers function; and
3 defining the specific attitudes, skills, and behavioral repertoire necessary for effective global management.

We call the various traits, attitudes, skills, and abilities that comprise global managerial expertise "global competencies." The extent to which these are present in any given manager is an indication of that person's general level of global managerial capability.

Later in this chapter we'll flesh out the components of global competency and address each competency in even greater depth in subsequent chapters.

Expert vs. Novice Global Managers

Experts are different from novices, not only because they do things better. Experts think differently.[2] When entering into a new situation they notice more and different types of cues, they interpret those cues differently, they choose from a different, wider range of appropriate actions than do novices, and then they execute/implement their chosen course of action at higher levels. In the case of global managers, these differences between novices and experts are magnified.

Dreyfus and Dreyfus[3] point out that novices begin by following rules; then, as they gain practical experience, they begin to understand general patterns. (Their framework is reflected in the evolution of mastery shown in table 3.1.) Once they become more competent, they recognize complexity and a larger set of cues. They are able to discern which cues are the most important and are able to move beyond strict adherence to rules and to think in terms of trade-offs. On attaining the expert stage, they can read situations without rational thought – they diagnose the situation unconsciously and respond intuitively because, over the years, they have developed the holistic recognition or mental maps

Table 3.1 The evolution of mastery

Stage	Level of mastery
Stage 1 Novice	Rules are learned as absolutes.
Stage 2 Advanced Beginner	Experience produces understanding that exceeds stated facts and rules.
Stage 3 Competence	Greater appreciation for task complexity. Recognition of larger set of cues and ability to focus on most important cues. Reliance on absolute rules begins to disappear; risk taking and complex trade-offs occur.
Stage 4 Proficiency	Calculation and rational analysis seem to disappear, and unconscious, fluid, effortless performance begins to emerge.
Stage 5 Expert	Holistic recognition and intuition rather than rules. Framing and reframing strategies as they read; changing cues that others do not perceive or read.

that allow for effortless framing and reframing of strategies and quick adaptation. Intuition is thus a "cognitive conclusion based on a decision-maker's previous experiences and emotional inputs"[4] and therefore a form of "compressed expertise." Klein calls this "recognition-primed decision-making": experts enter situations seeking cues that enable them to "recognize" the familiar from past experiences, thereby evoking expectations, goals, and responses.

The Effectiveness Cycle

To answer the question, "What's the difference between an expert and a novice global manager?," a more fundamental question must be addressed: "What is it that managers do?" The question isn't new. Managers and scholars have wrestled with it for at least a hundred years.[5] To cut through the myriad tasks – plan, organize, control, direct, and so forth – we adopt a process approach. At the most basic level, no matter what the task, the place or the people involved, what managers do can be broken down into a three-phase process. We call this the Effectiveness Cycle (see figure 3.1) because expert managers consistently perform at a high level in all three phases of the cycle. Conversely, novices may struggle with one or more of the phases, or encounter difficulty in performing the cycle consistently.

The first phase involves perception and analysis. An effective manager accurately decodes and diagnoses the situation, matching characteristics of the current situation to those experienced in the past, in the process scanning for relevant cues or their absence. Once the situation is "framed" in terms of experience and expectations, the manager

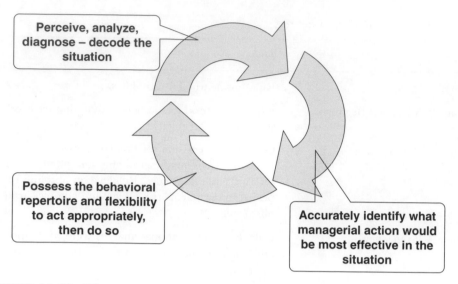

FIGURE 3.1 The Effectiveness Cycle: What effective managers do

establishes plausible goals that can be accomplished as an outcome of the situation. Based on the perception and analysis of phase one, and with one or more goals in mind, the manager moves into the second phase of the cycle: identification of one or more actions judged to be consistent with the situation and effective in achieving the goal. This phase involves knowledge about what managerial action will work in this specific instance. Such judgments are based on matching this situation with previous ones, along with the capacity to imagine and predict the results of various responses.[6] In this phase an expert manager draws upon a deep well of experiences, making fine-grained distinctions in the selection of subtly nuanced actions that exquisitely fit the specifics of the situation. The third phase shifts the activity from the cognitive processes in a manager's mind to the execution of the selected response. Knowledge of what to do, in and of itself, is insufficient here. A manager must possess the versatility and agility to carry out the chosen action successfully in a way that fits the demands of the situation.

The cycle repeats itself with each adjustment and adaptation that unfolds within the situation, and from one situation to the next. For example, a situation involving an interview with a low-performing subordinate may proceed along the lines of reprimand or admonition to work harder until it is disclosed that the subordinate has a recently developed medical condition, at which point the manager adjusts perceptions and analysis, and identifies and then implements a different course of action. Upon exiting the interview, in light of this new information, the manager may change his afternoon plans to include a consultation with the HR department about how to handle the employee's situation.

One final note: the Effectiveness Cycle can also be understood as a model of applied sensemaking. Considered in this way, managers perceive a situation, analyze it, select a response to the perceived situation, and implement the selected response. Their action prompts a response and alters the situation, thereby giving rise to new perceptions, analyses, and so on. Understood in this way, it is clear that the Effectiveness Cycle is affected by the panoply of perceptual biases and attributional errors that are even more pronounced in global settings.

GOING GLOBAL

The distinction between expert and novice managers is not the only one relevant to our topic. We must also recognize a fundamental distinction between domestic and global managers. That managers may be expert at operating within a single country is no guarantee that they will be equally talented when operating outside that country. The evidence is overwhelming that something more or different is required. Expert global managers are different from expert domestic managers, if for no other reason than that they are forced to adapt to the demands of significantly greater complexity. These demands include:

- a heightened need for cultural understanding within a setting characterized by wider-ranging diversity;
- greater need for broad knowledge that spans functions and nations;
- wider and more frequent boundary spanning both within and across organizational and national boundaries;
- more stakeholders to understand and consider when making decisions;
- a more challenging and expanded list of competing tensions both on and off the job;
- heightened ambiguity surrounding decisions and related outcomes/effects;
- more challenging ethical dilemmas relating to globalization.

Put simply, the transition from purely domestic to global is a quantum leap. Most managers don't notice the shift because there are few warning signs, companies do little to prepare them, and the jump often takes place over several years and a series of job rotations. As each new position or project moves a manager closer to the center of the global arena, the demands increase. Often the shift is most noticeable in the need to know more about more. Evolving global managers may feel overwhelmed by what they realize they don't know about other regions, countries, and cultures. They come to appreciate that they need "nuts and bolts" knowledge about how to do things or how to get things done across organizations, languages, and legal, political, and social systems. At the same time, they also come to realize that the specifics of "nuts and bolts" knowledge is only meaningful if it can be placed in a proper context, which calls for broad *and* deep understanding of cultural, religious, philosophical, and historical issues in a country or geographic region.[7] For example, in the opening vignette, the Germans and French undoubtedly had some prior knowledge of each other's culture and history; yet it was not enough to allow them to accurately interpret the cues available to them in this context.

In addition to the acquisition of an extensive knowledge base, global managers demand a more extensive scanning capability and behavioral repertoire. In particular, executives working 24-7-365 in an international context have more frequent, novel, significant, and emotionally intense international and intercultural experiences.[8] These experiences often crystallize into a form of expertise that is hard for novices to replicate.

To get a flavor of what is required of an expert global manager, apply the Effectiveness Cycle by imagining yourself in the following situation:

Phase One: You are meeting with the division head of one of your company's recently acquired Latin American subsidiaries. His name is Carlos Ramirez. You know nothing about him other than his name and position. As an IT manager, you have been sent from headquarters in Europe to convince the subsidiary to implement a new accounting system. You have heard that this subsidiary has a reputation for being fairly resistant to change. Warned by others at headquarters that Ramirez had agreed to previous corporate initiatives but failed to follow up, you are hoping your intermediate skills in Spanish are up to the challenge.

After arriving in Panama City the day before, you head out for the company offices early the next morning, arriving at 8:45 A.M. You take the elevator up to Senor Ramirez's floor where you are met by an attractive, young female receptionist who escorts you to his office.

The office is a private one with dark, carved colonial furniture and paintings that look as if they were produced by local artists. There are also pictures of Señor Ramirez shaking hands with VIPs, perhaps even Panamanian presidents, given the flags in the background. You pick up the heavy smell of tobacco in the air. As you walk across the thick carpet to greet Señor Ramirez, you note that he is a gentleman of about sixty years of age. He rises to shake your hand and then offers you a seat. Señor Ramirez asks about your plane trip and inquires whether this is your first visit to Panama. Upon hearing that it is, he extols the virtues of Panama, suggests several places of interest that you should visit, and offers to take you to see the Panama Canal. Señor Ramirez mentions several times that the canal is now in Panamanian hands and that there is no need for outsiders to run it. While wondering whether you really have time for field trips, you glance to the side and spot a computer sitting in total isolation on an adjacent table; the computer is not turned on. You decide you had better accept the invitation and immediately raise the issue of the new accounting system.

Señor Ramirez gives a vague response, and at this moment, the vice-president of marketing enters the office. What happens? There is no further opportunity to broach the subject, but on your way out you ask if you could meet with the people responsible for IT and accounting. You sent e-mails to these people two weeks ago and expected the subsidiary to have scheduled appointments with them. Señor Ramirez informs you that these people have been summoned to an unexpected meeting and cannot see you until tomorrow. Back in your hotel after the tour, you consider your next step, wondering all the way how to make sense of your first contact with Señor Ramirez and what his response really means.

Beginning with the first phase of the Effectiveness Cycle, how would you analyze the situation? Which cues would you select from the above description? What additional cues might you scan for? Do the cues confirm your expectations? How would you frame this situation? How should you interpret the office setting, or the fact that Señor Ramirez invited you to see the Canal yet did not give you the help you needed for your project? What experiences have you had in your past work in other cultures that might help you make an accurate assessment? Based on the framing you have done, and your own background, what attributions might you make about Señor Ramirez and this situation?

Let's return to the example and follow the trail of an expert global manager as she works through the situation.

The Expert in Phase One: Our expert global manager decided that, while it was tempting to be upset about the lack of progress on this first day, she needed to be patient and reserve judgment. She remembers that Panama is a culture that values establishing relationships before getting to work on tasks and is glad she accepted the canal invitation. There are several cues that indicate Señor Ramirez's pride in his country – the traditional furniture, the local paintings, and the photos. Furthermore, with his comments on the reversion of the canal to Panamanian hands, Señor Ramirez may be signaling his own feelings about the autonomy he wants for his division and his concerns about corporate initiatives. Our expert is not positive about this but will treat it as a hypothesis she can test in future interactions. She ponders the unused computer. Is Señor Ramirez simply very neat or is he computer-illiterate? She has received e-mails from Ramirez, but perhaps his secretary downloads and sends all his messages (as she observed with some older managers in Europe and the United States). This, too, becomes a working hypothesis, because it might explain the vagueness of his answer and could have implications for how open the office is to new technology.

Moving to Phase Two, what confidence do you have in being able to accurately identify an effective course of action? Does your behavioral repertoire include appropriate options from which to choose?

Let's see how our expert works through Phase Two.

The Expert in Phase Two: Based on the cues she interpreted, our expert global manager decides that she should be careful to treat Señor Ramirez with great respect and be especially careful to avoid making comments that denigrate Panama or his division. She knows from reading up on Panamanian history that sovereignty and outside intervention are sometimes touchy issues. She decides to develop a trusting relationship with Ramirez so he will feel free to tell her what he really thinks about the new accounting system. She also decides to have separate meetings with the IT and accounting managers to figure out who are the key players in this situation and identify the concerns and problems she has to confront. Our expert decides that she needs a cultural mentor to explain what's going on in this division and is going to be on the lookout for a likely candidate to fill this role.

In Phase Three, having selected a course of action, how confident are you in being able to implement it successfully? Will your limitations in Spanish be an obstacle? Do you have a strategy for working around it?

The Expert in Phase Three: Our global expert phoned an IT employee whom she had befriended when he went through a training program at headquarters. She peppered him with some questions about the division and asked who could provide the kind of inside information she needed to be successful at this project. He named a senior secretary who was plugged into networks all over the division. The expert asked Señor Ramirez if she could have this secretary assigned to her for the duration of her visit. He agreed, and the secretary was quite helpful in explaining what was happening and why, as well as giving other, more general advice to our expert. After the visit to the canal, the expert invited Señor Ramirez and his wife to dinner to reciprocate his hospitality. A few days later, Señor Ramirez felt comfortable enough to express his complaints about the way corporate imposed initiatives on subsidiaries without first ensuring that the changes would work in a foreign context. "We get these programs *precocinado* (pre-cooked) without ever being asked for our input." Our expert suggested having a focus group in the Panamanian subsidiary react to the proposed accounting system to see if local modifications were necessary or possible. As it turned out, her question about Ramirez's computer skills was answered; his hobby was building computers from scratch, and he hated a cluttered work area. She met individually with both the IT and accounting managers. She was able to do a favor for the IT manager by putting him in touch with the right person at headquarters. Her Spanish was good enough to allow her to establish a connection with the IT staff around technology issues. After figuring out how they managed the current accounting system, she was able to demonstrate the savings in both time and cost that would result from the new system. By the end of her visit, she had developed enough rapport with various employees and managers to be privy to their concerns about the new system. At Ramirez's request, she presented ways to resolve these issues in a final meeting, where Ramirez and the other managers gave their support to the project. She returned to headquarters and relayed the Panamanian suggestions for improving the new accounting system.

It should be clear from the exercise above that the work of a global manager is complex. Truly expert global managers are a rare breed. At the same time, the Effectiveness Cycle provides a model for identifying what competencies are required of effective global managers. Further, an understanding of the bases of expertise suggests that global managers can be developed.

This may be a good point at which to return to our troubled French and German managers and see if we can sort out their difficulties. French managers often seek to establish trust relationships through participation in "illicit" acts that serve to bind participants together in a shared transgression. Called *complicité*, participation in such an act tacitly signals to all involved a willingness to share a secret indiscretion, thereby tying them together. The suggestion over lunch to take the afternoon off was an offer to engage in such an act. The French accurately perceived, decoded, and analyzed the situation. The progress of the morning and the good feelings over lunch led them to conclude that the Germans were genuinely interested in partnering. Unfortunately, the French managers had a Phase Two breakdown when they failed to correctly identify an appropriate course of action. The course they chose may have been appropriate when working with other French managers, but not with the Germans. It is possible that the French managers lacked the behavioral repertoire to choose an appropriate course. In any case, having chosen the wrong action for this situation, Phase Three failed as well.

The cycle is iterative; it continues on from one situation to the next, which is to say that failures in working the cycle were not finished. The French managers then foundered in Phase One of the next iteration of the cycle. They misinterpreted German rejection of the offer as a sign that the Germans were not committed to the relationship. However the Germans *were* committed to the relationship, something they had signaled by indicating a desire to go back to the office and resume discussions.

The Germans had their own difficulties. They had a Phase One failure – misinterpreting the French offer to take the afternoon off as a lack of work ethic, rather than an attempt to build trust. Upon returning to the office after lunch, they failed again, this time to accurately interpret the change in French behavior, thereby making it nearly impossible to choose an appropriate response to the situation.

Once the German and French managers came to understand the nature of the problem, which involved their differing approaches to establishing and signaling trust, they were able to reduce their levels of frustration and establish trusting and committed relationships. These relationships became the foundation for successful negotiations and the eventual establishment of a joint venture. Equally important, for both groups the experience became a source of insight in understanding subsequent dealings with one another and in being sensitized to the challenges of accurately understanding and responding to dealings in other intercultural settings.

GLOBAL COMPETENCIES

Expert global managers combine the Effectiveness Cycle with a set of competencies that relate to all three phases. The identification of a core set of competencies, however, has not proved an easy task. Researchers and managers alike have struggled to come up with a comprehensive set.

On the corporate side, the range of competencies can prove intimidating. Chase Manhattan Bank developed a model for its global leaders that identifies 250 competencies.[9] Another MNC started with a list of 200 competencies, but was able to narrow it down to 160.[10] In contrast, some firms, such as IBM and 3M, have been able to winnow the list of competencies down to 11 and 12, respectively.

It should come as no surprise that academic researchers have found competency identification to be an equally challenging task. In their review of the relatively young field of research on global leadership, Mendenhall and Osland were able to identify 53 different competencies.[11] Noting that there were numerous areas of overlap across the various lists, they eventually settled on grouping competencies into six categories: traits and values, cognitive orientations, cross-cultural relationship skills, global organizing expertise, global business expertise, and visioning. In the separate, but related field of expatriate manager success, academic scholars have identified an even larger range of competencies. Efforts to synthesize research in this area have encountered similar problems in overlapping concepts and differing definitions and have settled on similar resolutions, grouping competencies into categories.[12]

One striking characteristic of both the expatriate and global leadership competency research is that it has, for the most part, taken a *content* approach. There is an unspoken assumption that effective managerial action will flow from an appropriate *content* of competencies.

We adopted a different perspective, choosing to focus on the *process* of global managing. Consequently, we have reviewed the work of academics and practitioners alike in search of competencies that support the *process* of managing.[13]

We begin by assuming that global managers, like anyone involved in cross-cultural work, should have certain threshold competencies. The foundation level comprises "global" knowledge. Managers can't function in the absence of knowledge, so in many ways this is the most basic element. Knowledge, however, doesn't represent a competence; rather, it is a resource. In that respect, knowledge is not only a foundation, but also a

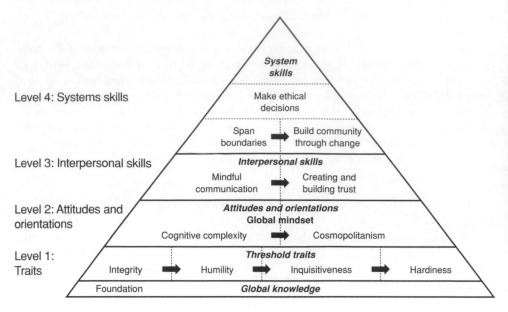

FIGURE 3.2 The building blocks of global competencies

leaven, to mix our metaphors, in that it pervades and is essential to all other competencies. The basic model for global competency is illustrated in figure 3.2 as a triangle with a foundation and four levels.

With knowledge as a foundation, Level 1 consists of four specific traits: integrity, humility, inquisitiveness, and hardiness. Level 2 of the triangle shifts to attitudes and orientations that influence how managers perceive and interpret the world. Attitudes are, in turn, followed by Level 3, which is associated with interpersonal interaction, with a particular focus on relationships within and among individuals and/or groups. The top of the triangle reflects upward movement to the level of systems – organizational and/or sociocultural. The central focus at this level is the ability to manage people and the systems in which they work. Taken as a whole, these competencies are meta-skills that encapsulate many others required for global work. The different levels of the model represent a progression from traits to attitudes, to interpersonal skills, and finally to systems skills, which involve interactions characterized by complex understandings and relationships. We'll briefly explain the logic of the framework, followed by a more in-depth introduction of each aspect.

The logic of the framework

The triangle, with its foundation and four levels, suggests a progression that is cumulative, advancing from bottom to top and left to right. Managers require a wide range and depth of various types of knowledge to work effectively. Without this knowledge they are unprepared to manage in a global context. They may be called upon to do so, and they may have some successes. But without a solid foundation of knowledge they cannot excel.

At the foundation, *knowledge* can be acquired, but knowledge alone is insufficient. What cannot be acquired or significantly changed is a core set of traits that facilitate the long-term development of global managerial abilities, skills, and knowledge. Though there are a variety of traits that contribute to making a good global manager, at Level 1 four are essential: integrity, humility, inquisitiveness, and hardiness. Without integrity managers cannot develop the respect they will need from both superiors and followers over the long haul. Without humility, managers are not open to learning from other cultures or organizations and are not willing to be taught by others. Humility, however, can be a passive trait unless it is combined with an inner curiosity, adventurousness or desire to learn. The desire to have new experiences and to learn from them, we call "inquisitiveness." The final trait that ties the other three together is hardiness. Without this persistence and resilience, it is difficult to preserve integrity, remain humble or maintain an inquisitive spirit. Without hardiness, managers find it difficult to rise to the unique challenges of global work.

The possession of the right types of knowledge, mixed with the four traits of Level 1, allow for the development of orientations and attitudes that contribute to managing effectively in a global setting. At Level 2, cognitive complexity reflects an ability to see multiple perspectives and consider ideas, people, and situations from a variety of angles. When cognitive complexity is joined with an awareness of the world and a positive orientation toward it, cosmopolitanism, then managers have acquired a global mindset that enables them to think outside the narrow confines of a single cultural view.

Knowledge, personality traits, and attitudes are of little worth unless they can be translated into action. In its most basic form, effective managerial behavior in a global context involves the ability to communicate across cultures. At Level 3, mindful, intercultural communication is predicated on an awareness of *self,* coupled with sensitivity to the situation and persons in it. Once mindful communication is established, effective managers are able to create and then build trust.

The capstone of the triangle, Level 4, is a set of skills that involve managing the systems of business. Effective global managers possess the ability to span boundaries, whether those boundaries be within the firm, between the firm and external others, or among other less obvious boundaries such as those among indirect stakeholders. The current environment also requires that managers be able to manage change. Sometimes the change is at the level of the individual, which usually involves some form of learning. On other occasions the focus of the change involves organizational units or targets that extend beyond the boundaries of the firm. In such instances, in addition to catalyzing learning on a larger scale, global managers need to create or build communities – of employees, and various stakeholders or organizations within and beyond the industry. The final system skill is more nuanced. It is the ability to make decisions and take actions that conform to a high ethical standard. How does this relate to a system? The answer is simple: to make ethical decisions a global manager must be able to see things from a larger perspective, must be able to think in terms of systems and in terms of the implications of individual and organizational actions for all parties that might be affected. Decision-making tends to violate ethical standards when it loses sight of the larger system and, instead, focuses on the narrow concerns or interests of individuals, organizations or industries. The system skill of ethical decision-making actually brings us back to the first threshold traits, because when decision-making is ethical, it reinforces integrity and humility.

In the following paragraphs, we will provide further explanations for the foundation and Level 1 of our pyramid. The top layers of the pyramid, Levels 2, 3, and 4, are the subjects of the remaining chapters in this part of the book.

Foundation: Global knowledge

Global managers require an exceedingly broad range of knowledge that includes, but is not limited to, the normal knowledge acquisition in the realm of function, organization, and business industry. While these categories are useful, they limit our ability to appreciate other types of knowledge that managers call upon in the various situations they confront. Recent research that visualizes careers as knowledge inflows and outflows uses a framework that more clearly describes the various types of knowledge that global managers require.[14] Kidd and Teramoto[15] have developed a four-class taxonomy of "knowings" that is useful in dissecting the knowledge content requirements for global managers. By using this typology, we can also distinguish between the knowledge sets of global managers and domestic managers.

Know who refers to a person's social capital, that is, the actual and potential resources embedded within, available through, and derived from the network of relationships an individual possesses. Examples of *know who* would include such knowledge as having a contact in a Korean *chaebol* (conglomerate) willing to make introductions on one's behalf to local firms, or having business-school classmates who are key decision-makers in Japan's Ministry of Trade, Economy and Industry. Knowing who involves not only an acquaintance with others but also an ability to draw upon various resources through those relationships. As one global manager stated, "It's all about collecting IOUs."

Know how refers to a person's set of skills and knowledge about how to do work or how to accomplish tasks. For example, techniques for giving *face* in Chinese negotiations would be one type of know how. Another variety of know how would be methods for structuring invoicing schedules to offset the effects of hyperinflation in Argentina.

Know what relates to the nature and extent of a person's understanding about specific projects, products, services, or organizational arrangements. A knowledge of Procter & Gamble's product offerings in German or an understanding of the structure of Volkswagen's US subsidiary constitute types of *know what*.

Know why relates to the nature and extent of a person's identification with the firm's culture and strategy: for example, knowing why the firm chose to set up an overseas operation in Chile rather than Brazil. Knowing why gives meaning and purpose to organizational and individual action.

This taxonomy provides insight into the interrelatedness of different types of knowledge and suggests additional considerations. First, while the demands of a given position or context may lead to an emphasis of one type of knowledge over another, effective global managers probably require significant development in all four. Indeed, the continued growth and development of a useful global knowledge base is probably predicated on a rough balance across the four types. A heavy emphasis on *know who*, for example, may be of little value when not used in conjunction with *know how*, *know what*, and *know why*.

Here's an example of an Indian manager-turned-entrepreneur who capitalized on the knowledge he acquired in years of international work with a large, high-tech firm. He saw the promise in a new invention to monitor people under anesthesia (know why). Rather than locating all the operations in one country, he organized a firm to bring together

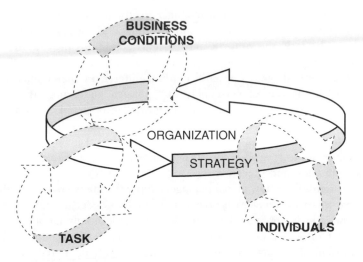

FIGURE 3.3 The global contexts of culture

people in his extensive personal network: mathematicians in Switzerland, R&D engineers and manufacturers in India, and sales people in Silicon Valley (know who). His lengthy experience working with different cultures made it possible to convince people to join him in this venture (know how). Because of his familiarity with technology and new products, all the IT and accounting functions are handled on the Web (know what). His experience with marketing led him to develop a marketing plan that focuses only on countries with either "lots of money" or "lots of people" (know why). Thus, his reliance on all four types of knowledge allows him to run successfully a worldwide company with a very small number of people.

When managers can appropriately apply the elements of these four types of knowing to a given situation, as our Indian manager did in his analysis of a business opportunity and the resultant innovative organization of the start-up, we call this *attributional knowledge*.[16] Attributional knowledge incorporates the range of knowledge necessary to accurately interpret a situation and to identify and select an appropriate response. In the Effectiveness Cycle, attributional knowledge is critical to accuracy in Phases One and Two. *Know what, know who*, and *know why* may be more relevant to Phase One, while *know how* is central to Phase Two. In some respects attributional knowledge is an outgrowth of increasing mastery of a range of global situations in that it demonstrates an ability to synthesize disparate pieces of knowledge into coherent configurations that enables accurate sense-making – perception, interpretation, and analysis.

As mastery of knowledge is combined with experiences in a range of situations, managers begin to recognize patterns and connect those patterns to successful responses. Managers can acquire attributional knowledge in three ways: from personal experience, vicariously from others' experience, and from cultural mentoring.

While managers often have proficiency in matters related to their organizations and industries, they may lack expertise and proficiency in the cultural or country-context area. Referring to the perspective introduced in the preceding part, figure 3.3 presents the general categories that a manager's knowledge must encompass. Even a moment's reflection on the types of knowledge a manager needs, however, reveals how vast the knowledge demands can become for the global manager. Knowledge about individuals, the organization, the task, the strategy, and business conditions provide the broadest of categories. For example, knowledge of individuals should also embrace knowledge of human nature in general, and aspects of cultural differences that influence individual variation, as well as aspects of personality and physical differences that also explain human variation. And of course, this type of knowledge of people as individuals must accompany knowledge about actual individuals – superiors, subordinates, colleagues and clients. In a similar fashion, managers must complement general knowledge about business disciplines, industries, and markets with knowledge of specific professional disciplines, specific industries, and specific markets.

Turning our attention to how global managers apply the knowledge bases they possess, we can observe them bringing to bear a variety of knowledge in any given situation. Often the knowledge is configured in complex, dynamic combinations of the general and the specific. Consider a performance appraisal interview between a British superior and an Indonesian subordinate in the accounting division of a manufacturing firm's Indonesian subsidiary. As the British manager approaches the interview, she must be knowledgeable about situation-general aspects of the interview; that is, what is the primary function of a performance appraisal? What are the different ways in which a performance appraisal may be conducted? What are the possible roles of superiors and subordinates in such an interview? At the same time, she must also be knowledgeable about the situation-specific aspects of this particular interview: What understanding and expectations do Indonesians in general and this Indonesian in particular hold regarding performance appraisals? What are the performance standards in the Indonesian subsidiary? Expert global managers diagnose the context and select the general or specific knowledge that matches the situation, and dismiss knowledge that is not applicable.

It is obvious that the knowledge requirements are enormous and the probability that novice managers will either possess the requisite knowledge or be able to configure it in a way that will allow accurate analysis and selection of appropriate response is low. Many talented managers with limited international experience have no doubt achieved expertise in some areas but attained only the novice or advanced beginner stage in other areas, particularly in terms of cultural relations and culture-specific knowledge.

With time and experience, the volume and value of each type of knowing may increase. It is important to recognize that, though global knowledge should increase over time, the rates of increase for particular types of knowing may vary according to the opportunities and demands of specific positions and personal disposition to learn. Finally, in considering knowledge evolution over time, it is important to recognize that not only will knowledge be acquired; it will also be lost. For instance, *know who* is lost or altered when acquaintances transfer to a new business unit, leave the company or retire. In a similar vein, *know how* may be lost when situations calling for certain skills disappear due to taking on a new assignment, receiving a promotion or joining a new project.

Level 1: Threshold traits

Nearly fifty years of research on expatriate managers, combined with recent work on global leaders, have generated a lengthy, if sometimes confusing, list of personality-based competencies. The term "personality-based competencies" is itself misleading, since it suggests that aspects of one's self are somehow skills. With this in mind, we set out two important distinctions. The first distinction we make is between competencies and traits. Competencies are abilities, skills or knowledge usually acquired through experience. In contrast, personality is a relatively enduring set of characteristics, tendencies and temperaments significantly formed by inheritance and by sociocultural and environmental factors.[17] For shorthand purposes, we'll use "trait" to denote the specific aspects of personality in which we are interested.[18] Traits may predict success, but because of their enduring nature, they cannot be easily or, in most cases, significantly altered. Competencies, however, can be taught or acquired. For example, people can learn how to interact effectively with people from other cultures. It is far harder to convert people who are pessimists into optimists.

The second distinction we make is between traits that may contribute to successful global managing versus those that are essential. From the 1960s, spurred in the United States in large measure by the establishment of the Peace Corps, a body of research has developed that focuses on traits associated with successful work overseas. Well into the 1980s much of this research remained anecdotal and prescriptive, often based on the personal experience of the writer. Not surprisingly, the lists of traits were as varied as the number of authors. Nor was there much agreement as to which traits should comprise the list.[19] Beginning in the 1980s, a new crop of researchers began to sort through the lists and conduct more systematic and rigorous research. Their efforts to synthesize the lists and organize what was known emerged in the form of a rough consensus as to which traits correlated with success.[20] We have chosen to focus on a subset that we label "threshold traits." The four threshold traits – integrity, humility, inquisitiveness and hardiness – are essential. Without them a global manager cannot succeed over time. While other traits also may contribute to managerial success in a global setting, these four are required.

These threshold traits – integrity, humility, inquisitiveness, and hardiness – show up in one form or another in each of the lists we have studied, stretching back through those developed from anecdote and experience and forward to current empirical studies and field research.[21] In several recent studies, investigators have examined how core aspects of the personality relate to effectiveness overseas.[22] This body of work focuses on the Big Five personality characteristics of emotional stability, extrovertedness, openness, agreeableness, and conscientiousness. Within the field of personality research, these five have been found to be the most stable and enduring traits. Some – openness, emotional stability, and extrovertedness – are particularly relevant to managing globally. Other researchers have worked with previously developed lists, confirming and clarifying relationships.[23] For example, Arthur and Bennett confirmed that integrity, tolerance, and flexibility were aspects of personality associated with success.[24] In 60 interviews, Wills and Barham identified core characteristics of successful international managers: a sense of humility; emotional self-awareness and resilience; psychological maturity, including the curiosity to learn and a present-day orientation to time; cognitive complexity, including cultural empathy and active listening; risk acceptance; and emotional support of the family.[25]

Each of the following subsections introduces one of the four threshold traits. Keep in mind that each of these traits encompasses a range of qualities and has myriad outward manifestations. The traits are sequenced to reflect the way in which they tend to complement and build on each other.

Integrity. Perhaps one of the greatest challenges that global managers confront is how to maintain integrity in their professional and personal lives across distance, time, and culture. Without integrity, the efficacy of other traits and competencies is compromised. As Black and associates note, "Integrity forms the bedrock of character and is essential in establishing genuine emotional connections with people."[26]

Integrity derives from the Latin *integritas*, meaning "whole," and is defined as "a steadfast adherence to a strict moral or ethical code; the state of being unimpaired; the quality or condition of being whole, undivided."[27] The absence of a clearly defined personal ethical code leaves managers susceptible to the pressures and vagaries of shifting situational demands and ambiguous standards. We can extrapolate from research on children of expatriate missionary couples, which concludes that a strong set of religious beliefs or moral principles serve as an important anchor in maintaining identity and mental well-being in another culture.[28] Kelley and Meyer suggest selecting people for international work based on their "personal autonomy," defined as a well-developed sense of self and a firmly rooted belief system.[29] In cross-cultural settings, where pressure to adapt or fit in are combined with incomplete and inaccurate understandings, integrity can help managers avoid making decisions or taking actions that would cause them pain and embarrassment further down the road.

For global managers, having integrity also means that they act with consistency. Consistency, as guided by a clear set of values, across all aspects of life and across all situations, enables others to trust managers. Integrity also implies *completeness* in the sense of being well-rounded and maintaining appropriate balance in what managers do and who they are.

The significance of integrity is borne out by research on its relation to success in cross-cultural, expatriate, and global assignments. After reviewing the literature and interviewing 101 executives chosen by their peers as the best at leading globally, McCall and Hollenbeck included honesty and integrity as critical key traits for global executives.[30] Another study of 300 expatriates hailing from 26 countries and assigned to working in 43 different countries also found integrity to be a critical factor in managerial success.[31]

Humility. Not a single study of effectiveness in global assignments has ever left the notion of openness off the list of key traits. However, the wide variety of terms used – flexibility, openness, humility, adaptability, curiosity, inquisitiveness, cross-cultural interest, open-mindedness, sense of adventure, and learning orientation, to name a few – led us to look more closely at what people meant by these terms. We discovered two types of openness traits; one we label humility, the other inquisitiveness.

Humility is an unusual term to use in a business context, perhaps because the word is often used to describe someone who is rather timid or unassuming. A thoughtful consideration of the dictionary definition led us to a different conclusion. Humility is thought and deed marked by meekness or modesty in behavior, attitude or spirit. Humility is the showing of deferential respect.[32]

Humility in the context of global managing refers to the willingness to learn from others and not assume that one has all the correct answers.[33] In other words, to have humility is to be teachable. Framed in this way, humility involves a sort of "passive" openness: open-mindedness in thought, and willingness to listen and learn from others. It is the opposite of the arrogance we associate with "the Ugly American" or "Ugly __(insert the appropriate nationality)".

Interestingly, the inclusion of humility in the list of success factors for cross-cultural and global assignments is relatively recent and still somewhat rare. McCall and Hollenbeck include it on their list of key competencies, culled from their review of the literature and interviews with 101 global executives.[34] Moreover, the emphasis on humility coincides with current findings on leadership in general. Recent articles on CEOs who have led companies through significant transformations and were subsequently viewed as global leaders point to the importance of humility in learning and leading, as well as in building trust and community.[35]

Inquisitiveness. The active variety of openness is inquisitiveness. Broadly defined, it is an inclination to investigate and to pursue knowledge, often conveying a sense of being unduly curious and inquiring.[36] For global managers, inquisitiveness refers to a deep curiosity about other peoples and cultures. It is an interest in what makes people similar and what makes people different, an interest in how other people live and work.[37]

Black and associates cite it as one of six key attributes they identified in successful global managers. They go on to note that managers who possess this trait "approach everyday business as an adventure and press beyond the horizon of everyone else's reality."[38] One can almost feel the excitement in listening to how one manager described what it means to be inquisitive: "I just itch to get to the next new place and learn what it is like. In fact, my work is like living in a big theme park and the theme park is the world."[39]

By contrast, global managers who lack inquisitiveness are what Mary Catherine Bateson calls those who "choose not to learn and therefore not to change except in superficial ways."[40] Managers without inquisitiveness may seek learning opportunities but, when offered, fail to take full advantage of them.[41] They go on global assignments, they live outside their own countries, but they lack a curiosity about the world beyond the narrow space they occupy.

Hardiness. The last of the four threshold traits, hardiness, is defined as being in robust and sturdy good health; being courageous and intrepid; capable of surviving unfavorable conditions.[42] If integrity is the bedrock foundation and humility and inquisitiveness the twin pillars that shape an outlook on the world, then hardiness is the capstone that fixes the first three firmly in place.

The concept of hardiness comes to us from the literature on stress and Big Five personality research. Within the Big Five, hardiness is usually referred to as emotional stability, a factor found to relate to expatriate performance.[43] It goes by other names as well. McCall and Hollenbeck call it "resilience."[44] Meyers & Kelly call it "emotional resilience"[45] and characterize it in this fashion: "The emotionally resilient person has the ability to deal with stressful feelings in a constructive way and to 'bounce back' from them. Emotionally resilient people . . . have confidence in their ability to cope with ambiguity . . . and have a positive sense of humor and self-regard." We can see a link to emotional intelligence in this description.

Hardiness also refers to a stress-resistant personality construct that influences how people perceive and experience stress. According to Maddi and Kobasa, hardy people perceive potentially stressful events as interesting and meaningful, see themselves as capable of changing events because they have control over them, and see change as normal and an opportunity for growth.[46] As a result, stress has less impact on hardy people.

Coping with stress and recovering from shocks and strains is an essential aspect of working globally.[47] Kuhlmann and Stahl propose that expatriates' ability to manage and cope with stress has a major influence on their adjustment and development.[48] In international work, the normal job stressors are joined by the uncertainty of dealing with another culture and different work practices. Furthermore, the broadened job scope of most global managers involves significantly more responsibility, more balls to juggle.

One source of stress, culture shock, is perhaps the most widely cited challenge to working effectively outside one's own culture. Befus defines culture shock as "an adjustment reaction syndrome caused by cumulative, multiple and interactive stress in the intellectual, behavioral, emotional, and physiological levels of a person recently relocated to an unfamiliar culture, and it is characterized by a variety of symptoms."[49] The resilience associated with the threshold trait of hardiness is valuable as the manager, either novice or expert, confronts culture shock.

Though a global manager may possess integrity, humility, and inquisitiveness in large amounts, without hardiness, failure is virtually guaranteed. The flux and flow of global work, the ubiquitous challenges, the tension of ambiguity, and the intensity of interdependence make short shrift of the brittle, emotionally unstable manager who finds these demands burdensome rather than energizing.

Selecting global managers

The next question for most managers is how to use the model levels we have described so far in terms of selecting the right people for global work.

Knowledge: We can test candidates' factual knowledge about global business and culture, and we can explore through interviews their ability to put that knowledge to use in practical situations.

Integrity: past actions and personal history are the best gauges of integrity. Actions speak louder than words, which points to the necessity of carefully checking references and eliciting critical incidents concerning ethical dilemmas in interviews.

Humility: checking references and in particular questioning others who worked below (rather than above) candidates about their willingness to learn and the level of respect they employ with others is one way to assess this trait. Almost everyone treats higher-ups with respect. Their general level of respectfulness to others is evident in how they treat everyone in the hierarchy. Asking for critical incidents about successes and failures, as well as humbling experiences, can also indicate the presence or absence of humility.

Inquisitiveness: job interviews can include questions geared toward what candidates have learned and figured out. In particular, we can look for efforts they have made to understand *why* things occur.

Hardiness: there is a 50-item instrument survey that measures hardiness, called the Personal Views Survey.[50] Additionally, there are a variety of instruments that measure Big Five personality characteristics, including hardiness. Candidates could also be asked for critical incidents related to stress and difficult times in their lives.

Finally, assessment centers could be used to determine whether candidates possess the necessary global knowledge and the four threshold traits.

It is possible to train executives to acquire the types of knowledge required for global managing. Threshold traits are less trainable; they can be nudged over time, but the presence or absence of such traits and the degree to which candidates possess them is more or less subject to change.

How the Global Competency Model Works

Let's return to the Effectiveness Cycle and consider how the various elements of the Global Competency Model's pyramid fit together. Table 3.2 shows the phases of the cycle and their relation to the global competencies framework. Global knowledge, humility, inquisitiveness, and hardiness contribute to accurately perceiving and analyzing the situation. Global knowledge, global mindset, integrity, and making ethical decisions play a role in identifying the most effective managerial action to take. Global mindset, mindful communication, creating and building trust, spanning boundaries, and building community through managing change – five of the six true competencies – come into play in the third phase, where managers must have the behavioral repertoire and flexibility to take action.

Outstanding global managers not only do a great job of working the effectiveness cycle – they also seek to develop greater skill at managing the process in themselves and others. In similar fashion, they are concerned with helping others develop the global competencies we've described in this chapter.

Over the course of writing this part of the book, we came to realize that the pyramid of global competencies first presented in figure 3.2, in a way, is both dynamic and interrelated. The building blocks metaphor is appropriate for initial description, but does not capture the dynamic way the global competencies interrelate in the process of managing. In reality, the competencies may be more accurately conceived of as being like a set of concentric circles (see figure 3.4). The knowledge, traits, and competencies of our framework originate inside the manager and extend outward. Traits and attitudes are internally

TABLE 3.2 Applying the building blocks within the Effectiveness Cycle and beyond

Phase 1 Perceive/analyze	Phase 2 Know effective action	Phase 3 Possess behavior repertoire and flexibility
Global knowledge	Global knowledge	Global mindset
Humility	Global mindset – Cosmopolitanism	Mindful communication
Inquisitiveness	Integrity	Create and build trust
Hardiness	Make ethical decisions	Span boundaries
Global mindset Cognitive complexity		Building community through managing change

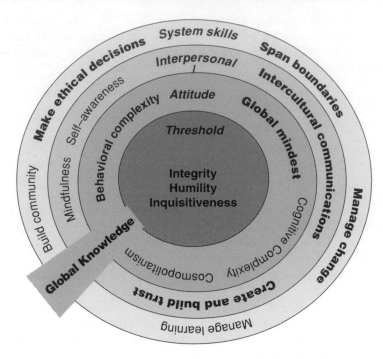

FIGURE 3.4 Global competencies

generated and comprehended, but externally manifested. Interpersonal skills involve the extension of the individual manager's influence through engaging others at the individual and group levels. System skills extend the manager's influence beyond the individual or group, branching out within the organization and beyond. Systems skills reflect the exercise of influence at a distance. As such, they have the potential to exert the greatest impact on the largest number of people. They can have this impact only if supported by expert interpersonal skills, which are in turn buttressed by appropriate attitudes and the right mix of traits.

Summary

In this introduction we have presented the Effectiveness Cycle, describing the process managers undergo when they are confronted with work situations, and we have pointed out the difference between expert and novice global managers. This led to the introduction and explanation of the model of global competency. We have reviewed its foundation level (knowledge) and explained the Level 1 threshold traits of integrity, humility, inquisitiveness, and hardiness. This introduction has begun the task of defining the specific attitudes, skills, and behavioral repertoires necessary for effective global management. The following chapters will complete the job by describing each global competency in greater detail. In exploring each competency,

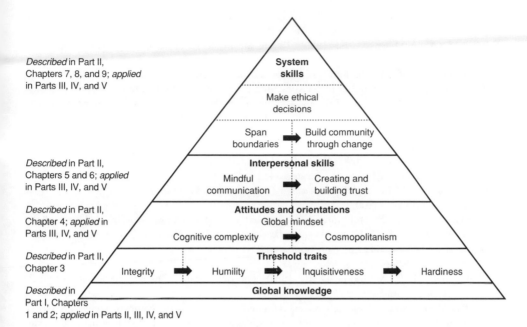

Described in Part II, Chapters 7, 8, and 9; *applied* in Parts III, IV, and V

Described in Part II, Chapters 5 and 6; *applied* in Parts III, IV, and V

Described in Part II, Chapter 4; *applied* in Parts III, IV, and V

Described in Part II, Chapter 3

Described in Part I, Chapters 1 and 2; *applied* in Parts II, III, IV, and V

System skills

Make ethical decisions

Span boundaries ➡ Build community through change

Interpersonal skills
Mindful communication ➡ Creating and building trust

Attitudes and orientations
Global mindset
Cognitive complexity ➡ Cosmopolitanism

Threshold traits
Integrity ➡ Humility ➡ Inquisitiveness ➡ Hardiness

Global knowledge

FIGURE 3.5 The relationship between global competencies and the *Handbook*'s structure

we define what it is, discuss the research that supports our knowledge base, and provide examples of how it contributes to effective global managing. We begin with a consideration of the attitudes and orientations that support a global mindset, Level 2 in the Global Competency pyramid. From there we move to Level 3, the interpersonal skills of mindful communication and the creating and building of trust. Lastly, we cover the Level 4 system skills of spanning boundaries, building communities by managing change, and making ethical decisions.

The global competencies that have been detailed in this part of the book will be referred to and seen in application in other chapters throughout the book, as shown in figure 3.5.

Notes

1 A review of global leadership research turned up over 200 different characteristics identified by corporations and researchers as important to effective global leadership. Mendenhall, M., & Osland, J. S. (2002), An overview of the extant global leadership research, symposium presentation, Academy of International Business, Puerto Rico, June. Cf. Cullen, J. B. (2000), *Multinational Management: A Strategic Approach*. Cincinnati, OH: South-Western Thomson Learning.

2 There is an extensive literature on differences between experts and novices. Though we reference several leading researchers in this part of the book, we find the work of Gary Klein and associates to be particularly insightful and consistent with our perspective. Klein, G. (1998), *Sources of Power: How People Make Decisions*, Cambridge, MA: MIT Press.

3 Dreyfus, H. L., & Dreyfus, S. E. (1986), *Mind over Machine: The Power of Human Intuitive Expertise in the Era of the Computer*, New York: The Free Press.

4 Burke, L. A., & Miller, M. K. (1999), Taking the mystery out of intuitive decision making, *Academy of Management Executive*, 13(4), 93.

5 While there are literally thousands of books that have been written on what managers do (or should do), there are a number of "classics" that have dominated much of the current thinking on management. A short list of the most influential authors would include: Bernard, Drucker, Follett, Sloan, Thompson, Weick, Luthans, Mintzberg, and Schein.

6 Klein (1998); Osland, J. S., & Bird, A. (1998), Trigger events and cultural sensemaking, unpublished manuscript.

7 Osland, J. S. & Bird, A. (2000), Beyond sophisticated stereotyping: Cross-cultural sensemaking in context, *Academy of Management Executive*, 14, 1–12.

8 Findings from the March, 2001 *Chattanooga Conference on Global Leadership*.

9 Mendenhall & Osland (2002).

10 Von Glinow, M. A. (2001), Future issues in global leadership development, in M. Mendenhall, T. M. Kulhmann, & G. K. Stahl (eds.), *Developing Global Business Leaders: Policies, Processes and Innovations*, Westport, CT: Quorum Books, pp. 264–271.

11 Mendenhall & Osland (2002).

12 Mendenhall, M. E., & Oddou, G. R. (1985), The dimensions of expatriate acculturation: A review, *Academy of Management Review*, 10, 39–47.

13 To date, the research on global managers is limited, and many of the competency lists are based on the accumulated wisdom of practitioners or scholars. Our own list, shown in figure 3.2, was developed in a series of facilitated sessions, similar to a modified Delphi technique, conducted over three days in February, 2001 at Northeastern University by the authors of this part of the book. Following that three-day exercise, the group retired to their studies, each to conduct their own review of the literature in light of the list developed in Boston. The group then met again in August, 2001 to further refine the list.

14 Bird, A. (2000), International assignments and careers as repositories of knowledge, in M. Mendenhall, T. Kuhlmann, & G. Stahl (eds.), *Developing Global Leadership Skills: The Challenge of HRM in the Next Millennium*, New York: Quorum, pp. 60–89.

15 Kidd, J. B., & Teramoto, Y. (1995), The learning organization: The case of the Japanese RHQs in Europe, *Management International Review*, 35(2), special issue, 39–56.

16 Bird, A., Heinbuch, S., Dunbar, R., & McNulty, M. (1993), A conceptual model of the effects of area studies training programs and a preliminary investigation of the model's hypothesized relationships, *International Journal of Intercultural Relations*, 17(4), 415–436.

17 Based primarily on a definition drawn from Maddi, S. R. (1989), *Personality Theory: A Comparative Analysis*. Homewood, IL: Dorsey Press, pp. 1–16.

18 The two words, "personality" and "trait," have different, more specific meanings in an academic setting than is usually the case in common daily usage. We are familiar with these differences, but have elected to use "trait" because in common usage it suggests a more limited concept than the broader "personality."

19 Spitzberg, B. (1989), Issues in the development of a theory of interpersonal competence in the intercultural context, *International Journal of Intercultural Relations*, 13, 241–268.

20 Mendenhall, M., Kuhlmann, T., Stahl, G., & Osland, J. (2002), Employee development and expatriate assignments, in M. Gannon & K. Newman (eds.), *Handbook of Cross-Cultural Management*, Oxford: Blackwell, pp. 155–184.

21 *Ibid.*

22 Cf. Caligiuri, P. M. (2000), The Big Five personality characteristics as predictors of expatriate's desire to terminate the assignment and supervisor-rated performance, *Personnel Psychology*, 53,

67–88; Ones, D. S., & Viswesvaran, C. (1997), Personality determinants in the prediction of aspects of expatriate job success, *New Approaches to Employee Management*, 4, 63–92; Lievens, F., Harris, M. M., & Van Keer, E. (2003), Predicting cross-cultural training performance: The validity of personality, cognitive ability, and dimensions measured by an assessment center and a behavior description interview, *Journal of Applied Psychology*, 88, 476–489.

23 Arthur, W., & Bennett, W. (1995), The international assignee: The relative importance of factors perceived to contribute to success, *Personnel Psychology*, 48, 99–114.

24 Arthur, W., & Bennett, W. (1997), A comparative test of alternative models of international assignee job performance, *New Approaches to Employee Management*, 4, 141–172.

25 Wills, S., & Barham, K. (1994), Being an international manager. *European Management Journal* 12(1), 49–58.

26 Black, J. S., Morrison, A. J., & Gregersen, H. B. (1999), *Global Explorers: The Next Generation of Leaders*. London: Routledge, p. 131.

27 Based on definitions in *The American Heritage Dictionary of the English Language* (2000), 4th edn., New York: Houghton Mifflin.

28 Meyer, J. E. & Kelley, C. (1993), *The Cross-Cultural Adaptability Inventory Manual*. Yarmouth, ME: Intercultural Press.

29 *Ibid.*

30 McCall, M., & Hollenbeck, G. P. (2002), *Developing Global Executives*, Cambridge, MA: Harvard Business School Press.

31 Will, S., & Barham, K. (1994), Being an international manager, *European Management Journal* 12(1), 49–58.

32 McCall, M. & Hollenbeck, G. P. (2002), These cites are wrong.

33 Based on definitions in *The American Heritage Dictionary of the English Language* (2000) and the compact edition of *The Oxford English Dictionary* (1970).

34 McCall & Hollenbeck (2002).

35 Cf. Churning at the top, *The Economist*, March 17, 2001, 67–69; Collins, J. (2001), *Good to Great*, New York: HarperCollins.

36 Based on definitions in *The American Heritage Dictionary of the English Language* (2000).

37 McCall & Hollenbeck (2002).

38 Black, J. S., Morrison, A. J., & Gregersen, H. B. (1999), *Global Explorers: The Next Generation of Leaders*, London: Routledge, p. 48.

39 *Ibid.*, p. 60.

40 Bateson, M. C. (1994), *Peripheral Visions: Learning along the Way*, New York: Harper Collins, p. 66.

41 Lievens, Harris, & Van Keer (2003).

42 Based on definitions in *The American Heritage Dictionary of the English Language* (2000).

43 Caligiuri, P. M. (2000), The Big Five personality characteristics as predictors of expatriate's desire to terminate the assignment and supervisor-rated performance, *Personnel Psychology*, 53, 67–88.

44 McCall & Hollenbeck (2002).

45 Kelly, J. E., & Myer, S. E. (1992), *The Cross-Cultural Adaptability Inventory Workbook*, Yarmouth, ME: Intercultural Press.

46 Maddi, S. R., & Kobasa, S. C. (1984), *The Hardy Executive: Health and Stress*, Homewood, IL: Dow-Jones-Irwin.

47 Stahl, G. K. (1999), Deutsche Führungskräfte im Auslandseinsatz: Probleme und Problemlöseerfolg in Japan und den USA, *Die Betriebswirtschaft*, 59, 687–703.

48 Kühlmann, T. M. (1995), Die Auslandsentsendung von Fach- und Führungskräften: Eine Einführung in die Schwerpunkte und Ergebnisse der Forschung, in T. M. Kühlmann (ed.),

Mitarbeiterentsendung ins Ausland, Göttingen: Verlag für Angewandte Psychologie, pp. 1–30. See also Stahl, G. K. (1998), *Internationaler Einsatz von Führungskräften*, Munich: Oldenbourg.

49 Befus, C. P. (1988), A multilevel treatment approach for culture shock experienced by sojourners, *International Journal of Intercultural Relations*, 12, 387.

50 This survey, the PVS, was developed by S. C. Kobasa at the Hardiness Institute in 1985.

4

The Crucial Yet Elusive Global Mindset[1]

Nakiye Boyacigiller, Schon Beechler, Sully Taylor, and Orly Levy

Global managers face challenges, dualities, and paradoxes of mammoth proportions for which structural solutions no longer are effective.[2] Building on the idea of requisite variety, researchers are beginning to conclude that only complex human behavior can match these complex demands of the global environment.[3] Managers need a mindset that enables them to think outside the narrow confines of a single cultural view. This *global mindset* comprises cognitive complexity, joined with an awareness of the world and a positive orientation toward it, cosmopolitanism.

What We Know About Global Mindset

A key difference between domestic and global managers is the need for global managers to deal with significantly greater complexity and to be open to the outside world. This global mindset thus builds on the four threshold traits that contribute to making a good manager, described at Level 1 of the Global Competency Model introduced in the preceding chapter: integrity, humility, inquisitiveness, and hardiness.

A global mindset has been defined as:

the ability to develop and interpret criteria for personal and business performance that are independent from the assumptions of a single country, culture, or context: and to implement those criteria appropriately in different countries, cultures, and contexts. (Maznevski & Lane, 2003, p. 4)

one that combines an openness to and awareness of diversity across cultures and markets with a propensity and ability to synthesize across this diversity. (Govindarajan & Gupta, 2001, p. 111)

As our definitions suggest, there are two dominant underlying dimensions of the global mindset: a cosmopolitan orientation and a cognitive complexity.[4]

Global mindset: An illustration

The President of TCC Latin America and Brazil Country Manager Gerald Schafer[5] offers us an example of a global mindset.

> Gerald Schafer is a Swiss national who has never really lived in Switzerland. He was born in Budapest to a Swiss foreign-service officer and his Hungarian wife. Mr. Schafer grew up in Africa and South America and studied in the United States. He speaks Portuguese (at home with his Brazilian wife), Spanish, French, German, English, and Hungarian. Given his role and background it is not surprising that Mr. Schafer spends approximately 40 percent of his time traveling outside of Brazil. He has a Master's degree in engineering, has been with TCC for close to thirty years and currently chairs an industry trade association.
>
> Mr. Schafer reflects many of the values of the company he works for, in that TCC has done a remarkable number of things to become a truly global company. The executive committee of the organization comprises four individuals – two Americans, one Englishman, and one Brazilian, with massive amounts of international experience amongst them. "I think there are very few companies where you can rise to the levels that you can rise in TCC where nationality is a non-issue. This allows a tremendous cross-fertilization of ideas. In the next decade, I expect to see a non-American CEO in this company."
>
> A quintessential boundary spanner when not traveling, Mr. Schafer makes a point of spending one day a week outside of the office with key customers, vendors, and government officials. He understands the chemical industry in Brazil to be built on relationships and gets much of his information and business while entertaining (on average, four nights a week). Mr. Schafer has an acute understanding of his local environment, from the complexities of its financial crises to the nuances of its political system. Within his organization, he employs people from many other Latin American countries. While English is the operating language of the company, Mr. Schafer argues that it is important not to make promotions based on language capabilities. He currently has a director of communications who, while very talented, has weak English. Recognizing that this is a likely impediment to her career, Mr. Schafer is making a practice of speaking English to this woman and sending her English-language e-mails, although both of them could communicate much more easily in Portuguese.

Cosmopolitan orientation

Cosmopolitans are individuals who are oriented toward the outside world, focused on their professions over their organizations, while locals are narrowly concerned with the affairs of the community and their organizations, to the exclusion of world affairs.[6] In a multinational context, cosmopolitans are characterized by a world orientation held by top management that downplays the significance of nationality and cultural differences, what Perlmutter first called a geocentric mindset.[7]

The cosmopolitanism themes of external orientation and openness resonate in the recent work on global mindset. People with a global mindset have time and space perspectives that extend beyond their personal surroundings, thus manifesting a patently external orientation.[8] They are a "social class defined by its ability to command resources and operate beyond and across wide territories."[9]

A transnational manager has a global perspective, knowledge of many foreign culture's perspectives, and simultaneous interaction with people of many cultures.[10] While this conceptualization emphasizes attitudes of openness and external orientation (cosmopolitanism), it also recognizes the importance of cognitive complexity and cognitive skills. This is the second characteristic of the global mindset.

Cognitive complexity

Cosmopolitanism by itself is not enough. A global manager also has to be able to see the complexity of things – markets, management issues, technological developments, political events – and make the connections between seemingly disparate pieces. Cognitive complexity has been associated with the capacity to balance contradictions, ambiguities, and trade-offs. It is also associated with an ideologically moderate world-view.[11]

The two primary components of cognitive complexity are differentiation and integration.[12] Differentiation is the number of dimensions or constructs used to describe a situation or issue, while integration refers to the number of links among the differentiated dimensions. Two key researchers on global competition and managers, Gupta and Govindarajan, borrow from cognitive psychology and knowledge structure to develop explicit ways to discuss managers with a global mindset: those who are high differentiators and high integrators – with differentiation being "the number of elements in the person or organization's knowledge base" and integration being "the person or organization's ability to synthesize the various elements."[13]

Because this is a new, developing area of research, quite a few authors talk about this aspect of global mindset, although only a few scholars have systematically researched the mindsets and cognitive maps of managers in MNCs.[14] Tom Murtha and his colleagues have conducted one of the few empirical studies of global mindset. They clearly take a *cognitive* approach, defining global mindset as "the cognitive processes that balance competing country, business and functional concerns." Other writers on global mindset, such as Stephen Rhinesmith, also strongly emphasize the importance of the cognitive complexity aspect of a global mindset, arguing that "a global manager must learn to live with conflict rather than resolution . . . global mindset . . . entails the simultaneous appreciation of contradictory ideas in a way that energizes rather than paralyzes."[15] Taken together, it is clear that both theory and research support the idea that cognitive complexity is a key component of global mindset.

Putting it all together, we suggest that global mindset comprises two critical features: cosmopolitanism and cognitive complexity. It can be thought of as a meta-capability, one that "permits an individual to function successfully in new and unknown situations and to integrate this new understanding with other existing skills and knowledge bases."[16] Important questions, however, are how an individual develops such a meta-capability, and what organizations can do to help.

DEVELOPING A GLOBAL MINDSET: HOW ORGANIZATIONS CAN HELP

While developing a global mindset may be elusive, the critical importance of global mindset has led to increased attention from corporations, as well as growing scholarly research. From this growing literature we can identify various critical issues, as well as emerging best practices regarding global mindset development.

Companies concerned about having a sufficient number of managers with a global mindset must look first and foremost at the human resource management (HRM) practices they use. Our research makes clear that HRM policies can either impede or undermine global mindset development. In the following section, we will briefly discuss the major HRM components that impact global mindset development, and incorporate these two questions into our discussion.

Selection practices and global mindset development

Cosmopolitanism and cognitive complexity can be used as important criteria when initially choosing potential candidates for managers in global companies. Individuals can be selected on their cognitive complexity, as this characteristic is probably one of the most difficult elements to change after hiring; it is the most innate of cognitive processes. To determine a job candidate's cognitive complexity capability, a company can add exercises to assessment center selection procedures that have been found to be effective in choosing candidates for international careers.[17] These exercises can be structured to identify people who see multiple dimensions of a problem as well as the interconnections among them. However, the company has to leverage the assessment-center selection experience to make sure that the candidate receives feedback concerning areas she needs to develop further.[18] In addition, identifying activities and accomplishments in the candidate's background that demonstrate an ability to differentiate and integrate across a great deal of information, such as running complex projects, could be used as indicators of potentially high cognitive complexity.[19]

The second component of global mindset, cosmopolitanism, or at least a propensity toward it, can also be seen in a candidate's background. Past research suggests that education in other countries, relatives (such as parents) from other countries, and foreign language ability are all associated with a more cosmopolitan orientation.[20] There are a variety of other ways in which people can demonstrate openness toward others and interest in the world, such as the travel they have voluntarily undertaken, the media they read, and the hobbies they pursue.

What *is* clear is that multinational organizations need to draw from a wide pool of candidates. A company that restricts itself to hiring candidates that are only of a certain nationality, gender or background will be at a disadvantage because such practices decrease the pool of candidates who are cognitively complex and cosmopolitan. As one of our colleagues notes, companies need to cast a wider net, to view the entire globe as a source of talent.[21] In addition, that a global mindset will develop within a management team that is not diverse itself is highly unlikely.

Training and global mindset development

Both before candidates have been selected to join the firm and after, the development process used with them to nurture a global mindset must be carefully considered. Initially, some kind of assessment should occur – in this vein, Govindarajan and Gupta provide a set of diagnostic questions to help organizations ascertain whether their employees have a global mindset:

1 In interacting with others, does national origin have an impact on whether or not you assign equal status to them?
2 Do you consider yourself as equally open to ideas from other countries and cultures as you are from your own country and culture of origin?
3 Does finding yourself in a new cultural setting cause excitement or fear and anxiety?
4 When visiting or living in another culture, are you sensitive to the cultural differences without becoming a prisoner of these differences?
5 When you interact with people from other cultures, what do you regard as more important: understanding them as individuals or viewing them as representatives of their national cultures?
6 Do you regard your values to be a hybrid of values acquired from multiple cultures as opposed to just one culture?[22]

There is a long history and a broad repertoire of cross-cultural training methods, many of which would be helpful for the development of a global mindset. Recent research suggests that living and working in a foreign country is probably the most powerful tool to develop global mindset.[23] Furthermore, Osland and Taylor suggest that there are four key aspects of a successful program to develop global leaders or managers with a global mindset. It should be multi-method, aligned with the organization, transparent, and inclusive.[24]

Multi-method. Perhaps the most important aspect of global mindset development is the recognition that it must draw on a myriad of methods in order to foster both cosmopolitanism and cognitive complexity. Research has shown that experiential learning is extraordinarily important – as much as 50 percent of learning occurs through work experience.[25] Companies from different countries will emphasize different methods for developing global leaders and their attendant global mindsets, yet despite these differing approaches, we make a recommendation that goes to the process: the company should look at a series of tasks or assignments that build in difficulty and impact on global mindset, starting with international business projects and building to global responsibility for a product.[26] The expatriate assignment must be carefully managed, however, in order for it to contribute to development of a global mindset. Simply posting managers overseas will not necessarily result in the development of a global mindset either in the individuals or in the organization. The expatriate assignment is just one, albeit an important one, of these progressively more global assignments that help to transform managers into leaders with global mindsets.[27]

In addition to overseas assignments, there are many other experiences that can be leveraged to build global mindset, including international business trips at the beginning of a manager's career.[28] In addition, managers can undertake exercises that help nurture greater cognitive complexity and work on multicultural teams to help increase their ability to work with people with different leadership or work styles – a critical factor for the development of global mindset.[29]

Black, Morrison, and Gregersen's research on global leadership found that travel, teams, training and transfers are the four primary development options firms can pursue to help create capable global leaders. While using all four types of experiences over the course of an individual's career is advantageous, the single most influential developmental experience reported by participants is living and working in a foreign country.[30]

Aligned and transparent. Alignment and transparency of HR policies are also important in the process of developing global mindsets. For example, given the need to develop a solid knowledge basis in the company's business and operations, as well as to preserve the social capital required to interact across global organizational boundaries, it is preferable to institute a long-term employment relationship. Global employees who feel they can trust and rely on the goodwill of others within the firm will be able to access information and coordinate more easily than when social capital is low. Employees who feel they are long-term employees of the firm are more likely to build the requisite relationships and trust, as is illustrated in Mr. Schafer's relationship with his director of communications.[31]

Inclusive. Finally, the global mindset development system must be inclusive. Including candidates from many nationalities signals the company's commitment to cosmopolitanism as an important value, that is, its own openness to the Other. As mentioned previously, firms that exclude candidates from development activities on criteria such as gender and nationality will create top management teams burdened by their homogeneity. In addition, as noted earlier, inclusiveness in the development process will foster a greater sense of equity and enlarge the pool from which to choose candidates with the requisite initial capabilities.

However, there is the potential of undesired consequences that creates a tension that companies feel from contradictory effects of HRM policies on global mindset development. For example, long-term employment can also undermine the cosmopolitanism of the management team if the system becomes impervious to recruiting outsiders. Another example of negative and positive effects is found with international assignments. While these assignments and other activities can be used to build cosmopolitanism, they can also lead to less desirable outcomes. Research shows that an international assignment does not necessarily lead to a global mindset. Unfortunately, it can lead to an increase in prejudice and cultural stereotypes.[32] A proactive HR function that doesn't leave employees solely to their own devices is likelier to lead to positive outcomes.

How Individuals Can Cultivate a Global Mindset

With the changing nature of the psychological contract between individuals and organizations, more responsibility than ever rests on individuals to ensure their own long-term development and employability. Organizations increasingly view international experience and the development of a global mindset as prerequisites to upward mobility.[33] Moreover, managers are increasingly seeking international assignments for the personal development and skills they may acquire as part of a "boundaryless" career, not necessarily to advance within a specific firm.[34]

Govindarajan and Gupta, building on work in cognitive psychology, human development, and technological innovation, argue that the development of a global mindset at either the individual or the organizational level follows a series of S-curves (see figure 4.1).

This model is similar to the novice–expert model depicted in the introduction to this part, and the implication of the S-curve thesis is clear: a global mindset develops over

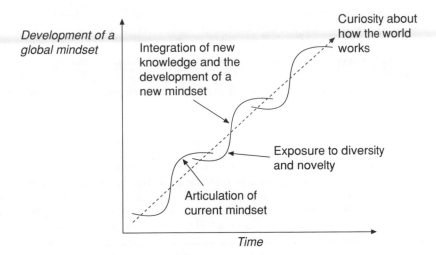

FIGURE 4.1 The development of a global mindset
Source: Govindarajan, V., and Gupta, A. K. 2001, *The Quest of Global Dominance*, San Francisco: Jossey-Bass, p. 125

time, and it is a nonlinear and somewhat uncertain process. Gupta and Govindarajan quote Jenny, an American married to a Frenchman:

> I have been here for seven years. In a most predictable manner, I have found that whenever I begin to get a sense that now I really do understand the French, something strange will happen that will throw me off completely. As I would reflect on the event and talk it over with my husband and friends, I would begin to develop a more complex view of the French. Then, things would seem to go fine for several months until the whole process would repeat itself in some other area.[35]

This quote, an illustration of a trigger event, reflects the process of thesis–antithesis and synthesis, the foundation of learning that needs to occur as a novice global manager develops the skills necessary to become an expert global manager.[36]

The development of global mindset, like the development of any cognitive schema, involves both assimilation and accommodation of new information.[37] It must be an ongoing process built on an articulation of self-awareness and other-awareness. As noted in the introduction to this part, novices begin by following rules, then, as they gain practical experience, they begin to understand general patterns.[38] As they become more competent, they recognize complexity and a larger set of cues. They are able to discern which cues are the most important and move beyond strict adherence to rules to think in terms of trade-offs. Once they reach the expert stage, they can read situations without rational thought – they diagnose the situation unconsciously and respond intuitively because over the years they have developed the holistic recognition, mental maps, that allows for effortless framing and reframing of strategies and quick adaptation. Their knowledge is, at this point, tacit.

Thus, the development of a global mindset is, in its dynamism, a sensemaking cycle that follows the three steps of our effectiveness cycle: (1) perceive and analyze the situation;

(2) select an appropriate response; and (3) act effectively. The first step involves the ability to decode and diagnose the context accurately. The second step involves knowledge about what managerial action will work in this instance. The third step is made possible by an adequate behavioral repertoire, as well as the behavioral flexibility to enact the script correctly.

Finally, and perhaps most importantly, the conscious development of a global mindset involves becoming more mindful of who we are. As Storti describes in *The Art of Crossing Cultures*, becoming aware, often retrospectively after an intercultural encounter, is a critical element of this mindfulness. Or as Hannerz states in his discussion of cosmopolitanism:

> A more genuine cosmopolitanism is first of all an orientation, a willingness to engage with the Other. It entails an intellectual and esthetic openness toward divergent cultural experiences, a search for contrasts rather than uniformity. To become acquainted with more cultures is to turn into an *aficionado*, to view them as artworks. At the same time, however, cosmopolitanism can be a matter of competence, and competence of both a generalized and more specialized kind. *There is the aspect of a state of readiness, a personal ability to make one's way into other cultures, through listening, looking, intuiting, and reflecting.* And there is cultural competence in the stricter sense of the term, a built-up skill in maneuvering more or less expertly with a particular system of meanings. (emphasis added)[39]

CONCLUSION

A global mindset is a significant advantage, given today's business environment. The global mindset is balanced on the foundation of a critical global competency characterized by two underlying dimensions – cosmopolitanism and cognitive complexity – and the threshold traits of integrity, humility, inquisitiveness, and hardiness. In this chapter, we have provided suggestions for how both organizations and individuals can develop and nurture a global mindset. In the following chapters, we turn to our Global Competency Model's next two levels: the interpersonal skills of mindful intercultural communication and creating and building trust; and the system skills of boundary spanning, building community through change, and ethical decision-making.

NOTES

1 This chapter contains material based upon work supported by the National Science Foundation under Grant No. 0080703. Any opinions, findings, and conclusions or recommendations expressed in this material are those of the authors and do not necessarily reflect the views of the National Science Foundation. The authors would also like to thank their home institutions for their support, and colleagues at ION, C4, the Academy of Management and the Academy of International Business for their earlier comments.

2 See Evans, Pucik, & Barsoux (2002).

3 See Bartlett & Ghoshal (1989); Prahalad & Doz (1987); Nohria & Ghoshal (1997); Ghoshal & Bartlett (1997); Ashkenas et al. (2002).

4 This work has its theoretical roots in organizational sociology.

5 TCC is a pseudonym to protect the identity of the company and Mr. Gerald Schafer is a pseudonym of the individual we interviewed at TCC during our research project.

6 The early research of Merton and Gouldner provides the foundation for our understanding of cosmopolitanism.

7 Perlmutter (1969); Heenan & Perlmutter (1979).

8 Kedia & Mukherji (1999). Flango & Brumbaugh (1974); Glaser (1963); Goldberg, Baker, & Rubenstein (1965); and Goldberg (1976).

9 Kanter (1995: 22).

10 Adler & Bartholomew (1992).

11 For work on cognitive complexity, differentiation and integration see Tetlock (1983); Bartunek et al. (1983); Weick & Bougon (1986).

12 In this context we are using differentiation and integration as an individual level construct, not as an organizational level construct. For an example of this see the classic work by Lawrence & Lorsch (1967).

13 Govindarajan and Gupta (2001), p. 110.

14 Kobrin (1994); Calori, Johnson, & Sarnin (1994); Murtha, Lenway, & Bagozzi (1998), p. 97.

15 Rhinesmith (1992), p. 64. Note once again that Evans and his colleagues expand and develop this notion of managing duality quite nicely in their book Evans, Pucik, & Barsoux (2002).

16 Maznevski & Lane (2004), p. 5, original emphasis.

17 Stahl (2001).

18 *Ibid.*

19 This builds on the work of Siegfried Streufert who, with his colleagues, defines a cognitively complex individual as one who employs "differentiation and integration as part of his or her information processing." Streufert & Swezey (1986), p. 18.

20 Birnbaum & Wong (1985).

21 Charles Vance presentation at the annual meeting of the Academy of Management, 2001. See also Rhinesmith (1996).

22 Govindarajan & Gupta (2001), p. 115.

23 Black et al. (1999).

24 Osland and Taylor (2001).

25 Dodge (1993).

26 Oddou et al. (2001); Dalton (1998).

27 Osland (2001).

28 See Dalton & Ernst (2003) and Oddou, Mendenhall, & Ritchie (2000) for examples.

29 See Maznevski & Lane (2004); Maznevski & DiStefano (2000); McCall, Lombardo, & Morrison (1988).

30 Black, Morrison, & Gregersen (1999).

31 See chapter 5B in this text, Adler & Kwon (2002) and Leana & Van Buren (1999) for excellent discussions of trust.

32 Bochner, S. (1982), *Cultures in Contact: Studies in Cross-Cultural Interaction*, New York: Pergamon (see pp. 53–54). Brislin, R. W. (1981), *Cross-Cultural Encounters: Face-to-Face Interaction*. New York: Pergamon. Klineberg, O. (1982), Contact between ethnic groups: a historical perspective of some aspects of theory and research, in S. Bochner (ed.), *Cultures in Contact: Studies in Cross-Cultural Interaction*, New York: Pergamon, pp. 45–76. Triandis, H. C. (1995), A theoretical framework for the study of diversity, in M. M. Chemers, S. Oskamp, & M. A. Costanzo (eds.), *Diversity in Organizations: New Perspectives for a Changing Workplace*, Thousand Oaks, CA: Sage, pp. 11–36.

33 Black et al. (1999).

34 Denise Rousseau has written extensively on the changing nature of the psychological contract in today's organizations. See Rousseau (1995) and Rousseau & Schalk (2000). See Black et al. (1999) for the importance of international experience in career mobility.

35 Govindarajan and Gupta (2001), p. 126.

36 This also dovetails nicely with Lambert's notion of "additive biculturalism" in Brislin (1981).

37 Maznevski & Lane (2003) cite Furth, H. (1970) *Piaget for Teachers*, New York: Prentice Hall (writing about the work of Jean Piaget) and note that, "in assimilation, new information is seen to be consistent with the schema and is incorporated readily . . . in accommodation, new information contradicts the schema to the extent that the schema is itself changed. . . . Or in organizational terms, single-loop and double-loop learning" (Argyris & Schon, 1978) and "evolutionary and revolutionary change" (Gersick, 1991, p. 6).

38 Dreyfus, Dreyfus, & Athanasiou (1986).

39 Hannerz (1996), p. 103.

BIBLIOGRAPHY

Adler, N. J., & Bartholomew, S. (1992). Managing globally competent people. *Academy of Management Executive*, 6(3), 52.

Adler, N., Brody, L., & Osland, J. (2000). The women's global leadership forum: Enhancing one company's global leadership capability. *Human Resource Management*, 39(2&3), 209–226.

Adler, P., & Kwon, S. (2002). Social capital: Prospects for a new concept. *Academy of Management Review*, 27(1), 17–40.

Argyris, C., & Schon, D. (1978). *Organizational Learning*. Reading, MA: Addison-Wesley.

Ashkenas, R., Ulrich, D., Jick, J., & Kerr, S. (2002). *The Boundaryless Organization: Breaking the Chains of Organizational Structure*. San Francisco: Jossey-Bass.

Bartlett, C. A., & Ghoshal, S. (1989). *Managing across Borders*. Boston: Harvard Business School Press

Bartunek, J. M., Gordon, J. R., & Weathersby, R. P. (1983). Developing "complicated" understanding in administrators. *Academy of Management Review*, 8(2), 273–284.

Beechler, S., Taylor, S., Levy, O., Boyacigiller, N., & Colton, C. (2001). Does it really matter if MNCs think globally? Paper presented at the Academy of Management Annual Meeting, Washington, DC.

Bennett, M. (1993). Towards ethnorelativism: A developmental model of intercultural sensitivity, in R. M. Paige (ed.), *Education for the Intercultural Experience*. 2nd edn., Yarmouth, ME: Intercultural Press, pp. 21–71.

Birnbaum, P. H., & G. Y. Wong (1985). Organizational structure of multinational banks in Hong Kong from a culture-free perspective. *Administrative Science Quarterly*, 30, 262–277.

Black, J. S., Gregersen, H. B., Mendenhall, M. E., & Stroh, L. K. (1999). *Globalizing People through International Assignments*. Reading, MA: Addison Wesley.

Black, J. S., Morrison, A. J., & Gregersen, H. B. (1999) *Global Explorers: The Next Generation of Leaders*. New York: Routledge.

Calori, R., Johnson, G., & Sarnin, P. (1994). CEOs' cognitive maps and the scope of the organization. *Strategic Management Journal*, 15, 437–457.

Conner, J. (2000). Developing the global leaders of tomorrow. *Human Resource Management*, 39(2&3), 147–157.

Dalton, M., and Ernst, C. (2003). Developing leaders for global roles, in C. McCauley and E. Van Velson, *The Center for Creative Leadership Handbook of Leadership Development* (2nd ed.), San Francisco: Jossey-Bass.

Denison, D. R., Hooijeberg, R., & Quinn, R. E. (1995) Paradox and performance: Toward a theory of behavioral complexity in managerial leadership. *Organization Science*, 6(5), 524–540.

Dodge, B. (1993). Empowerment and the evolution of learning. *Education and Training*, 35(5), 3–10.

Doz, Y. L., & Prahalad, C. K. (1991). Managing DMNCs: A search for a new paradigm. *Strategic Management Journal*, 12, 145–164.

Dreyfus, H. L., Dreyfus, S. E., & Athanasiou, T. (1986). *Mind over Machine*. New York: The Free Press.

Earley, P. C., & Erez, M. (1997) *The Transplanted Executive*. New York: Oxford University Press.

Evans, P., Pucik, V., & Barsoux, J-L. (2002). *The Global Challenge: Frameworks for Human Resource Management*. Boston: McGraw Hill.

Flango, V. E., & Brumbaugh, R. B. (1974). The dimensionality of the cosmopolitan–local construct. *Administrative Science Quarterly*, 19, 198–210.

Gersick, C. G. (1991). Revolutionary change theories: A multi-level exploration of a punctuated equilibrium. *Academy of Management Review*, 16, 1–32.

Ghoshal, S., & Bartlett, C. A. (1997) *The Individualized Corporation*. New York: Harper Business.

Glaser, B. G. (1963). The local–cosmopolitan scientist. *American Journal of Sociology*, 69, 249–259.

Goldberg, A. I. (1976). The relevance of cosmopolitan/local orientations to professional values and behavior. *Sociology of Work and Occupation*, 3(3), 331–356.

Goldberg, L. C., Baker, F., & Rubenstein, A. H. (1965). Local–cosmopolitan: Unidimensional or multidimensional?" *American Journal of Sociology*, 70, 704–710.

Gouldner, A. W. (1957). Cosmopolitans and locals: Toward an analysis of latent social roles – I. *Administrative Science Quarterly*, 2, 281–306.

Gouldner, A. W. (1958). Cosmopolitans and locals: Toward an analysis of latent social roles – II. *Administrative Science Quarterly*, 2, 444–480.

Govindarajan, V., & Gupta, A. (1998). Success is all in the mindset. *Financial Times* (London), February 27, 2–3.

Govindarajan, V., & Gupta, A. K. (2001) *The Quest for Global Dominance*. San Francisco: Jossey-Bass.

Gudykunst, W. B., & Kim, Y. Y. (1984) *Communicating with Strangers: An Approach to Intercultural Communication*. Reading, MA: Addison-Wesley.

Hall, E. T. (1976). *Beyond Culture*. Garden City, NY: Anchor.

Hannerz, U. (1996). Cosmopolitans and locals in world culture, in U. Hannerz, *Transnational Connections: Culture, People, Places*. London: Routledge, pp. 102–111 (originally published in *Theory, Culture and Society* (1991), 7, 237–251.

Heenan, D., & Perlmutter, H. (1979). *Multinational Organizational Development: A Social Architecture Perspective*. Reading, MA, Addison-Wesley.

Hooijberg, R. (1996) A multidirectional approach toward leadership: An extension of the concept of behavioral complexity. *Human Relations*, 49(7), 917–946.

Kanter, R. M. (1991). Transcending business boundaries: 12,000 world managers view change. *Harvard Business Review*, 69(3), 151–164.

Kanter, R. M. (1994). Afterword: What "thinking globally" really means, in R. S. Barnwik & R. M. Kanter (eds.), *Global Strategies*. Boston: Harvard Business School Press, pp. 227–232.

Kanter, R. M. (1995). *World Class: Thriving Locally in the Global Economy*. New York: Simon & Schuster.

Kedia, ?, & Mukherji, ?

Kobrin, S. J. (1994). Is there a relationship between a geocentric mind-set and multinational strategy? *Journal of International Business Studies*, 25(3), 493–511.

Lawrence, P., & Lorsch, J. (1967) *Organizations and Environments*. Boston: Harvard Business School Press.

Leana, C., & Van Buren, H., III. 1999. Organizational social capital and employment practices. *Academy of Management Review*, 24, 538–555.

Levy, O., Beechler, S. L., Taylor, S., & Boyacigiller, N. A. (1999) What we talk about when we talk about "Global Mindset": Managerial cognition in multinational corporations. Paper presented at the Academy of Management Annual Meeting, Chicago, August.

Maznevski, M., & DiStefano, J. (2000). Global leaders are team players: Developing global leaders through membership on global teams. *Human Resource Management*, 39(2&3), 195–208.

Maznevski, M., & Lane, H. (2004) Shaping the global mindset: Designing educational experiences for effective global thinking and action, in N. Boyacigiller, R. M. Goodman, & M. Phillips (eds.), *Teaching and Experiencing Cross-Cultural Management: Lessons from Master Teachers*. London and New York: Routledge.

McCall, M. (1992). Executive development as a business strategy. *Journal of Business Strategy*, January/February, 25–31.

McCall, M., Lombardo, M., & Morrison, A. (1988). *The Lessons of Experience*. Lexington, MA: Lexington Books.

McCall, M. (1994). Identifying leadership potential in future international executives: Developing a concept. *Consulting Psychology Journal*, 46(1), 49–63.

Mendenhall, M., Kuhlmann, T., & Stahl, G. (eds.) (2000) *Developing Global Business Leaders: Policies, Processes, and Innovations*. Westport, CT: Quorum Books.

Merton, R. K. (1957). Patterns of influence: Local and cosmopolitan influentials, in R. K. Merton, *Social Theory and Social Structure*. Glencoe, IL: The Free Press, pp. 368–380.

Murtha, T., Lenway, S., & Bagozzi, R. P. (1998). Global mind-sets and cognitive shift in a complex multinational corporation. *Strategic Management Journal*, 19(2), 97–114.

Nohria, N., & Ghoshal, S. (1997), *The Differentiated Network: Organizing Multinational Corporations for Value Creation*. San Francisco: Jossey-Bass.

Oddou, G., Gregersen, H., Black, S., & Derr, C. (2001). Building global leaders: Strategy similarities and differences among European, U.S., and Japanese multinationals, in M. Mendenhall, T. Kuhlmann, & G. Stahl (eds.) (2000) *Developing Global Business Leaders: Policies, Processes, and Innovations*. Westport, CT: Quorum Books, pp. 99–118.

Oddou, G., Mendenhall, M., & Ritchie, J. (2000). Leveraging travel as a tool for global leadership development. *Human Resource Management*, 39(2&3), 159–172.

Osland, J. (2001). The quest for transformation: The process of global leadership development. In M. Mendenhall, T. Kuhlmann, & G. Stahl (eds.) (2000) *Developing Global Business Leaders: Policies, Processes, and Innovations*. Westport, CT: Quorum Books, pp. 137–156.

Perlmutter, H. (1969). The tortuous evolution of the multinational corporation. *Columbia Journal of World Business*, January–February, 9–18.

Perlmutter, H. (1991). On the rocky road to the first global civilization. *Human Relations*, 44(9), 897–920.

Pfeffer, J. (1998). *The Human Equation*. Boston, MA: Harvard Business School Press.

Prahalad, C. K., & Doz, Y. L. (1987). *The Multinational Mission: Balancing Local Demands and Global Vision*. The Free Press, New York.

Pucik, V., Tichy, N., & Barnett, C. (eds.) (1992). *Globalizing Management: Creating and Leading the Competitive Organization*. New York: John Wiley.

Ready, D. (1999). Research report, International Consortium for Executive Development and Research. Boston, MA.

Rhinesmith, S. H. (1992). Global mindsets for global managers. *Training and Development*, 46(10), 63–69.

Rhinesmith, S. H. (1993) *Globalization: Six Keys to Success in a Changing World*. Alexandria, VA and New York: American Society For Training and Development and Irwin Books.

Rhinesmith, S. H. (1996) *A Manager's Guide to Globalization: Six Skills for Success in a Changing World*, 2nd edn., New York: McGraw-Hill.

Rosen, R., Digh, P., Singer, M., & Phillips, C. (2000) *Global Literacies*. New York: Simon & Schuster.

Rousseau, D. M. (1995) *Psychological Contracts in Organizations: Written and Unwritten Agreements*. Thousand Oaks, CA: Sage.

Rousseau, D. M., & Schalk, R. (2000) *Psychological Contracts in Employment: Cross-National Perspectives*, Thousand Oaks, CA: Sage.

Stahl, G. (2001). Using assessment centers as tools for global leadership development: An exploratory study. In M. Mendenhall, T. Kuhlmann, & G. Stahl (eds.) (2004) *Developing Global Business Leaders: Policies, Processes, and Innovations*. Westport, CT: Quorum Books, pp. 197–210.

Stahl, G. K., Miller, E. L., & Tung, R. L. (2002) Toward the boundaryless career: A closer look at the expatriate career concept and the perceived implications of an international assignment. Paper presented at the Annual Meeting of the Academy of Management, Denver.

Storti, C. (2001). *The Art of Crossing Cultures*. Yarmouth, ME: Intercultural Press.

Streufert, S., & Swezey, R. W. (1986). *Complexity, Managers, and Organizations*. New York: Academic Press.

Tetlock, P. E. (1983). Cognitive style and political ideology. *Journal of Personality and Social Psychology*, 45(1), 118–126.

Ting-Toomey, S. (1999). *Communicating across Cultures*. New York: Guilford.

Ting-Toomey, S., & Oetzel, J. (2001). *Managing Intercultural Conflict Effectively*. Thousand Oaks, CA: Sage.

Vance, C. (2001). Discussant, Academy of Management Annual Meeting, Washington, DC.

Walsh, J. P. (1995). Managerial and organizational cognition: Notes from a trip down memory lane. *Organization Science*, 6(3), 280–321.

Weick, K. E. (1979). Cognitive processes in organizations, in B. Staw (ed.), *Research in Organizational Behavior*, 1, 41–74. Greenwich, CT: JAI Press.

Weick, K. E., & Bougon, M. G. (1986). Organizations as cognitive maps: Charting ways to success and failure, in H. P. Sims and D. A. Gioia (eds.). *The Thinking Organization: Dynamics of Organizational Social Cognition*. San Francisco: Jossey-Bass, pp. 102–135.

Wills, S., & Barham, K. (1994). Being an international manager. *European Management Journal*, 12(1), 49–58.

Yeung, A., & Ready, D. (1995). Developing leadership capabilities of global corporations: A comparative study in eight nations. *Human Resource Management*, 34(4), 529–547.

5

Mindful Communication

David C. Thomas and Joyce S. Osland

To this point, we have introduced our model of global competency and explained the foundation Level 1 of the model, global knowledge and the threshold traits of integrity, humility, inquisitiveness, and hardiness. We then examined the global mindset, with its two main descriptors, cognitive complexity and cosmopolitanism. We are now ready to look more closely at the *skills* that we think are critical for global competency. In this chapter we look at interpersonal skills and in the following chapter, system skills.

Interpersonal skills are competencies that all people have to some degree. They have to do with how people understand the world. We think of them as interpersonal because they are related to how people exert influence over others on a one-to-one basis. In fact, exercising interpersonal influence over others requires a range of multidimensional and complex skills. We are focusing on the two most critical of these, mindful communication and creating and building trust.

Part A: Mindful Communication

Todd works for an American company in Korea. Sometimes he wonders why he ever accepted a position overseas – there seems to be so much that he just doesn't understand. Todd's secretary, Chungmin, speaks English with him because he is not fluent in Korean. Nevertheless, one incident in particular occurred the previous Friday when Chungmin made a mistake and forgot to type a letter. Todd considered this a small error but made sure to mention it when he saw her during lunch in the company cafeteria. Ever since then, Chungmin has been acting rather strange and distant. When she walks out of his office, she closes the door more loudly than usual. She will not even look him in the eye, and she has been acting very moodily. She even took a few days' sick leave, which she has not done in many years. Todd has no idea how to understand her behavior. Perhaps she really is ill or feels a bit overworked.

When Chungmin returns to work the following Wednesday, Todd calls her into his office. "Is there a problem?" he asks. " Because if there is, we need to talk about it. It's affecting your performance. Is something wrong? Why don't you tell me? It's okay."

At this, Chungmin looks quite distressed. She admits the problem has something to do with her mistake the previous Friday, and Todd explains that it was no big deal. "Forget it," he says, feeling satisfied with himself for working this out. "In the future, just make sure to tell me if something is wrong." But over the next few weeks, Chungmin takes six more sick days and does not speak to Todd once.

Adapted from Cushner, K., & Brislin, R. W. (1996), *Cultural Interactions: A Practical Guide*, Thousand Oaks, CA: Sage.

Communication involves significantly more than speaking the same language. Communication is the act of transmitting messages to another person who interprets the message by giving it meaning. In order for such exchange of meaning to occur, the sender and receiver must share common understanding. We call this shared understanding *grounding*. Such grounding is updated constantly over the course of any communication.[1] When individuals have less shared understanding, they lack common information, which explains why the difficulty of communication increases.

The miscommunication in the opening vignette also illustrates the transactional nature of the communication process.[2] Both Todd and Chungmin were sending and receiving messages, adapting their communication based on what they thought the other person was communicating to them, escalating the problem. Both have mistaken assumptions about the extent of grounding they share and expect the other person to communicate according to their own cultural script.[3] As a result, both Todd and Chungmin are communicating in a "mindless" manner. They are simply reacting to the situation in a semiautomatic way based on their own cultural grounding without considering possible cultural differences. For example, what Todd saw as giving constructive feedback, Chungmin perceived as a very rude public reprimand, which she attributed to Todd's thoughtlessness. She responded, mindlessly, by using a Korean script for expressing her displeasure through subtle cues. Because Todd was a novice at intercultural interaction, he failed to perceive this message accurately (he lacked knowledge of Korean culture and grounding) and had difficulty figuring out and making an accurate attribution for Chungmin's behavior. He tried to solve the problem by having an open and frank discussion with Chungmin, another US communication script that was not well received.

Once negative emotions were involved, Chungmin had even less motivation to decode Todd's communication accurately. She responded with more subtle cues to show her discomfort and began to stereotype Todd as an Ugly American. Like an airplane in an ever tightening spin, Todd and Chungmin's failure to correctly diagnose the situation and behave effectively resulted in a negative spiral that only an expert interculturalist could pull out of. The best way to recover from this type of situation is to avoid it in the first place, by learning to engage in mindful communication across cultures.

In this part of the chapter, we first explore what mindful communication is. The two most critical contributors to mindful communication are knowledge of the culture and communication skills, both of which we investigate. We then describe how to build competency in mindful communication and close with a brief summary.

What *Mindful* Communication Is

Mindfulness means attending to one's internal assumptions, cognitions, and emotions, and simultaneously attuning to the other's assumptions, cognitions, and emotions. It also involves learning to see behavior or information presented in the situation as novel or fresh: viewing a situation from several vantage points or perspectives; attending to the context and the person in which we are perceiving the behavior; and creating new categories through which this new behavior may be understood.[4] The antithesis of mindfulness, *mindlessness*, is exemplified in the following vignette.

Mindlessness

Yesterday, my wife called me at work and asked me to pick up some groceries for dinner on my way home. I have a carefully selected route home that I have designed to minimize traffic, and I follow it every day. In order to stop at the grocery store, I would have to make a slight adjustment to the route. Only after I arrived home to be greeted with the question, "Where are the groceries?", did I realize that I had automatically driven my normal route straight home.

The act of driving an automobile is a complex behavior, but most of us do it this semi-automatic way. And in this case, even when we have been cued to break out of our script, we fall back into it. Much of our behavior, including communication behavior, occurs in this scripted, seemingly mindless manner, which is a semi-reflexive response to the situation. As shown in the opening vignette, the adverse results of mindless communication across cultures are all too apparent. Someone who does not share the same cultural grounding easily misunderstands semi-reflexive communication guided by cultural norms. Mindfulness, on the other hand, puts us in a stage of readiness to interact with people who are different from ourselves. As such, it is a mediating step in linking knowledge with skillful practice.

Mindful communication can be judged by the criteria of appropriateness, effectiveness, and satisfaction.[5] Appropriate communication matches the expectations of both sender and receiver and is perceived as proper. Effective communication achieves mutual shared meaning and the goals desired by the communicators. Finally, satisfaction occurs when a communicator's desired identity image is affirmed rather than disconfirmed during the interaction. Competence in intercultural communication involves (1) the heightened mindfulness described above, which builds on (2) the acquisition of in-depth knowledge, and the development of (3) communication skills. We address both knowledge and communication in the following sections.

Knowledge of the Culture

An in-depth knowledge of the culture of the other party in a cross-cultural communication is an important first step in negotiating shared meaning. As argued in Section 1, understanding cultural values is the foundation for comprehending and decoding the behavior of others and ourselves. Cultural values result in different communication norms that individuals use to guide behavior in certain settings. Knowledge of cultural identities, values, attitudes, and communication practices such as those described previously makes for greater predictability and more accurate attributions. This knowledge allows a better grasp on the internal logic and modal behavior of another culture, which can serve as a first best-guess[6] about behavior in another culture. For instance, individualists tend to express themselves in low-context, direct communication because they value efficiency and are asserting an independent self-identity.

Developing cultural knowledge and sensitivity, a process supported by a global mindset, helps global managers understand the habitual verbal and nonverbal messages and the interaction styles they observe in the multicultural workplace and overseas. Global managers need general knowledge they can extrapolate to incidents to form hypotheses about cultural behavior. Knowledge provides the basic lesson that not all cultures communicate in the same way. Therefore, special attention and caution are required before accurate interpretations can be made. Key elements of knowledge that are important to mindful intercultural communication include knowledge about the communication process itself and about the effects of language, communication style, and nonverbal communication.

The communication process

Communication occurs within social systems, and each communicator has a personal context, a field of experience. These backgrounds cause people to encode and decode messages in a unique fashion, which makes it necessary to find a shared field of experience or common grounding. Like all behavior, much communication proceeds in a routine manner without much conscious thought and is consistent with the cultural field in which it is embedded. The communication process can be influenced, however, by "noise," anything that interferes with the intended communication, such as environmental, physiological, and emotional states.

The entire communication process is embedded in culture, which affects how messages are encoded (converted to symbolic form) and sent by some means (a channel) to the receiver, who then interprets (decodes) the message. In this chapter, we define mindful intercultural communication as *a symbolic exchange in which individuals interactively negotiate shared meanings*.[7] The effectiveness of this exchange is critical in a business environment characterized by an ever-increasing number of intercultural interactions. Mastering the intercultural communication process is a fundamental requirement of effective international management.

The basic model of intercultural interaction presented in this section provides a tool for examining the effects of culture on communication. As shown in figure 5.1, we can envision intercultural communication as involving three related stages, all affected by culture.

The first stage concerns how messages are sent, perceived, diagnosed, and decoded. Then, individuals must identify how to respond, which involves making attributions about the meaning of the message they have received. Finally, individuals must choose from their repertoire of possible responses and enact those that they think are most appropriate. This requires a degree of behavioral flexibility that often separates novices from experts. Expert intercultural communicators are better at diagnosing and decoding messages and more skilled at choosing and enacting effective scripts. The effectiveness of the communication depends on a lack of distortion, which can occur at any stage of the process. Common sources of distortion, explained in the following section, include language, communication style, nonverbal communication, social categorization and stereotyping, and the willingness to communicate.

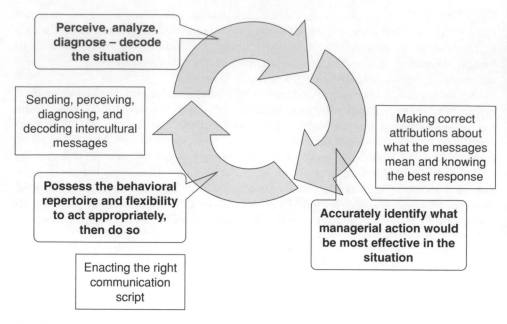

FIGURE 5.1 Effective intercultural communication

Language

An obvious consideration in intercultural communication is the language being used. Three aspects of language influence the ability to create shared meanings. These are language fluency, language accommodation, and second language use.

Language fluency. With reference to our basic model on intercultural interaction, fluency in a foreign language affects a global manager's ability to accurately perceive and diagnose the situation and limits the behavioral repertoire with which he or she can respond. However, the relationship between language fluency and effective communication is not so straightforward that we can simply say more fluency is always better. First, compared to a total lack of fluency, a small amount of language skill (knowing a few words) is beneficial to a manager. To reach a higher level of benefit in intercultural interactions, however, individuals need to develop a much more advanced degree of fluency that permits "conversational currency" (being able to make conversation about everyday things such as local sporting events, and so on).[8] Second, the willingness to communicate with others who are culturally different may be more important than fluency itself.[9] Finally, fluency in a foreign language creates certain perceptions among host-country nationals. Fluent foreign managers are perceived as having beliefs more closely aligned with the locals. Furthermore, host-country nationals may also assume that higher degrees of language fluency by a manager are linked to higher competency in other areas, such as knowledge of cultural norms. For example, cultural blunders by a foreign manager are more likely to be forgiven when people are less fluent; fluency sometimes brings higher expectations for culturally appropriate behavior.[10]

People often restrict their communication to those who speak their own language. For example, when large MNCs buy a local company in countries with a different language, they sometimes appoint as their liaison or local manager the host-country national who is most fluent in the language of the MNC. This person is not necessarily the most competent or best able to teach them about the local subsidiary and context; however, the transaction costs of communicating with them are the lowest.[11]

Language accommodation. In our opening vignette, Chungmin accommodated to Todd's inability to speak Korean and spoke English. Language accommodation often relates to the behavioral flexibility stage of our model and identifying the behavior that is most appropriate to the particular situation. Determining who will accommodate can be complex and depends on the motives of the parties in the interaction, the identities of the parties, and the situation itself.[12] Japanese managers, for example, tend to believe that it is not possible for foreigners to be really fluent in the Japanese language and will automatically switch to the foreigner's language. The effort that one party puts into accommodating the other's language is often appreciated and reciprocated. In business situations, the default language is often English, but as we will see in the next section, expecting people to work in a second language may have drawbacks.

Second language use. Most intercultural communication involves at least one of the parties switching to a second language. Often this means switching into English. Using a second or bridge language (second language for both parties) may be the most appropriate behavioral response, but the use of a second language has a number of implications for cross-cultural communication. First, working in a second language can create cognitive strain, requiring more effort on the part of second language users and putting them at a disadvantage. Over long periods of time, second language use can be exhausting. Second, if the native language speaker is unable to recognize signals that indicate lack of understanding or does not work to create an environment where it is acceptable to check for understanding, the second-language speaker may pretend to understand in order to appear competent or avoid embarrassment. To avoid distortion, both participants must devote more attention to the communication process in order to achieve a negotiated meaning.

Communication style

Having a language in common does not ensure mutual understanding. Todd and Chungmin spoke the same language, but the differences in their communication styles distorted their communication. Communication style differences are logical extensions of the internalized values and norms of their respective cultures. They are often a barrier to effectively perceiving, analyzing, and decoding intercultural interactions. To avoid misinterpretations and false attributions, managers who work across cultures must learn the culturally based rules that govern the style, conventions, and practices of language use. Some of the most common style differences are high-context versus low-context communication, direct versus indirect communication, succinct versus elaborate communication, and self-enhancement versus self-effacement. We now review each of these style differences.

High- and low-context styles.[13] Cultures vary in terms of the extent to which they use language itself to communicate the message. Low-context communication relies on explicit verbal messages to convey intention or meaning, whereas in high-context communication most of the information is either contained in the physical context or internalized in the person; very little is in the coded or explicit part of the message. In the opening vignette, Todd, in accordance with his low-context style, expected Chungmin to communicate in words, but given her high-context style, she expected him to read the meaning in her nonverbal communication and actions.

High-context communication

An Indonesian woman invited the mother of the young man who was courting her daughter to tea. The woman was not pleased with the possibility that her daughter might marry into a family that she viewed as having a lower socioeconomic status. During the visit she never mentioned the relationship of their children, but she served bananas with the tea, an unlikely combination. The message that her son did not belong with the woman's daughter any more than bananas go with tea was subtle and implicit; nonetheless, the young man's mother received the message loud and clear.

Source: Thomas, D. (2002), *Essentials of International Management: A Cross-Cultural Perspective*, Thousand Oaks, CA: Sage.

As shown in this example, high-context communication involves multilayered contexts (historical context, social norms, roles, situational and relational contexts), and the listener is expected to understand the nuances of the implicit messages. In contrast, in the low-context communication style, the onus lies on the sender to transmit a clear, explicit message that listeners can easily decode. High-context style is more likely in collectivist cultures such as Asia and Latin America and low-context style in individualist cultures such as Switzerland, Germany, and the United States.

Direct versus indirect communication. Cultures also vary in the extent to which their language and tone of voice reveal or hide intent. Speakers who use a direct style specify their intentions in a forthright manner, whereas in the indirect style nuances in verbal statements hide the speaker's meaning. People from cultures using indirect styles (typically collectivists, such as Chungmin in the opening vignette) may perceive those with a direct style as blunt or insensitive. Conversely, Westerners (such as Todd), who prefer a direct style, often perceive the indirect style of Eastern cultures as insincere and untrustworthy. This is understandable, because in collectivist cultures being polite and avoiding embarrassment often takes precedence over *truth*, as truth is defined in individualist cultures. For collectivists, the social setting determines the degree of directness or truthfulness that is appropriate.

Succinct versus elaborate communication. Communication styles also vary in terms of the quantity of talk (or silence) used to communicate. Styles range from succinct (low quantity of talk), to exacting (just the right amount of words), to elaborate (a high quantity of talk).[14] Failure to recognize these differences often results in misattributions that are barriers to negotiated shared meanings. People with a succinct style may discount elaborate speakers as illogical or inefficient and may even stop listening to them. Elaborate speakers may assume that succinct communicators have very little to say or contribute. The periods of silence used in Eastern cultures are often misunderstood by Westerners, who interpret them as a lack of understanding and then try to shorten them with further explanation or with moving on to the next point. In multicultural work groups, members of highly verbal cultures often fill in the silences and do not allow enough room for people with a more succinct style to talk.

Arab cultures have an elaborate style, involving detailed descriptions, repetition, verbal elaboration and exaggeration, and the use of metaphor, similes, and proverbs. In contrast, the exacting style, typical of England, Germany, Finland and Sweden, emphasizes clarity and precise meanings. These cultures perceive the use of too many words as exaggeration, while the use of too few words is viewed as ambiguity. The succinct styles of China, Japan, Korea, and Thailand are characterized by understatements and meaningful pauses. To some extent, the succinct style of collectivist cultures employs silence as a way of controlling the communication interaction in the same way that individualists use talking.[15]

Self-enhancement versus self-effacement. The self-enhancement verbal style emphasizes the importance of boasting about one's accomplishments and abilities. The self-effacement verbal style, on the other hand, emphasizes the importance of humbling oneself via verbal restraints, hesitations, modest talk, and the use of self-deprecation concerning one's effort or performance.[16] Failures to establish shared meanings occur when people from self-enhancing cultures do not perceive the accomplishments and real worth of people from self-effacing cultures. Furthermore, employees from self-effacing cultures find "selling themselves" to gain promotion in self-enhancing cultures difficult and even repugnant. For example, when counseled to explain why he was the best person for a promotion, a Chinese engineer opted instead to quit one US firm for another that was more cross-culturally sensitive and accustomed to working with Asians. Negative perceptions can also occur when the boastful mode of self-enhancers is not well received in self-effacing cultures. Collectivist Asian cultures are generally self-effacing, while Arab and African-American cultures are self-enhancing.

This style difference also relates to the use of praise – how frequently praise is used, what is praised, and the appropriate response to it. For example, Americans use praise frequently and are prone to praise people who are close to them such as friends or family; they are also likely to praise physical appearance. Japanese are more likely to praise strangers, and Arabs are more likely to praise skill and work than physical characteristics. Response to praise also varies across cultures. In cultures like China, where modesty is a virtue, praise may cause embarrassment. The Hong Kong Chinese, for example, tend to deflect praise, whereas British people are more likely to politely accept it.[17]

Nonverbal communication

Nonverbal communication (such as Chungmin slamming the door and avoiding eye contact) conveys important messages and is produced more automatically than words. It includes body movements and gestures, facial expressions and facial gazing, tone of voice, and the emphasis of certain words. According to some researchers, as much as 70 percent of communication between people in the same language group is nonverbal.[18] It is possible that people rely even more heavily on the nonverbal component in cross-cultural communications.

Nonverbal communication helps to regulate intercultural interaction by providing information about our feelings and emotional state, adding meaning to our verbal messages, and governing the timing and sequencing of the interaction. Nonverbal behaviors serve the same functions across cultures. As with language, however, nonverbal systems of communication have a significant amount of variation around the world. Failures in establishing shared meanings occur because the same nonverbal behavior can have very different meanings across cultures, and because the same meaning is conveyed by different nonverbal cues in different cultures. For example, in Samoa people sit down to show respect, whereas in many cultures they stand up; showing the sole of one's shoe in a Moslem society is a sign of great disrespect; and, while in North America repeatedly crooking the index finger with the palm up beckons another person to come closer, this same gesture is obscene in some cultures.

As with all intercultural behavior, individuals often fall into the trap of using their own cultural lenses to interpret and explain nonverbal gestures. The challenge is to interpret nonverbal communication as intended by the senders, not as it would be perceived in our own culture.

Table 5.1 outlines some of the most common categories of nonverbal behaviors and their influence in intercultural communication.

TABLE 5.1 Categories of nonverbal behavior

Tone of voice	Pitch, volume, speed, tension, variation, enunciation, and a number of other voice qualities such as breathiness or creakiness convey different meaning based on cultural norms.
Proxemics[19]	People follow predictable patterns when establishing distance between themselves and others that are consistent with cultural norms. However, what is appropriate in one culture may seem unusual or even offensive in another.
Body position	The way people position their body conveys information in all cultures. People learn which body position is appropriate in a given situation in the same way that they internalize other aspects of culture. The vast array of possible body positions is difficult to categorize in any systematic way.
Gestures	Hand gestures are used both intentionally and unintentionally in communication. Those gestures that are used as a substitute for words are called emblems. Because the hand can be configured in numerous ways and with great precision, the number of possible hand gestures is quite extensive. To further complicate matters, the same hand gesture can have different meanings in different parts of the world.
Facial expression	Underlying emotional states seem to be closely linked to facial expression. The six basic emotions of anger, fear, sadness, disgust, happiness, and surprise are evident in facial expressions around the world from a very early age. However, individuals often deliberately seek to override the link between their emotions and their facial expressions as a result of display rules appropriate to their culture.
Eye contact (gaze)	All cultures utilize eye contact (gaze) in nonverbal communication. Maintaining and avoiding eye contact communicate important messages. Cultural differences in gaze patterns seem to be fixed relatively early in life and persist regardless of subsequent cross-cultural experiences.

COMMUNICATION SKILLS

Intercultural communication skills are our ability to interact effectively in a given situation; they consist of mindful observation, mindful listening, identity confirmation, and collaborative dialogue.[20] They also include the willingness to communicate.

Mindful observation involves an analytical sequence of observing, describing, interpreting, and suspending evaluation when we encounter new behavior. Mindful observation and reliance on description of cultural behavior that is different from one's own is more effective than are reflexive and often evaluative attributions about this behavior. When a Samoan student visited one of the authors, he immediately seated himself without being invited to do so and averted his eyes. Instead of evaluating this behavior as casual and disrespectful, the mindful response would be to think "He sat down immediately upon entering the room and is not making eye contact with me. Perhaps this is appropriate behavior in Samoa, even though in my culture it is disrespectful. I need to check this out before making any judgments or reacting to this behavior." Investigation revealed that for Samoans to stare at or occupy a position physically above a person of higher status is exceedingly impolite. Mindful observation involves a reflective inner dialogue grounded in nonjudgmental description and interpretation. It also requires self-awareness so people can monitor and control their reactions to the "different" behaviors and interactions.

Mindful listening refers to hearing more than just the words that are said. It also involves checking for accurate perception and paraphrasing the speaker's message into one's own words. Checking for mutual understanding and shared meanings is critical in order to overcome all the possible barriers in an intercultural interaction.

Identity confirmation means addressing people by their preferred titles, labels and identities, and using inclusive rather than exclusive language. This behavior indicates a sensitivity to and respect for the perceptions people have of themselves. For example, in Latin American cultures, people of a certain rank usually expect to be addressed with the formal verb tense (*Usted* rather than *tú*) until they signal otherwise, with the title that reflects their occupation (*Ingeniero* [Engineer] Gonzalez) or educational degree (*Licenciado* Martinez [college graduate]), or with a deferential term of respect (*Don* or *Doña*). Ignoring these communication rules disconfirms their sense of identity or the way they see themselves.

Collaborative dialogue means suspending one's assumptions about culturally different people and refraining from imposing one's views on them. Engaging in collaborative dialogue is analogous to what has been called an ethno-relative perspective.[21] In contrast to ethnocentrism (viewing one's own culture as superior), an ethno-relative approach involves greater recognition and acceptance of cultural differences. It assumes that behavior can be understood only within a cultural context rather than judged on a universal standard of right or wrong.

Willingness to communicate is involved in both perceiving and decoding the intercultural situation and identifying appropriate behavioral responses to that situation. This willingness to communicate is influenced both by the way we view other groups and how receptive we are to communication. When people categorize others and themselves as members of particular groups, such as a cultural group, they make assumptions that affect their beliefs, attitudes, and behaviors. They see people less as individuals and more as members of the group to which they belong. They assume group members are relatively more similar with regard to their beliefs and behavior, and the group is believed to be a more important cause of their behavior than individual characteristics.[22]

The in-group out-group boundary that results from social categorization has several implications for the way individuals select, structure, and process social information. First, this categorization invokes a comparison of one's own group with other cultural groups, resulting in intergroup bias. While it can be either positive or negative, intergroup bias most often favors one's own group. People are more likely to respond favorably to information from an in-group member. Novices to international work are often heard making such negative comparisons between host-country nationals and their own culture ("People are more reliable, ethical, trustworthy, and so on, in my country"). Expert interculturalists avoid comparisons and sweeping generalizations, and use stereotypes only when they are helpful as a first "best-guess" about how others might act. Second, in-group members sometimes develop their own brand of communication, especially the nonverbal component, which can be very difficult for an out-group member to interpret correctly. Finally, when people categorize others as out-group members, they tend to rely on stereotypes when interacting with them. Stereotyping means assigning identical characteristics to all members of a group, regardless of the actual variation among them.[23] Based on relatively little information, stereotypes are resistant to change even in light of new information, and are rarely accurately applied to specific individuals.[24]

Stereotypes affect the senders' ability to communicate their messages because they interfere with their ability to be "heard" and accurately judged. The senders' stereotype about receivers also determines how much and what type of information they will share with them. Stereotypes create expectations of how out-group members will behave. These expectations, in turn, influence the way in which we interpret incoming messages and the predictions we make about out-group member behavior.

Early research on stereotypes indicated that people could nurture intense stereotypes about other national cultures even though they had never met a person from that culture.[25] These cultural stereotypes, however, are often associated with other groups with which one's culture has had a long (often negative) history. National stereotypes may also be susceptible to what is called social dominance theory,[26] which involves a hierarchy of nationalities based on generally accepted status. High status may be attached to a particular nation because of economic dominance or other desirable characteristics. For example, some cultures give Canadians and Norwegians high status because of their generous foreign aid and peacemaking roles. According to this theory, the extent to which one's national group has high status will influence the attitude of others toward a communicator. Their message is more likely to be attended to by others.

The final factor with regard to the willingness of individuals to communicate is receptiveness. Receptiveness involves both cosmopolitanism and satisficing behavior. As seen in our discussion of the global mindset in chapter 4, cosmopolitanism refers to the willingness to engage with others who are different.[27] People with a cosmopolitan mindset are more likely to seek out and communicate with "strangers," even when doing so requires extra effort.

One's willingness to continue making an effort to communicate across cultures can be affected by satisficing. Satisficing in decision-making refers to accepting a decision that is "good enough" because the costs of maximizing are too great.[28] In an intercultural context, we find satisficing in two areas, in the plateauing that occurs in both language acquisition and cultural understanding.[29] When these skills are good enough to get by, some people stop learning. There is no motivation to reach a higher level of cultural understanding or fluency unless an event occurs that initiates another round of cultural sensemaking or a return to the dictionary or language teacher.

Developing Competence in Mindful Communication

Communication competence is a strong predictor of job performance, psychological adjustment, overall intercultural effectiveness in living in the host culture, the extent of social interaction with host nationals, and transfer of technology.[30] We suggest the path to communication competence is through mindful communication. Experts in mindful intercultural communication possess these competencies: empathy, respect, interest in the local culture and people, flexibility, tolerance, nonjudgmental attitudes, initiative, open-mindedness, sociability, positive self-image, positive attitudes, and stress tolerance.[31] Kealey contends that effective intercultural communicators are characterized by adaptation skills, cross-cultural skills, and partnership skills,[32] all of which are necessary for global managers.

Intercultural communication training is generally carried out by external consultants with diverse backgrounds (experience of living and/or working abroad, being married to a spouse from a different culture, experience in international companies, and/or academic degrees in related fields). Some of the larger consulting companies provide culture training along with foreign language training or relocation services for expatriates.[33] The Society for Intercultural Education, Training, and Research (SIETAR) International is the professional organization responsible for the development of the field, and the Intercultural Communication Institute is a resource center for information about the profession.[34]

Intercultural communication training is often included within cross-cultural training programs geared at helping people work and live effectively in a foreign cultural environment. Such training is either culture-general (applicable to all cultures) or culture-specific (directed toward a particular country's culture), and consists of either didactic or experiential workshops.[35]

Research has shown that cultural assimilators (cultural dilemmas with alternative answers and detailed explanations for each answer) are effective and that integrated, multi-method training is more effective than a single approach.[36] There is a large body of research indicating that cross-cultural training can be effective in sensitizing individuals to cultural issues, enhancing cultural self-awareness and empathy, decreasing the use of negative stereotypes, developing complex rather than oversimplified thinking about another culture, and facilitating cross-cultural interaction.[37] Such training significantly increases employee productivity, business skills, and commitment to the employer.[38]

Conclusion

In this section we have explored mindful communication as a critical interpersonal skill and a component of global competency. Mindful communication competence rests on a global mindset and its development is supported by the acquisition of knowledge about different cultures, by the practicing of mindfulness in interacting with others who are culturally different, and by the development of communication skills that improve shared understanding. We now explore the process of creating and building trust, a process in which mindful communication skills are critical.

Notes

1 For a discussion of the concept of grounding see Clark, H. H., & Brennan, S. E. (1991), Grounding in communication, in L. B. Resnick, J. M. Levine, & S. D. Teasley (eds.), *Perspectives on Socially Shared Cognition*, Washington, DC: American Psychological Association.

2 J. T. Wood (1997) provides a good description of the transactional communication process in *Communication in our Lives*, New York: Wadsworth.

3 For a description of cultural scripts, see Triandis, H. C., Marin, G., Lisansky, J., & Betancourt, H. (1984), *Simpatia* as a cultural script of hispanics, *Journal of Personality and Social Psychology*, 47(6), 1363–1375.

4 For more on the concept of mindfulness see Thich, N. H. (1991), *Peace is Every Step: The Path of Mindfulness in Everyday Life*, New York: Bantam Books and Langer, E. J. (1997), *The Power of Mindful Learning*, Reading, MA: Addison-Wesley.

5 For a more complete discussion see Ting-Toomey, S. (1999), *Communicating across Cultures*, New York: The Guilford Press.

6 The idea of using stereotypical behavior as a first best guess is presented in Adler, N. J. (1997), *International Dimensions of Organizational Behavior*, 3rd edn., Cincinnati: South-Western.

7 Many of the ideas about the influence of culture on communication presented in this section are drawn from Stella Ting-Toomey's excellent book, *Communicating across Cultures* (1999).

8 The idea of "conversational currency" was first presented by Brein, D., & David, K. H. (1971), Intercultural communication and the adjustment of the sojourner, *Psychological Bulletin*, 76(3), 215–230.

9 Empirical evidence of this idea is presented in Benson, P. G. (1978), Measuring cross-cultural adjustment: The problem of criteria, *International Journal of Intercultural Relations*, 2(1), 21–37.

10 For a more complete discussion of this point see Hui, H. C., & Cheng, I. W. M. (1987), Effects of second language proficiency of speakers and listeners on person perception and behavioural intention: A study of Chinese bilinguals, *International Journal of Psychology*, 22, 421–30.

11 For more information on the relationship between intercultural communication and organizational learning, see Taylor, S., & Osland, J. S. (2002), The impact of intercultural communication on global organizational learning, in M. Easterby-Smith and M. A. Lyles (eds.), *Handbook of Organizational Learning and Knowledge*, Oxford: Blackwell.

12 A more complete discussion of language accommodation can be found in Gallois, C., & Callan, V. (1997), *Communication and Culture: A Guide for Practice*, Chichester: John Wiley.

13 The high- and low-context communication style was first identified by Hall, E. T. (1976), *Beyond Culture*, New York: Doubleday. Also see Ting-Toomey (1999), p. 272.

14 This style consideration is well documented in Gudykunst, W. B., Ting-Toomey, S., & Chua, E. (1988), *Culture and Interpersonal Communication*, Newbury Park: CA: Sage.

15 For more information about the cultural use of this style see Giles, H., Coupland, N., & Wiemann, J. M. (1992), Talk is cheap . . . but my word is my bond: Beliefs about talk, in K. Bolton & H. Kwok (eds.), *Sociolinguistics Today: International Perspectives*, London: Routledge, pp. 218–243.

16 For more information on this style difference see Ting-Toomey (1999).

17 Two empirical studies with regard to praise across cultures are Barnlund, D. C., & Araki, S. (1985), Intercultural encounters: The management of compliments by Japanese and Americans, *Journal of Cross-Cultural Psychology*, 16, 9–26 and Loh, T. W. C. (1993), Responses to compliments across languages and cultures: A comparative study of British and Hong Kong Chinese, research report no.30, City University of Hong Kong.

18 Based on Noller, P. (1984), *Nonverbal Communication and Marital Interaction*, Oxford: Pergamon.

19 *Proxemics* is the term that has been coined to describe the study the way in which people use personal space in their interactions with others. See Hall, E. T. (1966), *The Hidden Dimension*, Garden City, NY: Doubleday.

20 Ting-Toomey (1999).

21 See Bennett, M. (1993), Towards ethnorelativism: A developmental model of intercultural sensitivity, in R. M. Paige (ed.), *Education for the Intercultural Experience*, Yarmouth, ME: Intercultural Press, pp. 21–71.

22 For a more complete discussion of social categorization see Wilder, D. A. (1986), Social categorization: Implications for creation and reduction of intergroup bias, in L. Berkowitz (ed.), *Advances in Experimental Social Psychology*, New York: Academic Press, Vol. 19, pp. 291–355.

23 See E. Aronson (1976), *The Social Animal*, San Francisco: W. H. Freeman, for one of the original descriptions of stereotyping.

24 For more information on stereotypes see Ashmore, R. D., & Del Boca, F. K. (1981), Conceptual approaches to stereotypes and stereotyping, in D. L. Hamilton (ed.), *Cognitive Processes in Stereotyping and Intergroup Behavior*, Hillsdale, NJ: Erlbaum, p. 1–35.

25 For example, see Katz, D., & Braly, K. W. (1933), Verbal stereotypes and racial prejudice, *Journal of Abnormal and Social Psychology*, 28, 280–290.

26 See Sidanius, J. (1993), The psychology of group conflict and the dynamics of oppression: A social dominance perspective, in S. Iyenger & W. McGuire (eds.), *Explorations in Political Psychology*, Durham, NC: Duke University Press.

27 See Hannerz, U (1996), Cosmopolitans and locals in world culture, in U. Hannerz, *Transnational Connections: Culture, People, Places*, London: Routledge, pp. 102–111.

28 For more information on satisficing see Simon, H. A. (1955), A behavioral model of rational choice, *Quarterly Journal of Economics*, 69, 129–138.

29 For a more complete discussion of satisficing in an intercultural context see Osland, J. S. (1995), *The Adventure of Working Abroad: Hero Tales from the Global Frontier*, San Francisco, CA: Jossey-Bass and Osland, J., & Bird, A. (2000), Beyond sophisticated stereotyping: Cultural sensemaking in context, *Academy of Management Executive*, 14(1), 65–87.

30 These findings are located in Ruben, B. D., & Kealey, D. J. (1979), Behavioral assessment of communication competency and the prediction of cross-cultural adaptation, *International Journal of Intercultural Relations*, 3, 15–48; Hammer, M. R. (1989), Intercultural communication competence, in M. K. Asante & W. B. Gudykunst (eds.), *Handbook of International and Intercultural Communication*, Newbury Park, CA: Sage, pp. 247–60; Hawes, F., & Kealey, D. J. (1981), An empirical study of Canadian technical assistance, *International Journal of Intercultural Relations*, 5(3):, 239–58; and Clarke, C., & Hammer, M. R. (1995), Predictors of Japanese and American managers' job success, personal adjustment, and intercultural interaction effectiveness, *International Management Review*, 35(2), 153–70.

31 This list is compiled from the work of Kealey, D. J., & Ruben, B. D. (1983), Cross-cultural personnel selection criteria, issues, and methods, in D. Landis & R. W. Brislin (eds.), *Handbook of*

Intercultural Training, vol. 1: Issues in Training and Design, New York: Pergamon; Kealey, D. J. (1996), The challenge of international personnel selection, in D. Landis & R. S. Bhagat (eds.), *Handbook of Intercultural Training*, 2nd edn., Thousand Oaks, CA: Sage, pp. 81–105; and Chen, G. M., & Starosta, W. J. (1996), Intercultural communication competence: A synthesis, *Communication Yearbook*, 19, 353–83.

32　See Kealey (1996).

33　For a book that describes the field of intercultural communication, see Dahlén, T. (1997), *Among the Interculturalists: An Emergent Profession and its Packaging of Knowledge*, Stockholm Studies in Social Anthropology, Stockholm: University of Stockholm Press.

34　The Intercultural Communication Institute (ici@intercultural.org) was formerly located at Stanford University. The Institute maintains an extensive library and resource lists, as well as providing training and a Master's program in intercultural communication. See Wederspahn, G. (2000), *Intercultural Services: A Worldwide Buyer's Guide and Sourcebook*, London: Butterworth-Heinemann, for a description of programs and experts in this field.

35　Gudykunst, W. B., Guzley, R. M., & Hammer, M. R. (1996), Designing intercultural training, in D. Landis & R. S. Bhagat (eds.), *Handbook of Intercultural Training*, 2nd edn., Thousand Oaks, CA: Sage, pp. 61–80.

36　Gudykunst, W. B., Hammer, M. R., & Wiseman, R. L. (1977), An analysis of an integrated approach to cross-cultural training, *International Journal of Intercultural Relations*, 1(2), 99–109; Harrrison, J. K. (1992), Individual and combined effects of behavior modeling and the culture assimilator in cross-cultural management training, *Journal of Applied Psychology*, 77, 952–62; Early, P. C. (1987), Intercultural training for managers: A comparison of documentary and interpersonal methods, *Academy of Management Journal*, 30(4), 685–98; Mendenhall, M., Stahl, G., Kühlmann, T., Osland, J., & Oddou, G. (forthcoming, 2004), Evaluation studies of cross-cultural training programs: A review of the literature from 1988–2000, in D. Landis. J. Bennett, & M. Bennett (eds.), *Handbook of Intercultural Training*, 3rd edn., Thousand Oaks, CA: Sage.

37　Bhawuk, D. P. S., & Brislin, R. W. (2000), Cross-cultural training: A review, *Applied Psychology*, 49(1), 162–191; Hammer, M. R., & Martin, J. N. (1996), The effects of cross-cultural training on American managers in a Japanese–American joint venture, *Journal of Applied Communication Research*, 20(2), 161–182; Black, J. S., & Mendenhall, M. (1990), Cross-cultural training effectiveness: A review and a theoretical framework for future research, *Academy of Management Review* 15(1), 113–136.

38　Hammer, M. R. (1995), Making the case with the corporation: Tracking the effects of an international management development program, presentation given at the 21st annual congress of the Society for Intercultural Education, Training, and Research, Phoenix, AZ, May 14–17.

6

Creating and Building Trust

ELLEN WHITENER AND GÜNTER K. STAHL

Creating and building trust is the next interpersonal skill we find most critical for global competency. Here we establish the importance of trust in global management through an analysis of trust issues encountered recently by Ford and Firestone. We then look at the theoretical foundations for trust before we focus on how global managers can create and build trust.

THE IMPORTANCE OF TRUST IN LEADING GLOBAL ORGANIZATIONS: THE EXAMPLE OF FORD–FIRESTONE

Trust may be taken for granted until a crisis occurs. Ford and Firestone provide an interesting example of the importance of trust in leading global organizations – and the consequences of not appreciating the impact of cultural differences on building and maintaining trust. The comparison of the actions of the CEOs of Ford and Firestone provides some lessons about creating and building trust as global leaders.

Ford and Firestone faced serious challenges in restoring the trust that customers, suppliers, employees, and even the country, had in the companies in the wake of the Ford Explorer accidents and Firestone tire failures:

> When reports began to surface that the treads of Firestone tires on Ford Explorer sport utilities and Ranger pickup trucks were peeling off under pressure and causing fatal accidents, [Ford CEO Jacques Nasser] seized on the crisis as an opportunity to show that Ford was, in his words, not "just another car company." The tires are now related to over 1,400 accidents and other mishaps in the United States involving 88 deaths, and the federal government has launched an investigation. . . . Though the problems are not of Nasser's making, they are his responsibility. Says a Ford insider: "This is a test of character for Jac. He's been saying we're a consumer-focused company, and the way he handles this will determine his credibility going forward – both internally and externally."[1]

Indeed, trust in both Ford and Firestone would depend on how their leaders responded to the crisis.

After the giant Japanese tire manufacturer Bridgestone acquired US-based Firestone in 1988, it retained the American CEO, John Nevin. But it soon became clear that his straightforward and assertive leadership style didn't fit with the polite and reserved style of his Japanese bosses. In 1989, he was succeeded by a Japanese executive, who in 1993 was followed, as part of a regular rotation, by Masatoshi Ono. Ono had spent his whole career with Bridgestone, starting in 1959 as an engineer and working his way into management. His style sharply contrasted with Nevin's: in an interview with *Modern Tire Dealer*, he described his style of management: "See–Think–Plan–Do. I believe in getting a first-hand, on-site understanding of the actual situation – seeing and thinking about conditions . . . before making a decision or taking action."[2]

Nasser became CEO of Ford in 1998 after 30 years working for the company – all but six outside of Detroit in Australia, Thailand, the Philippines, Venezuela, Mexico, Argentina, Brazil, and Europe. Born in Lebanon, raised in Australia, he speaks five languages. He is "as close to zero percent American as you can get . . . but [he] has one distinctly American characteristic . . . a highly entrepreneurial, impatient, can-do mentality."[3]

Ford, with Nasser at the helm, became aware of problems with tire separations in 1997 and 1998 when reports of failures of Firestone tires on Ford vehicles began to filter through to the company from Saudi Arabia, Qatar, Kuwait, and Venezuela. Firestone blamed these incidents on customer misuse and refused to act. Taking its cue from Firestone, Ford did not explore the problems thoroughly. But at the instigation of its national affiliates, Ford replaced or upgraded tens of thousands of Firestone tires on its sport utility vehicles. Firestone did not participate in the replacement program in the Middle East, allegedly because it didn't want regulatory officials in the United States to find out.[4]

Neither company initiated further action until mid-2000, when evidence of similar problems started to accumulate in the United States. Despite a media and public outcry and an inquiry from the National Highway Traffic Safety Administration, Ford responded quietly, focusing on gathering information and waiting for its tire supplier, Firestone, to respond. Nasser did get the company organized to find out more about the problem, setting up a "war room" and designating a crisis management team, but avoided direct interaction with the public. He turned down invitations to testify before congressional committees and instructed Ford's researchers to study tire failure and separations at the company's test tracks, instead of gathering information in the field, directly from customers. Problems continued, pressure mounted, and Ford's credibility declined. So Nasser decided to quit waiting on Firestone and reach out directly to the public, participating in Internet chat rooms and starring in a series of print and TV advertisements in which he apologized for the problems.

Ono and his boss, Yoichiro Kaisaki, CEO of parent Bridgestone, practiced *fugenjikko* – no words, only action.[5] After stalling for several weeks, the company joined Ford in authorizing a recall of 6.5 million tires in August 2000. In addition, they initiated an advertising campaign focused, according to a Firestone spokesperson, on helping consumers get accurate information about which tires were involved in the recall.[6] Ono and Kaisaki stayed behind the scenes, pushing John Lampe, Corporate Executive Vice-President and President of the tire sales division, more visibly into the fray. He appeared in advertisements asserting Firestone's commitment to safety and product quality. Otherwise, Firestone's spokespeople denied knowing of any pattern of problems until early August 2000. Then they pointed fingers at Ford for recommending low tire pressures and at customers for poor maintenance, and did not apologize.

Although Nasser and Ono responded differently, both personally lost the trust of their customers, their employees, their suppliers, and their investors. Indeed, by fall 2001, both had been replaced (Nasser by a Ford grandson; Ono by American John Lampe). But more questions remain about whether Firestone can regain the trust of the public than Ford: "It takes a long time to build consumer trust in a brand, but a fraction of the time to destroy that trust. . . . It is possible to rebuild the brand, but it will be expensive. They [Firestone] may have done too little too late."[7] Indeed, numerous experts in crisis management allege that Firestone may not recover from its basic failure to accept responsibility and apologize: "America is a forgive-and-forget country. What America doesn't like is someone who doesn't own up;"[8] "The public is very forgiving for those institutions that will admit their shortcomings and really level with them all the way."[9]

The Ford–Firestone example illustrates the qualities global leaders need to possess and the managerial actions they need to take in order to avoid the mistakes made by Nasser and Ono and to create and build trust globally. What theory tells us about trust and trust building across cultures, found in the next section, provides a framework for identifying those qualities and actions in the third section.

BUILDING TRUST WITHIN GLOBAL ORGANIZATIONS: THE THEORY

Evidence of the importance of trust in leading global organizations comes from a large body of research on intra- and inter-organizational trust. Trust can be defined as "a psychological state comprising the intention to accept vulnerability based upon positive expectations of the intentions or behavior of another."[10]

Research on trust within organizations has suggested that trust is important in a number of ways: it can improve the quality of employee work performance, problem-solving, and communication, and can enhance employee commitment and citizenship behavior. Trust can also improve manager–subordinate working relationships, implementation of self-managed work groups, and the firm's ability to adapt to complexity and change.[11]

Trust also plays a central role in the formation and implementation of cooperative alliances between firms, such as joint ventures, R&D collaborations, or marketing partnerships.[12] For example, joint ventures or supplier–buyer relationships, communication and information exchange, task coordination, informal agreements, and low extents of surveillance and monitoring all require a willingness to be vulnerable, and, hence, trust, on the part of the parties.[13]

Third, trust is important in customer–organization relationships.[14] Customer trust in the service provider, the manufacturer, or the brand seems to be rooted in the actions of the organization or its representatives – such as the listening behavior of sales representatives[15] or the manner in which mistakes or complaints are handled.[16] Trust affects the level of customer loyalty, future intentions, mutual disclosure, and cooperative intentions.[17]

Finally, trust is of critical importance to the success of mergers and acquisitions, by overcoming employee anxiety and resistance, enhancing employee commitment and work performance, and increasing the quality of communication and cooperation between the members of merging or acquired organizations.[18]

The importance of personal relationships

Though represented as employees', suppliers', customers', joint venture partners' or merger partners' trust in the organization, trust is essentially rooted in the personal relationships among individuals (for example, the customer service representative, sales person, joint venture manager). Roger Mayer and his colleagues developed a framework representing the psychological process associated with building trust in relationships.[19] They proposed that individuals' trust in others is based on their propensity to trust and their perceptions of others' trustworthiness, rooted in their interpretation of the attributes and behavior of others. First, individuals vary in their general willingness to trust. Their propensity to trust is a stable within-person, dispositional factor of the trustor that affects the likelihood that they will trust others. At the most global and abstract level, this approach to trust relies on a process by which people develop generalized expectations about how others will treat them.[20] The expectations reflect the extent to which individuals have deep faith in themselves, others, systems, culture, or society,[21] possess an attitude that people are basically trustworthy, moral, responsible, and cooperative,[22] and can rely on the words, promises, and written or verbal statements of others.[23]

Second, the trust individuals have in others also depends on their perceptions of the attributes of the trustee. Many attributes have been proposed to be part of the assessment of trustworthiness (for example, competence, discreetness, integrity, openness, and receptivity);[24] they can be parsimoniously organized into three categories: perceptions of another's ability or competence, benevolence, and integrity.[25] These factors of perceived trustworthiness likely combine multiplicatively in determining the overall degree of trust that one party has with respect to another party.[26] That is, a very low level of trust in terms of any of the dimensions can undermine trust, and greater trust exists in a given referent when high levels of trust along several dimensions are present. For example, greater trust exists in a manager when that person is perceived to be both competent and concerned for the welfare of his or her subordinates. A manager who is either incompetent or does not care for his or her subordinates will likely not be trusted at all.

Does trust differ across cultures?

The question arises, then, whether individuals from different cultures see trust differently. Evidence exists through the World Values Survey that individuals from different cultures have different propensities to trust. In this survey, an international, cross-disciplinary team of researchers studied the basic values and beliefs of individuals in over sixty countries. In the 1990–3 survey, subjects in 43 countries indicated whether they agreed with the statement that "most people can be trusted." The differences in the responses across the 43 countries were significant. For example, almost 70 percent of respondents in the Scandinavian countries of Finland, Norway, and Sweden, approximately 50 percent of those surveyed in China, the United States, and Canada, 42 percent in Japan, and less than 20 percent in Latvia, Slovenia, Romania, Turkey, and Brazil agreed with the statement that most people can be trusted.[27]

These results provide rough evidence that individuals from different cultures have different generalized propensities to trust others; however, the results of comparative research using more sophisticated measures offer additional support. For example, using a survey instrument of trust versus suspiciousness that they carefully crafted and extensively pretested, a team of researchers found that managers in the United States had higher trust than managers from a cluster of regions (Scandinavia, central Europe, Thailand, Spain, South Africa, and Japan) and substantially higher trust than managers from Greece.[28]

People from different cultures therefore seem to start with different levels of generalized trust in others. The question then becomes whether individuals from different cultures view the factors of perceived trustworthiness as universally effective in facilitating trust in interpersonal relationships. One study specifically designed to explore this question found that the answer is yes, and no. After taking into consideration their different propensities to trust, managers in Norway, the United States, and the People's Republic of China all indicated that their trust in their managers was associated with two-way communication and benevolence/demonstration of concern. Integrity was related to trust only for managers in the United States; and delegation of control was related to trust only for managers in China.[29]

In a study of leadership, Bob House led a large team of researchers[30] in exploring implicit leadership theories in 62 countries. The team found that many of the elements of leader trustworthiness were seen universally as contributing to outstanding leadership. Specifically, different facets of leader integrity (justice, honesty, trustworthiness), competence (administratively skilled, win–win problem solver, communicative), and benevolence were found to be universal positive leader characteristics and attributes such as egocentricity, irritableness, or lack of cooperation were universally viewed as impediments to effective leadership. However, a common preference for a certain type of leadership does not preclude cultural differences in actual leader behavior. A shared preference for what has been described in the trust literature as attributes of managerial trustworthiness[31] does not mean these attributes will be enacted in exactly the same way across cultures or that similar meaning would be attached to all exhibited behavior across all cultures.

Indeed, members of international cross-cultural teams find that building trust is problematic.[32] Differing orientations toward trust and other values, rooted in cultural differences, may create conflict among the members, polarizing them into cultural subgroups and reinforcing ethnographic or cultural stereotypes. As discussed below, however, leaders who understand and address the tensions that cultural differences in propensity to trust and perceptions of trust-building behavior can create in building trust should bridge the differences and build trusting, cooperative, and high-performance relationships among management, staff, customers, and suppliers.[33]

CREATING AND BUILDING TRUST GLOBALLY

The Ford–Firestone example illustrates the qualities global leaders need to possess (or should not possess) and what managerial actions they need to take (or should avoid) in order to build and sustain trust globally. As shown in figure 6.1, global leaders need to accurately diagnose situations, identify effective managerial action, and act appropriately.

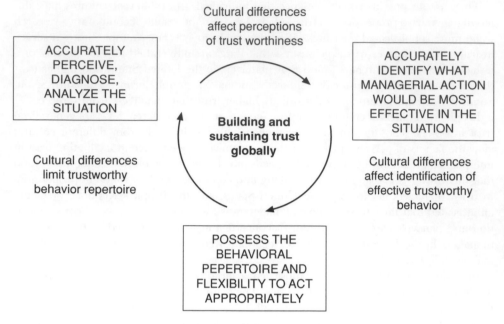

FIGURE 6.1 Building and sustaining trust globally

With regard to trust building, they need to recognize that cultural differences frame their own and others' perceptions of trustworthiness, affect determination of effective action, and limit their behavioral repertoire. A comparison of Nasser's and Ono's perceptions and actions illustrates the role of cultural differences in developing trust and suggests ways that leaders can understand and act to effectively build trust across cultures. We use the effectiveness cycle for our analysis.

Accurate diagnosis of the situation

Both Nasser and Ono made mistakes in handling the crisis that ultimately led to their dismissal, but Ono seems to have had more difficulty in diagnosing the issue, deciding to act, and then acting effectively. First, Nasser seems to have understood historical, legal, and cultural aspects of the crisis that facilitated his diagnosis of the situation. He recognized the power of historical precedent in framing others' interpretation of his response. He knew that customers and government regulators believed that car companies, including Ford, had blundered in previous crises (for example, exploding gas tanks in the Pinto, instability in the Corvair, rollovers with the Bronco). He appreciated the dilemma that this created – on the one hand, customers expected Ford to take responsibility and respond quickly to what they believed was a serious problem and on the other, they expected Ford to stonewall and dodge, like it and other companies had done in the past – and vowed to respond more swiftly and responsibly.[34] Nasser realized the situation encompassed more than the current crisis – and people's interpretation of their response would be compared against historical responses.

Firestone also has a history. In the 1970s, customers started to complain about tread separation on steel-belted radial tires. Firestone blamed the problem on inadequate maintenance and argued with the government for months before recalling over 13 million tires. At the time, Ono was not CEO and Bridgestone did not own the company; but because they responded in exactly the same way as Firestone had responded before, it appears that they did not understand that the situation was bigger than the current incident.

Nasser also understood that although the customer orientation in the United States has significant legal support when safety is threatened, Americans see the problem in ethical–moral terms. Interest groups and government agencies actively protect the safety and rights of consumers; and the legal system abounds with product liability lawsuits, primarily to ensure that companies respond ethically. Early on Nasser realized the moral and ethical tone of the crisis. When asked in an interview in *Fortune* how he felt about the crisis, he replied, "Well, the first one is sorrow about the defective tires and the fact that we have had deaths attributed to these faulty tires. I think whenever there is a break in trust it pulls at our heartstrings. We don't want to let anyone down. And when something unintended like this happens, it really doesn't matter whose fault it is. We feel morally and emotionally connected to the people who buy our vehicles."[35] Ono was really not available for comment, suggesting he may not have fully appreciated the legal or moral context. Consumers in Japan have few rights and product liability lawsuits are almost nonexistent.[36]

Finally, Nasser realized that Americans expect action and contrition. Americans tend to have a high propensity to trust. They are likely, therefore, to have high and significant expectations of others and a willingness to take risks and make themselves vulnerable to others. Yet they may also be quick to lower those expectations and abandon trust if they believe they are being taken advantage of: "Fool me once, shame on you; fool me twice, shame on me." The American public was wary of Ford and Firestone, because they had been "fooled" before. Yet Nasser seemed more aware of this than Ono, and acted quickly to try to fulfill rather than disappoint their positive expectations. After pressuring Firestone to respond and getting the brush-off, first in Saudi Arabia and then in the United States, Ford started to act on its own. Ford replaced tires themselves in the Middle East, and when the crisis spread to American shores, they initiated an advertising campaign in which Nasser himself apologized to the people for the problem. He also took the very visible action of temporarily closing three automobile assembly plants and using their tires for the recall. Ono's management style of See-Think-Plan-Do, coupled with a Japanese discomfort with public disclosure and repentance, led to delays and denials.

Interestingly, at the time the crisis started to unfold, Nasser had lived and worked in the United States for less time than Ono; perhaps, however, his experiences in many different cultures over the course of his career with Ford sensitized him to looking for the nuances in a culture's perceptions.

Identification and initiation of effective managerial action

With their long history of corporate crises, Americans have come to expect specific responses from corporate leaders: a crisis mentality, full disclosure, resources backing up the rhetoric, and top leader visibility. Nasser's mindful communication skills helped him recognize the list of responses that Americans expected, and he gave them most of these. If Ono recognized the list, he did not perform the responses, suggesting that he under-appreciated their role in maintaining his credibility and their trust and confidence in him and his company.

Once he realized that Firestone was not going to take the lead on the tire problem, Nasser acted swiftly. He created an organizational structure to manage the company's interaction with the problem, designating a crisis management team and assigning two executives as chairs. He set in motion several mechanisms for gathering more information, directing research engineers to study tire separations on their test tracks and, when that was inconclusive, sending them to the field to get data directly from customers. He also gathered information himself by logging onto chat rooms and interacting with concerned customers. He committed significant resources to replacing the tires, authorizing Ford to spend its own money (ultimately $3 billion) to replace Firestone tires and closing three automobile assembly plants to poach the tires originally destined for new cars. And he shared information with the public, meeting with members of the press and appearing in advertisements to explain what they were doing and to express his regret for the situation.

Ono went to his public relations firm, Fleishman-Hillard, to handle the crisis. But the agency resigned from the account when Firestone ignored its counsel to take "positive, dramatic steps to address the crisis."[37] Ono replaced them with another firm (Ketchum) with strong ties to Washington. In addition, Firestone said it didn't keep track of consumer tire failures and didn't describe any attempts to gather that information once the reports started to emerge. It did respond to specific consumer complaints by pointing out that most tire failures are a result of improper inflation at high temperatures. When finally pressured into the recall, Ono did get Bridgestone to fly more tires from Japan and to increase production. He also offered consumers up to $100 per tire if they wanted to purchase a competitor's tire. Finally, Ono assigned the job of spokesperson to Corporate Executive Vice-President John Lampe. Lampe appeared in several advertisements expressing Firestone's commitment to quality and safety. Firestone complemented this approach with a website and dedicated customer service hotline to provide consumers with recall information.

Finally, when congressional hearings convened in late 2000, both Nasser and Ono blamed each other. Observers described Nasser as poised and comfortable in the hearings and Ono as rattled, inconsistent, and uncomfortable. One senator reacted to Ono's performance: "What does it take to put a company on notice that perhaps they've got a defective product out there?"[38]

Behavioral repertoire and flexibility to act appropriately

Finally, global leaders need to recognize that cultural differences limit their behavioral repertoire and flexibility to act appropriately. The demonstration of integrity, for example, may differ significantly across cultures. Several analysts of the Ford and Firestone crisis indicated that Americans are forgiving if an offending official accepts responsibility and tells the truth. Nasser fairly quickly hit the advertising and print channels with that message. However, Japanese norms of integrity may differ; indeed, in October 2000, Ono followed a practice common in Japan, resigning from his position, symbolically accepting the responsibility for the company's problems.[39] Americans' assumptions that leaders with integrity would immediately and publicly accept responsibility clashed with the Japanese assumption that leaders with integrity try to fix the problem and then resign quietly. It may have been just as improbable for Ono to do what Nasser did as it seems to have been for Americans to trust Ono when he didn't apologize.

CONCLUSION

The example of the CEOs of Ford and Firestone in the tire separation crisis combined with research on trust provides a framework to guide global leaders in building and sustaining trust in their cross-cultural organizational relationships. Generally, global leaders need to recognize that individuals from different cultures vary in their propensity to trust. They also need to ascertain the historical, legal/moral/ethical, and cultural differences underpinning perceptions of interactions and situations, identify the expectations of interaction partners with diverse cultural backgrounds, and modify their behavior to fit those expectations.

As our reviews of culture and mindful communication suggest, individuals differ greatly in their perceptions of situations, preferences for certain behaviors, and predilections to act. Individuals with the same experiences and cultural backgrounds often share tendencies to understand situations and behaviors in similar ways. In contrast, individuals who don't share those experiences and backgrounds can struggle to connect with them. Therefore leaders must figure out how to bridge the cultural and individual differences in perceptions, preferences, and predilections to build and sustain trust. Leaders with a global mindset, perhaps rooted as is Nasser in a wide array of cross-cultural experiences, and with mindful communication skills, will be better equipped to successfully build and maintain trust in their cross-cultural organizational relationships.

NOTES

1 Taylor (2000), p. 123.
2 Stoyer (1993), p. 24.
3 Zesiger (1998), p. 80.
4 O'Rourke (2001).
5 Eisenberg (2000).
6 Cardona (2000).
7 Robert Kahn, director of a branding company as quoted in Lucas (2001), p. 22.
8 Bill Lyddan, CEO of an advertising company, quoted in Cardona (2000), p. 54.
9 Harold Burson, CEO of a public relations firm, quoted in Eisenberg (2000), p. 40.
10 Rousseau et al. (1998), p. 395.
11 For recent reviews see Kramer (1999); Mayer, Davis, & Schoorman (1995); Rousseau et al. (1998); Whitener et al. (1998).
12 Das & Teng (1998); Ring & Van de Ven (1992); Zaheer, McEvily, & Perrone (1998).
13 Doney & Cannon (1997); Inkpen & Currall (1998).
14 Berry (1995); Ganesan (1994); Garbarino & Johnson (1999).
15 Ramsey & Sohi (1997).

16 Tax, Brown, & Chandrashekaran (1998).
17 Crosby, Evans, & Cowles (1990); Singh & Sirdeshmukh (2000); Sirdeshmukh, Sing, & Sabol (2002); Swan, Bowers, & Richardson (1999).
18 E.g., Nikandrou, Papalexandris, & Bourantas (2000); Stahl & Sitkin (2001).
19 Mayer, Davis, & Schoorman (1995).
20 Stack (1978).
21 Erikson (1963).
22 Wrightsman (1992).
23 Rotter (1967; 1971).
24 Butler (1991).
25 Mayer, Davis, & Schoorman (1995).
26 Mishra (1996).
27 Inglehart (1997); Inglehart, Basanez, & Moreno (1998).
28 Harnett and Cummings (1980).
29 Whitener et al. (1999).
30 Den Hartog et al. (1999); House et al. (1999).
31 E.g., Mayer, Davis, & Schoorman (1995); Whitener et al. (1998).
32 Moosmüller, Spieß, & Podsiadlowski (2001); Smith & Noakes (1996).
33 Moosmüller et al. (2001).
34 Taylor (2000).
35 Taylor (2000), p. 128.
36 Eisenberg (2000).
37 O'Rourke (2001), p. 261.
38 Eisenberg (2000).
39 Griffin & Pustay (2002).

References

Berry, Leonard L. (1995). Relationship marketing of services – Growing interest, emerging perspectives. *Journal of the Academy of Marketing Science*, 23, 236–245.

Butler, John K., Jr. (1991). Towards understanding and measuring conditions of trust: Evolution of a conditions of trust inventory. *Journal of Management*, 17, 643–663.

Cardona, M. M. (2000). CEOs' summer fashion – The hair shirt; corporate contrition means execs must go beyond apologies: Pundits. *Advertising Age*, 71(37), 54.

Crosby, L. A., Evans, K. R., & Cowles, D. (1990). Relationship quality in services selling: An interpersonal influence perspective. *Journal of Marketing*, 54, 68–81.

Das, T. K., & Teng, B-S. (1998). Between trust and control: Developing confidence in partner cooperation in alliances. *Academy of Management Review*, 23(3), 491–512.

Den Hartog, D. N., House, R. J., Hanges, P. J., Ruiz-Quintanilla, S. A., Dorfman, P. W., et al. (1999). Culture-specific and cross-culturally generalizable implicit leadership theories: Are attributes of charismatic/transformational leadership universally endorsed? *Leadership Quarterly*, 10, 219–256.

Doney, P. M., & Cannon, J. R. (1997). An examination of the nature of trust in buyer–seller relationships. *Journal of Marketing*, 61, 35–51.

Eisenberg, D. (2000), September 18. Firestone's Rough Road: Facing the wrath of Congress and the Public, Can the Tiremaker survive? *TIME*, 156(12), 38–40.

Erikson, E. H. (1963). *Childhood and Society*. 2nd edn., New York: Norton.

Ganesan, S. (1994). Determinants of long-term orientation in buyer–seller relationships. *Journal of Marketing*, 58, 1–19.

Garbarino, E., & Johnson, M. S. (1999). The different roles of satisfaction, trust, and commitment in customer relationships. *Journal of Marketing*, 63, 70–87.

Griffin, R. W., & Pustay, M. W. (2002). *International Business: A Managerial Perspective*. 3rd edn., Upper Saddle River, NJ: Prentice Hall.

Harnett, D. L., & Cummings, L. L. (1980). *Bargaining Behavior: An International Study*. Houston: Dame Publications.

House, R., Hanges, P. J., Quintanilla, A., Dorfman, P. W., Dickson, M. W., Javidan, M., et al. (1999). Cultural influences on leadership and organizations: Project Globe, in W. H. Mobley, M. J. Gessner, & V. Arnold (eds.), *Advances in Global Leadership*, vol. 1, Greenwich, CT: JAI Press.

Inglehart, R. (1997). *Modernization and Postmodernization: Cultural, Economic, and Political Change in 43 Societies*. Princeton, NJ: Princeton University Press.

Inglehart, R., Basanez, M., & Moreno, A. (1998). *Human Values and Beliefs: A Cross-Cultural Sourcebook*. Ann Arbor: University of Michigan Press.

Inkpen, A., & Currall, S. C. (1998). The nature, antecedents, and consequences of joint venture trust. *Journal of International Management*, 4, 1–20.

Kramer, R. M. (1999). Trust and distrust in organizations: Emerging perspectives, enduring questions. *Annual Review of Psychology*, 50, 569–598.

Lucas, P. (2001). Is it the end of the road for Firestone? *Journal of Business Strategy*, 22(5), 21–22.

Mayer, R. C., Davis, J. H., & Schoorman, F. D. (1995). An integrative model of organizational trust. *Academy of Management Review*, 20, 709–734.

Mishra, A. K. (1996). Organizational responses to crisis: The centrality of trust. In R. M. Kramer & T. R. Tyler (eds.), *Trust in Organizations: Frontiers of Theory and Research*, pp. 261–287. Thousand Oaks, CA: Sage.

Moosmüller, A., Spieß, E., & Podsiadlowski, A. (2001). International team building. In M. E. Mendenhall, T. M. Kühlmann, & G. K. Stahl (eds.), *Developing Global Business Leaders: Policies, Processes, and Innovations*, pp. 211–224. Westport: Quorum.

Nikandrou, I., Papalexandris, N., & Bourantas, D. (2000). Gaining employee trust after acquisition: Implications for managerial action. *Employee Relations*, 22(4), 334–355.

O'Rourke, J. (2001). Bridgestone/Firestone, Inc. and Ford Motor Company: How a product safety crisis ended a hundred-year relationship. *Corporate Reputation Review*, 4(3), 255–264.

Ramsey, R. P., & Sohi, R. S. (1997). Listening to your customers: The impact of perceived salesperson listening behavior on relationship outcomes. *Journal of the Academy of Marketing Science*, 25(2), 127–137.

Ring, P. S., & Van de Ven, A. H. (1992). Structuring cooperative relationships between organizations. *Strategic Management Journal*, 13, 483–498.

Rotter, J. B. (1967). A new scale for the measurement of interpersonal trust. *Journal of Personality*, 35, 615–665.

Rotter, J. B. (1971). Generalized expectancies for interpersonal trust. *American Psychologist*, 26, 443–452.

Rousseau, D. M., Sitkin, S. B., Burt, R. S., & Camerer, C. (1998). Not so different after all: A cross-discipline view of trust. *Academy of Management Review*, 23, 393–404.

Singh, J., & Sirdeshmukh, D. (2000). Agency and trust mechanisms in consumer satisfaction and loyalty judgments. *Journal of the Academy of Marketing Science*, 28(1), 150–167.

Sirdeshmukh, D., Singh, J., & Sabol, B. (2002). Consumer trust, value, and loyalty in relational exchanges. *Journal of Marketing*, 66, 15–37.

Smith, P. B., & Noakes, J. (1996). Cultural differences in group processes. In A. West (ed.), *Handbook of Work Group Psychology*. Chichester: John Wiley, pp. 479–501.

Stack, L. C. (1978). Trust. In H. London & J. E. Exner, Jr. (eds.), *Dimensions of Personality*. New York: John Wiley, pp. 561–599.

Stahl, G. K., & Sitkin, S. (2001). Trust in mergers and acquisitions, paper presented at the Academy of Management Conference, Washington, DC, August 3–8.

Stoyer, L. (1993). Masatoshi Ono: Finally off to the races? *Modern Tire Dealer*, 74(9), 22–25.

Swan, J. E., Bowers, M. R., & Richardson, L. D. (1999). Customer trust in the salesperson: An integrative review and meta-analysis of the empirical literature. *Journal of Business Research*, 44(2), 93–107.

Tax, S. S., Brown, S. W., & Chandrashekaran, M. (1998). Customer evaluations of service complaint experiences: Implications for relationship marketing. *Journal of Marketing*, 62, 60–76.

Taylor, Alex, III (2000). Jac Nasser's biggest test. *Fortune*, 142(6), 123–124, 126, 128.

Whitener, E. M., Brodt, S. E., Korsgaard, M. A., & Werner, J. M. (1998). Managers as initiators of trust: An exchange relationship framework for understanding managerial trustworthy behavior. *Academy of Management Review*, 23, 513–530.

Whitener, E. M., Maznevski, M. L., Hua, W., Saebo, S., & Ekelund, B. (1999). Testing the cultural boundaries of a model of trust: Subordinate–manager relationships in China, Norway and the United States, paper presented at the 59th Annual Meeting of the Academy of Management, Chicago, August.

Wrightsman, L. W. (1992). *Assumptions about Human Nature: Implications for Researchers and Practitioners*. 2nd edn., Newbury Park, CA: Sage.

Zaheer, A., McEvily, B., & Perrone, V. (1998). Does trust matter? Exploring the effects of interorganizational and interpersonal trust on performance. *Organization Science*, 9: 141–159.

Zesiger, S. (1998). Jac Nasser is car crazy. *Fortune*, 137(12), 80–82.

7

Boundary Spanning

Schon Beechler, Mikael Søndergaard, Edwin L. Miller, and Allan Bird

Introduction to The System-Level Skills of Global Competency

The capstone of our global competency model is a set of skills that involves exerting influence over others by leveraging the organization's systems. Such ability to manage the organization's systems in order to exert influence relies heavily on the interpersonal skills of mindful communication and creating and building trust. The three systems skills are boundary spanning, creating and building community through change, and ethical decision-making. Effective global managers possess the ability to span boundaries, those within the firm, those between the firm and external constituencies, and those less obvious boundaries such as we find among indirect stakeholders.

Global managers also have to be able to manage change. Change may be at the level of the individual or group within the firm, which usually involves some form of learning. On other occasions the focus of the change involves constituencies that extend beyond the organization's boundaries. In most instances, in managing change, it is necessary to create or build communities – of employees and various stakeholders within and beyond the organization.

The third system skill is more nuanced. It is the ability to make decisions and take actions that conform to a high ethical standard. Ethical decision-making is a system skill because in the process of making ethical decisions, a global manager must be able to see a complex array of inputs from a broad perspective and to think in terms of systems to fully grasp possible consequences of the decisions. Decision-making is in danger of violating ethical standards when it loses sight of the larger perspective and, instead, focuses on narrower interests. The system skill of ethical decision-making actually brings us back to our model's threshold traits because ethical decision-making reinforces integrity and humility.

Our focus in this chapter is on boundary spanning as a system skill at the individual level. We begin, though, with a description of the current, organizational-level understanding of boundary spanning because this is the level at which boundary spanning is presently discussed among most researchers. We then examine boundary spanning at the individual level, including a review of the few studies that have been conducted from this perspective. Building on this approach, we introduce the framework we use to think about boundary spanning. Our focus then moves to an examination of the process of boundary spanning, including the role of boundary spanning in the communication or sharing of explicit and tacit knowledge, and how this process proceeds at the individual level. We then suggest ways to build boundary-spanning skills, first at the individual level and then at the organizational level. A brief conclusion summarizes our evolving understanding of the critical process of boundary spanning.

WHAT BOUNDARY SPANNING IS

Traditionally boundary spanning has been defined as the creation of linkages that integrate and coordinate across organizational boundaries. Boundary spanners, go-betweens, interfacers: they are the people who establish and maintain such organizational linkages.

As they work in multiple systems, managers face four types of boundaries: vertical, horizontal, external, and geographic.[1] For global managers to be effective at boundary spanning, they must:

1 Gather potentially relevant information; interpret, filter and communicate that information to units and individuals located within the organization's boundaries;
2 Represent the firm in an effective way to its various external clients and sources of influence;
3 Gain influence over the external environment while simultaneously communicating with their organizational constituents; and
4 Enable the firm to respond more rapidly to changes in environmental demands.

In this context, the boundary spanner cuts across functional, geographic, and external boundaries in order to move ideas, information, decisions, talent, and resources where they are most needed.

Such activities are important because they help to ensure that vertical, horizontal, external, and geographical boundaries do not hamper the flow of essential information and ideas. Boundary spanners are the people who establish and maintain such organizational linkages.

Today, channels of information have expanded both in scope and scale, owing to three developments: the nature of boundaries has become increasingly more permeable; the number of boundaries which require spanning has increased dramatically; and technology has developed more rapid and accessible means of communication. As organizations ready themselves to face global opportunities and challenges, they have learned that managing information and knowledge requires integrative activities and networking[2] of a sort that vastly extends the traditional notion of boundary spanning. As Rosen and his colleagues point out in their study of global literacy:

Walls are crumbling among markets, organizations, and nations. People, information, labor, and capital move freely as never before. Global media, international travel, and communications have eroded distance and borders, linking us instantly to one another from Prague to Shanghai, from Lima to London. A tightly woven fabric of distant encounters and instant connections knits our diverse world together.[3]

As the complexities that constitute globalization continue to transform the environment of business, multinational firms can no longer afford rigid, traditional organizational boundaries that separate employees, tasks, processes, and places. Rather, they need to establish more flexible structures and processes that span existing boundaries and allow greater fluidity throughout the organization and swifter coordination of action.

An example[4] of such boundary spanning is found in the Scandinavian Airline System (SAS) corporate management contribution of Michael Mertz Mørk. Mørk was a successful Danish career diplomat hired by SAS CEO Jan Carlzon[5] to establish linkages among the many areas that developed policy at SAS to ensure the continuity and appropriateness of their policies. This concern for coordination grew as the airline industry shifted from a government monopoly to a deregulated industry facing a competitive marketplace. The process involved negotiations with multiple public authorities. At SAS Mørk and two assistants, also hired from the Danish Foreign Service, implemented an information system modeled on one used in the Foreign Service. The goal of increased coordination was to strengthen the strategic position of SAS by building its ability to span divergent areas related to airline policy. Specific demands of the boundary-spanning information system at SAS involved increasing the quality of information and the content of documents, and increasing their flow as well.

Michael Mørk built his skills as a boundary spanner based on his service in the Ministry of Foreign Affairs, and was particularly well-suited to the boundary-spanning challenges SAS, a large, semi-public organization, faced. The boundaries that needed to be spanned were internal and external, with both private and governmental constituencies, plus a large public constituency, and the concern for boundary spanning grew as SAS shifted from a government monopoly to a deregulated industry facing a competitive marketplace. This process involved negotiations with multiple authorities. The goal of the boundary-spanning initiative was to increase coordination in order to strengthen the SAS strategic position by building its ability to span the divergent areas related to airline policy.

While at SAS, Mørk and his team established linkages, but more than that, they were successful in establishing a conduit system of *information flows* within SAS. This approach is based on *knowing who* in Kidd and Teramoto's terms.[6] However, *knowing who* is not enough, given the increasing complexity of globalization. Mørk did more than build *know who* at SAS. He established a network composed of people and conduits for information flow, a series of pipelines carrying two-way flows within SAS and between SAS and its external constituencies. The way of thinking he introduced at SAS was to focus on the process rather than the structure, on the flow of information rather than the architecture of the information network. His approach encouraged a more strategic and complex view of information and its processing at SAS: to know *what* relationships and their outcomes contributed to SAS; to know *why* this process was implemented and why its outcomes mattered; to know *how* to maintain the process flow.

Boundary spanning at the individual level

Boundary spanning is a complex phenomenon, often discussed at the organizational level as an important part of an organization's strategic capabilities. At the same time, boundary spanning is also an individual-level capability, as illustrated above. In this section, our focus is on boundary spanning at the individual-level competency, while boundary spanning at the strategic level is included in the focus of Part IV: Executing Strategic Initiatives Globally.

At the individual level, boundary spanning is a system skill that is built on the foundation of the threshold traits of integrity, humility, inquisitiveness, and hardiness. Global managers who are effective boundary spanners are able to ensure that boundaries do not hamper the flow of essential knowledge and information. Interpersonal networks are vital in this effort because they serve as the glue that holds these vast geographically dispersed and internally differentiated organizations together. Interpersonal links act as integrative mechanisms because they are conduits for information exchange that enable the various interconnected parts of the multinational enterprise to coordinate their activities with one another.[7]

The actual process of boundary spanning is implemented through the communication acts of individual members of the organization. Global managers who have the threshold traits described in the global competency model, especially inquisitiveness and humility, combined with the global mindset orientation (cognitive complexity and cosmopolitanism) and the interpersonal skills of mindful communication and creating and building trust are likely to be able to build and maintain the relationships necessary to support boundary-spanning activity in a global context.

Boundary spanning is a systems skill because, as a process, it builds and maintains connections both within the organization and beyond it. In addition, this system skill is a vital contribution to the global manager's ability to make ethical decisions. In the global context, ethical decision-making requires an understanding of community, an ability to build new community, and an appreciation of the many systems at work in the shaping of the community. Effective boundary spanning is the process through which the global manager gains all this information.

Boundary spanning: An evolving perspective

We find the traditional, linkage approach to boundary spanning too static in its imagery to capture the essence of the vitality Mørk fostered at SAS. *Knowing who*[8] was not enough for the SAS boundary spanners. Mørk focused on the information flows *between and among* the "*whos.*" The way of thinking he introduced led to establishing a process, rather than simply a structure, which in turn led to a focus on the flow of information rather than the architecture of the information network.

As described above, the traditional terminology to capture the idea of boundary spanning has been built on the idea of *linkage*, the underlying metaphor being links in a chain. This conceptual framework is somewhat limited in its ability to capture and describe the capabilities managers need to be successful in a global environment. Managers find themselves in the midst of a dynamic complexity in which structured and formalized linkages may actually impede boundary spanning. Given such complexity,

TABLE 7.1 Boundary spanning

Traditional, structure-based concept	*New, process-based concept*
Linkages as in a chain; connections	Conduit, flows
Structural aspects received focus	Container, content and flow are the focus
Static	Dynamic
Straddling boundaries	Joining knowledge flows
Gateway and gatekeepers	Knowledge flows among people, flow rates; information brokers
Relationships	Use of relationships

global organizations need to look beyond the rigid, traditional boundaries that separate employees, tasks, processes, and places. We suggest thinking of boundary spanning in a more fluid, evolving way, as the conduits or piping system and the information that flows through them.

Mørk saw these same challenges. His innovation at SAS was to establish flows of information among different systems of knowledge within the SAS organization and with a complex group of external stakeholder constituencies, to focus on content and flow as well as on the structural aspect, the linkages.

The new call is for flexible structures and processes that span existing boundaries and allow for fluidity throughout the organization and swift coordination of action. Table 7.1 summarizes our evolving approach to boundary spanning.

In the following sections we examine the process of boundary spanning. We then discuss how boundary-spanning skills can be fostered at the individual and organizational levels.

Focus on the Process of Boundary Spanning

When members span boundaries through their interpersonal contacts, they share knowledge and information. The value of such flows in achieving strategic goals is significant. These flows spread knowledge critical to the organization. Yet there are two additional advantages to boundary spanning: it allows the organization to achieve higher levels of efficiency because it allows parts of the organization to take advantage of arbitrage opportunities. It also stimulates innovation through chance discoveries and putting ideas together in novel ways.[9]

Let's examine the knowledge flows facilitated among people in an organization and in the organization's environment. Drawing on the distinction introduced in the opening of this section, the effective boundary spanner *knows how*, *knows who*, *knows what*, and *knows why*. These knowings require two types of knowledge: explicit and tacit. Explicit knowledge can be expressed in words and numbers and is easily communicated and shared. Hard data, scientific formulae, codified procedures, and universal principles are all examples of explicit knowledge.

Tacit knowledge is difficult to identify because it is knowledge we have which we *cannot* articulate or express. Subjective insights, intuitions, and hunches fall into this category of knowledge. Tacit knowledge is highly personal and hard to formalize, which makes it difficult to communicate or to share with others. It is also deeply rooted in our action and experience, as well as in our ideals, values, and emotions.[10] Tacit knowledge emphasizes the importance of learning from direct experience, including trial and error.

In the global context, much of the knowledge that the expert manager has about a foreign location, for example, is tacit, a result of experiential learning and meaning-giving based on these experiences. The value of such knowledge to an organization is great, and its role in boundary spanning is critical. For example, the expert manager in a global venture in a developing country will know almost intuitively on whom to call for advice, how to do so in a culturally appropriate way, why such relationships need to be built, and what the business situation is in this developing economy from many points of view.

Tacit knowledge encompasses the informal and hard-to-pin-down skills or crafts captured in terms of know-how and a cognitive dimension that includes schemata, mental models, beliefs, and perceptions so ingrained that we take them for granted. It reflects our image of reality (what is) and our vision for the future (what ought to be), and while these images cannot be articulated very easily, they are implicit models that shape the way we perceive the world around us.[11] An example of tacit knowledge would be an expatriate manager's intuitive sense of the best course of action on a disagreement with a joint-venture (JV) partner, given the JV's long-term goals. The expatriate's action/understanding is different from the headquarters manager's in this instance because the expatriate has built contextually relevant tacit knowledge about the JV's needs.

Tacit knowledge is communicated and shared within the organization through face-to-face interactions. Bearers of such knowledge meet with those who need to share such knowledge. These personal interactions allow the transferor and the transferee to reach shared understanding of the *hows*, *whys*, *whos* and *whats* in question. This creation of a shared understanding becomes organizational knowledge. Nonaka and Takeuchi sum this process up in their observation that "[c]reating new knowledge is also not simply a matter of learning from others or acquiring knowledge from the outside. Knowledge has to be built on its own, frequently requiring intensive and laborious interaction among members of the organization."[12]

Knowing how to do things requires that the boundary spanner have the set of skills and abilities about the craft of the practices of the professional field. *Knowing what* to do requires that the boundary spanner have knowledge about industries, organizations, products, and services, and other information useful to span boundaries. These are necessary but not sufficient knowledge categories to perform boundary spanning in the complex process of global organizing.

Knowing who and *knowing why* require both explicit and tacit knowledge. *Knowing who* to build and maintain a network with is an example of explicit knowledge. Such information is necessary to bring together a network of colleagues and acquaintances, as is the ability to leverage this network. In addition to *knowing who*, the boundary spanner needs to have a sense of the big picture, and an understanding of *what* is important and *why*, both within and outside the work setting.

Through boundary-spanning activities, effective global managers create the conduit for these intensive interactions to occur, not only among members of the organization, but also between organizational members and key stakeholders in the environment. For example, one way to understand the importance of golf in the practice of business in Japan is to understand it as an opportunity for the boundary spanner to build tacit knowledge about the people and the processes of the Japanese business partner. Then this boundary spanner can interact with the other managers to share what he or she has learned and can articulate both the explicit part of the knowledge and what may well be hunches and intuitions, the tacit knowledge of the Japanese business partner.

As a result of such boundary-spanning activities, boundary spanners develop networks of contacts, which give them social capital.[13] Social capital confers three types of benefits:

1 Benefits of access – such as the valuable information global managers receive from their contacts;
2 Benefits of timing – how quickly they learn information affects the speed with which they can take advantage of it; and
3 Benefits of referrals – such as an ability to provide and receive information on others from the global manager's contacts.[14]

Thus social capital is valuable to the individual, boundary-spanning global manager and to the organization, because it can be used to facilitate and leverage knowledge creation, which leads to continuous innovation and ultimately to competitive advantage for the organization.[15]

Clearly, boundary spanning is a complex system skill that facilitates the process of managing complexity. How this skill can be encouraged in managers throughout the organization is our next concern.

Boundary-spanning skills at the individual level

Much of the research on boundary spanning is at the organizational level of analysis, where it focuses on roles and system-level capabilities rather than on individual-level competencies. In this literature, expert boundary spanners are often described as having three broad competencies: (1) analytical ability; (2) the ability to think laterally; and (3) the ability to maintain a holistic point of view, which gets a deep understanding of the big picture.

In a recent study of boundary-spanning competencies,[16] Williams outlines five capability areas: personal relationships, communication and listening, conflict resolution, brokering, and personal attributes. The first of these is an ability to build and sustain personal relationships. This capability applies the interpersonal skills of mindful communication and trust building and is supported by the threshold traits of integrity, humility, inquisitiveness, and hardiness. The boundary spanners in Williams's study note that part of their process is an exploration, discovery, and understanding of people with different organizational, professional and social backgrounds. Such explorations are conducted in search of additional explicit and tacit knowledge about roles, responsibilities, problems, accountabilities, cultures, professional norms and standards, aspirations, and underlying values. In short, the boundary spanner needs to be able to build and maintain friendships with many people who have many differences. An ability to effectively manage these differences rests solidly on the cognitive complexity of the global mindset.

Williams's second competency is effective communication skills, including active listening skills. Effective communication and listening skills are built on the cornerstone of mindful communication. They enable the boundary spanner to discover shared meaning with others and to effectively transfer explicit knowledge within and outside of the organization. The ability to establish trust is critical to this process. The boundary spanner develops diverse sources of information about the business environment and local cultural practices, and the resulting knowledge, both explicit and tacit, can help to shape managerial views and provide organizations with a competitive advantage in the face of rapidly changing environmental conditions. A recent study of global managers by Stahl, Miller, and Tung[17] underscores the importance of these skills. These researchers found that global managers occupying boundary-spanning positions reported that the communication objectives of their current assignments were:

◆ To improve the communication and information processing between the subsidiary and the parent company;
◆ To link and coordinate the subsidiary's activities with the overall activity of the corporation;
◆ To transfer technical and administrative knowledge.

These findings suggest that at least among these global managers, their communication responsibilities represented an important factor linked to their performance.

Third, Williams suggests that to be effective boundary spanners global managers require conflict resolution skills. The ability to solve or manage conflicts and move on is necessary because, inevitably, relationships that span differences are tested by disagreements and unmet expectations.[18] Effective boundary spanners also develop an ability to anticipate conflicts and neutralize them before they happen.

Fourth, boundary spanners need to be able to broker solutions and to make deals with a number of parties. The boundary spanner needs to be able to perform the honest broker role, to have the perceived legitimacy to act objectively and openly for others while influencing the negotiation.[19] The boundary-spanning role also may place global managers in situations where there are conflicting accountabilities at the interface between the boundary spanner's organization and a network partner.[20] The boundary spanner as a broker who negotiates with a number of internal actors may also be significant. The boundary spanners of the Williams's study solved such role conflict by being loyal to the organization.

Fifth, the Williams study suggests that boundary spanners need to have certain personality traits. These include respect, honesty, openness, tolerance, approachability, reliability, and sensitivity.[21] These traits correspond to the threshold traits of integrity, humility, inquisitiveness, and hardiness, which are central building blocks for global competency. Williams found that the best boundary spanners use these traits to build sincere, trusting relationships that do not carry with them organizational and professional baggage.[22]

There is an additional aspect to the understanding of boundary spanning at the individual level. Boundary-spanning positions typically require taking risks and moving beyond the fulfillment of the day-to-day requirements or easily measurable attributes of the position. The very nature of a boundary-spanning position presents the individual with situations that will require professional, career, and sometimes personal risks. The risks relate to the boundary spanner's bridging activities. The boundary spanner connects decision-makers who may have different perspectives. The decision-makers may be so far apart, due to differing cultural values and behaviors and geographic distance, as well as disparate sources of information and perspectives, that the variance may create risk for the boundary spanner. Although risk-taking behavior has become essential in our turbulent economic and political times, risk-averse behavior is found to be relatively common and persistent among those global managers occupying boundary-spanning positions.[23]

The development of boundary-spanning skills: The individual

The organization can do much to develop boundary-spanning competencies at the individual level. Human resource management (HRM) philosophy and policies can also do much to support individual boundary-spanning activity. The research suggests that development of global boundary spanners should address both the recognition of threshold traits and the possibility of training.

One of the most powerful tools that an organization can use to enhance individual boundary-spanning skills is obvious: to move people across boundaries.[24] Today, many organizational positions represent a learning environment for employees who move across boundaries, and there is a growing expectation that the lessons learned, the social networks developed, and the acquisition of an international/global knowledge base will combine in such a way as to make the organization much more competitive within the global marketplace. For example, in a study of managers from the headquarters and subsidiaries of Philips, Matsushita, and NEC, expatriation did increase inter-subsidiary contacts.[25] In addition, formal training soon after hiring in these firms increased the interdepartmental ties of managers. Furthermore, the study found that having a mentor early in one's career decreased inter-subsidiary and interdepartmental ties, while having a mentor later in one's career increased these ties by a significant degree.[26] Expatriation, formal training, and getting a mentor at the right time are examples of what organizations can do to foster the growth of individual boundary-spanning skills.

The HRM system can facilitate or inhibit individual boundary-spanning behavior and ultimately the organization's competitive capability. As the firm strives to support boundary spanners, the HRM system will need to identify, support, and reward activities which develop boundary-spanning skills at the individual level. Such support requires that the organization know:

1 What unique skills and perspectives an individual needs to make sure the organization is a successful global competitor;
2 How employees are chosen for foreign boundary-spanning positions;
3 What incentive systems encourage qualified employees to accept an international assignment and to share ideas worldwide;
4 What it does to enable employees to gain global experience without the career liabilities sometimes associated with global manager assignments;
5 How it encourages the sharing of technical, political, social, and functional information relevant to the organization's goals globally;
6 How to create a global mindset culture that will permeate the management team members' strategic thinking and management practice;

7 How it capitalizes upon the expatriate manager's knowledge upon reassignment to other positions within the organization.

This knowledge will help HRM to develop support for the growth and exercise of boundary-spanning skills in individual managers. Note that successful performance in the boundary-spanning position is not limited to current performance, but more meaningfully to how that knowledge and experience learned in an expatriate assignment influence subsequent performance. Stated in slightly different terms, what does the former boundary spanner do with the experience and knowledge gained from the assignment to a boundary-spanning position? How does the organization capitalize upon this rich resource? Note that unfavorable attitudes of repatriates about their professional value or usefulness to the organization and its management may lead to a resignation and a position with a potential competitor who can use the individual's foreign experiences and skills.[27]

Development of boundary-spanning skills: The organization

The challenges facing the organization have to do with developing an environment that will reward and encourage global manager boundary spanners to contribute their acquired international experiences to the organization's global competitiveness during and after their boundary-spanning assignments. This will not be an easy task. Stahl, Miller, and Tung report that:

1 A substantial percentage of global managers resign upon repatriation and seek employment elsewhere.
2 Other global managers report that they have become professionally unproductive and personally dissatisfied because their companies fail to capitalize upon their overseas experience.
3 Global managers value an international assignment for the opportunity it brings for skill acquisition, personal development, and career enhancement, even though it may not help them within their company. This experience can help them with their next company.[28]

A common problem faced by many international managers responsible for managing boundary-spanning positions is, "I reward behavior A while hoping for behavior B." Essentially this phrase captures the management problem of having to reward one behavior while hoping for another.[29] Performance evaluation and reward structures need to be orchestrated so that they address this potentially damaging problem. The goal is "Reward behavior A while simultaneously expecting behavior A." To achieve the desired risk-taking behavior associated with boundary-spanning positions that allows expatriate managers to build trust with the local organization as well as fulfill the needs of the home organization, at least two HRM activities come into play: (1) accurate and timely performance evaluation and feedback, (2) development of reward practices that make work activities function in such a way as to promote the boundary spanner's self-interest. Considerable attention has been devoted to the means that management can use if they want to increase the risk-taking behaviors among those occupying boundary-spanning positions.

An organizational culture that encourages risk-taking behavior will not come easily. Considerable attention must be focused upon building trust, encouraging teamwork, stimulating flexibility, and stressing an external orientation. The process for encouraging risk-taking behavior begins with a committed senior management actively expressing their commitment by word and deed to the importance of risk-taking behavior. Implementation of a performance appraisal and a reward program that allows a boundary-spanning manager to develop deeper knowledge of customers, competitors, technological advances, and the political environment can lead to enhanced risk-taking and ultimately superior performance.

Conclusion

Boundary spanning is a complex skill that is found both at individual and organizational levels simultaneously. It is enacted through acts of individual communication and lies at the center of an organization's ability to know what it knows and build value from that knowledge. As globalization continues to increase the complexity of the business environment, multinational firms need to span more boundaries more effectively. In order to do that, they need to implement flexible approaches that integrate what has been traditionally separated, both inside and outside the organization. Organizational boundaries that separate employees, tasks, processes, and places need to be replaced by more flexible structures and processes. We suggest this new approach is to think of boundary spanning as a series of pipelines, conduits that carry and distribute information and knowledge throughout the organization, and to focus on the process at the individual level.

Global managers with well-developed boundary-spanning skills are likely to be able to build and maintain the relationships necessary to support effective boundary spanning. HRM systems that focus on building organizational cultures which support individual and organizational boundary-spanning skills will help position their organizations to manage the increasing complexity of their global businesses.

Notes

1 Ashkenas et al. (2002).
2 Cross & Prusak (2002), pp. 104–112).
3 Rosen et al. (2000).
4 Information from personal communication from Consul General Michael M. Mørk with Mikael Søndergaard, New York, February 2000.
5 Without using the concept of boundaryless organization, Jan Carlzon described the contingencies of such an organization in his book *Moments of Truth* (1987).
6 Kidd, J. B., & Teramoto, Y. (1995). The learning organization: The case of the Japanese RHQs in Europe. *Management International Review*, 35(2), special issue, 39–56.
7 Nohria & Ghoshal (1997).
8 Kidd & Teramoto, Y. (1995).
9 Nohria & Ghoshal (1997).
10 Nonaka & Takeuchi (1995), p. 8.

11 *Ibid.*
12 *Ibid.*, p. 10.
13 Burt (1992).
14 *Ibid.*
15 Nonaka & Takeuchi (1995).
16 Williams (2002), pp. 103–124.
17 Stahl, Miller, & Tung (2002).
18 Williams (2002), pp. 115–116.
19 Williams (2002), p. 117.
20 E.g., Lawrence, P., & Lorsch, J. (1967), *Organization and Environment*, Boston, MA: Harvard University Press; Lawrence, P., Kolodny, H., & Davis, S. (1977), The human side of the matrix, *Organizational Dynamics* (Summer), 47–62; Bartlett & Ghoshal (1990).
21 Williams (2002), p. 116.
22 *Ibid.*
23 Aldrich & Herker (1977).
24 E.g., Nohria & Ghoshal (1997).
25 *Ibid.*
26 *Ibid.*
27 See Black et al. (1999); Briscoe (1995).
28 Stahl, Miller, & Tung (2002).
29 Black et al. (1999); Kerr (1975).

Bibliography

Adams, J. S. (1976). The structure and dynamics of behavior in organizational boundary roles, in M. D. Dunnette (ed.), *Handbook of Industrial and Organizational Psychology*. Chicago: Rand McNally, pp. 1175–1199.

Adams, J. S. (1980). Interorganizational processes and organizational boundary activities, in S. J. Adams, *Research in Organizational Behavior*. Greenwich: JAI Press, pp. 321–355.

Aldrich, H., & Herker, D. (1977). Boundary Spanning Roles and Organization Structure. *Academy of Management Review*, 2, 217–231.

Ashkenas, R., Ulrich, D., Jick, T., & Kerr, S. (2002). *The Boundaryless Organization. Breaking the Chains of Organizational Structure*. San Francisco: Jossey-Bass.

Bartlett, C., & Ghoshal, S. (1990). Managing International Business. [A Multimedia Course Module]. Course Technology.

Black, S., Gregersen, H. B., Mendenhall, M. E., & Stroh, L. (1999). *Globalizing People through International Assignments*. Reading, MA., Addison Wesley.

Briscoe, D. (1995). *International Human Resource Management*. Englewood Cliffs. NJ.: Prentice Hall.

Burt, R. (1992). The social structure of competition. In N. Nohria & R. G. Eccles (eds.), *Networks and Organizations: Structure, Form and Action*. Boston: Harvard Business School Press, pp. 57–91.

Carlzon, J. (1987). *Moments of Truth*. Cambridge, MA: Ballinger.

Cross, R., & Prusak, L. (2002). The people who make organizations go – or stop. *Harvard Business Review*, 80(6), 104–112.

Kerr, S. (1975). On the folly of rewarding A while hoping for B. *Academy of Management Journal*, 18(4), 769–784.

Leana, C. R., & Van Buren, H. J. (1999). Organizational social capital and employment practices. *Academy of Management Review*, 24(3), 538–555.

Nohria, N., & Ghoshal, S. (1997). *The Differentiated Network*. San Francisco: Jossey-Bass.

Nonaka, I., & Takeuchi, H. (1995). *The Knowledge-Creating Company: How Japanese Companies Create the Dynamics of Innovation*. New York: Oxford University Press.

Rosen, R., Digh, P., Singer, M., & Philips, C. (2000). *Global Literacies. Lessons on Business Leadership and National Cultures*. New York: Simon & Schuster.

Stahl, G, Miller, E. L., & Tung, R. (2002). Toward a Boundaryless Career. *Journal of World Business*, 37, 216–227.

Tushman, M. L., & Scanlan, T. J. (1981). Boundary spanning individuals: Their role in information transfer and their antecedents. *Academy of Management Journal*, 24(1), 286–305.

Ulrich, D. (1996). *Human Resource Champions*. Boston, MA: Harvard University Press.

Williams, P. (2002). The competent boundary spanner. *Public Administration*, 80(1), 103–124.

8

Building Community through Change

Joyce S. Osland

Global managers play an important role in fostering the agility, adaptability, and rapid learning capacity that is so crucial to business survival and success. They face the challenges of steering the change efforts and aligning far-flung multinational corporations (MNCs) with thousands of diverse employees. The purpose of this part is to summarize what we are learning about change leadership in global organizations.

Building community is an essential part of the change process. Little has been written about the ability of global managers and change agents to build community, but we are starting to hear this theme repeatedly in our interviews with global leaders. The leaders of large, multicultural, and geographically distant organizations have to bring the members of their heterogeneous groups together before they can act in concert. A sense of community may be the "glue" that global organizations require to have enough consistency to risk major changes and survive the unanticipated consequences inherent in change efforts. Building work communities in organizations is a vital link to innovation, action, and change.[1]

We begin with an introduction to change and then examine both the leadership skills and organizational aspects of change that global managers will want to consider as they initiate the change process. Finally, we look at the implementation aspects of change management, which involves the behavioral flexibility to act appropriately, and then doing so.

INTRODUCTION TO CHANGE

Managing the change process well, so that it results in a stronger community, is just as important as coming up with a good analysis of the situation and an idea about what needs to be changed, the first two steps of the effective management cycle. Particularly on a global level, behavioral change is extremely challenging. Therefore, understanding the *process* of organizational change is important. In this introductory section we summarize models for change, outline what we have learned about the change process, and then examine a change case study.

Change process models

The process of change is often viewed in terms of unfreezing, moving, and refreezing.[2] *Unfreezing* is accompanied by stress, tension, and a strongly felt need for change. The *moving* stage refers to relinquishing old ways of behavior and testing out new behaviors, values, and attitudes that have usually been proposed by a respected source. *Refreezing* occurs when the new behavior is reinforced, internalized, and institutionalized, or rejected and abandoned. One study of multinational organizations modifies this framework to describe the sequence as follows: *incubation* (questioning the status quo), *variety generation* (middle-up experimentation) leading to *power shifts* (change in the leadership structure), and then the process of *refocusing*.[3] In successful large-scale strategic transformations at GE, ABB, Lufthansa, Motorola, and AT&T, Ghoshal and Bartlett observed the following sequential and overlapping process: *simplification, integration, and regeneration*. Simplification articulates a change such as GE's "being number one or two in the industry," which clarifies the strategy. The integration phase involves realigning cross-unit relationships, for example, bringing people together with shared values. A good example of this is GE CEO Jack Welch's focus on inter-unit collaboration and the sharing of best practices. The last phase, regeneration, attempts to build an organization capable of renewing itself. This was the purpose of Welch's "boundarylessness" push at GE.[4]

The order of sequential stages in the change process is refined into smaller steps by several models. Kotter's model is one example:

1 establish a sense of urgency;
2 form a powerful guiding coalition;
3 create a vision;
4 communicate the vision;
5 empower others to act on the vision;
6 plan for and create short-term wins;
7 consolidate improvements and produce still more change;
8 institutionalize new approaches.

Not everyone agrees with this view of change as an orderly progression, in part because the reality of change can be seen as more haphazard and dependent on luck and circumstance. Some see change in terms of a "strategic layering" process, in which firms continuously build capabilities in response to environmental demands.[5] Yet another school of thought views change as a spiral process wherein the management team focuses on a change initiative until it flirts with excess and then switches their focus to prevent the pathologies that could result from the initial change effort.[6] For example, a firm in the midst of decentralizing may switch its attention to integration mechanisms when decentralization begins to cause too many coordination problems.

Global change involves a broader range of action than does change in a firm's single location or in its operations in a single country. This broader range raises the necessity to anticipate changes to a greater degree than in the narrower, less complex range of the domestic environment. The process of looking ahead to predict future needs and adjustments is called anticipatory sequencing.[7] This somewhat daunting challenge involves building the future into the present. As the epitaph for a change agent read, "How are you supposed to change the tires on a car when it's going 60 miles per hour?"

Organizational change is usually categorized in terms of magnitude as either incremental or transformative. Incremental change, also known as first-order change, is linear, continuous, and targeted at fixing or modifying problems or procedures. Transformative change, also called second-order change or gamma change, modifies the fundamental structure, systems, orientation, and strategies of the organization.[8] Transformative change is radical and tends to be multidimensional and multilevel. It involves discontinuous shifts in mental or organizational frameworks. Whereas incremental change is analogous to rearranging the furniture in a room to make it more comfortable, transformative change means asking whether this is even the room or floor where we should be.[9] Organizational change experts such as Champy and Nohria maintain that incrementalism is a luxury businesses can no longer afford, given the complexities of a global organization; they recommend radical change and moving ahead quickly to avoid falling behind.[10]

What we know about managing change

There is no extensive body of literature to guide us on the management of large-scale global change. We can, however, begin with the following transferable lessons from our knowledge about successful domestic and international organizational change.[11] These lessons are categorized by the broad topics of leadership, communication, trust, context, tactics implementation, and resistance.

Leadership
- Top management support for the change, or at least benign neglect, is crucial.
- In addition to top management support, there needs to be a "critical mass" – the smallest number of people or groups who must be committed to a change for it to occur.
- Resistance to change is a natural response and requires thoughtful management.
- The more discretion managers have, the more changes they will make.

Communication
- The end result of the change must be clearly communicated, so people are willing to leave behind what they know for something new.
- It is almost impossible to "over-communicate" a change – people need to hear about it several times in a variety of media before the message is accurately received.

Trust
- Lasting change won't happen unless there is a sufficient level of trust within the organization.

Context
- Change almost always requires reexamining and rethinking the assumptions people hold about the environment, the way the organization functions, and their working relationships with other people. There is often a mourning period before people can let go of the way things used to be.
- Change requires new assumptions, attitudes, behaviors, and skills, which must eventually be institutionalized so the change can endure.
- Constant change is a source of stress for employees, so organizations have to balance both change and continuity.

Tactics
- Since tactics that work in one part of the organization cannot always be transferred successfully to another area, standardized change efforts may not be possible.
- Evaluation and incentive systems have to support the change and reward the desired behaviors.
- Changing one element in a system will not work unless we bring all the other elements into alignment to support the change.

Implementation process
- Change is a process rather than an event or a managerial edict.
- A good idea is not enough – the change process has to be skillfully managed for implementation to be effective.
- The change process occurs in multiple steps that cannot be bypassed.
- Changes require a fertile context – an organizational culture with values and norms that complement the change and a climate of renewal and growth.
- Changes need time to take root.
- Change is hard to sustain; some innovations succeed initially but conditions eventually revert to their previous state.
- There are costs associated with any change, and we can expect a predictable slump in performance before a successful change starts to show results.

Resistance
- Changes often upset the political system in organizations and come into conflict with the vested interests of people who prefer the status quo.
- Allowing people to participate in some aspect of the change process and educating them about the change are positive ways to reduce resistance.

The research on large-scale global change is less extensive and conclusive than is the research on more narrowly focused change management. Nevertheless, the data and personal reports from successful leaders of global changes show that the following factors are critical:

- vision that is clear, motivating and linked to performance goals;
- authority that is clearly understood;
- accountability for results;
- use of teams;
- measurement during the process;
- organizational learning;
- high standards; and
- a results-driven approach.

All of these factors are present in the following story of a change effort.

In 1998 Dick Shoemate, CEO of Bestfoods, studied the data from an employee survey and noticed that women had higher turnover rates at every management level and perceived less opportunity for advancement and career development than men. While the number of senior women (mainly in the United States), corporate officers, and board members at Bestfoods was respectable when compared to many companies, only 15 percent of "high-potential" employees worldwide were female. With women making more than 80 percent of purchasing decisions for Bestfoods' products, Shoemate saw promoting women into senior management positions as a matter of strategic competitive advantage. On numerous occasions, he reiterated his commitment to developing the most highly talented women and men from around the world.

Shoemate and Laura Brody, Director of Diversity and Development, faced two key challenges to their goal of increasing the number of women global leaders. First, in a highly decentralized multinational that values local independence, no CEO could simply mandate change. Regional and local management had the autonomy to adapt and modify changes suggested by corporate headquarters. "It's our strength," said Shoemate, "but it's also a challenge when we try to make changes."

The second challenge concerned the different cultural perspectives on the issue of women leaders and diversity. Since diversity is often viewed as a "US issue," the leadership of companies headquartered in the United States often treads lightly in this area until a consensus can be developed. Within some cultures, equity among women and men is not a well-publicized concern, and diversity is locally defined to refer to other groups within the population. Brody's background in organization development (OD) was a great advantage. She had laid the groundwork for change by developing a US Diversity Advisory Council composed of high-level executives and chaired by the CEO. This team established a common vision for diversity and a Balanced Scorecard for Diversity that mirrored the Corporate Balanced Scorecard. Brody also educated the council with benchmarking and best-practice studies from outside the firm. Her strategy was the "drip method" of change – small changes over time that eventually add up to real progress – since this method fit Bestfoods' traditional, conservative, and non-confrontational culture.

So when Shoemate looked at the survey data and asked, "If you could do one thing to improve things for women in this company, what would it be?", Brody pitched her best idea.

I really cannot speak for all women. But if I were the CEO, what I would want to do is to engage a significant number of women in this dialogue. What about sponsoring a global forum for high-potential and senior women representing all the businesses from around the world? They could help us better understand the environment and culture in the company and how it impacts women. We could do what we always do with a business issue that needs to be driven from the center – have an action-learning program with outside experts to design and facilitate it. We could receive both information and recommendations from participants on how to proceed and make progress, and we could also do some leadership training at the same time.

Although he'd never heard of a company doing this before, Shoemate immediately agreed and sent letters to the six members of the Corporate Strategy Council describing the Forum and requesting that they order their nominees by rank. Next, he personally sent the invitation to the Forum participants to attend.

Prior to the Forum, Brody's team carried out a survey-feedback process in hopes that the data would serve as a baseline and discussion catalyst, in addition to causing people to reexamine their thinking about the opportunities and barriers for women's career advancement and leadership. Brody also viewed the survey as a means of involving senior women and men in these issues and building their support for implementing the Forum recommendations.

The Forum's goals were closely tied to business issues: increasing global competitiveness; developing the women's global leadership skills; creating an internal women's leader network to facilitate their global effectiveness; and developing both global and local recommendations to support the career advancement and success of more women. The participants generated several recommendations, which Shoemate and the corporate officers responded to in real time. The immediate positive feedback from those in attendance indicated that the Forum had served as a successful catalyst in the change process. The next challenge, however, was to implement the proposed changes and then institutionalize them.

In response to widespread curiosity about the Forum, Brody prepared a communication pack, complete with overheads, for each participant. A week later, Shoemate sent a letter thanking participants for their input, responding in writing to each recommendation, and laying out the company's planned next steps. Shortly thereafter, the Corporate Strategy Council approved all the women's recommendations and added two of their own. They agreed to take responsibility for oversight of the company's global diversity strategy and establish diversity councils in their respective businesses, which they invited Forum participants to join.

With this decision, diversity became a global, rather than a US issue. Given the positive response, Shoemate set a new Corporate Balanced Scorecard goal: by the year 2005, 25 percent of high-potential employees would be women. Numerous local initiatives sprouted – such as benchmarking and regional strategies for retaining women – before the company was bought by Unilever.[12]

Like Shoemate and Brody, global managers need to be skilled at diagnosing an important corporate need for change and selecting the correct change target for their particular organization. Both were adept at scanning and reading the organizational mindset and culture and choosing the most effective change tactics. And equally important, both had the behavioral repertoire needed to push and gain acceptance for the change throughout the entire process.

CHANGE LEADERSHIP SKILLS

This section describes in greater detail the global competency of managing change to build community through a focus on leadership, vision, and communication.

Leadership and change management

John Kotter once noted that leadership, unlike management, is about coping with change.[13] Leaders are catalysts and managers of strategic and cultural change. According to Champy and Nohria, the new responsibilities of a global manager are to:

- establish a company's identity, which illuminates its purpose;
- nurture initiative, to tap the wellsprings of creativity within the organization;
- pursue integrity, which creates trust and serves as the basis of organizational control.

This presumes a leadership style characterized by authentic and mindful communication, empowerment, and tolerance of creative discord. Tolerance of ambiguity is also an important attribute. The command and control approach to management does not result in agile, proactive companies that are skilled at dealing with change. John Browne, CEO of

British Petroleum, reiterates this belief with his view on how leaders institutionalize break-through thinking.[14]

> The top management team must stimulate the organization, not control it. Its role is to provide strategic directives, to encourage learning, and to make sure there are mechanisms for transferring the lessons. The role of leaders at all levels is to demonstrate to people that they are capable of achieving more than they think they can achieve and that they should never be satisfied with where they are now. To change behavior and unleash new ways of thinking, a leader sometimes has to say, "Stop, you're not allowed to do it the old way," and issue a challenge.

Champy and Nohria claim that a leader must possess these personal traits to manage change:

- driven by a higher ambition;
- able to maintain a deep sense of humility;
- committed to a constant search for the truth;
- able to tolerate ambiguity, uncertainty and paradox;
- personally responsible for consequences of their actions;
- highly disciplined in their everyday lives;
- always authentic.[15]

This list speaks to our global competency model – the importance of humility, inquisitiveness, and cognitive complexity. Furthermore, authenticity relates to both trust and mindful communication. Global managers have to be able to inspire trust and promote collaboration for change to work. They also have to live with ambiguity and paradox. They don't always have the time to make as careful a diagnosis as they would wish, and switching tactics and directions is an inherent part of managing continuous change. Coming up with the right change goals and tactics at the right time often involves discontinuous thinking and draws on the global mindset attitudes and orientations. Good change agents know that they must first understand and then change employees' mental maps in order to implement a change. Articulation of a vision and the ability to communicate this vision both draw on the model's interpersonal skills and are important abilities in this regard, so we now focus on them.

The importance of vision

International studies of leadership find to some degree that cultures have different definitions of good leadership. One study, however, was able to identify six capabilities that were globally valued by respondents from eight countries.[16] The most important capability was *the ability to articulate a tangible vision, values, and strategy*. The other five capabilities all contribute to successfully managing global change: *being a catalyst for strategic change, being results-oriented, empowering others to do their best, being a catalyst for cultural change, and exhibiting a strong customer orientation.* For example, the closer managers stay to the customer, the better they become at managing change. As they listen to customers and scan the environment, they perceive the need for change. Larry Bossidy, of AlliedSignal, stated, "I think that the closer you come to the customers, the more you appreciate the need to change. And the more inwardly focused you are, the less you understand that need. As we get more and more customer focused, we don't have to preach about the need to change. People know it."[17]

Unless managers provide a clear vision for global change, employees will not change their behavior. Stories from successful global CEOs indicate that in their change efforts, they had a clear vision for change that seemed sound to followers, they communicated that vision over and over, and they laid out the process by which the vision could be achieved.

Selecting the right change target obviously depends on one's scanning capabilities. Global managers are not solely responsible for this stage – some companies use a group process to determine needed changes, but managers have to ensure that this analysis is taking place and that it is accurate. The change target should be results-driven, rather than activity-based, that is, "increase market share" rather than "train 1000 employees in emotional intelligence." The change should be tied to business issues and performance, as shown in the Bestfoods vignette. And finally, the change should fit the organization's history and core values (except when those values are part of the problem and the change effort involves modifying the organizational culture). An in-depth understanding of the organizational culture and history is crucial. It provides important insight into which change tactics will be most effective, and it also reveals aspects that should *not* be changed because they are the organizational glue or key success factors.

The capacity to envision a feasible and powerful future is one of the ways a single person can influence a large organization. Larry Bossidy provides a clear explanation of how a global manager can be a catalyst for change.

> I believe in the "burning platform" theory of change. When the roustabouts are standing on the offshore oil rig and the foreman yells, "Jump into the water," not only won't they jump but they also won't feel too kindly toward the foreman. There may be sharks in the water. They'll jump only when they themselves see the flames shooting up from the platform. Chrysler's platform was visibly burning; the company changed. IBM's platform was not visibly burning; it didn't.
>
> The leader's job is to help everyone see that the platform is burning, whether the flames are apparent or not. The process of change begins when people decide to take the flames seriously and manage by fact, and that means a brutal understanding of reality. You need to find out what the reality is so that you know what needs changing.
>
> I traveled all over the company with the same message and the same charts, over and over. Here's what I think is good about us. Here's what I'm worried about. Here's what we have to do about it. And if we don't fix the case problem, none of us is going to be around. You can keep it simple: we're spending more than we're taking in. If you do that at home, there will be a day of reckoning.[18]

The global manager's role in establishing a shared organizational vision involves increasing the perceived need for change. This can be done by highlighting what Peter Senge calls the "creative tension" that results from perceiving the gap between the ideal situation (the organization's vision) and an honest appraisal of its current reality. Global managers "turn up the heat" and create a sense of urgency by focusing attention on problems or opportunities and taking their message about the change to numerous groups of employees at all levels in the organization. The message about change is communicated more effectively when it contains a simple metaphor that travels well across cultures.

As consultant Richard Beckhard noted: "For change to be possible and for commitment to occur, there has to be enough dissatisfaction with the current state of affairs to mobilize energy toward change. There also has to be some fairly clear conception of what the state of affairs would be if and when the change was successful. Of course, a desired state needs to be consistent with the values and priorities of the client system. There also needs to be some client awareness of practical first steps or starting points toward the desired state."[19]

It is possible to increase the level of dissatisfaction with the status quo by sharing environmental analyses or productivity information about competitors with employees or by utilizing survey-feedback techniques that present employees with the aggregated results of their individual opinions, as Bestfoods did. In this manner, more people perceive the need for change and form the necessary critical mass.

Communication

Bossidy's earlier statement, "I traveled all over the company with the same message and the same charts, over and over," is repeated by numerous global leaders. Barnevik and his team spent 200 days a year communicating their vision and message and helping units operationalize the vision.[20] The message has to be consistent and has to be repeated endlessly so employees become personally convinced about the importance of what needs to be changed. Otherwise, they "sit out" change efforts, assuming that this is just another in a long line of management fads that will pass when a new CEO is named or when the current top management team's attention is drawn to a more pressing issue. Communicating dissatisfaction with the status quo, reiterating the perceived need for change, and painting a vivid picture of the desired end state are essential parts of the unfreezing process. Communicating new changes in large global firms sometimes has a great deal in common with the child's game of telephone – the message is distorted as it is passed along hierarchies and cultural borders.

Fortunately, personal communication is not the only tool global managers have for transmitting change messages. In addition to persuasive communication (speeches, newsletters, articles), change agents can influence and communicate change by:

- ◆ encouraging the participation of those who will be impacted by the change in the process;
- ◆ supporting HRM practices (hiring criteria, performance appraisal systems, compensation, employee development programs);
- ◆ giving importance to symbolic activities (rites and ceremonies, celebrations);
- ◆ instituting diffusion practices (best-practice programs and transition teams);
- ◆ establishing management of internal and external information; and
- ◆ instituting formal activities that demonstrate support for change initiatives (modified organizational structures and new job descriptions).[21]

CHANGE IMPLEMENTATION

We now examine aspects of change implementation that are central to the change process: organizational alignment, context for organizational change, change tactics, and organizational learning abilities.

Organizational alignment

Successful global change always requires a certain degree of alignment of organizational design components. For example, a new strategic thrust often requires concomitant changes in policies, employee skills, staffing, systems, cultural norms, and structure. Organizations are interdependent systems, so changing one component is usually insufficient. Ensuring the "fit" among components is a way to institutionalize change. For example, a study of 500 of the largest European firms found significant performance benefits only in firms that changed structures, processes and boundaries. Firms that changed only structures and boundaries but not processes, actually did worse."[22]

The evolutionary nature of organizations, however, means that global managers cannot expect their alignments to last. They face the paradoxical demands of "increasing the alignment or fit among strategy, structure, culture, and processes, while simultaneously preparing for the inevitable revolutions required by discontinuous environmental change."[23] Organizational evolution usually consists of periods of incremental change punctuated by discontinuous or revolutionary change. This means that global managers have to keep an eye on the future and be willing to tear apart what they've just painstakingly cobbled together.

With regard to organizational capability, Lew Platt stated, "We have to be willing to cannibalize what we're doing today in order to ensure our leadership in the future. It's counter to human nature, but you have to kill your business while it is still working."[24] Alignment can be a double-edged sword – both a necessity for institutionalizing change and a barrier to subsequent changes.

Context for organizational change

Organizational scholars have long believed in the idea of requisite variety, that organizations have to be as complex as their environments. With regard to the change process in a global context, the complexity of diverse views is extremely important. Heterogeneous perspectives help firms to perceive opportunities, problems, and solutions that a homogeneous mindset cannot see. The innovation and creativity so necessary to successful change will be stifled unless employees can add their diverse views, thereby improving the change effort.

Global managers have to create such a context for change so that the seeds they plant can flourish. The social architecture aspect of a global manager's job involves building an organizational culture with these characteristics that set the stage for change:

- *entrepreneurship* – to foster initiatives and a concern for performance;
- *diversity* – to attract and retain employees of all types so different views can be heard;
- *learning and innovation* – to promote renewal and growth and ward off stagnation and obsolescence;
- *participation* – so diverse views can be heard and employees can express their ideas and feel a sense of ownership;
- *trust* – so employees believe in the wisdom and fairness of their leaders and colleagues;
- *collaboration* – so that employees are willing to contribute their efforts to the change effort.

Two examples of firms that successfully affected their contexts for change are Honda and Johnson & Johnson. Honda created the necessary context for change through *waigaya* sessions.

Contrary to what many Westerners might think about the importance of consensus in Japanese culture, institutionalized conflict is an integral part of Japanese management. At Honda, any employee, however junior, can call for a *waigaya* session. The rules are that people lay their cards on the table and speak directly about problems. Nothing is out of bounds, from supervisory deficiencies on the factory floor to perceived lack of support of a design team. *Waigaya* legitimizes tension so that learning can take place.[25]

Johnson & Johnson improved the context for change in their firm when they came up with FrameworkS, a method for decreasing resistance to change. Although size is a competitive advantage in maintaining financial strength and market leadership, the company was concerned that its size (170 distinct operating companies) could prevent rapid adaptation to emerging opportunities and environmental changes. Its nine-member executive committee devised the FrameworkS management process because they wanted "frameworks" to better understand issues that cut across the company's decentralized structure, such as markets, customer expectations, and new opportunities. The capital S helps remind them that there are multiple frames through which they must view the diverse businesses in their global organization.

The company forms FrameworkS teams – task forces comprising members from various companies, countries, and functional areas who extensively research topics important to the company's future. Their findings are presented to and discussed by all the other FrameworkS teams and the executive committee. After including this input, the teams develop and implement action plans. The FrameworkS program has paid off in tangible results, such as setting up new businesses and entering new markets. The intangible results, however, are equally impressive. The executive committee is more in touch with how employees and customers think, operations has learned it can push ahead to take advantage of opportunities without waiting for edicts from the top of the hierarchy, and "there is a greater receptivity to deal with change that did not exist five years ago."[26]

Change tactics

The global change tactics of successful companies and change consultants are rooted in trial-and-error experience. Yet the tactics urged can be categorized in five broad ways:

1 draw from effective principles for effective change;
2 know what suits your company's particular needs;
3 understand the need for a solution to be universalist or particularist;
4 modify mindsets through the appropriate training; and
5 establish specific, measurable goals.

From their work as consultants with various firms, Goss, Pascale, and Athos provide the following advice to firms that want to "manage the present from the future" and stay ahead of the curve:

1 *Assemble a critical mass of key stakeholders.*
2 *Conduct an organizational audit* to identify assumptions, influential functional units, key systems that drive the business, core competencies or skills, shared values, and idiosyncrasies.
3 *Create urgency and discuss the undiscussable* so employees are motivated to question basic assumptions.

4 *Harness contention* to jump-start the creative process.
5 *Engineer organizational breakdowns*, like setting impossible deadlines, so organizational problems become visible.[27]

General tactics like these are useful, but successful global managers also adapt change tactics to suit the conditions of their particular organization and history. ABB's philosophy on making global change, for example, reflects what they have learned from their own experience with cross-border mergers.

1 Immediately reorganize operations into profit centers with well-defined budgets, strict performance targets, and clear lines of authority and accountability.
2 Identify a core group of change agents from local management, give small teams responsibility for championing high-priority programs, and closely monitor results.
3 Transfer ABB expertise from around the world to support the change process without interfering with it or running it directly.
4 Keep standards high and demand quick results.[28]

One of the paradoxes inherent in global change is the simultaneous need for a universal (global) and particularistic (local) solution. Even the best corporate-wide solutions have to be *contextualized* – modified to fit the local context. This is one of the major lessons about global change. Those who know the local people and culture best need the autonomy and discretion to tailor the change effort so it is appropriate. In the Bestfoods example, the regional and country units developed their own methods for increasing the number of female global leaders. Allowing for contextualization also fosters a community that values and tolerates diversity.

Many change efforts require a different mindset, new skills, or new ways of working that are best instituted via training programs. A key decision concerns the scope of the training – whether it should occur at all levels to ensure that the change is not bogged down at the middle-management level. Broad-scale training programs signal a deep commitment to the change effort on the part of the company, and send a strong message to employees.

Training programs in global firms have to be contextualized to ensure their relevance and acceptability to different cultures. Training designs should include room for learning to go in more than one direction. Global change and training are more than the transmission of knowledge from an expert source to a non-expert receiver. Instead, global change is a matter of knowledge creation among different communities; it involves mutual learning.[29] Global firms benefit most when training sessions produce general lessons, recommendations for the rest of the company, and knowledge about necessary local adaptations. The action learning format of the Bestfoods' Forum, for example, was designed to yield mutual collaborative learning.

Following the truism that "people do only what is measured," successful global change projects have a clear, understandable focus that can be measured. The use of metrics like the Balanced Scorecard allows MNEs to target the critical success factors and hold employees accountable for achieving them. Review processes that are carefully monitored allow global managers to keep tabs on the progress of change in far-flung MNCs.

Taking a long-term view of change is important since some changes are successful in the short run but eventually revert back to the status quo; other changes look like failures in the short term only to prove successful years later. Thus, "when" a change is measured makes a notable difference.

Organizational learning abilities

In addition to the social architecture involved in fostering a context for change, global managers also need to build learning organizations that encourage innovation. When companies are dedicated to organizational learning, the need for change becomes very obvious. According to John Browne, CEO of British Petroleum:

> Learning is at the heart of a company's ability to adapt to a rapidly changing environment. It is the key to being able both to identify opportunities that others might not see and to exploit those opportunities rapidly and fully. This means that in order to generate extraordinary value for its shareholders, a company has to learn better than its competitors and apply that knowledge throughout its businesses faster and more widely than they do.[30]

Before implementing major changes, some firms carry out empirical tests and pilot projects to determine which practices are successful. They then institutionalize those that work and cancel efforts that have not paid off. Such practices are rooted in organizational learning. Action learning is another example of organizational learning, as shown in the examples at Bestfoods and Johnson & Johnson.[31] These firms brought together diverse global teams to study and take action on specific issues.

In addition to programs such as these that structure and promote shared learning, learning organizations rely on flat structures, teams, networks to share knowledge, and decentralized decision-making. Flatter structures, which are more responsive than hierarchical, bureaucratic structures, are better suited to a complex, competitive global business environment.[32] This organizational design also fosters the related goal of innovation.[33] Since innovation and creativity, as well as change, often take place in the interfaces,[34] global managers need to devote special attention to developing networks and honing their boundary-spanning skills.

A word on cultural differences related to change

Cultures vary with regard to their comfort with change. When we look at the values described in Part I in the discussion of culture, we can make the following generalizations about change-related cultural differences. Few countries value change more than the United States. "In the Old World respect came from a valuable heritage, and any change from that norm had to be justified. In America, however, the *status quo* was no more than the temporary product of past changes, and it was the resistance to change that demanded an explanation."[35] Cultures that are high in uncertainty avoidance are more likely to avoid change and the risks that it involves. They will expect the change process to be very clearly delineated.

Cultures that place a higher value on the past and tradition are generally more resistant to change. In such cultures, managers will tend to be less proactive about making changes and change processes are likely to take more time. The same is true of cultures that believe more in fate than in human control of one's destiny.

Cultural values also affect the change implementation process. In cultures where human nature is viewed as unchangeable or evil, people are more likely to be skeptical about the success of a change effort, and it may take longer to build trust and commitment. Participation is the best way to allow employees to feel some sense of ownership of the change process in low power-distance cultures. Employees from cultures characterized by high power-distance, however, are more likely to expect leaders to make decisions without their input.

Influence is exerted in different ways in different cultures. Both formal and informal leaders play a major role in encouraging others to support a change effort. Determining who is the best person to communicate a change and who should be included in a coalition depends on the culture.

Cultures also vary in their beliefs about how change occurs. When most European and Japanese companies want to make a change, they begin by trying to change the attitudes and mentalities of their key people. Next, they modify the flow of communication and decision-making processes. Finally, they consolidate the changes by realigning the structure to mirror the changes that have already occurred. US companies, however, have opposite assumptions about change. They tend to assume that modifying the organizational structures results in organizational change. This line of thought presupposes that a new structure causes changes in interpersonal relationships and processes, which leads eventually to changes in individual attitudes and mentalities. Bartlett and Ghoshal note that these different national biases seem to be disappearing as global companies learn different approaches from one another.[36]

These are the stereotypical differences one looks for in multicultural change projects; however, global managers also need to take into consideration unique, indigenous cultural values, the country's history, and the organizational culture and the occupational culture of the particular group involved in the change effort. Brody's in-depth understanding of Bestfoods' organizational culture led her to model the change strategy on what was already effective in the company: action-learning programs. In doing so, she increased the likelihood of acceptance and legitimacy for the Forum. In other instances, historical issues from national culture might be more salient. For example, Hungary's political structure and state-owned companies exert a strong influence on views of change and its implementation, and one can expect special considerations in managing change in transition economies.[37]

Change efforts have a greater likelihood of success if global managers understand the various cultural values that influence change and recognize that change interventions that work in one country may not succeed elsewhere.[38] In many cases they have to adapt their own behavior to match the cultural scripts indigenous to different locations. An understanding of the communication style differences presented earlier in our discussion of mindful communication is important in managing global change.

One of the paradoxes of global management is that while successful managers understand and respect cultural constraints, they also know when and how to get around them. Percy Barnevik captured this expertise thus:

> Global managers have exceptionally open minds. They respect how different countries do things, and they have the imagination to appreciate why they do them that way. But they are also incisive, they push the limits of the culture. Global managers don't passively accept it when someone says, "You can't do that in Italy or Spain because of the unions," or "You can't do that in Japan because of the Ministry of Finance." They sort through the debris of cultural excuses. (Interview in Champy & Nohria, 1996)

Change and Building Community

Community is both a facilitator of change and one of its outcomes. Community building is a result of trust, shared values, shared language, and a sense of belonging and identification. Trust is an integral part of community-building and change efforts. The trust that results from community building increases the likelihood of transformation. Employees do not follow leaders whom they cannot trust. Furthermore, if the members of a team entrusted with a change effort do not trust one another, their chances of success are minimized. Transformational change is a treacherous journey best undertaken with trustworthy companions.

When Sir Colin Marshall announced his vision that British Airways would be "the world's favorite airline," BA was actually ranked among the worst in the world. Change targets like this unleash employee motivation, because most people want to be connected to a successful organization in which they can make a positive contribution.

When a sense of community is lacking in an organization, employees are less likely to make the effort or the necessary sacrifices to help a change succeed. Self-interest trumps a communitarian concern for the good of the organization, even when people recognize the need for change. Yet change can build community, as Steve Miller's experience with grass-roots change at Shell illustrates.

> Steve Miller, managing director at Shell, sent 6–8-person teams from six operating companies around the world to "retailing boot camp." These grass-roots employees were given the skills to identify and exploit market opportunities and then sent back home to apply them. Sixty days later the teams returned to present their analyses and plans to peer teams. They were given another 60 days to perfect their business plans, which were then presented in a fishbowl session with Miller and his direct reports while other teams looked on and learned vicariously. Miller and his staff approved plans and made financial commitments in exchange for promised results.
>
> The teams returned to the field to put their ideas into action and returned in another two months for a follow-up session. This process contributed $US300 million worth of audited results to Shell's bottom line and allowed the corporate culture to become more innovative and participative. However, it also built community – these employees were exposed to people at different levels from different locations in a way that had never occurred before in the 61,000-member company. Miller described the community-building outcome in this fashion:
>
>> The whole process creates complete transparency between the people at the coalface [Shell's term for its front-line activities in the worldwide oil products business] and me and my top management team. At the end, these folks go back home and say, "I just cut a deal with the managing director and his team to do these things." It creates a personal connection, and it changes how we talk with each other and how we work with each other. After that, I can call up those folks anywhere in the world and talk in a very direct way because of this personal connectedness. It has completely changed the dynamics of our operations.[39]

Building community helps change leaders and organizations avoid the dangers of change, about which Machiavelli has warned us:

There is no more delicate matter to take in hand, nor more dangerous to conduct, nor more doubtful in its success, than to be a leader in the introduction of changes. For he who innovates will have for enemies all those who are well off under the old order of things, and only lukewarm supporters in those who might be better off under the new.[40]

CONCLUSION

Given the relative youth of the field of global change, the best ways to develop this competence are to read descriptions of successful global change efforts and to work with and learn from expert managers and consultants in this area. In addition to the basic change agent skills (teambuilding, networking, tolerance of ambiguity, flexibility, good interpersonal skills including communication, political savvy, influencing and motivating skills, trust-building skills, and enthusiasm), global managers also require cultural knowledge and mindful intercultural communication skills. As they gain expertise, global managers learn to recognize the situational factors that promote or impede change and become more skilled at contextualizing change efforts and building community.

NOTES

1 In a small, exploratory study, L. W. Wellsfry interviewed 12 global leaders and reported this conclusion in *Global Leadership: A Hermeneutic Perspective on the Transnationalizing of Organizations*, dissertation, University of San Francisco, December, 1993.
2 Lewin, K. (1947), Frontiers in group dynamics, *Human Relations*, 1, 5–41.
3 Doz, Y. & Prahalad, C. K. (1987), A process model of strategic redirection in large complex firms: The case of multinational corporations, in A. M. Pettigrew (ed.), *The Management of Strategic Change*, Oxford: Basil Blackwell, pp. 63–83.
4 Ghoshal, S. & Bartlett, C. A. (1996), Rebuilding behavioral context: A blueprint for corporate renewal, *Sloan Management Review*, 37(2), 23–37.
5 Evans, P. & Doz, Y. (1989). The dualistic organization, in P. Evans, Y. Doz, & A. Laurent (eds.), *Human Resource Management in International Firms: Change, Globalization, Innovation*, London: Macmillan, pp. 219–242.
6 Evans, P., Pucik, V. & Barsoux, J. (2002), *The Global Challenge: Frameworks for International Human Resource Management*, Boston: McGraw-Hill Irwin. See also Eisenhardt, K. (2000). Paradox, spiral, ambivalence: The new language of change and pluralism, *Academy of Management Review*, 25(4), 703–705.
7 Evans & Doz (1989). See also Eisenhardt (2000).
8 Burke, W. W., & Litwin, G. H. (1992), A causal model of organizational performance and change, *Journal of Management*, 18, 523–545.
9 This analogy was created by Wilbur, K. (1983), *A Sociable God*, New York: McGraw-Hill.
10 Champy, J. & Nohria, N. (1996), *Fast Forward: The Best Ideas on Managing Business Change*, Cambridge, MA: Harvard Business School Press.
11 These lessons about change are found in several sources such as Armenakis, A., & Bedeian, A. G. (1999), Organizational change: A review of theory and research in the 1990s, *Journal of Management*, 25(3), 293–315; Cummings, T. C., & Worley, C. G. (1997), *Organization Development and Change*, Cincinnati, OH: South-Western University Press; Jick, T. & Peiperl, M. (2003), *Managing Change: Cases and Concepts*, Boston: Irwin; and Drucker, P. (forthcoming), *Change Leaders*.

12 For the complete story of this case, see Osland, J. (2001), Women and global leadership at Bestfoods, in J. Osland, D. Kolb, & I. Rubin, *Organizational Behavior: An Experiential Approach*, Upper Saddle River, NJ: Prentice-Hall, pp. 533–555). For an analysis of this change effort, see Osland, J., Adler, N. J. & Brody, L. W. (2002), Developing global leadership in women: Lessons and sense making from an organizational change effort, in R. Burke and D. Nelson (eds.), *Advancing Women's Careers*, Oxford: Blackwell, pp. 15–36.

13 Kotter, J. (1990) *A Force for Change: How Leadership Differs from Management*, New York: The Free Press.

14 Prokesch, S. E. (2000), Unleashing the power of learning: An interview with British Petroleum's John Browne, in J. E. Garten (ed.), *World View: Global Strategies for the New Economy*, Cambridge, MA: Harvard Business School Press, pp. 302–303.

15 Champy, J. & Nohria, N., The eye of the storm: The force at the center, in Champy & Nohria (1996), pp: 263–264.

16 For one of the first empirical studies of global leadership see Yeung, A. K., & Ready, D. A. (1995), Developing leadership capabilities of global corporations: A comparative study in eight nations, *Human Resource Management*, 34(4), 529–547.

17 Bossidy's quotation appears in Tichy, N. M., & Charan, R., The CEO as coach: An interview with AlliedSignal's Lawrence A. Bossidy, in Champy & Nohria (1996), p. 262.

18 *Ibid.*, pp. 247–248.

19 Beckhard, R. (1990), Strategies for large system change, in D. A. Kolb, I. M. Rubin, & J. S. Osland, *The Organizational Behavior Reader*, Upper Saddle River, NJ), p. 664.

20 Ghoshal & Bartlett (1996).

21 Armenakis, A., Harris, S., & Feild, H. (2001), Paradigms in organizational change: Change agent and change target perspectives, *Public Administration and Public Policy*, 87, 631–658.

22 Whittington, R., Pettigrew, A., Peck, S., Fenton, E., & Conyon, M. (1998), Change and complementarities in the new competitive landscape: A European Panel study, 1992–1996, *Organization Science*, 10(5), 583–600.

23 Tushman, M. L., & O'Reilly, C. A. (1996), Ambidextrous organizations: Managing evolutionary and revolutionary change, *California Management Review*, 38(4), 11.

24 Evans, Pucik, & Barsoux (2002), p. 423.

25 Goss, T., Pascale, R., & Athos, A., The reinvention roller coaster: Risking the present for a powerful future, in Champy & Nohria (1996), pp. 136–137.

26 Larsen, R. S. (1999), FrameworkS: Turning the challenges of change into opportunities for growth, *Chief Executive*, 144, 12.

27 Goss, Pascale, & Athos (1996), pp. 124–139.

28 Percy Barnevik, in an interview in Champy & Nohria (1996), p. 81.

29 Tenkasi, R. V., & Mohrman, S. A. (1999), Global change as contextual collaborative knowledge creation, in D. Cooperrider & J. E. Dutton (eds.), *Organizational Dimensions of Global Change: No Limits to Cooperation*. Thousand Oaks, CA: Sage, pp. 114–136.

30 This quotation appears in Dess, G. G. & Picken, J. C. (2000), Changing roles: Leadership in the 21st century, *Organizational Dynamics*, 28(3), 31.

31 For a good description of action learning programs, see Dotlich, D. A., & Noel, J. L. (1998), *Action Learning: How the World's Top Companies Are R e-Creating Their Leaders and Themselves*, San Francisco: Jossey-Bass.

32 Monge, P. & Fulk, J. (1999), Communication technology for global network organizations, in G. DeSanctis & J. Fulk (eds.), *Shaping Organization Form: Communication, Connection, and Community*, Thousand Oaks, CA: Sage, pp. 71–100.

33 Branscom, L. M., Florida, B., Hart, D., Séller, J., & Boville, D. (1999). *Investing in Innovation*, Cambridge, MA: MIT Press.

34 Evans, Pucik, & Barsoux (2002).

35 See Bridges, W. (1995), Managing organizational change, in W. W. Burke (ed.), *Managing Organizational Change*, New York: American Management Association, p. 20.
36 Bartlett, C. A., & Ghoshal, S. (2000), *Transnational Management*, Boston: Irwin McGraw-Hill.
37 Fehér, J., & Szigeti, M. (2001), The application of change management methods at business organizations operating in Hungary: Challenges in the business and cultural environment and first practical experience, in D. Denison (ed.), *Managing Organizational Change in Transition Economies*, London: Lawrence Erlbaum Associates, 2001: 344–361.
38 For a description of the various forms of organizational change efforts that emerge in different cultures, see Faucheux, C., Amado, G., & Laurent, A. (1982), Organizational development and change, *Annual Reviews of Psychology*, 33, 343–370. See also Weick, K. E., & Quinn, R. E. (1999), Organizational change and development, *Annual Review of Psychology*, 50, 361–386.
39 This description of Miller's change effort is found in Pascale, R. R. (1999), Surfing the edge of chaos, *Sloan Management Review*, 40, 83–94.
40 *The Prince*, 1513, Chapter 6 (1992, trans. K. W. Marriott, New York: Knopf).

9

Making Ethical Decisions

Jeanne McNett and Mikael Søndergaard

The area of ethics is the ultimate test of the ability to cope with the ambiguity of international business.

Evans, Pucik, & Barsoux[1]

Our focus on the process of ethical decision-making in a global context begins with mention of a well-known ethics problem, one about which most of us know and have opinions, Nike's labor issues in Southeast Asia. Nike faced criticism and boycotts on ethical grounds for their outsourced labor practices and work conditions. Although they moved to correct the practices once they realized and accepted their responsibility for them, Nike still faces the consequences of what reasonably can be called an error in ethical decision-making.

Nike's business model is centered on outsourcing all production in low-cost overseas labor markets. Nike owns no production facilities; it is essentially what critics call an empty box – a design and marketing company. In the early 1980s it outsourced with manufacturers in Japan, and then Korea and Taiwan. As these labor markets became more costly, as is expected with successful development, Nike moved on to the newer developing markets of China, Indonesia and Vietnam. Often their Korean and Japanese outsourcers moved into these markets as well, strengthening their relationships with Nike and maintaining their contracts.

The decision to outsource in Vietnam brought needed development dollars to a poor rural area whose political leaders had courted Nike's involvement. Nike contracted with a Korean business with whose work they were familiar.

In late 1997, a Vietnamese worker, a young woman, died when a machine exploded and her heart was pierced by shrapnel. This industrial accident brought the developed world's attention and judgment to work conditions, wage issues, and child labor conditions that had been endemic in many developing nations in the region.

Labor and political organizers built their case against Nike on the basis of labor conditions. By 1998, this case was being heard by an often incredulous and naive public, a public who did not understand how to apply purchasing power parity analysis to a daily wage in Vietnam of $1.67 for a sneaker that cost upwards of $150 in the US market. Nor did this public have any context for thinking about 14-year-old workers, capital punishment, and reduced bathroom privileges for assembly-line workers.

Earnings at Nike fell drastically near the end of 1998, in part because of the turmoil caused by the currency crisis in Asia, but also in part because of the public's decision not to purchase Nike products because of Nike's Asian labor practices. The developed country public's outrage over the working conditions and the treatment of workers in the Korean-owned, Korean-run production facility in rural Vietnam quickly became an ethical problem for Nike in all of Nike's developed world markets.[2]

Ethical decision-making is an especially complicated process in global management. It is a systems skill, we argue, because in order to make and implement ethical decisions, the global manager has to understand the environment and to make sense of it at a complex, systems level. We think that a good way to capture a sense of this complexity is to examine the process of ethical decision-making as a global management skill enacted by individual managers as they make decisions.

Our focus is on the individual manager faced with a series of decisions, both small and large, whose ethical content may not be immediately obvious yet whose ethical impact has significance for people beyond the usual stakeholder constituencies. Nike's experience with outsourcing decisions is a case in point. The novice manager, the manager with low levels of global competencies, may not grasp the deep and pervasive ethical content of decisions made in the global environment, both major decisions and the many small decisions that are a regular part of a global manager's day. Yes, there are international codes of conduct, such as the Caux Round Table Principles, the CERES Principles, and the ILO Standards. But their important contribution is at the broader, organizational values and practices level rather than at the individual manager's operations level.[3]

In this chapter, we set out to offer practicing managers various ways to think about and to approach the process of ethical decision-making. The first section contains a brief summary of ethics theory. We then examine ethical decision-making under conditions of global complexity, including an exploration of its place in the global competency model and its analysis using Kidd and Teramoto's taxonomy of knowings. This is followed by a third section that reviews approaches to ethical decision-making for the practicing global manager. A fourth section examines some of the barriers to ethical decision-making that mid-level managers would do well to be aware of because they exist in routine and broadly accepted organizational practices. We then look at some practical advice in a fifth section, and conclude with a brief summary.

Before we begin, we must acknowledge that each of us understands ethics based on our assumptions and cultural beliefs, factors which influence our perspectives and perceptions of phenomena in our world. Our assumptions may not always help us to describe and understand the world with accuracy. Our interpretations are the result of our cultural perspective and therefore may be ethnocentric and self-referencing. We remind ourselves that within any culture that differs from our own, ethical norms may be both subtle and markedly different, even contradictory, and yet still legitimate and authentic, understood to be widely accepted within that culture. For example, within the North American approach to ethical decision-making, the cultural bias is towards individualism and a doing mentality. These biases are relevant in the culture's approach to ethics. The Irish novelist James Joyce likened efforts to escape our own cultural conditioning to peeling

TABLE 9.1 Perry's ethical levels

Approach	Level	Description	Likely outcomes
Commitment in relativism	Advanced; coincident with expert global managers	Relativist understanding of the world is combined with a commitment to a set of values and principles within an expanded world-view	Manager assumes responsibility for actions and decisions based on analysis and reasoning
Relativism	More developed; frequently found in stage 2 and 3 global managers	Dualistic view is moderated by an awareness of context: knowledge and values are relative	May lead to a "When in Rome do as the Romans do" approach, a problematic basis for ethical judgment
Dualism	Least developed; often found in novice global managers	Bipolar model for ethical judgments. Assumption is there is a clear differentiation between right and wrong approaches; the manager's way is the right way	Leads to empire-style approach to ethical differences

back layers of an onion: the layers of cultural conditioning constitute our meaning. At the core there may be a spiritual essence, but not the neutral ground that would make addressing our own culture's influence on our perceptions easy.

The difficulty for global managers in addressing ethical issues in a global environment is thus often at the perception rather than the action level. Such managers may find a helpful approach to ethical variation across cultures by drawing on William Perry's scheme of intellectual and ethical development.[4] Perry's approach has been applied to help managers think about their positions on these issues,[5] as summarized in table 9.1.

ETHICS THEORY REVIEW

A brief review of ethics theory is helpful to remind the manager that the assumptions upon which we make ethical decisions are varied. Awareness of these assumptions is an important first step in understanding the complexities of what we consider to be right, good, and just actions. By tradition, ethics has been studied within the area of philosophy, and recently its study within business disciplines has begun to promise results that will be helpful to the global manager.

Ethics theory is either normative or empirical. Normative theory offers answers to questions about what constitutes correct action, and empirical theory helps us to understand what makes people do wrong and how bad consequences occur. Much as in philosophy itself, normative theory is by far the most predominant in the study of business ethics.[6] Empirical theory tends to focus on two questions: "What makes people do wrong?" and "How do bad consequences come about?"[7] This developing area may

TABLE 9.2 Matrix of ethics theories

Application	Deontology (Faith)	Teleology (Hope)	Caring (Charity)
Universalism	Universal duty: universal principles, the Way	Universal ends: Character ethic, utilitarianism, other-isms	Universal care love for humanity
Particularism	Particular duties: situation ethic, case-by-case approach	Particular ends: self-actualization	Particular care: personal relationships

Source: Brady, F. N. (1996), Ethical universals in international business, in F. N. Brady (ed.), Introduction: A Typology of Ethical Theories, Berlin: Springer.

be seen as approaching the border between psychology and philosophy, and it promises to help us better understand how to encourage and train managers for improved ethical conduct.

The normative philosophical approaches have received the most scholarly focus in recent years, and they can be further described by the generalizeability of their claims. F. Neil Brady has developed a matrix[8] for such a distinction that offers a cogent, helpful summary of the normative approaches. Its modification is in table 9.2. The horizontal axis describes the three main theoretical bases for ethical judgment, with Brady's suggested equivalents in parentheses. The first basis is deontological, stemming from duties and moral obligations (Greek deont, duty). Probably the most well-known deontological theory is Emmanuel Kant's categorical imperative, which dictates that one has a duty to "act only on that maxim by which you can at the same time will that it should become a universal law."[9] The popular paraphrase of Kant's categorical imperative is "Do unto others as you would have them do unto you." The second basis for ethical analysis is teleological, and addresses the good that comes from a focus on the ends achieved by a contemplated action (Greek telos, end). Utilitarianism, or the greatest good for the greatest number, illustrates such a teleological approach. Here, the ends can be seen to justify the means. The third basis is one of caring. In this category would be approaches that value relationship duties over other duties.

On the vertical axis the matrix based on Brady's work describes various ethical theories based on their application claims: is the theory universally applicable (the rule) or does it claim a situational focus (it all depends)? This dimension corresponds to the universalism–particularism dimension used to describe culture.[10] In cultures that measure high on the universalism dimension, such as the United States, Switzerland, Australia, and Canada, rules are seen to apply to all equally. In particularist cultures, such as China, Japan, Venezuela, Greece, and India, rules are seen as more variable, depending on the context and the actors.

Knowledge of these differing theoretical assumptions is of considerable value to global managers as they make decisions across cultures. For example, Chinese business ethics decisions tend to be particularist and relationship-based. Awareness that American business ethics decisions, in contrast, tend to be universalistic and rule-based would help an international partner from a particularist culture such as China understand the assumptions that underpin the US Foreign Corrupt Practices Act.

ETHICAL DECISION-MAKING AND GLOBAL COMPLEXITY

Often, in a global situation, the manager faces the opportunity to make decisions that bridge ethical values among cultural groups, for example, to pay a special, unofficial fee to speed up the import process into a developing country. An ability to make and then implement these decisions is important, and the implementation rests on the manager's ability to build support for the decision, which in many cases will bridge and reconcile divergent ethical positions.

Much of the complexity related to ethical decision-making in a global context stems from widely differing ethical standards among cultures. With decisions that span two or more cultures, even when there is remarkable similarity among their accepted, ethical business practices, the reasoning process used to get to that similarity may be quite different. As Donaldson suggests, there is "no international standard of business conduct."[11] Rather, ethical decision-making skills in the global arena are complex and situational.

We now look at the process of ethical decision-making under conditions of global complexity in two ways that we have found useful: first in terms of the global competency model, and second, using Kidd and Teramoto's four knowings.

Ethics and the global competency model

The individual global manager's ability to make ethical decisions depends on the decision-maker's beliefs about the world (how markets and organizations work), beliefs about others (their competence, motivation, ethical beliefs), and beliefs about themselves (competence, motivation, ethical beliefs).[12]

Interpersonal skills play significant roles in this process. Mindful communication and the ability to build trust greatly increase the likelihood that the global manager will have the knowledge and information necessary to perceive the situation in the local environment with a degree of accuracy. These interpersonal skills also support open communication channels and help to ensure an honest, two-way information flow that keeps the manager connected to understandings in the local environment as well as in the larger stakeholder environment. The local manager with such global understandings becomes an effective boundary spanner whose decisions can include knowledge of local ethical practices and of the ethical concerns and responses of the larger community.

How decision-makers decode the environment is influenced by their levels of complexity and cosmopolitanism: their global mindset. An in-depth example of this process, which goes to the maxim "We don't know what we don't know," may be helpful. A novice expatriate manager with low levels of cosmopolitanism might interpret a local cultural practice in the ways such behavior would be understood in the home culture and stop there rather than attempt to access the practice's meaning in the local culture also, and thereby extend the range of meanings, which would make the analysis more complex.

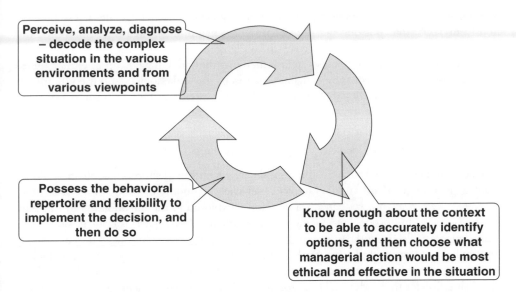

Perceive, analyze, diagnose – decode the complex situation in the various environments and from various viewpoints

Possess the behavioral repertoire and flexibility to implement the decision, and then do so

Know enough about the context to be able to accurately identify options, and then choose what managerial action would be most ethical and effective in the situation

FIGURE 9.1 Ethical decision-making in a global context

For example, if women's covering their heads and faces in conservative Muslim cultures is given meaning in a Western context, it would lead to different conclusions than were it given meaning with knowledge of the specific, local, Muslim context. Yet most global managers would not have access to this local meaning without quite effective boundary spanning, since most global managers, based on their gender, would not be able to interact with the covered women. Such limits on meaning-giving tend to constrain the level of complexity at which analysis takes place. High levels of cognitive complexity and cosmopolitanism would lead the manager to make inquiries to support any meaning-giving and to assign meaning in a tentative way.

Decision-making in the global context also depends upon how the decision-maker perceives, analyzes, and diagnoses the relevant business situation. When the novice global decision-maker is not adept at reading or decoding the local environment, the result is that the decision-maker may not be able to discern with accuracy what constitutes accepted, ethical practice in that local environment. In addition, the novice may not have the situational knowledge necessary to be able to generate ethical options, select from among them, and enact the chosen alternative in ways that will meet local, organizational, home culture and the larger stakeholder constituency's ethical standards. The final step is to have the behavioral flexibility be able to implement. This process is illustrated in figure 9.1.

That the Nike manager responsible for the outsourcing contract in Vietnam had limited knowledge about the labor conditions in practice at the Korean-owned and managed outsource facility is a reasonable assumption. Without the local knowledge, the decision-maker lacked the input required to diagnose the potential meanings that labor conditions may have encouraged in Nike's developed-nation consumers.

Such multileveled, complex awareness reduces the likelihood of decisions having unanticipated consequences because they are not aligned with the moral values of any of the various stakeholder constituencies. Nike painfully discovered, when its sales fell so precipitously in 1998, that outsourcing did not provide exemption from responsibility for the outsourcer's labor practices. Nor were the judgment criteria for those labor practices restricted to the local, Vietnamese environment, as they may have been in earlier times. The developed world's consumers defined themselves as stakeholders and used their own ethical criteria to judge the labor practices of Nike's suppliers. These consumers decided to hold Nike responsible for its contractor's labor practices.

Taxonomy of knowings applied to ethical decision-making

An equally helpful approach to the complexity of ethical decision-making in a global context is found in Kidd and Teramoto's four-class taxonomy of "knowings": *Know who, know how, know what, and know why*,[13] a taxonomy explored in the introduction to this part of the book. In the process of making ethical decisions, *knowing who* is critical, since such knowledge enables boundary spanning, which allows the decision-maker to learn about unfamiliar contexts and players. Such social capital takes time to build and is invaluable. With such social capital, the manager can call on influential contacts who understand the local situation for their advice. These contacts help the decision-maker to be able to assess what he/she does not know. We assume that the Nike decision-maker in the outsourcing contract in Vietnam did not know that there were pieces of knowledge about work conditions and stakeholders' potential readiness to judge workplace practices of a Korean outsourcer in rural Vietnam missing from the pre-decision analysis.

Knowing what allows the decision-maker to use product and organization knowledge as input for decision options. The Nike decision to outsource was cost-driven by an innovative business model that generated large margins that could be allocated to marketing. The contract could have been written to include salary and work condition safeguards, and still meet the cost targets.

Knowing why reflects an understanding of the basic business purpose and can be thought of as an ethical touchstone at the core of strategy: Why are we in this business? Why are we conducting business in this environment?

Finally, *knowing how*, having the behavioral skills and flexibility to carry out the decision, is important for the decision-maker's implementation. *Knowing how* allows the decision-maker to implement in such a way that the decision is understood as it is intended, and not misread. *Knowing how* connects to mindful communication and trust-building. *Knowing how* in a deep way connects to building community around the decision.

TOOLS FOR ETHICAL DECISION-MAKING

Researchers have developed useful tools to support ethical decision-making in the global environment. They include descriptions of ethical development stages, ethical styles, guidelines for making ethical decisions, and a decision tree focused on a process that will lead to an ethical result. Along with these tools are observations about the influence of culture on ethics and some practical advice about how to operate ethically, culled from the experience of international managers and researchers.

TABLE 9.3 Ethical development of international managers: Stages and characteristics

Manager stage	General characteristics	Operational approach to ethics
Stage 5 Expert	Able to read situation intuitively, understands purpose (what the business stands for)	The framing of an ethical approach happens automatically, based on values and knowledge of the local situation derived from experience. It is seemingly effortless.
Stage 4 Proficient manager	Calculation and rational analysis seem to disappear; fluid, seemingly effortless performance begins to emerge.	Ethical analysis is less mechanistic and increasingly more intuitive.
Stage 3 Competent manager	Recognizes the complexity of business situations.	Begins to think in terms of trade-offs and deeper-level values.
Stage 2 Advanced beginner	Can detect patterns.	Builds knowledge of local environment's underlying values. May see disconnect/gap between corporate codes and local needs.
Stage 1 Novice	May not be able to decode environment or to foresee potential issues. Relies on organizational codes and guidelines.	Follows the rules; local events are fit to corporate codes.

Manager's values: personal, organizational, and home culture

Source: Hosmer (1996).

Stages of ethical development

We begin with the stages, which describe ethical development found among global managers based on general characteristics of the stage and the operational approach to ethics in that stage (see table 9.3). This developmental typology describes the potential for development of ethical decision-making ability and, in that way, helps the manager appreciate alternatives and potentials. It also serves as a reminder of the variety of approaches possible, and at the same time offers a way to discuss these issues within the organization and with external constituencies.

These developmental stages illustrate the important role of experience and how it can build tacit knowledge, that is, a subtle, experiential, and not easily transmittable knowledge, about ethical decision-making. That novice managers realize that ethical decision-making rests on a complex model of global competency, some of whose aspects they are still building, is important because such awareness may help them avoid misperceptions and other errors in the processes of giving meaning, exploring options, and implementing.

The Stage 1 novice global manager can be encouraged to build mentor relationships with expert managers in the local environment, both within the organization and beyond the organization's borders, from whom they might seek advice as they develop their decision options. Local input into the discussion would also be a good option. Such boundary-spanning approaches help novices appreciate the local environment's complexity and anticipate some of its potential ethical issues.

Stage 2 and 3 global managers increasingly know that they may not know. This realization is a difficult step for novice managers who, after all, have been trained to analyze an environment, make decisions and, in a sense, impose their certainty on the environment. Once the manager realizes that complexity includes them, they can take precautions as they process their decisions and make efforts to understand the values of multiple environments, not simply their own, home headquarters' environment or the local one.

Stage 4 global managers increasingly operate from their tacit knowledge of the environment and their stakeholders. They have built trusting relationships in the local environment that have helped them learn how to read it with some accuracy. In a sense, the progression from Stage 1 to Stage 4 is a progression in the accumulation of tacit knowledge and the building of confidence to use it.

Ethical decision-making styles

The decision-making styles that managers use in the international environment vary greatly and depend to some extent on their organization's approach to ethical decision-making. Enderle has identified five distinct styles,[14] knowledge of which can help the global manager anticipate potential outcomes related to the decision's style and also can offer the decision-maker help in articulating and then exploring alternative approaches.

Foreign Country Style: the decision-making is based on the manager's perception of the values and norms of the local environment. This is the "When in Rome, do as the Romans do" approach. However, this approach may be a convenient justification for unethical behavior.[15] We have seen some of the additional problems such a localized approach may lead to in Nike's experience with their outsourcing decision in Vietnam.

Empire Style: the decision-making is based on the ethical and cultural values of the organization's *home country*. Such an approach may result in ethnocentric views of ethical behavior. Meaning-giving is a process that rests on cultural assumption, and awareness of these assumptions is critical to the giving of meaning.

Interconnection Style: Decision-making is based on values shared by other organizations such as the NAFTA, the EU, and groups of expatriate managers. This approach moves beyond the national level. It can be effective as a guide, especially in headquarters and at top management levels. Its helpfulness for the mid-level practitioner out in the field with imports to clear through customs, however, may be somewhat less direct.

Global Style: Decision-making is based on a *company's* articulation of principles, drawing on local and regional norms. This approach may impose the company's understanding of "truth" and its own norms on a local culture.

Creative Ethical Navigation Style: Decision-making is based on universally accepted norms (hypernorms) and local norms that do not violate the hypernorms. The Creative Ethical

Navigation Style[16] is based on social contract theory and was developed by Donaldson and Dunfee, who refer to it as "integrative social contract theory" (ISCT).[17] Local norms that are inconsistent with hypernorms are considered illegitimate. When the manager faces conflict between local norms and hypernorms, a gray area, possibilities exist to explore creative resolutions in a moral free space. This approach considers the widest possible array of stakeholders and prioritizes shared human values over locally held values if there is a values conflict.

The experienced international manager knows that the "When in Rome do as the Romans do" approach represented in the *Foreign Country Style* does not offer an adequate approach to ethical decision-making. The "When in Rome . . ." rule of thumb assumes that there is one ethical standard to which everyone subscribes and which they practice. We know from experiences in our own countries that people differ in their ethical behavior and that, more likely, there is a distribution of ethical standards in practice in all countries. Some people behave more ethically than others.

Given a world so connected that communication can be instantaneous, the values used to judge an organization's decision-making are at the same time both local and international. Such relativism as the "When in Rome" approach suggests is inappropriate. Consider, for example, the on-going ethics critique Nike continues to receive from developed country stakeholders because of its Southeast Asian outsourcing. Many of these treatment of workers, work conditions, pay levels, and outsourced production-monitoring issues are a result of the fully localized "When in Rome . . ." approach Nike initially chose. Yet "the CNN effect"[18] has taught Nike that local decisions, which may meet and even exceed some local ethical standards, are up for review by global stakeholders who hold norms and values that may be quite different from those found in the local culture.

The Empire Style and the *Global Style* of ethical decision-making, at the other end of the decision spectrum from the *Foreign Country Style*, are also problematic. Both styles impose outside values on the developing world. This standardized approach exports home values, an approach which may lead to ethically problematic decisions. A leading international ethics researcher, Donaldson, describes the decision-making of an American organization that was strongly committed to training aimed at reducing sexual harassment.[19] When the organization rolled out a global program that had been developed and tested in the US to the Saudi facility's workers, its reception was negative. Saudi managers were both baffled and insulted. Here some localization would have been appropriate. Jingoism such as this is one danger of the Empire Style. Its other costs are the missed opportunities to connect with the local environment to more fully grasp and appreciate its underlying cultural dynamic.

An *Interconnection Style* of decision-making accepts the values and norms followed by international organizations and multilateral groups. Following such global codes of conduct may raise the ethical bar across cultures. The Sullivan Principles in response to apartheid in South Africa are one such example. Yet this approach may be seen as an attempt to impose developed country values hegemony on the developing world. The Interconnection Style also may hold a manager back from uncovering creative opportunities to build common approaches with local values and from learning at deeper levels about the local culture.

The *Creative Ethical Navigation Style*, formulated by Donaldson and Dunfee as the Integrative Social Contracts Theory (ISCT),[20] offers a creative approach to building a shared values base, and in this way, may offer great potential to the global manager. This approach rests on the idea that the organization doing business in a foreign country has committed to a social contract with the host country. This contract requires that the organization act to increase the local welfare, recognize and respect the rights of all people, and minimize harm. ISCT suggests that local values, once understood, be included unless they conflict with more universal ethical values, called hypernorms. This approach incorporates the complexity of the global context, its multiple stakeholders and interested parties, and increased levels of ambiguity. In order to assess local norms, the global manager has to establish boundary-spanning relationships in the local environment, built on mindful communication, and build community through decision-making. Trust-building is essential to this process, which is supported by a global mindset. ISCT illustrates the value of the Global Competency Model in ethical decision-making.

Kohls and Buller's Ethical Decision Tree[21]

The individual manager's process of decision-making in a global context is the focus of work by Kohls and Buller, who have developed a decision tree to structure ethical decisions in this complex environment. The Ethical Decision Tree is useful to a manager because it structures a complex process while helping to ensure the consideration of multiple variables. Often, the Western global manager will be under considerable time pressure to show results, and may feel pushed to make a decision. This decision tree brings to the fore the decision-maker's strategic options. For example, under some conditions, Kohls and Buller suggest that a decision may be avoided; under other conditions, they suggest that the decision is best forced. Educating others so they share one's position may be an option, as may infiltrating one's values into the local context. Negotiation, accommodation, and collaboration are additional strategies for ethical decision-making.

Kohls and Buller warn that often in making ethical decisions across cultures, managers may be forced to sacrifice peripheral values in order to preserve core values.[22] This is another approach to priorities in case of conflict, in addition to the more local-, universal approach offered by ISCT. The focus on peripheral-core values offers managers another way to examine the values of their situation. Global managers need to be able to distinguish among these values, as Kohls and Buller suggest, so they do not, for example, sacrifice the core value of respect for others in order to preserve the peripheral value of consistency. See figure 9.2.

Decision rules for cross-cultural ethical conflict

Hamilton and Knouse[23] have outlined four principles for ethical decisions when there is cross-cultural ethical conflict, and from them, developed a decision process. Their decision rules are:

Decision Principle 1: Is the questionable practice in the host country less ethical than the global organization's usual practice? Then follow the usual practice. The challenge here is to decide if the questionable practice is less ethical or simply different. The conflict may be between a good and a bad practice or between two good practices.

Decision tree for selecting conflict resolution strategy

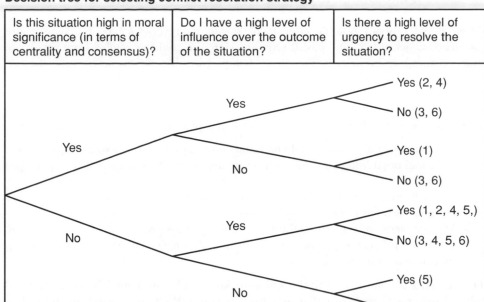

Is this situation high in moral significance (in terms of centrality and consensus)?	Do I have a high level of influence over the outcome of the situation?	Is there a high level of urgency to resolve the situation?

FIGURE 9.2 Strategies for coping with ethical conflict

Note: Numbers in parentheses indicate strategies that are feasible and arguably defensible: 1= avoiding; 2 = forcing; 3 = education; 4 = negotiation; 5 = accommodation; 6 = collaboration.

Decision Principle 2: If the questionable practice violates the organization's ethical minimums, follow the organization's minimum values. This suggests that first, organizations need to state clearly what the minimum ethical standard for its managers' conduct is, and second, that the organizations are able to state these ethical minimum standards in ways which carry meaning for the person implementing decisions.

Decision Principle 3: If Decision Principle 2 applies and the global organization has leverage in the host country to encourage local organizations to follow the global organization's practices, then it should influence local business standards for the better. Such leverage may not be possible.

Decision Principle 4: If the country's background institutions have prospects for improvement, then the global organization may have the obligation to follow its own ethical standards in order to support the improvement of local business institutions.

These principles offer some general guidance to the international manager based on the global organization's values. Note that these principles assume that the organization's leadership is able to articulate the organization's values and has done so, and that the international manager has a clear understanding of these values, both in and of themselves and as they would manifest in a foreign environment. We think that such an understanding is unlikely for the novice manager.

PRACTICAL ADVICE AND CULTURE OBSERVATIONS

When thinking about possible ethical challenges, many novice global managers are concerned about bribery and payoff requests. Here are guidelines culled from expatriate experience to help avoid such situations,[24] followed by observations on how specific cultural patterns might influence ethical decision-making for a novice Western manager.

When confronted with what feels like pressure to act unethically, don't assume that you have to do so. Look creatively for another approach by trying to understand what the need behind the request is. Perhaps a personal favor or a private donation would fill the need.

- You can say "no" without building antagonism by objectively explaining your personal and organizational values and by being polite. This approach may gain you respect.
- If you learn to read the contextual cues of the local culture, you will be able to recognize ways to evade bribery requests.
- Allocate plenty of time to establish relationships in support of your business goals. Avoid the temptation to buy your way out of perceived time pressures. Instead, allocate more time to the process.

The influence of culture on ethical decision-making can be substantial. There are several cultural patterns in particular that may present novice Western managers with predictable – yet frustrating – ethical challenges. These patterns involve cultures whose attributes are relationship-focused, hierarchical, and polychronic.

- In relationship-focused cultures (as found in many Asian, Middle Eastern, African, and Latin American countries), experienced international managers have learned to build relationships with the decision-maker or power broker in order to avoid paying to have their message carried forward in someone else's communication channel. This relationship-building takes time and is often a difficult area for the novice Western manager, who frequently is under time pressure to show results.
- Experienced managers have also learned that in hierarchical cultures, as found in many non-industrialized countries, going to the top from the very beginning leads to results. Again, this will require more time at the front end, but will pay off in the long term.
- If the culture is also polychronic, be aware that pushing on this time issue to ensure promptness may result in substantial increases in business costs in the long run.
- The experienced international manager learns the local culture at a sufficient enough depth to build a sense of what implicit values in the culture drive organizational performance.

ORGANIZATION-LEVEL CONSIDERATIONS RELATED TO ETHICAL PRACTICE

Mid-level managers would do well to be aware of some of the potential organizational barriers to ethical decision-making because these potential barriers exist in routine and broadly accepted organizational practices. Ethical values are embedded in an organization's strategy, structure, control, and motivation, whether they are explicit or implied. Global managers have to draw on these values to support their decision-making. How the organization at its core treats ethical issues is critically important to the global manager.

Strategy

An organization's values, including its ethical values, are found in the vision and mission statements, which drive the strategy. Strategy (What business are we in?) and ethics are linked via the idea of *purpose* (What is our purpose?). Freeman and Gilbert suggest that managers understand *purpose* in quite personal ways, as a guide for their personal action. They suggest that his action is activated by agreement with others, for the mutual benefit of the organization.[25] Yet the *purpose* line of questioning is often overlooked in strategy development, perhaps in part because one of the characteristics of the organization is to diffuse responsibility.

Freeman and Gilbert suggest that although managers may not discuss the underlying purpose of their work with colleagues, managers do understand the purpose of their organizational activities in terms of their own personal engagement with and responsibility for them. They also understand purpose as it applies to their connections to others, in and beyond the organization, people who agree to responsibilities related to their shared goals. These assumptions about an organization's underlying purpose are ethical in nature and are likely to be influenced by culture. To leave these assumptions tacit may result in deep-level misunderstandings.

To be effective, values have to reside at the operational levels, in the thoughts and actions of those who implement the strategy. Discussions within the company and with partners and customers, especially if they are from other cultures, is important in order to build understanding of the other's and the manager's own implicit, culturally influenced ethical assumptions. These dialogs can be a source of strength and resolution in times of moral uncertainty. A strategy development process which includes such an exploration of ethical considerations at its outset encourages ethical decision-making in the organization as a way of thinking.

Structure

Global organizations often are structured as a collection of divisions that have decentralized operational responsibility. Divisional managers are then held responsible for the division's performance. Hosmer[26] points out that such divisional structure may lead to a challenging ethical issue: corporate management has essentially no control over divisional strategies until they are either very good or problematic. Hosmer points out that once a division issue has become a problem, the organization may have missed the opportunity to make ethical decisions. They are in a response mentality. Moral action may be a part of the problem's solution, but this is of a smaller scope, of a different order than ethical decision-making. Hosmer's message here is that management by exception at the divisional level, because it tends to be problem-oriented, may confound ethical problems in the global organization. This condition suggests, once again, the need for ethical values to permeate the organization.

Control and motivation

Organizations may encourage global managers to be unethical in forceful, implicit ways, through disincentives. Among the most commonly mentioned disincentives in the literature are the reward of quantity over quality; the bottom-line pressure for profits at any cost; open-door policies but closed-door practices; punishment for reporting policy violations; uncertainty about ethical standards; promotion of managers known to be less ethical; and patterns of deception throughout management.[27]

The way performance is measured in US-style organizations may put pressure on managers to act for the short term rather than to choose what might be the right approach for the company in the long term. Given the time that may be required to build relationships and to understand the context in other cultures, the global manager should be particularly cautious in this regard. Hosmer suggests that motivated for the short term, managers find ways to show higher profits (recording issues), lower costs (labor moved from fixed to negotiated; altered product designs, neglected service warranties), and higher overhead rates (labor moved from indirect to direct) by managing for what is measured.[28] The message here for global managers is to set and manage reasonable performance expectations.

In summary, managers in US-style organizations, because of the way organizations develop strategy, structure, control, and motivate, may often understand ethics to represent a conflict between the economic and social performance of their organizations. In organizations which do not value ethical decision-making as central to the strategy process, this perceived conflict may pressure mid-level managers to take ethical shortcuts. In a global environment, such shortcuts may be especially tempting to the manager who may be under time pressure, who may be frustrated with progress rates, and who may be dealing with culture shock. Note, too, that other cultures may differ considerably in the ways to which their implicit ethical values drive these organizational activities.

SUMMARY

Making ethical decisions is the skill at the pinnacle of the global competency model, building as it does on the model's *traits* of integrity, humility, inquisitiveness, and hardiness; the *attitudes and orientations* of cognitive complexity and cosmopolitanism captured in the Global Mindset; the *interpersonal skills* of mindful communication and creating and building trust; and the *systems skills* of boundary spanning and building community through change. Often, seen from a distance, the ethical dimensions of decisions made by global managers are the one visible characteristic of the global enterprise, emblematic of the complexity that is at the core of globalization. If Nike had recognized the meaning their localization and delegation could have had, the conditions of their decision to outsource to a Korean firm in Vietnam may have been different. That difference might have been captured in a six-line work conditions clause in the contract. Because the global manager did not anticipate that the results of this agreement would not meet the ethical standards of many of their developed-world consumers, Nike, a company filled with people who care about others in good and ethical ways and apply such care to their business decisions, became described by this global managerial action in what for the company was a costly and painful nightmare. Nike has certainly learned from this ethics crisis, but at what a cost!

In this chapter, we began with a vignette based on Nike's outsourcing decision in Vietnam, and went on to briefly review ethical theory as applied to business. We then considered the place of ethics in the global competency model. Drawing on the work of ethics researchers, we then discussed tools for ethical decision-making and examined organizational barriers and disincentives to ethical decision-making. Ethical decision-making in the global context, sitting as it does at the top of the global competencies model, is increasingly the acid test applied by a multiplicity of stakeholders to judge global management competency.

NOTES

1 Evans, Pucik, & Barsoux (2002), p. 198.
2 See /www.corpwatch.org/nike/ and Spar, D. L. (2002), Hitting the wall: Nike and international labor practices, *Harvard Business School Review*, September, case no. DOI:10.1225/700047.
3 For the reader interested in these codes of conduct, see Williams, O. F., CSC (ed.) (2000), *Global Codes of Conduct: An Idea Whose Time Has Come*, Notre Dame, IN: University of Notre Dame Press.
4 Perry, W. G. (1970), *Forms of Intellectual and Ethical Development in the College Years: A Scheme*, New York: Holt, Rinehart & Winston. Perry's scheme has nine stages; Lane's version uses the three higher-level stages.
5 Lane, DiStefano, & Maznevski (2000), p. 438.
6 Very generally, in philosophy, ethics as a discipline was stagnant in the early part of the twentieth century. Philosophers were preoccupied with moral skepticism and problems in the philosophy of language With the Vietnam war, philosophers became dissatisfied with this work. There was a revitalized interest in classical, modern normative theory – Mill, Kant, and the social contract. John Rawls was a mover this revitalization. My thanks to my philosopher colleague Gavin Covert at Assumption College for his willing discussions on these matters.
7 Margolis (2001), p. 30.
8 Brady, F. N. (1996), Ethical universals in international business, in F. N. Brady (ed.), *Introduction: A Typology of Ethical Theories*, Berlin: Springer, p. 6.
9 Kant, I. (1785), *The Foundations of the Metaphysics of Morals*, Section One (trans. Lewis Beck, New York: Macmillan).
10 Hampden-Turner, C., & Trompenaars, F. (2000), *Building Cross-Cultural Competence*, New Haven: Yale University Press.
11 Donaldson (1996), p. 52.
12 Messick & Bazerman (2001).
13 Kidd, J. B., & Teramoto, Y. (1995), The learning organization: The case of the Japanese RHQs in Europe, *Management International Review*, 35(2), special issue, 39–56.
14 Enderle, G. (1995). Suggested in Donaldson and Dunfee (1999).
15 Lane, DiStefano, & Maznevski (2000), pp. 438 ff.
16 Weiss, J. (2003), *Business Ethics: A Stakeholder and Issues Management Approach*, 3rd edn., Mason, OH: Thompson South-Western, p. 295. Weiss developed the term; the concept was developed by Donaldson and Dunfee (1999).
17 Donaldson & Dunfee (1999).

18 This apt phrase was suggested by Allan Bird.
19 Donaldson (1996), p. 49.
20 Weiss (2003).
21 Buller, Kohls, & Anderson (1991).
22 Kohls & Buller (1994), p. 33.
23 Hamilton & Knouse (2001).
24 Greatly influenced by Gesteland (1999).
25 Freeman (1991), p. 17.
26 Hosmer (1996), p. 159.
27 Freeman (1991), p. 130.
28 Hosmer (1996), p. 165.

BIBLIOGRAPHY

Bartlett, C. A., & Ghoshal, S. (1989). *Managing across Borders: The Transnational Solution*. Boston: Harvard Business School Press.

Buller, P. F., Kohls, J. J., & Anderson, K. S. (1991). The challenge of global ethics. *Journal of Business Ethics*, 10, 35–43.

Buller, P. F., Kohls, J. J., & Anderson, K. (1997). A model for addressing cross-cultural ethical conflicts. *Business and Society*, 36(2), 169–93.

Donaldson, T. (1996). Values in tension: Ethics away from home. *Harvard Business Review*, September–October, 48–62.

Donaldson, T., & Dunfee, T. W. (1999). *Ties that Bind: A Social Contracts Approach to Business Ethics*. Boston, MA: Harvard Business School Press.

Dreyfus, H. L., Dreyfus, S. E., & Athanasiou, T. (1986). *Mind over Machine*. New York: The Free Press.

Enderle, G. (1995). What is international?: A topology of international spheres and its relevance for business ethics. Paper presented at the International Association of Business and Society, Vienna, Austria.

Evans, P., Pucik, V., & Barsoux, J. (2002). *The Global Challenge: Frameworks for International Human Resource Management*. Boston, MA: McGraw-Hill Irwin.

Freeman, R. E., ed. (1991). *Business Ethics: The State of the Art*. New York: Oxford University Press.

Freeman, R. E., & Gibert, D. R. (1998). *Corporate Strategy and the Search for Ethics*. Englewood Cliffs, NJ: Prentice Hall.

Gesteland, R. R. (1999). *Cross-Cultural Business Behavior*, 2nd edn., Copenhagen: Copenhagen Business School Press.

Hamilton, J. B., & Knouse, S. B. (2001). Multinational enterprise decision principles for dealing with cross cultural ethical conflicts. *Journal of Business Ethics*, 31, 77–94.

Hosmer, L. T. (1996). *The Ethics of Management*. 3rd edn., Boston MA: Irwin McGraw-Hill.

Kohls, J. J., & Buller, P. F. (1994). Resolving cross-cultural ethical conflict: Exploring alternative strategies. *Journal of Business Ethics*, 13, 31–38.

Lane, H. W., DiStefano, J. J., & Maznevski, M. L. (2000). *International Management Behavior*, 4th edn., Oxford: Blackwell.

Margolis, J. D. (2001). Psychological pragmatism and the imperative of aims: A new approach for business ethics. In J. Dienhart, D. Moberg, & R. Duska (eds.), *The Next Phase of Business Ethics*. Amsterdam: JAI Elsevier, vol. 3, 27–50.

Messick, D. M., & Bazerman, M. H. (2001). Ethical leadership and the psychology of decision-making. In J. Dienhart, D. Moberg, & R. Duska (eds.), *The Next Phase of Business Ethics: Integrating Psychology and Ethics*. Oxford: JAI Elsevier, pp. 213–238.

Nike ethics URL sites include /www.corpwatch.org/trac/nike/ and www.caa.org.au/campaigns/ nike/

Prahalad, C. K., & Doz, Y. (1987). *The Multinational Mission: Balancing Global Demands and Global Vision*. New York: The Free Press.

Weiss, J. (2003). *Business Ethics: A Stakeholder and Issues Management Approach*, 3rd edn., Mason, OH: Thompson South-Western.

Part III

LEADING AND TEAMING

INTRODUCTION

The focus of this part of the book is leading and teaming in a global context. In today's firms, leading and teaming are two highly interdependent components of organizing. Leaders are faced with the difficult task of convincingly presenting the organization's vision to a multicultural and diverse workforce in a highly uncertain and unpredictable environment, and the challenging task of executing the vision often lies with teams at different levels in the organization. To be effective in today's global environment, leaders need the knowledge and skills to act and decide appropriately, and to do so in a culturally sensitive manner; in other words, they need what Javidan and House call "cultural acumen."[1] Managers need not only a comprehensive technical knowledge base but also a well-developed set of relational and cross-cultural skills. A global leader needs the ability to define and solve problems in the face of increasing levels of uncertainty and an equally keen sense of how and when previous experience is relevant in new cultural settings.[2]

In many multinational firms, teams have become the basic organizing structure for accomplishing work in the global business environment. Hence, leading and working increasingly takes place through global teams, groups of people who interact across geographic, organizational, and cultural boundaries to achieve common goals for which they are mutually accountable. Members of global teams are often very diverse, representing different functions, organizations, and national cultures. Since the 1990s, the growth in global teams has increased exponentially as companies have invested resources in people and in organizational and technological infrastructure to connect technical expertise and local knowledge for the purpose of achieving shared global business objectives. Global teams, especially teams that work virtually across distance and time, are a fact of life today for managers and employees working in multinational companies.

Yet, how to lead and work in a global team, and how to evaluate, recognize, and reward performance to create positive outcomes both for the people who work in these teams and for the organizations that support them, is problematic for two reasons. First, research is only now beginning to uncover the differences between traditional or conventional teams who do most of their work face-to-face, and global teams who may do a large portion of their work virtually. Second, while managers have been quick to create global teams, many of these teams have been overwhelmed by the complex challenges that working globally brings to teaming, and they have failed, or have fallen short, in achieving their objectives. Managers, team leaders, and members must all understand more about the dimensions of complexity they face in global teaming and what strategies, skills and processes will help them manage this complexity to keep the team members working productively to achieve their goal.

Leading and Teaming

Chapter 10 is a discussion of the broad topic of leadership in a global context. We examine visionary leadership, leading teams, perceptions of leadership across cultures, diversity of people in leadership roles, leadership's consequences, and the future of leadership in the virtual age. In the remaining three chapters of this part, our discussion turns to leading and teaming specifically, and to the dimensions of complexity leaders and team members must manage through task and social process to produce successful outcomes.

Figure 10.1 illustrates leading and teaming in a global context. Leading and teaming involves managing *dimensions of complexity* through *interwoven task and social processes* in *designing* and *forming* teams, as leaders and members are *interacting* to accomplish the team's goal, and in managing how teams are *performing* throughout the team's work together. Leaders and team members also work to develop trust and to form a set of shared team perspectives and habitual work practices that are unique to the team and that consistently orient the team members to their task, a kind of collective team identity.[3] Trust and team identity can be thought of as *emergent states* that support the achievement of the team's goal.

Task processes represent *what* teams are doing, whereas social processes involve *how* they are doing it in relation to one another and to their task environment.

Task processes depend largely on the professional competencies of the leaders and team members and comprise primarily the processes that structure their roles and work practices, such as problem-solving, decision-making, and executing tasks. Teams move through task processes as *resources* are acquired and *members* are selected, as the members decide upon their *mission* and their *goals* as they *negotiate roles and responsibilities*, as they *manage project work*, often using *communication technologies*, and as they *evaluate, recognize, and reward performance*, *training and developing* team members as necessary.[4]

Social processes are interpersonal in nature and are directed at aligning members with one another. They include *creating a safe environment* for team members to work, and *developing shared mental models* and a *sense of community* among team members. Social processes also comprise the *sharing of information and learning* among team members, *differentiating*

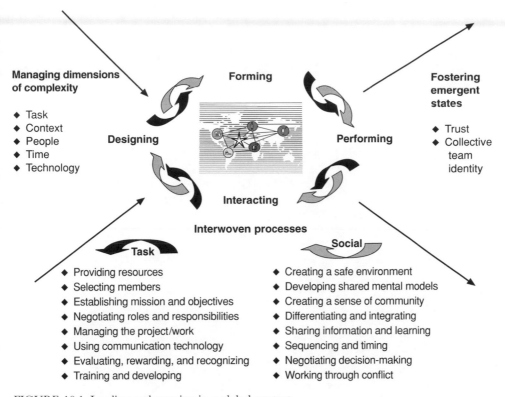

Managing dimensions of complexity

- Task
- Context
- People
- Time
- Technology

Designing

Forming

Performing

Fostering emergent states

- Trust
- Collective team identity

Interacting

Interwoven processes

Task

- Providing resources
- Selecting members
- Establishing mission and objectives
- Negotiating roles and responsibilities
- Managing the project/work
- Using communication technology
- Evaluating, rewarding, and recognizing
- Training and developing

Social

- Creating a safe environment
- Developing shared mental models
- Creating a sense of community
- Differentiating and integrating
- Sharing information and learning
- Sequencing and timing
- Negotiating decision-making
- Working through conflict

FIGURE 10.1 Leading and teaming in a global context

and integrating perspectives and approaches, and *negotiating the sequencing and timing* of members' interactions, as well as negotiating a process for *decision-making*, and for *working through conflict* when it occurs.[5]

Global teaming processes do not take place in a linear or unrelated manner. Rather, they are intertwined in an iterative or cyclical manner as team members do their work together over time. Teams develop a pattern of interaction that evolves in accordance with the team's task, the demands of the task environment, and the team members' competencies and the dynamics of their interactions. For example, team formation is itself cyclical and nonlinear. Events can precipitate re-formation processes, such as when members join or leave the team, or when the team faces an ethical dilemma, moving the team to revisit their values and working norms. Flux in the task environment, for instance when executives alter corporate strategy or when competitors engage in actions that significantly impact the team's purpose or objective, can lead team members to reexamine their purpose, goals, and options for decisions.

The chapters in this part are intertwined. However, each emphasizes a different aspect of leading and teaming and provides an in-depth perspective of these processes that every manager and employee engaged in global work can identify with and learn from.

10

Leading in a Global Context: Vision in Complexity

Deanne N. Den Hartog

The growing importance of world business creates a strong demand for leaders who are sophisticated in international management and skilled at working with people from other countries.[1] As described in Part I, "Globalization: Hercules Meets Buddha," a high level of complexity is inherent in this global business arena. Leaders in the global context need to be able to effectively deal with such complexity. Many different stakeholders from vastly different backgrounds play a role in the global arena. Ambiguity is common because words, intentions, and behaviors may be interpreted differently by different groups; and because conflicting interests may exist. Dealing with such high levels of complexity requires that leaders have an overarching and appealing vision that allows for the integration of different perspectives. Global leaders need the skills that allow them to develop such a vision and derive concrete strategic objectives and plans from it. Leaders are also faced with the difficult challenge of convincingly presenting their vision to a multicultural and highly diverse workforce and implementing it in an uncertain environment. This requires the ability to decide, communicate, and interact in a culturally sensitive and appropriate manner.

This chapter focuses on several aspects of leadership in a global context. Central to this chapter is the importance of the leader's vision. Other aspects that are crucial for leading teams at different levels in the organization are also discussed. For any person to gain influence, he or she needs to be seen as a leader. However, visionary leaders may "look" different in different cultures. What does it take to be seen as a leader in the United States? And in the Netherlands? Or India? We discuss similarities and differences in such images of leadership around the world. We then briefly touch on three challenges organizations face in the area of leadership: the possible unintended consequences of visionary leadership, the development of leadership capacity, and how organizations can increase the diversity of those who are suited for leadership roles. The chapter concludes with a discussion of several different scenarios for the future of vision and leadership.

Visionary Leadership

The study of leadership performance traditionally focused on how leaders can facilitate group maintenance and what they must do to ensure task accomplishment. Both task- and relationship-oriented behaviors are highly important for effective group leadership.[2] However, another important leadership function was traditionally not studied as often, namely, providing a vision or overarching goal. However, for leaders, this sense of direction, of knowing where one is going, is crucial to integrate and align followers' efforts. Through formulating a vision, a leader interprets reality for listeners and gives meaning to events.[3] Thus, for followers, the ideas expressed in the vision can act as a compass, guiding them in the daily decisions they make. The sense of purpose that an attractive vision of the future inspires acts as a powerful motivating force for those who share the vision.

Visionary leadership is highly important for leaders in an increasingly global context. The increasingly global business world "demands an unwavering commitment to change and a clear sense of direction. Visionary leadership is the mechanism for such change, providing the ideals to shape strategy and the energy to make it happen."[4] An example of a company built on a vision is The Body Shop. Former CEO Anita Roddick founded The Body Shop in the UK in 1976 out of her personal disappointment with the cosmetics market. She had strong views opposing the testing of cosmetics on animals, excessive packaging, and unfair trade. Roddick's vision focused on environmental and social issues. This is still expressed via the company's campaigns (for example, "Against Animal Testing," "Reuse, Refill, and Recycle," "Trade not Aid"). It is also reflected in their mission statement, part of which reads: "to dedicate our business to the pursuit of social and environmental change and to courageously ensure that our business is ecologically sustainable by meeting the needs of the present without compromising the future." The company Roddick built from scratch now has over 1,900 outlets in 50 countries.

Vision is seen as highly relevant in today's global strategic context. The dynamics of visionary leadership are therefore of interest here. How does vision relate to strategy in a global context? What constitutes an effective vision? Beyond foreseeing a better future, a visionary leader also needs to articulate, communicate, and implement ideas. In order to achieve goals following from the vision, different leader behaviors are needed, depending on the context. Thus, besides visionary and strategic leadership at the top of the organization, we will also briefly look at team leadership at lower hierarchical levels. Here, leadership generally has a more operational and relational focus, thereby ensuring task performance and social integration. First, we turn to global strategy and vision.

Vision and global strategies

As was stressed in the Introduction to this book, for most businesses the question is no longer *whether* to do business abroad, but to determine the desired *degree* of international involvement. Many hold that corporations nowadays must develop "global strategies" to succeed. But what is a global strategy? What types of international involvement exist? And how and where does leadership come in? More information on strategic initiatives in a global context can also be found in Part IV. Some aspects of strategy are discussed here as they relate to visionary and strategic leadership. Yip describes three separate processes for developing what he calls a "total global strategy."[5] The first step is developing the *core strategy*, in other words, the basis of a sustainable strategic advantage. The core strategy includes elements such as types of products, services, investments, and customers. The second step is *internationalizing* the core strategy through international expansion of activities and adaptation of the core strategy. *Globalizing* the international strategy occurs through integrating the strategy across countries. Organizations can be in different stages of this strategy process and the fit between strategy and organizational structure has received much attention.[6] Many factors complicate the relations between strategy, structure, and the degree of international involvement of organizations. An example is that large internationally operating firms can pursue different types of worldwide strategies for each of their businesses or products.[7] Also, many researchers question whether strategy development is indeed such a rational and sequential process. Strategies are often emergent and reactive rather than planned well in advance.[8]

Different strategies may lead to differences in the kind and degree of international involvement of firms. Based on their kind and degree of international involvement, different types of firms can be distinguished. For instance, Bartlett and Ghoshal describe the multinational, global, and international firm and add a fourth type, the "transnational."[9] The latter is most interesting from a global management perspective. "Companies following a transnational strategy recognize they should pay attention to global efficiency, national responsiveness and worldwide learning at the same time. In order to do this their strategy must be very flexible."[10] From the early 1990s, some convergence was seen among the leading multinationals from the different continents toward global operating divisions and a transnational perspective.[11] The transnational is not so much a specific strategic posture or a particular organizational form; rather, it describes a mode of management or management mentality in which flexibility and shared organizational purpose play key roles.[12]

Vision and leadership are highly important in transnational firms. The transnational perspective implies a rejection of the notion of a clear fit between strategy and structure in favor of the idea of seeking the strategic and organizational flexibility needed to face complex and dynamic environments. In such dynamic and complex environments, leadership processes and management attitudes are the key to the successful implementation of strategy. The large potential for fragmentation and dissipation, which inevitably comes with increased flexibility, is the greatest problem of this type of organization. A strong force of unification is needed in such a context. A strong, attractive, and shared corporate vision may provide such a force. Bartlett and Ghoshal noted that the most successful firms they studied had developed a common understanding of a clear and consistent corporate vision. The understanding and acceptance of the vision and the increased identification and commitment that follow from this can act as a kind of "global glue" in these diverse environments. "At its most effective, a carefully crafted and well-articulated corporate vision could become a beacon of strategic direction and . . . an anchor of organizational stability."[13]

The role of the top management team and especially the CEO in crafting and propagating this corporate vision is crucial. As Fombrun puts it, "effective leadership at the corporate level increasingly calls for personable executives skilled in the fine art of communicating across boundaries."[14] The CEO's or top management team's vision is the starting point of strategic thinking and articulates basic organizational values. The management mentality and attitudes toward internationalization are examples of such basic values where doing business in a global context is concerned. Basic attitudes toward international involvement can vary. Perlmutter's classic work describes different states of mind regarding attitudes toward "foreign people, ideas and resources, in headquarters and subsidiaries, and in host and home environments."[15] The three states of mind he distinguished are "ethnocentric" (home country-oriented), "polycentric" (host country-oriented) and "geocentric" (world-oriented).

Rephrasing such attitudes, one could say that the strategic assumption following from the ethnocentric perspective implies believing there is one best way to manage and do things. A polycentric perspective implies the company holds there are many good ways, leading to local responsiveness dependent on the nation involved. A geocentric attitude combines local responsiveness with global integration and fits the ideas of a transnational corporation.[16] One would expect such basic perspectives and values to be reflected in organizational visions. An example of a corporation with a geocentric attitude is Asea Brown Bovari (ABB). Led for a long time by Percy Barnevik, their often repeated adage was to "become global and local, big and small, decentralized but with central control." This adage articulated both the strategic imperative to be close to the nationally based customers while capturing global scale and the organizational requirement to manage the inherent conflicts. The transnational mentality with its recognition for these issues resulted in the implementation of a global matrix structure. However, ABB realized that structuring the organization to be geocentric would not be sufficient to make such a multidimensional, complex, and flexible management process happen. Thus, as CEO, Barnevik traveled around the globe to bring the message of why the company had to be managed this way, and how it could be done, to the front lines of ABB worldwide. As Barnevik indicates: "Thinking – the strategies and designs – only gets you five or ten percent of the way. Ninety percent is in the execution."[17] Below we will first focus on what visions are about, then come back to the issue of the execution of the ideas following from strategic visions.

Visions that work: What are they about?

As was shown above, corporate visions and articulate visionary leaders are often thought to play a key role in the formulation and implementation of international strategies. Leadership scholars have also emphasized the importance of articulating an attractive vision and providing an idealized image of the future as a means to profoundly influence followers.[18] The vision describes a better future in ideological terms and is congruent with the dearly held values of followers. By articulating a vision, leaders instill pride, gain respect and trust, and increase a sense of optimism and hope for the future in followers.[19] The leader communicates this vision through words as well as actions. A leader's personal example serves as a model of the kind of behavior required for attaining the vision. In other words, leaders act as role models. Modeling desired behaviors is important as the leader provides an ideal, a point of reference, and focus for followers' emulation and vicarious learning. Through demonstrating their courage and their moral conviction, leaders earn credibility and serve as a role model of the values inherent in the vision.[20] A powerful way to demonstrate conviction is self-sacrifice. Self-sacrifice on the part of the leader may demonstrate the leader's loyalty, model their dedication to the cause, and help build trust. Self-sacrificial behaviors in a business setting include denying oneself privileges, giving up resources, refraining from using position power, sharing hardships with followers, volunteering for the most arduous tasks, assuming blame for failures, giving up or sharing rewards (for example, taking a temporary salary cut). In a recent study, self-sacrificial leader behaviors were shown to have strong effects on followers. Followers attributed charisma and legitimacy to a self-sacrificial leader and they intended to reciprocate such behavior.[21]

A strategic vision can have an external orientation (product/service innovation) or an internal orientation (organizational transformation), and a broad (contribution to society) or a more narrow focus (contribution to the workforce).[22] A vision should ideally be attractive, flexible, and describe what could be achieved. It should also indicate *why* it is relevant to achieve that ideal, and give a first indication of *how* it can be done. Visions may be more general or more specific. However, visions need to go beyond specific short-term performance targets or directives. Such more specific targets may be based on the vision. A recent descriptive study on the content of organizational visions found that few organizations had well-developed visions. Most of the visions in the study were expressed as a brief, strategic, and future-oriented value statement or performance objective.[23]

Visions may focus on creating new opportunities or on a solution for an existing crisis in the organization or environment. As mentioned above, The Body Shop is an example of a company focusing on societal and environmental issues. An example of implementing a vision that is in response to a crisis can be found in the history of electronics giant Philips. In 1990 Philips undertook a highly ambitious program for restructuring and renewal. This turnaround process was called Centurion and was led by former CEO Jan Timmer. The process of change at Philips still continues. The first step of Centurion was to identify what the company stood for. "The Philips way" was defined in five values and beliefs that were meant to capture the spirit of the new company and, in doing so, bring Philips people together. These values were: delight customers, value people as our greatest resource, deliver quality and excellence in all actions, achieve return on equity, and encourage entrepreneurial behavior at all levels. The vision emphasized a renewed focus on customers and excellence. The creed "Let's make things better" captured this new focus on continuous improvement. Timmer expressed the importance of this creed to the employees by stating "It's a pledge to ourselves, to each other, and to the world at large."[24]

The content of a vision is obviously highly context-specific. Because of the central role of context, giving general directives for creating a compelling vision or an attractive content is difficult. Nutt and Backoff give four more general design criteria for crafting a vision for the organization that could help improve its performance, namely: *possibility*, *desirability*, *actionability*, and *articulation*. The first criterion of *possibility* refers to the innovative features of the vision; does the vision offer an exciting new order? The possibilities it offers should be unique, vibrant, and inspirational. Visions should be sufficiently future-oriented to show opportunities with potentially important consequences. Desirable visions draw on the organization's values and culture, and connect the future possibilities with these values. *Actionability* means that realizing the vision seems doable. This criterion means describing activities that people can undertake to move toward the desirable future possibilities that are envisioned. The vision meets the reality test. Finally, *articulation* refers to getting the message across to followers.[25]

Articulation is a key aspect of visionary leadership. Without effective communication, ideas are not likely to influence the listeners and their behavior in a pervasive way. Communicating the vision can be done on a one-to-one basis, but getting the message across to large audiences is often done in leaders' speeches. Gifted orators are able to gear their language to the audience at hand and use imagery and powerful rhetoric to persuade others of their views.[26] Anita Roddick, former CEO of The Body Shop, is strongly aware of the importance of vividly and imaginatively communicating one's vision. As she puts it in one of her speeches:

> What we do well at The Body Shop is communicate with passion because passion persuades. We also know that in this decade, to educate and communicate you have to be daring, enlivening and different. We go into the highway with our messages; our lorries are like moving billboards. I believe in promoting our products through global culture and linking them to political and social messages. . . . We see any empty space as an opportunity to create an atmosphere, deliver a message, make a point. Allow me to leave you with a favorite ethos printed on a T-shirt, given to members of staff: head in the clouds, feet on the ground, heart in the business.[27]

There are different styles to articulate visions, ranging from the quiet, softly spoken manner of leaders such as Gandhi and Mandela to the more "macho" oratory of a J. F. Kennedy or a Jack Welch. Profound differences exist across cultures in the preferred use of language, style of communication, and typical nonverbal cues. These differences are described in Part II's "Mindful Communication" and "Creating and Building Trust." In line with this, the preferred style to articulate a vision varies between cultures. In China, for instance, a vision is normally expressed in a non-aggressive manner. Confucian values stressing kindness and benevolence may play a role here. People are usually wary of leaders who engage in pretentious speeches without taking subsequent action and dislike leaders who are arrogant and distant.[28] In contrast, although Indian leaders must be flexible in this regard, and Gandhi was an exception, bold, assertive styles are generally preferred to the more quiet, soft, and nurturing styles.[29]

Regarding vision content, Sashkin defines three key content dimensions underlying effective visions of organizational leaders: *dealing with change, ideal goals,* and *people working together*.[30] Visions that work should help the organization deal with change; change in the environment, markets, and technology, for instance. Stressing the ongoing search for innovative ideas and new products is an example of this dimension. International strategy and the accompanying management mentality, as well as the approach to increasingly global markets and competitors, can also be seen as part of this dimension of vision.

Next, as mentioned above, effective visions incorporate goals in terms of ideal conditions or processes rather than explicitly defined final ends or specific production standards. Finally, effective visions also rely on their focus on people, both people within and outside the organization, such as members of the organization, possible investors, and customers. Visions become real through people. Coordinating and integrating activities of the collective is essential both to gain acceptance and commitment and to actually execute the vision.[31] The aforementioned Body Shop and Philips visions provide examples of these dimensions. In both cases we see the focus on change, the use of idealized conditions and goals, and the emphasis on those who can make it happen.

Some general guidelines that can be kept in mind when developing a vision are:[32]

- involve key stakeholders in the process;
- identify strategic objectives with a wide appeal that may serve as a basis for the vision;
- identify relevant elements in the old ideology that should be preserved and link the vision to core competencies to ensure the relevant elements remain; and
- evaluate the credibility of the vision and continually assess and refine the vision.

Clearly, just having and expressing a vision is not sufficient for success. Leaders also need to make their ideas happen. As ABB's CEO Percy Barnevik pointed out in the earlier quote, most work is in the execution of the ideas. Implementing the ideas from a new vision involves strategic planning and resourcing, but also abilities in other areas, such as timing (knowing when to do what), creating a sense of urgency, and social and political skills (being able to convince people, build coalitions; and knowing whom to involve). Implementation involves determination, the ability to learn fast, and persuasive abilities. Both ABB's Barnevik and Philips' Jan Timmer spent an enormous amount of time traveling around the world to explain to employees what the new course was and why they felt this was the right course to take. Philips, for example, organized internal "customer days" all over the world in which Timmer explained the new focus to employees across the globe in speeches and personally answered their questions in long question-and-answer sessions.

Boal and Hooijberg highlight the importance of three aspects of strategic leadership, namely the ability to learn (absorptive capacity), the ability to change (adaptive capacity), and managerial wisdom.[33] Absorptive capacity refers to the ability to learn: recognizing new information, assimilating it, and applying it to new ends. It involves reactively and proactively trying to improve the fit between the organization and its different environments. Absorptive capacity refers both to individuals and to the distribution of learning and knowledge throughout the organization as a whole. Learning occurs through studying (know how), doing (know why), and using (know how).[34] Creating an emphasis on continuous learning throughout the organization can also be the core of a vision of organizational change. For instance, Matthew Barrett, former CEO of the Bank of Montreal, initiated a dramatic change in the corporate culture at the bank several years ago, placing a heavy emphasis on learning at all levels of the organization. As he put it in one of his speeches:

> Our strategy is to embed into the organization a set of capacities, capabilities and competencies that will position and enable the organization to respond to whatever it may confront in an uncertain, turbulent world. . . . At the Bank, we see our culture of learning as our most distinctive trait and also our key competitive advantage. It differentiates us strongly today and over time it will do so even more. It is alive and open, our vital intelligence network that allows us to identify trends and absorb and incorporate them into our culture.[35]

The second aspect of strategic leadership is having the capacity to adapt and be flexible so that one can change when needed. Organizational flexibility derives from the abilities and openness of the leaders at the top of the organization. The third aspect is wisdom. Managerial wisdom involves two central aspects. The first is being able to take the right action at the critical moment. The second is discernment, the ability to perceive variations and patterns in the environment and to build an understanding of others and their relationships.[36] Such wisdom goes beyond simply being analytically smart or "having the brains." Sternberg shows that managerial intelligence has more components than the purely analytical aspects of intelligence (IQ) we usually refer to when we use the term *intelligence*. Although analytical intelligence obviously plays a crucial role in such a highly complex job, creative intelligence and practical intelligence (tacit knowledge and common sense) are also needed.[37]

Executing the vision: Other key leader behaviors

In addition to developing and articulating an exciting vision of future opportunities, other leader behaviors contribute to achieving desired results. Depending on their hierarchical level, leaders also have an important role in diverse activities such as translating vision into strategic directives and task requirements, monitoring progress and performance (of teams or larger units), deciding on the use of resources and budgets, adapting strategies and objectives, supporting and individually developing followers, maintaining high-quality relationships within the group, and stimulating critical thinking and innovation.

A leader inspires followers through articulating an attractive vision, and then, in the process of implementing these ideas (and meeting other important goals, such as the development of followers), usually will need to use a range of task and relationship oriented behaviors. Transformational leadership is seen when leaders have vision, and inspire and motivate followers to perform beyond expectation; when they stimulate followers intellectually to see problems in new ways and use individualized consideration and mentoring to help individual subordinates develop to their full potential. Individualized consideration implies treating each individual as valuable and unique, not just as a member of the group. It involves confidence building and expressing trust in followers' abilities to contribute to attaining the vision as well as providing for continuous feedback and linking the current needs of individuals to the organization's mission.[38] Intellectual stimulation of followers is important for innovation and change. An intellectually stimulating leader provides subordinates with a flow of challenging new ideas to stimulate rethinking of the old ways of doing things. This involves raising awareness of problems, obtaining subordinates' own thoughts and imagination, and recognizing their beliefs and values. Intellectual stimulation is evidenced by subordinates' conceptualization, comprehension, and analysis of the problems they face and the quality of solutions they generate.[39] Some guidelines for transformational leadership are:[40]

- ◆ articulate a clear and attractive vision and explain how it can be attained;
- ◆ lead by example and show optimism and confidence;
- ◆ use dramatic symbolic actions to emphasize core values and reward desired behavior;
- ◆ express confidence in followers' abilities to achieve goals and provide support for them where needed;
- ◆ empower others to achieve the vision; and
- ◆ create an intellectually stimulating environment in which criticism and ideas for improvement are expressed and seen as opportunities to learn.

Team leadership

At operational levels, the role of a team leader is not an easy one, especially in a global context. Individual team members and the organization have high and sometimes conflicting expectations of team leaders. Team leaders are expected to translate the strategic vision of the organization into team objectives and decide on the nature of the team task. They need to skillfully navigate the organizational and political context to ensure the team's interests are served. They are expected to create motivated, cohesive teams, even when working with people from diverse cultural backgrounds, even virtually and across time zones. They need to manage resources, balance conflicting interests, and deliver results that satisfy the demands from multiple stakeholders.[41]

From a functional perspective, team leaders are responsible for diagnosing problems that could potentially impede group and organizational goal attainment, generating and planning appropriate solutions for such problems, and implementing these solutions within typically complex social domains. Fleishman listed several leader performance functions that help team leaders perform these tasks:[42]

- *Information search and structuring.* This includes: acquiring information; organizing and evaluating information; and feedback and control.
- *Information use in problem-solving.* This includes: identifying needs and requirements; planning and coordinating; and communicating information.
- *Managing personnel,* including: obtaining and allocating personnel resources; utilizing and monitoring employees; and developing and motivating employees.
- *Managing material resources,* including: obtaining and allocating material resources; maintaining, utilizing and monitoring material resources.

Information search and structuring refers to the leader's systematic search, evaluation, and organization of information on team goals and operation. Information use in problem-solving refers to the leader's application of acquired information to problem-solving related to the team's goal attainment. The leader's role in boundary spanning is clear here. Vigilance, environmental scanning and forecasting are important. The team leader is usually responsible for interpreting tasks assigned to the team. This includes the translation of the vision and strategic intent of company executives into a workable plan for collective team action. It also involves acquiring information relevant to the team's mission and the resources that will be needed to complete it. This information is used to design a workable plan that fits the problem situation and will lead to team goal attainment. The action plan, including the way task execution ought to be handled and coordinated, must be communicated to team members.[43]

The other two areas of leadership performance involve the management of personnel and material resources. This is especially central at operational levels of the company. Managing personnel involves the whole spectrum of recruiting, selecting, coordinating, developing, motivating, and monitoring one's team members. From this description it is clear that this role is more difficult to fulfill when teams are not co-located. The changing nature of work and leadership in tomorrow's flexible organizations is discussed later in this chapter. Managing material resources includes procuring adequate resources for team action. Although not often described, this is a critical area in that not having sufficient resources will usually make it much harder for teams to attain specified goals within the agreed time frame even when solution quality and motivation are high.[44]

As is clear from the above, leaders can have a decisive impact on team effectiveness. They may affect different processes in teams (cognitive, behavioral, emotional, coordination, and motivational processes). For example, leaders may stimulate or hinder reflection and learning; they may affect interpersonal trust and shared emotions and impact on team members' motivation. Leadership also affects emotional processes in teams. Leaders who themselves feel excited, energetic, and enthusiastic have been shown to be more likely to positively energize their group of followers, whereas leaders feeling negative and hostile likely have a negative impact on the affective tone in the team.[45]

Effective team coordination and performance are partially dependent on the emergence of accurate shared mental models that describe requisite team strategies and interaction tactics among team members.[46] Shared mental models organize information about systems and their environment (for example, describing team purpose and expected team and member actions). Such shared models help team members anticipate each other's actions, which makes coordination easier and reduces the time needed to process and communicate during the task execution. Leaders play a role in the development of such models. Schein, for instance, states that "leadership is originally the source of the beliefs and values that get a group moving to deal with its internal and external problems. If what a leader proposes works and continues to work, what once was only the leader's assumption gradually comes to be a shared assumption."[47] An important function of leadership is the creation, management, and sometimes the destruction of such shared meanings and mental models.

Another important role leaders can have in the area of team cognitive processes is to facilitate team learning. Tannenbaum and colleagues stress the importance of facilitating learning through providing critical performance feedback to team members and encouraging collective reflection upon team processes. A list of helpful leader behaviors includes:

- Post-action reflection needs to take place in the context of pre-performance plans and goals. Thus, conduct "pre-briefs" and refer to these later when evaluating performance during or in post-action reviews.
- Provide a self-critique early in the post-action review.
- Guide briefings to include discussions of social processes or teamwork as well as taskwork processes.
- State satisfaction when the team or individual members demonstrate improvements.
- Provide specific, constructive suggestions in giving feedback. Avoid person-oriented feedback; rather, focus on task-related feedback.
- Accept ideas and feedback from others. Encourage active team member participation during briefings and reviews and avoid simply stating one's own observations and interpretations of the team's performance.[48]

In research, teams with leaders who were trained to act according to this list were found to be more likely to engage in collective reflection (that is, more likely to have discussions on topics such as teamwork and more likely to offer suggestions). Teams with a leader who encouraged such reflexive processes outperformed teams whose leaders did not engage in such behaviors.[49] Two aspects of the team context can make such processes even harder, namely when the team is virtual rather than co-located, and when it is international in the sense that its members have very diverse cultural backgrounds. These aspects often go hand-in-hand nowadays. Team members from different cultural backgrounds may have different rules and expectations in communication. Seeking harmony, communicating indirectly, and saving face are norms in some cultures, whereas openly criticizing each other and speaking up against leaders may be common in others. The degree to which the communication process is expected to be structured and formal is also influenced by culture. These team processes such as learning and developing shared mental models are discussed in more detail in subsequent chapters of this part.

Effective team leader behavior

Summarizing, effective team leader behavior encompasses several broad and overlapping areas, several of which are discussed in more detail in subsequent chapters:

◆ Vision development and attainment, including: envisioning an attractive future for the team that contributes to organizational goals; communicating this vision and translating it into realistic performance targets and strategic objectives; helping the team understand assumptions; learn, and develop shared mental models that help ensure vision attainment; creating an intellectually stimulating environment in which creativity and innovation are appreciated.

◆ Facilitating high-quality relationships and social integration, including: encouraging mutual trust and cooperation within the team; ensuring open communication and tolerance for dissenting views; helping team members in their personal development.

◆ Organizing and coordinating work (functional behavior), including: planning and scheduling activities; conducting meetings to inform others and make decisions; managing resources; monitoring progress and performance.

◆ Ensuring the environment is monitored (external boundary spanning), including: ensuring that client needs and emerging problems are clear; promoting a favorable image of the team to others; influencing others to provide adequate resources and assistance.[50]

So far, this chapter has described some aspects of executive and team leader behavior with a focus on the crucial role of vision. Much of these ideas are based upon Western views of leading and managing others. Research has shown that in order to be able to influence others, one needs to be seen and recognized as a leader.[51] However, what does it take to be seen as a leader? And, does it take the same thing in different cultures?

IMAGES OF LEADERSHIP AROUND THE WORLD

We are all confronted with leadership almost daily, in our job context and through the media. As a result, we all have ideas about what makes a leader effective. Different cultural groups may have different ideas regarding what leaders typically look like and how they should or should not behave. In some cultures a leader is thought of as typically an autonomous, strong, and decisive person; whereas in other cultures other images of ideal leaders may prevail. For instance, the ideal-typical leader might be an older person whose experience and wisdom rather than speed and boldness are admired and valued. Also, the evaluation and meaning of many leader behaviors and characteristics vary across cultures. For instance, in a culture endorsing a more authoritarian, tough, and assertive style of leadership, leader sensitivity might be interpreted as a sign of personal weakness. In contrast, in cultures endorsing a more soft, open, and nurturing style of leadership, the same sensitivity may be a prerequisite to be effective in a leadership role.[52]

A question that is especially relevant here is whether characteristics associated with visionary leadership are seen as important in different cultures. A recent research study called GLOBE provides more insight into such questions. GLOBE involves over 15,000 middle managers from 60 countries from all major regions of the world. These managers answered questions about culture and indicated which leader attributes and behaviors they thought would enhance or impede outstanding leadership in their context.[53] Several leader characteristics were found to be universally valued. These include many attributes reflecting visionary leadership. For instance, in all countries involved in the study, an outstanding leader is expected to be encouraging, positive, motivational, a confidence builder, dynamic, and to have foresight. Such a leader is excellence-oriented, decisive, and intelligent. Team-oriented leadership is also seen universally as important; outstanding leaders need to be good at team building, communicating, and coordinating. An outstanding leader is also trustworthy, just, and honest. Also, several attributes were universally viewed as ineffective, as impediments to outstanding leadership. These include being non-cooperative, ruthless, non-explicit, a loner, irritable, and dictatorial.[54]

Interestingly, the importance of many leader attributes varied across cultures. For instance, being unique and status-conscious are considered desirable characteristics for leaders in some cultures, but undesirable in others. Cultural differences play a role here. The differences that were found in appreciation of characteristics such as *subdued* and *enthusiastic* reflect differences in cultural rules regarding the appropriate expression of emotion. In many Asian cultures, displaying emotion is interpreted as a lack of self-control, and thus a sign of weakness. Not showing one's emotions is the norm. In other cultures, such as Latin cultures, it is hard to be seen as an effective communicator and leader without expressing emotions in a vivid manner. Also, several of the leader attributes that were found to vary across cultures reflect preferences for high power distance versus egalitarianism in society. For example, *status* and *class-conscious*, *elitist*, and *domineering* are attributes that are appreciated in leaders in some but not in other cultures.

Other leader characteristics that varied strongly across cultures reflect uncertainty avoidance, which as a cultural dimension refers to the tolerance for ambiguity. Being perceived as a risk taker, habitual, procedural, able to anticipate, formal, cautious, and orderly impedes outstanding leadership in some countries and enhances it in others. Finally, being autonomous, unique, and independent are found to contribute to outstanding leadership in some cultures and to be a barrier to leadership in others. These attributes seem to reflect different cultural preferences for individualism.[55] These differences show that although images of outstanding leaders around the world share some characteristics, there are also vast differences in what is seen as desirable for leaders.

Enacting leader attributes

The characteristics described above show a universal appreciation of certain leadership attributes and a more varied appreciation of others. However, even when attributes are universally valued, this does not mean such attributes will necessarily be enacted in the same way across cultures. The behavior that reflects an attribute may vary in different cultural contexts. In other words, *visionary* is seen as a positive attribute in most cultures, but what one needs to do to be seen *as visionary* may still vary strongly from one culture to another. As Bass puts it: "Indonesian inspirational leaders need to persuade their followers about the leaders' own competence, a behavior that would appear unseemly in Japan." However, even though it can be expressed in different ways, the concept of inspiration appears "to be as universal as the concept of leadership itself."[56]

An example of differences in such enactment is that what is perceived as sensitive or compassionate in one country may be seen as weak or inappropriate in another. For instance, Martinez and Dorfman describe the high degree of involvement of outstanding Mexican leaders in the private lives of their employees. An example was a manager calling the doctor when a family member of an employee was in hospital to make sure an operation was legitimate. This behavior was highly valued by the Mexican employees.[57] Similar behavior may also be valued and seen as an expression of compassion in other more collectivist societies. However, such behavior may not be seen as an appropriate expression of compassion and might even be interpreted as an invasion of privacy in less collectivist contexts. A more appropriate expression of compassion in such cultures might be inquiring after the situation or perhaps a temporary reduction of job duties so as to be able to care for the relative. Such examples clearly show that even though consideration and compassion may be evaluated positively in many cultures, the behaviors that are appropriate and will be seen as indicative of such consideration and compassion may vary strongly across cultures.[58]

Vision versus empowerment across cultures

Developing and communicating an attractive vision is an important aspect of leading in a global context. The media in many countries strongly emphasize the need for, and often, the dearth of, visionary leadership. For example, leadership is an important and popular topic in India. Whereas discussions of political leaders in India are often filled with cynicism and disdain owing to the perceived self-serving actions of these leaders, business leaders are mostly portrayed in a more positive light. Founders of businesses are usually admired and respected. A recent article in an Indian newspaper proposed five "leadership qualities and behaviors that CEOs should demonstrate, namely vision, inspiration, influence, empowerment, and expertise."[59] Similarly, the media in Austria also emphasize vision. However, the portrayal of business leaders is not always positive. Newspapers hold that although many leaders talk about vision, only a few are able to translate it into action. The reasons for this are said to be threefold: the leaders themselves (their being too "fearful" to pursue the vision), the followers (their unwillingness to go along) and/or structural constraints on realizing the visions.[60]

A tension exists between a leader disseminating a vision and cultural values stressing egalitarianism. Visions are often developed and communicated in a relatively leader-centered and directive manner, which may not always be the most effective style. In countries such as the Netherlands and Australia, a high value is placed on egalitarianism. In such cultures, employees usually feel equal to superiors and want to have their say in matters. Such egalitarianism may place higher demands on striving for consensus and taking employees' perspectives into account when developing a vision. The Dutch media, for instance, show a strong emphasis on the need for consensus and acceptance of visions by lower-level employees. This is reflected in remarks by Dutch CEOs such as "ideas need acceptance, otherwise they will not be realized" and "consensus is an important prerequisite to realize goals."[61] In egalitarian societies, processes emphasizing the collective development of shared ideals may prove most effective. In contrast, in high power-distance countries such an emphasis on acceptance and consultation of subordinates in developing a vision may be less important.

As described above, transformational leadership is seen when leaders have vision, inspire and motivate followers to perform beyond expectations, stimulate followers intellectually to see problems in new ways, and use individualized consideration and mentoring to help individual subordinates develop to their full potential. Bass has proposed that transformational leadership can take either a more directive or a more participative form.[62] In the Netherlands, participative leadership (consultation of followers in decision-making, especially where decisions affect their own work) was found to be important for transformational leadership.[63] Similarly, transformational leadership in Australia seems to be somewhat distinct from its North American counterpart, based on the ubiquitous value placed on egalitarianism by Australians. In Australia there is a tendency to denigrate high achievers. Feather refers to this as the "Tall Poppy syndrome" (to cut down the tall poppy that absorbs the sun while depriving the shorter poppies of exposure to the sun). Australian leaders are expected to inspire high levels of performance, but must do so without giving the impression of charisma or of not being anything more than "one of the boys."[64] The idea of *mateship*, the leader being "one of the boys," reflects the high value placed on egalitarianism in Australia. Thus, in strongly egalitarian societies, in order to be seen as transformational leaders and have transformational effects, leaders may need to be more participative and consensus-oriented (allowing subordinates a say in the objectives to be achieved) and act less elitist than in high power-distance societies.

Recently, "empowerment" seems to have come into vogue in business.[65] Empowerment in business involves managers giving employees more responsibilities, letting them work more autonomously, and sharing information with them, while at the same time encouraging employees and expressing trust in their abilities in a non-defensive manner. Benjamin Zander, conductor and director of the Boston Philharmonic Orchestra, started to think about his own empowering role as a leader when he realized that conductors themselves make no sound. The audience may love the music they hear, but the conductor has contributed no sound and "depends for his power, entirely on his ability to make other people powerful". An experimental study on empowerment among MBAs from different cultural backgrounds (high and low power-distance cultures) showed that participants were all more satisfied in the empowered rather than the disempowered condition. No differences in performance in the empowered or disempowered condition were found for the group from low power-distance cultures. However, individuals from high power-distance cultures did not perform as well when empowered as when disempowered. This group may be used to a much more structured and formal work environment in which decisions and task directives and guidelines are typically provided from above, access to information is limited, and responsibilities are explicit and few.[66] Individual differences within societies are likely to be large. However, these findings suggest that when implementing principles of empowerment and self-management in a high power-distance context, employees may need some more time and guidance in initial phases to get a clear understanding of expectations, processes, and performance criteria that characterize the new way of working.

CURRENT CHALLENGES FOR ORGANIZATIONS

Many challenges face organizations concerning global leaders. Here we will briefly describe three of these. First, we go into possible unanticipated negative consequences that may result from strong visionary leadership. Next, we discuss leadership development and increasing diversity of those in and preparing for leadership roles.

Dealing with unanticipated consequences

Leadership is often portrayed in a positive light and visionary leaders have indeed achieved great things. However, leaders are not always a force of positive change. As dramatic examples in history show, visionary leadership may also have unanticipated and negative consequences. One danger of visionary leadership lies in its possible misuse to work toward immoral ends. A leader's acts that on the surface appear selfless may actually serve fundamentally selfish and manipulative purposes. Thus, such leader behavior may result in exploitation and oppression rather than the empowerment of others.[67]

However, positive visionary leadership may also have unintended consequences. The effects of visionary and charismatic leadership are powerful and can increase followers' dependency on the leader rather than empower them. Also, followers may become less critical of the leader and vision than they should be. Enthusiastically working on achieving a mission one believes in may then become unquestioning obedience. The sense of urgency and strong dedication to the cause that often accompany vision create a strong pressure to keep performing at the highest possible level. This may in time result in increased levels of stress and burnout. Such prolonged stress decreases creativity and productivity and may even cause health problems.[68] Another problem may be that the vision may be overly dependent on one person. Succession planning is needed and the vision needs to be shared and embedded in the policies, processes, and structures of the organization to ensure it is not dependent on a single leader.

Visionary leaders need to demonstrate conviction in their own beliefs and self-confidence to convince others of the viability of their vision. However, the high level of self-confidence of such leaders can also have unanticipated negative consequences. Leaders can become overconfident, no longer seeing the flaws in their plans or adapting to changing circumstances. An example of this process is the behavior of the creator of the Polaroid camera, Edwin Land. He had previously been successful in designing the instant Polaroid camera and decided to develop a radically new and perfect instant camera. Ignoring feedback that the market for this new product would be too small, he invested an estimated half-billion dollars in the development and production of the camera. The strategy was not successful. Sales did not go well, and price cuts and years of redesign that took out most of the new features were needed to launch the camera. Land's personal vision of the camera had missed what the market wanted.[69]

Developing global leaders

All over the world, organizations need to think about how they can develop young managers and prepare them for future senior leadership roles. Organizations use different kinds of practices in developing their future leaders. These practices can often also be used for other purposes and be embedded in the work: to improve performance management (for example, 360-degree feedback), to facilitate corporate socialization (for example, mentoring and networking), and to enhance productivity (for example, job assignments).[70]

People learn through different processes. Some things can be learned through studying and then applying the new knowledge in context. In learning skills, observing others can be helpful, and much is learned through the process of practicing, receiving feedback, and reflecting on experiences. Existing leadership development programs can use a mix of methods to help different kinds of learning occur. For example, 360-degree or multi-source feedback involves collecting systematic perceptions of an individual's performance from relevant sources (subordinates, supervisors, peers, and even customers). When done sensitively, this information can be used to help people gain more insight into their performance as a leader and identify areas for further development. Such information on which behaviors are in need of further development can sometimes also be gathered in assessment centers. Training programs or one-on-one executive coaching are often used (as the follow-up on assessment) to develop specific areas of knowledge and behavior. Formal mentoring systems are also in place in many organizations. Most approaches couple a junior manager with a more senior executive outside the direct reporting line. Activities aimed at developing and fostering broader individual networks can help develop future leaders. Much is also learned on the job, for instance through participation in different projects, on committees, and through more formal systems of job rotation and job assignments.

Across countries, marked differences exist in typical approaches used for the development of leaders and managers. A study by Stewart and colleagues compared the career patterns and educational background of German and British middle managers. In Germany, vocational education was emphasized and formal qualifications were tied more strictly to functional responsibilities of middle managers than in the United Kingdom. Britain has a tradition of recruiting graduates of any discipline for many jobs, whereas in Germany the management task is perceived in more functional terms and a direct relationship between vocational training and the job to be done was more common. Regarding career development, in Britain more emphasis was placed on mobility. Large companies prepare their potential future senior manager by changes of jobs, tasks, and functions. In contrast, in Germany less emphasis was placed on mobility and development through exposure to different situations. Managers spent more time in a single job and development of expertise rather than variety was valued at middle management level. This example illustrates that companies can have different approaches to address the challenge of developing their managers, and that differences in traditions and preferences are found between countries.

Owing to globalization, many organizations nowadays are facing an even more daunting challenge. How does an organization develop managers so that they can become effective global leaders? Global leaders need knowledge about other regions and cultures of the world and need to understand what managing and doing business effectively in drastically different locations entails. They need strong conceptual skills, as they need to be able to effectively and constructively deal with the many ambiguities and complexities that come with the strategic management role in the global environment. Changes in the global environment are drastic and the pace is high, and global leaders must be able to adapt their minds at the same pace. Such leaders need to be experts at managing relationships and, clearly, culture plays an important role there. Managing relationships in an intercultural context requires cultural awareness and high levels of sophistication in adapting to different styles with different people.[71] We describe these issues at the individual level in Part II, "Global Competencies."

Leadership development in global firms is not only individual human capital development (leader development), but also the development of leadership capacity within the organization in a broader sense (social capital development). Increasingly, business leaders around the world recognize the value of diversity at the top. In an interview, Cor Herkströter, former chairman of Shell, stated: "With such a high percentage of British and Dutch men in senior positions we're not a multinational." He stresses that diversification at the top is a must, a business necessity. "Otherwise you run the risk of missing out on certain talents." Increasingly firms are including groups that were traditionally not often found in corporate boardrooms, such as women and ethnic minorities, in leadership development programs. Below, we will briefly go into diversity in the context of the leadership role.

Diversity in the boardroom

A global executive survey conducted by *The Economist* Intelligence Unit and sponsored by executive search firm Korn/Ferry International found that executives expect that the leadership ranks are likely to become more culturally diverse and gender-diverse over the coming decade. Of those senior executives surveyed, 66 percent expect corporate boards of directors to become more diverse in nationality and gender over the next ten years, while 84 percent anticipate greater diversity among the top 100 management positions at corporations. With respect to the CEO position at companies, however, nearly half of those surveyed expect little if any change.[72]

Where diversity at the top is concerned, one area that has received much attention is gender. Increasing numbers of women around the globe are preparing themselves for managerial careers. Women are getting management and business degrees, working long hours, and obtaining the experience needed for entering the executive suite. Child-rearing and household tasks are increasingly seen as a couple's joint responsibility. However, figures compiled by the International Labor Organization (ILO) indicate that, still, precious few women actually reach higher management levels around the globe. Different explanations for this phenomenon have been proposed. For instance, women may lack training and experience to qualify, corporate policies and procedures may make it more difficult for women to succeed, and the existence of discrimination and sex bias may play a role.[73]

Men are often seen as more assertive, achieving, and dominant and women as more socially responsive, passive, and submissive. Such characteristics refer to sex-trait *stereotypes* and do not imply absolute differences between the sexes. The *real* differences in behavior between the sexes seem to be less pronounced than the *beliefs* about those differences.[74] Also, in research, successful managers are stereotypically viewed as more similar to men than to women on attributes considered critical to effective work performance, such as leadership ability, self-confidence, ambition, assertiveness, and forcefulness.[75] This pattern has been found in different countries (China, Japan, Great Britain, Germany, and the United States). Such stereotypes may provide a hurdle for women pursuing a career in management. "If a managerial position is viewed as a 'masculine' one, then, all else being equal, a male candidate appears more qualified by virtue of such sex typing than the female candidate."[76]

Stereotypes are only part of the story, however. Fagenson assessed the interplay between gender and the position held in the organizational hierarchy. She found no relation between gender and the possession of masculine characteristics (such as assertiveness and dominance). Instead, masculine characteristics were related to individuals' perceived power and position in the organizational hierarchy. Both men and women in upper levels were reported to be more masculine than people at lower levels. In contrast, feminine characteristics (such as nurturance and warmth) were not affected by hierarchical level. Overall, women scored themselves higher on "feminine" characteristics than men. The perception of feminine characteristics was also affected by educational level, with less educated people reporting to be more feminine.[77]

Thus, while gender and gender stereotypes matter to some degree, other characteristics, such as hierarchical level, perceived status and power, and education may prove even more important. In line with this, the self-perceptions of men and women are found to be less stereotypical in more economically and socially developed countries.[78] In such countries, higher proportions of women attend university and are gainfully employed and the ideology regarding the status of women is more egalitarian. Also, a blurring of the sex differences in child-rearing has begun and women and men perceive themselves to be more similar. "In many societies, as modernization proceeds, traditional patriarchal patterns of female seclusion and male dominance are replaced by women's greater civil equality and political participation."[79] Thus, such differences are expected to decrease over time. This may also extend to other groups that traditionally have held positions of lower power and status in society. As levels of education and experience of different groups rise, their inclusion in leadership roles is also expected to increase.

In the final part of this chapter, we focus on the future of leadership in the global arena. As waves of change are fundamentally changing how we think about organizations, we need to ask whether our current ideas on leadership remain relevant in this changing world.

Leadership in Tomorrow's Organizations

Increasing globalization, with its concurrent developments in IT and other currents of change, are influencing the nature of work and organizations in a pervasive and long-lasting manner.[80] Among the fundamental changes in organizations is the increased importance of teams and other lateral organizing mechanisms.[81] The next three chapters will focus on such teaming in a global context. To meet increased customer demands and growing competition, organizations need to become increasingly flexible. Nowadays, organizations often comprise temporary systems whose elements (people as well as technology) are assembled and disassembled according to the shifting needs of specific projects. People shift from team to team or work in multiple teams at the same time. In such situations, organizations can no longer rely on the traditional hierarchy, nor can leaders rely on the same level of formal power they previously derived from their position in the former strict hierarchies.

The content of work itself is changing as well. Much twenty-first-century work, especially in the more economically developed countries, will be intellectual rather than physical. Owing to the technological possibilities, such work is no longer necessarily performed in the office building and people working together no longer need to be together physically. Software applications such as groupware have made non co-located work a more realistic option.[82] Such a virtual work environment creates new challenges for managers, who can no longer literally oversee subordinates' efforts. Observing, monitoring, and controlling the direct supervision of such intellectual tasks performed at various locations will be very difficult.[83]

If organizations are indeed becoming increasingly flexible, will a single person taking on the leadership role in teams or even larger units become obsolete? There are several scenarios describing potential developments that imply such a reduced importance of the leadership role.[84] One such scenario is what Shamir calls *disposable leadership*. As organizations increasingly rely on temporary arrangements such as virtual project teams, leadership itself may become such a temporary arrangement. Leadership would then be limited in scope and duration. Any team member with relevant task-related knowledge and experience could act as leader for a specific project. People may work in multiple teams simultaneously, possibly in a team leader role on one project and as team member on another.

Another scenario that reduces the importance of single-person leadership is the idea of shared, distributed, collective leadership. The common element in this idea about leadership is that the leadership will not be concentrated in the hands of one single person or even a limited group. Instead, the leadership role may be divided and performed by many or all team members simultaneously or sequentially.[85] The idea behind self-managed teams also implies such a transfer of the leadership responsibility from an individual to the team as a whole.[86]

A third scenario that implies a reduction of the importance of leadership is teleleadership.[87] The increasing use of computer-mediated technologies and group decision-support systems may enhance the importance of leadership functions that relate to the transmission of information between leader and group members. It may also reduce the distance between top and lower hierarchical levels in the organization by enabling more effective communication between these layers. The role of leaders may then be reduced to more cognitive elements (such as managing information flow) rather than the more social, human, and emotional elements of leadership. Whether it is possible to really identify with or trust leaders with whom one only communicates electronically is yet unclear. This problem becomes especially pertinent in global virtual teams. We will discuss the changes that this increasingly virtual work environment brings in more detail in our focus on global teams in this part.

There are some problems with these scenarios. For instance, self-management has not always yielded positive results in organizations. Also, identifying with a professional group, organization or team increases commitment to that group and its goals and implies adherence to a pattern of values shared within such a group. Belonging to multiple groups with unclear boundaries may lead to identity problems.[88] In addition to affective problems such as not knowing where one belongs or to whom one is supposed to be most loyal, team members may also experience role ambiguity. Different team leaders may place conflicting demands on team members. Criteria for performance evaluation may be ambiguous and who evaluates such performance may also be unclear in such structures. Self-management in teams, as well as boundary issues, are discussed in more depth in the following chapters.

The intellective, complex, non-routine tasks of the future will require problem solving, individual initiative, and innovative behavior, as well as a willingness to take on personal responsibility for getting the task done on the part of employees.[89] The increased pace of change may be accompanied with a sense of uncertainty and anxiety for organization members. A sense of psychological safety is essential for individuals. Creating such a sense of safety and clarity, as well as increasing motivation, identification, and commitment, seem likely to remain important leadership functions in tomorrow's organizations.[90]

Shamir states: "flattened, flexible, project-based and team-based organizations that employ temporary, externalized and remote workers, whose tasks are more intellectual and less routine, and cannot be controlled and coordinated by structure or direct supervision, need mechanisms of coordination through shared meaning systems, a shared sense of purpose, and high member commitment to shared values."[91] Therefore, such organizations are likely to need strong leadership for integrative functions. Such integrative functions are less likely to be performed by movable or disposable leaders. Leaders have played an important role in promoting change and innovation and challenging the status quo in stable environments. In contrast, it may well be that in tomorrow's international, uncertain, and volatile environments the role of leaders is different. In such an environment leaders may have to balance the emphasis on change with providing a sense of stability, continuity, and integration. Some research suggests that that when one's world is unstable and unpredictable, being coherent may be more important than being visionary.[92] To us, this statement seems too strong. Although the content of effective visions in the future may emphasize stability and coherence as much as change, the potentially positive role of well-conceived, well-articulated, and well-implemented ideological visions for organizational effectiveness remains a strong, core part of the leadership process in the complex global environment.

NOTES

1 Adler, N. J. (1991), *International Dimensions of Organizational Behavior*, Boston: PWS-Kent Publishing.
2 For extensive overviews of studies in this area, see Bass, B. M. (1990), *Bass and Stogdill's Handbook of Leadership: Theory, Research and Managerial Applications*, (3rd ed.), New York: Free Press or Yukl, G. (2002), *Leadership in Organizations* (5th ed.), Englewood Cliffs, NJ: Prentice Hall.
3 See, e.g., Conger, J. A. (1989), *The Charismatic Leader*. San Francisco: Jossey-Bass; Den Hartog, D. N., & Verburg, R. M. (1997), Charisma and rhetoric: The communicative techniques of international business leaders, *Leadership Quarterly*, 8, 355–391.
4 Whittington, R. (1993), What Is Strategy and Does It Matter?, London: Routledge, p. 60.

5 Yip, G. S. (1995), *Total Global Strategy: Managing for Worldwide Competitive Advantage* (Business school ed.), Englewood Cliffs, NJ: Prentice Hall.

6 See, e.g., Pralahad, C. K., & Doz, Y. L. (1987), *The Multinational Mission: Balancing Local Demands and Global Vision*, New York: The Free Press.

7 Yip (1995).

8 E.g., Mintzberg, H., & Waters, J. A. (1985), Of strategies, deliberate and emergent, *Strategic Management Journal*, 6, 257–272.

9 Bartlett, C. A., & Ghoshal, S. (1989), *Managing across Borders: The Transnational Solution*, Cambridge, MA: Harvard Business School Press.

10 Harzing, A. W. (1995), Strategic planning in multinational corporations, in A. W. Harzing & J. Van Ruysseveldt (eds.), *International Human Resource Management*, London: Sage, pp. 25–50, p. 38.

11 See, e.g., Mabey, C., & Salaman, G. (1995), *Strategic Human Resource Management*, Oxford: Blackwell.

12 Bartlett & Ghoshal (1989).

13 *Ibid.*, p. 176.

14 Fombrun, C. J. (1992), *Turning Points: Creating Strategic Change in Corporations*, New York: McGraw-Hill, p. 177.

15 Perlmutter, H. V. (1969), The tortuous evolution of the multinational corporation, *Colombia Journal of World Business*, 4, 9–18, p. 11.

16 Den Hartog & Verburg (1997).

17 Ghoshal, S., & Bartlett, C. A. (1998), Managing across borders: The transnational solution (2nd ed.), London: Random House.

18 See, e.g., Bass, B. M. (1985), *Leadership and Performance Beyond Expectations*, New York: The Free Press; Bennis, W. G., & Nanus, B. (1985), Leaders: The strategies for taking charge, New York: Harper; Sashkin, M. (1988), The visionary leader, in J. A. Conger & R. N. Kanungo (eds.), *Charismatic Leadership: The Elusive Factor in Organizational Effectiveness*, San Francisco: Jossey-Bass.

19 Shamir, B., House, R. J., & Arthur, M. B. (1993), The motivational effects of charismatic leadership: A self-concept based theory, *Organization Science*, 4, 1–17.

20 E.g., House, R. J., & Podsakoff, P. M. (1994), Leadership effectiveness: Past perspectives and future directions for research, in J. Greenberg (ed.), *Organizational Behavior: The State of the Science*, Hillsdale, NJ: Lawrence Erlbaum, pp. 45–82.

21 Choi, Y., & Mai-Dalton, R. R. (1999), The model of followers' responses to self-sacrificial leadership: An empirical test, *Leadership Quarterly*, 10, 397–421.

22 Conger (1989).

23 Larwood, L., Falbe, C. M., Kriger, M. P., & Miesing, P. (1995), Structure and meaning of organizational vision, *Academy of Management Journal*, 38, 740–769.

24 Den Hartog & Verburg (1997).

25 Boal, K. B., & Hooijberg, R. (2000), Strategic leadership research: Moving on, *Leadership Quarterly*, 11, 515–549; Nutt, P. C., & Backoff, R. W. (1997), Crafting vision, *Journal of Management Inquiry*, 6, 308–328.

26 Willner, A. R. (1984), *The Spellbinders: Charismatic Political Leadership*, New Haven, CT: Yale University Press.

27 Den Hartog & Verburg (1997).

28 Fu, P. P. (forthcoming), Chinese leadership and culture, in R. J. House & J. Chhokar (eds.), *Cultures of the World, A GLOBE Anthology of In-Depth Descriptions of the Cultures of 14 Countries* (vol. 1).

29 Chhokar, J. S. (forthcoming), Leadership and culture in India: The GLOBE research project, in R. J. House & J. S. Chhokar (eds.), *Cultures of the World, A GLOBE Anthology of In-Depth Descriptions of the Cultures of 14 Countries* (vol. 1).

30 Sashkin (1988).

31 *Ibid.*

32 Based on Yukl (2002).

33 Boal & Hooijberg (2000).

34 *Ibid.*; Garud, R. (1997), On the distinction between know-how, know-why, and know-what, in Walsch, J. P., & Huff, A. S. (eds.), *Advances in Strategic Management* (vol. 14), Greenwich, CT: JAI Press, pp. 81–101.

35 Den Hartog & Verburg (1997).

36 Boal & Hooijberg (2000).

37 Sternberg, R. J. (1997), Managerial intelligence: Why IQ isn't enough, *Journal of Management*, 23, 475–493.

38 Bass (1985).

39 See, e.g., Bass (1985); Bass, B. M., & Avolio, B. J. (1990), The implications of transactional and transformational leadership for individual, team, and organizational development, *Research in Organizational Change and Development*, 4, 231–272.

40 Based on Yukl (2002).

41 Canney-Davison & Ward (1999).

42 Fleishman, E. A., Mumford, M. D., Zaccaro, S. J., Levin, K. Y., Korotkin, A. L., & Hein, M. B. (1991), Taxonomic efforts in the description of leader behavior: a synthesis and functional interpretation, *Leadership Quarterly*, 2, 245–287.

43 Zaccaro, S. J., Rittman, A. L., & Marks, M. A. (2001), Team leadership, *Leadership Quarterly*, 12, 451–483.

44 *Ibid.*

45 George, J. M. (1996), Group affective tone, in M. West (ed.), *Handbook of Work Group Psychology*, Chichester: Wiley.

46 E.g., Cannon-Bowers, J. A., Salas, E., & Converse, S. (1990), Cognitive psychology and team training: Training shared mental models of complex systems, *Human Factors Society Bulletin*, 33, 1–4; Mathieu, J. E., Heffner, T. S., Goodwin, G. F., Salas, E., & Cannon-Bowers, J. A. (2000), The influence of shared mental models on team process and performance, *Journal of Applied Psychology*, 85, 273–283.

47 Schein, E. H. (1992), *Organizational Culture and Leadership* (2nd ed.), San Francisco: Jossey-Bass, pp. 26–27.

48 Tannenbaum, S. I., Smith-Jentsch, K., & Behson, S. J. (1998), Training team leaders to facilitate team learning and performance, in J. A. Cannon-Bowers & E. Salas (eds.), *Making Decisions under Stress: Implications for Individual and Team Training*, Washington, DC: American Psychological Association, pp. 247–270. See also Yukl (2002).

49 Tannenbaum, Smith-Jentsch, & Behson (1998).

50 Based on Yukl (2002).

51 Lord, R. G., & Maher, K. J. (1991), *Leadership & Information Processing*, London: Routledge.

52 Den Hartog, D. N., House, R. J., Hanges, P., et al. (1999), Culture specific and cross-culturally endorsed implicit leadership theories: Are attributes of charismatic/transformational leadership universally endorsed?, *Leadership Quarterly*, 10, 219–256.

53 House, R. J., Hanges, P. J., Ruiz-Quintanilla, S. A., et al. (1999), Cultural influences on leadership and organizations: Project GLOBE, in W. Mobley (ed.), *Advances in Global Leadership* (vol. 1), Greenwich, CT: JAI Press.

54 Den Hartog et al. (1999).

55 *Ibid.*

56 Bass, B. M. (1997), Does the transactional-transformational paradigm transcend organizational and national boundaries?, *American Psychologist*, 52(2), 130–139, p. 132.

57 Martinez, S., & Dorfman, P. (1998) The Mexican entrepreneur: An ethnographic study of the Mexican *empresario*, *International Studies of Management and Organizations*, 28, 97–123.

58 Den Hartog et al. (1999).

59 Chhokar (2003).

60 Szabo, E., & Reber, G. (forthcoming), Culture, organizational practices and leadership in Austria, in J. Chhokar, F. Brodbeck, & R. J. House (eds.), *Managerial Cultures of the World: GLOBE In-Depth Studies of the Cultures of 25 Countries*, Thousand Oaks, CA: Sage.

61 Thierry, H., Den Hartog, D. N., Koopman, P. L., & Wilderom, C. P. M. (forthcoming), Leadership, politics and culture in the Netherlands, in J. Chhokar, J. F. Brodbeck, & R. J. House (eds.), *Managerial Cultures of the World: GLOBE In-Depth Studies of the Cultures of 25 Countries*, Thousand Oaks, CA: Sage.

62 E.g., Bass, B. M. (1990b), Editorial: Toward a meeting of minds, *Leadership Quarterly*, 1, p. i.

63 Den Hartog, D. N. (1997), Inspirational Leadership, VU doctoral dissertation, KLI-dissertation series, 1997-nr 2, Enschede: Ipskamp.

64 Ashkenasy, N. M., & Falkus, S. (forthcoming), The Australian enigma, in R. J. House & J. Chhokar (eds.), *Cultures of the World, A GLOBE Anthology of In-Depth Descriptions of the Cultures of 14 Countries* (vol. 1); Feather, N. T. (1994), Attitudes towards high achievers and reactions to their fall: Theory and research concerning tall poppies, in M. P. Zanna (ed.), *Advances in Social Psychology* (vol. 26), pp. 1–73, New York: Academic Press.

65 E.g., Eylon, D., & Au, K. Y. (1999), Exploring empowerment cross-cultural differences along the power distance dimension, *International Journal of Intercultural Relations*, 23(3), 373–385. Shipper, F., & Manz, C. C. (1992), Employee self-management without formally designated teams: An alternative road to empowerment, *Organizational Dynamics*, Winter, 48–61.

66 Eylon & Au (1999), p. 381.

67 Carey, M. R. (1992), Transformational leadership and the fundamental option for self-transcendence. *Leadership Quarterly*, 3, 217–236.

68 Conger, J. A. (1990), The dark side of leadership, *Organizational Dynamics*, 19(2), 44–55; Den Hartog, D. N., & Koopman, P. L. (2001), Leadership in organizations, in Anderson, N., Ones, D. S., Kepir-Sinangil, H., & Viswesvaran, C. (eds.), *Handbook of Industrial, Work and Organizational Psychology* (vol. 2), London: Sage.

69 Conger (1989).

70 Day, D. V. (2000), Leadership development: A review in context, *Leadership Quarterly*, 11(4), 581–613.

71 Maznevski, M. L., & DiStefano, J. J. (2000), *Human Resource Management*, 39(2/3), p. 195.

72 http://www.kornferry.com/Library/Process.asp?P=ART_002

73 McKeen, C. A., & Burke, R. J. (1994), The woman friendly organization: Initiatives valued by managerial women, *Journal of Workplace Learning*, 6(6), 18–26.

74 E.g., Segall, M. H., Dasen, P. R., Berry, J. W., & Poortinga, Y. H. (1990), *Human Behavior in Global Perspective: An Introduction to Cross-Cultural Psychology*, New York: Pergamon Press, p. 255.

75 E.g., Schein, V. E. (1973), The relationship between sex role stereotypes and requisite management characteristics, *Journal of Applied Psychology*, 57, 5–100.

76 Schein, V. E. (2001), A global look at psychological barriers to women's progress in management, *Journal of Social Issues*, 57, 675–688.

77 Fagenson, E. A. (1990), Perceived masculine and feminine attributes examined as a function of individuals' sex and level in the organizational power hierarchy: A test of four theoretical perspectives, *Journal of Applied Psychology*, 75, 204–211.

78 Williams, J. E., & Best, D. L (1989), *Sex and Psyche: Self Concept Viewed Cross-Culturally*, Newbury Park, CA: Sage.

79 Segall, M. H., Dasen, P. R., Berry, J. W., & Poortinga, Y. H. (1990), p. 255.

80 See, e.g., Davis, D. D. (1995), Form, function and strategy in boundaryless organizations, in A. Howard (ed.) *The Changing Nature of Work*, San Francisco: Jossey Bass.

81 E.g. Mohrman, S. A., & Cohen, S. G. (1995), When people get out of the box: New relation-ships, new systems, In A. Howard (ed.), *The Changing Nature of Work*, San Francisco: Jossey Bass.

82 Andriessen, J. H. E. (2002), *Group Work and Groupware: Understanding and Evaluating Computer Supported Interaction*, London: Springer.

83 Den Hartog & Koopman (2001).

84 Shamir, B. (1999), Leadership in boundaryless organizations: Disposable or indispensable?, *European Journal of Work and Organizational Psychology*, 8, 49–71.

85 Ibid.

86 See, e.g., Barker, J. R. (1993), Tightening the iron cage: Concertive control in self-managing teams, *Administrative Science Quarterly*, 38, 408–437.

87 Shamir, B., & Ben-Ari, E. (1999), Leadership in an open army? Civilian connections, inter-organizational frameworks, and changes in military leadership, in J. G. Hunt, G. E. Dodge, & L. Wong (eds.), *Out-of-the-Box Leadership: Transforming the 21st Century Army and Other Top Performing Organizations*, Stanford, CA: JAI Press.

88 Den Hartog & Koopman (2001).

89 House, R. J. (1995), Leadership in the 21st century: A speculative enquiry, in A. Howard (ed.), *The Changing Nature of Work*, San Francisco: Jossey Bass.

90 Den Hartog & Koopman (2001).

91 Shamir (1999), p. 59.

92 Lissack, M. R., & Roos, J. (2001), Be coherent, not visionary, *Long Range Planning*, 34, 53–70.

11

Designing and Forming Global Teams

Julia C. Gluesing and Cristina B. Gibson

There are many reasons why companies form global teams to work internationally and interdependently toward a common goal. Global teams can be created to develop global strategies, or to work locally to execute these strategies, or both. Multinational corporations often create global R&D teams to benefit from site-specific scientific expertise that is not available in one location, but is spread around the world. Still other companies create global teams in specific functional areas, like sales and marketing, and then have representatives of that function from around the world collaborate in teams. This enables the organization to benefit from a diversity of perspectives and services that can match or fulfill the needs of a global client, wherever that client might be located.

No matter what the reason for the formation of a global team or what form the team takes, leaders and team members must address the complexity of global teamwork by architecting new ways of collaborating. This chapter is about how managers can create conditions in the pre-start and start-up phases of global teaming that will enhance the chances that a team will succeed.

DIMENSIONS OF COMPLEXITY

Whatever the type of global team an organization creates, the complexity the team faces in meeting its objective can be characterized along five different dimensions: task, context, people, time and technology.[1] This section of the chapter contains a discussion of these five dimensions and how they interact with one another to contribute to complexity in global teams. A series of suggested actions for designing global teams to help manage complexity follows the discussion.

Task

The primary tasks that global teams undertake can be grouped into a typology according to their complexity.[2] Task complexity is a continuum that comprises four major elements:

workflow interdependence, task environment, and external and internal coupling. The degree of workflow interdependence varies according to the structure of the activities that need to be performed to accomplish a task. Tasks are at the low end of interdependence when they can be performed separately by team members and then pooled into a finished product. Moving up the continuum of interdependence, work activities can become sequential and flow unidirectionally from one member to the next. When activities flow back and forth between members they take on a reciprocal character over time and become even more interdependent. At the high end of the continuum, when team members must make sense together of events or issues, problem-solve or collaborate together simultaneously to complete a task, workflow becomes intensely interdependent.

A team's task environment can also be placed on a continuum that varies from static to dynamic. A static environment is one that is predictable and stable and is one unlikely to disrupt team tasks or to require much monitoring. Many manufacturing settings have static environments. At the other end of the continuum, a team's task environment can be very dynamic and contain many uncertainties. R&D teams and new product development teams often face very dynamic environments. The environment has to be monitored constantly and new information must be brought into the team for interpretation and action on a continuing basis. A dynamic environment can greatly affect a team's ability to accomplish its task.

External coupling refers to how tightly a team is linked to or affected by what goes on in its task environment, varying on a continuum from loose coupling to tight. For example, firms can purposely shield teams in what are known as "think-tanks" or "skunkworks" so they can work on special R&D projects protected from the disruptions that might arise from fluctuations in day-to-day operational demands, organizational politics, and customer requirements. Or teams may be loosely coupled to their environments because they are working on routine functions, such as some accounting or financial reporting, that need to be performed on a regular basis regardless of what happens in the external organizational or marketplace environment. Teams working on new product introductions, new work ventures, or customer-driven initiatives could be characterized as tightly coupled with their external environments because they would be greatly affected by consumer and economic trends or changes in the organization, such as changes in personnel, internal politics or strategies.

Internal coupling describes the team members' relationships with one another, and can vary from weak to strong. Team members who are weakly coupled do not have to integrate with one another socially to accomplish their task. Many software development teams are weakly coupled, especially those working on open-source software. Individuals working separately complete the great majority of the team's tasks (as much as 80–90 percent) without exchanging information with other team members.[3] The organization of work allows for coordination through code repositories that are shared across boundaries and provide a common context even if individuals focus on separate aspects of the programming. On the other end of the continuum are teams whose members must make an effort to understand one another well, uncovering, negotiating, and integrating different perspectives to resolve a complex problem. A top management team responsible for creating a joint venture is an example of a strongly coupled team. Another example of a strongly coupled team is a new product development team in the auto industry that is working across national and organizational boundaries on a new vehicle platform design. The team members must work closely with each other to understand different perspectives and get to know local practices. They have to negotiate a common global architecture to achieve economies by sharing basic components of the vehicle, yet the common architecture must still allow for customization in local markets and distinct brand identities.

These four characteristics – workflow interdependence, task environment, external and internal coupling – together make up task complexity. Interestingly, teams who are at the low end of one continuum generally are also on the low end of the others. For example, teams that work on low-complexity tasks are generally working in a relatively static environment, are loosely coupled to that environment, and have members who are weakly coupled with one another and whose workflow is characterized by independent tasks that are pooled or done sequentially. An international team responsible for tracking and reporting sales in different regions in a standardized format could be called a team with a low-complexity task. As long as all the members of the team are working independently to gather data, and as long as each of them delivers their part of the report, their overall task requires little collaboration. On the other hand, in a team with high task complexity, like a new product development team in a high tech industry, the team is likely to be tightly coupled with an environment that is quite dynamic with innovations and new competitors entering the marketplace daily, affecting the nature and the pace of work. Workflow is likely to be highly interdependent, requiring greater levels of knowledge-sharing and real-time collaboration.

Task complexity puts demands on team structure and processes and therefore influences the leadership functions and membership interactions that will be critical for the team's effectiveness. As team tasks become more complex, the effective coordination of knowledge and carefully interrelated actions among team members become more important.[4] Complex work requires managers to pay careful attention to the selection of team members, to the organizational support systems within which the team will work, to the training and development and reward and recognition systems they put in place, and to the technical resources, particularly IT, they make available to the team so that these systems will encourage rather than work against collaboration.

Complex tasks mean information needs to be gathered, the task needs to be well defined and the scope of work has to be clearly outlined. Complex and uncertain tasks take much more interaction and collaboration than tasks that are more routine. This impacts the processes the team members will need to engage in, the efficiency with which they are able to work, and the outcomes that are likely. Successful interaction and outcomes are more likely when teams are able to achieve an equilibrium between too much complexity and uncertainty on the one hand and too much routine on the other.[5] If a task is too complex it can paralyze a team because members are unable to determine or agree on what actions to take. Or too much complexity can result in chaos when team members are doing so many different things in an attempt to get control of their work that they are no longer able to coordinate their activities. It is easy for team members to quickly experience information overload and shutdown when faced with more complexity than they can handle. In contrast, too much certainty and routine can cause team members to lose interest and motivation, making them complacent. Processes can become too rigid and team members may stop seeking out or paying attention to necessary information, slowing or halting progress on their task. They may even stop interacting altogether if they see no need for coordination.

Context

In addition to task characteristics, global teams are also complex based on context differences. Context is a way of life and work in a specific geographic area with its own set of business conditions, cultural assumptions, and unique history.[6] Some of the dimensions of context are climate, nationality, education, politics, judicial systems, economic systems, corporate governance, management systems, and incentive, motivation or reward schemes.[7] Context greatly influences how teams operate, and can quickly become problematic in global work that requires team members to work together, synchronously or asynchronously, across boundaries of many types.[8] The greater the number of contexts team members must cross to accomplish their tasks, and the greater the differences represented on the team, the more complex their work becomes. Crossing context increases complexity in many ways. Figure 11.1 offers a comparison on the dimension of context between traditional teams, that typically work within a single context, and global teams, that are likely to work across multiple contexts.

It is easily apparent how working across context adds dramatically to the complexity of work in global teams. When team members work in a single or common context, they share a taken-for-granted set of working conditions that form the backdrop for their work. They share common physical conditions, corporate work environments, and economic and political conditions; and a single national culture frames their work, for example, US, Chinese, and French. Even when team members themselves may come from diverse national cultures, their working conditions and general business situation are shared. It is also likely that team members share a common language. Tasks are generally contained within organizational and national boundaries, and team members have the opportunity for frequent, face-to face and informal interactions that allow them to share knowledge which requires an understanding of the context and to stay abreast of events as they occur. In this way, they can maintain alignment around the task and environmental challenges they face.

Complexity increases dramatically when team members primarily live – and thus work – in different contexts. Multiple work environments, national cultures, and economic and political conditions can affect team members differentially and have varying relevance and impact on the team's task. Team members are often constrained by distance, language differences, and restricted IT in their ability to communicate with one another frequently or informally. Because context is generally taken for granted, they may not even consciously consider the impact of context on their work and, therefore, are unlikely to share important or relevant information. Contextual knowledge is not easily transferred; thus cross-cultural competence and adaptability can be more important to the team's ability to achieve its task than professional expertise. A major challenge in global teamwork is making multiple contexts explicit and then co-creating a new "hybrid" context all team members can share.[9] This contextual complexity means that work in global teams is significantly more challenging than in traditional teams. Balancing multiple perspectives and demands in continuously fluctuating circumstances, and keeping the team members integrated and focused on a common objective are the real challenges.

Traditional teams work in a single context	Global teams work across multiple contexts
Characteristics 1 Common physical location and work environment	**Characteristics** 1 Multiple physical locations and work environments
2 Common national culture in a single geography	2 Multiple national cultures in multiple geographies
3 Common economic and political conditions	3 Multiple and dissimilar economic and political conditions
4 Native language speakers	4 Native and non-native language speakers
5 Professional expertise and communication skills	5 Cross-cultural competence and adaptability in addition to professional expertise, communication skills
6 Task is generally contained within organizational and national boundaries	6 Task generally involves crossing organizational and national boundaries
7 Opportunity for frequent, face-to-face and informal interactions and information sharing	7 Opportunities for informal interaction are infrequent and interaction is generally structured and mediated by technology
8 Work within a single time zone	8 Often work across multiple time zones

FIGURE 11.1 Summary of differences in context between traditional and global teams

These challenges are compounded when the team task is complex (highly interdependent, dynamic) which, as per the previous part of the book, is generally the case in global teams.[10]

People

A primary strategy for creating global teams is to involve a variety of expertise and perspectives that are likely required to accomplish the work and achieve objectives. This requirement means that the people who design and support, lead or work in global teams bring with them varying degrees of commitment, motivation, expectations, skills, and identities that come from their own (unique) work roles and their national, occupational, and organizational cultures. As a result, global teams are internally diverse on many dimensions, and these differences can add considerable complexity to the teaming situation in multiple ways.

People who work in global teams often do so on a part-time basis and have commitments not just to the global team, but also to other organizational roles or jobs, including primary functional assignments and even other teams. People are motivated to participate in the team to varying degrees depending upon their workload, the degree of organizational support they receive, the level of endorsement from others to whom they are linked organizationally, or their own personal interest in the work to be done. For example, motivation for members to participate can be based more on their professional influences, through their organizational network, than on any shared allegiance to the team.[11] It is often the case in virtual teams that members are required to perform numerous tasks and hold various roles to facilitate more flexible responses across different organizational contexts. These multiple demands can create role conflict and ambiguity and make decision-making responsibility unclear. This is similar to the effects found in matrixed organizations and further adds to the complexity in global teams, especially when people do not have the opportunity to interact frequently.[12] Therefore, motivating the team members means first recognizing the importance of their own unique network. Understanding the priorities and values of the members' networks can be key to achieving early commitment from the members, as well as support from the networks for the benefit of the team's overall objectives.

Likewise, individuals come to the global team with different skills and abilities related both to professional expertise and to interpersonal and cross-cultural communication competencies. People's experiences with international work, especially in global teams, can vary widely as well. In many cases, complexity is created due to the fact that members are selected simply because they are the only people with available time to work on the team when it is formed! Or members may be selected because they are in a particular formal job role within the organization, regardless of whether or not they have the skills necessary for the task, or for working with diverse people in uncertain situations. Status differences in the team may result from differential expertise or formal and informal organizational roles, which further exacerbates an already complex teaming situation.[13] As a result, authority and power may not be distributed clearly or rationally. People's language skill is another personal attribute that influences the team's ability to work together well and which can add considerably to the complexity the team has to manage. In addition to the obvious difficulties in understanding, there are also complications created by differences in speaking norms, for example in turn-taking, in the use of silence, or in when it is appropriate to speak up.

As discussed in previous chapters, belonging to different cultural groups has a significant impact on what people think is important in their work and how they interact with and relate to others in a work situation.[14] People's identities are formed in large part through the influence of membership in cultural groups both at work and outside of work, such as national culture, religious groups, occupational groups such as engineering, or organizational groups, such as the purchasing or sales and marketing departments. People carry these multiple identities with them when they come to the team. Culture exerts subtle influences that create expectations about leadership and status, about appropriate work practices, such as communication with superiors or subordinates or meeting participation, about the use of time and what constitutes a deadline, about quality, decision-making, and problem-solving.

Culture even has an impact on what it means to be a team.[15] Different cultures and organizations can have different models of teamwork, or "metaphors" that influence team members' behaviors, for example, a family, community, military or sport metaphor that coincides with national and organizational values. In countries like Mexico and Brazil which might have a family or community model of teamwork, a good team member is expected to help teammates and be very involved in their lives. The model is "all for one and one for all," and suggests that team members are nurturing, supportive, and depending on the urgency and importance of the task, may directly jump in and perform the task for a member in need. In countries like the United States and Australia, workers might conceive of a team using a sport metaphor, and good team members are expected to focus on their area of responsibilities (their own "position"). The motto of the team might be something like, "Let everyone take care of their own tasks and we will win against the competition." These differing expectations in what good teamwork looks like means that members are likely to disagree on the best way to structure work, set objectives, and reward and monitor performance. Without some negotiation and compromise, someone on the team will likely be unsatisfied and possibly unproductive, since their expectations are not being met.[16]

Thus, while there are clear benefits of increased diversity on teams for accomplishing complex work, there are drawbacks as well. Diversity among team members can make integration especially difficult, resulting in poorer rather than improved performance. However, as we will discuss later, if diversity is handled appropriately, the benefits can be realized.[17]

Time

A fourth component of global team complexity is time. Specifically, the amount of time a global team will be working together has an effect on team performance, so it is an important contingency in global team design.[18] Groups operating under tight time constraints have little room to adjust to the interaction styles of others or negotiate new norms for working. Further, when the pace of work is accelerated, often less attention is given to interpersonal relationships.[19] Global teams also experience time compression due to time-zone differences, and this restricts communication. Distance can very well equal delay in providing needed information or acting on decisions.[20] Because of these factors, global teams ironically may need more time than a traditional co-located team to accomplish the same task, although the likelihood is that they will have less time, given their role in the multinational firm.

The duration of global teams varies, and some have a very dynamic membership. A global team can have a very short life cycle of just a few days or weeks, such as a temporary task force team formed to solve a specific global customer problem. Or global teams can work on projects that take more than a year to complete, such as new product development teams. Some global teams are permanent, such as those within a specific function, but crossing numerous country subsidiaries of the same company. The life cycles of global teams are largely determined by the nature of tasks these teams perform.[21] Less complex tasks requiring less interdependence usually take less time to complete and can accommodate a more dynamic team membership. The more complex a task becomes, the more a stable membership and continuous life cycle becomes important to team functioning.

Global teams who have only a short time together (less than six months) in which to accomplish a complex task pose the greatest challenges to team design, because they are not likely to have the luxury of time to sort out differences and problems as they arise, nor can they take their time to develop processes or an infrastructure of resources to support their work. Therefore, it is especially important for these teams to pay careful attention to putting in place a structure that will minimize the complexity that they will have to manage.

Technology

Almost all workers in today's IT-rich environment and knowledge-based economy use communication technologies.[22] Thus, we cannot say that the distinguishing feature that differentiates traditional teams from global teams is the use of IT to communicate. Rather, it is the team's position on a continuum of virtuality, how much of the team's work is accomplished using virtual technologies, that distinguishes global teams.[23] A global team can be considered highly "virtual" (at the extreme end of the virtuality continuum) when members must rely on IT to communicate. That is, they have little or no choice, and are restrained (often by resources or design) from meeting face to face. Team members who are more distributed will have to rely more on communication technologies than on face-to-face interaction; however, not all global teams are highly virtual. Some meet face to face regularly, and most global teams use a mix of information technologies as well as face-to-face communication, depending upon the number of contexts that a team crosses and the time zones it spans. Many global teams are composed of members who interact according to the needs of the moment through a differing mix of media (e-mail, telephone, videoconferencing), with the amount of face-to-face contact determined by their own adaptations and the structures they create in their teaming processes.

A team's patterns of technology use result from the interplay between the structures and capabilities provided by the technology, the demands of the task, the characteristics of the people in the team, and the circumstances in the team's task environment or contexts.[24] As task complexity increases, communication and collaboration demands increase dramatically, and information richness (the depth and intricacy of the knowledge) becomes critical.[25] The team's life cycle can also have an effect on the appropriateness of the technology. Teams with short life cycles may rely only on simple technologies that are tried and true like the telephone or e-mail, simply because they do not have time to put into place or learn anything more complex.[26]

In addition, a team's technology needs may change as the team progresses through the life cycle. In R&D teams, for example, IT demands early in a project are for establishing informal networks and promoting creativity, while in the later phases the demands are more likely to be information exchange and coordination support.[27] Particularly early in a team's life, members' familiarity and skill levels with technology will constrain technology use, as will people's cultural preferences for communicating.[28] If a team crosses several contexts that are very different from one another, for example, teams which include members both from developed and developing countries, selecting the right technology can become especially complex, since infrastructure and access issues can restrict team members' ability to use technology. Status-related technology issues can also be created in crossing contexts. People who know how to use the technology can achieve dominance quickly. Status differences that arise from cultural membership or organizational role create complexity as well. In some cases status differences are not as noticeable when people are communicating through technology because culture is not as visible; however, studies indicate that status differences can persist in both face-to-face and electronic groups. Status labels and impressions based on them can have a larger impact on participation and influence than do communication media.[29]

Encouraging people to work together effectively in global teams involves more than simply connecting them via hard technologies. The telephone, fax, videoconferencing and other technologies are important means of facilitating communication from one team member to the next, but these electronic communication devices cannot (and are not intended to) deal with the social and behavioral issues that arise when individuals from multiple cultures are asked to work together. While some problems still exist with respect to hard technologies (especially with respect to videoconferencing), the major stumbling blocks that remain revolve around finding means of facilitating interpersonal interaction among team members.[30]

Media choices in global teams are complex and illustrate perfectly the dynamic interaction of the design dimensions discussed above: task, context, people, time, and technology. When it comes to technologies for information-sharing and collaboration, the old axiom "one size fits all" does not apply. Rather, a more apt expression might be "it depends." Good technology choices depend on uncovering the contextual and task issues a team is facing, and learning to avoid the technology pitfalls that can derail a global team.[31] However, effective teams do display some common characteristics in their use of communication technologies. They choose media and the content of their messages based upon the nature of the task and the characteristics and preferences of the group members. When the need for collaboration increases as tasks become more interdependent, global team members interact more frequently and need to use richer and more synchronous technology (audioconferencing) to accommodate the need for more complex messages. As the number of different contexts to be spanned (cultural, professional, organizational or country boundary) increases, effective global teams choose richer media, and generally begin their interactions together face to face. Successful global teams focus primarily on building relationships and on increasing trust to develop a shared view of their task and a hybrid culture to achieve that task. As team members become more comfortable with one another and with their work, however, they can often rely on less rich media to communicate (e-mail) because their shared frameworks and working norms help them make the correct interpretations of both messages and interpersonal relationships. At the same time, matching technology to task is a dynamic process. Time pressure and deadlines may necessitate rich technologies at some future juncture in the team's life.

Team Design Pre-Start

Given the dynamic complexity of the five key design considerations, structuring a team to manage complexity is the first and most important step to achieving successful teaming outcomes. Research has shown that managers should create a design that will keep the team "at the edge of order and chaos." Waves of disorder, catalysts to change, restructuring, and again disorder will likely unfold in global teams.[32] Managers should strive to help teams regain an equilibrium between an inflexible, rigid structure, and a disorderly, tumbling foundation. If task complexity is likely to be high, managers may need to do more to structure the task and determine workable expectations at the outset, before the team members are brought together for the first time. Some initial structure can reduce the anxiety and frustration that will arise if team members feel they are being asked to undertake a task that is unbounded, and perhaps impossible to achieve. Managers should be careful not to make the team too large in an effort to match the complexity of the task. It is tempting to assign too many different people, representing all possible organizations or groups. However, the more the people, the more the resources required – and all of this means much more coordination, increasing complexity. Adding too many people or resources can actually make things worse, not better. Managers should provide enough structure and diversity of membership to provide the team direction but also allow the members enough flexibility to develop an emerging structure that will address changing conditions and new information as they arise. Even if the overall strategy teams are asked to tackle is very complex, managers are advised to limit complexity of the team initially so that coordination will be manageable with the resources available. Start simply and increase complexity as the team develops. Managers should avoid "biting off more than they can chew" initially, allowing the team to seek progressively more complex activities as the team can handle them.[33]

So how can a manager structure a global team to manage complexity? There are four key design techniques that help create a supportive environment for global teams: (1) clearly specify the task objective and align it with organizational strategic initiatives; (2) make appropriate resources available; (3) select team members who have the skills, abilities, and experience to work in a global team, including the team leader, if appropriate; and (4) create a sense of urgency.[34]

Clearly specify the task objective and align it with organizational strategic initiatives

It is important to establish a clear task objective and to align it with organizational initiatives, whether those initiatives are tied to global efficiency, local responsiveness, organizational learning or knowledge creation. If team members do not know how their task fits with overall objectives as well as with their own priorities, it will be more difficult for them to commit, and hence to participate fully in the team's task. As emphasized earlier in this chapter, it takes time for team members to come to an understanding of their task, especially when the task is complex and diversity in the team is high. The more clearly and specifically managers can define the task, the greater the likelihood that teams with short life cycles and urgent deadlines meet with success. Organizational leaders who will have a stake in the outcome of the team's work should be identified early and should all participate in the task definition to achieve alignment across organizational boundaries. For example, in a cross-functional global team charged with process improvements, the key stakeholders may be each of the functional department heads who will be responsible for implementing the solutions generated by the team. One of the most difficult challenges for a global team to overcome is conflict among the various stakeholders about the team's objective. Prior to the start of a team, stakeholders and leaders should come together and agree on the team's objective, particularly if that objective will require the team to cross several boundaries to complete their work. It can be an insurmountable hurdle and a death knell for teams, as well as an unprofitable venture for the organizations involved, if the team's direction is not clearly supported and articulated before team members begin their work together, to the greatest extent possible based on the mandate of the team. Realistically, some objectives may be loosely structured by their very nature, but the point remains that even in these circumstances, the overall mission of the team should be clear. Stakeholders should also be actively involved in explaining the team's objective and its strategic intent to the team leader and members. Endorsement and involvement that is visible, especially if it comes from organizational leaders that team members know and respect, can create a strong message that the task is important, which can create quick buy-in among members and sustain the team during difficult times.

Some basic task boundaries and process guidelines can help teams begin their work with reduced complexity. Managers should provide the team with a basic outline for their scope of work and offer some teaming templates and recommended processes that team members can start with. Particularly if they are new to global teaming, team members need to begin their work with some minimal structure and then adapt it to their needs. Offering guidelines that can help team members understand where decision authority lies and what their reporting relationships are helps to avoid the confusion that ambiguous reporting relationships can create. These boundaries are important even if the team members will be working together on a part-time basis or only for a short while. In fact, more structure may be necessary when teams will be of short duration and with tight deadlines since the team does not have time to create this structure themselves. In sum, as a first step in pre-start-up, organizational leaders can manage task complexity by taking four key steps:

- provide the team with a well-defined, strategically aligned objective;
- actively endorse the team's objective;
- offer a minimal structure for the team's scope of work and some general process guidelines; and
- give the team basic guidance regarding organizational responsibility and decision-authority related to their objective.

Make resources available

Global teams are embedded not just in one, but in many contexts that may possess quite different systems of organizational support, including budgets, work processes, human resource policies and support people, such as facilitators and administrative support, and IT tools and facilities. Incompatible or insufficient resources are a major source of complexity and frustration for global team collaboration. To manage this complexity before a team is formed, the appropriate stakeholders or managers should conduct a resource assessment to determine the state of available resources, including the degree of overlap in the type and availability of resources across organizational and country boundaries. If there is a great deal of disparity or imbalance, with "rich" and "poor" resources in different contexts, managers may want to invest in resources before the team begins or reallocate resources that are available elsewhere. For example, perhaps facilitators or other support people for training and ongoing help are available in one context and could be shared with other contexts in which they are not readily available, prior to start-up. A substantial initial investment may be necessary, and companies will need to evaluate whether the objective is worthy of the expense in time, money and energy if resources are clearly a problem.[35] In a globalized world, however, if the firm wants to remain competitive, investment in global collaboration support systems will eventually be necessary. While it is not always possible to level the playing field entirely, managers should attempt to secure as many resources as possible in advance of the team's formation, or specify a clear path to accessible resources, so that team members do not have to spend valuable time searching for essential support people, information or technology, or worse yet, become so frustrated they are unable to execute their objective.

There is one caveat about resources: while IT is a critical resource for global teaming, the availability of technology resources is not sufficient for successful performance. Members must also be comfortable with the technology, and it should be reliable in each location where it is deployed. Simple technologies like e-mail and audioconferencing may suffice, and constitute the best technology choices for teams, especially when time is short. Team members do not have time to learn new technology if they are under pressure. At start-up, team members should be well acquainted with the technology and have enough "media dexterity" to use the technology effectively to avoid the technology downtime that can distract team members from their task. At the same time, technology use is a process of adaptation. Team members must be allowed to negotiate and come to a set of shared norms about how to communicate and which technology to rely on most heavily. In fact, the eventual performance of short-term teams working on high-stakes tasks is strongly influenced by members' ability to come to early agreement on communication processes. Ideally, they need to have a number of readily accessible communication channels that allow them to match their communication needs with the media available.[36] In summary, managers can control resource complexity, especially the complexity that can result from incompatible or imbalanced human resource and IT systems, if they keep these points in mind:

- ◆ conduct a resource and IT assessment prior to the start-up of the team;
- ◆ make an investment decision to acquire or reallocate support resources if necessary, or if resources are not available, postpone the team start-up if possible;
- ◆ specify for the team a path to available resources;
- ◆ it is management's job to make resources available to the team; however, the team should make the decision about the best match of resources and technology to match their needs as circumstances require and as team member skills, abilities, and preferences are negotiated.

Select team members who have the skills, abilities, and experience to work in a global team

Global team members need to be adept at working with task uncertainty, member diversity, and a variety of team situations.[37] Team members too often are selected based on professional expertise or job roles alone, or upon their availability to do the technical work. However, whenever possible, it is advisable to select team members who have already demonstrated the global competencies discussed in Part II. Research indicates that employees tend to be more comfortable and effective in a global teaming situation if they are capable of performing the core tasks for their roles, are self-disciplined and goal-directed, are flexible, collaborative, and willing to share and exchange information, and remain open to feedback.[38] Global team members should be perceptive and receptive to differences in people and culture, ways of thinking, and alternative approaches to processes. They need to be capable of handling the uncertainty. They should also be committed and connected to the business and competent in using the technology required for their roles. These skills, while desirable in many work settings in multinational corporations, are particularly crucial to the viability of global teamwork.[39]

There are selection tools, such as the *Global Personality Inventory* (GPI), which is a measurement tool specifically developed for work-related use by psychologists working in or with global organizations.[40] It was designed for applications such as pre-employment selection, developmental assessment, coaching, and succession management. Measures such as this one can help managers to select team members who can work well at the global level. The *Cross-Cultural Adaptability Inventory* (CPI) is a self-assessment tool that can help team members determine the likelihood that they will adjust well to a global teaming situation.[41] Team members can assess themselves on four dimensions that research has shown to be important in adapting to cross-cultural situations: flexibility–openness, emotional resilience, personal autonomy, and perceptual acuity. The instrument offers suggestions for what team members can do to increase their abilities on these dimensions as well.

It is particularly important to select people to be members of global teams who are capable intercultural communicators, because effective communication is especially critical for integrating diversity in global teams. Team members should be motivated to communicate with unalike individuals and be able to take on each other's perspectives so they can make correct interpretations of behavior, especially when they encounter difficulties.[42]

In selecting people for work in global teams it is important to remember that cultural biases, especially those derived from national culture, can have marked effects on team performance. There are taken-for-granted assumptions in every culture about the desirable qualities of the global manager and about how a good team member behaves, with some particularly strong contrasts between Eastern and Western cultures in the criteria for what constitutes an effective team member. Even the most sophisticated global executives are subject to biased assessments of these criteria. It is necessary to get more than just a monocultural perspective on the selection criteria and to use differences of opinion as a way of exposing implicit biases.[43]

When managers are designing a team for short-duration or temporary task work, it is especially important to select the right team members. Members who already know one another, who may have worked together well on previous projects and are comfortable with one another, are more likely to have some shared understanding of each other as people. A precondition for a fast start is enough of a shared reality among team members to enable effective communication without spending too much time surfacing differences and negotiating a shared resolution, especially when the differences have to do with how people relate to one another. There is also likely to be a foundation of trust and shared knowledge of each other's work habits if people have worked together previously. They do not have to spend time getting to know one another's working styles. Even if not all of the team members know each other, if a core group has had previous experience working together successfully, they can get off to a speedy start. If the team members do not know one another at all, it is possible for "swift trust" to develop and a "swift start" to occur if channels and norms for communication are pre-specified. For example, team members can draw upon shared occupational or functional rules or processes to help develop trust and norms.[44] Having a common language about process in product development has allowed automobile manufacturers to bridge many other differences as they partner across contexts. Among other things, they share values around the importance of process to quality events and outcomes.

A shared cohort culture can also help to develop swift trust. This was a key element in a short-term team (with a two-month life cycle) that the first author worked with. They had a complex project to do across several national boundaries. The fact that all the team members were high-potential managers who had been highly socialized in the same manner (although separately), allowed them all to come together and understand one another very quickly. Without this common frame of reference, it would have taken a lot longer for them to get started on their work. Finally, team members will have to spend less time planning their task if they already know who knows what, who is good at what, and who does what.[45] Being able to adapt quickly to one another, to changing circumstances, and to a quick exchange of ideas is a prerequisite for successful short-term teams, especially when the stakes are high and the task is complex.

To maximize their chances of successful teaming outcomes, organizational leaders and managers should remember these key points when they are selecting people to work in global teams:

- ◆ Select team members for professional expertise and roles related to the task, but also on their ability to handle task uncertainty, to integrate diverse perspectives and work practices, and to adapt to a variety of team situations.
- ◆ Engage the help of human resource professionals who can use selection tools that will provide some measure of an individual's global competencies and also allow team members to assess their own level of comfort with a global team assignment.
- ◆ Be especially mindful to select members who are effective communicators, particularly interculturally.
- ◆ If at all possible, select team members who know one another or who have worked together well on previous assignments, especially if the team will have a short deadline and a high-priority task.

Create a sense of urgency

Managers can maintain task focus and reduce complexity if they structure the team to convey a sense of urgency. There is nothing like a deadline to help focus minds. Research indicates that tight deadlines can get a group moving.[46] As with complexity and uncertainty, however, managers must be careful not to assign so much urgency that the members feel anxious about their ability to achieve.[47] Pressure from outside the team that has the potential to affect members' livelihoods, careers or rewards can be a motivating force if it is not extreme. A significant challenge with significant consequences, tied directly to everyone's interests, skills, abilities, and professions, has the capacity to concentrate team members' attention and to motivate them to work together. Pressure can push people to find solutions to differences and to come to an agreement for the sake of protecting their mutual self-interest. A sense of urgency can come from environmental factors in the marketplace or in the organization, such as new competitive pressures, new requirements from higher-level managers, poor business results, or pressure from a global customer everyone serves. Managers can convey a sense of urgency in the way they frame the goals for the team, by obtaining top-level endorsement for the goals, by bringing the voice of a credible customer into the task rationale, or by making a good business case for the goals, such as demonstrating a large investment that may be at risk. However, it is important that managers realize that it may take multiple sources of evidence to achieve a shared sense of urgency. This is due to the different understandings and perspectives about the task, different values or priorities, and different perspectives about time horizons that team members likely bring with them based on their cultural, professional, and organizational backgrounds. Understanding what is likely to appeal to team members' sense of urgency and then exerting positive pressure to engage in collaborative work are key to framing the goals to energize global teamwork.

In summary, managers can help team members align with their task objective by taking the following actions:

- frame the objective as important to the organization by selecting credible sources to endorse the objective;
- connect the team's objective to pressure from outside organizational boundaries, from competitors or customers in the marketplace;
- provide deadlines;
- connect the objective to people's careers or to rewards that will motivate participation.

Team Formation at Start-Up

At team formation the leader of a team plays a significant role in getting the team off to a positive start. Because leadership of a global team is highly related to a team's ultimate performance, team leaders are generally chosen by managers and other stakeholders who have a direct interest in the team's objective. New teams are merely a collection of individuals. The leader's functional role is to develop them into a well-integrated and high-performance work team. However, the ability of team leaders to perform key leadership functions in global teams is limited by the fact that team members are usually spread across space and time and therefore have fewer opportunities to meet face to face with the leader. This limitation means that leaders of global teams are more likely than leaders of traditional teams to create structures and routine processes that substitute for many of the usual leadership functions and to distribute a good deal of leadership to the team members themselves. Leaders are likely to create self-managing teams by providing direction and specific goals, monitoring environmental conditions, updating and revising goals and strategies as environmental contingencies require, and facilitating collaboration and cohesion among team members.[48] Habitual routines are necessary early on in the team's life cycle. They have to be established and reinforced by leaders at team formation. Leaders who set explicit objectives, create a clear mission, and develop an appropriate climate or tone can enhance team member self-regulation by creating a team context that forms the backdrop for the team's work.[49]

Establishing the right team context at start-up is critical to later team performance. The leader and team members together must build a context that includes internal norms, structures for coordination and collaboration, and a negotiated "hybrid culture" that bridges multiple cultural boundaries and allows team members to take advantage of their diversity for goal accomplishment.[50] Social processes are those that motivate team members to commit to a shared goal, that create a positive working climate, and that connect team members to each other and to the team's mission. Task processes include the development of individual goals that are linked with one another, strategies for executing tasks, and expectations for roles that are compatible across team members.

Global team members need to develop their own methods of working together in order to deal with the uncertainty and complexity inherent in their work. Since the rules for collaboration are not embedded in the operating procedures or shared cultural norms of a given organization, team members cannot take their collaboration for granted.[51] The processes that leaders and team members actively negotiate together will help them cut across multiple boundaries to develop a common focus and will provide the dynamic interdependencies that are the context for self-management as the team members move from start-up to ongoing collaboration.[52]

There is clear and strong evidence that to create conditions for effective global team performance, it is necessary for team members to spend time together face to face when the team is first formed.[53] It is particularly critical when the team's task is complex, diversity is high, team members have not worked together previously, and there is time pressure. Global teams may need to "slow down to speed up,"[54] spending more time in formation activities to ensure their continued development and their ability to withstand environmental changes that can disrupt the team and cause disintegration. Providing teams with an enriched environment at start-up can actually speed development.[55]

The stakeholders and team members will also need to decide whether to employ a skilled, cross-culturally competent facilitator to help them with their negotiation of taskwork and teamwork processes. At the first face-to-face meeting, facilitators can be helpful in structuring early discussions of the team's mission, roles, and responsibilities and in the development of norms for interaction, surfacing salient cultural differences and other contextual influences that the team will need to negotiate. They can support the teams in managing their organizational context by providing ongoing skill development through coaching of the team leader and members. Ideally, facilitators help team members learn skills for communicating and interacting effectively and can take on the facilitator's role themselves as they work together over time. In some cases, when there is conflict, flux or turbulence in the task environment, facilitators may need to remain part of the team to help the team stay aligned and make progress on their task objectives. Facilitators can also add considerable value to the team, especially when team members are inexperienced with global teaming or when there is time pressure and team members need to focus right away on the content of their taskwork. The team members may not know how to go about team integration or may not be able to pay sufficient attention themselves to teamwork processes.[56]

In many global teams it may be advisable to begin work with some form of organized training that is blended with work on defining the mission and team goals.[57] Conducting "immersion training," when team members come together face to face at formation, especially if team members have never worked together before, can expose team members together to formal instruction that is designed to build shared knowledge of the organization's vision for the team, of how the team fits with larger strategic objectives, and of expectations for how the team members are to work together. Training can provide explicit instructions about how team members are to conceptualize a problem and how to work together to accomplish an objective.[58] Initial training can also include skills training that can enhance collaboration, particularly cross-cultural communication, and culture-specific training to surface differences and similarities and to negotiate teaming processes.

Task processes

A team's performance and successful completion of its tasks is largely dependent on the team members' ability to make sense of the complexity they face and to come to a shared understanding early on about what their work entails and how they will accomplish it. Specifically, there are three key components of taskwork that the team leader and members need to put in place at the start of the team: (1) the vision for the team, the team's mission and objectives that will guide their interdependent taskwork; (2) team members' roles and responsibilities in relation to their objectives and their norms for interacting with one another as they work to complete tasks; and (3) the selection and adaptation of appropriate communication technology.

Establishing the team vision, mission, and objectives. Establishing a clear and inspiring shared purpose and accompanying goals and performance expectations that are consistent with the business strategy of the organizations in which the global team operates is critical.[59] This requires taking initiatives to ensure that all members are involved in creating or understanding the purpose and vision of the group or a specific project. That members have sufficient opportunity to voice their respective opinions and feel that the reasons for these differences are clearly understood is important. Leaders need to be skilled facilitators themselves or employ a skilled facilitator to help the team focus on a common goal that can unite team members and be inspiring enough for team members to move beyond differences and commit to achieving objectives.

Team members should be encouraged to talk explicitly about factors in their context that support the team's objectives or that can become barriers. For example, the availability of resources or the support of managers in different contexts can be a determining factor in team members' participation. It may be especially difficult to bring sensitive or difficult issues into open discussion when there are cultural norms that inhibit this type of open discussion. A leader or facilitator may be able to engage in one-on-one discussions with team members to uncover these issues. The leader or facilitator can reframe issues for later discussion by the group in an impersonal and non-threatening manner.

Above all, it is important for team members to feel collectively that they can carry out their tasks and that they have some chance of success in achieving their objectives. They are likely to perform better if the leader can set expectations for realizing a team's object-ives in the initial start-up phase.[60] Team members' early perceptions of likely success can bring about improvements in both short-term performance and in factors affecting long-term effectiveness and viability. People will be more willing to continue working as a team over a long period of time, to learn from each other and from the context of their work, and to work independently while they are within the team context, especially when they encounter obstacles, if they have a collective understanding of the team's objectives and feel they are achievable.[61] Team leaders can play a critical role in establishing buy-in and positive attitudes in the way they frame the team's task and bring about collective knowledge and understanding of what it will take to achieve it by engaging in the follow-ing actions:

- share information about the organization's strategy;
- clarify the rationale and intent of strategies and goals;
- provide clear expectations for team members' contributions to achieving objectives;
- ensure that team members are involved in decisions that affect their work;
- seek ideas and opinions from all members;
- focus on a subordinate goal that team members can share in common;
- if possible, use the organization's core values to guide the members' planning, decisions, and objectives;
- promote creativity and innovation in undertaking new goals or opportunities;
- help members develop positive approaches to the needs of the organization;
- challenge assumptions that may inhibit progress;
- demonstrate flexibility in adapting to changes in goals and expectations.

Determining roles/responsibilities/interaction norms. One of the factors that can contribute to smooth coordination early in the existence of the team is a clear definition of responsib-ilities. A lack of clarity may lead to confusion, frustration, and actually discourage people from participating, particularly if the work is only part of the team member's organiza-tional responsibilities. It is helpful for the leader or facilitator to know about team mem-bers ahead of time, about both their professional and interpersonal skills, to provide guidelines in negotiating roles and responsibilities. Team members should also have the opportunity to offer ideas about how they would like to contribute to achieving the team's objective. In many cases, it may be difficult for the team to sort out detailed roles and responsibilities at their first meeting because they are grappling with the complexities and uncertainties of their task, but if members can agree on short-term responsibilities, they can begin working and continue negotiating as they conduct further data gathering sensemaking.

If the team leader, perhaps with the help of a facilitator, can engage in a "contracting" discussion to establish norms for interaction, it will increase the predictability, and reduce the uncertainty, of the team's coordination across distance and time.[62] Contracting can help prevent the occurrence of haphazard or halfhearted participation, and can help teams resolve conflict when it occurs.[63] Team members should continue talking until there is mutual agreement. If time is short and there is pressure from deadlines, the leader or facilitator can help with ongoing discussion through individual meetings while the team members continue to work on tasks.

Global teams can jump-start their collaboration by understanding their roles and negotiating their responsibilities and expectations for interaction. Leaders and team members can establish clarity in the face of complexity and uncertainty by doing the following:

♦ link roles and team contributions to the organization's strategy and goals;
♦ ensure that all members know how their contributions affect the team objective;
♦ discuss how and with what frequency members expect to be in contact with one another;
♦ determine the acceptable hours for contacting each other and what length of time constitutes an acceptable response;
♦ determine priorities for responsibilities;
♦ be concrete and specific about expectations: "I'd like a weekly check-in" instead of "I'd like you to communicate";
♦ establish a process for getting in contact if a crisis arises.

Select and adapt appropriate communication technology. At start-up, it is important to collectively choose the appropriate communication media.[64] As mentioned earlier, different technologies are appropriate at different times as the team carries out its work. However, the technology choices at the start of the team and how they are chosen will impact the comfort team members have with mediated communication and how effective this communication will be. For example, using audioconferencing that permits synchronous (real-time) dialogue between team members is important for developing trust early on. Audioconferencing can establish a baseline safety zone that can get technology use off to the right start. On the other hand, using computer conferencing at the start of a team project may be a poor choice because language differences and inexperience can restrict the free flow of information necessary to the formation of relationships. Because conversations may be recorded in computer conferencing, team members may be more guarded in what they say, especially if trust is not yet established.[65]

"Leveling the electronic playing field" at start-up is important to fostering a baseline of trust within a global team that will be working virtually. It is necessary to ensure that less knowledgeable team members are not disadvantaged in an environment that has already been stripped of traditional visual cues. Where there is a large gap among team members' knowledge and familiarity with a technology or their access to technology, training for members who are unfamiliar with a particular technology is necessary, or selecting a technology that all can use comfortably is recommended.[66]

These are some key issues and questions for consideration in selecting the appropriate communication technologies for the team:

♦ *Availability* – to what extent are the various technological options readily available to everyone involved in a geographically dispersed work group? Which technologies can be used regularly without putting anyone at a disadvantage?
♦ *User skills* – how skilled are the team members and how comfortable are they with the different technological options?
♦ *Culture* – what are the cultural requirements or preferences?
♦ *Sense of community* – how well do people who are communicating know one another, and is there enough of a sense of shared understanding to keep misinterpretation of messages at a minimum?

◆ *Importance of the message* – the more important the message, the richer should be the communication medium.

◆ *Virtual context* – are there ways to create a shared virtual context that can enhance participation and help develop shared mental models, such as multiple media, ways to communicate formally and informally, and virtual facilitation?

◆ *Regular pattern* – have team members agreed on a regular pattern of virtual messaging, when to expect them, and in what form?

◆ *Language* – if one language is used as the team language, are the native speakers considerate in their speech and transmission of written materials to non-native speakers?

◆ *Time* – do team members know and respect the most convenient times to send and receive messages across time zones? Are there ways to share private contact numbers that will improve communication while respecting people's personal lives?

◆ *User choice* – have team members been given the opportunity to say how they would prefer to communicate in a given transaction?[67]

Social processes

First impressions are critical in global teamwork because there is little opportunity for informal personal interaction when most of the communication is restricted and mediated by technology.[68] Initial messages need to be handled well. Face-to-face initial interactions are important for this reason alone. They set the stage for the development of trust in ongoing interactions and help establish the shared understanding and a shared team identity that will sustain team members when they can be pulled in different directions by demands in their local work contexts. When a team is formed and first comes together at start-up, leaders need to pay particular attention to accomplishing three things that can significantly affect teamwork, either positively or negatively, through their initial interactions together: (1) create a safe environment; (2) develop shared "mental models"; and (3) create a sense of community.

Creating a safe environment. In teams that develop high levels of trust, there is usually a willingness to express ideas openly and there are explicit verbal statements about commitment, support, and willingness to do the work. If this kind of expression can be achieved, it increases the attraction to the group and the tendency for agreement and cooperation.[69] However, for expressions of ideas and commitment to occur, a safe environment must be created first, whether that environment occurs in a face-to-face setting or in a virtual environment. While people are first getting to know one another, ideas are being tested, and options are being discussed, team members may be reluctant to share work in progress, especially if it is in an "electronic place" that is open to all members of the team. To do so means that they expose themselves by testing ideas or admitting a lack of knowledge in public.[70]

Team members may also have different ideas about when it is appropriate to share information. Some cultures, such as the French, place a great deal of emphasis on thinking through ideas thoroughly and writing well, making it unlikely that French team members would feel comfortable sharing an idea that is less than completely formulated. There is always a risk in sharing ideas or work in teams; nevertheless, the team environment requires that members feel a certain level of security and safety for them to express ideas and offer to share their knowledge or their work with others.

In global teams, creating a safe environment may take more time and multiple approaches. If possible, the team leader should try to understand what criteria the team members believe distinguish between "safe" work and "risky" work by talking with them individually. This requires getting to know something of the team members' cultural values and practices regarding work. However, this may not be possible in many global team situations. In most cases, safe work involves more objective tasks such as helping to establish the project goals and management process – schedules, for example. Initially, risky work might be the presentation of a new approach or idea, or engaging in a creative problem-solving task, or anything for which the team member will be held personally accountable, requiring that the team member trust that the others will receive the work positively. It is also risky to present ideas in a public team forum before team members have enough knowledge of one another to correctly interpret the responses of others. There may be too much uncertainty for some team members to feel comfortable enough to share ideas fully.

Creating a safe environment for the expression of new ideas and commitment to following through on task work means doing the following:

- Start out with "safe" work, and then move to "risky" work, especially if people have not yet had the opportunity to interact face to face and get to know one another.
- Allow team members to work in smaller groups initially, with people of their own choosing with whom they feel most comfortable, to flush out ideas.
- Create and take every opportunity to socialize face to face in initial interactions. Socializing increases shared experiences, which more fully integrates the people into the team and helps them to better interpret each other's behaviors when they are apart.
- If team members cannot meet face to face initially, the team leader should engage in inclusive social messages at the start of the team's virtual interaction. Social communication that complements task communication may help strengthen team bonds and significantly increase the likelihood that people will develop a level of trust that will support the exchange of ideas.[71]

Developing shared "mental models." In many global organizations, teams that cross boundaries do so in order to create knowledge that will provide solutions to pressing business problems or that will foster development of new products and services. Research indicates that the development of shared team "mental models" or shared frameworks, a kind of "collective mind," is a critical step in facilitating the team learning that allows team members to come together to contribute their diverse knowledge and expertise to solve problems. Mental models of the external task environment, of the organization and organizational strategy, and of the definition of the team's situation are necessary for effective team functioning. So are models of team knowledge, and the skills and abilities of teammates. Team members need knowledge about work, about the group, and about group members to develop organized knowledge and shared expectations.[72]

If team members are unaware of similarities or if they do not know what their colleagues "know," they will not be able to develop a team mental model. Just having every member independently recognize a problem is not sufficient for problem identification at team level. Team members need to do a lot of communicating with one another in the early stage of teaming to share knowledge about their task, their contexts, and themselves. This shared knowledge then becomes the basis for developing shared team mental models that will contribute to successful performance. These team models become a point of reference for sensemaking and for incorporating new information into the team's processes, enabling team members to work more efficiently and effectively together in later stages of their work without the need to communicate with one another quite as much or as often.[73]

One of the most important tasks a team leader or facilitator can perform at team formation is directing group interaction to surface what people know, who they know, what their differences and similarities are in perspectives and practices, and what their shared understanding of their situation is. Teamwork is likely to proceed in a well-coordinated manner if group members' definitions of the situation are alike. Similarly, shared situation models ensure that all participants are solving the same problem and help exploit the capabilities of the entire team. Common expectations of the task and the team allow team members to predict the behavior and resources needs of team members more accurately.[74] Shared mental models are assumed to enhance the quality of teamwork skills and team effectiveness. Common expectations of the task and team allow members to predict each other's behavior and resource needs more accurately.[75]

It is easier to develop team mental models if the people who are selected to be members of the team are similar in their orientation toward work and working, based around shared values and work habits. However, in most global teams such member recruiting and selection that will ensure shared perspectives is not possible. It may not even be desirable, if taking advantage of diverse perspectives is one of the reasons the team is being formed. Stakeholders and team leaders can draw on strong corporate cultures in global companies, or strong occupational cultures when possible, to facilitate the development of a common work orientation. Yet it is most likely that team members need to come together face to face in the early formation stage, particularly if they have no history of working together, if they are to have an opportunity to create for themselves shared team models. This takes time. Time that would ordinarily be spent on task will have to be diverted and used to allow team members to surface their mutual perceptions, assumptions, options, and preferences. If teams do not take the necessary time for initial face-to-face interactions in "real time" to surface and discuss perceptions, assumptions, options and preferences, there is an increased likelihood that false starts will occur and that added costs will occur, quality will suffer, and valuable time will be lost. Team members with critical information may not be heard. Inferior or inefficient strategies for work accomplishment may be adopted. The chances are great that conflict will arise later in the team's work and interpersonal relationships might be damaged, and the team's collective effort will be lower as a result.[76]

The team leader can provide guidance, and the facilitator, with the help of other human resource professionals, can provide training that will help shape expectations through direct instruction or through the modeling of behavior. The leader's central function in helping the team develop shared mental models is to engage team members in information-gathering activities and then to help the team integrate and interpret, negotiating their disagreements. The team needs to focus on articulating explicitly what is generally taken for granted and implicit within the members' individual work contexts. Developing shared team mental models will facilitate the creation of a team context for their interdependent work and ongoing team processes. With the support of stakeholders and a facilitator or other trainers, the leader can engage in the following activities to foster the development in team mental models at team formation:

- ◆ Create public rituals for the team, such as a ceremony to inaugurate the formation of the team, or formal announcements or training events at which all are present, even if they are not face to face. Team training at start-up, when everyone is present and knows who else is there, can accomplish more than just the transmission of important information or knowledge. These activities let team members know what other team members know. They help solve coordination problems in which taking action requires knowing that other people know what you know and that you know that they know that you know.[77]
- ◆ Use storytelling to allow team members the opportunity to share knowledge that may be implicit, complex or embedded in context and therefore difficult to communicate, especially when language difficulties may be present.
- ◆ Use metaphors that all team members will understand to help create team mental models that will guide action. For example, a metaphor that involves food or food preparation and consumption is one whose meaning can be unifying across contextual boundaries and can help team members talk about planning (creating recipes), gathering information or resources (shopping for ingredients), executing tasks (cooking), and delivering results (putting the meal on the table). Metaphors can help uncover similarities and differences in assumptions, knowledge, and habitual practices in a non-threatening way and can facilitate the development of a shared framework. Metaphors, because they contain both symbolic and emotional content, allow for social sharing at the same time they allow for the sharing of knowledge, creating the opportunity for informal bonds among team members to develop.[78]

Creating a sense of community. A key to effective global teams is developing a sense of community that demonstrates sensitivity to differences, establishing ground rules and project team etiquette or agreement among the members for how the team will work together. Recruitment and selection of team members, defining the vision, mission, and objectives, developing group working agreements, and a project management process are all positive steps that will aid the development of a sense of community in the team. However, in the unstable global environment, leaders especially have to work actively to establish and maintain a collective team identity because traditional identity-forming boundaries are no longer useful and may not even be present.[79]

Again, face-to-face communication at the start of a diverse global team which is undertaking a complex task is essential to begin establishing mutual trust between members at the beginning of their work relationship.[80] It is a particularly important choice when the task is sensitive; when there is anxiety in the team, when performance is in question, or when confusion or dissatisfaction exist. In all cases when there is high emotional content, face-to-face communication, when properly positioned and managed, can build community and connections to the business, and is especially essential at team formation.[81]

Team leadership can play a significant role in influencing commonality of values.[82] The leader, and ideally one who has a facilitator to help, can model the desired behavior for the team, use language that will frame the task in common terms, subtly interrupt patterns of dysfunctional behavior, and redirect actions that will orient the team's values. The leader can reinterpret task activities, issues, and problems to highlight desirable team values while respecting and preserving the integrity of diverse perspectives and knowledge.

Engaging diverse people as team members requires the leader to understand that not all kinds of team member diversity influence team processes in the same manner and that members come into the teaming situation with inequalities in experience, access to resources, and ability to influence others. Demographic diversity (differences in age, gender, race, professional background, and education) can produce preconceptions in team members that can affect interpersonal relationships. Diversity that is job-related, such as functional differences and status differences in the organization, can affect the levels of positive functional debate (task-related conflict) in the group.[83] Certain types of values have a stronger relationship with particular team processes. Focusing on the development of potentially shared work values may lessen the tendency of group members to make undesirable comparisons on the basis of demographic differences. In actual team settings, similarity in work values may supplant the impact of demographic diversity in producing effective and satisfying relationships and a sense of community in the team. Here are some ways a leader can work to build community in the team:

♦ Surface cultural, social, and functional differences by using a value checklist in the initial start-up phase of teamwork to consciously establish which differences, such as diverse knowledge, experience, creativity, and skills, are relevant to the team's objective.[84]

♦ Allow team members to negotiate and agree upon their own structures for working so that team members will own these structures together as a group. If team members feel their viewpoints and preferences are considered equally, and they have had the opportunity to be part of the decision, rather than have structures imposed from outside the team, they will be more likely to engage constructively in team processes.

♦ Work with the team to develop a symbol, a kind of team logo, that can signify the work values the team will hold in common. The process of creating this symbol together can in itself create a feeling of community.

Conclusion

This chapter has reviewed the key dimensions of complexity – task, context, people, time, and technology – that interact to produce challenges for global teams beyond those in traditional teams. These factors must be considered and managed in designing and forming global teams to perform successfully. Stakeholders, team leaders, and team members can actively participate in creating conditions prior to the start-up of a team that can provide and enhance the likelihood that the team will achieve its objective. They can also structure task and social processes when team members first come together that will establish a positive foundation for their ongoing work together. The next chapter will discuss ongoing task and social processes and what leaders and team members can do to sustain their development and reach their goals.

Notes

1 Cohen, S. G., & Bailey, D. E. (1997), What makes teams work: Group effectiveness research from the shop floor to the executive suite, *Journal of Management*, 23, 239–290. These authors, among many others, have identified that team effectiveness is a function of factors related to task, group, and organizational design factors, environmental factors, internal processes, external processes, and group psychosocial traits.

2 Bell, B. S., & Kozlowski, S. W. J. (2002), A typology of virtual teams: Implications for effective leadership, *Group & Organization Management*, 27(1), 14–49.

3 Yamauchi, Y., Yokozawa, M., Shinohara, T., & Ishida, T. (2002), *Collaboration with Lean Media: How Open-Source Software Succeeds*, Department of Social Informatics, Graduate School of Informatics, Kyoto University.

4 Weick, K. E., & Roberts, K. H. (1993), Collective mind in organizations: Heedful interrelating on flight decks, *Administrative Science Quarterly*, 38(3), 357–381.

5 Earley, P. C., & Gibson, C. B. (2002), *Multinational Work Teams*, Mahwah, NJ: Lawrence Erlbaum.

6 Gluesing, J., Alcordo, T., Baba, M., Britt, D., Harris Wagner, K., McKether, W., Monplaisir, L., Ratner, H., & Riopelle, K. (2002), The development of global virtual teams, in C. Gibson and S. G. Cohen (eds.), *Virtual Teams That Work: Creating Conditions for Virtual Team Effectiveness*, San Francisco, CA: Jossey-Bass, pp. 353–380.

7 Doz, Y., & Santos, J. (1997), On the management of knowledge: From the transparency of collocation and co-setting to the quandary of dispersion and differentiation, unpublished paper.

8 Mohrman, S. A. (1999), The contexts for geographically dispersed teams and networks, in C. L. Cooper and D. M. Rousseau (eds.), *Trends in Organizational Behavior, Volume 6, The Virtual Organization*, New York: John Wiley, pp. 63–80

9 Gluesing et al. (2002).

10 Earley & Gibson (2002).

11 McDonough, E. F. III, & Cedrone, D. (2000), Meeting the challenge of global team management, *Research Technology*, 43(4), 12–17.

12 Bell & Kozlowski (2002).

13 Gluesing, J. G. (1995), Fragile alliances: Negotiating global teaming in a turbulent environment, doctoral dissertation.

14 Hambrick, D. C., Canney Davison, S., Snell, S. A., & Snow, C. C. (1998), When groups consist of multiple nationalities: Towards a new understanding of the implications, *Organization Studies*, 19(2): 181–205.

15 Gibson, C. B., & Zellmer-Bruhn, M. E. (2001), Metaphors and meaning: An intercultural analysis of the concept of teamwork, *Administrative Science Quarterly*, 46(2), 274–303.

16 Laroche, L., & Bing, C. M. (2001), Technology, protocol keep global teams going without face-to-face meetings, *Canadian HR Reporter*, 14(18), 17–19.

17 Maznevski, M. L. (1994), Understanding our differences: Performance in decision-making groups with diverse members, *Human Relations*, 47(5), 531–532.

18 McCollom, M. (1990), Reevaluating group development: A critique of the familiar models, in J. Gillette & M. McCollom (eds.), *Groups in Context: A New Perspective on Group Dynamics*, Reading, MA: Addison-Wesley, pp. 35–48.

19 McGrath, J. E. (1991), Time, interaction, and performance (TIP): A theory of groups, *Small Group Research*, 22(2), 147–174.

20 Fineholt, T. A. (2000), Global software development, productivity and trust in virtual teams at Lucent Technologies, paper presented at Effective Virtual Teams Conference, Collaboratory for Research on Electronic Work, School of Information, University of Michigan, October.

21 Bell & Kozlowski (2002), pp. 32–33.

22 Griffith, T., & Neale, M. A. (2001), Information processing in traditional, hybrid, and virtual teams: From nascent knowledge to transactive memory. In R. Sutton and B. Staw (eds.), *Research in Organizational Behavior*, Vol. 23. Stamford, CT: JAI Press, pp. 379–421.

23 Cohen, S. G., & Gibson, C. B. (2002), Virtual teams: A framework and introduction, in C. Gibson and S. G. Cohen (eds.), *Virtual Teams that Work: Creating Conditions for Virtual Team Effectiveness*, San Francisco: Jossey-Bass, pp. 1–19.

24 DeSanctis, G., & Poole, M. S. (1994), The hidden complexity in advanced technology use: Adaptive structuration theory, *Organization Science*, 14, 157–176.

25 Hollingshead, A. B., McGrath, J. E., & O'Connor, K. M. (1993), Group task performance and communication technology: A longitudinal study of computer-mediated versus face-to-face work groups, *Small Group Research*, 24, 307–333.

26 Gluesing et al. (2002).

27 Earley, C. P., & Mosakowski, E. (2000), Creating hybrid team cultures: An empirical test of transnational team functioning, *Academy of Management Journal*, 43(1), 26–49.

28 Nunamaker, J. F., Jr., Briggs, R. O., Mittleman, D. D., & Vogel, D. R. (1997) Center for the Management of Information, MIS Department, Karl Eller Graduate School of Management, University of Arizona and Balthazard, P. A. (1997), *Lessons from a Dozen Years of Group Support Systems Research: A discussion of lab and field findings*, University of North Carolina, *Journal of Management Information Systems*, 13(3), 163–207.

29 Weisband, S. P., Schneider, S. K., & Connolly, T. (1995), Computer-mediated communication and social information: Status salience and status differences, *Academy of Management Journal*, 38(4), 1124–1151.

30 McDonough, E. F., & Kahn, K. B. (1997), Using "hard" and "soft" technologies for global new product development, *IEEE Engineering Management Review*, Fall, 66–75.

31 Riopelle, K., Gluesing, J., Alcordo, T., Baba, M., Britt, D., McKether, W., Monplaisir, L., Ratner, H., & Wagner, K. (2002), Context, task, and the evolution of technology use in global virtual teams, in C. B. Gibson & S. G. Cohen (eds.), *Virtual Teams that Work: Creating Conditions for Effective Virtual Teams*, San Francisco: Jossey-Bass.

32 Waldrop, M. M. (1992), *Complexity: The Emerging Science at the Edge of Order and Chaos*, New York: Touchstone.

33 Gluesing et al. (2002).

34 Canney Davison, S., & Ward, K. (1999), *Leading International Teams*, Maidenhead: McGraw-Hill International. See also Gluesing et al. (2002).

35 Levenson, A., & Cohen, S. G. (2002), Return on investment in virtual teams, in C. B. Gibson & S. G. Cohen (eds.), *Virtual Teams that Work: Creating Conditions for Effective Virtual Teams*, San Francisco: Jossey-Bass, pp. 145–174.

36 McKinney, E. H., Jr., Barker, J. R., Davis, K. J., & Smith, D. (2000), Getting swift starting teams off the ground. What airline flight crews can tell us. Working paper.

37 Townsend, A. M., DeMarie, S. M., & Hendrickson, A. R. (1998), Virtual teams: Technology and the workplace of the future, *Academy of Management Executive*, 12, 17–29.

38 Thompson, J. A. (2000), Effective leadership of virtual project teams, *Futurics*, 24(3/4), Sciences Module, 85–90.

39 Jarvenpaa, S. L., & Leidner, D. E. (1998), Communication and trust in global virtual teams, *Journal of Computer-Mediated Communication*, (3)4, 791–815, http://www.ascusc.org/jcmc/vol3/issue4/jarvenpaa.html

40 Hazucha, J. F., Schmit, M. J., & Tillman, P. T. E. (2002), Variations in personality at work across cultures, paper presented at the 17th Annual Conference of the Society for Industrial-Organizational Psychology, Toronto, Ontario.

41 Kelley, C., & Meyers, J. (1992), *Cross-Cultural Adaptability Inventory*, Minnetonka, MN: NCS Assessments.

42 Maznevski, M. L. (1994), Understanding our differences: Performance in decision-making groups with diverse members, *Human Relations*, 47(5): 531–532.

43 Franke, J., & Nicholson, N. (2002), Who shall we send? Cultural and other influences on the rating of selection criteria for expatriate assignments, *International Journal of Cross Cultural Management*, 2(1): 21–36.

44 Dose, J. L. (1999), The diversity of diversity: Work values effects on formative team processes, *Human Resource Management Review*, 9(1), 83–109.

45 Rulke, D. L., & Rau, D. (2000), Investigating the encoding process of transactive memory in group development, *Group & Organization Management*, 25(4): 374–396.

46 Gersick, C. J. G. (1989), Marking time: Predictable transitions in task groups, *Academy of Management Journal*, 32(2): 274–309.

47 Baba, M., Gluesing, J. C, Ratner, H., & Wagner, K. (2002), The ecology of development in globally distributed teams, *Journal of Organizational Behavior*, in press.

48 Bell & Kozlowski (2002).

49 Gersick, C. J. G., & Hackman, J. R. (1990), Habitual routines in task-performing groups, *Organizational Behavior and Human Decision Processes*, 47, 65–97.

50 Mohrman, S. A. (1999), The contexts for geographically dispersed teams and networks, in C. L. Cooper & D. M. Rousseau (eds.), The virtual organization, *Journal of Organizational Behavior*, 20, special supplement to *Trends in Organizational Behavior*, 6, 63–80.

51 Mohrman (1999).

52 Kozlowski, S. W. J., Gully, S. M., McHugh, P. P., Salas, E., & Cannon-Bowers, J. A. (1996), A dynamic theory of leadership and team effectiveness: Developmental and task contingent leader roles, in G. R. Ferris (ed.), *Research in Personnel and Human Resource Management*, 14, 253–305.

53 Maznevski, M. L., & Chudoba, K. M. (2000), Bridging space over time: Global virtual-team dynamics and effectiveness, *Organization Science*, 11: 473–492. See also Gluesing et al. (2002).

54 Canney Davison & Ward (1999).

55 Gluesing et al. (2002).

56 Canney Davison & Ward (1999).

57 Gluesing et al. (2002).

58 Kozlowski, S. W. J., Gully, S. M., Nason, E. R., & Smith, E. M. (1999), Developing adaptive teams: A theory of compilation and performance across levels and time, in D. R. Ilgen & E. D. Pulakos (eds.), *The Changing Nature of Work and Performance: Implications for Staffing, Personnel Actions, and Development* (SIOP Frontier Series), San Francisco: Jossey-Bass, pp. 240–292.

59 Thompson (2000).

60 Gibson, C. B. (1999), Do they do what they believe they can? Group-efficacy beliefs and group performance across tasks and cultures, *Academy of Management Journal*, 42(2), 138–152.

61 Pescosolido, A. T. (2001), The effects of group efficacy: Group efficacy and overall group effectiveness, paper presented at the Academy of Management Annual Meeting, Washington, DC.

62 Platt, L. (1999), Virtual teaming: Where is everyone?, *Journal for Quality and Participation*, 22(5), 41–43.

63 Gibson, C. B. (1994), Team mental model: construct or metaphor?, *Journal of Management*, 20(2), 403–437.

64 Maznevski, M. L., & Chudoba, K. M. (2000), Bridging space over time: Global virtual-team dynamics and effectiveness, *Organization Science*, 11: 473–492.

65 McDonough & Cedrone (2000).

66 *Ibid.*

67 Gundling, E. (1999), How to communicate globally, *Training and Development*, 53(6), 28–31.

68 Coutu, D. (1998), Trust in virtual teams, *Harvard Business Review*, May–June, 20–21.

69 Fulk, J. (1993), Social construction of communication technology, *Academy of Management Journal*, 36(5), 1993, 921–950.

70 McDonough & Cedrone (2000).

71 Cascio, W. F. (2000), Managing a virtual workplace, *Academy of Management Executive*, 14(3), 81–90.

72 Weick, K. E., & Roberts, K. H. (1993), Collective mind in organizations: Heedful interrelating on flight decks, *Administrative Science Quarterly*, 38(3), 357–381.

73 Yoo, Y. (2001), Developments of transactive memory systems and collective mind in virtual teams, *International Journal of Organizational Analysis*, 9(2): 187–208.

74 Cannon-Bowers, J. A., Salas, E., & Converse, S. A. (1993), Shared mental models in expert team decision-making. In N. J. Castellan (ed.), *Individual and Group Decision Making*, Hillsdale, NJ: Lawrence Erlbaum, pp. 221–246.

75 Klimoski, R., & Mohammed, S. (1994) Team mental model: Construct or metaphor?, *Journal of Management*, 20(2), 403–437.

76 *Ibid.*

77 Chwe, M. S-Y. (2001), *Rational Ritual*, Princeton, NJ: Princeton University Press.

78 Gibson & Zellmer-Bruhn (2001).

79 Den Hartog, D. N. (2001), *Leadership as a Source of Inspiration*, Inaugural Addresses Research in Management Series, Rotterdam: Erasmus Research Institute of Management.

80 Thompson (2000).

81 *Ibid.*

82 Dose, J. L. (1999), The diversity of diversity: Work values effects on formative team processes, *Human Resource Management Review*, 9(1), 83–109.

83 Pelled, L. H. (1996), Demographic diversity, conflict and work group outcomes: An intervening process theory, *Organization Science*, 7(6), 615–631.

84 Canney Davison & Ward (1999).

12

Effective Team Processes for Global Teams

SUE CANNEY DAVISON AND BJØRN Z. EKELUND

The previous chapter outlined how to design and create effective start-up processes for global teams. We now examine team processes with special attention to how the complexities of these global teams play out as the team's work evolves. This chapter begins with an introductory section that focuses on three fundamental aspects of teams we use to describe internal team dynamics (for best practices in boundary spanning and managing external boundaries, see Part II: Global Competencies). Our focus then moves to the two aspects of team processes whose understanding is especially important for global team members and leaders: process building blocks and process flows, as outlined in figure 12.1. It is well appreciated that in reality, many teams work under conditions of extreme urgency and expediency. Under those conditions a team needs to focus particularly on the processes that build trust and create fast feedback loops that quickly resolve conflicts and create decision-making processes that suit the context. Based on a fuller exploration of all the important processes shown in figure 12.1, this chapter provides recommendations for global team leaders and concludes with a summary of the key success factors for global teams.

Different types of team processes	Building blocks	Team process flows
Task processes	Building trust	Differentiating and integrating
Social processes	Differentiating	
Emergent states	Integrating	Face-to-face and virtual
Coordinating mechanisms	Managing conflict	Phases and transitions
	Creating and sharing knowledge	

FIGURE 12.1 Process building blocks and process flows

BASIC ELEMENTS OF TEAM DYNAMICS

We begin with a look at three fundamental aspects of teams: their task and social processes, their emergent states, and their team coordinating mechanisms.

Task and social processes

Healthy team processes usually involve multiple modes of exchange and high levels of internal and external responsiveness. This means maintaining fast feedback loops where the energy remains positive and aligned with the team's task despite changes, arguments, and difficulties. Team processes describe *how* the team interacts. They are the interdependent acts that convert inputs to outcomes.[1] *Task processes* are those intellectual and physical processes that directly assist the team to achieve its tasks, and *social processes* are those that govern the pattern of interaction among the team members and between the team and the organization. These two types of processes are closely linked and in fact usually happen simultaneously. Task processes influence performance directly and quickly, while social processes influence outcomes indirectly, through their influence on task processes and, in the long term, through their influence on the team's ability to work together. The task processes may lead to completion of the task and the social processes to a sense of community, to team members seeing themselves as integral parts of a whole team consciousness. If an organization is to capture all the learning from a team, the organization needs to be able to identify and measure the quality of both the task work and the social processes. It may be the case that there is valuable learning in the social processes even when the task itself is not successful. For example, clinical trials may reveal serious side effects to a certain drug. The drug is shelved, but the team responsible for its development may have much to teach other teams about effective international coordination and cross-cultural interaction.

Team members and leaders must work hard at creating effective social and interactive processes that will support, fuel and, to some extent, craft, the deep and complex intellectual activities needed to build new knowledge, find news ways of doing things, and so achieve the task. The way a task is coordinated will affect the quality of the team members' relationships.[2] For instance, if the task is organized such that most team members relate mainly with the team leader, who coordinates and decides based on individual input, there is little need for the team members to interact in any significant way.

Emergent states

Team members collectively create a broad mental environment for their interaction. Internal predispositions and assumptions set the stage for the dynamics. We refer to these as *emergent states*: they are conditions that shift and evolve as the team works together. The three most important emergent states are mutual trust, collective team identity,[3] and confidence in the team's ability to achieve its tasks. Each of these states is a collection of the attitudes held by the team members about the team itself. Emergent states influence and are influenced by the team interaction in a synergistic way.

When the team starts, each member will attribute differing degrees of these states to other team members and to the team as a whole. If the task and social processes evolve well, these states are increasingly enhanced, until high levels are shared by all or most of the team members.[4]

Good task and social processes support the evolution of positive emergent states, which in turn support positive task and social processes. Together they can increase each team member's level of participation, openness, honesty, and commitment. With positive task and social processes in place, team members are more likely to engage fully in the task and interaction and take the risks that can lead to greater flexibility and adaptation within the team. Ineffective task and social processes, based on alignments, power differences, unexplored value differences, and lack of communication and coordination, can quickly undermine trust, confidence, and cohesion.

Coordinating mechanisms

Coordinating mechanisms are the formal processes that teams use to bring together the different contributions, make decisions, and move forward. The main coordinating mechanism for most teams is meetings, where the patterns of individual interaction planned are significant. Most teams establish a rhythm between face-to-face meeting and individual work, and between off-line and on-line work. The increasing use of communication technology has changed the scope, type, speed and pattern of coordination mechanisms for many teams. These mechanisms cut across the task, the social process, and the emergent states within a team and need aligning to them.

TEAM PROCESS BUILDING BLOCKS

Having reviewed these basic elements of team dynamics, we now are ready to address the key ways in which global teams can craft their task and social processes mindfully. In this section, we identify the building blocks of team processes: those processes that every team must be able to engage in well. In the following section, we discuss how the process building blocks should be sequenced – which ones should be drawn upon when – creating a productive flow for the global team. The five process building blocks are: building trust, differentiating, integrating (including decision-making), managing conflict, and creating and sharing knowledge.

Building trust

Trust has been well discussed as an interpersonal skill in Part II, and we refer the reader to that part for more details. Here we briefly explore its application to global teams in three ways: addressing the question of how much trust is needed and why, describing how trust is built over team dynamics, and identifying some important practices for building trust in virtual teams.

High levels of trust allow global teams to work together, especially when they are geographically distributed. Trust provides a safe environment in which team members can surface and explore values and sensitive issues, and make decisions for each other. Different team tasks demand different kinds and levels of trust. Some simple, routine tasks, such as organizing meetings and serving routine customers, demand reliability, whereas more complex tasks, such as product development, demand confidentiality, discretion, and openness. Teams with long life cycles will build up more social and interpersonal bases of trust, where temporary teams are far more likely to operate around action-based trust focused specifically on the particular short-term task.

Building trust is more difficult in teams where there are higher levels of risk, lower levels of interdependence, membership distributed over wide geographic areas, and greater cultural differences. In these situations special attention to trust-building is critical. Some important processes include creating safe boundaries for interaction and establishing constructive norms around collaboration, inclusive decision-making, and conflict resolution.

In a global team, each team member starts with varying levels of an initial preponderance to give trust, the swift trust that creates a narrow field of safety. Team members can surface some relevant assumptions about how they can interact to support trust and then negotiate the first set of working agreements, as described in the previous chapter. These agreements release and direct the energy of the team members to get the team started. The better these processes work, the deeper the next layer of trust that is created. With this deeper layer established, teams can then take the next set of risks as they develop more meaningful, conscious working agreements.

Establishing trust on-line

Trust is all the more important in teams working across large distances on communication technology. Tasks are often more fluid and emergent, roles are less clear, and there is less direct supervision and fewer social controls. Team members know less about each other's situation and contexts, and can interpret each other's actions as personal rather than seeing them in context. This diminishes the levels of trust. The process for developing trust in groups described in the previous paragraph – from swift trust to deeper trust – also applies on-line. The only difference is that the process is much more difficult on-line and takes much longer to move to deeper trust. Face-to-face interaction at a relatively early point in the team's life gives the on-line process an important boost.

In order to establish trust, it is helpful if team members:

- intentionally discuss what trust means to them;
- remember that different people understand and reciprocate trust differently;
- take actions to sustain and develop whatever swift trust is initially developed;
- use trust to delve deep in order to unleash blocked energy for task or social processes.

Differentiating

Differentiation is the process of diverging by revealing understanding and even creating differences. Multiple layers of difference are a fact in any team: members represent different disciplines, cultures, time zones, personalities, styles, roles, physical and social realities, and organizations. Whatever the pattern of differences among team members, the differences immediately present the team with a challenge: they can force change and create learning opportunities. Teams that grasp this opportunity can outperform most other teams. Those that do not rise to the challenge and either ignore or suppress their differences will at best be mediocre, or at worst, fail. Some argue that recognizing that someone else is different is what motivates people to communicate in the first place, and indeed, good communication about differences is key to turning them into an advantage.

Differences can bring both higher performance and conflict to a team, depending on how team members respond to them. Table 12.1 presents the opportunities and challenges that the most common differences in global teams present.

Having recognized differences as a challenge, one way to work constructively with them is to *map* and then *bridge* them.[5] Mapping is the process of identifying which differences are most relevant to the team's purpose and task, then describing the differences and their impact in a careful, insightful way, with extensive dialogue. The team leader and members need to take the time to identify the differences that will bring strength, flexibility, and speed, as well as those that may cause communication and emotional difficulties, then explore those differences deeply. For example, if team members come from different cultural backgrounds, then exploring their cultures and the implications for how the team works together is critical (see Part II).

Bridging is communicating in a way that takes differences into account effectively. With effective bridging processes, team members understand each other's different ideas from each team member's own perspective. They do not necessarily agree with each other, but they understand each other. The most important aspects of bridging are decentering and recentering. Decentering is trying to see things from the other's viewpoint: suspending judgment and adapting to the other's preferred needs. Listeners then reframe their own assumptions and preferences and strengthen relationships. Out of this process comes recentering, in which the team members can find shared ground and define those parts of knowledge and working agreements that need to be commonly held and shared.

Team members must deeply acknowledge that most differences are directly linked to differences in power and influence. The dynamics of prejudice are complex. For example, having the same mother tongue as the working language, being part of an advantaged subgroup, or being perceived to have more access to sources of power in the organization all act to increase the level of likely involvement and influence in an international team.[6] There can be strong dysfunctional stereotypes about those in positions of advantage: they can be assumed to be arrogant and closed-minded.[7] Yet many team exercises have demonstrated that for those with advantage to see the world from the point of view of the disadvantaged can be difficult. When those with less power do speak up, they may be labeled as "full of anger," "whistle-blower," or "folks with chips on their shoulders."[8] People who feel disempowered may try to gain power by aligning with those who are more powerful, often shunning their "own" group to work with others.[9] And those in power can feel envious if those traditionally seen as having less power do better, for example, calling such success "reverse discrimination."[10]

Countering the negative effects of differences is usually easier if everyone is different from each other rather than if there are distinct subgroups.[11] Coalitions based on issues tend to disband soon after a decision is made, but those based on sub-group membership tend to endure and influence dynamics throughout a team's life.[12] Because people from the majority are more likely to agree with minority views in private than in public,[13] it is

TABLE 12.1 The impact of differences in global teams

Source of difference	Opportunity presented	Impact on	Experienced as	Integrating mechanisms
Preferred leadership styles.	To question assumed leadership style and make leaders and members actively search for the most effective leadership role(s) and style where both adjust and align their expectations.	Effective leader/team member interaction, decision-making, levels of satisfaction.	Frustrations, disagreements on form. Disappointment due to failed expectations.	Openness about leader style and leader–team member expectations. Identification of conflicts and the best ways to handle them.
National and organizational culture of origin and leadership of the organization.	Can give core identity and sense of cohesion that can be adjusted/improved through experience in other cultures. Social cohesion can allow flexibility in other areas.	National culture can deeply affect HR policies and organizational culture. People who share nationality of organization and its leadership are perceived as more influential than others.	Perceived bias in accepted norms and levels of influence and access to resources. Glass ceiling based on nationality.	Well-structured participative processes and inclusive policies.
Preferred ways of resolving conflicts.	To access different approaches and adapt them to different contexts and communication modes. Confronts team with need to find synergistic solutions.	Ability to address difficult challenges and conflicts.	Denial of conflict. Displaced frustrations. Lack of trust. Lack of group efficacy.	Joint definition of which conflicts need to be addressed and how. Which conflicts to be avoided.
Preferred ways of decision making.	Creates variety; highlights need to make decision-making processes explicit and suitable for different contexts.	The quality of, involvement in, and follow up/implementation of decision-making processes.	Lack of loyalty to decision and team. Dissatisfaction and lack of respect.	Collective training on which type of decisions are fit for different purposes.

Different languages yet working in one. (often English).	Brings the possibility of different mindsets and cognitive styles if they can be accessed and integrated. May force native speakers to improve communication styles. May be a hindrance for second language speakers.	Interruption patterns. Use and interpretation of silence. Meaning of gestures and body language. Use of in-jokes/humor. Dominant patterns of logic. Placing of key information.	Inability to participate. Frequent misunderstandings. Exclusive patterns of humor. Translation can be clumsy when building relationships.	Choosing a working language and/or translators; maintaining steady rhythm and active listening skills.
Different professions.	Brings requisite variety of knowledge, skills, and approaches to complex problems. Speeds things up. Improves quality, relevance of output.	Values and where to focus. Common professions can act as a large integrating factor. If different, team members need bridges and translation among the different languages.	Power struggle. Ignorance. Misunderstanding.	Definition of the uses of different functions in relation to the goal. Respect and positive acknowledgment.
Expectations and values around interaction and team behavior.	Forces awareness of differences, assumptions, the tensions that they bring and the need to acknowledge and work with them.	Levels of participation. Misunderstandings.	Missed timing, anger at inappropriate reciprocity. Feeling misunderstood. Things not happening "in the right way."	Value checklist-type exercises to make differences explicit and legitimate and then negotiate them into inclusive working agreements.
Cultural preconceptions.	Increased awareness of these. Approaching them with humor, not acting on them. A learning opportunity that there are many different ways of seeing the world, each of which is real to each individual.	Preconceived perceptions of more or less relevant experience, education.	Stereotypical comments or implicit behavior toward "disadvantaged" people or about those "in charge."	Highlighting team members' different strengths and relevant experiences up front and using the strengths.

TABLE 12.1 (cont'd)

Source of difference	Opportunity presented	Impact on	Experienced as	Integrating mechanisms
International experience.	Can bring empathy, flexibility, humbleness, self-reflection. People with international experience can act as bridges between core and local sites. Gives recognition to those from different cultures.	Ability to understand implicit unwritten rules and working norms. Ability to speak different languages. Ability to empathize with other team members and understand the working realities of their contexts.	Bias that wide international experience and linguistic skills are more essential for people from "other" nationalities than for those whose mother tongue is working language of firm. Bias that "going native" in developing countries is bad, yet adapting to developed lifestyle is good.	Insist on international experience as part of international career path and selection criteria for international team leaders. Role-model lack of bias based on different cultural, social, political, and economic levels. Create participative mechanisms to appreciate and value different contributions.
Different geographical locations.	Access to much wider intellectual, financial, and social resources. Allows global efficiencies, local responsiveness, and knowledge transfer and learning across the organization.	Who meets face to face and who does not. Coordination, timing understanding of importance of required actions. Whether some are seen as more central than others.	Impenetrable in groups in certain locations. Lack of loyalty, invisible agendas.	Stress integrated team model spread across geography, not hub and spoke. Give extra support to those out there alone and create inclusive processes through available technology. Create hyper-attractiveness and virtual team visible locally and globally.

best to legitimate private conversations around issues rather than have all discussions in the public view.

High-quality participatory processes help teams take advantage of differences rather than be derailed by them. Ironically, *structured* processes can create the *freedom* for all to contribute and prevent dominant people or norms prevailing. For example, going around the meeting table and having each person speak for two minutes on a topic increases the surfacing of differences and makes them available for everyone. Other structured processes will be described later in the section on process flows.

Differences on-line

On-line dynamics relate to differentiating in two ways. First, team members will have different preferences for how they engage on-line, such as a preference for information through pictures or words, or for linear or synchronous sequencing. These differences can be accommodated with flexible on-line design of multicultural team spaces.

Second, the nature of on-line spaces can alter the context and power dynamics. Therefore, if they are well used, they can change the quality and frequency of participation and communication in positive ways. On-line spaces can be anonymous and asynchronous, and can be more comfortable for those who feel invisible in face-to-face settings, particularly with respect to hierarchy; those who are shy in face-to-face settings, but have a great deal to say; those who defer in face-to-face settings (because of culture, gender); those who need more time to formulate thoughts and words (because of language, style); and those who appreciate social interaction but in face-to-face reality operate in a more formal setting. Such people can find on-line spaces warmer and more congenial, which can lead to great intellectual work in the play or café spaces.[14]

Global team members will benefit from differences if they can:

- recognize that differences force change, so they need to be proactively acknowledged and developed into a strength;
- examine in detail (map and bridge) the complex patterns of both off-line and on-line differences within the team, paying attention to the different ways in which inequalities can emerge and prevent creative participation;
- put in as many participatory processes as possible to access all contributions;
- consciously use different media and strategies to bring out the different voices in the team.

Integrating and decision-making

Integrating is bringing the team's ideas and perspectives together to a shared understanding. Integrating is a group event, and the whole team must engage in choosing a response through a process of dialogue, negotiation, compromise, consensus, voting, and whatever other processes the team considers appropriate. Integration is also often designed to move the team from one context into another, for example from a pre-decision to a post-decision mode, often with little option to turn back. As such, integration has significant consequences for the team's success. The content, context, social implications, and consequences all need to be considered simultaneously.

It is relatively easy to find a few points in common and stick to discussion around those. But high-quality integration is a multilayered and more difficult task than is differentiation. Such integrative synergy usually comes about when three conditions are present:

1 Team members are wholly dependent on each other to complete the task.
2 There is a strong core team with the requisite variety of skills to match the complexity of the task.
3 Team members are stretched to make up the necessary skills by combining together.

Because the whole team needs to agree, integrative tasks usually need much denser social ties and patterns of interaction than do differentiative tasks. Many face-to-face teams ask for facilitated help and structured processes at this point. On-line, creation of the necessary structured spaces where teams can move simultaneously among these different levels of integration is quite difficult. It demands planning, the patience to get used to new technologies, skill, strong social relationships, enough trust and commitment, good structure, and supportive facilitation.

Decision-making is one of the most common and most important integrative processes, and it has been well researched.[15] The main elements are information-gathering and sensemaking, bringing contextual issues into consideration, and reaching agreement. Different cultures approach each of these aspects very differently, and in a multicultural team, there will be a wide range of diversity in how each team member interprets the issues to be decided.[16] If the team engages in good differentiating processes, members are likely to accept each other's viewpoints as legitimate and incorporate them into their own frames of reference rather than to rely by default on the majority interpretation.[17]

Once the team has framed the different interpretations of the broad issues, there are still likely to be very different understandings on a suitable process of how to reach a decision. For some, voting is a reasonable solution; for others, building consensus is key; and for others, the preference may be that the team leader decides. Different tasks and situations call for different types of decision-making. Global teams must decide explicitly on, for example, what type of decisions need full discussion and argument and which are fine to poll. Which decisions can anyone take? Which need total team consensus? Which are okay to decide with a quorum? In what circumstances does only the team leader make the decisions?

Key principles of effective global team decision-making include visibility, awareness, explicit structure, and accountability.[18] The more visible the flow of the task work through an effective on-line project management system, the better the teams can collectively structure and interweave their decision-making. This in turn will strengthen the social processes and emergent states. If the task is high-risk, ambiguous, and urgent, with very short time lines, often the team leader may need the freedom to move fast and be fairly directive. Good leaders manage to keep the balance between consultation and fast decision-making even in times of crisis. If the team membership is fairly stable, it is easier to delegate decision-making powers to individuals according to capabilities and roles. In many ad hoc, short-term teams of peers, maintaining consensus can be the key to success and flexibility. To prevent information overload, a team with high levels of trust, confidence, and identity can involve as few people as possible in active decision-making, as long as they maintain transparent input and feedback processes.

Integrating and decision-making on-line

The on-line process of integration is more difficult than face-to-face integration. This is especially true when the on-line integrative process aims to be consensual. Teams performing integrative tasks will benefit from richer modes of communication, such as face to face, and rich bandwidth combined synchronous technologies, so long as they keep a record for the group memory. On-line integrative processes can be frustratingly slow and can push team leaders to be more directive and less participatory. Many teams resort to simpler participatory processes such as polling, ranking, and voting to speed things up. On the other hand, the absence of visual and verbal cues and the reduced social presence and lower social conflict can result in higher-quality decisions. Individuals on-line often share more of their unique information, pay more attention to others, and are more influenced by the views of socially different team members.[19]

Global teams find that some types of decision-making work well on-line and others do not. A simple rule of thumb is that if decision-making is not working well in one medium, then try another. Mix and match technologies to the task and the emotional, social, and internal needs of the process. To manage multiple decisions on-line, spaces can be also be created where subteams can process decisions in parallel. Although only a subteam is involved in the active decision-making, everyone on the team can have access to the process, thus increasing visibility in the process.[20]

Over time, a team may find that having members who explicitly engage in making the interface between the technology and each team member, and who contribute actively to the social processes that can give a sense of relationship even on-line, can greatly influence the chances of success.[21]

With respect to integrating and decision-making, we suggest that members and leaders remember to:

- appreciate the depth of culturally different expectations and preferences around integrating and decision-making processes;
- decide who needs to be involved in what types of decisions and on what decision-making processes to use for different types of decisions;
- be prepared to sequence decisions that feed into each other as well as organize for some to be taken simultaneously;
- appreciate that some aspects of decision-making may work better on-line and others may be more difficult;
- develop integration and decision-making processes to maximize visibility, awareness, explicit structure, and accountability.

Managing conflict

Conflict is a difficult but important process in a team. There are specific times when constructive conflict is healthy and probably essential to high performance, but conflict can reduce team members' satisfaction, level of participation, liking of each other, and intent to remain on the team. Sometimes conflict is not even recognized by team members, and it is important to remember that over-generalizing, losing one's cool, gossiping, back-stabbing, over-adherence to rituals, not responding to e-mails, and spreading one's own version of events are all signs that conflict may be latent.[22]

Different cultures see and respond to conflict in very different ways. Some cultures prefer very indirect ways of working out difficulties. In others, it is important to "give it to them straight." One study suggests that Chinese managers rely more on an avoiding style of conflict because they place relatively high value on conformity, whereas US managers rely more on a competing style of conflict because they place a relatively high value on individual achievement.[23] In Finland, silence is often the response to public conflict. In Kenya, rebuking or arguing with someone in earshot of anyone else is a mistake that can result in an employee's resignation. In Italy showing intense emotions demonstrates to the other that you care, even though you disagree. Moreover, each individual in any culture will also have developed preferred styles of conflict management. Different responses to perceived conflict include avoidance, confrontation, accommodation, aggressiveness, passive resistance, and collaboration.

Informational or cognitive conflict is usually much more constructive than relationship-based conflict that arises from personal disaffection. Explicit task disagreement can force a team to evaluate and critique what it is doing, create new frames of reference, find new ways of doing things, and so lead to better decisions and outcomes. Managing task conflict in an integrating conflict management style, taking all perspectives into account and working towards win–win solutions, creates perceptions of greater equality and increases the trust, confidence, and identity within the team. Perceptions of inequality in treatment, rather than differences themselves, increase relationship conflict, resulting in lower levels of satisfaction. Avoiding conflict usually leads to higher levels of relationship conflict in the future.[24]

Fostering constructive cognitive conflict is easier when teams are small and have a propensity to tolerate, encourage, and engage in an open and frank expression of views. A sense of shared accountability also helps. Bigger, less open teams are more likely to experience relationship conflict. Some teams encourage sharing emotions openly, discussing what members feel about each other, but this can actually increase the degree of relationship conflict without helping members manage such conflict.[25] Such openness should only be practiced in teams that have strong abilities to redirect the conflict into the task.

Global leaders must learn to recognize, defuse, and redirect affective conflict, and to structure and guide teams through cognitive conflict. The cultural and personality instrument tools that we discussed previously can greatly assist in diffusing personality clashes, saving face, and giving people a constructive way out. To resolve task conflicts, teams can ask for facilitation, mediation, or arbitration. They can also establish key principles and criteria, and defuse personality attacks with working norms that make issues specific and work-related.

Conflict on-line

Team members who often work virtually soon learn that frequently they need to communicate the same message in two or three different ways to make sure the receiver understands. When writing something controversial, it is important to set the stage, tone and context, to consciously frame the message for the reader in order to prevent the fast escalation of conflict that can happen on-line (*flaming*). The listener or reader should practice the active listening techniques of asking or clarifying specific questions, paraphrasing and summarizing, and playing back what they have understood. Such active listening helps avoid unnecessary escalation of conflict.

Interestingly, conflict can sometimes be defused more quickly in virtual interaction. With the lack of visual contact, it is easier to keep conflict on a cognitive or task level, especially if relationships are strong in the first place. On-line, people may perceive the willingness of team members to share their unique information and debate ideas as signs of engagement and commitment to the team. On-line, the receivers of e-mail tend to read a communication more than once before responding, which can reduce quick reactions to messages that are not completely understood in the first place.

On-line teams need deeper levels of trust to withstand the uncertainties and anxieties produced by conflict in asynchronous, written, on-line communication. Most team members intuitively pick up the phone when they feel things are getting out of sync or are in crisis, and try to get together face to face if possible. But waiting until emotions subside and people reflect can be wise. Teams should stay flexible and mix and match technologies to what the individuals concerned think may work best. Everyone is learning and experimenting across this relatively new medium.

In summary, global team members and leaders can manage conflict effectively if they:

- appreciate the very different cultural perceptions of what constitutes conflict and how to address conflict;
- understand when cognitive conflict can be constructive and when relationship conflict is destructive;
- are prepared to surface and work through interpersonal conflicts in a collaborative way rather than to let them simmer;
- remain aware of the ways in which conflict evolves on-line.

Creating and sharing knowledge

Organizations are increasingly seen as knowledge systems, and global teams are an important vehicle for accessing, gathering, combining, and transferring knowledge within global organizations. Knowledge is defined as information in context, or information that is meaningful.[26] Information, in turn, is data that are organized to facilitate such interpretation. Knowledge can be categorized based on what it can achieve and how contextually dependent it is.[27] Knowledge is strategically important if it serves as a precondition for action, achievement, creativity, and innovation. Knowledge that resides within the organization is often more accessible than are hard assets, resources or financing. This ready accessibility of knowledge means that repackaging and learning from current knowledge can be the fastest source of regeneration within an organization. Failure to communicate contextual information, uneven information distribution and speed of access, difficulties in understanding the relevance and importance of information, and the different interpretations of silence, can all prevent the effective build-up of mutual knowledge.[28]

As explained in Part II, we know more than we can tell. In order to become knowledge, information needs context. It requires making more meaning from the information than is in the information itself, by attaching to it context and accumulated wisdom. This "knowledge beyond information" is often called tacit knowledge. Accessing and sharing tacit knowledge is critical in global teams, as their performance depends on turning information into knowledge that is valuable for the organization.

Creating tacit knowledge is a social process. Team members must bring tacit knowledge into consciousness and transmit it in a way that receivers can understand. This requires strong social interrelationships, ties, and trust within a team. To share tacit knowledge, team members need to have credibility with each other and find some common basis of understanding. Effective knowledge transfer requires two-way dialogue in which team members share, question, and clarify the objects of knowledge as well as their own contexts and understandings, all within supportive social relations and interactions. It is best done in a face-to-face environment, with the richness, immediacy, and opportunity for dialogue in this medium.[29] However, under any conditions, setting communication norms and agreements up front is key. These communication norms evolve as relationships deepen and the need for accessing more tacit and contextualized knowledge increases.[30]

To share and create valuable knowledge, global teams must pay special attention to how they use face-to-face and on-line modes. It is important not to assume that being together will automatically result in establishing relationships and sharing tacit knowledge. People in the same room can be mentally and emotionally very distant from each other.[31] Many global teams use face-to-face time together to socialize or to make decisions without taking the time to engage in deep conversations around the knowledge brought to the table. Teams should use expensive, valuable, rich face-to-face time to build a similar understanding of their team relationships and to build a shared view of their knowledge base and task. Knowledge of the start-up factors outlined in the previous chapter: the organizational context and environment, the overall team purpose, goals, milestones, individual tasks, roles, responsibilities, accountability and agreed principles, procedures and working agreements, need to exist as shared mental models within the team. However individual technical and detailed knowledge and expertise can remain dispersed within individuals so long as it is accessible as and when needed. This understanding allows them to share and build on tacit knowledge, and to work more effectively at a distance.[32]

Occasionally, teams can develop the relationships and knowledge base described above without meeting face to face. In such rare situations, team members usually have such a "positively anchored relationship"[33] that they are able to intuit the tacit elements of what they are communicating effectively. This happens more easily when two people find that they have similar mental models and values about their tasks and relationships. For example, they may be alumni of the same engineering school but have never met in person.

Certain types of knowledge and information can be more easily exchanged on-line than others. If innovative information is easy to analyze and not very complex, it can be shared more easily across technology than if it is very complex and hard to analyze independently.[34] Explicit packages of procedural and intellectual knowledge, such as schedules and lists of publications, also travel easily on-line. The virtual space is also helpful for creating a collective memory.[35] Not everyone needs to remember everything, but team members rely on each other to remember different pieces of information, and the virtual space coordinates this process.

Teams use electronic technology for knowledge-sharing in four ways: synchronous communication technologies such as the telephone and videoconferencing; asynchronous communication technologies such as e-mail, interactive websites, and share databases; Internet and Intranet technologies to gain access to different information sources such as on-line libraries and websites; and database and other software that help to structure a team's activities.[36] Synchronous technologies have more social presence than do asynchronous, but they tend to go unrecorded. Asynchronous technologies tend to record the interaction and can begin to act as a pool of memory, helping the team to turn individual knowledge into group performance. For example, team members just down the corridor from each other use e-mail not just because it is sometimes easier than getting up or telephoning, but because it offers a way of sharing, sequencing, recording, making visible and filing interactions, and information exchange. Knowing when to switch modes, create a compact disc, pick up the phone, or meet face to face in order to share more contextual and tacit types of knowledge is crucial to success in a globally distributed team.

A specific type of knowledge-based global team is the community of practice.[37] These communities, often on-line, consist of groups of people who connect across some common point of identity or common experience, knowledge, or discipline. Members often keep a loose network and sense of cohesion among themselves that builds a sense of shared context. Companies that encourage participation in these communities of practice may well find that geographically dispersed teams are able to form and disband much faster and can quickly access extra expertise, because there is already a strong network of interpersonal linkages and understandings spread across the geography of the organization.

With respect to knowledge-sharing, global teams and leaders should:

- recognize that knowledge-sharing involves a lot more than more than distributing information;
- accept the importance of tacit and context-dependent knowledge and learn to access it through strong relationships and rich modes of communication;
- build up the necessary shared context, relationships, and mental models by articulating as much context, identifying purpose, roles and responsibilities, and sharing as much relevant documentation as possible;
- share, question, and create a dialogue about their contexts and reframe their knowledge for other team members on an ongoing basis as the team evolves.

In the virtual space:

- create a dedicated on-line team space with many tools: cafés for socializing; instant messaging and chats; libraries for documentation; structured task spaces with specific questions, outcomes, and deadlines; schedule records, project planning tools, and so on;[38]
- include social interaction from the start through introductions, sharing photos, on line cafés, fun icebreakers;
- mix and match communication modes to the situation and switch modes when one is not working, being aware to not lose the benefits of each one.

Team Process Flows

While all of the team process building blocks are critical to any global team, equally important is their sequencing over the life of a team's work together. Engaging in conflict resolution, differentiating, and integrating at the right time leads to performance; at the wrong time it can force decisions and actions that are less than optimal, and create poor relations. In this section we identify three types of process flows: differentiating and integrating; face-to-face and virtual; and phases and transitions.

Differentiating and integrating flows

As described above, differentiating is exploring and working with differences, and integrating is coming together to make decisions, get closure, and move ahead. Effective teams develop a rhythm of actively seeking out and highlighting the differences in their approach, knowledge, assumptions, and understanding, then weaving these differences into rich, jointly agreed solutions and decisions. This flow of differentiating, integrating, differentiating, integrating drives many key team processes at different levels.

Once a team has clarified its common vision and purpose, agreed on the task, and allocated roles and responsibilities, the members need to elicit their relevant differences on how they will work together in order to reach effective working agreements and dos and don'ts, the agreed, safe field for their interaction and social processes. All the team members need to actively differentiate, sharing as much of their differences as trust will allow.

In a team setting, most creativity is at the point of maximum cognitive dissonance, a strategic moment when there may be a heavy silence. If the team can hold this tension/dissonance open, new insights, issues, and ways of doing things can emerge into the team's explicit and conscious field of work. This process of staying with the tension is often easier in a period of high-density interaction, in small teams (of up to five),[39] and during face-to-face interaction. Holding tension open in large teams, on-line, and asynchronously is possible, but difficult. Such teams will need even stronger safety nets of deeper trust, emotional maturity, and latitude, or a strong sense of common identity that can simultaneously contain and hold open the tension, so that team members can withstand the discomfort and uncertainty at the edges of potential conflict as they await unknown replies.

Once the team has accessed new emergent knowledge, the time comes to choose, negotiate, weave, and argue the different opinions, viewpoints, and perspectives into useful working agreements and task distributions. In other words, they need to integrate again. Consciously differentiating (for example, highlighting cultural differences, brainstorming options for problem-solving) and then integrating (negotiating working agreements, making a group decision) is a process that builds the team's confidence that they can handle differences in a mature and open fashion on a reasonably level playing field. With each cycle of effective differentiating and integrating, the team enhances its trust, confidence, and identity, and maximizes decision-making quality.

For example, once initial agreement on group process is clear (integrating), a team needs to access its members' diverse knowledge and expertise while they analyze the problem and create multiple options as solutions (differentiating). If these potential conflicts are managed well, a shared model of the task work forms (integrating). The integrative arguments that arise around which option(s) to pursue may be heated and intense, and should forge a shared mental model from a wide variety of ideas. This fine balance between cognitive conflict and shared understanding maximizes the exchange and active combination of tacit and explicit knowledge. Good facilitation and leadership move the team past sticky moments of relationship conflict and focus on cognitive conflict (differentiating then integrating). The team members may next draw apart to check that the decision will work in a wide variety of contexts (differentiating). Then the team may come together again to finalize and agree on the outcome (integrating).

Different tasks require different emphasis within the differentiating–integrating flow. Some tasks, by their nature, have differentiation as an intended outcome, while others have integration. Teams focused on differentiation (for example, creating local responsiveness) can allow more differentiating and less integrating than those focused on integration (such as creating global efficiencies and economies of scale).[40] Globally distributed teams can outperform co-located teams on differentiation tasks, such as drawing knowledge from the organization or from the external environment, or executing a decision by adapting it in different parts of the organization. Their composition, distribution, and virtual communication modes fit well with differentiating processes once the members know each other. Globally distributed teams are not so well set up for integrative tasks, though, and must find ways to compensate for their structure in order to integrate well.[41]

When team processes take place in cyberspace rather than in meeting rooms, the cycles become more stark and visible. They are often driven by short-term, medium-term, and final goals and deadlines. Just as in a meeting room, in cyberspace people usually start cutting in and interrupting just before a major decision, so team activity usually spikes just before an immovable deadline. As outlined in the previous chapter, a good project management system should include a team task analysis so that multi-tasking in different phases can be tracked and resources and training budgeted for.

In summary: global team members and leaders will benefit by:

◆ recognizing the rhythm of differentiation and integration as the major pulse that drives many team processes;
◆ seeing how the repeated cycles of these processes build up knowledge within the team and strengthen the emergent states;
◆ seeking out the best processes to surface differences and move through the bridging zone into fair, integrative mechanisms.

Face-to-face and virtual flows

Over time, most teams must also sequence their face-to-face meetings, interspersing them with virtual communication using a variety of modes. The most effective way is to create a regular rhythm of face-to-face meetings – a heartbeat.[42] Face-to-face meetings can be scheduled up to a year in advance, say once a quarter or once every four months. The meetings can even be combined with sales meetings or visits to customer or supplier sites for greater economies.

During the face-to-face meetings, the team should engage in all the relationship-building and tacit knowledge-sharing described earlier. This process builds the emergent states of trust, identity, and confidence, and creates a strong environment of safety. In the face-to-face environment, teams should both differentiate and integrate, but they should do both by focusing on topics that require a lot of tacit knowledge-sharing.

Between face-to-face meetings, while the team is working virtually, the team members can build on the relationships and shared tacit knowledge they already have by working through the task. Again, both differentiating and integrating will take place, but generally without pushing the bounds of the relationships or creating new tacit knowledge. Team members can collect more knowledge, share it with each other in databases, discuss implications of the knowledge, select the most fruitful directions for further study, and so on.

This rhythm of face-to-face and virtual interaction sets an important pace for the team. If members know that a regular meeting is coming up, then conflicts can be addressed "temporarily" in the virtual setting so people can move on, then readdressed when the team is face to face. In this way, not having the richness of face to face does not stall the team's progress.

The spacing between meetings depends on the health of the team and the type of task. Regular face-to-face meetings should be more frequent (for example, every six to eight weeks) the less strong the team members' relationships are and the more tacit the knowledge that must be created is. Face-to-face meetings can be four or even six months apart with a team whose membership is stable, whose relationships are strong, and whose stock of shared tacit knowledge is very high. The frequency may need to change over time, for example, as the task or environment changes, or as membership changes. If a team's budget does not stretch to meeting face to face, then it is important to mimic the social, integrative, and conflict-resolution processes as closely as possible in rich, interactive on-line environments.

Between face-to-face meetings, as described above, members will use a variety of virtual modes, depending on the needs of the task, constraints of the environment, and preferences of the members. Subsets of members will communicate with each other differently, and with different intensity, according to the same contingencies. The goal is to make sure the team continues the flow of differentiating and integrating, while resolving conflicts and sharing knowledge, using whatever technology works well for them. This process is usually much more effective with the guidance of the leader or facilitator who reminds team members to stick with the processes, and supports them as they do.

The key action for team leaders and members is to focus on developing the social relationships and working/communication norms that will support what the team does face to face and on-line, in order to create a blended, hybrid pattern of interaction which makes the best use of each communication mode and environment, a multimedia "hybrid vigour."[43] Global team members and leaders will benefit by:

- developing a regular rhythm of face-to-face meetings interspersed with virtual communication;
- using face-to-face time to build relationships for trust, confidence, and identity and to share and develop tacit knowledge;
- adjusting the rhythm depending on characteristics of the task and the team;
- providing a portfolio of technology to be used virtually between face-to-face meetings and supporting members' use of the technology in subgroups and as they believe is appropriate.

Phases and transitions

All teams have life cycles, even if their task is ongoing without a foreseeable end. The team composition and design, their types of tasks, and their contextual environment all affect the sequence, pattern, and timing of the patterns of integration and differentiation within a team's life cycle. These patterns can be seen in Tuckman's team model,[44] *forming* (integrating), *storming* (differentiating), *norming* (integrating), *performing* (both), and *adjourning* (differentiating). A more multifaceted approach to team development is to think of it as cycles of action followed by transitional phases.[45] Scanning, sourcing, monitoring, co-ordinating, and integrating are the action-phase activities. Transitions in the midst of these action phases (mid-phase transitions) are times of reflection and review in order to refocus and decide on future action. They often occur at the mid-point or later of an action phase, and serve to launch the end of the action phase and guide the beginning of the next action phase. An example of a mid-phase transitional process would be using feedback to re-establish the vision, renegotiate targets and resources, and revitalize through external input from other teams.

During a mid-phase point, teams can often hit deadlock, controversy, apathy and disengagement and need to be brought back on track. Reminding the team of the initial working agreements and offering to renegotiate important ones can provide a powerful mechanism for realigning everyone's energies. Teams are more likely to succeed if they review and reorient themselves toward the objective at this mid-phase point.[46] This is easiest done at face-to-face meetings, but on-line survey tools now make possible the use of structured cultural-value checklists, different types of inventory, and tailor-made "half-time health check" questionnaires for review, reflection, bringing in new members, and learning.

Constructive conflict is essential in mid-phase transitions, such as around the time when a team has to narrow down their multiple options to one or two that everyone can agree to go forward with. If there is no constructive conflict at half-time, a number of things could be happening. There could be unanimous agreement that one option naturally stands out as much better than all the rest. However, it could also be that an individual or subgroup have so dominated the process that alternative options have not been properly generated or considered, or the team processes have been so badly handled, or there has been so much interpersonal conflict, that many team members have lost passion and interest in the task. The latter two possibilities are problems. They can be made less likely by fully engaging in the start-up processes, splitting very large teams into smaller teams to generate options, fostering open, collaborative norms, using an integrative conflict management style and open decision-making processes, or choosing to change the dynamic.

The difficulty with most mid-phase conflicts is that first, time is running out and second, they are often about the deeper and more sensitive issues that no one wanted to talk about right at the beginning. These can range from the fact that in some areas of their work, team members are actively competing against each other, either for resources or territory. Mid-phase crises or "strategic moments" usually demand staunch, centered, and persistent leadership and facilitation. The better the team's start-up working agreements have anticipated these issues and engendered a commitment to make the team work, the more likely the team is to get through these difficulties in a reasonably constructive way. This can prove cathartic and release the energy previously taken up in covert, under-the-table conflict, thereby adding significantly to positive emergent states.

We recommend that global teams and leaders:

- anticipate mid-phase transitions and facilitate them actively;
- use mid-phase transitions to help the team move through one phase to the next;
- encourage cognitive, task-related constructive conflict at mid-phase transitions while helping the team move beyond relationship conflict.

CONCLUSION

Often global teams are called on to create value by making and implementing important decisions. This chapter demonstrates that teams create such value by actively engaging in rhythms of differentiating and integrating, face to face and virtually, through phases and transitions, while building trust, resolving conflicts, and creating knowledge. It is the real-life, everyday team experiences of team leaders and members that create the color, timbre, rhythms, and chords of what each of these processes can achieve and how they play out. Doing them well enables the necessary levels of trust, cohesion, and confidence to emerge, which in turn allows the team to contain the tensions and difficulties inherent in these processes and determines the success of the team. This success needs to be measured in the team's performance and in the capacity of the team to learn.

Good team leadership entails developing both the technical aspects of the task and the character and competency of the team's social processes. Leaders who keep in touch with the needs of their team members and who are able to find collaborative solutions to personality conflicts, all while staying sensitive to the perceptions and needs of external stakeholders, can continue to be effective through team change and transition. The style of leadership suitable for the team will need to change as the team progresses through different phases. The advocacy, entrepreneurial, "busting the boundaries and bargaining for budgets" style that may be needed to get a team started usually needs to evolve into a supportive, morale-boosting, consistent, steady learning pattern in mid-life. Leaders may be able to adapt, or a change of leadership may be required in long-term project teams.

To summarize the major points of this chapter's message, global team members and leaders will benefit by:

- using the basic elements of task and social processes, emergent states, and coordinating mechanisms;
- creating the right conditions, norms, and agreements for trust, identity, and confidence to emerge;
- differentiating by understanding and leveraging differences in the team;
- integrating by coming together and making effective decisions;
- resolving conflicts constructively, working through task-related cognitive conflicts and preventing relationship conflicts;
- understanding the relationships between tacit and explicit knowledge and the importance of tacit knowledge in global teams;
- engaging in the rhythm of differentiation and integration that will bring in fresh perspectives, and create synergies, new knowledge, and learning;

- engaging in the flow of face-to-face and virtual interaction that will build the relationships and tacit knowledge that connect people with the rest of the organization;
- working through the phases and transitions with a view to the end goal;
- understanding the special leadership skills needed to lead a team from a distance and working together to evolve the best set of skills for each individual team and task.

Now that we have reviewed important global team processes, we turn our attention to another critical area whose mastery and successful implementation contribute to the success of these teams, global team performance management.

NOTES

1 Hackman, J. R. (2002), *Leading Teams; Setting the Stage for Great Performances*. Cambridge, MA: Harvard Business School Press.

2 Quinn, R. W., & Dutton, J. E. (2002), Organizing through energy-in-conversation: A process theory of coordination, Ph.D. thesis, University of Michigan Business School.

3 See chapter 8.

4 Marks, M. A., Mathieu, J. E., & Zaccaro, S. J. (2001), A temporally based framework and taxonomy of team processes, *Academy of Management Review*, 26(3), 356–376.

5 DiStefano, J. J., & Maznevski, M. L. (2000), Creating value with diverse teams in global management, *Organizational Dynamics*, 29(1), 45–63.

6 Canney Davison, S., & Ward, K. (1999), *Leading International Teams*. London: McGraw Hill, p. 44; see www.pipal.com; Canney Davison, S. (1995), Multicultural processes in international teams, Ph.D. thesis, London Business School.

7 See Ely, R. (1995), The role of dominant identity and experience in organizational work on diversity, in S. Jackson & M. Ruderman (eds.), *Diversity in work teams*, Washington, DC: American Psychological Association, pp. 161–186.

8 Aquino, K., & Bryon, K. (2001), Dominating interpersonal behavior and perceived victimization in groups: evidence for a curvilinear relationship, paper presented at the Academy of Management, Washington, DC.

9 DiTomaso, N., Cordero, R., & Farris, G. (1996), Effects of group diversity on perceptions of group and self amongst scientists and engineers, in M. Ruderman, J. Hughes, & S. Jackson (eds.), *Selected Research on Work Team Diversity*, Washington, DC: American Psychological Association, pp. 99–120.

10 Timmerman, T. (2001), Do majority team members welcome or envy high performing minorities?, paper presented at the Academy of Management, Washington, DC.

11 Lau, D., & Murnighan, J. (1999), Demographic diversity and faultlines, *American Management Review*, 23, 325–340. Earley, C. P., & Mosakowski, E. (2000), Creating hybrid team cultures: An empirical test of transnational team functioning. *Academy of Management Journal*, 43(1), 26–49. Moss Kanter, R. (1977), *Men and Women of the Corporation*, New York: Basic Books. A classic book on different types of inequality is Blau, P. M. (1977), *Inequality and Heterogeneity*, New York: The Free Press.

12 Polzer, J. T., Mannix, E. A., & Neale, M. A. (1995), Multi-party negotiation in its social context, in R. M. Kramer & D. M. Messick (eds.), *Negotiation as a Social Process*, Thousand Oaks, CA: Sage, pp. 123–142.

13 Moscovici, S. (1985), Innovation and minority influence, in S. Moscovici (ed.), *Perspectives on Minority Influence*, Cambridge: Cambridge University Press, pp. 9–52.

14 Insights posted by Nancy White (www.fullcirc.com) in a virtual teams course, November 2002.

15 For example, Guzzo, R. A., Salas, E., et al. (1995), *Team Effectiveness and Decision Making in Organizations*. San Francisco: Jossey-Bass.

16 Bettenhausen, K. L. (1991), Five years of groups research: What we have learned and what needs to be addressed, *Journal of Management*, 17, 345–381.

17 Mohammed, S., & Ringsies, E. (2001), Cognitive diversity and consensus in group decision making, *Organizational Behavior and Group Decision Making*, 85(2), 310–336.

18 Brown, R. (1988), *Group Processes; Dynamics within and between Groups*. Oxford: Blackwell, p. 144.

19 Bhappu, A., Meader, D. K., Erwin, C. R., & Crews, J. M. (2001), Conflict and communication media in diverse teams: To see or not to see when we disagree, paper presented to the Academy of Management, Washington, DC, August. Duarte, L. D., & Snyder, N. T. (1999), *Mastering Virtual Teams*, San Francisco: Jossey-Bass; Maznevski, M. L., & Chudoba, K. M. (2000), Bridging space over time: Global virtual team dynamics and effectiveness, *Organization Science*, 11, 473–492.

20 Erickson, T., Halverson, C., Kellogg, W. A., Laff, M., & Wolf, T. (in press). Social translucence: Designing social infrastructures that make collective activity visible. *Communications of the ACM*, special issue on supporting online communities, ed. J. Preece. See http://www.research.ibm.com/people/w/wkellogg/publications.html

21 Orlikowski, W. J., Yates, J., Okamura, K., & Fujimoto, M. (1995), Shaping electronic communication: The meta-structuring of technology in the context of use, *Organization Science*, 6, 423–444.

22 Kolb, D. M., & Putnam, L. L. (1992), The multiple faces of conflict in organizations, *Journal of Organizational Behavior*, 13: 311–324.

23 Morris, M., Williams, K. Y., Leung, K., et al. (1998), Conflict management style: accounting for cross-national differences, *Journal of International Business Studies*, 29(4), 729–748.

24 Wall, V. D., & Nolan, L. L. (1987), Small group conflict. A look at equity, satisfaction and styles of conflict management, *Small Group Behaviour*, 18(2), 188–211.

25 Jehn, K. A. (1995), A multimethod examination of the benefits and detriments of intragroup conflict, *Administrative Science Quarterly*, 40, 256–282.

26 For an in-depth and intellectually challenging exploration of turning data into information and then into knowledge in different cultural settings, see Boisot, M. (1995), *The Information Space*, London: Routledge. Also Fisher, K. & Fisher, M. D. (1998), The distributed mind: achieving High Performance through the collective intelligence of Knowledge Work Teams. New York: Amacom (American Management Association); and Doz, Y., & Santos, J. F. P. (1997), On the management of knowledge: form the transparency of collocation and co-setting to the quandary of dispersion and differentiation, INSEAD working paper 97/119/SM.

27 See *ibid.*; also Mohammed, S., & Dumville, B. (2001), Team mental models in a team knowledge framework: Expanding theory and measurement across disciplinary boundaries. *Journal of Organizational Behavior*, 22, 89–106.

28 Crampton, C. D. (1999), The mutual knowledge problem and its consequences in geographically dispersed teams, working paper, Fairfax, VA: George Mason University.

29 Negroni, F., & Colombo, C. (2001), Managing knowledge in R&D dispersed teams, paper presented for the European Group for Organizational Studies 17th Colloquium, Lyon, July 5–7.

30 *Ibid.*

31 Pinto, M. B., Pinto, J. K., & Prescott, J. E. (1993), Antecedents and consequences of project team cross-functional cooperation, *Management Science*, 39(10), 1281–98.

32 Gibson, C. B., & Cohen, S. G. (eds.) (2003), *Virtual Teams That Work: Creating Conditions for Virtual Team Effectiveness*. San Francisco: Jossey-Bass; see www.Josseybass.com

33 Goffman, E. (1972), *Interaction Ritual*. London: Allen Lane

34 De Meyer, A. (1991), "Tech talk": How managers are stimulating global R&D communication, *Sloan Management Review*, 33, 49–58.

35 Griffith, T. & Neale, M. A. (1999), Information processing and performance in traditional and virtual teams: The role of transactive memory, Stanford University Research Papers series, no 1613, 7/22/1999.

36 McGrath, J. E., & Berdahl, J. L. (1998), Groups, technology and time: Use of computers in collaborative work, in R. S. Tindale et al. (eds.), *Applications of Theory and Research into Groups to Social Issues*, New York: Plenum, vol. 4, pp. 205–228.

37 Wenger, E., McDermott, R., & Snyder, W. (2002). *Cultivating Communities of Practice*. Cambridge, MA: Harvard Business School Press.

38 http://www.kmnews.com/Technology/technology.htm has a run down of some current packages. Also see Loops on http://www.pliant.org. For an atlas of different cyberspaces visit http://www.cybergeography.org/atlas/atlas.html

39 Bales, R. F. (1953), The equilibrium problem in small groups, in T. Parsons, R. F. Bales, & E. A. Shils (eds.), *Working Papers in the Theory of Action*, New York: The Free Press, pp. 111–162; Canney Davison, S. (1995), Multicultural processes in international teams, Ph.D. thesis, London Business School; and Hackman, J. R. (2002), *Leading Teams*, Cambridge, MA: Harvard Business School Press, p. 117 all found that five seems to be an optimal number of many teams processes.

40 Snow, C. C., Canney Davison, S., Hambrick, D., & Snell, S. (1996), Use transnational teams to globalize your company, *Organizational Dynamics*, 24(4), 50–168.

41 Maznevski, M., & Athanassiou, N. (2003), Designing knowledge-management infrastructure for virtual teams: Building and using social networks and social capital, in C. B. Gibson & S. G. Cohen (eds.), *Virtual Teams That Work: Creating Conditions for Virtual Team Effectiveness*, San Francisco: Jossey-Bass, pp. 196–213.

42 Maznevski, M., & Chudoba, K. L. (2000), Bridging space over time: Global virtual team dynamics and effectiveness, *Organization Science*, 11(5), 473–493.

43 A term coined by Jochan Rockstrom, a CGIAR manager on a virtual teams course, November 2002.

44 Tuckman, B. W. (1965), Developmental sequence in small groups, *Psychological Bulletin*, 63(6), 384–399. Jensen, M. A. C. (1977), Stages of small-group development revisited, *Group & Organization Studies*, 2(4), 419–427.

45 Marks, M., Mathieu, J., & Zaccaro, S. (2001), A temporally based framework and taxonomy of team processes, *Academy of Management Review*, 26(3), 356–376.

46 Gersick, C. G. (1989), Marking time: Predictable transitions in task groups, *Academy of Management Journal*, 32(2), 274–309. Gersick, C. G. (1988), Time and transition in work teams: Toward a new model of group development, *Academy of Management Journal*, 31(1), 9–41.

13

Performance Management in Global Teams

BRADLEY L. KIRKMAN AND DEANNE N. DEN HARTOG

When organizations globalize, most of the work dedicated to this effort gets done through the collaboration and coordination of many people located in different nations. Often this collaboration takes the form of global work teams. In fact, teams form the basic building blocks of most global organizations. Globalization rarely occurs without teamwork. The "global" aspect of teamwork in organizations adds another layer of complexity to the complicated overall globalization process. Thus, there is a pressing need to understand the role of teamwork in globalization and what factors account for successful global teams.

Previous global team-related parts of this book have covered such areas as the leadership of teams, the design and formation of global teams, and the creation of effective processes for global teams. The purpose of this chapter is to discuss the next logical phase of global team development: the performance management of teams in an international context. Performance management is problematic in teams of this type because members are likely to bring widely disparate viewpoints about appropriate ways to reward, recognize, evaluate, and train and develop global team members. In this chapter, we first discuss the issue of global team-based rewards and recognition. Second, we highlight the difficult task of evaluating contributors in global teams. Finally, we discuss the importance of training and development in global teams. We also note that many of the issues we discuss in this chapter could be applied to other organizational units in addition to teams, such as work units, departments, divisions, whole organizations, or even one-on-one manager–employee relationships. We focus specifically on teams here due to their widespread use in global organizing.

REWARDS AND RECOGNITION IN GLOBAL TEAMS

If the many failures of implementing global teams and other organizational forms worldwide could be traced to one single factor, that factor would most likely be inappropriate reward and recognition strategies. Key management decisions related to reward and recognition include:

- Should rewards be based on individual performance, team performance, or both?
- What are the important factors to consider when using team-based pay?
- How can recognition be used in addition to, or instead of, monetary rewards?

Rewarding global teams

Managers have many choices for rewarding global teams, but generally the issue comes back to two major strategies: rewarding team members based on individual performance and rewarding team members based on team performance as a whole. Whether organizations are team-based or individual-based, most US managers continue to reward organizational contributions individually. Managers and employees set individual goals and develop individual action plans, and individuals are held accountable for their progress toward their goals. This approach becomes problematic in a team setting because often tasks are accomplished by people working together, interdependently, and individual contributions cannot be identified or, in some cases, are nonexistent. Consider the example of a software design team whose members frequently exchange the latest versions of a software program. Software may undergo hundreds or even thousands of iterations; and keeping track of specific, individual contributions neither makes sense in this context nor is feasible. This effect may be exacerbated in many global teams because of their reliance on electronic rather than face-to-face communication, which makes assessing individual contributions even more problematic. As Charles Handy stated when discussing virtual organizations, "How do you manage people whom you do not see?"[1]

Individual-based rewards

Individual rewards, in most cases, do just what they are designed to do. They elicit behaviors that are consistent with an individual's focus and persistence toward his or her own goals, not those of a team, especially in individualist contexts. For example, the piece-rate pay system, so often used in manufacturing settings worldwide, compensates individuals for the number of units they produce daily. The more an individual produces, the more he or she gets paid. Consider what happens, however, when a team-based work system is implemented in such an environment. Imagine the reaction of a piece-rate-compensated worker being asked to step away from his or her work area for an hour or two to help a new team member learn a task. While helping a new team member, the piece-rate worker produces nothing that will be counted and monetarily rewarded. The new team member who needs the help might as well be reaching into that person's wallet or purse and removing money while being helped! Simply put, individual-based pay motivates individual-based behavior. Unless there is an incentive for teamwork, most human beings won't react positively to simply being told to "act like a team."

Team-based rewards

At the other end of the spectrum are team-based rewards. Incentives are not based on individual output, but on the output or performance of the team as a whole. Such plans might range from 100 percent team-based pay to as little as 5 to 10 percent, but the intent is the same: to reward team members for performing well as a team. As with individual pay, team members receiving team-based pay will likely be motivated consistent with the manner in which they are paid. Unfortunately, what looks good on paper often does not translate well in the workplace. Some companies that have transitioned to team-based pay systems, such as the apparel maker Levi Strauss in the United States, have fared no better, and in some cases, worse than companies retaining their individual-based pay systems. The underlying reason for much of the failure may be social loafing.[2]

Social loafing is a phenomenon best described by the "tug-of-war" example. Tug-of-war usually involves two groups of individuals pulling in opposite directions on a rope, sometimes across an unpleasant middle ground such as a mud pit or pool of water. One team wins when it successfully pulls the other team into or across the unpleasant middle ground. Studies have shown, however, that as more and more individuals are added to either side of the rope, individual pulling efforts decrease.[3] That is, team members who initially used 100 percent of their pulling strength reduce their efforts to, say, 80 or 90 percent, once new team members are added. Team members simply see no reason to continue exerting maximum effort once their comrades have joined the fray. Social loafing effects have been found in a variety of countries.[4]

The same phenomenon can and does occur in the workplace, and team-based pay can be the culprit. When Levi Strauss abandoned their piece-rate pay system and transitioned to 100 percent team-based pay in the United States, chaos erupted.[5] Slower workers and those who took long lunch breaks or slacked off on the job were verbally assaulted and threatened with physical violence. To maintain order, law-enforcement officers were stationed at one Levi Docker's trouser-producing plant in Powell, Tennessee. Higher-performing team members reacted very negatively to fellow members whom they held responsible for reducing the overall compensation of the team. What's worse, the workers who were most negatively affected by team-based pay were the highest performing under the old piece-rate system. Many saw their take-home pay decrease as rewards were tied to team, not individual, performance. Levi's lost many of these high-performing workers to rival factories before abandoning team-based pay.

Combining individual and team-based rewards

So, if the lesson above is not to use either purely individual-based pay or purely team-based pay in global teams, then the answer must lie somewhere in between. Indeed, most team researchers and compensation specialists argue that a combination of individual- and team-based rewards provides a better solution (even though some research has not supported this claim).[6] Companies can use global team-based pay to encourage teamwork, and individual-based pay to stimulate individual accountability and decrease social loafing. However, such a solution raises another question. What is the best combination of individual- and team-based rewards? Should companies strive for a fifty-fifty balance or lean more heavily in one direction or the other? And, if the latter, how does one decide the direction of emphasis? There is no easy answer here, but part of the answer lies in at least five distinct areas: the nature of the task, the stability of team membership, the national culture of the team members, the national and local labor laws affecting employee compensation, and reward options.

Nature of the task

By nature of the task, we refer specifically to how *interdependent* the tasks are that the team performs. As defined earlier, task or workflow interdependence is defined as the degree of communication and coordination required between team members to get their jobs done.[7] Low task interdependence might occur in a group of project managers who perform their tasks relatively autonomously in different regions of the world, rarely interacting or exchanging information. High task interdependence would be characteristic of a surgical team or a globally distributed team of software design engineers who constantly exchange information and materials to accomplish tasks. A rule of thumb would be the more interdependent the task, the higher the level of team-based rewards relative to individual-based rewards. This rule of thumb also applies to larger work units (as in the case of unit-based pay), such as departments or divisions.

Membership stability

The stability of team membership is another important factor affecting the proportion of team-based rewards used. If there are frequent composition changes in a global team, it will be difficult to accurately assess the contributions of various members and, in turn, reward based on global team performance. For example, Eastman Chemical (Kodak) abandoned team-based rewards because the company found it impossible to draw indisputable lines around "the team."[8] Managers will likely have to move to a higher level of rewards such as unit-level or organization-level rather than team-based rewards to ensure fair compensation when firm team boundaries cannot be drawn. Perhaps team members themselves can be a part of the design and administration of a rewards and recognition program, especially in countries in which employee participation is commonly used and valued.

National culture of team members

One of the strongest points we can make is that the whole concept of performance management will vary across different countries and cultures. For example, reward and recognition systems are often designed based on Western-oriented notions of goal- and task-oriented conceptualizations of work. These work concepts are unlikely to hold up in Eastern cultures or those cultures in which work is not considered a central life interest.[9] It should come as no surprise that in countries like the United States, Great Britain, and Australia, cultural individualism pervades rewards and recognition programs based on individual performance. The notion of "sharing" rewards or credit for an accomplishment is as foreign a notion in individualistic countries as, say, an "employee of the month" award would be in collectivistic countries like Japan, China, or Malaysia.

Should the managers at Levi Strauss have been surprised at the reaction of their US workers when the company tried to implement team-based rewards? Perhaps hindsight is a luxury here, but not only were Levi's operating in what many consider to be the most individualistic country in the world,[10] they hired workers who assumed they would be working in a piece-rate system. It doesn't take a lot of imagination to guess what type of worker is attracted and selected into this compensation system: individualistic workers who like to work autonomously and be responsible solely for their outcomes. Simply put, a piece-rate system rewards the fastest individual workers. So, not only did Levi's try to implement team-based pay in a highly individualistic country, they tried to implement it in a facility in which they had hired individualistic workers from the most individualist country in the world.[11]

The impact of individualism–collectivism on team and other unit-based reward strategies can also be seen in more collectivist-oriented countries such as China. In China, harmony is seen as a key element in relationships among workers. Maintaining such harmony ensures smoothly running work processes. A research study on human resource management in China showed that few companies in China implement individual-based rewards, as these types of rewards could lead to so-called "red-eye disease" among workers, an expression commonly used in China to refer to jealousy.[12] Jealousy emanating from individual-based pay could constitute a disruption of harmony and, as such, have a negative impact on working relationships and performance.[13] Such interpersonal dynamics in the workplace may undergo some changes in the coming years owing to China's fast paced economic development and increased openness to Western organizations and management styles. However, paying attention to the different meanings and effects that recognition and reward for performance may have in different cultures is important.

Thus, where global teams are concerned, in addition to looking at tasks, managers need to take into account the heterogeneity level or diversity of individualism–collectivism of the team members. That is, if a global team or work unit comprises primarily members from individualist countries such as those in North America, Western Europe, and Australia (all the members are basically the same on the individualism–collectivism dimension), rewards should be based more on individual performance rather than on team or unit performance.[14] Similarly, if a global team or work unit comprises mostly members from collectivist countries such as those in Asia, Latin America, and Africa (again, the members are basically the same on the individualism–collectivism dimension), managers can use a higher proportion of team- or unit-based rewards compared to individual-based rewards. Reinforcing this strategy, there is evidence that supports the link between one's degree of collectivism and a preference for team-based rewards[15] and between individualism and resistance to team-based work systems in general.[16] One could argue, however, that using a large proportion of team-based rewards might again lead to higher levels of social loafing in collectivistic countries. Research does not support this contention, however. In fact, in an experiment designed to compare social loafing between US and Chinese managers, Americans performed less effectively when working in groups compared to working alone.[17] Chinese managers, on the other hand, never demonstrated a social loafing effect and, in fact, performed better in a group than working alone. These results suggest that the lack of a social loafing effect in collectivistic countries provides additional support for using a high proportion of team- or unit-based rewards.

Perhaps the trickiest reward scenario is for a global team that is characterized by a high level of cultural value heterogeneity on the individualism–collectivism dimension. For example, team members comprising a global team from countries such as those in Asia, Europe, Latin America, and North America would likely bring completely different assumptions and beliefs about the appropriateness of team-based rewards. Team leaders should seek the input of heterogeneous teams before designing and implementing a team-based reward system. It is likely that the parameters of such a system will have to be negotiated among team members with such diverse viewpoints on reward appropriateness. The greater the cultural diversity on a global team, the more likely will be the need for team leaders and members to think through the design and implementation of team- or unit-based reward systems. Taking action quickly on these issues may lead to problems.[18]

Labor laws

Local labor laws on compensation issues must be considered when deciding between individual-based and higher-level rewards. For example, Genencor International, the second largest biotechnology company in the world and a joint venture between Eastman Chemical and Finland's Cultor, has operations in Argentina, Belgium, Finland, and the United States (with headquarters in Rochester, New York). In an attempt to streamline their human resource practices worldwide, managers at Genencor wanted to implement team-based pay at all of their facilities. They were not successful in Finland, however, because of local labor laws and active union involvement at the facilities.[19] Finnish labor unions control and regulate salaries by job levels. Managers found that they were required to conform to national and state labor laws and the industry union-based collective bargaining agreements. While some companies, such as General Electric, have been very successful in dealing with unions, especially in Europe, managers should keep in mind that their ability to manipulate compensation to stimulate teamwork and to establish other performance-related pay plans might be constrained by national labor laws.

Reward options

A final key point is the role of recognition as it relates to team performance. Employees often value gestures of recognition more than pure financial rewards. For example, when asked what is important in a job, most US workers ranked a "full appreciation of work done" and a "feeling of being in on things" much higher than good wages.[20] Many managers all over the world often overlook recognition as a relatively inexpensive way in which to reinforce desired team-related behaviors. Guidelines for using recognition should be similar to those for designing reward systems for teams. Richard Daft tells the story of an American executive in Japan who offered a holiday trip to the top salesperson, but employees showed no interest. After changing the individual recognition program to group recognition in accordance with the collectivist values of the Japanese employees, the entire group reached the sales target.[21] Thus, recognizing teams or units when the members have, on the whole, collectivist values and recognizing individuals when the members have individualist values are good rules of thumb.

In summary, when designing and implementing global team-based reward systems, managers should be certain to:

- ◆ use a combination of individual- and team-based rewards to motivate team-related behavior but avoid social loafing (the balance of this combination will vary by culture);
- ◆ use a higher level of team-based (relative to individual-based) rewards the higher the level of task interdependence in a global team;
- ◆ use a higher level of individual-based (relative to team-based) rewards as the instability of global team membership increases;
- ◆ use a higher level of team-based rewards the more collectivistic the global team; use a higher level of individual-based rewards the more individualistic the global team;

and when the heterogeneity level of individualism–collectivism in the team is high, reward systems will be best negotiated among team members with such diverse viewpoints on reward appropriateness;

♦ pay attention to national and state labor laws and the collective bargaining agreements established with industry unions when designing and implementing reward systems for global teams;

♦ take into account the importance of recognition to supplement or complement tangible reward systems for global teams, tailoring recognition to the cultural values of each global team member.

PERFORMANCE EVALUATION AND APPRAISAL IN GLOBAL TEAMS

As with the reward and recognition of global teams and work units, evaluation of individual global team members and teams as a whole has presented many challenges to those who lead global teams. In most organizations, evaluations are often tied to important rewards such as promotions or highly visible assignments. Thus, there is a clear link between performance evaluation and rewards: in order to be able to design effective performance-related pay systems, one must first be able to measure performance. This holds for both global team and individual-based systems. One of the most frequently observed reasons why performance-related pay systems fail to reach the desired results is that the criteria for performance evaluation are unclear or unfair.[22] Key decisions in global team-based performance appraisal include:

♦ On what additional knowledge, skills, and abilities (KSAs) should workers be evaluated when they are working in a global team versus individually?

♦ Who should have input into global team member evaluations (supervisor, peers, customers)?

♦ How can managers ensure the perceived fairness of the performance evaluation process in multicultural global teams?

Appraisals

Taking the knowledge, skills, and abilities decision first, evaluating global team members on team-relevant KSAs is another way to reinforce and motivate teamwork in organizations in addition to monetary rewards and recognition. There is a link between good reward systems and appraisals: timely and appropriate rewards require an appraisal system that ensures performance is measured adequately. As such, appraisal acts as a basis for the reward.

Effective appraisal systems enable the assessment of task performance and monitor whether people are good team players whose behavior is conducive to the effectiveness of the entire team. Effective appraisal systems should both reward good team players and discourage behaviors that are not conducive to global team effectiveness.[23] Each organization is responsible for conducting job analyses to determine the specific KSAs needed for each global team. Beyond task-specific KSAs are the more general, process-oriented ones such as conflict resolution, collaborative problem-solving, communication, decision-making, and team member support. In most studies of team effectiveness, these KSAs have been found to be critical to team success.[24] Such processes vary by culture and country.

US researchers have found that conflict about task-related issues (rather than interpersonal-related issues) enhances team performance, especially the quality of team decision-making.[25] Thus, for teams composed predominantly of US and other Western members, managers would be encouraged to stimulate and encourage this type of conflict to increase team performance. There are cultural differences, however, that might make this advice problematic for non-Western global team members. For example, the concept of "face-saving" is related to group harmony and conversational indirectness. In Eastern cultures such as China, Japan, and the Philippines, the loss of face, or public humiliation, can result from receiving negative feedback.[26] Thus, while team members in the United States might openly confront one another in meetings and question the rationale behind decisions in order to enhance decision-making, such behaviors in cultures that value face might be cause for extreme shame, ending in retaliation or possibly physical violence such as the Indonesian ship-worker who chased his boss into his quarters with an axe after being publicly berated in front of other crew members.[27]

Evaluation input

Another key decision in global team-based performance appraisals is who should have input into the evaluation process. Accompanying the increase in the use of 360-degree feedback, or getting evaluation input from one's boss, peers, and subordinates, in the United States has been the use of peer evaluations in teams.[28] The logic for their use is, who can better assess the performance of team members than the people who work with each other on a daily basis?

Rather than relying solely on just one source of feedback for team member evaluations, many companies integrate multiple sources similar to a 360-feedback program. Nancy Kurland and Diane Bailey, researchers who study telecommuting, or workers who do their jobs from remote locations and communicate electronically, stated:

> A major challenge for [global team] managers is their inability to physically observe their employees' performance. They question, "How do you measure productivity, build trust, and manage people who are physically out of sight?" If a manager can't see her subordinates in action, then she can't note where the employee is struggling and where he is strong . . . monitoring and measuring [employee] performance remain problematic and a source of concern.[29]

Clearly, assessing the performance of global team members who are geographically dispersed is a challenge. One company on the cutting edge of global virtual team performance evaluation and assessment is Sabre, Inc., the Dallas/Fort Worth, Texas-based travel reservation company.[30] Sabre provides computer reservation systems for American Airlines, United Airlines, and over 60,000 travel agents in 114 countries. Sabre is also a majority owner of Travelocity.com, the on-line reservation service, and uses global virtual teams in part of its North American (Canadian and US) operations. Sabre has built a comprehensive performance review system, which uses actual customer satisfaction ratings as part of an overall "balanced scorecard"[31] measure, or a measure that includes both financial and non-financial performance indicators, of global team effectiveness. Managers assess individual contributions to team effectiveness by monitoring electronic communications and by systematically collecting data from peers and direct reports using the 360-degree format. Performance data provide a solid foundation for recognizing and rewarding team and individual performance, developing new training programs to assist virtual teams, and identifying individual team members who could benefit from off-line mentoring and coaching. As one manager at Sabre stated, "Most everyone's work is measured in the results they produce and through statistics, and it can all be pulled out systematically for each individual."[32] For global teams at Sabre, US and Canadian team members can be judged more on what they actually do rather than on what they appear to be doing.

Assessment across cultures

Cultural values that would be likely to affect how global team members in different countries give each other feedback are the individualism–collectivism, power distance, and uncertainty avoidance dimensions and the concepts of harmony, assertiveness, and face. Research has shown that collectivists give more generous evaluations to fellow team members than do individualists, and this is especially true if the team member is an in-group rather than an out-group member.[33] In-group members are similar others such as family and close friends while out-group members lie outside these preferred groups. Thus, fair and unbiased peer evaluations may be more difficult to obtain when collectivistic global team members have to rate members of their in-group, especially in face-to-face, rather than virtual teams in which the pressures for conformity may be higher.

Power distance is the second cultural value likely to affect peer evaluations in global teams. Power distance refers to the extent to which power differences and status inequalities in a society are tolerated. In high power-distance countries such as China, Mexico, and the Philippines, subordinates are typically more reluctant to challenge their supervisors than are employees in low power-distance countries such as Finland, Israel, and the United States. In line with this, employees in high power-distance cultures were shown to be more fearful in expressing disagreement with their managers.[34] If global teams are composed of members of different status levels, and lower-status team members are asked to evaluate the performance of higher-status members, evaluations are likely to be positively skewed, especially for face-to-face teams. People in high power-distance cultures are likely to be reluctant to provide negative feedback to superiors, and the acceptability of the idea that subordinates would be allowed to provide such ratings is likely to be less in high power-distance cultures, as this may be perceived to threaten status positions.

Uncertainty avoidance refers to cultures in which members shun ambiguity.[35] People in such cultures want things to be predictable and easy to interpret; and rituals such as elaborate planning and control systems are put into place to ensure this. The concept of lifelong employment in Japan is a good example of how organizations can reduce uncertainty. Looking at performance appraisal, one would expect a much higher degree of formalization in high uncertainty avoidance cultures. The performance appraisal system is likely to be spelled out in more detail, and there are more regulations and procedures in place, ensuring that complaints or grievances are handled through a predesigned structure. For example, German culture ranks high on uncertainty avoidance and research has shown that German employees typically prefer formalized performance evaluations such as clear goals, time frames, and exact measurements.[36]

The emphasis on maintaining harmony found in several Eastern cultures may lead to skewed peer and subordinate ratings in a positive direction, since global team members would be reluctant to jeopardize their relationships with fellow members. Similarly, team members from cultures that are typically highly assertive, aggressive, and dominant in social relationships are more likely to provide negative feedback than those in less assertive cultures.[37] People in highly assertive cultures such as the United States prefer direct feedback and communication and have a "tell it like it is" mentality. For example, at General Electric, all employees are ranked from the top to the bottom of the organization. The bottom 10 percent may be given either an opportunity to improve, or outplacement services. Former CEO Jack Welch argues that such a system is appropriate because softening feedback for under-performing workers is unfair to them and akin to outright lying because it might prevent them from finding opportunities that are more suitable. In contrast, in many Asian cultures the subtleties of conversational indirectness are preferred.[38] We do not want to give the impression that directness is the one best way to provide feedback in order to enhance performance in global teams. The real issue here is maintaining harmony and how that may affect peer and subordinate ratings in global teams. Directness may not be as appropriate in Eastern cultures, but subtle approaches may be just as effective because the elaborate networks that exist in these cultures will ensure that everyone will already know relevant performance feedback.

Similar to the effect it has on open conflict, saving face will likely prevent open discussion of individual global team member performance by fellow members, especially in face-to-face teams. However, this does not mean that peer feedback cannot be used on teams that have members that value saving face. At Motorola in the Philippines, for example, issues regarding team performance are raised in more general form in team meetings.[39] No one is singled out personally, but often this is enough to motivate the under-performing team members to step up their efforts. When performance appraisal data must be collected from global team members, it can be collected anonymously and presented in summary form to mask authorship. Such a strategy has worked very effectively for Motorola's teams in the Philippines and in other countries that value face-saving.

Fairness across cultures

The third and final issue for performance evaluation and appraisal in global teams is ensuring perceptions of fairness or justice in the performance appraisal process. In Western management thought, justice in organizations has generally been conceived of as having three dimensions:

◆ *Distributive justice* – the perceived fairness of the distribution of outcomes. This type of justice emanated from equity theory.[40]
◆ *Procedural justice* – the perceived fairness of the criteria used to make decisions regarding the distribution of outcomes, including voice, or the opportunity for the employee to have a say in decisions.[41]

◆ *Interactional justice* – the perceived fairness of how decisions are communicated, including adequate explanations and consideration of employee welfare by managers.[42]

While the perceived fairness of evaluation procedures has received considerable attention in dyadic manager–employee settings,[43] there has been considerably less attention paid to the perceived fairness of *team-based* evaluation settings.[44] One recent study did examine general employee justice concerns during an implementation of self-managing work teams in two US Fortune 50 organizations.[45] Many employee concerns centered on issues of the fairness of team-based performance appraisals. Open-ended comments from the study included: "Will peer reviews be fair and objective?"; "Who will fairly judge my contribution to the business?"; and "I hate peer ratings because it is a personality contest and not a question of merit." Clearly, employees in the United States were very concerned about the fairness of team-based performance appraisals. In addition, these employees expressed the desire to have voice in the performance appraisal process. This finding was echoed at the dyadic level by Jerald Greenberg who found that US employee perceptions of procedural justice in the appraisal decision were based on, among other elements, the ability to rebut or challenge a supervisor's appraisal.[46]

Owing to cultural differences, there are reasons to believe that global team members may have different mental models regarding what constitutes a fair team-based performance appraisal. In other cultural contexts, employees may not conceive of distributive, procedural, and interactional justice in the same manner.[47] For example, while Western conceptualizations of procedural justice include the ability to challenge or rebut decisions, research has shown that in China, procedural justice does not include this component.[48]

The most likely explanation for this difference is the cultural value of power distance.[49] While power distance was originally conceived of as a country- or nation-level phenomenon,[50] like many of the other cultural values, researchers have adopted this dimension to explain variations in individual behavior. For example, Joel Brockner and his colleagues found that when employees did not have a say in managerial decisions, they were less committed to their organizations. However, this effect was much more pronounced in lower power-distance cultures such as the United States and Germany than in high power-distance cultures, such as China, Mexico, and Hong Kong.[51] It has also been shown that the relationships between procedural justice and trust in supervisors and between distributive justice and psychological (implied) contract fulfillment were stronger for those lower, rather than higher, in power distance.[52] Simon Lam and his colleagues found similar results with justice–work outcome relationships with the effects of fairness stronger for those lower, rather than higher, in power distance.[53]

These findings suggest that managers should pay attention to cultural value differences, especially power distance, when designing and implementing global team-based performance appraisal systems if team members are to perceive them as fair. This is important because a number of studies have shown that employees who perceive managerial decisions as unjust will react unfavorably.[54] Unfortunately, at times there may be very little managers can do to ensure fairness in employee work assignments in global teams. For example, at ItemField, a New York-based business-to-business software developer, new-hire Israeli team members located in Israel (who typically do not work on Fridays) were told that they had to be on call on Fridays to support the US sales force.[55] Even though Israeli employees were alerted in advance, business demands limited the actions that US managers took to enhance fairness perceptions among their Israeli global team members.

There is also evidence that the performance evaluation process may be fairer (less biased) in globally distributed teams versus face-to-face teams. Differences in such demographic factors as race, gender, and age can lower performance ratings for employees who differ in these aspects from their bosses[56] and for team members that are different from team leaders.[57] However, when team leaders do not see team members on a daily basis, the opportunities for bias to enter the performance appraisal process may be fewer. In addition, contamination of evaluations by perceptual biases is less likely when team leaders have extensive objective data at their disposal.[58]

When designing and implementing global team-based performance evaluation and appraisal systems, managers should be certain to:

- reward good team players but also discourage behaviors that are not conducive to global team effectiveness;
- in addition to determining task-specific KSAs, include evaluations of global team processes such as conflict resolution, collaborative problem-solving, communication, decision-making, and team member support;
- use multidimensional, balanced performance evaluation systems that include a mixture of objective and subjective ratings such as 360-degree feedback and altering peer feedback systems based on cultural differences, along with technology-based measures to document global team member achievements such as e-mail and electronic team meeting archives; customer surveys and team member input;
- enhance the fairness of global team peer evaluations by: (1) attempting to broaden team member in-groups by stressing value similarity among members; (2) standardizing the appraisal system by training peer raters and using job-relevant rating scales; (3) enhancing the fairness of peer evaluations by informing employees of when and how ratings will be collected; (4) rewarding team members on their ability and willingness to provide accurate ratings that differentiate between low and high performers; and (5) assessing team members on the individualism–collectivism dimension in order to anticipate potential bias in peer ratings.[59]

TRAINING AND DEVELOPMENT IN GLOBAL TEAMS

One of the most important facets of effective global team implementation is the effective use of team training and development. Working in global teams can be a very foreign concept to many employees, and if managers decide that teams are appropriate, they need guidance in order to effectively shape appropriate global team behaviors. One facet that is often missing from global team training is the inclusion of the whole team in hands-on capability development.[60] Global teams should be treated as a whole unit and training should be applied as the team performs actual job-related tasks.[61] As a result, the value of the training is established in the context of the work that the team does. Key questions to consider with regard to training and development include:

- What are the best methods for training and development in global team-based organizations?

- ◆ What should global team members be trained to do?
- ◆ How can training be leveraged to increase the amount of global team learning and flexibility?

Best methods

Regarding methods or techniques for global team training and development, there are at least three general techniques used by training specialists to enhance team member abilities. First, there is the cognitive style, which normally involves traditional classroom instruction in which a trainer covers basic principles of team operation such as forming a team charter, setting ground rules for teams, or managing conflict. Second, there is the behavioral style, or experiential learning, which can involve immersing team members in situations similar to those they are likely to face in their actual jobs. Such simulations might include performing a complex task in a limited amount of time, purposefully engaging in conflict over a valued resource, or role-playing a key event in a team's life cycle. Finally, there is the affective style, which typically involves some level of emotional involvement on the part of team members. This may take the form of heart-to-heart talks between team members such as intimate self-disclosure, or intense personal feedback between global team members guided by experienced facilitators.

With at least three possible methods of training and development, the question still remains: What is the best method to use? The answer is, not surprisingly, all three. Since human beings differ in the manner in which they learn most effectively, that is, some are classroom learners, some have to experience it before they understand, and still others need to be moved emotionally to internalize key learnings, most training and development specialists advocate a combination of these three techniques to enhance the transfer of training for all global team members.

As stated, people differ in the way they learn most effectively. An individual's learning strategy can be seen as a predisposition to use certain types of learning behavior.[62] For example, one can distinguish between *surface* (instruction-oriented) and *deep* (meaning-oriented) learning strategies, the latter fostering managers' career success.[63] The different ways in which people learn reflect different existing modes of thought or cognitive styles. The most widely recognized distinction in this area is between *analytical*, that is, logical, sequential information processing, and *intuitive*, in other words, more integrative and nonlinear thinking styles.[64] There are also cross-cultural differences to be considered in the way people think and prefer to learn; however, the evidence regarding cross-cultural differences in these cognitive styles is somewhat mixed. Whereas some propose a contrast between the "analytic West" and the "intuitive East," many studies find different patterns. In a six-nation study among managers from organizations in both the public and private sectors and management students, the most integrative and nonlinear thinking was seen among managers from the most developed countries (UK, Australia, Hong Kong, Singapore), whereas an emphasis on logical and sequential thinking was seen in the developing and Arab countries (Jordan, Nepal).[65] The explanation for the differences may lie in the increasing complexity of management problems in many organizations in highly developed countries. Such high complexity may call for integrative, nonlinear thinking.

What about cross-cultural differences in learning preferences? According to Hofstede, people in uncertainty avoidant cultures have been programmed from childhood to feel comfortable in structured environments.[66] Such differences in the need for structure are also reflected in the learning environment. In cultures high on uncertainty avoidance (Germany) one thus often finds structured learning situations with precise objectives, detailed arrangements, and strict timetables. People prefer tasks with a correct answer that they can find and like to be rewarded for accuracy. On the other hand, those from cultures low on uncertainty avoidance (UK) are more likely to prefer less structure. They prefer open-ended questions, vague objectives and no timetables. They do not believe that there should be a single correct answer and expect to be rewarded for originality.[67] Similar patterns may be expected in a training situation, where people from cultures high on uncertainty avoidance are likely to prefer much more structured processes and assignments compared with people from cultures low on uncertainty avoidance.

Another cultural dimension to consider is power distance. In cultures high on power distance, the role and status of the teacher or trainer are likely to be different from such a role in cultures low on power distance. In cultures high on power distance, the teacher–student relationship is essentially an unequal relationship, in which the more powerful party (teacher) is treated with respect and hardly ever openly receives uninvited criticism from the less powerful party (students). The process is likely to be teacher-centered, with the teacher initiating conversation and deciding on what is to be taught. In contrast, in cultures low on power distance, teachers and students have a more equal relationship. The process is more student-centered; students take more initiative and decide on and pursue what they want to learn. Open communication, questioning teachers, and arguing their opinion is the rule rather than the exception.[68] Again, similar patterns may be expected in a training situation.

Training content

Beyond the methods and techniques used for training and the learning styles of trainees, the second key issue is the actual content of the training for team members. As discussed in our section on evaluation (performance appraisal), team-relevant knowledge, skills, and abilities (KSAs) must be identified by each organization for each job, so that global team members will know and can be trained for the most job-relevant KSAs. Also relevant are interpersonal processes such as communication, decision-making, and conflict resolution, all critical for global team success. In addition to KSAs and global team processes, development of self-management skills among global team members is important. Since the purpose of many global teams is to be proactive and take on the many responsibilities traditionally reserved for management, starting team members down the path of self-management to increase global team effectiveness is critically important.

The main question then becomes: How much autonomy is appropriate for most global teams? There are several contingency factors that are crucial to consider here. First is the type of global team. Research has shown that autonomy is highly effective for line-level work teams but can have detrimental effects on cross-functional project teams that have a high level of complexity and rich information-processing requirements.[69] In these types of teams, strong leadership is needed to help team members manage complexity.

Second, there is the level of task interdependence, defined earlier in this chapter as the degree of coordination and communication needed between members to perform a task. Granting teams high autonomy when tasks are interdependent results in higher levels of team effectiveness; in contrast, for tasks low in interdependence, giving autonomy to a team can actually result in lower team effectiveness.[70]

Third, there are several cultural values that are likely to affect initial acceptance of training on self-management. Global team members from high power-distance countries such as Mexico, China, and the Philippines may have difficulty engaging in self-management-related activities such as setting their own goals or taking initiative without asking for supervisory permission. Also, management in such countries may be less likely to allow the global team members a high level of autonomy. As discussed in Part I, a being orientation refers to the extent to which people in a society focus on non-work activities. People in high being-oriented societies work only as much as they need in order to live and would likely resist taking on the additional responsibilities associated with a high degree of self-management. Also as discussed in Part 1, determinism refers to the extent to which people in a society believe that their outcomes are determined by forces outside of their control such as luck, fate, or a deity. Because self-management requires that employees set their own goals and take actions to bring them closer to achieving their goals, employees high in determinism would likely resist self-management in teams.[71]

Recent research has supported a link between these cultural values and employee resistance to self-management in teams in different countries.[72] So, does this mean that managers should not try to train employees on self-management in countries that are high in power distance, being orientation, and/or determinism? The answer is not so much whether employees are trained on self-management or not but *how* such training occurs and gets carried out.[73] For example, employees in high power-distance countries are likely to need more reinforcement that organizational authorities support their taking on more self-management in their global teams. Perhaps having high-level keynote speakers during training sessions would encourage high power-distance employees to internalize the self-management training. Training modules could be designed around more routine tasks that would become self-managing, rather than higher-level tasks such as hiring and firing fellow team members or initiating management-level decisions. Self-management training and development need to be adapted to fit the cultural values of team members in different countries.[74]

Leveraging global team training

A final key issue for training and development involves leveraging global team training and development for maximum team learning and flexibility. In a true team-based organization, learning is required across functions, levels, and even organizations.[75] Such learning requires norms that are very different to those present in traditional organizations. For example, true team learning requires that organizations encourage team members to surface bad news and act on it.[76] However, if the organizational *status quo* maintains the typical reaction of negatively evaluating the messenger of bad news, organizational learning will not take place. Only organizations that encourage experimentation and innovation and set up mechanisms for shared team reflection, or what Amy Edmondson calls a climate of psychological safety,[77] will be likely to be able to successfully capitalize on this learning.[78]

In this respect, differences among people as they deal with errors are of interest. In organizational life, errors are unavoidable. Even with the best checks and procedures, there is almost always some margin for error. Focusing too much on error prevention, through bureaucratic procedures and checks, and having a negative approach to errors, by punishment of those responsible, may lead global team members to low levels of risk-taking and exploration.[79] In such circumstances, people may cover up errors or blame others rather than take responsibility for their errors and share their experiences so others can learn from them. In describing his role in the Barings Bank disaster in 1993, for instance, Nick Leeson noted that a major reason he started an unauthorized shadow account was that he was afraid to admit errors.[80] Leeson found a way to hide errors and their negative consequences and make up for them without having to admit to them. Barings had a very punishing culture, quickly firing those that made mistakes or were not successful enough, which apparently reinforced covering up mistakes.[81]

As Peter Senge notes, a learning organization needs to have a positive attitude toward exploration and errors.[82] Thus, an important management issue becomes "the design and nurture of work environments in which it is possible to learn from mistakes and to collectively avoid making the same ones in the future."[83] In order to be able to learn from errors, it is necessary to use active rather than passive approaches.[84] Thus, a strategy that ensures negative consequences of errors such as loss of time, accidents, and faulty products are minimized (a control goal) and at the same time fosters the potential positive side of errors (learning, innovation, resilience – a learning goal), seems optimal.[85] Error orientations are shared within teams and even organizations. The above example of the punishing culture at Barings that resulted in Leeson's trying to cover up errors illustrates the reinforcement outcomes of covering up errors. In a Dutch study, error aversion (feeling strained by and covering up errors) was negatively related to team performance; and a mastery orientation (taking on the challenges of error occurrences) was positively related to organizational performance.[86] A link between dealing with errors and uncertainty avoidance seems likely.[87] Cultures high on uncertainty avoidance are likely to be low on risk-taking and probably have a more negative view of errors. In line with this, these cultures may then be high on error strain and covering up errors and low on learning from them.[88] The concept of saving face is critical for how global team members handle the discussion of errors. If team members are concerned about admitting mistakes to avoid humiliation, this could severely hamper global team learning. On the other hand, if the global team members knew how to decode and design for this dynamic, conceivably they might understand what was going on, take appropriate actions, save face, and promote team learning.

As stated above, to reflect on one's actions and surroundings is crucial to organizational learning. For example, reflection can be important for recognizing how certain present ways of operating can be obsolete, owing to environmental changes.[89] Teams often use "habitual routines" to guide team behavior. Habitual routines exist when groups repeatedly exhibit a functionally similar pattern of behavior in similar situations without explicitly selecting this pattern over alternative ways of behaving.[90] Although having some "ground rules" on what to do in certain circumstances seems helpful to smooth interactions and effective functioning, groups tend to stick to the patterns of interactions that are set early in their life, even when circumstances have changed and these patterns are no longer adequate. Reflexive behavior in teams seems important to counteract the tendency to rely on routines that may be no longer effective.

At the team level, reflexivity is defined as the extent to which group members overtly reflect on and communicate about the group's objectives, strategies (decision-making), and processes (communication), and adapt these to current or anticipated circumstances.[91] Differences between people in reflexivity are also important. As was seen above, teams need to reflect on errors, but also analyze their success, think about whether current group composition is adequate to meet objectives, talk about their use of time and resources, and decide how to deal with changes in the environment.[92] Besides reflecting on such issues, teams also need to engage in action planning to ensure that envisioned changes are acted upon. Reflexivity can thus be seen as an iterative three-stage process of reflection, planning, and taking action. Reflexivity is especially important for the effective functioning of teams involved in complex decision-making. Such teams have high autonomy and work in highly uncertain and unpredictable environments.[93] Research has found reflexivity to be positively related to subjective as well as objective measures of team performance in the UK as well as in the Netherlands.[94]

A trusting and open team climate and non-authoritarian leadership styles are conducive to reflexivity in teams. However, only few teams actually take the time to reflect on their strategies and actions on a regular basis.[95] Given the fact that in many organizations global teams are increasingly autonomous and need to make increasingly complex decisions, more attention to the creation of work environments that are conducive to reflexivity and learning seems relevant to help improve global team functioning.[96] For example, the US, Brazilian, and Italian team members on Whirlpool Corporation's North American Appliance Group developed a chlorofluorocarbon-free refrigerator using a global team. To enhance team learning, the team met face to face every four months to discuss the project and the ground rules necessary to stimulate creative, out-of-bounds thinking. A key to the project's success was the informal social gathering that took place allowing team members to build relationships and develop a climate for freedom of expression.[97] Similarly, Mobil Corporation has its global team members huddle in one location at the launch of a new product so the members can build the relationships necessary for true learning to take place.[98] Beyond anecdotal evidence, to date levels of team reflexivity have not been thoroughly compared across different cultures. However, reflexivity seems most likely to occur in cultures that are relatively low on power distance. In high power-distance cultures, team members are less likely to speak up or disagree with team leaders or other higher-status members. This may hamper reflexivity and global team learning in general.

The planning aspect of reflexivity is likely to be linked to uncertainty avoidance. For example, Rauch and colleagues compared German and Irish small enterprises.[99] Germany and Ireland are similar on all but one of Hofstede's culture dimensions. Whereas the German culture is high on uncertainty avoidance, Ireland ranks as one of Europe's lowest on uncertainty avoidance. Thus, Germany has a culture in which one would expect business owners to plan more and in greater detail. Customers will expect such planning and doing things "right," and meeting customer expectations in such an environment should be linked to careful and detailed planning. In contrast, in Ireland planning is seen as less necessary. Customers will have less respect for plans, show unplanned behavior themselves, and expect high flexibility. Planning too much will render small business owners inflexible. Thus, Rauch and colleagues expected and found that planning had a positive influence on small business success in Germany and a negative influence on small business success in Ireland. The cultural appropriateness of planning will influence its success.

Training and development systems aimed to maximize global team learning and success need to take cultural values such as those ensuing from power distance and uncertainty avoidance into account. Culture differences will lead to different expectations of the role of the trainer or teacher, differences in the likelihood of people "speaking up" during the learning process, different preferences in structure and planning approaches, and different approaches to errors – all variables that may play a role in designing effective learning environments for global teams. When designing and implementing global team-based training and development systems, managers should be certain to:

♦ use a combination of training techniques to enhance the transfer of training for all the members of a global team (cognitive, behavioral, and affective styles);
♦ use structured learning situations with precise objectives, detailed arrangements, and strict timetables for team members high in uncertainty avoidance cultural contexts; and open-ended questions, vague objectives, and few timetables for team members low in uncertainty avoidance contexts; use teacher-centered training for team members in cultures high in power distance and student-centered training for team members with cultures low in power distance;
♦ train global team members to be self-managing when appropriate (as with work teams versus project teams, highly interdependent versus highly independent teams that have relatively low levels of power distance, being orientation, and determinism);
♦ leverage global team training and development for maximum team learning and flexibility (increase global team psychological safety, avoid a focus on error prevention, and increase team reflexivity).

CONCLUSION

We have discussed global team performance management in the areas of rewards and recognition, performance evaluation and appraisal, and training and development. In each of these areas, we have seen how the cultural values of those belonging to global teams had important implications for the design and administration of global team performance management. Clearly, there is not one ideal way to manage global team performance or the performance of other work units such as departments or divisions. Implementing a best practice without regard for culture would likely result in a high level of employee resistance to such initiatives.[100] To increase the chances for effective global teams and work units, managers should take into account the complexity of the cultural differences represented on the team. Only then will organizations be able to realize the true global team effectiveness.

NOTES

1 Handy, C. (1995), Trust and the virtual organization, *Harvard Business Review*, 73, 40–48.
2 Latane, B., Williams, K. D., & Harkins, S. (1979), Many hands make light the work: The causes and consequences of social loafing, *Journal of Personality and Social Psychology*, 37, 822–832.
3 Moede, W. (1927), Die richtlinien der leistungs-psychologie, *Industrielle Psychotechnik*, 4, 193–207; Ringelmann, M. (1913), *Aménagement des fumeriers et des purins*, Paris: Librarie agricole de la Maison rustique.

4 Thompson, L. (2000), *Making the Team: A Guide for Managers*, Upper Saddle River, NJ: Prentice-Hall.

5 King, R. T., Jr. (1998), Jeans therapy: Levi's factory workers are assigned to teams, and morale takes a hit, *Wall Street Journal*, 232, A1, A6.

6 Wageman, R. (1995), Interdependence and group effectiveness, *Administrative Science Quarterly*, 40, 145–180.

7 Shea, G. P., & Guzzo, R. A. (1987), Groups as human resources, in G. Ferris & K. Rowland (eds.), *Research in Personnel and Human Resources* Management, Greenwich, CT: JAI Press, Vol. 5, pp. 323–356.

8 Lipnack, J., & Stamps, J. (2000), *Virtual Teams: People Working across Boundaries with Technology*, 2nd edn., New York: Wiley.

9 Trompenaars, F. (1993), *Riding the Waves of Culture: Understanding Diversity in Global Business*, Chicago: Irwin.

10 Hofstede, G. (1980), *Culture's Consequences: International Differences in Work-Related Values*, Beverly Hills, CA: Sage.

11 *Ibid.*; Au, K. Y. (1999), Intra-cultural variation: Evidence and implications for international business, *Journal of International Business Studies*, 30, 799–812.

12 Verburg, R. M. (1996), Developing HRM in foreign-Chinese joint ventures, *European Management Journal*, 14(5), 518–525.

13 Verburg, R. M., Drenth, P. J. D., Koopman, P. L., Van Muijen, J. J., & Wang, Z. M. (1999), Managing human resources across cultures: A comparative analysis of practices in entrepreneurial organizations in China and the Netherlands, *International Journal of Human Resource Management*, 10(3), 391–410.

14 Kirkman, B. L., Gibson, C. B., & Shapiro, D. L. (2001), "Exporting" teams: Enhancing the implementation and effectiveness of work teams in global affiliates, *Organizational Dynamics*, 30(1), 12–29.

15 Cable, D. M., & Judge, T. A. (1994), Pay preferences and job search decisions: A person–environment fit perspective, *Personnel Psychology*, 47, 317–348; Kirkman, B. L., & Shapiro, D. L. (2000), Understanding why team members won't share: An examination of factors related to employee receptivity to team-based rewards, *Small Group Research*, 31, 175–209.

16 Kirkman, B. L., & Shapiro, D. L. (2001a), The impact of employee cultural values on productivity, cooperation, and empowerment in self-managing work teams, *Journal of Cross-Cultural Psychology*, 32(5), 597–617; Kirkman, B. L., & Shapiro, D. L. (2001b), The impact of cultural values on job satisfaction and organizational commitment in self-managing work teams: The mediating role of employee resistance, *Academy of Management Journal*, 44(3), 557–569.

17 Earley, P. C. (1989), Social loafing and collectivism: A comparison of the United States and the People's Republic of China, *Administrative Science Quarterly*, 34, 565–581.

18 Maznevski, M. L., & Chudoba, K. M. (2001), Bridging space over time: Global virtual team dynamics and effectiveness, *Organization Science*, 11(5), 473–492.

19 Kirkman et al. (2001).

20 Kovach, K. A. (1987), What motivates employees? Workers and supervisors give different answers, *Business Horizons*, 30, 61.

21 Daft, R. L. (1987), *Management*, Chicago: Dryden Press.

22 Richardson, R. (2001), Performance-related pay: Another management fad?, *Inaugural Addresses Series in Research in Management*, EIA-2001-01-ORG, Rotterdam: Erasmus Research Institute of Management, Erasmus University.

23 Gibson, C. B., & Kirkman, B. L. (1999), Our past, present, and future in teams: The role of human resources professionals in managing team performance, in A. I. Kraut & A. K. Korman (eds.), *Evolving Practices in Human Resources Management: Responses to a Changing World of Work*, San Francisco: Jossey-Bass, pp. 90–117.

24 Campion, M. A., Medsker, G. J., & Higgs, A. C. (1993), Relations between work group characteristics and effectiveness: Implications for designing effective work groups, *Personnel Psychology*, 46, 823–850; Campion, M. A., Papper, E. M., & Medsker, G. J. (1996), Relations between work group characteristics and effectiveness: A replication and extension, *Personnel Psychology*, 49, 429–452; Hyatt, D. E., & Ruddy, T. M. (1997), An examination of the relationship between work group characteristics and performance: Once more into the breech, *Personnel Psychology*, 50, 553–585.

25 Pelled, L. H., Eisenhardt, K. M., & Xin, K. R. (1999), Exploring the black box: An analysis of work group diversity, conflict, and performance, *Administrative Science Quarterly*, 44, 1–28.

26 Earley, P. C. (1997), *Face, Harmony, and Social Structure: An Analysis of Organizational Behavior across Cultures*, New York: Oxford University Press.

27 Daft (1987).

28 Saavedra, R., & Kwun, S. K. (1993), Peer evaluation in self-managing work groups, *Journal of Applied Psychology*, 78, 450–462.

29 Kurland, N. B., & Bailey, D. E. (1999), Telework: The advantages and challenges of working here, there, anywhere, and anytime, *Organizational Dynamics*, 28(2), 53–67.

30 Kirkman, B. L., Rosen, B., Gibson, C. B., Tesluk, P. E., & McPherson, S. O. (2003), Five challenges to virtual team performance: Lessons from Sabre, Inc., *Academy of Management Executive*, 16(3), 67–79.

31 Kaplan, R. S., & Norton, D. P. (1996), Using the balanced scorecard as a strategic management system, *Harvard Business Review*, 74, 75–85.

32 *Ibid.*

33 Gomez, C. B., Kirkman, B. L., & Shapiro, D. L. (2000), The impact of collectivism and ingroup/outgroup membership on the evaluation generosity of team members, *Academy of Management Journal*, 43(6), 1097–1106.

34 Adsit, D. J., London, M., Crom, S., & Jones, D (1997), Cross-cultural differences in upward ratings in a multinational company, *International Journal of Human Resource Management*, 8(4), 385–401.

35 Hofstede (1980); Hofstede, G. (2001), *Culture's Consequences: Comparing Values, Behaviors, Institutions, and Organizations across Nations*, Thousand Oaks, CA: Sage.

36 Lindholm, N. (1999), National culture and performance management in MNC subsidiaries, *International Studies of Management & Organization*, 29(4), 45–66.

37 Den Hartog, D. N. (2003), Assertiveness, in R. J. House, P. J. Hanges, M. Javidan, P. W. Dorfman, V. Gupta, & GLOBE Associates (eds.), *Cultures, Leadership, and Organizations: A 62 Nation GLOBE Study*, Thousand Oaks, CA: Sage, vol. 1.

38 *Ibid.*; Holtgraves, T. (1997), Styles of language use: Individual and cultural variability in conversational indirectness, *Journal of Personality and Social Psychology*, 73, 624–637.

39 Kirkman et al. (2001).

40 Adams, J. S. (1965), Inequity in social exchange, in L. Berkowitz (ed.), *Advances in Experimental Social Psychology*. New York: Academic Press, vol. 2, pp. 267–299.

41 Lind, E. A., & Tyler, T. R. (1988), *The Social Psychology of Procedural Justice*, New York: Plenum.

42 Bies, R. J., & Moag, J. S. (1986), Interactional justice: Communication criteria of fairness, in R. Lewicki, M. Bazerman, & B. Sheppard (eds.), *Research on Negotiation in Organizations*, Greenwich, CT: JAI Press, vol. 1, pp. 43–55.

43 Cropanzano, R., & Greenberg, J. (1997), Progress in organizational justice: Tunneling through the maze, in C. L. Cooper & I. T. Robertson (eds.), *International Review of Industrial and Organizational Psychology*, New York: John Wiley, vol. 2, pp. 317–372; Greenberg, J. (1986), Determinants of perceived fairness of performance evaluations, *Journal of Applied Psychology*, 71(2), 340–342; Greenberg, J. (1990), Organizational justice: Yesterday, today, and tomorrow, *Journal of Management*, 16, 399–432; Korsgaard, M. A., & Roberson, L. (1995), Procedural justice in perform-

ance evaluation: The role of instrumental and non-instrumental voice in performance appraisal discussions, *Journal of Management*, 21, 657–669.

44 Colquitt, J. A., Noe, R. A., & Jackson, C. L. (2002), Justice in teams: Antecedents and consequences of procedural justice climate, *Personnel Psychology*, 55(1), 83–109.

45 Kirkman, B. L., Shapiro, D. L., Novelli, L., Jr., & Brett, J. M. (1996), Employee concerns regarding self-managing work teams: A multidimensional justice perspective. *Social Justice Research*, 9(1), 47–67.

46 Greenberg (1986).

47 Lind, E. A., & Earley, P. C. (1992), Procedural justice and culture, *International Journal of Psychology*, 27(2), 227–242; Greenberg, J. A. (2001), Studying organizational justice cross-culturally: Fundamental challenges, *International Journal of Conflict Management*, 12(4), 365–375.

48 Kirkman, B. L., Lowe, K. B., & Peng, D. (2000), The role of procedural justice, perceived organizational support, and individualism-collectivism in motivating organizational citizenship behavior of employees in the People's Republic of China, paper presented at the annual meeting of the Academy of Management, Toronto, Canada, August.

49 Pillai, R., Scandura, T. A., & Williams, E. A. (1999), Leadership and organizational justice: Similarities and differences across cultures, *Journal of International Business Studies*, 30(4), 763–779.

50 Hofstede (1980).

51 Brockner, J., Ackerman, G., Greenberg, J., Gelfand, M. J., Francesco, A. M., Chen, Z. X., Leung, K., Bierbrauer, G., Gómez, C., Kirkman, B. L., & Shapiro, D. L. (2001), Culture and procedural justice: The moderating influence of power distance on reactions to voice, *Journal of Experimental Social Psychology*, 37(4), 300–315.

52 Lee, C., Pillutla, M., & Law, K. S. (2000), Power-distance, gender, and organizational justice, *Journal of Management*, 26, 685–704.

53 Lam, S. S. K., Schaubroeck, J., & Aryee, S. (2002), Relationship between organizational justice and employee work outcomes: A cross-national study, *Journal of Organizational Behavior*, 23, 1–18.

54 Cropanzano & Greenberg (1997).

55 Alexander, S. (2000), Virtual teams going global,. *Infoworld*, 22(46), 55–56.

56 See, e.g., Kraiger, K., & Ford, J. K. (1985), A meta-analysis of rater race effects in performance ratings, *Journal of Applied Psychology*, 70(1), 56–65. See also Pulakos, E. D., Oppler, S. H., White, L. A., & Borman, W. C. (1989), Examination of race and sex effects on performance ratings, *Journal of Applied Psychology*, 74(5), 70–78.

57 Baugh, S. G., & Graen, G. B. (1997), Effects of team gender and racial composition on perceptions of team performance in cross-functional teams, *Group & Organization Management*, 22(3), 366–383. See also Kirkman, B. L., Tesluk, P. E., & Rosen, B. (in press), The impact of demographic heterogeneity and team leader-team member demographic fit on team empowerment and effectiveness, *Group & Organization Management*.

58 Kirkman et al. (in press).

59 Gomez et al. (2000).

60 Gibson & Kirkman (1999).

61 Mohrman, S. A., Cohen, S. G., & Mohrman, A. M., Jr. (1995), *Designing Team-Based Organizations: New Forms for Knowledge Work*, San Francisco: Jossey-Bass.

62 Biggs, J. B. (1993), What do inventories of students' learning processes really measure? A theoretical review and clarification, *British Journal of Educational Psychology*, 63, 3–19.

63 Hoeksema, L. H., Van de Vliert, E., & Williams, A. R. T. (1996), The interplay between learning strategy and organizational structure in predicting career success, *International Journal of Human Resource Management*, 8, 307–327.

64 Allinson, C. W., & Hayes, J. (2000), Cross-national differences in cognitive style: implications for management, *International Journal of Human Resource Management*, 11(1), 161–170.

65 *Ibid.*

66 Hofstede, G. (1991), *Cultures and Organizations: Software of the Mind*, London: McGraw-Hill.

67 *Ibid.*

68 *Ibid.*

69 Cohen, S. G., & Bailey, D. E. (1997), What makes teams work: Group effectiveness research from the shop floor to the executive suite, *Journal of Management*, 23, 239–290.

70 Langfred, C. W. (2000), Work-group design and autonomy: A field study of the interaction between task interdependence and group autonomy, *Small Group Research*, 31, 54–70.

71 Kirkman, B. L., & Shapiro, D. L. (1997), The impact of cultural values on employee resistance to teams: Toward a model of globalized self-managing work team effectiveness, *Academy of Management Review*, 22(3), 730–757.

72 Kirkman & Shapiro (2001a, 2001b).

73 Elenkov, D. S. (1998), Can American management concepts work in Russia? A cross-cultural comparative study, *California Management Review*, 40, 133–156; Kirkman & Shapiro (2001b); Nicholls, C. E., Lane, H. W., & Brechu, M. B. (1999), Taking self-managed teams to Mexico, *Academy of Management Executive*, 13, 15–27.

74 Kirkman, B. L., Lowe, K. B., & Gibson, C. B. (2002), Two decades of *Culture's Consequences*: A review of the empirical research on Hofstede's cultural value dimensions, working paper, Georgia Institute of Technology.

75 Mohrman et al. (1995).

76 Edmondson, A. (1999), Psychological safety and learning behavior in work teams, *Administrative Science Quarterly*, 44, 350–383; Kasl, E., Marsick, V. J., & Dechant, K. (1997), Teams as learners: A research-based model of team learning, *Journal of Applied Behavioral Science*, 33(2), 227–246.

77 Edmondson (1999).

78 Gibson & Kirkman (1999); Mohrman et al. (1995).

79 Edmondson (1999).

80 Leeson, N. (1996), *Rogue Trader*, London: Little, Brown.

81 Rawnsley, J. (1995), *Total Risk: Nick Leeson and the Fall of Barings Bank*, New York: Harper; Van Dyck, C. (2000), *Putting Errors to Good Use: Error Management Culture in Organizations*, Amsterdam: KLI Dissertation series, 2000–3.

82 Senge, P. M. (1990), *The Fifth Discipline: The Art and Practice of the Learning Organization*, New York: Currency Doubleday.

83 Edmondson (1999), p. 25.

84 Frese, M. (1995), Error management in training: Conceptual and empirical results, in C. Zucchermaglio, S. Bandura, & S. U. Stucky (eds.), *Organizational Learning and Technological Change*, New York: Springer.

85 Van Dyck (2000).

86 *Ibid.*

87 Hofstede (1991).

88 Rybowiak, V., Garst, H., Frese, M., & Baltinic, B. (1999), Error Orientation Questionnaire (E.O.Q): Reliability, validity, and different language equivalence, *Journal of Organizational Behavior*, 20, 527–547.

89 Tjosvold, D. (1991), *Team Organization. An Enduring Competitive Advantage*, New York: John Wiley.

90 Gersick, C. J., & Hackman, J. R. (1990), Habitual routines in task-performing groups, *Organizational Behavior and Human Decision Processes*, 47, 65–97.

91 West, M. A., Garrod, S., & Carletta, J. (1997), Group decision-making and effectiveness: Unexplored boundaries, in C. L. Cooper & S. E. Jackson (eds.), *Creating Tomorrow's Organizations: A Handbook for Future Research in Organizational* Behavior, Chichester: John Wiley, pp. 293–316.

92 West, M. A. (1996), Reflexivity and work group effectiveness: A conceptual integration, in M. A. West (ed.), *Handbook of Work Group* Psychology, Chichester: John Wiley, pp. 555–579.

93 *Ibid.*

94 Carter, S. M., & West, M. A. (1998), Reflexivity, effectiveness, and mental health in BBC-TV production teams, *Small Group Research*, 29, 583–601; Schippers, M. C., Den Hartog, D. N., & Koopman, P. (2001), Reflexivity in Teams: The Development of a Questionnaire and the Relationship with Trust, Leadership, and Performance of Work Teams, manuscript submitted for publication.

95 West (1996).

96 Maznevski & Chudoba (2001).

97 Geber, B. (1995), Virtual teams, *Training*, 32(4), 36–40.

98 Solomon, C. M. (1998), Building teams across borders, *Global Workforce*, November, 12–17.

99 Rauch A., Frese, M., & Sonnentag, S. (2000), Cultural differences in planning/success relationships: A comparison of small enterprises in Ireland, West Germany, and East Germany, *Journal of Small Business Management*, 38(4), 28–41.

100 Kirkman & Shapiro (1997).

Part IV

Executing Strategic Initiatives Globally

14

Managing Knowledge in Global Organizations

Tatiana Kostova, Nicholas Athanassiou, and Iris Berdrow

As discussed in the previous chapters, global organizations are faced with enormous complexity with regard to their external environments and customers, their internal structures and arrangements, as well as the mindsets and cultural milieu of their employees and partners. The environment in which they operate is characterized, on one hand, by high uncertainty and ambiguity, and on the other hand, by significant and complex interdependence. In response, firms engage in a series of strategic initiatives that can help them address these challenges and achieve stable competitive advantage in the complex global marketplace. Increasingly, global companies are beginning to implement large-scale initiatives such as knowledge management, innovation management, external sourcing of knowledge, global account management, and joint ventures and alliances. There is a growing consensus that the focus on knowledge, relationships, and intellectual resources that these initiatives take can in fact provide sustainable superior performance.

Furthermore, both management research and business practice are approaching a realization that, because of the nature of these organizational initiatives, they cannot be managed effectively through more traditional mechanisms and approaches. Instead, they require newer and more complicated approaches and tools. It is clear that formal structures, budgeting and control practices, and top-down autocratic leadership fall short of providing the necessary means to handle these highly complex organizational tasks. Coordination, control, and communication under conditions of dynamic complexity cannot be structured and formalized, but instead have to be guided in a much more fluid and evolving way. Similarly, knowledge sharing, for example, requires much more than expensive information technologies. Among other supports, it needs an appropriate mindset, culture, and organizational environment conducive to this activity. It also requires good relationships among people, trust, openness, and many other elements that do not lend themselves easily to formalization.

As a result, the management of organizational processes is becoming critical for the successful implementation of strategic initiatives. The emphasis is shifting away from creating formal structures and institutionalizing fixed (albeit "best") routines and procedures toward more informal, fluid, dynamic concepts that can handle the complexity of the tasks at hand. Critical processes that successful global firms seem to be focusing on include the building and nurturing of productive global social networks; using boundary spanning across cultural, national, and organizational boundaries; building social capital and managing relationships within the organization as well as across organizations with customers, communities, and partners; and promoting continuous learning and renewal.[1] These processes transcend tasks, functions, and initiatives, and have developed into a common platform for effective management under complex conditions.

Managing Knowledge

The term *knowledge management* is becoming increasingly popular and meaningful among both practicing managers and businesses researchers. Although knowledge has long been recognized as an important value-creating resource in organizations and often referred to as intellectual capital, companies have focused their attention on its formal management only recently. Organizations from a variety of industries are now beginning to view knowledge as a distinct strategic asset and to design organizational structures, processes, and systems aimed at its effective management.[2] Following the example of the pioneers, such as GE and McKinsey, a growing number of companies are involved in initiatives related to knowledge management. New job titles are beginning to emerge on the organizational charts; new departments and units are being added with the particular task to manage knowledge; new, sophisticated information systems are being developed and purchased to facilitate this function; and creative ways are being sought to motivate employee involvement.

Despite the significant attention, resources, and efforts devoted to managing knowledge, the field is far from being able to formulate a "best practice" of knowledge management. Different companies are experimenting with different models and approaches; most are experiencing setbacks and challenges, and very few seem to be completely satisfied with the results. Part of the problem lies in the fact that the function of knowledge management is relatively recent and we have not been able to accumulate enough understanding of how it should be done. More importantly, knowledge management is among the most complex tasks within an organization and requires an equally complex learning process through a cumulative and multidisciplinary effort. The purpose of this chapter is to discuss the importance of managing knowledge for achieving sustained global competitive advantage and to highlight why this task is distinct and more challenging in the multinational organization than in an organization that does not span national boundaries. We outline the current perspectives on the subject of knowledge management. In addition to describing various initiatives in different companies, we provide an integrated discussion of these experiences and address several important questions. First, why is knowledge management appearing on the radar screen of management professionals? Is it just a fad and fashion that will eventually fade away, or is it a fundamental management task of strategic importance that will stay on the agenda of managers for years to come? Second, what is distinct about the management of knowledge compared to other organizational resources? Third, how are companies dealing with this task? What are some of the "better" practices that have been implemented in organizations? Fourth, what are the critical factors for success of developing and implementing knowledge management systems, and what are some of the most typical problems, challenges, and pitfalls? These questions, although relevant for all types of organizations, will be discussed here in the more complex context of multinational companies.

Why manage knowledge?

There are several reasons knowledge has been brought to the forefront of organizational resources, necessitating its formal management. At a very broad level, the nature of the economy has changed dramatically in the last decade, and experts are now talking about the *"knowledge-based"* economy. A number of significant developments, including radical innovations in technology, revolutionary changes in communications, massive liberalization of markets, and an unprecedented scale of globalization, have caused a major shift in the main sources of strategic competitive advantage. The traditional value-producing resources such as materials, capital, and labor, while still very important, are becoming more readily available and accessible to all. As a result, they are less frequently a sustainable source of distinct *competitive advantage* for any particular firm. Access to global markets makes it possible for organizations to find the cheapest and best natural resources anywhere in the world and to secure needed financial capital in the global financial marketplace. As a result, the focus is shifting toward the *knowledge resources* that exist in the various geographically distributed parts of the firm, which are far less imitable and accessible. Because of its specific characteristics, such as tacitness and embeddedness, knowledge is difficult to acquire in the open marketplace, to share with a different part of the multinational organization, and to turn into a unique source of competitive advantage for the entire firm.

Embeddedness describes organizational knowledge that is created and interpreted within a particular social context, for example, in a given country.[3] Different social contexts are likely to lead to the creation of different types of organizational knowledge that reflect the specific contextual conditions. For instance, a firm operating in Brazil will have to learn how to deal with hyperinflation, while a firm in China will have to develop some competency in dealing with *guanxi* types of relationships. In addition, the same piece of information or knowledge may have different meanings in different contexts owing to cultural and cognitive differences. Even the notion of business relationships may have a different meaning as we cross cultural borders. In the West, business relationships are primarily the means by which you get things done. In contrast, in countries like China, Japan, Greece, and many others, the notion of business relationships is much more encompassing; it implies a long-term connection based on loyalty, trust, and reciprocity.[4] In that context, business relationships are guided by strong social norms and are a goal in themselves rather than a way to reach a goal. Companies have to be aware of these challenges and learn how to effectively manage this resource.

Since knowledge is partly shaped by the external environment of the organization, the subsidiaries in each host country, characterized as they are by a distinct economic, institutional, educational, cultural, and technological environment, will produce distinct knowledge and competences. This may result in pockets of differentiated and possibly fragmented knowledge, which may not be utilized throughout the organization. Among the reasons for such underutilization of organizational knowledge are an unawareness that this knowledge could indeed be useful and an inability to see how the knowledge could be applied properly. Consider, for example, a situation where engineers in the German subsidiary of a US multinational corporation (MNC) know the solution to a technical problem. A well-functioning knowledge-management system in the MNC would identify this piece of knowledge, assess its potential value for other subsidiaries in other geographical locations, and provide a smooth and effective transfer and possibly modification and adaptation of this solution to all relevant units. In the absence of such a system, these intellectual resources will be underutilized and misapplied, if not wasted. The ability of MNCs to leverage their distributed capabilities is their main source of competitive advantage over their domestic competitors. Thus, knowledge management is a critical task of strategic importance for MNCs.

Finally, knowledge management in MNCs is becoming increasingly critical because of the changing nature of multinational corporations as they progress from the multinational to the transnational model.[5] While the local operations in the multinational model are pretty much adapted to, and contained within, the host country, the transnational model is characterized by a high level of complex interdependence amongst the dispersed local operations, an interdependence reflected in intensive and multidirectional flows of all types of resources. Such transnational interdependence increases the importance of leveraging, sharing, and utilizing the MNC's intellectual resources that are distributed around the world.

In summary, knowledge management in MNCs is becoming more important because of the knowledge-based economy, the nature of the knowledge in MNCs (differentiated by unit and distributed widely), and the increasing and more complex nature of interdependence among the dispersed operations of MNCs as they move toward the transnational model. Thus, the practice of knowledge management in organizations, while relatively new and possibly appearing faddish, is brought forward by powerful underlying macro- and micro-dynamics which are in no way temporary and likely to fade away. Managing knowledge is becoming a critical task for MNCs because knowledge is an important strategic resource that needs nurturing and development. It should be noted that MNCs, and all companies, for that matter, have always been involved in some way or another in knowledge management. However, in the last several years, organizations have taken these activities to a new level. Knowledge is increasingly being viewed as something that needs to be managed in a more professional, conscious, deliberate, organized, formal, and structured way, to the extent that this is possible.

What is distinct about managing knowledge?

Knowledge management is the systematic, explicit, and deliberate process of creating, identifying, and organizing important information and expertise within the organization, disseminating and applying it to wherever it is needed to enhance organizational effectiveness and achieve organizational objectives.

Managing knowledge is one of the most challenging and complicated tasks involved in managing an organization. Knowledge itself is a very complex resource that is difficult to define and describe. It includes data and information but goes beyond them because it also consists of ideas, rules, procedures, intuition, experiences, and models that have been developed over time and that guide action and decisions. Knowledge can be individual, but it can also be collectively held. It is contextual in that it often derives its meaning from the specific context within which it has been developed.[6] For example, knowledge about gift giving in business interactions has different meanings in different cultural contexts within which the MNC operates. These differences may create problems when the practice of gift giving is taken out of one cultural context and transferred to another. For instance, giving gifts to clients may be not only acceptable, but the norm in countries like Morocco, while it may be viewed as inappropriate or even illegal in the United States.

The knowledge base of an organization is extremely rich and diverse. It includes knowledge about the "whos" of the organization (those who have social capital and what social capital they may have, a subject further explored in chapter 19 of this volume, "Managing Complexity in the Global Innovation Process: A Networks and Social Capital Solution"); the "whats" of the organization (resources, facilities, customers, markets); the "hows" (process, procedures, "getting things done"); the "whys" (strategic reason, logic, meaning); as well as the "wheres" and "whens" of different tasks, activities, and functions. Knowledge differs from financial and material resources in that it is more difficult to quantify, qualify, transfer, create, and share. For example, raw materials can be accounted for through some unit of measurement. While raw materials diminish with consumption, knowledge actually grows through consumption. It is possible for multiple people to use the same bit of knowledge understood in very different ways in uniquely distinctive activities. In the end, more people hold and can reuse that knowledge. Knowledge can evolve without investment in retooling or retraining. Knowledge cannot be stored or moved in the same way as money or tangible resources. Furthermore, as a resource, knowledge does not follow normal market behavior. For example, it has limited property rights, disclosure of its attributes is difficult, and so, too, is recognizing knowledge-related trading opportunities. Finally, organizational knowledge contains a tacit component which is implicit, taken for granted, difficult to communicate, and is thus almost impossible to quantify, formalize, and transfer. Experts, even if they are willing to share, are often incapable of communicating their knowledge on a subject. The information critical for transfer is automatic or subliminal. Ikujiro Nonaka,[7] a leading scholar of knowledge management, points out that "to convert tacit knowledge into explicit means finding a way to express the inexpressible." In fact, tacit knowledge cannot be transferred. Michael Polanyi,[8] the philosopher of science, tells us that two people can share the interpretation of their respective tacit understanding through face-to-face interactions much as an apprentice learned the tacit nuances of a master's genius over many years of collaboration in Renaissance Florence. Tacit knowledge cannot be articulated.

The complexity of knowledge management is further increased by the fact that it requires a number of organizational components to be specifically designed into an *integrated system*. Among the main critical components for such a system are technology, organization, and people. Creating each of these components is a difficult and novel task by itself, but achieving internal consistency among them and ensuring their co-evolution as time progresses is even more difficult. Some companies have been more successful in developing the technological component (Eureka in Xerox), others in designing the proper organization or culture (McKinsey, GE). However, few companies have succeeded in building an integrated system for knowledge management capable of self-sustaining and self-renewing over time.

The complexity of the knowledge-management function is also increased as a result of *wide organizational scope* and *wide distribution*. As our field research shows, activities related to knowledge management (creating and sharing knowledge) span functional areas and hierarchical levels and cross-departmental and country boundaries. For example, the global R&D units in one large pharmaceutical company are involved in knowledge creation and sharing by and among a number of specialists, including world-renowned pharmacologists and other scientists as well as lab technicians, database administrators, and computer modeling experts, among others. Added to this differentiation are the geographical distribution and the variety of cultural and educational backgrounds of the participants.

Finally, many activities of knowledge management are characterized by high *ambiguity and uncertainty*. For example, it is difficult to predict exactly what knowledge will be created, needed or shared, who will be involved in these tasks, and how, where, and when they will occur. This ambiguity presents serious problems for the *a priori* design of a formal structure and a comprehensive description of all related procedures.

In summary, knowledge management is a highly complex function owing to the characteristics of the knowledge resource, the multitude of organizational components that need to be integrated into a knowledge-management system, the broad organizational scope of the task in terms of functions, units, and hierarchical levels, and the inherent uncertainty and ambiguity of the related activities. Knowledge management becomes even more complex across national and cultural borders.

How do companies manage knowledge?

As discussed above, the knowledge-management function is extremely multifaceted and complex. Companies are just beginning to create the building blocks of appropriate systems. Amongst the wide variety of approaches, we identify three common perspectives: the process perspective, the systems perspective, and the evolutionary/organic perspective.

First, from a *process perspective*, knowledge management is seen as a process consisting of several distinct yet interrelated tasks: identifying, generating or acquiring knowledge; codification, documentation, and storing; and use by distributing, transferring, and sharing. It should be noted that this process conceptualization is useful for design and analytical purposes. In reality, the process may not be linear, may include recursive loops, and may begin at different places. For example, pieces of knowledge that are already stored in the system may be retrieved for reuse and combined in some novel ways, thus creating new units of usable knowledge. The different stages represent different types of organizational activities, have different characteristics, and, accordingly, require distinct approaches and techniques to be managed. For example, the creation of knowledge is a highly idiosyncratic and creative task that is difficult to manage through formally structured processes. Storing and organizing knowledge, on the other hand, is seen to be much more structured, thus lending itself to a formal management approach. Presumably, there will be limitations to this task, as tacit knowledge cannot be easily identified, stored, organized, and shared. The different tasks also place different emphasis on the technology, organization, and people components of the knowledge-management system.

Second, effective knowledge management is possible only if approached from a *sociotechnical* orientation. The main components of such a system include the organizational components of knowledge management described above, technology, organization, and people. A number of *technologies* enable and facilitate the various knowledge-related tasks. For example, to organize, develop, and store knowledge requires database management systems; to transfer, share, and disseminate knowledge requires messaging and communications technologies, such as e-mail, Intranet, conferencing technologies, and groupware. The creation, acquisition, and development of knowledge, although mostly requiring human expertise and cognitive abilities, are enhanced by decision-support and expert systems. Companies are investing significant resources in the acquisition and development of sophisticated information systems. For example, Accenture (formerly Andersen Consulting) has put in place a system called Xchange, which is based on Lotus Notes and contains 3,000 databases. Xerox has developed a system called DocuShare to support their Eureka project. DocuShare's technology component is largely limited to explicit and codified knowledge because tacit knowledge cannot be managed through databases.

The *organization* component of the systems perspective includes the formal structure responsible for carrying out these tasks. It consists of specialized knowledge-management units and specific job positions such as Chief Knowledge Officer (CKO), knowledge managers, knowledge engineers, specialists, and champions. Additional elements here include communication infrastructure and networks for interaction throughout the organization. McKinsey has created Centers of Competence, which are responsible for building the knowledge base within a particular functional or industry area. KPMG has Shared Knowledge Centers, a Web Council, and designated job positions, such as knowledge champion and knowledge master.

Technologies and organization are necessary for an effective knowledge-management system. They provide the ability, the means, and the infrastructure for knowledge management. None of this matters, however, if employees lack the motivation to participate in these initiatives. All companies launching a knowledge-management initiative quickly recognize that *people* are the most critical component of knowledge management. At Accenture, for example, they began their knowledge-management efforts at the beginning of the 1990s, but by the end of the decade they continued to be dissatisfied with the degree of usability of the systems that they had in place. They had indeed invested heavily in the technology of the information systems and had created the organizational structure to support it (project knowledge managers). What Accenture lacked were the interpersonal networks that would give life to the information systems and would utilize them to their maximum potential. The *"people"* component provides the necessary motivation for employees to actively engage in using and contributing to the system. It also facilitates the transfer of tacit and embedded knowledge. It includes elements like specific knowledge-related incentive mechanisms, training, and support by leadership at the highest levels.

Finally, from an *evolutionary/organic* perspective, the development and implementation of a knowledge-management system should be gradual, evolutionary, and interwoven with the other activities of the organization. It is recommended that companies start small and slowly and gradually expand the system to the boundaries of the whole organization and then possibly beyond, as described in Chapter 15, "External Sourcing of Knowledge in the International Firm."

One multinational pharmaceutical company that we studied, for example, started with one particular task – knowledge sharing, and one division – pharmacology. They created the organizational infrastructure by forming global cross-functional research teams organized by therapeutic areas. They also modified the performance appraisal system to reflect the contribution of each team member to the knowledge-sharing initiative. In the process of implementation, they uncovered a series of technical and organizational barriers to knowledge sharing. For example, they realized that their units in different countries were using different and often incompatible forms for documentation of their work. Standardizing the documentation and the procedures was one particular step toward achieving the goal of integration through knowledge sharing.

Another problem that surfaced very early in the knowledge-management process in the pharmacology division was the reluctance of people, especially the scientists, to participate in the system. The most common problems clustered around complaints and excuses – most frequently that others were "speaking a different language" (they meant scientific language) because of the different education and training that people from different countries had gone through; that others had a "different pace of work"; that there was a "lack of flexibility" of the other party; and that the others "think they know better." Management realized that the root cause of all these problems might be more subtle and deep. Of course, the organizational structures, modifications to the reward and incentive systems, and standardization of the processes and documentation that were implemented were all positive steps toward the goal. However, what was missing was a commonly held culture of knowledge sharing across the company's operations that spanned many national and cultural boundaries. People did not understand the value of sharing and collaboration; there was not a norm of sharing in the organization; there was very limited past history of sharing and working together across unit boundaries. It was clear that the pharmacology department was *dis-integrated*, that there were many boundaries along country of operation, function, hierarchical level, and project.

In an attempt to solve these problems, the pharmaceutical company's management started a series of initiatives fostering cross-boundary communication and interaction. One of the most successful events was an annual global meeting of all employees that was held in a different location every year. The results were very positive as many of the misconceptions, stereotypes, and resistances were slowly removed. People got to know each other on a personal level. They developed their social networks and started feeling a part of a common entity. Furthermore, a common culture of collaboration and sharing started to emerge as a result of the involvement of all employees and the extensive opportunities for formal and informal interaction, including face-to-face. The elements of the knowledge-sharing system were integrated into the current activities and processes rather than appended to them. They slowly became part of the pharmacology division's culture. Perhaps the most critical factor in all of this was the absolute commitment of top management to this initiative. The approach that the management in this pharmaceutical company had taken – a bottom-up, gradual, organic process of careful development of different aspects of the system and modification of them as the process evolved – started to pay off.

Unfortunately, not all companies understand the importance of nurturing and maintaining a system of extensive cross-border interactions. In another example, the president of the international division of KFC International spent three years fostering knowledge sharing across business units, levels, and borders. Around forty key managers from headquarters, regional headquarters, and major subsidiaries would gather in one of the company's different locations around the world at least twice a year. The location was selected in a way that allowed these managers to experience a particular national market with which they were not familiar or to understand a successful new product/process innovation within its natural context. The formal purpose for these meetings was to discuss and accept strategic plans and marketing plans. Beyond that, enough time was allocated for social interactions. By the end of the three years, the international division had become hugely successful in terms of growth and profits. It had also turned into a well-oiled machine that exchanged information informally and fostered an environment of cross-border cooperation. This was done in a proactive manner, as some of the more affluent subsidiaries would offer others their knowledge and people to help them transfer best practices and new products. At the end of the president's third year, the company changed ownership. One of the first actions of the new parent organization was to replace the president of the international division with one of their own managers, who happened to have limited international business experience. The new president communicated only at the highest level, with his four direct reports and his four regional vice-presidents. He immediately cut himself off from the other thirty or so senior managers who had been key to managing the transfer of the company's knowledge across global units and across hierarchical levels. This new president did not understand that instead of fostering knowledge sharing, he was laying the grounds for knowledge Balkanization. He did not recognize the importance of the informal face-to-face global meetings as a knowledge-management tool for transferring tacit knowledge. He himself was cut out of the knowledge loop. The result was immediate and negative to both division growth and profits. Further, the international corporate culture of collaboration and knowledge sharing that had been in place previously was destroyed and not reconstituted until a full decade later.

What are the critical success factors?

Dealing with tacitness

One of the biggest challenges in knowledge management is effectively eliciting tacit knowledge (or know-how) from a source, once it has been identified. Some of the approaches that are being used include storytelling and using metaphors and analogies. These tools facilitate the process of describing, formulating, and codifying the tacit and subtle aspects of a piece of knowledge by prompting experts to make sense of what they know and communicate the subtleties via these richer forms. These forms work as proxies for the more implicit, tacit levels of knowledge. Codification does not allow for the inclusion of the tacit aspects. Once the knowledge has been codified, so it can be transferred and disseminated across units, the tacit aspects have been left behind. In addition to implementing what has been already codified, the recipient of the codified knowledge must internalize and master the knowledge by gradually attaching meaning and adding back to it the tacit component lost during the codification and transfer process. An issue related to this is the contextual embeddedness of knowledge. We know that knowledge derives much of its meaning and value from the specific context in which it has been created. Transferring to a new context (organizational or cultural) may require some adaptation of the knowledge itself or its interpretation in the new place. Some scholars refer to this process as "recontextualization." Tacit and contextual knowledge are best transferred by people and through intensive interaction between its source and recipient.[9] In fact, this is perhaps the only possible way in which transfer can occur.[10]

The Danish pharmaceutical company Novo Nordisk A/S provides an interesting example of the transfer of knowledge.[11] In the late 1990s the company was struggling with inefficient management, lack of a shared company culture, and insufficient collaboration and integration. In an attempt to address these issues, the company developed a set of documents and initiatives that spelled out the vision, mission, and philosophy of management. The "Ten Fundamentals of the Novo Nordisk Way of Management" summarized the new management philosophy and system that they were trying to implement. Among the main objectives was transfer and utilization of best practices throughout the organization. While providing the technology and the organizational infrastructure for cross-unit interaction and communication, the main tool that management used to implement the new systems was the "Facilitator" initiative. A group of 14 facilitators was selected from around the company, reflecting its functional and cultural diversity. The task of the facilitators was to help units implement the new management systems. After extensive training, the facilitators began their visits, audits, and consults throughout the organization. They helped "translate" the new philosophy and systems into the "language" of the recipient units; that is, they helped recontextualize this knowledge with the help of the local managers. The facilitators were effective at transferring knowledge by first extracting it from the source experts, codifying it into transferable pieces, and then implementing it into the recipient units while adding back the tacit components that give meaning and value to the explicit knowledge they were transferring.

The human factor

The importance of the human element in building effective knowledge-management systems cannot be overstated. Owing to the complexity and ambiguity of the task, it is critical that people at all levels and in all types of functions get actively involved in the identification, documentation, organization, transfer, and use of organizational knowledge. Much of what knowledge management entails cannot be mandated. There needs to be a *motivation* on behalf of employees to create, offer, and use knowledge, so, in an attempt to motivate such behavior, many companies are adjusting their *performance evaluation* systems accordingly. For example, when Novartis launched their global knowledge-sharing initiative, they added four new knowledge-related items on which employees from all ranks were evaluated as part of their 360-degree feedback process. Some of the specific items included: "this person proactively shares his/her knowledge with the other members of the team"; "this person achieves work goals better as result of communicating with the rest of the team"; "I can rely on him/her for information that I need in my work." At McKinsey, knowledge-sharing orientation and behaviors are at the heart of the performance evaluation system. Each consultant is assessed on their contribution to knowledge creation, dissemination, sharing, and use in the company. As a McKinsey associate says, "There is no such thing as not returning a phone call from a colleague who is seeking some type of information or knowledge." The above examples illustrate organizations' efforts to increase employee motivation to share knowledge and its linking to the formal evaluation and compensation processes.

Monetary rewards, however, are not the only effective means of motivation. Xerox had an interesting experience with their Eureka project. The objective of Eureka was to create a system for organizational learning where the experience and expertise of each individual service technician around the world would be documented and added to the knowledge base of the company. Then other technicians facing similar technical problems would be able to use this knowledge. Service technicians were encouraged to post tips describing their experience onto the system. Surprisingly, when the technicians were surveyed with regard to how they would like to be given incentives to participate, they chose *non-monetary rewards*. They wanted to be recognized publicly for their contribution by posting their names with each tip submitted to the system. Over time, certain people gained an expert reputation and became well known and respected among their colleagues. In addition to being highly motivating, this initiative facilitated the knowledge-transfer process because everyone knew whom they should contact if they needed additional clarification and guidance in applying a piece of knowledge.

A similar approach is used at McKinsey, where practices and solutions are documented in their practice bulletins. Each bulletin contains a brief description of a problem and the solution that was developed for it, as well as the contact information of the expert to contact for further details. These systems are valuable because they motivate participants through fostering a sense of ownership and authorship. What is significant is that they are also extremely effective for fostering personal interaction, which allows for the transfer of the tacit aspects of organizational knowledge.

Personal interaction can be formalized with some organizational positions. There is a special role in the knowledge-management initiatives in organizations for the *boundary spanner*, an individual who is connected to more than one organizational entity in some way or another. For example, an expatriate manager transferred to a foreign subsidiary is someone who should be able to span the boundary between the subsidiary and headquarters and facilitate the process of translation and transfer of organizational knowledge between the two entities. The following excerpt from an interview with a manager from the UK subsidiary of a large US multinational illustrates this point. The manager was on a six-month assignment to corporate headquarters.

> I have been asked and pressured by headquarters, for years now, to adopt the teamwork concept in our operations in England. And I have been reluctant to do so. I just thought that teamwork is highly inefficient and does not fit our culture. The skeptics would even say it is a waste of time. I have been here at headquarters for over three months and have been involved in teamwork on a daily basis. I feel I now understand the value of teamwork and I am ready to go back to my unit and make it work.

As we see in this example, a boundary spanner has emerged who, once placed in the proper context, has been able to make sense of the very tacit notion of teamwork and is ready to serve as its champion at his own location.

In addition to country, cultural, and language barriers, boundary spanners are also important for overcoming departmental, functional, and other organizational boundaries. For example, employees may become boundary spanners and facilitate the knowledge transfer between departments as a result of a job-rotation program or a training event that has brought them in contact with representatives of other organizational units. It should be noted that boundary spanners do not necessarily hold formal positions as such.

On many occasions certain individuals will come to play a boundary-spanning role as a result of their personal networks, personalities, or other circumstances. What is important though, from a knowledge management perspective, is that the organization nurtures and fosters boundary spanning as a constructive activity and values boundary spanners as valuable for knowledge transfer. Managers should identify individuals who have the potential to play this role and provide them with opportunities to do so.

Organizational context

GE is a leader in knowledge management and has been the trendsetter in management practice. GE creates new practices, such as workout sessions, and has been successful in diffusing these practices throughout its many divisions and locations. Furthermore, the company is effective in institutionalizing its knowledge: GE employees throughout the organization gradually internalize GE practices. Most of the people at GE believe that their organizational knowledge is superior and that it is this knowledge and competence that create a sustainable source of competitive advantage. There is a lot to be learned from GE's experience in knowledge management, especially in terms of creating a holistic system and a strong organizational context underlying and fostering the knowledge-management task.

There are two main initiatives that illustrate GE's approach and success in knowledge management, "best practices" and the Crotonville Center. "Best practices," a formal system for identifying, documenting, and formalizing, and then disseminating and implementing the "best practice" in different areas throughout the organization, was launched by former CEO Jack Welch in 1989. In search of a best practice, the company audited all of its divisions and businesses and even went outside, by forming a consortium with other interested companies that were known for their competence in various areas (Wal-Mart in customer satisfaction, Honda in new product development). The best practices initiative resulted in a major improvement in management throughout the organization and helped set benchmarks and channel the energy of management toward searching for, learning about, and implementing the best way to conduct certain functions. A strong knowledge-oriented mentality started to emerge.

The Crotonville Center, another initiative, has had an even greater impact on knowledge management at GE. GE built this $40-million executive leadership facility in the late 1980s, at a time when the company was focused on the bottom line. Since then, thousands of managers have attended seminars and programs at Crotonville. Today, it continues to serve as a major vehicle for personal and professional development. The vision for Crotonville goes beyond individual training and learning: it is an important vehicle for organizational learning. Through a variety of tools such as workout sessions, the center serves as a place where new organizational knowledge is continuously created and existing knowledge is effectively identified and disseminated to all participants and to the diverse units that they represent. Most importantly, the Crotonville phenomenon is an effective vehicle for shaping the mindset and philosophy of the managers and for creating and diffusing the strong GE organizational culture, an essential component of which is a knowledge orientation. Managers from all levels of GE are involved in the generation of new ideas and the development of new organizational knowledge. As a result, the tasks of knowledge creation, dissemination, and sharing have spread throughout the company, permeating functions, businesses, and hierarchical levels. Strong personal networks are created that are not limited to the top managers from each facility but include a large number of different specialists at all levels. This multilevel characteristic is a major factor in precluding top managers from becoming the gatekeepers in their facilities by filtering all information exchanges and limiting the access of the other employees to knowledge outside of their unit. The Crotonville experience creates and instills an organization-wide mindset that carries out knowledge management in a forceful, effective way.

Finally, we can draw some wisdom of how critical it is that the very top manager of the organization is completely devoted and committed to the initiative. For reference, Jack Welch personally taught at Crotonville for two days every single month until his recent retirement. The personal involvement of senior managers is a tremendous factor for communicating the strategic value of the initiative and for creating an environment of trust and shared, knowledge-oriented organizational culture. These are the building blocks of the very complex task of managing knowledge.

The objective is to create a system that is organic in nature, that is well integrated with all parts of an organization and is capable of renewing itself as conditions change. As Yoshio Maruta, Chairman of Kao Corporation of Japan suggests: "If anything goes wrong in one department, those in other parts of the organization should sense the problem and provide help without being asked."[12] Knowledge management is far more than information systems. At its very heart is the network of individuals with a shared mindset of attending to and proactively contributing to the knowledge resource of the organization.

NOTES

1 Ghoshal, S., & Bartlett, C. A. (1995), Changing the role of top management: Beyond structure to processes, *Harvard Business Review*, January–February, 86–96; Kostova, T., & Kendall, R. (2003), Social capital in multinational corporations and a micro-macro model of its formation, *Academy of Management Review*, 28(2), 297–318.

2 Zack, M. H. (1999), Developing a knowledge strategy, *California Management Review*, 41(3), 125–46.

3 Kostova, T. (1999), Transnational transfer of strategic organizational practices: A contextual perspective, *Academy of Management Review*, 24(2), 308–24.

4 Hall, E. T., & Hall., M. R. (1989), *Understanding Cultural Differences*, Yarmouth, ME: Intercultural Press.

5 Bartlett, C. A., & Ghoshal, S. (1989), *Managing across Borders: The Transnational Solution*, Boston: Harvard Business School Press.

6 Doz, Y., Santos, J., & Williamson, P. (2001), *From Global to Metanational*, Boston, MA: Harvard Business School Press.

7 Nonaka, I., & Takeuchi, H. (1995), *The Knowledge-Creating Company*, New York: Oxford University Press.

8 Polanyi, M. (1966), *The Tacit Dimension*, London: Routledge & Kegan Paul.

9 Athanassiou, N., & Nigh, D. (2000), Internationalization, tacit knowledge and the top management team of MNCs, *Journal of International Business Studies*, 31(3), 471–488.

10 McKenney, J. L., Zack, M. H., & Doherty, V. S. (1992), Complementary communication media: A comparison of electronic media and face-to-face communication in a programming

team, in N. Nohria & R. G. Eccles (eds.), *Networks and Organizations*, Boston, MA: Harvard Business School Press; Davenport, T. H., & Prusak, L. (1998), *Working Knowledge: How Organizations Manage What They Know*, Boston, MA: Harvard University Press.

11 Holden, N. (2002), *Cross-Cultural Management: A Knowledge Management Perspective*, Harlow: Prentice Hall.

12 Bartlett & Ghoshal (1989).

15

External Sourcing of Knowledge in the International Firm

Julian Birkinshaw

The importance of knowledge as an underlying source of competitive advantage for international firms is now well recognized. As discussed in the first chapter in this part, "Managing Knowledge in Global Organizations," many firms now work very hard on identifying and transferring their best practices, and others invest heavily in IT-based systems for codifying their proprietary knowledge and making it available on an international basis. This topic will be addressed in the next chapter.

But while the ability to share knowledge within the international firm is clearly important, this ability is only half the story. Equally critical is the ability to tap into external sources of knowledge – knowledge held by suppliers, customers, competitors, universities, and other institutions. The underlying logic here is almost simplistic – no firm can possibly own or control all of the knowledge it requires to succeed in today's fast-changing world, so it has to seek out new knowledge in its business environment on a continuous basis. And this is particularly the case in an international firm, because new customer demands and new technologies can potentially emerge in any part of the world.

While few would argue that external sources of knowledge are not important, there is surprisingly little research concerned directly with this issue, and even less that focuses on external sourcing of knowledge in an *international* setting. The purpose of this chapter, then, is to briefly review the existing literature, to develop an organizing framework that makes sense of the different approaches firms use to source external knowledge, and to delineate the pros and cons of each.

BACKGROUND

While it is only since the mid-1980s that we have developed a way of thinking about knowledge management *per se*, the broad ideas about tapping into external sources of knowledge have been around for much longer. One line of thinking is concerned with environmental scanning,[1] which refers to the gathering of information about trends, opportunities, and threats in the marketplace. This is done for the most part on an informal basis, for example, through individuals going to conferences or reading trade journals. But many firms today also have specialized "business intelligence" departments whose role is to actively seek out information about competitors and customers.

A second line of thinking is concerned with obtaining access to the specific knowledge of other firms through vehicles such as alliances, joint ventures, and acquisitions. Here again, the idea that there is a process of knowledge exchange between partner firms is an old one, even though the older literature did not refer explicitly to knowledge. The so-called Uppsala School, for example, centered on the idea that there was a process of mutual adjustment between suppliers and customers over time so that new capabilities were developed within the relationship.[2] There is research on how alliance partners learn from one another,[3] and on the processes of learning in joint ventures.[4] And there is some discussion of the processes of knowledge transfer and assimilation in mergers and acquisitions.[5] While it is impossible to draw any general conclusions from such a diverse body of literature, a common theme is that transferring knowledge across firm boundaries is difficult to do and takes a long time. Often, the focus of an alliance or acquisition is on other issues, so the transfer of knowledge ends up getting neglected. And often the ability of the firm to internalize the partner firms' knowledge is not very good; often firms lack absorptive capacity.[6]

In terms of the international aspects of knowledge acquisition, there is a limited body of existing literature. Vernon (1979) argued that multinational corporations should become "global scanners," with certain subsidiary companies having the explicit role of identifying and tapping into new opportunities in the local market. A number of studies have built on this basic insight and explored the ways that subsidiary companies gain access to local knowledge.[7] The ability to tap into foreign markets is particularly important for multinationals that are "born in the wrong place," far away from the leading-edge clusters of activity.[8] For example, most of the European players in the information technology industry have had to find ways of tapping into what is happening in Silicon Valley to be sure that they stay on the leading edge of technology.

Finally, there is a separate body of literature concerned with the acquisition of "market knowledge" in foreign locations, knowledge about customer needs, competitive offerings, and laws and regulations for serving those markets. This work is concerned with the overall process of learning about foreign markets and with the specific modes of entry used, such as acquisitions, joint ventures, and greenfield investments.[9]

THE ORGANIZING FRAMEWORK

The external knowledge-sourcing framework organizes the approaches to external sourcing found in international firms. Its two dimensions are, first, the type of knowledge being sought; and second, the approaches that firms can use to access external knowledge.

One well-used approach to categorizing the type of knowledge being sought is to distinguish between "home-base-exploiting" knowledge and "home-base-augmenting" knowledge.[10] This approach builds on the assumption that most of the international firm's core knowledge base is developed in the home country. If a firm wants to sell its products or services abroad, it needs to develop a certain amount of knowledge about its foreign markets – knowledge about local customers, competitors, and regulations, for example. This sort of knowledge is classified as home-base exploiting because it enables the firm to exploit its existing knowledge, as embodied in products or services developed at home.

Home-base-augmenting knowledge, in contrast, adds value to the core products or services of the corporation. Much of this knowledge is developed in the home base of the firm, but increasingly it is being generated in foreign locations as well. For example, Ericsson has around fifty "design centers" involved in the development of its mobile systems technology, fewer than ten of which are in Sweden. Where these design centers are located overseas, they are not interested in the state of the local market; instead, they want access to the latest technological thinking in local universities or in their competitors' R&D sites. So the knowledge they access is said to augment the firm's core knowledge base rather than exploit it.

There are four basic ways for the firm to access external knowledge.

- *Scanning* is getting access to external knowledge from what you read or hear. This can operate in a very dispersed way, in that every employee is potentially open to new ideas. But it can also work in a very specific way, in that particular units may be created to undertake scanning of certain technologies or trends. Scanning takes many forms – business intelligence, spying, attending conferences, reading trade journals, and general openness to new ideas.
- *Partnering* sources external knowledge through the creation of a deep relationship with another firm. As the relationship with the other firm develops, it becomes possible to gain access to knowledge of a more specific and tacit nature than would be possible through a scanning activity. Partnering takes a variety of forms such as alliances, joint ventures, industry consortia, and long-term buyer–supplier relationships.
- *Contracting* is essentially an outsourcing strategy. Rather than attempting to develop knowledge in-house, the firm instead chooses to contract with an outside expert that has the relevant knowledge and will apply it to solve a particular problem for a fee. This can be an efficient way of gaining access to knowledge that does not exist in-house, and it is typically very fast. But the net result is that the knowledge is never developed in-house. Again there are a variety of forms of contracting, including many supplier relationships, consulting contracts, and individual contractors.
- *Acquiring* is a way to access knowledge that brings it into the firm from the outside on a permanent basis. It includes both hiring individuals from competitor firms or universities and buying up whole firms. To some extent it is like contracting, in that it involves "buying," not "making" knowledge. But the difference is that by acquiring an individual or firm on a permanent basis, their knowledge then becomes part of the firm's knowledge base, and can, if used effectively, be applied to many different opportunities.

When we juxtapose these two dimensions, the type of knowledge being sought and the access approach, we have eight distinct scenarios for external knowledge sourcing. This chapter explores each one in turn; as outlined in figure 15.1.

Approach used to source external knowledge	Type of knowledge being sourced	
	Home-base-exploiting	Home-base-augmenting
Scanning	1 Market reconnaissance visits	5 "Scanning" unit, created to tap into new knowledge and ideas in local milieu
Partnering	2 Market-focused joint venture with local firm	6 Local university partnership; alliance with key supplier, customer, or other partner
Contracting	3 Licensing or franchising; paying for a market survey by local consultant	7 Contracting relationship with local supplier; buying local consulting expertise
Acquiring	4 Acquiring local competitor to gain access to market knowledge	8 Acquiring local firms to gain access to new or leading-edge knowledge

FIGURE 15.1 Approaches to external knowledge sourcing

Home-base-exploiting knowledge

1 Scanning

While some companies such as Shell and Coca-Cola have operations in every corner of the world, the vast majority of international companies have much more limited activities outside their home countries. For such companies, the first requirement as they consider entering or developing a new market is to collect information about that market – about social demographics, the political and economic situation, channels to market, existing products, existing competitors, and so on. This basic information-gathering process can best be thought of as scanning. Some information can be gained through public sources such as the Economist Intelligence Unit, but detailed information can typically only be generated through in-person reconnaissance visits.

A good example of this comes from Prêt à Manger, a UK-based sandwich shop.[11] "Prêt" grew very rapidly in London during the 1990s and started to look at the opportunities for growing internationally in 2000. New York was identified as the most exciting overseas location and one that was close to London on a number of important dimensions. However, the owners of Prêt were reluctant to consider a franchise or acquisition approach to market entry, for fear that they would lose control of their business model. So they decided to do it the hard way. One of the two founders, Sinclair Beecham, moved to New York in October 1999, and spent many months reconnoitering the city – identifying the areas where traffic flow was greatest, watching where people went for lunch, and then talking to city officials, real-estate dealers and potential suppliers about getting started. One year after moving to New York he opened the first Prêt shop, and within a couple of months it was already operating on a break-even basis.

The Prêt example highlights the importance of an effective scanning process in developing foreign market knowledge. Perhaps the key point is that it was one of the company's founders who moved to New York because he realized how important it was to learn about the market at first hand. While much of the necessary market knowledge can be gained in codified form, there is also a significant tacit component.

2 Partnering

A second approach to developing foreign market knowledge is by partnering with a local company. This is a very common approach to market entry – witness the large numbers of joint ventures with local partners formed by Western companies to enter Russia and China. For example, Svetozor was a joint venture between Polaroid and the Russian ministry of machine building, and the rationale from Polaroid's perspective was in large part to learn about the Russian marketplace (Fey, 1995).

Partnering has important benefits and costs as a way of developing local market knowledge. The primary benefit is that by building a long-term relationship with a partner company through a joint venture or alliance, it is possible to develop a very rich understanding of the local market. Unlike scanning, in which the primary flow is of codified knowledge, partnering allows tacit knowledge about the local market to gradually be developed by the international firm. For example, the local partner can provide help in negotiating with government officials and in evaluating potential suppliers. A potential cost of partnering is that your knowledge becomes available to your partner. While the international firm is learning about the local market, the local company is developing knowledge about the international firm's products and services. This is often called a "race to learn," and it is not unheard of for the local company to abandon its joint venture and set up in competition with its former partner, or for the international firm to abandon its partner, so partnering is not without risk.

3 Contracting

Contracting is a very different approach to knowledge sourcing in that the international firm essentially decides that it does not want or need to internalize knowledge about the local market. Instead, it contracts with an independent company to develop or apply the market knowledge in question, and then seeks to exploit that knowledge through a commercial arrangement.

A couple of examples will clarify this logic. When first entering a foreign market, an international firm will often commission a market-entry study by a consulting company that knows the market. This is a form of contracting for market knowledge – the consulting company undertakes the study and writes a report for its client, but much of the knowledge developed in the course of the study stays with the consultancy. All the client gets is a condensed interpretation of this knowledge, in the form of advice about what market segments to target or which local companies to work with. Obviously there are good reasons for commissioning such studies, often based around speed, but ultimately such studies are an unsatisfactory way of developing local market knowledge.

The contracting model is also evident in the various modes of arm's-length market entry such as franchising and licensing. Again, in such cases the international firm elects not to develop the market knowledge itself, but instead chooses to work with an independent company that has the knowledge already. Licensing and franchising are both effective ways of expanding quickly overseas, but with a corresponding loss of control over how the product or service ends up being sold in the foreign market. Contracting of this form also makes future build-up of local market knowledge very difficult, because it puts the international firm in a dependent position vis-à-vis its contractor.

4 Acquiring

The fourth approach to sourcing local market knowledge is by acquiring it. Acquiring market knowledge takes two forms. One is to buy a local company or distributor that has an existing position in the market. If all that is needed is the local market knowledge, acquiring a company is a rather expensive way of obtaining such knowledge. The other way to acquire knowledge is through the individuals that are hired. Both of these are commonplace activities, and they do not require a great deal of elaboration. However it is worth noting a couple of points. The risk with *acquiring* market knowledge, rather than developing it, is that it never gets applied or contextualized in a manner that is useful for the international firm. To use a simple example, if Wal-Mart were to buy a high-end supermarket in France, the knowledge that it acquired would be of little use in rolling out the Wal-Mart business model in France. Clearly the executives running this supermarket chain would be immensely knowledgeable about the market, but it would be difficult for this knowledge to be applied in a way that Wal-Mart would find useful.

The other problem with acquiring knowledge is that it can be very expensive. When e-trade, the online broker, entered the Nordic countries, it hired as its chief executive one of the founders of Icon Medialab, a successful Swedish Internet company. Clearly this individual had relevant and valuable market knowledge, but he also reputedly negotiated himself a very lucrative package.

In summary, the four approaches to sourcing external market knowledge (or "home-base-exploiting" knowledge) are well known, so they have been discussed relatively briefly. The important point to emerge from this discussion that is not so well understood is that each approach has very different implications for the sort of knowledge that ends up residing within the company. Once the other four approaches to knowledge sourcing have been discussed, we will revisit this significant issue.

Home-base-augmenting knowledge

The other major category of external knowledge that is of interest to international companies is home-base-augmenting knowledge, which refers to knowledge about technologies, products, or services that can be incorporated into the company's core offering and used in multiple markets around the world. In other words, it refers to any knowledge picked up in a foreign country that has value outside that location. Again, we can identify four different approaches to accessing this sort of knowledge.

1 Scanning

The concept of establishing some sort of scanning unit in leading-edge market regions around the world is well known. For example, Ericsson has created "Cyberlabs" in New York, Palo Alto, and Melbourne, Australia, that are charged with monitoring developments in those markets and building relationships with local companies. Intel has a small R&D unit in Stockholm that is concerned primarily with tapping into the latest thinking in wireless technology. Volkswagen has a design center in Simi Valley, California, because it recognizes that many sociodemographic and environmental trends start there before working their way to Europe.

The underlying logic for such scanning units is that competition is global, so international companies need to have an early warning device to pick up on trends and ideas at the same time as do their competitors. Particularly for companies that are born in the wrong place, a long way from the epicenter of technology in their chosen industry, scanning units are a vital competitive tool.

However, scanning units of this sort are rarely successful. There are two typical problems. First, the scanning unit is usually a rather small entity that is an observer rather than a participator in the local technology cluster. As a result, it struggles to develop the deep relationships, based on reciprocity and trust, that allow it to become a true insider. Second, scanning units are usually a long way from the home base, both geographically and in terms of the worldview of the respective "scanners' people." As a result, even if good ideas are picked up by the scanning unit, they rarely get acted on back home. Volkswagen's Simi Valley design center became very knowledgeable about changes in Californian legislation and new auto trends, but they struggled to get the ear of the relevant groups back in Wolfsburg. They were eventually given a major role in designing the new Beetle, and this proved to be a great success in North America, but even here it is possible to question whether their learning was ever internalized by the corporate headquarters.

Scanning, then, works well at a superficial level and with primarily codified knowledge, but is less effective as a means of developing tacit or highly specific knowledge. For these forms of knowledge to be developed, partnering and acquiring, both of which are more expensive, are likely to be more effective.

2 Partnering

Many international companies develop joint ventures, alliances, or partnerships in overseas countries, with a view to learning more than just local market knowledge. Such partnering relationships are typically an attempt to build highly specific and deep knowledge about something happening in that local market that can then augment the company's core technologies. Partnering takes many forms. Siemens, Nokia, and Alcatel all have corporate venturing units in Silicon Valley, for example, who identify and invest in exciting start-up companies where they see technological complementarities with their core business. Ericsson has developed relationships with around a dozen US universities, and more specifically with professors who are working on various aspects of communications research. In a more specific example, Cadence, the US chip-design company, worked with Scottish Enterprise on "Project Alba," a state-of-the-art R&D center near Edinburgh.

This involved investment from a number of other companies, and it also involved two local universities developing new Masters degree courses in electronic engineering.

Partnering is an attractive way to develop knowledge because it involves a much deeper level of interaction than do the other approaches. The problems, as observed earlier, are first that it is a slow process, and second that partnering involves opening up one's own knowledge base to external parties. A famous example of this is Toyota and GM's NUMMI joint venture in Fremont, California. For GM, this was intended as a way to develop knowledge about Toyota's lean manufacturing techniques, but in practice the company was never able to transfer this knowledge to its other plants, while Toyota benefited enormously from their greater knowledge of the US market.

3 Contracting

Of the eight approaches to external knowledge sourcing, a decision to use contracting is the most difficult to make sense of. Indeed, one could argue that contracting for home-base-augmenting knowledge is an oxymoron, in that the process of contracting prevents the home-base knowledge from being augmented. However, there are some examples that may be considered a part of this category.

The first is the technology-sourcing approach that many European companies use in Silicon Valley. To provide a specific example, Ericsson's fixed-network business has a purchasing group based in Silicon Valley whose role is to identify companies to which certain components or processes can be subcontracted. One such company was ACC, a Santa Barbara-based company working in IP technology. Initially, Ericsson and ACC signed an OEM/software agreement. However, two years later, Ericsson recognized the strategic value of what ACC was doing and acquired them. In this case, Ericsson's original approach was contract-based, in that no attempt was made to internalize ACC's knowledge in IP. And yet at the same time the knowledge in question was clearly of the home-base-augmenting type.

A related – and less convincing – example is Ericsson's decision to work with the Chasm Group, a Silicon Valley-based consulting company founded by Geoffrey Moore. Moore is well known for such books as *Crossing the Chasm* and *Inside the Tornado*, and he works closely with many Silicon Valley companies. It could be argued that Ericsson's decision to employ the Chasm Group to help it with strategy is a way of contracting for external knowledge that is home-base augmenting. Of course, Ericsson would surely argue that this relationship is more of a partnership and that Moore's ideas will subsequently be internalized by people in Ericsson, but it is often the case that consultant–client relationships do not deliver the intended level of knowledge transfer.

Contracting, in other words, is an unusual arrangement for accessing home-base-augmenting knowledge because typically the company wants to build the knowledge itself rather than contract it out to an independent company. As the above examples show, contracting may be either a temporary measure, leading to an acquisition, or it may be a failed partnering model.

4 Acquiring

Acquiring either companies or people in order to access home-base-augmenting knowledge is very common and needs little explanation. There are some well-known successful examples, such as Deutsche and Dresdner banks buying into the City of London banking sector through the acquisitions of Morgan Grenfell and Kleinwort Benson respectively. Northern Telecom's acquisition of Bay Networks was likewise regarded as an effective way to build a presence in Silicon Valley, notwithstanding the subsequent problems the company has experienced. Well-known failures include Sony and Matsushita's disastrous acquisitions of Hollywood studios in the early 1990s.

The pros and cons of acquiring knowledge have been discussed earlier. Acquisition is typically a fast and effective way of accessing external knowledge, but it is often very expensive, and the knowledge that has been acquired requires contextualizing and applying before it can be used by the acquiring company. The other major risk of this approach is that the individuals – who own the knowledge that is being acquired – are often prone to leave if the acquisition is not handled carefully. Ericsson purchased a Silicon Valley-based company called Raynet some years ago, but by handling the transfer of power badly, they faced a net result of all the valued employees leaving, so Ericsson gained very little of value from their acquisition.

DISCUSSION AND CONCLUSIONS

There are several broad themes that emerge from our review of external knowledge sourcing. The first point to make is that while these are distinct approaches, they are often used in combination. For example, a foreign R&D unit will often be involved in scanning (attending local conferences, hanging out in local bars), partnering (working with local university professors), and acquiring (hiring staff from competitors). So in terms of trying to identify appropriate knowledge-sourcing strategies, these should never be seen as either – or approaches; they should be thought of as complementary and, indeed, are often more valuable when used in combination.

The second broad theme to emerge from our review is that the type of knowledge being sourced in each case is rather different. One way of thinking about this is to use two established dimensions – the extent to which knowledge is tacit, or learned through experience, rather than explicit and codified; and the extent to which it is specific to a particular company or context. Using this frame, scanning typically yields relatively codified and generic knowledge, partnering yields more tacit and company-specific knowledge, contracting gives access to but not ownership of relatively tacit and relatively generic knowledge, and acquiring gives access to both tacit and codified knowledge that is typically industry-specific but not company-specific. Figure 15.2 illustrates this line of thinking. Note that our hypotheses are based on anecdotal data, so there is room for discussion as to exactly how each one is positioned on the grid. But the broad insight that each approach yields different types of knowledge should be clear.

Two further themes should be noted in our conclusion. First, the approach a company takes to external sourcing of knowledge cannot be properly understood without also considering its internal knowledge management strategy. Indeed, as the Volkswagen example hinted, the problem with external knowledge sourcing is often *not* about getting access to external knowledge in the first place. It is about subsequently making use of that knowledge inside the international firm. As a rule,

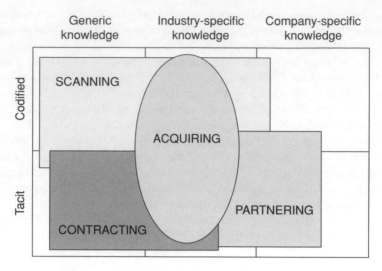

FIGURE 15.2 Types of external knowledge being sourced through each approach

the stronger the links that the foreign subsidiary company has within its local market, the weaker its links with headquarters are likely to be. A classic example of this is Xerox's Palo Alto Research Center (PARC) which, through its deep connections in Silicon Valley, became highly innovative and successful, but increasingly detached from the business units located in Rochester and Stamford. So external knowledge sourcing is evidently important, but it has to be combined with a process for transferring or sharing that knowledge internally.

Finally, it is worth underlining that the company's chosen approach to external knowledge sourcing is only ever part of the picture. Important decisions such as those about joint venture partners, foreign acquisitions, and such, are made on the basis of multiple and often conflicting criteria, including financial returns, speed to market, likely competitor reaction, and government relationships. The impact of the decision on the company's knowledge base is important, but it is often less critical than some of the other criteria. This is why, for example, we see so much contracting despite the clear evidence that it is detrimental to knowledge development. The purpose of this chapter, in other words, is not to suggest that companies rethink their international investment decisions around the development of knowledge, but rather that they enable themselves to explore the ways that external knowledge can be sourced through a *variety* of approaches.

NOTES

1 Aguilar (1967); Hambrick (1982).
2 Håkanson & Johanson (1992).
3 Badaracco (1991); Hamel (1991); Inkpen & Dinur (1998).
4 Berdrow (1997).

5 Bresman, Birkinshaw, & Nobel (1999); Haspeslagh & Jemison (1991).
6 Cohen and Levinthal (1990).
7 Birkinshaw & Solvell (2000); Kummerle (1996); Westney (1990).
8 Porter (1990).
9 Johanson & Vahlne (1977).
10 Kummerle (1996).
11 Worth (2001).

REFERENCES

Aguilar, F. (1967). *Scanning the Business Environment.* New York: Macmillan.

Badaracco, J. (1991). *The Knowledge Link.* Cambridge, MA: Harvard Business School Press.

Berdrow, I. (1997). Learning in joint ventures. Doctoral dissertation, Richard Ivey School of Business.

Birkinshaw, J., & Solvell, O. (2000). Guest Editor's introduction: Leading edge clusters and leading edge multinationals. *International Studies of Management and Organisation*, 30(2), 3–10.

Bresman, H., Birkinshaw, J. M., & Nobel, R. (1999). Knowledge transfer in acquisitions. *Journal of International Business Studies*, 30(4), 439–462.

Cohen, W. M., & Levinthal, D. A. (1990). Absorptive capacity: A new perspective on learning and innovation. *Administrative Science Quarterly*, 35, 128–152.

Fey, C. (1995). Success strategies for Russian–foreign joint ventures. *Business Horizons*, November–December, 49–54.

Håkanson, H., & Johanson, J. (1992). *Industrial Networks: A New View of Reality.* London: Routledge.

Hambrick, D. C. (1982). Environmental scanning and organizational strategy. *Strategic Management Journal*, 3, 159–173.

Hamel, G. (1991). Competition for competence and inter-partner learning within international strategic alliances. *Strategic Management Journal*, 12, 83–104.

Haspeslagh, P. C., & Jemison, D. B. (1991). *Managing Acquisitions: Creating Value through Corporate Renewal.* New York: The Free Press.

Inkpen, A., & Dinur, A. (1998). Knowledge management processes and international joint ventures. *Journal of International Management*, 9(4), 454–468.

Johanson, J., & Vahlne, J-E. (1977). The internationalization process of the firm – A model of knowledge development and increasing foreign market commitments. *Journal of International Business Studies*, 8, 23–32.

Kummerle, W. (1996). The drivers of foreign direct investment in R&D. Doctoral dissertation, Harvard Graduate School of Business Administration.

Porter, M. E. (1990). *The Competitive Advantage of Nations.* New York: The Free Press.

Vernon, R. (1979). The product cycle in the new international environment. *Oxford Bulletin of Economics and Statistics*, 41, 255–267.

Westney, D. E. (1990). Internal and external linkages in the MNC: The case of R&D subsidiaries in Japan, in C. A. Bartlett, Y. L. Doz, & Hedlund, H. (eds.), *Managing the Global Firm.* London and New York: Routledge, pp. 279–299.

Worth, J. (2001). Prêt lightens up New York lunch-break. *Management Today*, January, 73–76.

16

Seeking Global Advantage with Information Management and Information Technology Capabilities

Donald A. Marchand

Senior managers face a series of business and competitive challenges in globalizing their enterprises, and, at the same time, not diluting the historical ingredients and business capabilities that have made their companies successful. The challenges facing senior managers, particularly regarding information technology (IT), are often best captured in their own statements or questions that they pose to their colleagues or external advisors:

Chairman, owner and CEO, large Asia-Pacific industrial group:

"How can my group of 20 diversified companies provide flexibility for each operating company to grow and innovate and, at the same time, leverage scarce functional knowledge, reduce administrative overheads, and employ information and IT across the group?"

President, large regional division, leading elevator company:

"Our business focuses on providing local services to customers in 22 countries. Will our biggest foreign competitor enter our region with a business architecture that relies on 22 country operations with high local focus and higher costs of operations across our region? No way!

CEO, global food products company:

"We are on a course to nurture internal sources of growth in addition to strategic acquisitions. To do so, we must provide our country markets with high flexibility to operate effectively on a local basis. Yet, to compete with global brands against regional and global competitors, we must adopt common processes in our supply chain, reduce the costs of non-value-added activities, and learn to leverage information and IT on a global, regional, and local basis. The challenge is not *if*, but *how* we will do so."

> **Managing board member, global cement group:**
>
> "Differentiating our concrete and cement products locally requires using product, customer, market and operational information better than our competitors to grow market share and profitability. Historically, we have employed a bottom-up, local approach to managing change and innovation in our group companies. Today, one of our biggest competitors has a global, top-down approach to managing information, people, and IT capabilities. How do we compete using information and knowledge across our decentralized group companies and achieve the cost and information-sharing efficiencies of greater standardization by leveraging our information, people, and IT capabilities regionally and globally?"

As these examples indicate, there are four essential elements of organizational design and transformation that face companies as they seek to globalize. First, companies seek paths for growth that emphasize new sources of innovation balanced against efficiencies in operations locally, regionally, and globally. Total cost of operations and growth are not perceived as *or* but *and*. Both are necessary for success in product and service industries where growing commoditization and price pressures on products and services are economic realities.

Second, the managers quoted above are concerned also about recalibrating the organizational pendulum between operating in a decentralized and a more centralized manner. The language of standardization, flexibility, shared services, and common processes points in the direction of finding right balances rather than swinging the pendulum to the extremes of centralization and decentralization.

Next, these managers also recognize that regardless of which path they take, transitioning their companies from a product-oriented, inward focus to a more customer-centric and outward focus is critical for growth in market share, profitability, and company reputation. Behind these concerns are deep changes in management mindsets that drive the search for better and different business results.

Finally, these managers recognize that being a smarter company requires deploying the right mix of information, people, and IT capabilities. Their concerns about sharing scarce expertise and best practices as well as customer and operational knowledge depend on nurturing the right organizational culture (employee behaviors and values) to seek and use information effectively, as well as having the right customer, product, operational, and market information available to anyone who needs it in the company at any time, regardless of structural boundaries.

The managerial mindset represented in these examples is concerned about using information and knowledge effectively and perceives a clear need for the appropriate enabling support of IT services and infrastructure. Thus, a precondition for repositioning the company for going global is the transformation of the IT organization, infrastructure and services that are essential to how information and knowledge will be used by people in the company.

Balancing Flexibility and Standardization

This chapter presents five approaches (figure 16.1) to balancing business flexibility and standardization in globalizing companies, focusing on the criteria and trade-offs that

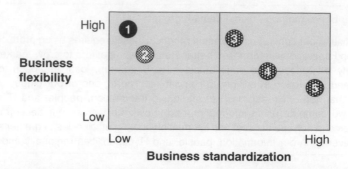

Approach
1 Pursuing business flexibility and standardization country by country, business unit by business unit
2 Realigning business and functional IS with IT infrastructure from the corporate center
3 Managing a global IT infrastructure in a decentralized business application environment
4 Defining a regional approach to business flexibility and standardization
5 Leveraging a global approach to business flexibility and stanndardization

FIGURE 16.1 Balancing business flexibility and standardization

general managers must consider in finding the "right" balance in their companies over time.[1] The chapter will also discuss the transitions between these approaches that companies make in various industries and the key competitive factors that lead some companies to implement the right balance between business flexibility and standardization. Finally, the chapter will address how some companies are able to achieve improved business performance from making these transitions over time.

First, globalizing the enterprise today requires managers to implement an "information-oriented" view of the industry in which the company is competing, based on how their employees use information and IT to achieve business results.[2] This is a key strategic priority. Second, achieving the right balance between business flexibility and standardization cannot be implemented without a corresponding transformation of how the IT organization and resources are deployed across the company. Third, companies that increase their maturity in developing their information, people, and IT capabilities over time are best positioned to reap the business benefits of using information and knowledge effectively, sharing best practices and new knowledge, and moving rapidly to make business changes in response to market and customer demands. Fourth, globalizing the company is fundamentally a matter of managerial mindset and leadership that perceives the dynamic relationship between going global as a strategic concern and building the right business capabilities to leverage information, people, and IT practices over time.[3] Finally, achieving the appropriate balance between business flexibility and standardization cannot be executed equally well by all companies and, therefore, this ability is a source of competitive advantage.

Why getting the balance between business flexibility and standardization counts

Companies that aspire to operate globally have a range of options for balancing business flexibility and standardization. Finding the right balance affects how the company is able to create business value with customers by being flexible in delivering services and products. However, the company also must manage its business processes and infrastructure to reduce demands on working capital, by adopting common processes and information systems (IS) or building capabilities to leverage the company's human knowledge and information across markets, time zones, and geography.

In addition, implementing the right balance is not a one-time choice for most companies but a journey influenced by their product and service mix and the business processes and information required to deliver them. Most companies begin their journey by establishing themselves in many local markets and focusing product and service delivery on local customers. Over time, companies establish relationships with customers or develop brands on a regional and then global basis that require business processes and information to be managed regionally and globally, not just locally. In other cases, companies (such as bulk chemical companies and consumer products companies) sell essentially the same products or services globally and require business processes and information sharing to be global as well.

On the one hand, business *flexibility* provides the business unit or product manager in global companies with the choice of how to tailor their products and services, as well as their demand/supply chain processes and information management practices, to fit the unique needs of local markets. As long as these managers can operate profitably by creating customer value in their business unit (BU) or country, they decide how their business processes, information systems, and information technology infrastructures are configured and managed.

However, business *standardization* reflects the need to find ways to reduce operating costs by seeking to share information about best business practices or by adopting common business processes, information systems, and IT infrastructure wherever feasible. In addition, business standardization may be necessary for a company to leverage its human knowledge across the business and product units, or to share product, customer, and operational information, or to collaborate on projects for the benefit of the global company.

At the center of senior management decisions about the appropriate business architecture for their global company are their perceptions about how information and knowledge should be employed in the company, and the appropriate role and investments in IS and IT infrastructure. Under-invest in IS and IT and the company lacks the capabilities to compete in a networked business environment where speed, flexibility, and quality of information sharing is critical; over-invest and the global company raises its operational costs and, therefore, its use of working capital. Additionally, efforts to implement business standardization may be resisted by the very business units that shared, or common, IS and IT systems are intended to benefit.

Finding the right balance between business flexibility and standardization

Figure 16.2 provides an overview of five approaches to balancing business flexibility and standardization that are discussed below. Each approach, as table 16.1 indicates, has certain strengths and weaknesses associated with its deployment in a company.

Business applications and IT deployment	Approach				
	Multinational 1	International 2	Transnational 3	Regional 4	Global 5
Business Information Systems (BIS)	Local	Local	Local	Regional	Global
Functional Information Systems (FIS)	Local	Local	Global	Regional	Global
IT infrastructure	Local	Local and global	Global	Regional and global	Global

FIGURE 16.2 Approaches to balancing business flexibility and standardization locally, regionally, and globally

Approach 1: Pursuing business flexibility and standardization country by country, business unit by business unit

At some time in their history most global businesses started with this approach. The business is organically grown or developed through numerous mergers and acquisitions country-by-country or business unit by business unit, with a focus on local autonomy and flexibility. Since the company produces, delivers, and sells products locally, the key processes of a company and its business information systems (BIS) such as manufacturing, distribution, marketing, and sales, as well as its functional information systems (FIS) such as the general ledger, accounting, payroll, and purchasing, are also developed and deployed locally. Not surprisingly, with this approach, the company configures its IT infrastructure for data, document, voice, video, and mobile networking to support the local business with little need to achieve any synergies across country units or product lines.

The result of this diversity in BUs or country-based operations is often viewed by senior managers as providing the required flexibility to grow and run the business locally, uninhibited by control or interference from the corporate center. The latter normally plays a more passive role in terms of financial reporting, brand management, and finance and control. Local unit managers define and execute strategies for their businesses and develop their own local people cultures, information practices, and IT infrastructures. In this context, flexibility often leads to *ad hoc* variation in management practices and a strong "not invented here" syndrome.

TABLE 16.1 Five approaches to balancing business flexibility: their strengths and weaknesses

Possible approach	Strengths	Weaknesses
1 *Multinational* Pursuing business flexibility and standardization country by country, business unit by business unit	Country and BU managers are able to configure their organization according to the local market and customers. Corporate (central) managers are able to focus on issues other than IT as these are the responsibility of local managers.	Global business costs are much higher as costs of BIS and FIS can be duplicated many times over. IT systems and infrastructure are incompatible, again leading to higher costs, reduced communication, or both. Poor information sharing across business units.
2 *International* Realigning business and functional IS and IT infrastructure from the corporate center	The corporate center can *enable* business units to exploit synergies and share business and functional information systems. Some costs can be reduced as economies are achieved. The corporate center develops an awareness of IS/IT best practice, which is then more widely disseminated.	Greater bureaucracy can result and consequently decisions take too long, reducing flexibility. If IS/IT is perceived as a cost center then there can be pressure from the center to reduce service levels to local business units (sometimes quite arbitrarily).
3 *Transnational* Managing a global IT infrastructure in a decentralized business environment	The IT infrastructure is provided on a pay-as-you-go basis. IT costs are billed to BU managers and there is an increased awareness of costs at the point where they are incurred. The managers of business units make decisions relating to information systems, but the company's decentralized culture promotes the spread of best practice. A global IT infrastructure provides a platform for business units to use as they grow: therefore businesses can focus on creating value rather than maintaining systems. Business flexibility is maintained with high levels of IT standardization; as a result value creation and growth benefit and costs are lowered.	A company culture of "managed consensus" is required, with the ability to balance global priorities with local business needs. The time needed to establish this delicate balance and company culture can be years. The central IT infrastructure needs to be standardized on a global basis whilst also meeting the constantly evolving needs of local BUs.

TABLE 16.1 (cont'd)

Possible approach	Strengths	Weaknesses
4 *Regional* Defining a regional approach to business flexibility and standardization	Costs are reduced as the regional focus allows companies to reduce costs by adopting standard BIS and FIS across regions (rather than countries). Time is saved and information is standardized as one system in one region needs to be implemented, rather than several (or many) across a number of countries. People, cultures, and processes are aligned to operate in regional mode, often closely mirroring the markets and customers that they are serving.	Considerable top-down management is needed to make this system work effectively. Changes in company culture and management authority are needed. A regional focus can take a long time to implement (often because of resistance from entrenched country managers). Because of the time required to change to a regional focus, it can be difficult to adapt quickly to market changes at the same time.
5 *Global* Leveraging a global approach to business flexibility and standardization	The business's strategy, culture, processes, information, systems, and IT infrastructure worldwide are completely aligned. This matters where markets, products, and brands are global and business flexibility is largely unimportant. Cost economies and productivity – often crucial in these types of business (such as fast-moving consumer goods) – are greatly enhanced. The worldwide business infrastructure facilitates speed and effectiveness.	Business uniformity and consistency are emphasized, and this requires a strong company culture and top-down leadership. The system is less suited to changes in business conditions and markets, where a more flexible approach to local operations may be needed.

What is important to remember about this approach is that it works very well for companies over long periods of time. For Nestlé, this approach dominated its growth until the 1990s. For Microsoft, this approach influenced its international growth through the 1980s and 1990s. In industry after industry, if we closely examine the early development and growth of leading global or international companies, we find that Approach 1 is the dominant one in many successful businesses for many years.

Strengths of this approach   The strengths of this approach stem from the flexibility that it gives to country or BU managers to configure their business architecture to the local market and customers. The country or BU management team perceives IS/IT either as a support function where costs can be minimized, or as a service, providing valued information services to the local company. Corporate management in such companies focuses on financial performance, management of brands internationally, or perhaps centralized R&D, but rarely on IS/IT concerns, since these are included in the management responsibilities of local managers.

Potential weaknesses   There are basically three weaknesses to this approach.

1 There are high costs of doing business globally since BIS and FIS are duplicated in each BU.
2 There are incompatible systems for IT infrastructure and information from BU to BU.
3 There is poor communication and information sharing about customers across BUs.

These weaknesses surface in companies in three ways. Some companies need to reduce the costs of duplicated functional or business processes and IS/IT in local business units, but are frustrated in their efforts by incompatible IT infrastructures and a mélange of internally developed or externally tailored software. Each BU manager defends his BU's uniqueness even in functional areas such as payroll systems, general ledgers, and accounting.

For companies that want to share standard financial reporting measures across all BUs, such efforts are stymied by inconsistent business languages and data definitions, incompatible databases or locally customized applications software, and, of course, locally focused management practices. Finally, for companies that need to deal with global customers or suppliers requiring coordination and information sharing across business units, a range of factors hampers these companies. These include local unwillingness to share customer, product, or operational information with other BUs, incompatible e-mail and messaging networks, and locally organized customer, product, and operational files and databases whose quality varies with the customer relationships of the local company sales team.

Common complaints cited by managers in such companies include the following:

We have 156 of everything – general ledgers, payroll systems, data centers – regardless of value added to the company or of costs of doing business!

Our BU managers do not share best practices across BUs: we have lots of reinvention of BIS, FIS, and IT in our company.

How many different spreadsheet packages, Enterprise Resource Planning Systems (ERP) and Customer Relationship Management (CRM) systems does a global business need? When is *flexibility* counterproductive?

To confront the weaknesses of the highly decentralized BU-by-BU approach, corporate managers in global companies have had to challenge the local authority and prerogatives of the country managers without losing the benefits of a locally focused company. During the 1980s and 1990s, these concerns led companies to pursue a second approach to finding the right balance between business flexibility and standardization.

Approach 2: Realigning business and functional IS and
IT infrastructure from the corporate center

Recognizing that local BUs tend to concentrate on short-term business results and local operating concerns, corporate managers of global companies appointed senior IS/IT managers at the corporate center with several important responsibilities to implement the second approach (figure 16.2). First, the Chief Information Officer (CIO) was responsible for monitoring trends in the business and the IS/IT industry that could lead to opportunities for BUs to develop shared or common systems. Since the mid-1990s, this has led many companies to standardize with one Enterprise Resource Planning systems vendor, such as SAP, or one Customer Relationship Management vendor, such as Siebel Systems. Second, the CIO needed to develop and maintain standards across operating units for voice, video, data, and mobile networking to enable regional and global communications and information sharing. Third, the CIO was charged with lowering the costs of operating voice and data networks as well as consolidating data centers among operating units through shared services initiatives.

While typically the corporate directors of IS/IT reported to the Chief Financial Officer, their operating authority was based on persuasion, not on a top-down mandate. They had to build coalitions among local BUs for setting company-wide IS/IT directions and standards. Rarely could they compel a local BU managing director to adhere to a decision, since the BU manager could cite authority and prerogative to run their BU as they deemed appropriate as long as the BU's financial targets were met.

Strengths of this approach   There are three strengths to this approach.

1 Companies that operate in a very decentralized business culture can maintain their local flexibility, but at the same time can also work toward shared BIS, FIS, and IT services enabled, but not mandated, by the corporate center.
2 Some companies are successful at reducing the overall costs of IT operations by reducing the number of data centers and economizing on voice and data networks locally and globally.
3 Awareness develops from the corporate center about best practices that can be used by local BUs.

Potential weaknesses   However, these strengths are often counterbalanced with three significant weaknesses.

1 Decisions take too long to make. A corporate director of IT complained that "it took us six years to reduce the number of general ledgers in the company from 160 to 30 and may take another 5 years to go from 30 to 4."
2 In most companies, IS/IT continues to be perceived as a cost center where there is continuous pressure from senior corporate managers to lower the cost of IT by

reducing local BU service levels. In one company, the CEO was proud of saying that IS/IT costs were less than 1 percent of sales and would stay that way: "We are not in the IT business, but in manufacturing."

3 The development of IS/IT standards is driven by committees of BU managers and corporate staff which require long decision cycles that often result in preventing rather than facilitating the adoption of IS/IT standards for networking, hardware, operating systems, and common application software.

Approach 3: Managing a global IT infrastructure in a decentralized business application environment

The third approach represents a hybrid among the other four approaches. As we have seen, the first two rely predominantly on managers of BUs deciding how IS/IT should be managed in a global company. The final two depend on strong top-down, regional, or corporate leadership to implement. However, this third approach tries to balance two sets of needs.

Strengths of this approach

1 It aims to meet the needs of a *bottom-up business culture*, where flexibility in deploying BU-specific business processes and systems is needed for growth and innovation.

2 It tries to satisfy the need for *company-wide synergies* to reduce the costs of functional processes and systems while maintaining a transparent, interconnected global IT infrastructure that permits anyone in the company to communicate with anyone else, in any place, at any time.

3 Decisions over BISs are specific to each business unit, enabling BUs to tailor systems to their key business processes to maximize growth and profits. However, decisions about IT infrastructure and FIS are made on a global basis through a process known as *managed consensus*, where open debate is encouraged up to a point, after which a top-down decision is made and local BU managers are expected to implement the decision.

In the 1980s and 1990s, HP employed this approach to decision-making to develop a model for how to balance decentralized business needs for flexibility with a global approach to functional information systems and IT infrastructure.[4] A number of other companies, such as ABB and BP in the late 1990s, adopted aspects of this model to develop global IT infrastructures in decentralized business areas globally. The model continues to attract managerial attention since it seems to reconcile the apparent dilemma of maximizing business flexibility and standardization at the same time, giving a company huge cost savings in IT and FIS across its enterprises while also providing local BUs and country managers flexibility to design their business processes and systems in line with their business strategies.

This model has four additional strengths:

1 It provides the company with transparent voice, data, and video IT infrastructure on a pay-as-you-go basis. All IT costs are billed to the BU managers. The company's senior managers believe that every employee should be aware of the costs of doing business.

2 Although BU managers still make BIS decisions, the company's culture is marked by a strong spirit to beg, borrow, and steal best practices among BUs. This culture promotes the transfer of best BIS practices from one unit to another without top-down decisions over common systems.

3 A global IT infrastructure provides a platform for the business units to use as they grow and change, without reinventing FIS and IT infrastructures each time. BUs can focus on creating value in the business rather than on maintaining functional systems and IT infrastructure.

4 This approach attempts, wherever possible, to maximize high levels of business flexibility with high levels of business and IT standardization, with the aim of promoting growth and value creation in the business and lower costs.

Potential weaknesses The third approach to balancing business flexibility and standardization does have its weaknesses, however. It requires the development of a company culture of managed consensus where global priorities are balanced with local business needs. In a company with a very decentralized, country-by-country culture, this may take many years to develop. Secondly, the approach creates a powerful IT infrastructure function on a global basis that must balance IT standardization with the constantly changing needs of its local BUs. The dangers are twofold: either the IT people will fall behind the rapidly changing needs of the BUs, or the business units will outsource the IT infrastructure to external providers and thus move back from the third to the first approach.

Approach 4: Defining a regional approach to business flexibility and standardization
The fourth approach to finding the right balance between business flexibility and standardization represents a clear move to a *regional focus for the company*. In companies that take this approach, the intent of senior managers in these companies is to treat a region, Europe, for example, as one country, thus moving away from the country-based model.

These global companies perceive their customer supply chain as regional rather than country-specific and want to align their key processes, information management, IS, and IT infrastructures to reflect regional leadership, direction, and operations, rather than a more fragmented and costly collection of local operations. These companies may be in business-to-business industries such as white goods or appliances, where the markets are more regional than global, or in fast-moving consumer goods industries, such as consumer electronics, where retail chains expect their suppliers to operate on a regional rather than local basis.

Strengths of this approach

1 Regional operations allow these companies to reduce costs by adopting standard BIS and FIS across regions, rather than within each country. To the extent that these companies adopt common processes and systems, they save on the time implementing BIS and FIS since they have to install only one system in each region.

2 These companies align their people, cultures, and processes to operate in a regional mode, closely mirroring their markets and customers. Treating Europe as one country accommodates specific regional concerns and business climates that are different from those found in the North American or Asian regions. Thus, the company can

manage information sharing and communication on a regional basis to respond to local market diversity.

Companies such as Dell Computers who have adopted a consistent direct model of business globally, have done so largely through adopting a regional approach to deploying their people, information, and IT capabilities.[5]

Potential weaknesses

1 To work successfully, this approach needs considerable top-down management.
2 Important changes in company culture and power distribution among managers are also required. This is a potential weakness when local and regional differences appear that delay the implementation of this approach.
3 The regional focus takes a long time to implement.

Managers in such companies speak about breaking the country dominance and displacing the country kings or, in the case of Dell, adhering to a consistent direct business model no matter where in the world the company is growing. Clearly, changes in company culture and power distribution among managers are needed, as occurred with Dell in Europe in the 1990s or with bulk chemical companies in the 1980s, when they shifted their business in Europe from a country to regional approach. These changes take time, in some companies up to ten years. These companies must align their whole business system to reflect the regional focus, which requires a consolidation of organization, authority and culture in one consistent direction. If markets change quickly, such commitments to business regionalism may be difficult to change rapidly.

Approach 5: Leveraging a global approach to business flexibility and standardization
The fifth approach extends the fourth from the regional to the global level. In this case, a global company has moved from Approach 1 or 2 in the 1980s to Approach 4 in the late 1980s and 1990s. It is now moving again, from Approach 4, to the globalization of its business processes and systems.

Companies in this category possess very strong top-down cultures. In some cases, such as the Mexican-based CEMEX, the third largest cement producer in the world, CEO Lorenzo Zambrano has since 1987 been the inspiration and guiding force behind taking a global approach to what is normally considered a very local business.[6] For companies using this approach, senior managers want to operate in global markets where selling their products, in France, for example, is basically the same as selling their products in South-East Asia, and where they can use an 80/20 approach, where 20 percent of the value-creating activity needs genuine tailoring to local and customer needs while 80 percent can be standardized across business units and functions. Such companies want to roll out a new business practice, such as Web sales in the US market, and three months later in the Philippine market. To do so requires consistent and accurate information for global decision-making, common processes, information and systems to reduce costs, to eliminate time delays, and to minimize complexity. In addition, new business and functional information systems have to be implemented only once worldwide, rather than in every region and country. This approach saves substantial money and time in FIS and BIS implementations as well as in the deployment of one standard, global IT infrastructure.

Strengths of this approach

1 The company's business strategy, culture, processes, information, systems, and IT infrastructure are aligned worldwide.
2 Speed and effectiveness of doing business globally are facilitated by worldwide IT infrastructure as well as common business and functional systems.

Business flexibility, in the sense mentioned here, is not so important, since business value is created with global brands and a global approach to business practices and information sharing. Cost economies and productivity are critical, especially in low-margin and highly competitive industries such as fast-moving consumer goods or cement. Assuming common markets, products, and brands worldwide, such a company is in an excellent position to maximize profitability and business opportunity globally and locally.

Potential weakness   There is, however, a weakness in this approach: the necessary business uniformity and consistency requires a strong company culture with top-down leadership. Again, the good news is that the whole company has a consistent way of doing business, which is also a potential vulnerability if business conditions or markets change, requiring a more flexible model of global business operations. To overcome this weakness, companies such as CEMEX seek to make their use of information, people, and IT capabilities a competitive advantage by leveraging common processes, systems, IT, and people practices globally, while also seeking to incorporate local innovation and best practices in a consistent way. The logic here is compelling: if a company is better at proactively using information and knowledge both globally and locally than are its more decentralized competitors, then the company can achieve tremendous cost savings from a global approach to processes, systems, and IT; yet its cultural values and behaviors can motivate its people to use information and knowledge wherever in the company it is needed.

Key Competitive Factors in Globalizing the Company with the Right Mix of Business Flexibility and Standardization

Common sense suggests that senior managers choose an approach to business flexibility and standardization that best fits their business environment. However, in some cases, senior managers can seek some combination of five different but related types of competitive advantage when they undertake these transitions from one approach to another in their companies.

The total cost leadership advantage

The first type of competitive advantage arises from attempting to lower the total cost of operations of the global enterprise through increased business standardization, while balancing the need for business flexibility in creating value in local markets. Companies that have moved from Approaches 1 and 2 to Approaches 3 and 4 in their industries have sought to achieve total cost efficiencies and yet still satisfy local needs where they genuinely can create value and growth in their businesses.

An obvious question that arises is: what is the point of being part of a global group of companies, if there are no cost efficiencies coming from the way the group can leverage its resources regionally or globally across its business units? The CEO of a leading beer company in Europe captured this point in a comment he made about why a truck full of his branded beer with multi-country labeling on cans and bottles somehow could not cross from one European country to another in the common market. His company had historically succeeded in building a strong business regionally and globally based on Approach 1 and managers in the business did not see or look for opportunities to reduce the cost of operations locally by adopting the common processes, systems, and information flows that would permit the delivery of beer across borders in the same region. Such stories among senior managers of large companies tell of their frustrations in not seeking more cost *and* value synergies in the locally focused, global company.

The execution advantage

The second type of competitive advantage arises when two or more competitors in an industry seek to redefine the balance between business flexibility and standardization by moving from Approaches 1 and 2 to 3, 4 or 5; but not all are equally successful in doing so. This execution advantage arises from the fact that these transitions by companies are complex and involve significant changes in not just IT capabilities, but also in information management practices and in shared or common people behaviors and values that affect the ways information and knowledge will be deployed in the company under the new approach. For example, American companies such as Wal-Mart and many others have been very successful in defining a standard approach to information, people, and IT capabilities in their home markets. But, in the process of growing internationally by mergers and acquisitions, they have had great difficulty in transitioning their people practices and information management practices with equal effectiveness in overseas operations. Companies like these have moved from Approach 1 to 2 and back to 1 since they have had limited success in translating their model of doing business into their acquired companies. This is in contrast to companies like CEMEX and Banco Bilbao Vizcaya Argentaria (BBVA) in Spain, who have used the criteria of cultural proximity and attractiveness for acquiring and integrating companies with "IBERIO" cultural traits into their way of expanding their business reach to Latin America, Portugal, Spain, and even the United States.[7] In addition, unlike Wal-Mart, companies like BBVA and CEMEX have been very attentive to rapidly and systematically integrating their acquisitions into the BBVA or CEMEX way of doing business. Today, both BBVA and CEMEX are moving beyond cultural proximity to organizational proximity as a criterion for seeking acquisitions globally and rapidly assimilating them into the BBVA or CEMEX way of doing business, a globally standard way of deploying information, people, and IT capabilities.

The contrarian advantage

The third type of competitive advantage arises when one company in an industry decides to adopt a contrarian approach to business flexibility and standardization. The senior managers of the company consciously choose to adopt approach 3, 4 or 5 when all other leading companies in their industry are taking approach 1 or 2. In this case, senior managers perceive that the appropriate fit in their industry to business flexibility and standardization would lead to a form of competitive necessity that does not give any one player any differentiated advantage. So, over time, they go for an approach that runs contrary to where the pack of business competitors is going. For example, in the 1980s and 1990s, the first bulk chemical company to achieve regional and then global standardization in business processes, systems, and IT enjoyed a competitive advantage until all other competitors caught up over the next five to seven years. Starting in the early 1990s, Hewlett Packard (HP) enjoyed a major cost advantage in IT and functional information systems by operating its decentralized business following Approach 3 rather than 2 or 1, which is where most of its competitors were. Similarly, Michael Dell has chosen to implement the direct business model in the PC and peripherals industry on a regional basis, leveraging highly centralized regional business processes, information practices, and people behaviors and values, while most of his competitors have adopted locally based approaches to international expansion. Finally, in the cement industry, Lorenzo Zambrano of CEMEX started with Approach 1 in the Mexican market in the 1980s, adopted Approach 4 in the 1990s with Latin American expansion, and now has moved to Approach 5 as the company has sought to grow on a global basis.

In each of these cases, senior managers are developing their approach to business flexibility and standardization with a careful eye to differentiated fit relative to other competitors in their industry over time. Their advantages in this case can be both short and long term. In the short term, they can enjoy cost and value advantages that their competitors cannot replicate with Approaches 1 and 2. In the longer term, these contrarian companies can extend their business models globally in ways that their competitors can talk about but not execute.

The information orientation advantage

The fourth type of competitive advantage develops when a company's vision for making these transitions extends beyond standardizing operational processes and IT services/infrastructure in order to lower the total costs of operations toward how the company uses information and knowledge across its employees, customers, partners, and suppliers more effectively than do competitors. This managerial approach is driven by a desire to be more agile, flexible, and swift in using market, customer, product, operational, and best practice information effectively across a business than any other competitors locally or globally. Managers in these companies recognize that regional or global IT standardization and practices are necessary but not sufficient to extract business value from the ways information and knowledge are used internally by their employees and externally with customers, partners, and suppliers. They are also looking to instill the appropriate values and behaviors such as integrity, transparency, sharing, and proactiveness in their people and the appropriate information management practices to sense, collect, organize, maintain, and process useful information in their companies.

These managers are seeking high maturity in the Information Orientation[8] of their companies to achieve superior business performance not just locally, but regionally and globally as well. As figure 16.3 suggests, by working on all three information capabilities at the same time, information, people, and IT, and achieving higher effectiveness in information and knowledge usage across their companies, these managers are seeking to use effectiveness in information and knowledge use to differentiate their companies from

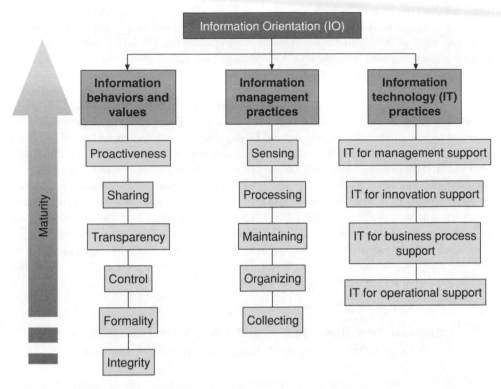

FIGURE 16.3 The Information Orientation (IO) maturity framework
Source: Marchand, D. A., Kettinger, W. J., & Rollins, J. D. (2001), *Information Orientation: The Link to Business Performance*. Oxford: Oxford University Press.

their competitors.[9] The source of competitive advantage in this case arises not just from the deployment of effective IS/IT practices regionally and globally, but more importantly, from the ability to develop and deploy a consistent set of values, behaviors, management incentives, and training that focuses on developing information practices effectively across the enterprise locally, regionally, and globally. Achieving regional and global maturity on all three sets of capabilities is what provides these companies with significant information and knowledge advantages over their more locally focused competitors. Research has demonstrated that the thread that runs through the development of companies as diverse as Dell Computers, CEMEX, and BBVA, among others, is this commitment to building information, people, and IT capabilities over time on a regional and global level that helps them to know more than their competitors about their customers, products, services, markets, and best practices, and to use that information more effectively wherever in the enterprise can create business value.[10]

The leadership advantage

The fifth type of competitive advantage arises from the mindset and consistent leadership of senior managers to envision the need for transitions from Approaches 1 and 2 to Approaches 3, 4 or 5 before their own people and their competitors clearly perceive the need for this type of transformation in their industry. This leadership advantage is crucial in developing the lead time to execute changes that may take two to five years to move from one stage of development to the next. In companies like CEMEX, BBVA, and Dell, this commitment to the evolution of the company as a global enterprise has taken many years and has evolved in a series of strategic moves linked to building the appropriate information capabilities, as noted earlier. Each company in its early years moved from developing an information-oriented business model in its domestic market and in the next stage sought regional rather than global development. Each company has consistently pursued building information, people, and IT capabilities linked to each stage of its development. And each company has emerged as an industry leader in the face of competitors that claimed they, too, could replicate the company's business model and capabilities. In fact, this persistence to evolutionary change and transition from one approach to another in the balancing of business flexibility and standardization, coupled with a commitment to using information, people, and IT capabilities better than other firms in their industries, provide these companies with significant sources of advantage that cannot be in the short term copied by competitors who pursue more locally based visions of their enterprise or who do not understand that the evolution from Approaches 1 or 2 to 3, 4 or 5 is not inevitable, but rather requires a disciplined journey.

ACHIEVING THE BENEFITS OF *BOTH* BUSINESS FLEXIBILITY AND STANDARDIZATION IN GLOBALIZING THE COMPANY

While there may not be one best approach to achieving the right mix of business flexibility and standardization in a company, how is it that some companies have been able to achieve the benefits of local flexibility to promote market responsiveness and global standardization to achieve lower costs simultaneously? How do some companies turn what appears to be a business paradox into a business advantage by achieving flexibility and standardization benefits at the same time? We offer ten principles that have guided the decisions of senior executives in globalizing their companies to achieve both business flexibility and standardization (see also figure 16.4).

1 Senior managers seek to reduce the total cost of business operations and create business value at the same time. They use as a decision criterion the notion that business activities can be standardized according to an 80/20 rule where 20 percent of the value-creating activity needs genuine tailoring to local and customer needs while 80 percent can be standardized across business units and functions. They are willing to apply this rule to value chain functions from manufacturing to logistics through to market, sales, and customer services. Thus they search for common or shared information, processes, and systems across all business activities of the enterprise.

2 Senior managers understand that IT infrastructure services and functional information systems do not add direct value to their businesses and therefore should be unified across the enterprise regionally or globally. This substantially reduces the total cost of operations across the company, and can work toward leveraging the best functional and technical knowledge anywhere it is needed in the company. Thus, operating centers of excellence for functions such as finance, human resources,

legal matters, and public communications as well as IT provides the company an opportunity to reduce headcount and still use the best people in support activities that do not create direct business value.

3 Senior managers are focused on the rapid diffusion of best practices anywhere they are needed in the company. In the traditional company using Approach 1 or 2, managers can act as if they did not know best-practice information was available to solve operational problems, whereas in the global enterprises managers must act on the knowledge of best practices in solving problems, since the company information and IT practices make this information available anywhere, any time.

4 Senior managers understand the difference between acting in a globally flexible way versus a locally flexible way. While local flexibility is useful, it often inhibits the pursuit of global or regional flexibility by placing too much attention on local differences at the cost of commonalties. Thus, local managers can insulate themselves from seeking synergies and shared practices across the enterprise by claiming local differences where they do not exist. "Not invented here" is often the safeguard of local flexibility.

5 Senior managers encourage and support proactive IS/IT leadership to work toward standardizing IT infrastructure and support services across the enterprise so that the business managers can focus their attention on the deployment of effective business information and people practices to drive information use in their businesses. Globalizing the IT organization and services makes a company more rather than less flexible, since information and knowledge can be communicated and shared anywhere in the enterprise it is needed.

6 Senior managers seek to build a shared, action-oriented culture around the integrity, quality, and use of information and knowledge anywhere in the company they are needed and can be put to use to improve the business. For these managers, a company must act on what it knows every day or it could be blindsided by smarter competitors. Managers in the globalizing company understand that these attitudes toward proactive information use must be cascaded throughout every level of the company.

7 Senior managers are focused on building an information-oriented business where organizational and structural barriers to information and knowledge use are no longer tolerated and are actively assaulted. Releasing the power of information in their companies involves removing the barriers to using information and knowledge anywhere in the company they are needed. Such practices encourage more rather than less standardization of information, people, and IT capabilities across the company, as structural barriers to information use are actively discouraged.

8 Senior managers practice decisive management styles that encourage debate, decision, and action and discourage management styles based on debate, decision, and more debate. Managers recognize that top-down leadership is required to pursue standardization among well-intentioned people who would like to protect local prerogatives and local flexibility. Channeling the bottom-up energy and initiative in a company is what achieving the right balance between flexibility and standardization is about.

9 Senior managers do not shy away from complexity and ambiguity in business, but recognize that simplifying and standardizing the information, people, and IT capabilities of the company best prepares it to deal with the inevitable diversity, complexity, local variations, and differences in its business environment.

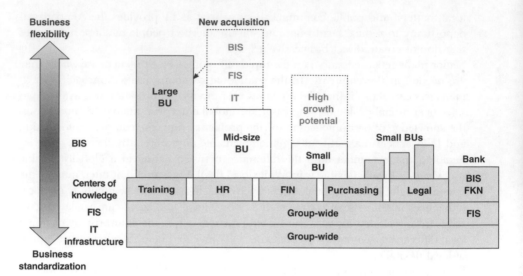

FIGURE 16.4 Balancing group and individual company flexibility and standardization

10 Finally, senior managers recognize that achieving the right balance between flexibility and standardization is a managed journey rather than a destination. It must be taken in doable time frames with initiatives that show real business results. Companies that embark on this journey focus on evolutionary change since their managers believe that building global flexibility and standardization contributes to a company whose business capabilities depend on the rapid and targeted use of information, knowledge, people, and IT capabilities to achieve business results. Business results are a measure of the effectiveness with which their companies use information and knowledge to cope with rapid change, increasing complexity, and high uncertainty.

Conclusion: Competing Globally with Business Flexibility and Standardization

In closing, it is useful to return to where we began. What did the four senior managers who posed the hard questions about business flexibility and standardization actually do to address the questions that they raised at the beginning of this chapter?

Case 1: Chairman, owner and CEO, large Asia-Pacific industrial group

This senior manager decided to transition his group of companies from Approach 1 to Approach 3, as figure 16.2 suggests. The first step involved hiring a business-oriented IT Director at group level to manage the transition from company-specific IT to a group-wide IT infrastructure. The second step was to adopt standard functional information systems in HR, finance, and purchasing that were either bought externally or chosen from the best of internal company systems. The third step was to establish centers of excellence in functional knowledge in six key areas to support all companies with the best expertise rather than limit functional experts to supporting only one company, as in the past. For a company that operated in emerging markets, such a move was critical since it was difficult if not impossible to hire highly competent functional experts in each company. The fourth step was to encourage all business units to modernize their business information systems in line with the needs of their core business using the 80/20 rule, so best practices in business processes and information management could be shared across the different units. The only exception was the group's bank, since there were certain legal requirements to operate business and functional systems at arm's length from the group companies. Finally, the group was able to develop a post-integration merger and acquisition strategy that permitted the group to rapidly integrate the acquired company's IT and functional systems into the group in weeks and months rather than years. While the group remains quite diverse in business interests, nonetheless, today, the group operates from a shared platform that reduces the total cost of operations, provides expertise and technology to small companies at a higher level than in the past, and focuses management attention on deploying information, people, and IT capabilities to create value for the business and the group as a whole.

Case 2: President, large regional division, leading elevator company

Within months of making his statement quoted above in front of his 22 country managers, this company acquired a new CEO and the decision was made to divide the 22 country operations into 3 regions operating in a more regional rather than country orientation. The president became head of one of the three regions. The CEO moved the company from Approach 2 to Approach 4 over the next three years as he sought to reduce the total operating costs of the company against its foreign competitors that were now building better elevators at lower costs and supporting them through regional approaches to IT, functional information systems, and even business information systems. Having regained its profitability through lowering its cost structure, the company is better positioned to leverage its reputation, deep business knowledge, and human capabilities to target real sources of competitive differentiation locally in elevator markets and at the same time leverage regional and global expertise where it creates technological, product, and operational advantages. Thus the company was able to achieve a better balance between flexibility and standardization to respond to substantial competitive threats. Ironically, this was all done in a region where country managers adopted different payroll, general ledger and purchasing systems just to be different.

Case 3: CEO, global food products company

For most of its distinguished history, this company grew and operated successfully using Approach 1. From the mid-1980s to the late 1990s the company operated under Approach 2, treating IT standardization as necessary, but only by voluntary compliance. The CEO at that time considered IT an operational support function and cost center and so IT budgets were kept to a minimum company-wide. During the late 1990s, the current CEO decided to move the company from Approach 2 to Approach 4 over a seven-year time frame. An ambitious project organization was launched from the corporate center with the objective to standardize the IT infrastructure regionally and globally, as well as adopt common functional and business information systems on a regional and local basis. This dramatic move to transform the balance of business flexibility and standardization in the company is aimed at making the company more and better able to share and use information, people, and IT capabilities anywhere in the world they are needed. This story remains unfinished.

Case 4: Managing board member, global cement group

As the former CEO of a country operating company, this senior executive focused on making information and knowledge use sources of differentiation in the local cement market by increasing the company's information, people, and IT capabilities and making the company more market- and customer-centric. After three years of improved business results, the country CEO was appointed to the managing board of the global, but highly decentralized group. Recognizing that success in the cement business required lowering the total costs of operations in his region, the manager sought to move his region from Approach 1 to 4 over two years. However, in adopting the regional approach, he employed a "copy and paste" approach[11] to standardizing IT and business information systems in the region by using the templates and IT systems that had worked in his earlier company. With no history of top-down decision-making in the group, this manager has sought to adapt the approach of managed consensus from Approach 3 while developing a shared vision of leveraging information and knowledge competitively across the region and locally as well. The success of his efforts depend on managing a growing consensus among managers in the region that operating on a regional and local basis to leverage information, people, and IT capabilities for growth is not an *or*, but an *and*. By sharing information capabilities and best practices, the operating companies can collaborate and better serve their local markets at a lower total cost of operations with regional capabilities.

Each of these cases illustrates that the challenge for senior managers to find the right balance between business flexibility and standardization to improve business performance and use information, people, and IT capabilities effectively requires continuous learning and adjustment. However, not addressing this challenge may prohibit the globalizing company from navigating in a complex, ambiguous world where not seeking new knowledge and using what a company knows are perhaps the biggest competitive dangers that a company now faces.

NOTES

1 Marchand, D. A. (2000), The IT advantage: Competing globally with business flexibility and standardization, in D. A. Marchand (ed.), *Competing with Information: A Manager's Guide to Creating Value with Information Content*, London: John Wiley, pp. 283–298.

2 Marchand, D. A., Kettinger, W. J., & Rollins, J. D. (2001a), *Information Orientation: The Link to Business Performance*, Oxford: Oxford University Press.

3 Jeannet, J-P. (2000), *Managing with a Global Mindset*, London: Financial Times and Prentice-Hall.

4 Marchand, D. A., & Oliver, D. (1997), *Hewlett-Packard (HP): Competing With A Global IT Infrastructure*, Lausanne, Switzerland: International Institute for Management Development, Case Study GM 653, 14 pp.

5 Marchand, D. A., Boynton, A., & Shaner, J. (1999), *DELL Direct in Europe: Delighting the Customer With Every Order*, Lausanne, Switzerland: International Institute for Management Development, Case Study GM 785, 14 pp.

6 Marchand, D. A., & Chung, R. (2002), *Cemex: Global Growth through Superior Information Capabilities*, Lausanne, Switzerland: International Institute for Management Development, Case Study GM 1081, 13 pp.

7 Marchand. D. A., Kettinger, W. J., & and Rollins, J. D. (2001b), *Making the Invisible Visible: How Companies Win with the Right Information, People and IT*, London and New York: John Wiley.

8 Marchand, Kettinger, & Rollins, 2001a.

9 Marchand, Kettinger, & Rollins, 2001b.

10 *Ibid.*

11 Szulanski, G., & Winter, S. (2002), Getting it right the second time, *Harvard Business Review*, 80(1), 62–69.

17

Global Account Management: New Structures, New Tasks

Julian Birkinshaw and Joseph J. DiStefano

In most multinational corporations today, global account management is high on the strategic agenda. While the concept was initially developed in the 1980s as a way to manage increasingly complex relationships with global customers in the professional services sector, it has now found widespread acceptance in industrial and high-technology companies, and is even beginning to take hold in the consumer goods sector.

But while global account management sounds alluring in principle, its practice creates enormous challenges and complications. Global account management typically requires a new organizational overlay on top of what is already a complex, multidimensional structure. It demands new ways of working for anyone involved in marketing and selling to international customers. Last but not least, the process of *implementing* a global account management structure can be long and painful, because implementation involves shifting responsibilities and power balances within the global organization. In short, global account management reflects a response to the fluctuating complexities of interdependence, ambiguity, and multiplicity that are the underlying themes of this book.

This chapter presents a detailed discussion of global account management and the main challenges facing multinational corporations as they work with and implement these structures. Our discussion is in five sections. Section 1 looks at the drivers of global account management, the changes in the business environment that have led so many corporations to create such structures. Section 2 describes the organizational structures and roles typically used in global account management, while Section 3 examines the process of implementing such a structure. Section 4 focuses on the impact that global account management has on performance. Section 5 integrates the previous parts by reviewing the experience of a major industrial manufacturing company that adopted global account management in stages over a period of years.

1 Drivers of Global Account Management

The emergence of the global customer

The single most important trend driving global account management is the emergence of global customers, customers who are purchasing their inputs on an integrated basis worldwide, and who are therefore looking for a single global point of contact with their suppliers.

In which industries do we see such global customers? A recent survey of a wide range of companies that were either undertaking or considering global account management identified three broad categories:

- *Industries in which global customers are the core of the business*. Telecom equipment manufacturers such as Ericsson and Nortel, for example, sell most of their products nowadays to global operators such as Telefonica and Vodafone. Automotive component manufacturers sell almost exclusively to auto giants such as Ford, Volkswagen, and Toyota.
- *Industries in which global customers are an important and profitable segment*. This is currently the most common category, including industries such as banking, insurance, computers, chemicals, and industrial products.
- *Industries in which global customers are an emerging segment*. This is particularly evident in the consumer products sector, where food and household products companies are selling to the big retailers such as Carrefour, Wal-Mart, and Tesco, which themselves are starting to become global in scope.[1]

There are also several industries in which global customers are not yet an issue. The automotive industry sells through dealers that are predominantly owned and run on a local basis. The pharmaceutical industry sells primarily through channels that are state controlled. While these and others are likely to change in future, they currently have little or no concern about global customers. As in the case of the automotive industry, though, they may well have global account relationships with their suppliers, as we will see in Section 4.

While the globalization of customers is the single most important driver of global account management, there are also many other factors at work that make it both possible and desirable for a company to sell on a globally integrated basis. Table 17.1 lists a complete set of drivers.

From global customers to global account management

Just because a customer is global in scope does not mean that they should be managed as a global account. As observed already, the key factor that drives the creation of global accounts is the extent of the *demands* placed on the vendor by the customer. Six sets of such demands are: (1) coordination of resources for serving customers; (2) uniform global prices; (3) uniform terms of trade; (4) standardization of products and services; (5) consistency in service quality and performance; and (6) service in markets in which the company has no customer operations.[2] Survey evidence has shown that demand for all of these had increased dramatically during the 1990s and that the most important was consistency in service quality and performance.

TABLE 17.1 Drivers of global account management

Global customers Customers who are global in their scope of operations, and who have to some degree integrated their purchasing activities.

Global channels Channels to market that are global in scope, even if the final customer is locally focused. For example, Tamro and Alliance-Unichem are international pharmaceutical distributors.

Transferable marketing Many marketing elements, such as brand names and advertising, require little adaptation and are readily transferable across countries.

Lead countries New ideas and innovative practices are often concentrated in a few countries, and global account management helps to ensure that customers in these lead countries get special attention so that the company learns.

Global economies of scale Global account management provides a way of coordinating activities so that facilities achieve their necessary economies of scale.

High product development costs Product development costs can be amortized across many markets if there is a system in place to ensure that the same product is sold on a global basis.

Competitors globalized A company's approach to globalization has to be driven as much by the competitive realities of the industry as by its innate globalization potential. So if competitors have moved toward global account management, the company has little choice but to follow.

Source: Yip, G., & Madsen, T. (1996), Global account management: The new frontier in relationship marketing, *International Marketing Review*, 13(3), 24–42.

The second factor that appears to be important in determining whether a global account management structure is used is the *strategic importance of the customer*. One measure of this is the percentage of all customer inputs the vendor sells to them. To consider a hypothetical example, Vodafone may buy a third or so of all its inputs from Ericsson, but well under one percent of its inputs from 3M (miscellaneous office products) or ISS (a global cleaning company). While Vodafone may decide to push for reduced global prices from all three, the broader set of demands listed above is likely to make sense only for Ericsson.

Considering these two factors together, the strategic importance of the product to the customer and the customer's global integration (see figure 17.1) gives a sense of the customer's demands on the vendor and hence the likelihood that a global account arrangement will be valuable.[3] The shaded area on figure 17.1 represents the area in which global account management is most worthwhile. The further toward the top right quadrant, the more critical global account management becomes.

Vendor objectives in creating global accounts

The discussion so far has focused mostly on the customer's demands. But clearly the vendor's objectives are also important. Indeed, evidence suggests that not all vendors wait

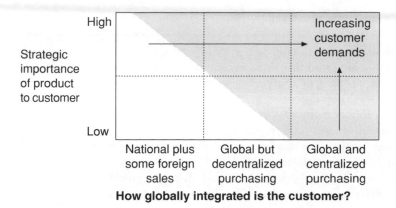

FIGURE 17.1 Identifying which customers require global account management
Source: Birkinshaw, Arnold & Toulan (2000).

for their customers to demand global account relationships; some proactively seek out customers with whom they can develop such relationships on their own terms.

The question of whether global accounts are set up by the vendor in a reactive or proactive manner is important because the objectives of the two parties are typically very different. The proactive customer typically sees global account management as a way of reducing prices. The proactive vendor is typically looking for ways to differentiate itself from its competitors (for example, with better service) or increase its sales volume. Of course, relationships have to be structured in a win–win way if they are to survive in the long term. The implicit agreement appears to be that global accounts involve lower prices in return for higher volumes, but with many other elements as well. Table 17.2 lists objectives typically mentioned by companies in their global account relationships.

The other important issue for vendors is to figure out how many global account relationships to create. Anecdotal evidence suggests that companies with large global account programs have gone through an analysis of their customers and ended up with some sort of 80–20 split, whereby 20 percent of their customers provide 80 percent of their revenues. This makes it easy to establish the approximate numbers of global accounts that deserve special attention. The number varies from a couple of accounts (typically a pilot program) through to just over one hundred, though 20 or 30 are more common. The common criteria used to select global accounts are listed in table 17.3.

One important point in making this assessment is to recognize that global accounts are not synonymous with *key accounts*. For example, one of HP's biggest customers is Boeing, but because it has an almost exclusively US presence it is handled as a national key account that reports exclusively to the US sales organization. This arrangement allows them to avoid the complex global structures described below.

What happens to the customers that are not designated as global accounts? Some companies have established a multi-tiered system of global accounts, international accounts, prospective accounts, and so on. Others have explicitly created new support systems for serving their non-global accounts. Many companies already had "key account" systems for accounts that were handled on a national level.[4] But the point is that for global account management to work from the vendor side it has to be exclusive, because the

TABLE 17.2 Vendor objectives in establishing global accounts

Growth in sales to customer worldwide
Cross-selling into new divisions of customer operation
Greater control of relationship with customer
Increased responsiveness to customer's specific needs
Matching of competitor moves
Joint innovation projects with customer
More efficient use of salespeople's' time in serving customer
Reduced administrative costs
Access to leading-edge practices undertaken by customer
Tapping into new product ideas suggested by customer
Avoiding trade diversionary practices
Creation of a long-term relationship

Source: Birkinshaw, Toulan, & Arnold (2001).

TABLE 17.3 Commonly mentioned criteria for selecting global accounts

Size of global sales to customer
Global sales potential of customer
Customer buys from multiple vendor businesses
Focus on certain sectors
Customer is market leader in its segment
Customer open to close relationship with vendor
Opportunity for learning or innovation by vendor
Customer has centralized purchasing
Customer views vendor product as "strategic"

Source: Birkinshaw, Toulan, & Arnold (2001).

selection represents a commitment to the customers that are designated as global accounts. One manager noted that he gets one call a week from a salesperson asking for his customer to be upgraded to a global account. And 90 percent of the time he says no, because if the program becomes too big, it becomes impossible to retain focus.

2 GLOBAL ACCOUNT MANAGEMENT STRUCTURES

Reporting structure

Every company has its unique structure for global account management that takes into account the existing organization as well as the need for global customer coordination. Three broad approaches can be identified, based around the balance of power between the global account manager (GAM) and the country sales manager. This is the key issue,

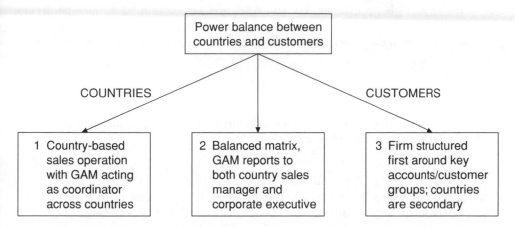

FIGURE 17.2 Options for structuring the global sales organization

because often there will be conflicts between what is best for the local country and what is best for the global customer, and the power balance is what tips the decision one way or the other. Three generic situations can be envisaged, as indicated in figure 17.2.

1 *The balance of power lies with country sales managers.* Under this structure, global account managers act as coordinators across countries, but the ownership of the account stays at the local level. Ericsson, for example, has traditionally had very strong local companies, and up until 1999 these companies retained ownership of all sales in their national market. Global account managers acted as information providers, influencers, and coordinators, but they did not have decision-making power over sales to their account. British Telecom (BT) is another example of this structure. Many of BT's overseas operations are joint ventures, which means that all local sales are legally owned by the joint venture, not by BT. Thus, as in the case of Ericsson, BT's use of global account management represents a way of coordinating across strong local sales organizations.

2 *There is a "matrix organization" in which global account managers report to both their local sales manager and to a corporate executive responsible for global accounts.* This is probably the most common arrangement, seen in such companies as ABB, 3M, HP, and Intel. In cases of conflict, such as the GAM spending time building sales to the global customer in another country, it is up to the local sales manager and the corporate executive responsible for global accounts to agree on a solution. The matrix is typically not completely balanced, in that the local may usually take precedent over the global, or vice versa, but the point is that the GAM has someone to turn to in each direction. And that is the essence of matrix management.

3 *The balance of power lies with the global account managers.* This structure is currently fairly rare, but it is starting to emerge in a few companies. The logic of this structure is that global customers are more important than local sales, so the company is organized first and foremost around those customers. The best examples are top-tier automotive suppliers such as Magna and Bosch and contract electronic manufacturers such as Solectron and Flextronics, because their activities are defined around a few large

customers. Others, including HP and ABB, are starting to think in such terms, but because sales has historically been a local-for-local activity, there is a strong administrative heritage to overcome before the global customer organization can emerge.

Supporting systems

The reporting structure gives an overall sense of how global account managers fit with the rest of the sales and marketing organization, but to work effectively it has to be backed up with a range of supporting systems.

Evaluation and reward systems

Traditionally, salespeople are evaluated and rewarded on the basis of their sales quota. Global account management creates some difficulties with the quota system. To take a hypothetical example, when Electrolux makes a sale to Shell in Germany, should that sale be attributed to the German sales manager or to the global account manager for Shell? The answer for most companies is that the sale is double counted, that is, both individuals get credit for it. For this approach to work, the bonus system has to be adjusted accordingly, otherwise the company ends up paying out too much in bonuses. But most companies seem to have figured out how to make it work. The alternatives – not paying bonuses, or trying to figure out who did the work on each sale – are less attractive.

Double counting sales is not the whole answer to the question of evaluation and reward for global account managers. An equally big issue is how to motivate the global account manager to act in the long-term interests of the customer, rather than just for short-term gain. This is always an issue in sales reward systems, but it is particularly acute in the case of global account management because the relationships are often intended to be long-term strategic partnerships. Many companies have, in fact, moved toward a compensation system for global account managers that is mostly fixed salary and a relatively small bonus for making the sales quota.

Head-office support

Many companies have built a head-office support function to provide specific help or extra resources to global account managers. The services they offer include: pooled support services, corporate-wide marketing programs that have to be standardized across global accounts, internal marketing for the global account structure, funding one-off or special projects, and providing consultancy services to local sales organizations. Some also hold annual forums or conferences, so that global account managers from around the world can get together to share their experiences.

Global account executives

These are senior individuals in the company given an overview responsibility for specific accounts. They can be called on to support the global account manager in a critical sales meeting or if conflicts arise with the local sales organization. Particularly when the global account program is relatively new, this is an important way of giving it support and visibility.

Information technology (IT) support systems

Of course every company uses IT, but the important issue here is the extent to which those IT systems can track information by customer. As companies first establish global account programs, they typically realize that their existing IT systems are not configured in such a way that sales or profitability by customer can be calculated. Today, some companies have solved this problem, as has been explained in the preceding chapter on information management and IT capabilities. HP, for example, can now draw up P&Ls for each of its global accounts.

Customer councils

Some companies, such as BT, have developed customer councils, at which senior executives from the global accounts are brought together with the global account managers and executives. These events provide an opportunity for the vendor to learn more about their customers' demands and for the customers to hear about the vendor's latest products and services.

This may not be a comprehensive list, but it gives a good sense of the kind of support services that companies are offering to their global account managers. Whether all these additional services can be justified is not clear at the present time. It is always easy to identify new services that should be offered or to add resources, but the challenge is to cut costs elsewhere at the same time. One of the fundamental challenges that global account management faces is to achieve its objectives *without* becoming a massive new overhead on the global sales organization.

The role of the global account manager

The global account manager can be one person, a whole team, or a fraction of a person. For example, Skandia, the Swedish insurance company, has global account managers each of whom manages five or more global accounts. At the other extreme, one of Ericsson's global accounts has eight people working on it full time. In addition, many companies use a system with one account manager, plus a variety of technical and administrative support people also working on the account.

In terms of experience level, the global account manager is typically at approximately the level of a national sales manager and with a background in sales. This gives him or her sufficient seniority to deal with a global purchasing manager. For key meetings, global account managers typically have a senior "global account executive" on whom they can call.

The global account manager's network

Global account managers are seen first and foremost as employees of their local sales organization. Some companies have toyed with the idea of establishing a "global" team of global account managers that have affiliation only to their customers, but they all ended up giving their global account managers a home wherever it made most sense, typically near the head office of the customer. The local sales organization pays the global account manager's salary, manages his or her career, conducts performance appraisals, and provides administrative support.

Where there is a considerable amount of variation is in the way global account managers spend their time. As noted in one recent study,[5] at one extreme there were a couple of Ericsson account managers who spent the vast majority of their time in the customers' offices or working with the customer on bids for telecoms licenses. These individuals were far more conversant with their customers' strategy than with Ericsson's. At the other extreme was one Johnson & Johnson global account manager who ended up spending large amounts of his time working with his internal network of sales managers, coordinating their actions and spreading information about the opportunities afforded by the global customer.

3 Implementing a Global Account Structure

This section considers the issues multinational companies face in implementing global account structures. Just as with any other form of organizational change, the creation of a global account structure is highly complex. As a result, many companies have taken many years to implement their global account structures, and others have even given up on their global account efforts and opted instead for a simpler or more easily executed arrangement. Three broad sets of problems can be identified.

Lack of recognition of country sales managers' interests

The biggest single challenge in creating global accounts is that country sales managers lose control of some of their largest customers. Unless efforts are made to ensure that country sales managers are comfortable with the new arrangements, the whole process can be disrupted.

Ericsson offers a good example of how important working with the country sales managers can be. Traditionally, Ericsson sold telecoms equipment exclusively to national operators, or "PTTs." As a result, its country sales operations became highly autonomous. Ericsson in the UK, for example, bought products from the business units in Sweden but had a local development group who undertook customization work to meet the particular needs of BT.

With the deregulation and globalization of the telecommunications industry, equipment companies like Ericsson realized that they had to start coordinating sales on an international basis. BT, Telefonica, and other PTTs were starting to develop international operations; and new operators like Worldcom (fixed) and Vodafone (mobile) were emerging all the time. In the early 1990s, Ericsson therefore launched a pilot global account program focused on coordinating sales to three of their most international customers. However, this global account initiative was resisted strongly by the local market companies (the country units). They saw these nascent global accounts as a threat to their autonomy.

Rather than push such an unpopular program, corporate management decided to rethink their global account structure, opting instead for a much looser arrangement, whereby certain individuals were given the task of coordinating the *relationship* between Ericsson and its key customers. These account managers initially spent most of their time facilitating the flow of information internally, so that pricing and service levels were consistent across countries. Gradually, these account managers also built relationships with the customers, to the extent that the local market companies allowed it. That the local market company owned the account in its country of operation was made very clear.

This global account structure was used during most of the 1990s, but gradually the role of the global account managers was increased as everyone realized how critical global sales were to Ericsson's success, particularly on the mobile side. In the late 1990s, the structure was formally changed so that the global account managers had the primary accountability for their customers on a worldwide basis. This change has been successful, but it took the organization the best part of ten years for the shift in the balance of power to occur.

Too much change, too quickly

A second major challenge that many firms encounter is that their existing organization is simply not capable of delivering on the demands of global customers. Electrolux provides a good example of this problem. Electrolux became the biggest international player in the white goods industry through a series of acquisitions during the 1980s and 1990s. However, its acquisitive model of growth resulted in a fairly fragmented organization with hundreds of different brands selling across dozens of product lines into most of the major national markets around the world.

A major part of Electrolux was the professional appliances group, which was divided into five separate businesses: commercial and dynamic preparation. Each business was largely autonomous, with responsibility for developing, manufacturing, marketing, and selling its product line on a global basis. Thus, even in foreign markets there were typically separate sales forces for each professional appliance business.

The customer base for the professional appliance business was highly international. Some customers bought predominantly from one business (Shell buying refrigerator units for its gas stations), while others bought from many businesses (Hilton Hotels). As a result, there were various initiatives during the 1990s aimed at coordinating the sales of the professional appliances group for its large customers. The commercial refrigeration group created a few global account managers (for Shell, BP, and Coca-Cola); and in Norway and France, *key* account managers were established to coordinate sales across the five business units.

In the mid-1990s, the professional appliances group launched a global account initiative. The individual in charge of the initiative was told to work with certain key customers (Hilton, McDonald's) on a worldwide basis, to identify their global needs and to coordinate with the business units to deliver on them. But this initiative never took off. The business units were suspicious because the global account initiative appeared to be undermining their relationships with some of their most important customers. But more importantly, the global account director realized that the organization was simply too fragmented to be able to deliver on a coordinated "global solution" to Hilton Hotels. As a result, the initiative foundered. Instead, the group decided to work on building global accounts on a business-unit basis (following the commercial refrigeration lead), and then subsequently bring them together on a group level.

Lack of top-level support

The third challenge that is often encountered is a lack of support for the global account management program at the corporate level. This is important because it facilitates buy-in across the entire organization, and in particular from the national sales managers who would otherwise be likely to resist.

ABB provides an example of this point. ABB was organized as a business–country matrix when it was formed in 1988, largely because so many of its customers were national power and energy companies that demanded a strong local presence. However, as these industries were deregulated, the need to serve customers on a global basis started to emerge. A feature of ABB is its entrepreneurial management style, and perhaps as a result of this there were two initiatives in the mid-1990s that attempted to create global account programs. However, both of these foundered, not because they were bad ideas but essentially because they did not have top-level support. In 1998, when Goran Lindahl took over as CEO, he recognized the need to address global customers' needs properly, and he asked the former president of ABB Germany to lead a task force to implement a global account system. This has now become a centerpiece of the new ABB structure.

As these examples show, implementing a global account management program is far from straightforward. A number of consistent themes emerge from these examples. First, the country sales manager needs to be co-opted into the program if it is to work, because he or she has the most to lose. Second, the balance of power between country sales managers and global account managers should be altered very gradually. And third, the goals for the program have to be realistic. There is clearly no point in offering a "global solution" to customers if the organization cannot deliver on it.

4 IMPACT OF GLOBAL ACCOUNT MANAGEMENT ON PERFORMANCE

The final issue to consider in detail is the impact of global account management on performance. Unfortunately, the evidence here is far from complete. Virtually all studies of global account management have focused, for obvious reasons, on the vendor organization, and most of these focus on one or a few case studies, so the generalizability of their findings is limited.

Four studies have attempted to measure the performance effect of global account management. A survey of 191 executives from 165 multinational companies showed that the demands of global customers led to greater use of global account structures, which in turn led to higher vendor performance, in terms of customer satisfaction, revenues, and profits.[6]

A different approach focused primarily on the global account manager, rather than the company as a whole.[7] A sample of 107 global account managers showed that high performance was associated with five factors: the level of dependence of the customer on the vendor, the extent to which the vendor's activities were coordinated internationally, the scope of the relationship with the customer (the number of hierarchical levels covered), the extent of communication with the customer, and the use of support systems in the vendor organization.

A related study focused on 55 national sales managers who sold their output, to varying degrees, through global accounts.[8] The key finding from this study was that in comparison to local accounts, global accounts appeared to result in a lower average selling price. In other words, the effect from the vendor side is not entirely positive. Sales volumes typically rise, but at the expense of the sales margin.

Finally, the results of a survey of 200 sales, marketing, engineering, and purchasing managers in multinational companies showed that customer satisfaction was positively affected by three sets of factors: (1) the building of long-term global relationships between vendor and customer; (2) the development of consistent products and services worldwide; and (3) the provision of a global network infrastructure.[9]

While these studies all appear to support the idea that global account management is good for both vendor and customer, it is worth noting that there is little in the way of definitive evidence. All of these studies focus on the vendor side of the relationship, and all of them involve highly subjective measures of performance. There is a need for more systematic and definitive data before this question can be answered with any confidence.

5 SCHNEIDER ELECTRIC'S EXPERIENCE WITH GLOBAL ACCOUNT MANAGEMENT[10]

To take a close look at the evolution of the customer-oriented global account management approach, this final section offers a description of the global account management experience of a large manufacturing company, Schneider Electric, which has its headquarters in Paris. It illustrates the integration of many of the elements covered previously and clearly underscores the point that building an effective global account management organization depends on sustained leadership and commitment. Leadership and commitment are necessary in order to achieve the required collaborating, learning, aligning, and balancing informed by systems thinking, as is described in the introductory chapter of this book.

The discussion of Schneider's experience with global account management begins with a description of the environment and Schneider's strategy, and then examines the evolution of organizational structure, tasks, people, and systems that Schneider developed in order to implement global account management. At the time of the emergence of its first global account in the early 1990s, Groupe Schneider had purchased its largest competitor, Square D, in the United States. Previously it had bought several other well-established brands, all manufacturers of products involved in the distribution of electricity, from fuse boxes in private homes and electrical systems inside machinery to distribution controls for large-scale power generators. The success of Schneider Electric's global account management comes from the fit of the elements of its organizational design, a congruence represented in figure 17.3.

Environment and strategy

The industry was characterized at this time by consolidation (as exemplified by Schneider's strategy) and competitiveness on product characteristics, innovation, service, and price. As noted in Section 1, Schneider's customers were starting to globalize, too, and this

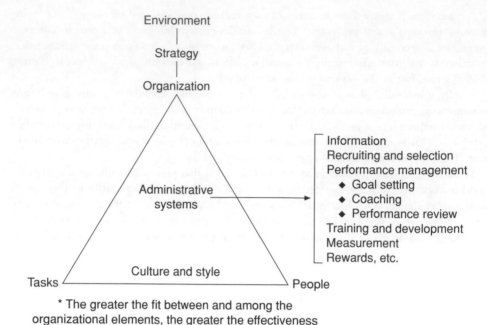

FIGURE 17.3 The organizational effectiveness framework*
Source: Adapted from Lane, DiStefano, & Maznevski (2000).

represented a significant opportunity for growth. The origin of Schneider's global account management was based on seeing the potential with a major customer and *leading* the relationship as distinct from *reacting* to it, an innovative development on the typical vendor objectives in establishing global accounts outlined previously in table 17.2. A champion for coordinating the existing customer's requirements emerged among Square D's sales staff, the salesperson responsible for their Xerox account. This individual's leadership led to a series of annual workshops held with Schneider and Xerox executives during which additional cooperation was planned. These activities earned the two companies Arthur D. Little's international award, "Best of the Best Supply Chain Management Practitioners," in 1994.[11] The champion took advantage of an existing international management development program inside Schneider to advance his idea and, through this program, organized a project team to work on expanding their approach. Recognizing both the changing industry dynamics and the drive and leadership of this forceful personality, senior management agreed to establish a few additional global accounts on an informal basis.

Schneider added more international account managers and accounts, and by the mid-1990s had 25 international account managers (IAMs) and had set up a separate unit, Schneider Global Business Development (SGBD), to run this part of the business.

Organizational structure

As this specialized unit grew in influence and power, it employed each of the three structural options shown previously in figure 17.2. The country-based sales operations

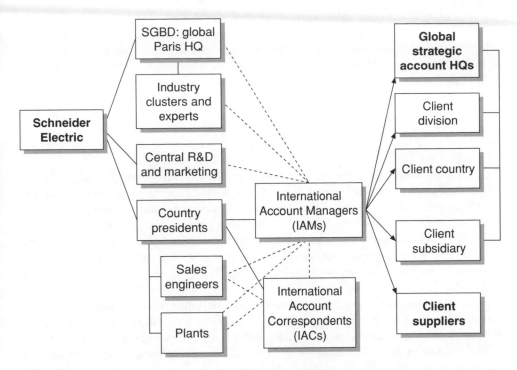

FIGURE 17.4 The organizational structure and role of Schneider international account managers

continued to have significant power and influence in the company. In fact, the customer-focused IAMs reported directly to the geographic presidents. The matrix is also in evidence, since these IAMs had a reporting relationship with an executive in the Paris-based SGBD as well.

Even *within* the SGBD organization there is a matrix structure, with four industry clusters on one side, and geography on the other. A member of the senior executive team also maintained a relationship with the CEO of each global account and mentored the IAM, providing additional influence when needed. The IAM was responsible for one or two global accounts and worked from the country base of the account's headquarters. But to serve the needs of the customers' operations around the world, most large countries also had international account correspondents (IACs). These individuals, who also report to the country presidents where they are located, worked on the local relationships of several global accounts in their countries and coordinated with several different IAMs located in different countries. The complexity of this structure and the role of the ensuing relationships are depicted in figure 17.4.

Currently Schneider has about sixty global accounts and plans to expand significantly. In the process of growing its global account management structure to this size, it has organized increasingly around its customers, reflecting a shift among the alternative alignments shown in figure 17.2. Yet, while the SGBD structure has a substantial set of centralized services in Paris, and while Schneider's most senior executives commit significant portions of their time and the company's resources to this customer group, it still maintains its country operations. How long Schneider can sustain this balance of power across all three of the organizational forms of country, matrix, and customer is an open question. But Schneider has not made countries secondary, choosing to describe the dedicated SGBD unit as operating in parallel to the country sales structure. One reason Schneider can maintain this balance is described below in the section on measurements and rewards.

Tasks

The key tasks necessary to the success of this complex structure depend primarily on the IAMs and IACs. There are multiple relationships that need to be maintained for the global account system to work. IAM task requirements go beyond *relationship management*, however. The IAM needs to be able to solve customer problems, anticipate how Schneider can help the global account in ways that even the account doesn't see, and deliver all the knowledge of 60,000 people in Schneider's worldwide organization to the customer. This requires significant influence in the organization. Yet there is very little power at the IAM's disposal. In many ways the IAMs are to country managers, R&D, production, and service units in Schneider, as brand managers in a consumer goods company are to their functional units. That is, they are responsible for critical tasks, and exercise them largely through good will and information. Willing collaboration by all parties is key.

One of the most critical tasks for global account management is the screening of potential global accounts. From Schneider's perspective it is important that global account designation be seen as exclusive, because of the priority and level of commitment Schneider makes. In the case of Xerox, for example, by the end of the second annual workshop, the R&D heads of each company were providing each other with highly sensitive information about research programs, and Schneider was being asked to match R&D activities of Xerox and to anticipate product requirements that hadn't even been developed yet.[12]

Schneider developed a set of guidelines to qualify its global accounts that include most of those criteria listed in table 17.3. In particular, a company had to have a minimum of several million dollars in potential annual sales from Schneider. It also was expected to offer the potential of sourcing at least 50 percent of its global business from Schneider within four to five years. These criteria allowed the IAM to show that an interested customer had more commitments to make before it would be considered seriously as a global account.

Schneider worked hard to screen out companies that were primarily interested in price discounts. Obviously, one of the motivating factors for the customer is price consideration for the increased volumes and commitments being made. But Schneider's IAMs point out the immense savings from solutions brought to the global account at Schneider's initiative and from cost reductions through the elimination of long and costly bidding processes.

Of much greater sensitivity is the problem of de-listing an account that doesn't maintain Schneider's global account criteria. Senior executives acknowledge that this process is not invoked as often as it should be. Most companies share this reluctance to alienate a large customer. Schneider uses their senior executives to prod the customers in the areas of shortfall.

People

Schneider seeks a rare combination of ability and motivation in the people who execute these tasks within such a complex structure.[13] Strong relational skills are obvious as a requirement, along with a drive to engage in them. IAMs need to have very high energy to sustain the necessary initiatives and persistence. They have to be focused on the mission to serve their customer, yet wide-ranging in their sources of information and inspiration for how to do it. Balancing other dualities is demanded of them, too. They have to be independent; in Schneider they report to a country head who provides hardly any of the resources they need to be successful. Yet they are dependent on a network of cooperation from people in all functions of the company, located around the world. All these abilities are in addition to substantive knowledge about Schneider's products and the ability and location of Schneider people who can solve customer problems. Finally, given the multinational operations of both Schneider and the global accounts they serve, IAMs have to have great cultural sensitivity and adaptability. In fact, IAMs require all of the global competencies described in Part II of this book, with an emphasis on trust building and boundary-spanning skills.

People who can meet these demanding requirements are rare. Not only must they be found and retained, they must be rewarded sufficiently to stay in the same job for a sustained period of time. That the IAM be associated with the same global account is important, since so much understanding of both sides of the relationship resides with the IAM. After all, one of the major advantages for the customer is to be able to deal with one representative from Schneider for all its needs. One characteristic common to all the successful IAMs is extremely high job satisfaction because of the intrinsic nature of the role. The IAMs take great pleasure from learning more and more about the global account. Fritz Keller, the IAM from Switzerland, takes great delight in telling how he often provides the global account with information about their own operations that they didn't know and saves them money by solving problems that they had yet to recognize. He is less motivated by the thought of being promoted to a different job than by getting more IACs to help him in other countries and persuading his country manager to fund an additional IAM to join him in growing yet another global account in Switzerland. Schneider's design of its global account measurement and reward systems, described next, helps to retain these crucial IAMs and to maintain their enthusiasm.

Systems

Recruiting and selection systems for identifying IAMs, measurement systems for tracking IAM and global account performance, reward systems for recognizing accomplishments, and information systems for supporting IAM activities are the most important systems we have found to support global account management in the experience of the companies with whom we have worked. These systems are all clearly identified in Schneider's organizational design.

Once the SGBD unit was established in Paris, the recruiting and selection processes for IAMs was formalized. Starting in the mid-1990s, annual training and development workshops were added for the IAMs so they could come together to trade ideas and experience and add to their management skills. At the annual workshops held by the IAMs with

executives from their global account companies, the IACs and SGBD executives from
Paris also contributed training and development components. These benefited the managers
from both organizations. The IAMs organized the agenda for most of these activities,
further adding to their satisfaction and loyalty to Schneider.

In global account management, measurement and reward systems are often problematic. However, Schneider has dealt with both their internal allocations of credit
for sales and the assessment of the performance of the global accounts in fairly simple
ways. They provide incentives to cooperate with the IAM by dividing the credit for sales
based on actual effort contributed by various parts of the organization. Consider, for
example, the following range of efforts involved in the execution of a major additional
sale to the Mexican subsidiary of Schneider's global account with its headquarters in
Switzerland:

- the Schneider IAC in Mexico assists in identifying the project and helps the IAM in
  Switzerland prepare an analysis and proposal;
- a design team of specialists for the industry based in France (one of four subgroups
  maintained in different locations by SGBD) assists in solving a difficult problem of
  an unusual specification by the customer;
- manufacturing of the equipment for the sale takes place in a US plant and after-sales
  service is supplied by yet another group in the United States.

The credits for the sale are allocated according to general policies established by the
SGBD organization, but the details of each deal are set by the IAM within these guidelines. In case of disputes, the IAM negotiates a settlement; in the rare case when that
process falters, a committee of the SGBD makes the final decision. What is useful to note
here is that the establishment of *a completely specified solution* to the complex accounting for
rewards could be a nightmare. Instead, Schneider has chosen to establish a *process* within
some general parameters, an excellent example of the process-oriented model for dealing
with global complexity described in Part I of this book.

Each IAM is evaluated based on performance against objectives for growth in the
account agreed to in annual planning with the Paris-based SGBD geographic manager. Both qualitative and quantitative criteria are part of the evaluation for bonuses
and salary. Although conventional wisdom puts heavy emphasis on the right reward
system, especially in sales organizations, our observation of Schneider and other organizations with global account management leads us to suggest that the more important decision is the selection of IAMs whose sustained performance depends more on
their personal motivations and job satisfactions than on the marginal effects of annual
bonuses.

This is not to suggest that financial rewards are not important, but the best incentive
system fails if the wrong people are put in the jobs. And as was seen in the sections on
Tasks and People, global account management's success is heavily dependent on the
continuity of self-motivated IAMs.

The tension in the Schneider matrix relative to rewards arises from the fact that
most of the country presidents' rewards are based on strictly local profit performance.
Hence the IAM's natural push for more resources allocated to the global account, which
adds to the country manager's cost base, is resisted unless the country manager can see
benefit to the country bottom line. Inevitably there is a lag between expenditures and

bottom-line impact, so this tension is an ongoing issue at Schneider and in the other organizations with whom we have worked. In short, it is another area requiring continuing balancing.

Another measurement issue of more importance to the SGBD unit in Paris is how to evaluate the benefits to Schneider of any given global account. The additional revenues stemming from the global account are fairly easy to track. The temptation is to install an elaborate cost allocation system to determine the profitability of the accounts. But this would generate endless debates, constant negotiations about transfer prices, and hairsplitting which would add considerably to delays and costs with no additional value to the customer. So for most accounts, major attention is directed to the growth in revenues. Each year, for two or three accounts where there may be questions about profitability, a special audit is done and a more elaborate examination of costs is undertaken. As the former CFO who set up these procedures reported, Schneider did not want to waste time and energy arguing about cost allocations when an account's revenues are growing by multiples year-to-year. He observed that, given no unusual deals, such growth is a sign that the system is performing as intended. Eroding margins would be signaled by complaints from the manufacturing plants.[14]

Other organizations take a more complicated approach to measurement. Schneider's simpler method seems to make good sense, because it gets the overall assessment desired without undue pain and expense.

Schneider's information system for supporting the operation of its global account management concentrates primarily on customer data. Basic information about the customer such as names, addresses, titles, and contact data, are available for access on Schneider's secure Intranet. The IT "shell" also contains more elaborate information including new projects, special studies, and latest contacts by the IAM and the IACs. Once again, however, the critical element in the information equation is the people. If the system is too difficult to access or there are too many entries or reports to make, the IAM and the IACs will stop supplying information. Therefore, Schneider's SGBD IT group in Paris pays very close attention to advice from the IAMs and IACs in the field, often incorporating shortcuts and simpler data summaries developed by these people.

The maintenance of an up-to-date, useful database on the global accounts is often a source of major frustration for the IACs and IAMS. The IT system itself and the need for key people to enter important customer data quickly are constant sources of irritation, regardless of the industry.[15] Approaches to avoiding these problems are described in the previous chapter.

In the case of Schneider Electric there is strong corroboration of the key factors identified in the earlier parts of this chapter. But what their experience also illustrates is the importance of having a high degree of congruence among the organizational characteristics. The various parts of the organizational design all support the global account management activities. This may seem obvious, but at Schneider this design wasn't the result of a deterministic study of the best design to put in place. Rather, Schneider developed its strategy, structure, key tasks, willing and able people, and systems over time. Starting from a single global account with the energy of a champion who still is a powerful force in mentoring new IAMs, Schneider progressed slowly over the first five years, feeling its way and avoiding premature commitment of resources until it developed both competence and confidence.

CONCLUSIONS

Examination of research literature, observation of an example of one company over a ten-year period, and extensive discussions with global account managers from a large variety of companies suggest a few conclusions. Successful design and implementation of global account management results from a *set of interrelated factors*.

- A strategy which emphasizes relationships which lead to added value for both customer and vendor on several dimensions (not just financial).
- A structure organized to serve the needs of global account management, with acceptance of both the complexity and ambiguity required to meet such needs.
- Key tasks defined as identifying and addressing the problems and opportunities of the global accounts.
- Global account managers and their allied correspondents selected and developed as key resources.
- Administrative systems designed to provide measurements, information, and rewards to support the global account managers and customers worldwide (with strong inputs from the users of systems).
- Executive leadership at the top of the organization, including personal time and attention to the global accounts and support to the global account managers.
- A corporate culture of openness and a bias toward action.

Putting the example together with the research literature reveals the complexity of this strategic initiative. The interdependence and multiplicities inherent in global account management explode: networks of relationships to be maintained, geographies and functions to be integrated, costs and revenues to be allocated, and so on. Continuous learning and aligning and realigning, recognizing ambiguities and balancing contradictions and dualities, all are part of making global account management work. These, and other realities described in this chapter, underscore the need for *systems thinking* as a way to address the increasing levels of complexity that accompany globalization.

NOTES

1 See Birkinshaw, Arnold, & Toulan (2000).
2 See Montgomery and Yip (2000).
3 This diagram is taken from Birkinshaw, Toulan, & Arnold (2001).
4 See McDonald, Millman, & Rogers (1997), Shapiro & Moriarty (1984); Weilbaker & Weeks (1997).
5 See Birkinshaw, Toulan, & Arnold (2001).
6 See Montgomery, Yip, & Villalonga (2000).
7 Birkinshaw, Toulan, & Arnold (2001).
8 Arnold, Birkinshaw, & Toulan (2001).
9 Senn and Arnold (1999).
10 DiStefano, J. J., & Ohlsson, A. V. (2001), Schneider Global Account Management, IMD Case GM #968, Lausanne: Switzerland: IMD International Institute for Management Development.

11 See Lane, DiStefano, & Maznevski (2000), pp. 201–202, 215.

12 The fundamental importance of the relationship between buyer and seller in both parties' product innovation process is an underlying theme of the chapter on innovation by McDonough, Spital, and Athanassiou in chapter 19 of this book. See that chapter for details of how the relative emphasis between the parties and the formality of their relationship shifts as the product development process becomes more sophisticated.

13 The list of characteristics included in this section are amply demonstrated by "Fritz Keller" in the Schneider case study. But the authors note these characteristics in all the successful global account managers they have met across all industries.

14 As reported by a Schneider executive who was attending the Senior Executive Forum at IMD on October 4, 2001.

15 For example, in an eight-month period, executives from a supplier of Internet electronics, from one of the "Big Four" professional services firms, from heavy equipment manufacturing, and from an advertising/PR agency, and CEOs from several different industries, all reported that the information systems in their own global account management gave them the most headaches. Most credited Schneider's approach as a likely source of competitive advantage for the company. There is a certain irony in the fact that the organization that complained the most about its information system's shortfalls was itself in the business of supplying IT equipment. Our observation is that it is Schneider's ability to make it work, rather than the system architecture or technology, that makes the difference.

BIBLIOGRAPHY

Arnold, D., Birkinshaw, J., & Toulan, O. (2001). Can selling be globalized? The pitfalls of global account management. *California Management Review*, 44(1), 8–20.

Birkinshaw, J., Arnold, D., & Toulan, O. (2000). How to Manage Your Global Customers, working paper, London Business School.

Birkinshaw, J., Toulan, O., & Arnold, D. (2001). Global account management in multinational corporations: Theory and evidence. *Journal of International Business Studies*, 32(2), 231–248.

Lane, H. W., DiStefano, J. J., & Maznevski, M. L. (2000). *International Management Behavior: From Policy to Practice*. Oxford: Blackwell.

McDonald, M., Millman, T., & Rogers, B. (1997). Key account management: Theory, practice and challenges. *Journal of Marketing Management*, 13, 737–757.

Momani, F., & Richter, T. (1999). Standardization versus differentiation in European key account management: The case of Adidas-Salomon AG. *Thexis*, 4, 44–47.

Montgomery, D., & Yip, G. (2000). The challenge of global customer management. *Marketing Management*, Winter, 22–29.

Montgomery, D., Yip, G., & Villalonga, B. (2000). An Industry Explanation of Global Account Management, working paper, Stanford Business School.

Senn, C., & Arnold, M. P. (1999). Managing global customers – Benchmarks from an international research project. *Thexis*, 16(4), 36–41.

Shapiro, B., & Moriarty, R. (1984). *Support Systems for National Account Programs: Promises Made, Promises Kept*. Cambridge, MA: Marketing Science Institute.

Weilbaker, D. C., & Weeks, W. A. (1997). The evolution of national account management: A literature perspective. *Journal of Personal Selling & Sales Management*, 17(4).

18

Barriers and Bonds to Knowledge Transfer in Global Alliances and Mergers[1]

HENRY W. LANE, DANNA GREENBERG, AND IRIS BERDROW

INTRODUCTION: SEARCHING FOR COMPETITIVE ADVANTAGE

The trade liberalization, deregulation, and privatization that have taken place as part of globalization have created new market opportunities. Many companies have responded by entering into more international joint ventures (IJVs) and engaging in more cross-border mergers and acquisitions (M&As). From the late 1980s through the 1990s there was a dramatic increase in the number of strategic alliances and mergers and acquisitions.[2]

This increase in activity was driven by many factors, including corporations' need to grow, to develop economies of scale, to share investment risk, and to gain access to new products, processes, and markets.[3] Although the traditional lists of reasons for using alliances often included extending or accelerating R&D capabilities, "enrich[ing] their technology base" and procuring "time to learn,"[4] the learning function tended to be implicit and taken for granted. More recently, M&As and alliances have been seen explicitly as part of a company's knowledge management strategy,[5] as platforms for inter-organizational learning,[6] and as a means to access knowledge, which is not yet widely distributed or exploited.[7]

Knowledge is a key resource, particularly for global companies. Their stock of knowledge includes technical knowledge as well as knowledge about how to function in global markets, knowledge of local conditions, how to protect intellectual property, and how to operate successfully in various forms of partnerships. This package of knowledge resources is critical for creating value for the company's shareholders, customers, and employees. Some researchers suggest that knowledge is a source of inimitable competitive advantage and economic rents (abnormal financial returns).[8]

Knowledge transfer has increased in importance as a growing number of firms have been using global alliances and mergers as a strategy for acquiring or gaining access to innovative technology and processes.[9] In many industries, technological change is occurring so rapidly that no single firm has been able to develop the required knowledge or technology internally. In the report of their study of international knowledge transfer in acquisitions, Bresman, Birkinshaw, and Nobel commented:

It is increasingly difficult to attain and sustain a competitive advantage through the realloca-
tion of capital and other assets of the balance sheet. Meanwhile, those who have gained a
competitive edge over their rivals, have increasingly done so through innovative recombina-
tion of knowledge. To put it somewhat more dramatically, there is evidence suggesting that
the winners in tomorrow's market place will be the masters of knowledge management.[10]

Knowledge management is the conscious and active management of locating or creating
and assimilating, disseminating, and applying knowledge to strategic ends. It is a dynamic,
interactive *process* supported by technology with the purpose of enhancing strategic advantage. It is not "the implementation of a technology; rather, it is a multidisciplinary approach
that integrates business strategy, cultural values and work processes."[11]

Yet executives often don't think about managing knowledge. Learning or transferring
knowledge is an implied outcome of other processes, such as creating a joint venture. But,
in an environment where knowledge is a key success factor, managers must manage
knowledge itself, just as any other resource. Although mergers and alliances may provide
rich opportunities for learning, obtaining competitive advantage in the knowledge race by
this route can be a challenge.

The performance problem

When Helmut Maucher was Chairperson of Nestlé SA, a company with substantial M&A
experience, he supported the idea of mergers as a competitive strategy but warned that
success was not automatic and that knowledge transfer was not easy. He wrote:

> If implemented properly M&As are an important and efficient strategic instrument for en-
> hancing the competitiveness of a company. . . . M&As do not automatically generate success.
> Management should give its undivided attention to aspects of the actual integration process
> itself during the period when all contractual and financial aspects have been taken care of.
> These aspects include, *inter alia*, motivating the new employees, ensuring equal opportunity
> for all, and achieving a two-way transfer of knowledge – all aspects that are much more
> difficult to deal with than, for example, handling a property transfer.[12]

As strategically justified as a joint venture, merger or acquisition may be, however,
companies are painfully learning that these activities are not easy to implement and that
success is not guaranteed. The literature on M&As supports the perception that large
numbers of M&As "fail" in the sense that they do not increase shareholder value or
profitability.[13] Depending on the particular financial or accounting measures tracked,
researchers have found that between 50 and 80 percent of M&As fail to create significant
shareholder value or generate their promised strategic and financial goals.[14] A similar
pattern of poor performance has been found in IJVs.[15] Some reports claim that up to 70
percent of IJVs and other alliances fail.[16] Piero Morosini, writing broadly about alliances
and mergers, observed:

> Although the pace of cross border M&A, JV and alliance activity has continued to increase
> at a torrid pace during the last three decades of the 20th century, extensive evidence suggests
> that their performance has been far from successful. Indeed since the early 1970s, a growing
> number of empirical studies carried out by academicians, management consultants and
> practitioners have consistently reported high failure rates for M&As, JVs and alliances.
> Remarkably, these studies cover a broad array of performance measures and methodological

approaches, including diverse industry sectors, time periods and country samples, and embracing both domestic and cross-border types of deals.[17]

Academics and practitioners alike have found that the problems in combining firms and alliances often have less to do with strategic fit and more to do with implementation. Insufficient attention usually is given to execution of the strategy, management of the integrated employees, and differences in organizational and national culture.[18]

National differences as they manifest themselves in organizational culture, language, and organizational practices significantly increase the difficulties of succeeding in cross-border ventures. Differences in national culture have led people in different countries to develop their own philosophies on how to best manage people and organizations. Because of these differences, there is a diversity of human resource practices in organizations (e.g., planning and staffing, performance evaluation and compensation, and job design).[19] Since organizational culture is directly influenced by national culture,[20] global alliances and mergers are more likely to have diverse organizational cultures and, hence, a greater potential for culture clash, which can affect learning and knowledge transfer.[21] Mowery, Oxley, and Silverman found support for this argument in their research, which showed lower levels of inter-firm knowledge transfer in alliances between US firms and non-US firms than among alliances involving only US firms.[22]

In their research, Pekar and Alio found that successful alliances could be differentiated from unsuccessful ones by the focus of their activities at the "complexity boundary," the place where the skills needed for successful change are. They state: "Careful examination of complex firms suggests that successful alliance management places greater emphasis on the human and cultural side of the process."[23]

Firms operating in simpler environments tend to focus more on analytical and operational concerns. Organizations operating on different sides of the complexity boundary need to be cognizant of this condition and the fact that they may not share the requisite skill bases for working on the human and cultural issues.

Successful learning and knowledge transfer require an appropriate combination of organizational characteristics and social processes. For example, some characteristics that have been found related to organizational learning and knowledge transfer in alliances include clearly articulated goals, adequate training, distinct partner contributions, and absorptive capacity.[24]

However, learning and knowledge transfer are also social processes – a "collective endeavor" open to social and political maneuvering that can result in conflict between different organizational subcultures and ideologies.[25] Learning from partners requires connecting people in relationships so that complex knowledge can be shared, understood, interpreted and leveraged. Managers in complex domestic organizations told Pekar and Alio "that relationship building is tough and not easy to maintain over the long haul."[26] Building relationships can be even more challenging in the presence of organizational and national boundaries that may inhibit knowledge flows. And the tacit knowledge, the unarticulated and non-codified knowledge that is so important in any operation, is context-specific. In these cases, learning has to be facilitated through personal interactions, which are often inhibited by differences in language, norms, and worldviews.

Learning can occur across these differences in IJVs or acquisitions.[27] However, many IJV partners do not recognize the potential of active learning from IJVs for the parent organization. Beamish and Berdrow found that accessing knowledge and learning new skills were not the primary motives for entering into IJVs.[28] Even among those that do have learning as a strong motive, knowledge transfer and learning is not necessarily achieved. Similarly, many companies engaged in M&As only see the products and markets that come with the companies that they are acquiring, and not their knowledge bases.

For example, in a study of 40 North American–Japanese JVs among automotive suppliers, Inkpen and Crossan found that learning was an explicit objective for 32 of the North American parent companies. Under tremendous competitive pressure, they wanted access to the transplant factories. JVs with Japanese automotive suppliers were about the only way they could obtain access. The JVs also provided them the opportunity to learn the "secrets" of Japanese success and would allow the North Americans to improve their own skills and capabilities. Despite unhindered access, "learning often proved to be a difficult experience for American managers and their firms."[29] This study also pointed to a "transmission loss" in learning between the individual who actually did the learning and the institutionalization of this knowledge.

In this chapter we explore why many organizations don't seem to learn from their global alliances or mergers to develop the synergies that were anticipated. Combining barriers and bonds theory with a conceptual framework for organizational learning, we examine ways to facilitate more effective knowledge flow and learning in global alliances and mergers.

Crossing boundaries

In global alliances there are various areas in which the transfer of knowledge can, and should, occur. In this section we briefly look at the boundaries that knowledge must cross in global alliances and mergers, particularly in cross-border IJVs and M&As.

IJVs

A network perspective helps to identify the players and relevant boundaries in the creation of cross-border IJVs and provides an understanding of how knowledge can move between partners and the IJV. There are usually at least three separate entities, two parent companies and the IJV, which means that there are multiple organizational and national boundaries across which knowledge must flow and learning must take place. The flow of knowledge between each of the players is different and calls for related yet unique knowledge management processes. These flows are as follows:

1 Transfer (paths AB, BA, AC, and BC) is the migration of existing knowledge between parent firms and from parents to the IJV. This migration can happen through activities such as buying technology, observing and imitating technology used by the partner, or changing existing technologies according to directions given by a partner. Basically, transfer means accepting what the partner does, integrating it into one's own systems or changing one's own resources to imitate it. The importance of knowledge acquisition between parent firms has been discussed in the literature,[30] and Lyles and Salk found support for the relationship between knowledge learned from parents and IJV performance.[31]

2 Transformation (within C) is the integration, application, and leveraging of contributed knowledge and the creation of new knowledge as a result of joint activities. The

potential for knowledge transformation exists any time individuals are placed in new situations or are presented with new challenges and ideas. Transformation also occurs whenever existing knowledge is challenged by new contextual realities. For example, understanding what constitutes an efficient and effective plant layout may be challenged by the realities of space and utility costs, and the availability of building materials. These challenges force reassessment of existing knowledge to solve problems and, in the process, learn something new.

3 Harvesting (paths CA and CB) is the capture of transformed and newly created knowledge from the IJV by the parents. Of the three types of learning identified – transfer, transformation, and harvesting – the third is least understood and may be the most difficult or overlooked, as evidenced in the research by Inkpen and Crossan.[32] Harvesting involves the flow of knowledge from the IJV to the parent, where it can be applied to other internal activities or external alliances. Unfortunately, the "not invented here" syndrome often prevents managers from considering the validity or usefulness of the knowledge developed within the IJV.

This network perspective is diagrammed in figure 18.1, which identifies organizational boundaries and knowledge flows.

M&As

The acquisition process can be divided into three general phases: pre-combination, combination, and post-combination.[33] In each of these phases there are boundaries that can prevent learning from taking place and there are boundaries that also can hinder learning between phases.

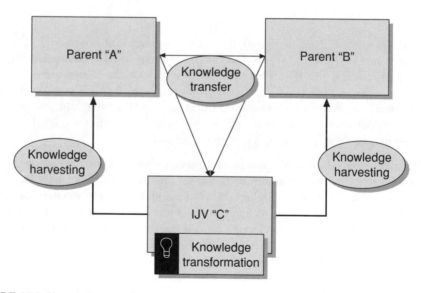

FIGURE 18.1 Knowledge transfer in an international joint venture network
Source: Adapted from Berdrow, I., & Lane (2003). International joint ventures; creating value through successful knowledge management. *Journal of World Business*, 38(1), pp. 15–30.

1 In the pre-combination phase, prior to completing the acquisition, due diligence is conducted and final deals are negotiated. In larger firms, M&A activity is typically planned and initiated by a specialized business development group. These M&A specialists have the training, background, and experience needed to conduct the complex process of evaluating M&A targets.[34]

2 The driving force during due diligence is to avoid an "acquisition disaster" that could occur if key liabilities went unnoticed until after the deal were finalized.[35] A team of financial and legal specialists and business development advisors scrutinize accounting data and investigate potential legal liability associated with environmental conditions, employee benefits, and other issues.

3 Many authors have argued that there is a need for an expanded due diligence process that places greater emphasis on some of the less quantifiable, intangible aspects of a firm.[36] It also has been proposed that an assessment of cultural issues be added to the due diligence process to develop an awareness of the cultural differences and to begin to plan integrative efforts to bridge such differences.[37]

4 In the combination phase, one of the key challenges is to efficiently hand off responsibility from the business development team to the integration teams that will have responsibility for planning and executing the integration strategy. This hand-off is often problematic since important information gathered during due diligence that is likely to affect the integration process may not be passed forward.

5 Although it may be clear what needs to be done during the combination phase, this period of actual execution is the most challenging phase of the acquisition process. Politics, cultural differences, and individual pressures and uncertainty make integrating two organizations highly problematic.[38] This situation is further exacerbated in cross-border mergers. Employees are often more apprehensive when they are being acquired by, or are acquiring, a foreign firm. Uncertainty regarding the differences between the firms and how the newly integrated organization will manage across these differences is great. If these challenges are not successfully managed, it is highly unlikely that information will flow easily in the newly merged organization. As a result it is unlikely that the organization will achieve the synergy that was initially anticipated.

6 In the post-combination phase, the new organization is expected to capitalize on the synergies that were identified during earlier phases. Unfortunately, problems that occurred during the pre-combination phase and the combination phase often prevent the integrated organization from achieving anticipated synergies.

7 Reflecting back on the three phases, we can see an outline of the learning and knowledge transfer barriers emerging. Different groups (M&A specialists, financial and legal specialists, integration teams) are interacting with different parts of different organizations in different countries and with people of different backgrounds, languages, and cultures.

Complexities in knowledge transfer

There are a number of complexities in knowledge transfer. Szulanski identified four factors that can influence transfer, including the *type of knowledge* being transferred, the *organizational capabilities* of the *source* of knowledge as well as the *recipient* and the organizational *context* within which the process takes place.[39] One of the most discussed complexities in knowledge transfer is the type of knowledge. Much of the knowledge associated with innovation, new product development, and other organizational procedures is tacit rather than explicit, or codified.[40] Tacit knowledge is not documented. It resides in the understandings and memories of organizational members. Codified knowledge, in contrast, resides in documents and models. Further, Hakanson notes that much knowledge is context-dependent and, as a result, may lose value in cultures or settings in which it was not developed unless certain bridging functions are performed.[41]

The second complexity relates to characteristics of the organizations involved in the transfer. Less research has been done on the characteristics of the source than on those of the recipient. On the former topic, Szulanski identified motivation and trustworthiness as characteristics of the source of knowledge. On the latter topic, substantial research has been done on the absorptive capacity of firms engaged in learning and knowledge transfer.[42] Lane and Lubatkin reconceptualized the construct as relative absorptive capacity in recognition that not all firms have the same capacity to learn and utilize knowledge from other firms. Relative absorptive capacity includes the similarity of the firms' knowledge bases, their organizational structures and compensation policies, and the recipient firms' dominant logic for utilizing or commercializing knowledge.

A third complexity is the organizational context of the process itself, which is influenced by structure, systems, and sources of coordination and the quality of communications and relationships between units.[43] Trust[44] also plays a role.[45] In order for organizational members to engage in knowledge-transfer activities they need to feel a sense of belonging and trust with their colleagues. A "community" needs to be created among organizational members. The challenge of creating a community in cross-border alliances and mergers is further complicated when organizational members differ in their languages, national cultures, and institutional and social contexts.

The predominant approach for overcoming differences and creating a new social community is by building connections across the organizational boundaries. Lyles and Salk suggested "grafting" individuals with specialized expertise in IJVs. Their emphasis, however, was on knowledge transfer.[46] Another approach is to engage boundary-spanning managers who also can help build community. Tushman and Scanlan describe the important role that boundary-spanning managers can play in the knowledge-transfer process.[47] Boundary spanners typically bring a unique combination of technical and interpersonal skills, which enable them to facilitate the knowledge-transfer process, as was discussed in chapter 7. A similar approach for facilitating knowledge transfer and the development of a new social community involves counterparts, organizational members assigned from one firm to the other firm, and vice versa.[48] All of these approaches enable connections to be created across differences, which facilitate the building of a shared community and the transfer of knowledge, particularly if it is done with the explicit intention of building community and learning.

While boundary spanners and redeployment of people are potentially valuable tools for facilitating knowledge transfer, they may not be enough if other barriers exist as well. Because much of the research is not based on a conceptual framework of the learning process, it does not provide insight into how organizational factors inhibit or facilitate learning or knowledge transfer. We believe that learning in global alliances and mergers is fundamentally about the exchange that must occur between individuals, groups, and organizations. If the combining organizations are not designed to support learning in the early phases of the process, then the knowledge transfer that supports value creation in the later phases is not likely to occur.

Global alliances and mergers provide both opportunities for and barriers to organizational learning. To address the question "Why don't organizations seem to learn in their global alliances and mergers?," we believe that identifying, understanding, and managing the potential barriers and bonds to learning can offer significant value in achieving anticipated synergies from global alliances and mergers. We will now explore a learning model that has potential application in the transfer of knowledge across boundaries, and then we will link the barriers and facilitators of learning to it in the following section.

A learning model for knowledge transfer in global alliances and mergers

As we think about the use of alliances and M&As to gain access quickly to proprietary knowledge for corporate competitive advantage, the challenge seems clear – communicating well in order to move knowledge across organizational and cultural boundaries. Some recent studies have pointed to communication as being important in the knowledge-transfer process.[49] Positive connections and relationships enabling the flow of information can be fostered, as Bresman, Birkinshaw, and Nobel discovered in their study of acquisitions. They found that the quality and quantity of post-acquisition knowledge transfer increased over time as companies consciously fostered the development of a communication process and other ways of enhancing integration.[50]

Developing an understanding of the other organization's people, products, processes, and capabilities means acquiring and disseminating information in different systems organized by different logics of action and using this understanding to motivate people in a common direction.[51] This is a dynamic process and, ideally, not simply a one-way transfer from the acquired to the acquirer or from the parent to the IJV. One model that has been developed to understand the organizational dynamics of learning is the 4I theory of organizational learning.[52] It identified four processes: intuiting, interpreting, integrating, and institutionalizing, that occur over three levels: individual, group, and organization. In an ideal world the innovative ideas that occur to individuals are shared with others, actions are taken, and common meaning developed (interpreting and integrating). This shared understanding developed by groups becomes institutionalized in organizational processes and routines.

The model has been extended and elaborated in the following ways:[53]

1 To link it more directly to the environment through the process of attending, which is an externally oriented search or scanning process (see chapter 15 for a discussion of external sourcing of knowledge).

2 To include sociopolitical processes which have been identified as having a role in organizational learning, such as championing and coalition building.

3 To specify the feedback processes of encoding institutional procedures and enacting the organization's procedures and principles by individuals.

A conflict can develop between assimilating new learning (feed-forward) and exploiting, or using, previous lessons (feedback). The former is the process that facilitates the flow of information and ideas from an individual to a group and to the organization, fostering change and innovation. The latter is the process that facilitates structure and routine, thus affecting how people think and behave. These routines become the organizational logic of a company (the way things should be done) and contribute to the development of a distinctive corporate culture.

Although this dynamic theory of learning primarily focuses on intra-organizational learning, the model also has been extended to serve as a framework for analyzing inter-organizational learning. In particular it was applied to an historical analysis of the inter-organizational learning that took place among Xerox PARC (Palo Alto Research center), Apple Computer, IBM, and Microsoft.[54] Meyer argued that inter-organizational learning also takes place through the processes of intuiting, interpreting, integrating, and institutionalizing.

The model highlights the complexity of the psychological, social, and political processes that can be involved in organizational learning and knowledge transfer. Learning in cross-border ventures requires communicating across different personal cognitive maps, organizational cultures, and national cultures, and integrating these differences in a way that develops a shared, collective understanding. This is not easy or always successful.

Within firms there are barriers to communication as people try to communicate between groups and functional entities, and communication choke points develop which block the flow of information and knowledge. If communicating across functional boundaries within an organization can be difficult, there are potentially many more challenges in learning across organizations. Since many aspects of our logics of action and culture are tacit, communicating them requires a process of surfacing and articulating ideas and concepts or making tacit knowledge explicit. Even if this is accomplished, it does not mean this information will be shared. The language and logic that form the collective mindset of the organization, or national culture as well as existing investment in assets, may present formidable physical and cognitive barriers to change and realization of synergies. These barriers, which exist within a single organization, are that much greater when they are between firms. In a cross-border deal the complications escalate even further with national culture as an added factor in the dynamic of the process, the complexities of which were outlined in chapter 2.

A dynamic theory of organizational learning provides a means to understand the fundamental tensions that are inherent in learning and knowledge transfer in global alliances and mergers: the tension between exploration and the possible creation of synergies or the imposition of the ways of the acquirer or parent.

We now examine the human and organizational features that can facilitate or hinder communication, learning, and knowledge transfer. A number of these factors such as structure, compensation, training, values, and mindsets, have been referred to in various research projects on international joint ventures, mergers and acquisitions, and inter-firm knowledge transfer. However, the framework just presented, combined with the barriers and bonds to be discussed in the next section, pulls these factors together conceptually within an organizational learning framework. We believe it also begins to address the calls for richer conceptual frameworks to map the learning capacities and processes of organizations involved in inter-firm knowledge transfer in search of competitive advantage.[55] The framework, shown in figure 18.2, illustrates that factors such as culture, language, structure or organizational systems, for example, can affect the interpersonal and social processes so critical to communication and can function as barriers to learning and knowledge transfer or become bonds, or bridges, across which knowledge can flow.

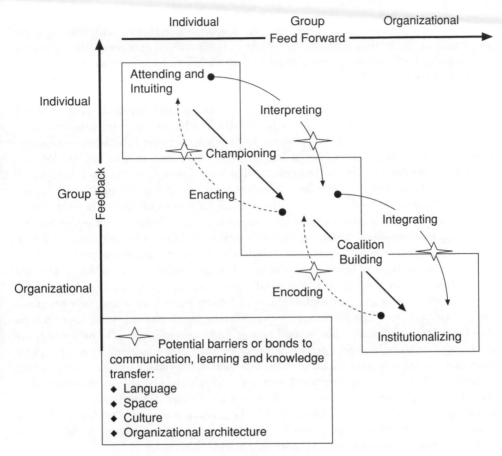

FIGURE 18.2 The framework of organizational learning
Source: Adapted from Crossan, M. M., Lane, H. W., & White, R. E. (1999). An organizational learning framework: From intuition to institution. *Academy of Management Review*, 24(3), 522–537, p. 532, and Kleysen, R. F., & Dyck, B. (2001). Cumulating knowledge: An elaboration and extension of Crossan, Lane & White's framework of organizational learning, in M. Crossan & Olivera, F. (eds.), *Organizational Learning and Knowledge Management: New Directions*, Ivey Publishing, Richard Ivey School of Business, London Canada 2001, p. 387.

Barriers and bonds in communication and knowledge transfer

One of the requirements for knowledge development and learning is communication. Four of the key factors that help or hinder the flow of information across boundaries are language; space; culture, particularly as it affects motivation; and organizational architecture. These factors are central to the type of communication needed to stimulate learning and innovation.[56] They can be used by an organization to consciously facilitate the flow of information or, if they are not recognized, may impede the flow of information. In the following sections, we describe in more detail these four factors to show how they can affect learning and knowledge transfer and provide examples from mergers and acquisitions to illustrate them.

Language

The first barrier or bond is language. In general, if organizational members do not share a common language they cannot share ideas or build on one another's ideas, and they cannot learn. For example, previous studies of cross-border M&As have shown that cross-national differences can lead to miscommunications and misunderstandings, which further impede learning as well as the development of positive relationships that support learning.[57] Lack of a common language may stem from the merging partners having different national languages. For example, when BMW acquired Rover, language problems arose as organizational members at BMW, whose first language was German, tried to communicate with organizational members at Rover, whose first language was English. When a merger involves different lines of business, such as Sears Roebuck's acquisition of Coldwell Banker and Dean Witter, language differences may arise from different logics.[58] Even when the merging partners share the same national language and are in the same line of business, other types of language barriers can exist. In these instances, language barriers may emerge from organizational cultures, functional cultures, or professional cultures, arising from differences in scientific or technical backgrounds and experience.

There are two types of language differences that can hinder communication. The first is the difference in the actual words used to communicate an idea. For example, a software programmer may use slightly different terminologies than a hardware programmer. A German speaking English may use different words to convey an idea than an American speaking English. The second type of language difference is in how words are used and how thoughts, feelings, and information are communicated. This aspect of a language barrier is more difficult to overcome because it relates to differences in tacit knowledge. As a result, organizational members may not even be able to recognize when they do not understand how a concept is being communicated. Furthermore, the organizational members may not be able to explain the subtlety of how they communicate even when asked. This could be particularly true if one of the firms is from a high-context culture in which communication is more subtle and indirect.

Some of the problems in due diligence that have been highlighted include an overemphasis on legal and financial information and a lack of emphasis on more critical factors, such as human resources, operational strategies, infrastructure, and external relationships with customers and suppliers. As a result, the experts who are conducting the due diligence may misunderstand the value-creation potential of the acquisition along with the critical success factors that are needed to obtain that value.[59] We believe that specialized language barriers may be one of the reasons underlying these misunderstandings and the lack of learning that often occurs during due diligence.

These misunderstandings may stem from the specialist groups' use of specialized language and from not understanding the language being used by the target's human resource or technical staff to discuss the value-creation potential of the M&A. Or they may arise because the technical experts from the acquirer simply to do not understand the language that is being used by the technical experts from the target. Without a common language between members of the merging organizations, the acquirer cannot learn about the value creation potential of the target and whether it can mine this potential.

As the organization moves into the integration phase, language barriers may then hinder the merged organization's ability to successfully manage the integration process. If the merging organizations are not able to learn basic information about one another's structures and operating procedures, they will not create a realistic plan for integrating the two organizations and obtaining value from the merger.

Space

Physical space can be a barrier or bond to the effective flow of information and learning. If individuals or groups are not co-located, space can create a barrier to information flow. One of the criteria Cisco uses to identify a potential acquisition target is whether the company is located in Silicon Valley or near one of Cisco's remote sites.[60] Physical proximity is particularly important as it enables informal networks and relationships to develop between the target and the acquirer's staff. This proximity can facilitate the flow of information. Although meetings and conference calls may be used as a way to communicate, these mechanisms are not as useful for building relationships. Through relationships, more sensitive and complex information can be shared.

It is important to note that this barrier or bond is co-location and not just close physical proximity. Relationships will develop faster and more information will be shared when organizational members are co-located. For example, when EMC acquired Data General, one of the factors that was expected to ease the acquisition process was the close geographic proximity of the two companies (both companies were located 30 miles west of Boston). However, because this geographic distance was coupled with major organizational culture differences (motivational barriers to be discussed in a later section), it created a chasm across which information sharing and learning did not take place. Two barriers existed together until EMC created a bond by relocating people, so that former DG and EMC employees were in the same building where they could share information. Only then did they start learning about what the two organizations might be able to accomplish together.

Culture: Its influence on motivation

Culture and its impact was the focus of chapter 2. Among other effects, culture influences motivation, management styles, and organizational structures and systems.[61] In this section we will discuss primarily culture's relationship to motivation and leave its influence on organizational systems to the next section. In our discussion of culture, we include both organizational culture and national culture. Understanding motivation basically means understanding the relationship between particular individuals and the situations in which they find themselves. Organizational members have beliefs about the relationship between their context, their actions, and their desired outcomes. It is necessary to understand the relationship between personal and organizational objectives to explore why and how learning occurs during the alliance and merger process.

Positive motivation fuels the desire among organizational members to want to learn about each other with the goal of creating an integrated organization. Unfortunately, following an acquisition, organizational members are often demotivated as they worry about the security of their jobs, their new roles, and the policies of the new organization. Organizational members are motivated to look out for their own best interests as they try to preserve their jobs and their sphere of influence. Because of this territorial reaction to uncertainty and change, many organizational members are actually motivated not to share knowledge with colleagues, which means learning cannot take place.

National culture is a motivational factor to consider. In domestic acquisitions, differences in organizational culture can increase the complexity of the integration process and make it more difficult for the merged company to achieve anticipated synergies. In cross-border mergers and acquisitions, national culture is added to the equation. Hofstede defined culture as "the software of the mind that distinguishes one group from another."[62] It is a commonly held body of beliefs and values which define the *shoulds* and the *oughts* of life for those who hold them. These beliefs influence people's actions.

Cultural differences often deter learning from occurring during most acquisition processes. One of the key issues that must be worked through during the acquisition process is culture clash.[63] As the two organizations learn more about each other's norms and values, a competitive "us versus them" environment often develops, as organizational members become biased toward the good of their culture and nostalgic over what they may lose as the new organization forces this culture to change.[64] Organizational members often are ethnocentric, seeing their culture as superior to that of the merging partner.[65]

Culture clash, whether it is due to organizational culture or national culture, may demotivate organizational members from learning from their partner and from learning new ways to work together. Organizational members become territorial about their culture and are resistant to adopting new ways of doing things that come from the other organization's culture. Furthermore, if they see their culture as superior to that of their merging partner they are demotivated from learning about their merging partner since they are biased toward seeing the knowledge and norms of their partner as inferior.

To counteract the demotivation of organizational members toward learning and knowledge sharing following an alliance or merger, organizations need to purposefully encourage a different type of behavior, such as teamwork (See Part III for a detailed discussion of teams and teamwork). Organizations need to find ways to motivate people to see the value in sharing knowledge and to learn from their colleagues to create a new organization. They also need to find ways to help organizational members reframe their views of culture and the process of cultural change. There are many ways organizations can do this. First, and foremost, it is critical that major changes regarding jobs, responsibilities, new structures, new policies, and layoffs should be made as quickly as possible following a layoff. When these changes are made quickly, a new, stable order can be created which helps organizational members focus on the real work of developing the newly formed organization.[66] Organizational members will worry less about their stability and will see the value in sharing their knowledge and learning from their counterparts as they work to support the new organization.

Organizational architecture

Managers use various systems to organize employees, to focus them on their tasks, and to link them with other groups and departments. Structure creates reporting relationships between people at various levels of responsibility and facilitates the completion and coordination of critical tasks. It sends messages to organization members about what behavior is expected of them, what behavior is appropriate or inappropriate, what tasks to work on and toward what goals, whom to work with, whom to obey, and whom to direct. Structure includes established subunits, such as departments or divisions of the organization, the management hierarchy that delineates authority, and linking mechanisms such as committees and task forces that ensure that the groups work together.[67]

Managers also use a variety of other administrative mechanisms to align people with organizational goals. The range of administrative systems includes employee selection criteria, training and development programs, reward systems, information and control systems, and performance evaluation methods. These organizational systems should help to promote an alignment, or "fit," internally between strategy, structure, work tasks, and people, and externally between the organization and its environment, in order to be effective and successful.

A complexity arises for managers who must work across boundaries: managers don't necessarily give much thought to national culture in their domestic context, but they must learn to do so when crossing national borders. They need to be able to judge the impact of their national or headquarters' organizational culture on management systems and practices.[68] They need to have a global mindset and recognize the ethnocentric assumptions that must be abandoned when operating across boundaries. See chapter 4.

Management concepts and practices may be "culture-bound," working well in one culture but not others, if they are based on assumptions that reflect one culture's practices. These practices may work well in the culture that developed them because they are based on local cultural assumptions and paradigms about the right way to manage. Hofstede asked the question: "To what extent do theories developed in one country and reflecting the cultural boundaries of that country apply to other countries?"[69] For example, what are the cultural assumptions underlying practices such as empowerment, self-directed work teams, and 360-degree feedback? Can structures, systems, and practices developed in one country or organization be transferred to another, where assumptions and paradigms about the "right way to do things" may be different? Or do they need to be modified?

Most acquisition research that discusses organizational structure highlights the need to create a structure following an acquisition that enables the two organizations to work together effectively to achieve anticipated synergy.[70] Organizational structure can inhibit or facilitate learning right from the due diligence phase in assessing the "fit" between the target and the acquirer. Fit includes both strategic fit, the degree to which the merging companies' resources, goals, and strategy are complementary, and organizational fit, the degree to which the merging companies' structures, operating processes, and culture are compatible.[71] Depending on how the target and the acquirer are structured, learning the necessary information to assess both strategic and organizational fit may be more or less difficult. When organizations have different R&D or innovation processes, for example, it may be more difficult for each partner to assess the potential complementarities of its current processes if they do not fully understand each other's structure.

Many researchers have advocated that organizations that rely on frequent acquisitions to grow and compete would benefit from having a separate subunit that oversees pre-acquisition decision-making and due diligence.[72] For example, one of the strengths of Cisco's acquisition process is it has a permanent new business development department that is responsible for identifying and assessing the fit of acquisition targets.[73] This department is a permanent group comprising members who have prior experience with acquisition decision-making and integration and who are able to learn from their prior experiences and apply these lessons to their assessment of new acquisition candidates.

Part of the strength of the new business development department stems from the fact that it remains well connected with the other departments at Cisco.

Even when the due diligence team is structured to facilitate learning there are components of the target's organizational structure that may create a barrier to learning. For example, organizations that are highly centralized may have formal or informal policies that inhibit lower-level employees from communicating and sharing information. Such a policy will make it difficult for knowledge to be shared easily and quickly during due diligence. In addition, if there are no strong linking mechanisms that enable different units to share information with one another, then it would be unlikely that the representatives from the target's side would have the necessary information to enable the due diligence team to accurately assess strategic fit. This was clearly the case when AT&T acquired NCR. The capabilities that AT&T thought it was acquiring were not in fact the true capabilities of NCR. Although there were many factors that influenced this poor assessment, part of the issue was that representatives from NCR could not provide the due diligence team with accurate information to learn about the potential fit.

A critical component relative to learning during a merger involves the selection and structuring of the integration team whose goal is to manage the integration process.[74] There needs to be a way of connecting the integration team to the due diligence team which has information about financial and legal situations, as well as about strategy, culture, and structure. When this information is not shared, as is true in most cases, the integration process is slow and costly and often much less effective.[75] Hence, there needs to be a structural linkage, such as a boundary spanner, between the due diligence team and the acquisition team so that valuable information is not lost.

Selection of members of the integration team will affect learning. For example, following Compaq's acquisition of Digital in 1998, the services group created an integration team and an integration process that included individuals from the services divisions at Compaq, Digital, and Tandem (a Compaq acquisition from six months before). Organizational members from each of the merging companies were included in this process because these individuals were best positioned to share with the team their knowledge about their current organizational structure, processes, and expertise. By including members from all three merging partners, at least one double barrier was avoided (space and organizational structure). The team was better positioned to learn about the existing processes, create an integration process, and create a new organizational structure that would best fit with the company's capabilities. Because the different members of the integration team were also knowledgeable about their own organizational cultures and human resource systems, these members were then well positioned to help educate their respective organizations on the changes.

Finally, the integration team must facilitate learning among executives and employees in order to execute the integration process. It needs to put into place structures and processes that enable the rest of the organization not just to buy in, but to understand and create the actual integration team. Although the integration team sets the stage, it is the rest of the organization that will actually carry out the integration and establish the structure that will emerge in the new organization. Communication is one component of this process, but communication alone will not facilitate the necessary organizational learning. Instead, the integration team would benefit from focusing on creating linking mechanisms that enable other organizational members to participate in the integration process. These quick results are essential for helping an organization establish new patterns following an organizational change. GE Capital, for example, used this approach when it acquired a Japanese financial services company.[76] It created short-term projects (100 days) for the Japanese and American employees to work on *together*, thus avoiding the double barrier of structure and space while providing a common motivational goal that had a direct impact on the bottom line. Members of the newly merged organizations were able to experience the value of integration. This experiential process will foster organizational learning much faster than one-way communication and will begin to create bonds that will transcend the barriers of space, structure, and language.

Systems such as performance appraisal and reward systems can support or destroy the motivation to share and learn. New performance appraisal systems and compensation systems may need to be created that reward behavior that supports greater integration. Organizations can motivate employees toward knowledge sharing and learning by ensuring that incentive systems support this learning. Existing systems that may demotivate learning about the other organization need to be altered. When EMC acquired Data General it had a sales incentive program that "disincented" people from selling Data General products. This system prevented sales people from learning about the Data General product line and from finding innovative sales tactics to support both lines. EMC salespeople only started to learn about the Data General products when this system was changed.

When managers actively work to motivate organizational members to cooperate and design their organizations to encourage and support cooperation, employees will be motivated to share knowledge and learn from each other.

CONCLUSION: ENHANCING ORGANIZATIONAL LEARNING AND KNOWLEDGE TRANSFER

By understanding how the four factors described above affect communication and knowledge transfer, managers can create bridges across communication chasms to stimulate the flow of knowledge using barriers and bonds in a complementary way: if two barriers exist together then a bond needs to be created.[77] We saw this technique used in some of the examples provided above:

- GE Capital used short-term projects for Japanese and American employees to work on *together*, thus avoiding the double barrier of structure and space while providing a common motivational goal.
- EMC's acquisition of Data General, in which geographic distance, coupled with major organizational culture differences, created a chasm across which information sharing and learning did not take place. Two barriers existed together until EMC created a bond by relocating people so that former DG and EMC employees were in the same building.
- Compaq's acquisition of Digital, in which they created an integration team and an integration process that included individuals from the services division at Compaq, Digital, and Tandem, avoided at least one double barrier of space and organizational structure.

Success in global alliances and mergers and achievement of anticipated synergies depend on learning and the effective transfer of knowledge – preferably a two-way transfer. However, to achieve these learning outcomes, we believe learning must also occur throughout the venture process. Managers who are involved in the various phases of the acquisition process or who are putting together IJVs for the purposes of knowledge transfer must pay attention to the barriers and bonds that can affect learning during this process. By identifying these barriers and bonds and consciously managing them, firms stand a better chance of avoiding the chasms across which information cannot flow. They should build the bridges required to permit learning and knowledge transfer. By increasing information flow and learning from global alliances and mergers, managers increase their chances of achieving the anticipated benefits for which they entered into the relationship in the first place.

Notes

1 We will use the term "global alliances and mergers" as shorthand to denote cross-border mergers and acquisitions (M&As), international joint ventures, and non-equity global alliances. We would like to recognize the contributions of Keith P. Bahde to an earlier paper, which helped us frame the issue in the context of cross-border M&As. We would also like to thank Mark Lehrer and David Wesley for their comments on this chapter.

2 *World Investment Report: Cross-border Mergers and Acquisitions* (2000), New York and Geneva: United Nations Conference on Trade and Development, pp. 110–111; Beamish, P. W., & Berdrow, I. (forthcoming, 2003), Learning in IJV's: The unintended outcome, *Long Range Planning*; Gonzalez, M. (2001), Strategic alliances: The right way to compete in the 21st century, *Ivey Business Journal*, September/October, pp. 47–51; Inkpen, A. C., & Crossan, M. M. (1995), Believing is seeing: Joint ventures and organization learning, *Journal of Management Studies*, 32(5), 595–618; Pekar, P., & Alio, R. (1994), Making alliances work – Guidelines for success, *Long Range Planning*, 27(4), 54–65.

3 Hitt, M. A., Hoskisson, R. E., Ireland, R. D., & Harrison, J. S. (1991), Are acquisitions a poison pill for innovation?, *Academy of Management Executive*, 5(4), 22–34; Berdrow, I., & Lane, H. (2003), International joint ventures: Creating value through successful knowledge management, *Journal of World Business*, 38(1), 15–30.

4 Pekar & Alio (1994), p. 63.

5 *Ibid.*, pp. 455–457.

6 Inkpen & Crossan (1995); Simonin, B. L. (1999), Transfer of marketing know-how in international strategic alliances, *Journal of International Business Studies*, 30(3), 463–490.; Lane, P. J., Salk, J. E., & Lyles, M. A. (2001), Absorptive capacity, learning and performance in international joint ventures, *Strategic Management Journal*, 22(12); and Lyles, M. A., & Salk, J. E. (1996), Knowledge acquisition from foreign parents in international joint ventures: An empirical examination in the Hungarian context, *Journal of International Business Studies*, Special Issue.

7 Zack, M. H. (1999), Developing a knowledge strategy, *California Management Review*. 41(3), 125–145.

8 Schendel, D. (1996), Knowledge and the firm, Editor's Introduction to the winter special issue, *Strategic Management Journal*, 17, 1–4.

9 Mowery D. C., Oxley, J. E., & Silverman, B. S. (1996), Strategic alliances and interfirm knowledge transfer, *Strategic Management Journal*, 17, special issue.

10 Bresman, H., Birkenshaw, J., & Nobel, R. (1999), Knowledge transfer in international acquisitions, *Journal of International Business Studies*, 30(3), 439–462, 440.

11 Harris, K., Fleming, M., Hunter, R., Rosse, B., & Cushman, A. (1999), *The Knowledge Management Scenario: Trends and Directions for 1998–2003*; Strategic Analysis Report, Gartner Group, {HYPERLINK http://gartner4/gartnerweb.com:80/gg/purchase/0/0/775/40/doc/00077540/}, March 18.

12 Maucher, H. O. (1998), Mergers and acquisitions as a means of restructuring and repositioning in the global market? Business, macroeconomic and political aspects, *Transnational Corporations*, 7(3) December 1998. United Nations Conference on Trade and Development, Division on Investment, Technology and Enterprise Development. Geneva.

13 World Investment Report (2000), p. 139.

14 See, e.g., Ashkenas, R. N., & Francis, S. C. (2000), Integration managers: Special leaders for special times, *Harvard Business Review*, 78, 130–145; Sirower, M. L. (1998), *The Synergy Trap: How Companies Lose the Acquisition Game*, New York: The Free Press; Hitt et al. (1991); and Ravenscraft, D. J., & Scherer, F. M. (1987), *Mergers, Sell-offs and Economic Efficiency*, Washington, DC: Brookings Institution.

15 Beamish & Berdrow (forthcoming, 2003), referencing a study by Park, S. H. (1996), When competition eclipses cooperation: An event history analysis of joint venture failure, *Management Science*, 42(6), 875–889.

16 Gonzalez (2001), p. 48.

17 Morosini, P. (1999), *Managing Cultural Differences: Effective Strategy and Execution Across Cultures in Global Corporate Alliances*, Oxford: Pergamon, p. 5.

18 Cogan, G., A. T. Kearney Canada (1998), Creating a winning combination: Best practices in post-merger integration, presentation to the Ivey Consulting Club, London, Ont., September 24; Morosini (1999), p. 5; *Seven Steps to a Successful Merger or Acquisition*, Towers Perrin, Company Report.

19 Schneider, S. C. (1988), National vs. corporate culture: Implications for human resource management, *Human Resource Management*, 27(2), 231–247.

20 *Ibid.*

21 Lane, Salk, & Lyles (2001).

22 Mowery, Oxley, & Silverman (1996).

23 Pekar & Alio (1994).

24 Lane, Salk, & Lyles (2001); Lyles and Salk (1996); Lane, P. J., & Lubatkin, M. (1998), Relative absorptive capacity and organizational learning, *Strategic Management Journal*, 19(5), 00–00.

25 DeLong, D., & Seeman, P. (2000), Confronting conceptual confusion and conflict in knowledge management, *Organizational Dynamics*, 29(1), 34–44.

26 Pekar & Alio (1994), p. 63.

27 See, e.g., Lane, Salk, & Lyles (2001) and Lyles & Salk (1996); Bresman, Birkenshaw, & Nobel (1999).

28 Beamish & Berdrow (forthcoming, 2003).

29 Inkpen & Crossan (1995), p. 607.

30 Kogut, B., & Zander, U. (1992), Knowledge of the firm, combinative capabilities and the replication of technology, *Organization Science*, 3(3), 383–397.

31 Lane, Salk, & Lyles (2001); Lyles & Salk (1996).

32 Inkpen & Crossan (1995).

33 Marks, M. L., & Mirvis, P. H. (1998), *Joining Forces: Making One Plus One Equal Three in Mergers, Acquisitions, and Alliances*, New York: Jossey-Bass; Kogut & Zander (1992).

34 Bentley, T. (1996), Putting the right people on in-house M&A teams, *Mergers & Acquisitions*, 30(6), 30–36.

35 Begley, T. M., & Yount, B. A. (1994), Enlisting personnel of the target to combat resentment, *Mergers & Acquisitions*, 29(2), 27–32.
36 Harvey, M. G., & Lusch, R. F. (1995), Expanding the nature and scope of due diligence, *Journal of Business Venturing*, 10(1), 5–21.
37 Marks, M. L. (1999), Adding cultural fit to your diligence checklist, *Mergers & Acquisitions*, 34(3), 14–20.
38 Marks & Mirvis(1998).
39 Szulanski, G. (1996), Exploring internal stickiness: Impediments to the transfer of best practices within the firm, *Strategic Management Journal*, 17, special issue.
40 Singh H., & Zollo, M. (1998), *The Impact of Knowledge Codification, Experience Trajectories, and Integration Strategies on the Performance of Corporate Acquisitions*, Fontainebleau, France: INSEAD.
41 Hakanson, L. (1995), Learning through acquisitions: Management and integration of foreign R&D laboratories, *International Studies of Management & Organization*, 25(1, 2), 121–157.
42 See, e.g., Cohen, M. D., & Levinthal, D. (1990), Absorptive capacity: A new perspective on learning and innovation, *Administrative Science Quarterly*, 35(1), 128–152; Lane & Lubatkin (1998); Szulanski (1996); and Lane, Salk & Lyles (2001).
43 Szulanski (1996); Inkpen, A. C., & Dinur, A. (1998), The transfer and management of knowledge in the multinational corporation: Considering context, working paper 98–16, Carnegie Bosch Institute.
44 See chapter 5 for a detailed discussion of trust.
45 Kostova, T. (1999), Transnational transfer of strategic organizational practices, *Academy of Management Review*, 24(2), 308–324; Janowicz, M., & Noorderhaven, N. (2002), paper, Department of Organization and Strategy, Tilburg University, the Netherlands.
46 Lyles & Salk (1996).
47 Tushman M. L., & Scanlan, T. J. (1981), Boundary spanning individuals: Their role in information transfer and their antecedents, *Academy of Management Journal*, 24(2), 289–305.
48 Berdrow & Lane (2003).
49 Nobel, R., & Birkinshaw, J. (1998), Innovation in multinational corporations: Control and communication patterns in international R&D operations, *Strategic Management Journal* 19(5), 479–496; Szulanski (1996); Bresman, Birkenshaw, & Nobel (1999).
50 *Ibid.*
51 Lane, H. W., Beddows, R. G., & Lawrence, P. R. (1981), *Managing Large Research and Development Programs*, Albany: State University of New York Press; Lane, H. W., Beddows, R. G., & Lawrence, P. R. (1981), The technical logic of research and development, *R&D Management*, 11(1).
52 Crossan, M. M., Lane, H. W., & White, R. E. (1999), An organizational learning framework: From intuition to institution, *Academy of Management Review*, 24(3), 522–537.
53 Kleysen, R. F., & Dyck, B. (2001), Cumulating knowledge: An elaboration and extension of Crossan, Lane & White's framework of organizational learning, in Crossan, M., & Olivera, F. (eds.), *Organizational Learning and Knowledge Management: New Directions*, Richard Ivey School of Business, London, Canada: Ivey, pp. 383–393. See http://groups.ivey.uwo.ca/conference/Authors.htm
54 Meyer, J. P. (2001), Embrace and Extend: A Case of Inter-organizational Learning, paper presented at the Eastern Academy of Management.
55 Szulanski (1996); Mowery, Oxley, & Silverman (1996).
56 Morton, J. A. (1967), A systems approach to the innovation process, *Business Horizons*, Summer.
57 Schoenberg, R. (2001), Knowledge transfer and resource sharing as value creation mechanisms in inbound continental European acquisitions, *Journal of Euromarketing*, 10(1), 99–114.
58 Prahalad, C. K., & Bettis, R. A. (1986), The dominant logic: A new linkage between diversity and performance, *Strategic Management Journal*, 7, 485–501.
59 Marks & Mirvis (1998).

60 Cisco Systems, Inc.: Acquisition integration for manufacturing (A), Wheelwright, S. C., Holloway, C. A., Kasper, C. G., & Tempest, N., Case no. 9-600-015, Harvard Business School California Research Center, January 1999.

61 See Hofstede, G. (1980), Motivation, leadership and organization: Do American theories apply abroad?, *Organizational Dynamics*, Summer; and Lane, H. W., DiStefano, J. J., & Maznevski, M. M. (2000), *International Management Behavior*, 4th edn., Oxford: Blackwell.

62 Hofstede (1980).

63 Buono, A. F., Bowditch, J. L., & Lewis, J. W. (1985), When cultures collide: The anatomy of a merger, *Human Relations*, 38(5), 477–500; Shrivastava, P. (1986), Postmerger integration, *Journal of Business Strategy*, 7(1), 65–76.

64 Buono, Bowditch, & Lewis (1985); Marks & Mirvis (1998).

65 Hambrick, D. C., & Cannella, A. A, Jr. (1993), Relative standing: A framework for understanding departures of acquired executives, *Academy of Management Journal*, 36, 733–762.

66 Ashkenas, R. N., DeMonaco, L. J., & Francis, S. C. (1998), Making the deal real: How GE capital integrates acquisitions, *Harvard Business Review*, Jan.–Feb., 165–178.

67 Greenberg, D. N. (2002), Designing effective organizations, in A. R. Cohen (ed.), *The Portable MBA*. New York: John Wiley, pp. 243–276.

68 See Lane, H. W., DiStefano, J. J., & Maznevski, M. M. (2000). Part 2: Implementing strategy, structure and systems, in *International Management Behavior*, 4th edn., Oxford: Blackwell.

69 Hofstede (1980).

70 Marks & Mirvis (1998).

71 *Ibid.*

72 Ashkenas et al. (1998).

73 Cisco Systems, Inc. (1999).

74 Ashkenas et al. (1998).

75 *Ibid.*

76 *Ibid.*

77 Morton (1967).

19

Managing Complexity in the Global Innovation Process: A Networks and Social Capital Solution

EDWARD F. McDONOUGH III, FRANCIS C. SPITAL,
AND NICHOLAS ATHANASSIOU

New products are a major source of competitive advantage for companies. Yet managing new product development has never been more complex. Not only have firms become more widely dispersed around the globe, but so too have the resources and knowledge that are needed to successfully develop new products. This complex global innovation process has four elements that are particularly important: managing tensions, building networks, facilitating drivers, and achieving outcomes (see figure 19.1).

During the global innovation process, managers are faced with a series of tensions, the most pervasive of which is, "How do you develop and deliver state-of-the-art products and, at the same time, minimize demands on corporate resources?" These tensions are managed by building a network of informal, interpersonal relationships with customers and with companies that have complementary technologies. Such a network allows the

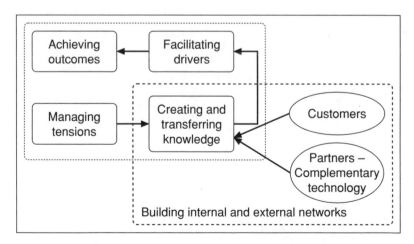

FIGURE 19.1 The global innovation process

company to access, create, and transfer the knowledge needed to develop the competencies and capabilities that the company needs to execute its primary tasks, which we call drivers. Successfully executing these drivers lets the company achieve its desired outcomes. While the global innovation process is clearly much more complicated than simply these four elements – managing tensions, building internal and external networks, facilitating drivers, and achieving outcomes – we think these often have the greatest impact on whether a global project succeeds or fails.

In this chapter we discuss one organization's experience with managing global innovation. Our insights are based on an 18-month investigation of HGO, an organization in Ireland.[1] HGO is a subsidiary of the US-based Compaq Computer Corporation, which itself merged with Hewlett Packard in 2002. HGO transformed itself, in seven years, from a non-player in the high-performance computing market to the market-share leader.

Dynamic complexity is inherent in the global innovation process and is created by a variety of interacting forces: multiple evolving technologies that need to be integrated; globally distributed technology sources that need to be tapped; and globally distributed customers. HGO's success can be attributed to their ability to manage this dynamic complexity. For instance, HGO built a flexible network of relationships, supported by stocks of social capital, which allowed them to adapt their innovation strategy quickly – both as they searched for new technologies, products, and customers, and as they implemented their new product strategy. The informality of the network they created also enabled their success. As noted by a senior Compaq manager, "There is a formal organization and an informal organization. The importance of operating in both is that it's in the informal organization that you get to take your largest risks. In the formal organization, you can't." HGO managers were able to take considerable risks because they thoroughly understood the informal organization within Compaq, and built and leveraged an informal network within this formal organization that extended to customers and vendors. As we shall see, HGO's ability to absorb practically the entire risk for innovating globally through the use of this informal network allowed Compaq's top managers to assume no risk during the early and uncertain stage of new product development.

Our exploration of HGO's successful global innovation process is divided into three main sections. The first discusses the story behind HGO's success, while the second analyzes the key factors that led to this success; specifically, how HGO managed critical tensions across three phases of the innovation process: *wandering through the wilderness, heroic experimenting*, and *stable commercializing*. The final section summarizes key lessons on global innovation and suggests steps that managers should consider when facing global innovation challenges.

THE STORY

In 1993, several senior managers in the United States were trying to get supercomputing started as part of an effort to create a market for one of their key technologies. At this same time, however, the company started significant downsizing and consolidation. Any obvious attempt that exposed the company to additional risk by creating a new organization, building capabilities, and developing and delivering new products would almost certainly fall victim to severe budgetary constraints. These senior managers chose instead to hide the supercomputing effort where it would go virtually unnoticed – in Ireland. The subsidiary in Ireland (HGO) was managed by highly qualified technologists who lacked expertise in supercomputing. However, what these technologists lacked in expertise was more than made up for by the motivation to survive. Because of declining sales, Compaq had recently transferred HGO's manufacturing function to other parts of the global operations, leaving HGO with little work and dim prospects for survival.

Thus, while HGO had the support of several senior managers at the company's US operations, they had no corporate mandate to enter the target market. In addition, they had no established customer contacts and insufficient technology prowess in supercomputing to interest customers. Further, they had neither a business plan nor a development plan. Indeed, the only deliberate strategy was what one manager referred to as a "stealth" strategy to keep their product innovation team below the corporate "radar horizon" while it developed knowledge and competencies. As they had no budget, their work had to be funded by culling resources from approved projects and their cost had to be kept sufficiently low to avoid corporate attention. Despite these constraints, they were able to put together a core team of 15 people within 6 months. Some of these people were former employees of organizations that could become customers, and others were included purely for their technical capabilities.

Driving their efforts was a broadly stated goal to become a significant competitor in the supercomputer market and to "do something important." As one senior engineer pointed out:

> the goal for the group was to do something interesting that looked good to make sure that our employers in the U.S. looked kindly upon us. We weren't really focused around product or profit. We just wanted to keep pulling stunts and hopefully to get people to buy more of Compaq's stuff. The strategy of the group was to become stronger and become a big leader in supercomputing, but the way of getting there wasn't clear.

In the longer term, HGO managers were interested in developing products that would ultimately generate profits for the corporation. Thus, it was necessary to understand customer needs and problems so that accumulating technological expertise could be directed toward the development of a commercially viable product.

In the first two years of its existence, the first phase of the global innovation process, HGO did a considerable amount of "wandering about in the wilderness" looking for opportunities to make money, to help the company, to develop its own technical competence, and to begin to understand the needs and problems of customers. For example, HGO's senior manager developed relationships among the members of his core engineering team and purposefully engaged the interest and expertise of selected engineers in the US operations. Further, he assigned his Ireland-based engineers to work on selected projects of US-based development teams. He also recognized the importance of developing relationships with potential customers early on. Customers in this business require "benchmarking" tests before purchase so that they can evaluate the performance of products in their particular environment and for their specific task. HGO provided this service free to customers. Through this benchmarking activity, customers described their needs, so the organization could begin to understand them. In short, HGO managers sought to learn about what they didn't know.

After two years of "wandering about," HGO moved into a second phase in the global innovation process. This was the "heroic experimenting" phase. Compaq had recognized its existence by then and it was formally assigned to report to a senior executive in the United States who would oversee the entire supercomputing effort, both in the United States and Ireland. This executive had three decades of experience in Compaq. At the same time a technical director, who also had worked for Compaq for many years in the United States, was brought to Ireland to work as part of the HGO team. These two executives dramatically changed the goals. The new goal was to build a reputation, both among the customers and internally within the corporation. They believed it was important to generate revenues to enhance credibility in the corporation. As a first step, the technical director decided that a good way to focus the team and announce its capabilities to customers would be to build a working machine and demonstrate it at the annual supercomputing trade show that was scheduled in approximately seven months' time. In response to this challenge, the engineers integrated Compaq's existing technologies to assemble a very high-performance computer, and unveiled it at the trade show in November of that year. This prototype high-performance machine made a huge impression and a number of copies were subsequently sold to customers.

Coincidentally, a lead user[2] in supercomputing initiated discussions with Compaq in an attempt to solicit a bid for the next-generation supercomputer that would meet this user's future needs. To initiate these discussions, a director from the lead user approached a Compaq hardware manager, whom he knew. That hardware manager happened to know HGO's new technical director and asked him to meet the lead user and help develop the relationship. Lead users in the supercomputing market are customers who buy products that incorporate the very latest technological advances; they also understand that these products rarely come completely "bug"-free. Thus, a vendor has to work closely with these lead users to debug the machine and respond to other problems that may arise. At the same time, by working closely with these lead users, a vendor learns a great deal about how to improve its technology to meet customer needs and problems, about competitors' technologies, and about ways to improve upon existing machines. Finally, these lead users had development funds to apply to the project; HGO could not secure such funding from Compaq while it was still proving itself.

HGO's first lead user needed a machine with performance far superior to that developed for the trade show. The lead user's managers identified the bottleneck element in that design, and introduced HGO to a vendor located in England, WFI,[3] that possessed a complementary technology that was far superior. In the fall of 1999, by working closely with this lead user and with WFI, HGO was able to develop and produce a computer faster than any other on the market. Within three years of the first delivery of this machine, they had sold and installed four of the five fastest machines in the world. They had also won contracts for the biggest computers in Japan, Europe, and Australia. When they secured a new contract to build the most powerful computer in the world, its technical complexity went beyond what anyone could have imagined only a few years earlier. These machines provided a strong reputation in the supercomputing market. Meanwhile, HGO's reputation had become even stronger within Compaq because its huge contracts for new computers had begun to generate significant revenues.

Beginning in 2000, focus once again shifted. In this third, "stable commercializing" phase, the "sane, scaling" phase of HGO's innovation process, the goals evolved to include making a commercial profit by manufacturing and selling standardized products. To achieve sufficient profitability, they had to scale the business to produce machines that were manufactured in volume to a set of specifications. These machines were sold to commercial customers who were not interested in the most leading-edge technologies as much as they were in machines that were dependable and reliable. In this third phase, commercial versions of these machines were being manufactured in Compaq facilities in the United States, Scotland, and Singapore. So HGO had to modify some of their behaviors to match the business models that drove Compaq volume manufacturing and service globally. At the same time, they needed to maintain the development processes that had allowed them to innovate so successfully and get them to this point. Within two years, several hundred machines had been sold to customers in countries as far-flung as France, Japan, Australia, and the United States, with each of these machines being serviced by Compaq's after-sales service organization. As of the end of 2001, they had acquired a dominant market share in the supercomputing market and, perhaps most importantly, had begun to contribute significantly to corporate profits. HGO's sales had increased to account for two to three of all servers produced by Compaq.

The discussion to this point shows how HGO's successful global innovation story breaks down into three phases: *wandering through the wilderness, heroic experimenting,* and *stable commercializing* (figure 19.2). In the next section of this chapter we discuss the key factors

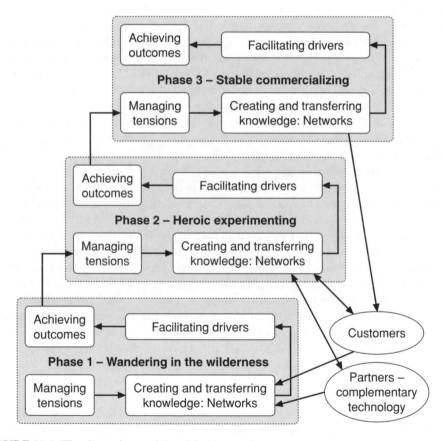

FIGURE 19.2 The three phases of the global innovation process

that contributed to their successful global innovation. In each phase, these key success factors involve managing conflicting tensions by building and modifying a successful social network.

Managing Tensions by Building Networks and Social Capital

Within and between each phase in the global innovation process, managers are faced with the need to manage a series of tensions, such as: "How do you develop and deliver 'state-of-the-art' products and, at the same time, minimize demands on corporate resources?" Successfully managing such tensions allows the organization to effectively gain access to and leverage the knowledge, information, and resources needed to achieve the goals of each phase of the global innovation process. But because global innovation itself, and the process of managing these tensions, are dynamically complex, they require nimbleness and flexibility in execution. HGO's experience suggests that much of the work of global innovation relies on building a network of informal, interpersonal relationships, most often through frequent, face-to-face interactions among pairs or small groups of individuals. This informal, fluid network is an important vehicle for managing the global innovation process because it enables access to resources that would otherwise be unavailable. As we shall see, the purpose and nature of this network change from phase to phase.

But how does such a network function? It is based on relationships that are built between individual network members who make up its nodes. Because these relationships are based on the notion of reciprocity, a prerequisite to their development is trust. Each person who is in the relationship has to believe that the other person is trustworthy, that they will reciprocate in some fashion. There is an assumption within the relationship that if I go to you and ask for information, advice, or assistance and you grant my request, I will help you when you come to me with an equivalent request, whenever that may be. Reciprocal exchange builds stocks of social capital. These stocks represent assets that can be used to achieve specific goals that are embedded in relationships among people. Like any other asset, social capital can lose its value if it is not maintained through a nurturing of the underlying relationship, or not used over a period of time.

Because the relationships that form the basis of a network are personal and often require face-to-face interaction, particularly when they involve network links across national borders and cultures, they take time to build. However, as we discuss below, it is possible for a manager to speed up the development of a network and to take actions that will facilitate the development of the "right" network. In fact, we shall see that in Phases One and Two HGO's network is built through face-to-face interactions. In these two phases innovation is at the early, creative, and undocumentable stage, and managers need to develop a deep, personal, tacit understanding. A shared tacit understanding can only be gained with others through face-to-face interactions.[4] By Phase Three, at which time the new product has been commercialized globally, most of HGO's network nodes that link the original innovators to the commercial customers are connected through other means (memos, procedures manuals, e-mails), because the knowledge being transferred by now to such customers is totally explicit.

Key Factors of HGO's Success

Phase One: Wandering in the wilderness

Broadly stated, HGO's goal in Phase One was to become a significant competitor in high-performance technical computing. To achieve this, management was confronted with the tension of how to generate a variety of ideas on what technologies to pursue and what products to develop. These choices had to solve customers' needs *and, at the same time,* ensure that these ideas were focused and could be linked together in ways that would result in useful new products.

Management was able to generate a variety of ideas by hiring individuals with different backgrounds and broad experience. At the outset, managers hired individuals based solely on the technical skills that they possessed, but quickly changed their focus to hiring individuals who were former employees of companies that were potential customers for the products that HGO thought it might develop. The head of HGO commented:

> Spreading our net in terms of the background that we hired from resulted in a better overall team of people in terms of capability. The corporation had typically been quite narrow in terms of looking at electronic engineering or computer science backgrounds and hiring people from physics and chemistry. By taking people from a wider pool, we just ended up with a brighter and better group of people.

Despite their diverse backgrounds, these individuals all viewed new ideas as interesting and problems as challenges, and they all enjoyed working on interesting problems with the other members of the team. This "common context," along with continual face-to-face interaction, created a safe environment for generating, sharing, and listening to the ideas of other team members. This, in turn, created high levels of trust between team members.

To extend the team's thinking, the network, which was composed initially of HGO's core team members, was expanded to include engineers in the United States (figure 19.3).

> I deliberately created connections between different locations. We set up a development team where I deliberately had people here [Ireland] working for an engineer in the US. Social capital was deliberately built through making people talk on a regular basis by having them work very intimately on a joint project. It created relationships between the U.S. engineer and people here that are very enduring.

Social capital accumulated in this network of relationships as people got to know each other, when they identified mutual interests and needs, when they did things together, and when they worked together. As social capital accumulated, knowledge about technologies and customers also accumulated, and this intellectual capital[5] was shared. Thus, exposing team members to different perspectives and to people who viewed the same problems through a different lens was also an effective means of generating ideas.

While all of these actions had the effect of generating a variety of new ideas, some way had to be found to focus team members' thinking around a manageable set of ideas. HGO needed to constrain these ideas in a way that provided focus for subsequent development efforts. One approach was to hire individuals who were more interested in developing a successful and profitable product than in developing new technologies, so that knowledge creation and transfer were focused on developing commercially viable products.

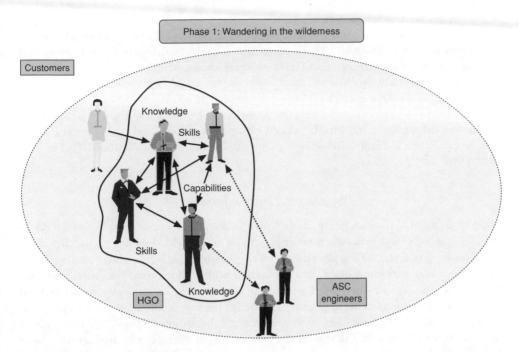

FIGURE 19.3 The network is born

Managers also imposed focus by deciding to build upon existing Compaq technologies in developing their new products. HGO did this by taking on work "that [Compaq] couldn't get done or didn't want to do, to sort of insinuate our way into the business." Doing so required that HGO build strong relationships with Compaq. However, this was particularly difficult because HGO was separated from corporate headquarters, where the existing technology resources were located, near the ocean. To overcome this difficulty, relationships were developed through selected individual travel and working together on challenging tasks. "In the end, it came down to time spent with people. You just need to spend a lot of time, one-on-one in the same place, working with them." Whenever individuals who did not know each other were going to begin to work together, an initial face-to-face meeting was set up. These face-to-face contacts increased HGO team members' stock of social capital by providing value to the engineering group in the United States.

Lastly, HGO ensured that ideas were focused on useful products by having the team develop an understanding of customer needs and problems by conducting benchmarking for customers. HGO's network thus expanded to include these customers. Customers in this business require benchmarking tests before purchase so that they can evaluate the performance of products in their particular environment and for their specific task.

> We made a definite decision, initially, to do things that were close to customers. One of the obvious things to do was benchmarking. Any competitor procurement would involve a competitive benchmark. It was a good way for us to get started and to get some connection with the customers and the people actually selling to those customers. Because we were doing it for free, people were delighted to come to us.

Through this benchmarking activity, customers described their needs, so the organization could begin to understand them and narrow the technological issues to consider in the development of new products. These customers were located in the United States and Europe. At the same time, because HGO was providing a valuable service at no charge, social capital was built up between the customers and HGO engineers.

In sum, in Phase One a series of quite deliberate steps was taken to build social capital, technological competence, and customer knowledge. In doing so, HGO's network expanded to include the core team, US-based Compaq engineers, and customers in Europe and North America. Figure 19.3 illustrates the network of relationships that HGO built in Phase One.

Phase Two: Heroic experimenting

Despite being able to wander for its first two years of existence, pressure on HGO to develop products and generate a revenue stream intensified. In Phase Two, the *heroic experimenting* phase, HGO's goals shifted to emphasize building products and revenue. Doing so was important to build their reputation both with external customers and with internal constituents in Compaq. The tension, of course, is, how do you get started? In the absence of customer deliverables, how do you get the team committed to developing and delivering tangible outcomes *and, at the same time*, deal with internal resource constraints?

In answer to the first half of this tension, the technical director, who had recently been hired from elsewhere in Compaq, created a "marshalling event,"[6] a *"raison d'être"* around which the team could rally their efforts and focus their attention. This marshalling event was the development of a machine for an upcoming supercomputing trade show. As noted by one manager, "It was a signal to the marketplace, but also to the company that we could actually do this. People were very impressed that we were able to do it. Team members still talk about it." The marshalling event was an effective device to provide focus and confidence in HGO's ability to generate results.

In the absence of "real" deadlines such as sales delivery dates, it is important to create deadlines that can be used to ensure that engineers won't endlessly tweak and tune new products. Deadlines can also inspire a team to overachieve, and they can develop deep commitment to the project. But, in order for this to happen, it is necessary that the deadline stretches the team. The supercomputing trade show served as just such a deadline for the HGO team. In fact the trade show deadline was very nearly unrealistic, requiring an heroic effort on the part of the team to complete it. Development began in the spring and the show was in November of that same year. The team's heroic effort bonded the team members and built a great deal of cohesiveness and commitment among members. The effect was strengthened since management decided to build a working machine, something that was almost unheard of. Most of the "machines" at these shows were simply boxes with nothing inside. The deadline thus required them to solve technological problems and develop technological competence at a faster rate than they might otherwise have had to do. Lastly, the deadline demonstrated to the team, to the corporation, and to prospective customers that they were capable of building a product, they were able to work as a team, and the technology was feasible.

While the development of virtually every new product is done under budgetary constraints, flying under the corporate radar horizon meant that HGO had access to even fewer resources than in a normal product development situation. Thus the other side of the tension arises: How did they manage to develop extremely resource intensive products under severe resource constraints? The answer was to use other people's resources. But how did they tap into these resources? Part of the answer was to expand their network.

This was accomplished in two ways. First, a technical director from elsewhere in Compaq was hired by HGO. Second, a senior executive with three decades of experience in Compaq was brought in to head up supercomputing in Compaq, of which HGO formally became a part. Both individuals brought extensive tacit knowledge: how to leverage important resources in the corporation, market savvy, and their own pre-existing networks that included links with other groups in Compaq. These managers had had many years of successful assignments within Compaq. Because they were quickly convinced of the unique opportunity with supercomputing and of HGO's motivation and expertise, these two managers were willing to bring their own networks and social capital to bear on the innovation. Thus HGO's network and social capital immediately grew in terms of quality, quantity, and geographic/global reach (figure 19.4).

To obtain resources for the development of the trade-show machine, the senior executive built upon his existing relationships and existing stocks of social capital with an executive in Compaq customer service who was excited by the challenge posed by the marshalling event. That executive was able to siphon resources from within her budget that could be used to develop the machine.

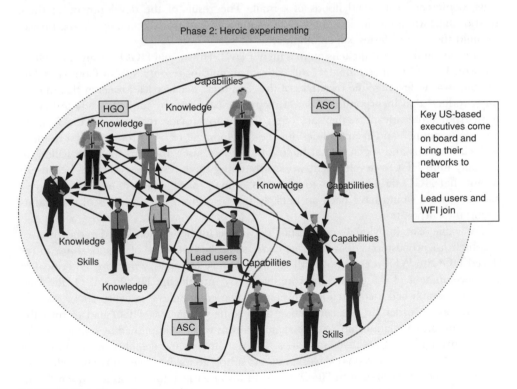

FIGURE 19.4 The network evolves

While the development of the trade-show machine was a major step, the real goal was to become a player in building the world's fastest machines. This goal required resources far in excess of anything they had been able to obtain thus far. Here again, the broad reach of the networks that the technical director and senior executive brought with them were instrumental in securing resources. In this case, a lead user, who had become aware of some recent technological developments by Compaq, approached a manager at Compaq with questions concerning their developments. This manager was in the lead user's network and also in the technical director's network. The link between HGO and the lead user was thus created (figure 19.4).

While the network connections enabled an initial meeting between HGO and the lead user, it was necessary to build meaningful and productive relationships and social capital among multiple individuals within each organization. These relationships were built through intensive face-to-face interactions. The frequency and intensity of contact with the lead customers was, naturally, lower than that within the core team. Yet this contact led to development of commitment by the core team to the customer and product and to a culture of "heroic success" in which engineers worked ferociously hard to meet deadlines and specifications that had been previously developed within the core team. These tight links would not have developed if HGO's engineers had not been perceived as being technically capable. Thus, the technological competence that HGO developed in Phase One was an important prerequisite in building social capital and expanding the network in Phase Two. Relationships were subsequently maintained by frequent travel, telephone calls, conference calls, and floods of e-mail. The result of the development of these relationships was an invitation to HGO from the lead user to bid on an upcoming project to build the world's fastest supercomputer.

This invitation raised the tension to a higher level. How could HGO design and deliver the world's fastest supercomputer, still without significant resources from Compaq? The solution was to leverage the resources of the lead user. Because lead users in this market buy products that incorporate the latest technological advances and are likely to benefit most from those advances, they are often willing to provide resources (in the form of money, personnel, and even facilities) for the development of new products. As a result of the relationships and social capital built with the lead user, the lead user was willing to partially fund HGO's development work. Obtaining these resources was vital because it meant that HGO didn't have to go back to Compaq management to ask for resources; such resources would have been an unlikely prospect given the severe fiscal constraints facing the corporation.

The value of an individual's pre-existing network is further demonstrated in the instance in which a lead customer, based on its own established network of relationships, introduced HGO to WFI, a company with complementary technology that proved critical to the development of these fast supercomputers. By introducing HGO to WFI, the lead customer established a connection between the two companies (see figure 19.4).

However, in order for this connection to become productive, HGO had to turn the connection into a relationship. We see again that this was accomplished by building social capital through a series of deliberate steps. Team members and engineers from WFI were temporarily co-located to do real work, not just simply to meet to "get to know each other better." Senior managers from HGO and WFI also met face-to-face on a frequent basis, alternating their meeting sites between companies. As noted above, face-to-face interaction results in building understanding and trust and contributes to building stocks of social capital. Subsequently, real work continued at their respective locations through frequent e-mails and phone calls.

However, relationships degrade when people don't meet face-to-face. Therefore, when a long-term relationship is important, it is necessary to replenish the relationship and stocks of social capital through face-to-face meetings. Management was careful to maintain stocks of social capital over time by holding regular face-to-face meetings every six months or so with engineers from both companies.

Building and maintaining stocks of social capital is especially important when developing global innovations. These stocks provide a buffer that alleviates the frictions caused by the dynamic complexity of working collaboratively across organizations at the leading edge of multiple technologies. Once they had accumulated social capital, HGO and WFI sought joint solutions to problems created by missed deadlines rather than blame each other.

As HGO succeeded in meeting their goals in Phase Two, they confronted other challenges. They had created a number of impressive products, which built their reputation. Installing and supporting these products, however, required significant time from their engineers. The architect and designer had to be at the customers' sites, sometimes for several weeks, and there was a constant flow of telephone calls and e-mail. These commitments called on engineering resources that were also needed to develop the next-generation machines that customers required. In addition, their internal reputation had created visibility. They were no longer below the radar, but thus far they had generated revenues, not profit.

Phase Three: Stable commercializing

Having achieved the goals of revenue generation and reputation in the *heroic experimenting* phase (Phase Two), HGO's goal in Phase Three, the *stable commercializing* phase, changed to achieving profitability. This third phase was characterized by an effort to achieve a "sane scaling" for this new business. Achieving this goal required that HGO manage another key tension, the need to implement and maintain a routine process for manufacturing and delivering new products to customers *and, at the same time*, the need to maintain the focus on innovating that predominated in Phase Two.

To achieve profitability required selling products in volume, and this meant selling products to commercial customers. These customers did not require the very latest technology. Instead, they preferred technology that was two or three years behind the state of the art, but that was stable and reliable. Also, they needed only a fraction of the power of the products that had been developed for lead users. To sell these "scaled-down" products at a profit, however, required a routine production process that was dependable and efficient, and which could deliver products to customers on time.

The difficulty for HGO was that the skills they had worked so hard and successfully to develop through Phase Two were not the skills required to implement this new business model. While HGO had been able to use its informal relationships with other parts of Compaq to convince them to help with the production of a handful of products for lead users, scaling the business required a much more significant commitment of time and resources by these groups. To gain commitment meant that HGO needed to somehow bring these other organizations into their network. But to make these people part of the network, HGO had to make the product attractive to their business model. As noted by one senior HGO manager, these constituents "want the excitement of the revenues that are generated, but they want that excitement delivered in a sane, repeatable fashion."

To get manufacturing to sign up to build products, HGO had to conform to the processes that manufacturing required and develop the discipline of volume manufacturing. This required that HGO radically alter its way of functioning and its mindset. As HGO's senior manager described it:

> Early on, the core team was essentially responsible for doing everything. Literally, pre-sales, obviously development, building machines, installing at the customer site, making it work, supporting it. You have that heroic phase where they're doing everything.
>
> In order to scale the business, you've got to put in place the structures that allow you to do things through normal company channels. You go into a phase where you have to engage people who don't have the same emotional stake in the product as you have. You're a little frustrated because you can't believe that they're not as motivated as you are. Who wouldn't be? But, they have disciplines that they require you to follow which can be strange to us. They would tell us that, "If you're going to go through volume manufacturing, these are the rules." And we would say, "Our product is different." Their response was, "No, it's not; these are the rules. If you want us to support it, these are the rules. . . ." The way to become respectable is not by saying, "Look how heroic we are. Come be heroic with us." Rather it's, "This is easy. It's easy to build these products repeatedly."

HGO also needed to bring the services organization into the network. They began to develop the relationship by bringing members of the services organization to Ireland to work with HGO's fledgling support team for three weeks fixing problems. Having people work face-to-face, intensively, for weeks at a time built solid interpersonal relationships between HGO and the services group. As these relationships blossomed, services came down squarely in HGO's camp as champions of the supercomputers they were developing.

HGO also hired a program manager from a group in corporate. His job was to guide projects through the corporate new product development process: to involve all of the key functions at the appropriate time and to ensure that Compaq processes were followed. This person had lengthy experience with the process and was also well connected with key constituents in corporate. He was a forceful and credible presence who was able to stand up to any attempts from the development team to subvert the process.

Success in scaling the business, however, raises the critical Phase Three tension. HGO needed to be successful at two very different tasks. On the one hand, they needed a high degree of routine in the manufacturing and delivery process in order to build a "sane, repeatable" business selling stable technology to commercial customers for normal commercial margins. On the other hand, they needed to maintain an innovative focus, drawing on the skills, networks, and social capital that had provided the state-of-the-art technology in Phase Two to continue to produce leading-edge products for lead users. Delivering state-of-the-art supercomputers to those lead customers generated a reputation that fueled subsequent commercial sales and provided the technology that would be delivered to commercial customers after two or three years. The commercial customers, in turn, provided the profit margin needed to sustain the business. HGO's challenge was to meet the needs of both lead users and commercial customers and to let neither the innovative nor the routine system overwhelm the other.

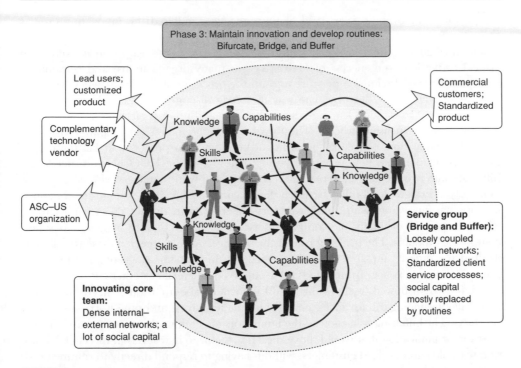

FIGURE 19.5 The network matures

To ensure that the needs of both were met, HGO's network bifurcated into two relatively distinct network clusters that pursued different goals (see figure 19.5). One network cluster was composed of the innovating core team, the complementary technology vendor, lead users, and a few individuals within the United States. This network cluster was essentially the original Phase Two network. It needed to maintain dense ties with high levels of social capital among network members and a strong focus on innovation in order to foster the fast, frequent exchange of knowledge among members and, ultimately, the development of state-of-the-art products. The second, newer network cluster was a commercial customer service group composed primarily of Compaq individuals from manufacturing, sales, and service. It linked the commercial customers to the innovating group. To be as efficient and cost-effective as possible, this newer network cluster's members needed to be as loosely coupled as possible. They also needed to be focused on using routine processes to interface with customers. This service group network cluster maintained a high level of social capital with the innovating group in order to be able to solve the occasional extraordinary challenge. However, with most commercial customers the cluster as a group had little need to use social capital to get its job done. The intense social capital, which oiled the frictions among the different actors in the innovative cluster of the network, was not required in the service-group network. In the service group network, established procedures and rules made interactions formal and predictable to a great extent. The reduced need for social capital was for the infrequent task of smoothing out occasional disruptions. For these infrequent situations, the service group acted as a bridge to the innovating group and at the same time buffered the innovating group's resources from multiple routine enquiries.

The dual goals, generating profits and developing state-of-the-art products, were both critical to the long-run success of HGO. Yet, at many organizations, and certainly in Compaq, there is also intense pressure to routinize processes, increase efficiency, and seek cost savings. Doing so, however, can sow the seeds of long-run failure. The innovation that is required to develop leading-edge technology and products is sometimes a messy, inefficient, and expensive process. The forces for routine, unless kept separate from the forces for innovation, can easily overwhelm the innovation process and kill the engine driving reputation and new product development. Thus, the HGO network needed to bifurcate into two distinct clusters that were connected with managers who acted simultaneously as bridges and buffers between the two (figure 19.5). The first cluster contained the original innovators whose task was very different from that of the second cluster, which contained members of Compaq's services group who were assigned to supercomputing products. The bridging role of the managers who connected these two clusters assured the orderly and free flow of knowledge, which at this stage of the innovation process was very explicit, from the HGO group to commercial customers. It also ensured that information flowed freely to the HGO innovators about customer needs and problems, new technological advances, changes in market forces, and time horizons for new products. The buffering role allowed the innovators to continue their messy search for the next major innovation that would move the HPC sector to new levels in direct collaboration with old and new lead customers, without having to respond directly to routine needs of commercial customers.

INNOVATION MANAGEMENT LESSONS

Our study of HGO's experience allows us to suggest actions that managers involved in global innovation can take:

♦ *Encourage and accept innovation from parts of the organization that are willing to show the initiative to take charge of the process.* Innovation does not necessarily come from a formal "new product development" department. In Compaq's case, initiative was taken by a small core of motivated managers who (a) wanted to find a new *raison d'être* within the corporation; (b) identified a potential market niche; and (c) did something about it in an innovative and persistent way.

♦ *Build social capital-based networks that span national borders and serve the firm's global objectives to fuel and protect the innovation process.* HGO's ability to build social capital and enduring relationships provided its primary competitive advantage. Although its parent corporation, Compaq, certainly had technology that was important, HGO's primary competitive advantage was organizational, not technical. Innovation occurs by integrating available multiple technologies from diverse sources. Turning initial introductions and connections that are provided by networks into social capital, that is, enduring relationships that can be leveraged to achieve organizational objectives, is a critical capability to assure that lead users, complementary technology vendors, and other partners make critical contributions. These enduring relationships and the knowledge created by them provide competitive advantage. There are several conditions that have to be nurtured for the development of such social capital-based networks.

1 *Be certain that social capital-based networks allow innovating groups to access resources that may reside in various parts of the organization, its partners, and its clients.* In the case of HGO, as the innovation process took shape it became important to bring individuals into the innovating group's network from globally dispersed parts of its parent organization, from the organizations of key vendors, and from the organizations of lead clients. Such an expanded network provides competitive advantage because these networks are not easily replicable owing to the nature of the networks themselves – they are extensive and include the "right" people – and because of the time it takes many key members to develop the social capital they bring to the expanded network. In the case of HGO, much of the capital had been built up over 20–30 years. Such social capital is impossible for competitors to duplicate. This unique, inimitable, and valuable network[7] is a device for keeping in continuous contact with the broader technological environment and enables a company to understand which technologies are emerging. Such a network also allows contact with the broader customer environment and enables managers to understand what customers want, which leads to continued profitability in the future.

2 *Co-location is not always the right answer to achieving knowledge transfer. Though several researchers have advocated co-location as a means of facilitating new product development, HGO's case suggests that this is not always an appropriate model.*[8] Most importantly, the talent that is needed is not found in one location and those that are located elsewhere, often in another country, frequently cannot be persuaded to relocate to a single location.[9] Even if they did agree to co-locate, this may not be the desirable action because the source of the person's continued expertise improvement may reside in the remote location itself. In HGO's case, the challenge was to integrate many different technologies that already existed in locations in different parts of the world, each of which had its own development trajectory. HGO managers realized that if they co-located experts in these different technologies, then soon they would not be up to date with rapidly evolving technologies.

3 *To ensure that the innovating group has allies in key positions in the firm's hierarchy, it must develop social capital-based networks that access the managers in these key positions of authority.* These alliances are needed particularly in the early non-revenue generating phases of the innovating process. Such a network allows understanding of the ever-changing corporate environment and enables nurturing of corporate support, securing needed resources, and buying time to achieve profitability.

4 *The innovating group must develop the right networks and the right social capital stocks for each phase of the innovating process.*[10] For example, in a *wandering in the wilderness* phase (figure 19.3, Phase 1), when the primary task is to build technical competence and understanding of technical customer needs, the innovating group's network essentially consists of engineers and technical people from the innovating

firm and its potential customers. In an *heroic experimenting* phase (figure 19.4, Phase 2) the primary task is to build products and revenue and the resource requirements increased significantly. Here the innovating group's network must expand to include other sources of critical technology, customer needs information, and financial resources. Lastly, in a *stable commercializing* phase (figure 19.2, Phase 3), when the primary task is to scale the business and provide profitability on volume sales of repetitive solutions, the innovating network must be reconfigured. Now, the network needs to expand to include people and groups with established skills to achieve the new set of goals that characterize an ongoing volume business. But because a network is created to solve the tensions that arise in a particular phase, that network will only be appropriate to that phase, and inappropriate to prior or subsequent phases. As we have seen in the case of HGO, networks and social capital were expanded at each consecutive phase. Yet, the networks that existed in the *stable commercializing* phase would have been completely destructive had they been imposed in *wandering in the wilderness* phase.

NOTES

1 We would like to thank the managers of the company that became the focus of this study for their enthusiastic help, and the Center for Innovation Management Studies for the funding that supported the initial interviews. Finally, we want to acknowledge the support and assistance provided by Northeastern University's Center for Global Innovation Management.

 Our investigation was based on 26 face-to-face interviews with 22 executives based in 3 countries and in 5 geographic locations. These interviews led to follow-up face-to-face and telephonic discussions. The transcripts of all these interactions were content analyzed. The executives interviewed were from HGO, key collaborator companies, and client organizations crucial to HGO's GPI process. HGO and ASC are pseudonyms.

2 Lead users are customers who need and demand products containing the very latest technological advances.

3 WFI is a disguised name.

4 Polanyi, M. (1966), *The Tacit Dimension*, London: Routledge & Kegan Paul.

5 Intellectual capital consists of (1) knowledge about customers, technologies, and competitors; (2) skills regarding how to work with technologies and customers, and compete effectively with competitors; and (3) capabilities concerning which resources and systems are critical.

6 Ralph Katz uses the term "marshalling event." Katz, R. (1997), How a team at Digital Equipment designed the "Alpha" chip, in R. Katz (ed.), *The Human Side of Managing Technological Innovation*, New York: Oxford University Press, pp. 137–148.

7 See Barney, J. (1991), Firm resources and sustained competitive advantage, *Journal of Management*, 17(1), 99–120.

8 Edward McDonough and David Cedrone elaborate on other reasons why co-location is often not a feasible solution. See McDonough, E. F. III, & Cedrone, D. (2000), Meeting the challenge of dispersed team management, *Research Technology Management*, July–August, 12–17.

9 See *ibid*. for more discussion of this issue.

10 This point is substantiated by Ross Ashby's argument for requisite variety. He proposes that the control system for any organization must reflect the variety in the organization itself. See Ashby, R. (1956), *Introduction to Cybernetics*, New York, John Wiley.

Part V

SPECIAL ISSUES IN DEVELOPING AND TRANSITIONING ECONOMIES

Introduction

JOYCE S. OSLAND AND SUE CANNEY DAVISON

Throughout this book, we have endeavored to unpack the complexity of global management. The last step in our progression from Hercules to Buddha is to add another layer of
complexity from the vantage point of developing and transitioning economies. One of the
most common analogies used in global work is that of the six blind men who each had a
different understanding of an elephant given the part of its anatomy they happened to
touch.[1] In the context of this book, the realities of different economies, different national
contexts, different management styles, and even different perceptions of the global economy
depend on where one sits and what one experiences. For various reasons, most of what's
written on global management comes from developed nations, but that's not the whole
story. Fully 80 percent of the world's population resides in developing countries. Effective
global managers have to be aware of and understand as many views of the elephant as
possible – to avoid costly mistakes as well as to take full advantage of global resources and
opportunities. Given that no one book can capture all the important local knowledge
from around the globe, our purpose in this part is to distill the key lessons and bring the
reader a sampling of voices and views from developing and transitioning economies.

DIFFERENT PERSPECTIVES ON GLOBALIZATION

One of the major discrepancies between some developed and developing countries is the
view toward globalization itself. Business and government leaders in the developed world
tend to view globalization as a *fait accompli* and a positive force. Although developed
countries may well be home to anti-globalization protesters who are concerned about
issues such as inequity, job displacement, labor standards, and environmental sustainability,[2]
by and large the focus is how to succeed at globalization and how to take advantage
of this opportunity for economic growth and prosperity without excessive job loss for
workers and excessive risk to contracting industries.

The view of globalization as an opportunity to enhance wealth is also shared by some
segments of society in certain developing countries. However, one also hears globalization

portrayed as a threat to prosperity and political sovereignty; in particular, some developing countries are often concerned about losing control of their economies[3] and, to some degree, their culture.[4]

In reality, globalization is neither a panacea nor an unmitigated plague.[5] Given the complexity and scope of the topic, it is difficult to determine with precision whether some of the problems attributed to globalization would exist independently and in what degree. National policies and institutions are often critical factors in whether globalization succeeds or fails in a particular country.[6] Nevertheless, globalization in its current state often involves serious trade-offs for nations, and they perceive and react differently to those trade-offs.

The disparate mindsets toward globalization are rooted in ideology as well as experience. Objective experts agree, however, that globalization has resulted in both winners and losers. Globalization is blamed for increasing the chasm between new groups of haves and have-nots – between the well educated and the poorly educated, between the technologically skilled and the unskilled, and between those living in countries that compete successfully in the global economy and those that do not.[7] Globalization has resulted in more jobs in some developing countries, creating another group of winners depending on the level of wages they receive. Other developing countries have suffered job losses in local industries that could not compete with foreign multinationals once formerly protected markets were opened.[8] There have been examples of spectacular development, like the Asian Tigers (Singapore, Taiwan, Hong Kong, and South Korea) and China, as well as examples of countries that are marginalized from the global economy, such as parts of sub-Saharan Africa. Amidst the sometimes contradictory economic findings on globalization's impact, one piece of incontrovertible evidence stands out: There is more inequality across and within countries today than in the past.[9]

Critics argue the structure of the global economy favors developed countries over developing countries. Some of the reasons they give include:

- Relative commodity prices for many products grown in developing countries have fallen, resulting in the need for developing countries to sell more commodities to purchase the industrial goods made by developed nations.
- Western countries have pushed poor countries to eliminate trade barriers but retained some of their own barriers and stringent regulations owing to pressure from special interest groups. This prevented developing countries from exporting their products and left indigenous companies vulnerable to competition from multinationals based in developed countries.[10]
- Workers in developing countries often lack the rights, legal protections, and union representation enjoyed by their counterparts in rich countries. Lacking in bargaining power, workers do not benefit from an increase in the demand for their labor. Their wages do not go up. They may have no choice but to work in sweatshops, suffering unhealthy or dangerous conditions, excessive hours or even physical abuse. In the worst cases, children as well as adults are the victims.
- Industrialized countries continued to subsidize agriculture while insisting that developing countries eliminate subsidies on basic foodstuffs and agricultural and industrial goods.[11]

- The World Trade Organization was founded to help trade flow smoothly, freely, fairly and predictably, but critics claim that some prices and agreements are less favorable to developing countries.[12]
- The world's financial centers, located in developed nations, determine the policies of international bodies such as the International Monetary Fund and the World Bank. These policies have not been universally successful and do not fit the needs of all countries.[13]
- Western banks profited from decreased capital market controls in developing countries, but speculative hot money (money that comes into and out of a country, often overnight, often little more than betting on whether a currency is going to appreciate or depreciate) resulted in economic crises.[14] These speculative activities can readily overwhelm the reserves of almost any government attempting to maintain a fixed exchange rate. Since 1997, there have been massive involuntary devaluations of the fixed currencies of Thailand, Indonesia, Malaysia, South Korea, and Russia.
- Closely linked to devaluations have been huge declines in financial markets in developing and transitional economies, as the fear of devaluations has driven portfolio capital in a search of safer havens. Investors are more likely to place their money in developed nations than in developing countries where investment risks are higher due to economic, social, and political instability.

A country's state of development has far-reaching impacts that global managers should take into consideration. It influences how its citizens see themselves and foreign business, and determines whether they view themselves as operating at an impossible disadvantage or participating in an exciting chance to carve out a place for their nation on the international stage. A country's state of development can also influence the attitudes and policies of global managers toward the country, its government, its workers, and even their suggestions.[15] For these reasons, understanding the unique situation and placement of each country and region in the global constellation is the first step in working with developing nations.

An example is Botswana, a landlocked former British colony in a region marked by poverty and a very high incidence of HIV/AIDS. It has had the fastest growth in income per capita over the past 35 years. Botswana may serve as a useful case study in getting the details right but sadly, this defies simple prescriptions. Some on the political Left might attribute Botswana's success to egalitarianism. Not quite: inequality there is as severe as it is in Colombia, Brazil or Kenya. Those on the Right would like to point to a laissez-faire regime. Wrong again: the government spends a hefty 40 percent of GDP.

In many African countries, such as Congo, Sudan, and Sierra Leone, gems, hardwoods, oil, and other natural resources, as well as easy access to small arms, can fuel years of bloody civil war. In Botswana, valuable minerals have had benign effects: diamonds enriched the elite enough to discourage further profit seeking.

Perhaps Britain's most valuable legacies in Botswana were the law and contract procedures. Botswana's politics have developed along the lines of a single dominant ruling party, closer to Japan's pre-recession LDP than to Europe's ideas of multi-party democracy. But minority parties do exert pressure. Wealthy and secure, the elite pursued sensible policies, such as a customs union with South Africa, and a currency pegged to the rand. The country never tried to oust most of its expatriate labor as some other countries did. Foreign mining companies were welcomed, and the country dealt with them fairly but firmly: it even renegotiated its contract with South Africa's diamond giant, De Beers, when it realized the scale of its reserves.

Botswana's experience suggests that poor countries must try to align the incentives of the elite with those of the masses, much as companies in rich countries try to tie managers' rewards to those of shareholders. One lesson from Botswana is that history shapes countries. Another is that good management is at the center of growth, and that the rule of law is as important as the laws of economics.

If Botswana is a success story, Argentina is a well-known example of a country in economic crisis. At the beginning of the twentieth century, Argentina was the sixth wealthiest country in the world. Political instability, and the resulting turnover in leaders and governments, kept the country from establishing consistent economic policies. Another factor in Argentina's economic history was the populist mindset that President Perón encouraged in labor unions. He rewarded them for their political support, and they came to expect short-term economic gain.[16] Labor unions viewed foreign multinationals as "villains," or at best "a necessary evil," when it became apparent that the country desperately needed to open its borders to foreign investment. Unlike Costa Rica, where the solidarity movement encouraged unions to partner and share profits with foreign firms,[17] union relationships with multinationals in Argentina tended to be adversarial.

Argentina was formerly called the International Monetary Fund's Poster child because of its strict adherence to their advice and conditions. The country underwent privatization, opened its markets, pegged its national currency to the US dollar, cut social spending, reduced wages, raised prices, and balanced the budget to attract foreign investment. Indeed, Argentina's structural reforms in the 1990s reduced rampant inflation and encouraged impressive growth rates. Nevertheless, economic crises elsewhere (Mexico, Asia, Russia, and Turkey) jolted Argentina into recession in 1998.[18] For varied and complex reasons, the country has not yet recovered from this recession. The strength of the US dollar made Argentina's exports uncompetitive, and, unlike Chile, it had inadequate policies for protection against speculative inflows of capital. Government corruption contributed to Argentina's problems and the inability to control government spending. Shrinking GDP eventually caused the country to default on its public debt. Increasingly tough demands on the populace (reduced wages and pensions, increased taxes, a freeze on bank deposits) led to a loss of confidence in the politicians' ability to manage the economy and resulted in riots and civil unrest. As one observer noted, Argentina entered "social, political and economic bankruptcy."[19] Argentina went from boasting a sizeable middle class to having 60 percent of its population living in poverty, and an unemployment rate of over 20 percent. This has been a shocking slide for a proud country.

Despite agreement on this recital of facts about Argentina's economic crisis, there is no overall consensus about what went wrong. Some argue that Argentina should have gone farther with its reforms; in contrast, others blame monetary and fiscal orthodoxy hampered by a rigid exchange rate.[20]

As in Botswana, Argentina's experience with globalization reflects the unique constraints and opportunities found in a country's history and institutions,[21] which are a part of the complexity that global managers need to understand. Another lesson to be drawn from Argentina's example is the need for contextualization. The "one size fits all" approach to globalization is coming under greater scrutiny; multinationals must also apply this lesson with regard to business strategies and practices and remember to adapt to the local environment. And finally, the rapid change in fortune for Argentina is a clear warning about the need to manage political and financial risk and exposure in volatile economies.

This part focuses on some issues that effective global managers need to consider when dealing and working in developing countries. We begin with a balanced overview of the developing world – its opportunities and characteristics in terms of economics, demographics, culture, politics, and corruption. The second chapter describes the socio-cultural context in developing countries and its implications for effective leadership and teamwork. The third chapter highlights the need for foreign managers to understand the country-specific context when framing and implementing strategic decisions. Gaining legitimacy, for both foreign managers and their firms, is a primary goal for long-term success in transitioning economies. Finally, the fourth chapter describes five managerial competencies needed in developing countries, supported by African examples.

NOTES

1 This Indian legend was the topic of a poem written in 1963 by John Godfrey Saxe, entitled "The Blind Men and the Elephant."

2 For a good description of anti-globalization protest issues, see Kobrin, S. (2001), Our resistance is as global as your oppression: Multinational corporations, the protest movement and the future of global governance, paper presented at the meeting of the International Studies Association, Chicago; February.

3 Champlin, D., & Olson, P. (1999), The impact of globalization on U. S. labor markets: redefining the debate, *Journal of Economic Issues*, 33(2), 443–451.

4 For different views on the impact of globalization on culture, see Tomlinson, J. (1999), *Globalization and Culture*, Chicago: University of Chicago Press; Hamelink, C. (1993), *Cultural Autonomy in Global Communications*, New York: Longman; and Guillén, M. F. (2001), Is globalization civilizing, destructive or feeble? A critique of six key debates in the social science literature, *Annual Review of Sociology*, 27, 235–260.

5 For a balanced view of globalization, see Lechner, F. J., & Boli, J. (eds.) (2003), *The Globalization Reader*, 2nd edn., Oxford: Blackwell, and Osland, J. (2003), Broadening the debate: Pros and cons of gobalization, *Journal of Management Inquiry*, June, 137–154.

6 Olson, M. Jr. (1996), Big bills left on the sidewalk: Why some nations are rich, and others poor, *Journal of Economic Perspectives*, 10(2), 3–24.

7 Frank, R. H., & Cook, P. J. (1997), *The Winner Takes All Society*, New York: The Free Press; Pritchett, L. (1997), The once and future distribution of world income, *Economie Internationale*, 0(71), 19–42; United Nations Development Programme (1999), *Human Development Report 1999*, New York: Oxford University Press.

8 Lee, E. (1996), Globalization and employment: Is anxiety justified?, *International Labour Review*, 135(5), 486–497. For a critique of the policies enacted by the IMF and the World Bank by a former insider, see Stiglitz, J. (2002), *Globalization and Its Discontent*, New York, Norton.

9 United Nations Development Programme (2001), *Human Development Report 2001*, New York: Oxford University Press.

10 Stiglitz (2002).

11 *Ibid.*

12 *Ibid.*

13 *Ibid.*

14 *Ibid.*

15 In addition to occasional stories about stereotypes and condescending attitudes toward people in developing countries, there is evidence that the relative status of countries influences the direction of organizational learning in multinationals – e.g., lessons and innovations flow more readily from headquarters and developed country subsidiaries to developing countries than vice versa. See Bonache, J., & Brewster, C. (2001), Knowledge transfer and the management of expatriation, *Thunderbird International Business Review*, 43(1), 145–168; Inkpen, A. C., & Dinur, A. (1998), Knowledge management processes and international joint ventures, *Organization Science*, 9(4), 454–468; and Gupta, A., & Govindarajan, V. (1991), Knowledge flows and the structure of control within multinational corporations, *Academy of Management Review*, 16(4), 768–792.

16 See Guillén, M. F. (2000), Organized labor's images of multinational enterprise: Divergent foreign investment ideologies in Argentina, South Korea, and Spain, *Industrial and Labor Relations Review*, 53(3), 419.

17 See Sheppard, N. Jr. (1997), AFL-CIO asks U.S. officials to revoke Costa Rica's special trade privileges, *Journal of Commerce and Commercial*, 397(28–35), August 10, 4A; and Bejarano, O. (1997), La fuerza del solidarismo, *La Nación*, July 18.

18 See Kiguel, M. A. (2002), Structural reforms in Argentina: Success or failure?, *Comparative Economic Studies*, Summer–Fall, 83–103.

19 This statement is attributed to MIT professor of Economics Rudi Dornbusch.

20 Kiguel (2002).

21 Guillén, M. F. (2001), *The Limits of Convergence: Globalization and Organizational Change in Argentina, South Korea, and Spain*, Princeton: Princeton University Press.

20

The Developing World: Toward A Managerial Understanding

BETTY JANE PUNNETT

This part focuses on approximately 80 percent of the world's population, the people who live and work in countries characterized as developing. These people represent a large, growing market and labor force, spread among countries that are extremely diverse and which produce a wide array of products and services. These products and services are largely unknown, yet have potentially high demand in the developed world. For example, the Canadian company President's Choice has a very successful food line called "Memories of . . . ," and includes products from around the world – jerk sauces from Jamaica, marinades from Hong Kong, dressings from Malaysia, and so on – illustrating the range of specialty foods in demand in Canada. A look at the specialty shelves of any super-market in Canada, Europe, or the United States serves to reinforce this, as so many products from developing countries around the world are found there.

A recent article in the *New York Times*[1] noted that David Coleman, the chef at Atlas on Central Park South, tasted a $3 glass of sorrel at Gary's Jamaican Hot Pot, a restaurant in Harlem. Sorrel is a traditional West Indian drink, made from edible hibiscus. Coleman was so impressed that a hibiscus sauce is now used at Atlas as a glaze for a foie gras ballottine dusted with pulverized dried hibiscus petals, part of the restaurant's $68 three-course tasting menu. Hibiscus has now become part of the menu at several high-end New York restaurants, among them the brand-new Cinnabar, at 235 West 56th Street, and Citarella, at Avenue of the Americas and 49th Street, where every dinner ends with a shot glass of "Exotic Hibiscus Cocktail."

In addition to providing products and services, the developing world is potentially a very large market. Many discussions of global economic development assume that growth will be fueled by Europe, Japan, and the United States. Real growth is more likely to be fueled and sustained by the developing countries – 80 percent of the world's population. If incomes increase in these countries, the average person will be able to afford many of the goods and services currently only available to the rich. This increased consumption can stimulate economic growth in the developing as well as the developed world.

The workforce in the developing world is another potential strength of these countries. The workforce is young, an attribute which has the potential to provide an enthusiastic and hard-working group of employees for many years. In contrast, the developed world's workforce is aging. The developing world has been exposed to developed-country products and services, and embraces many of them. At the same time there are products and services from the developing world that the developed world needs and wants. For example, Blue Mountain coffee, grown in the Blue Mountains of Jamaica, is considered by many to be the best coffee in the world, and sells at a premium price everywhere. There are many opportunities on which managers from both sets of countries can capitalize, but they need to understand each other to be able to do so.

Managers from the developed world are often attracted to the developing world by its numbers: large potential markets, a large potential workforce, and available resources. Managers are unsure, however, of the reality of doing business in developing countries because they expect a business environment very different from what they know. Managers from the developing world also see the advantages of their own large markets, workforce, and potential to supply the rich world with new and unique products and services, but these managers are also unsure of the reality of doing business in an environment different from what they know. This chapter examines some of these differences between developed and developing countries, and considers how they impact effective management. This chapter's purpose is to help all managers build a realistic understanding of business opportunities, and how they might explore these, in the context of the realities of the differences between developed and developing countries.

Developing countries have received little attention from management writers, yet understanding management in these countries is particularly relevant in today's global business environment. There are concerns that managers should note. First, as one researcher has recently pointed out, because the evolution of a global marketplace is redefining the arena for international business, managers should be aware that "since prior examinations have focused primarily on locations in the industrialized regions of North America and Western Europe, our theories, models, and practices [of management] exhibit a significant 'Western' influence,"[2] which means they may not be applicable in the rest of the world. Second, as noted in a recent evaluation of research publications in the cross-cultural management field, "there is a risk of creating two distinct branches of management literature: global and North American."[3] This chapter seeks to provide information relating to managing in the "rest of the world" – the 80 percent that is now generally called "developing."

The specific aim of this chapter is to identify potential variations associated with level of development and to explore how managers are likely to experience these variations. It examines the opportunities in the developing world, then considers what the term *development* actually means, and continues with an exploration of a variety of factors that characterize development. The chapter is followed by other chapters that consider global competencies, teams, and leadership, and managing strategic initiatives, all in the context of the development issues identified.

DEVELOPING WORLD OPPORTUNITIES

Many people think first of poverty when developing countries are mentioned. According to a report on the BBC in April 2002, a poll of Europeans showed a negative view of developing countries, predominantly focused on poverty and illness.

There is another side to developing countries that managers should recognize – their substantial potential. Consider the following:

- The developing countries, together, account for 80 percent of the world's population, representing a substantial market and workforce. China and India together have a population of over 2 billion.
- Per capita incomes have been growing in developing counties, albeit not as quickly as in the developed world, and there is a growing middle class in many countries.
- A substantial number of developing countries achieve high scores on the United Nation's Development Index, a composite index which indicates the presence of good education, health care, and quality of life. These countries are recognized as good places in which to live and do business. Countries as diverse as Barbados, Singapore, and the United Arab Emirates are among these.[4]
- Some developing countries, such as India, have large numbers of highly trained and qualified people. Others, such as Zimbabwe, have good infrastructures. Still others, such as Barbados, have stable governments and high literacy rates. Cuba is an example of a developing country with excellent medical facilities. These are all characteristics that provide an environment for both inward and outward business opportunities.
- The current emphasis by a wide range of development organizations is on support of developing countries in their efforts to make the most of their resources in a global business environment. Such support provides opportunities for both indigenous and foreign companies. Many development agencies from Europe, Japan, and North America provide resources in the form of loans, grants, and insurance aimed at initiatives in developing countries.
- A number of developing countries – Argentina, Brazil, China, India, and Nigeria, for example – are physically large and may offer access to substantial reserves of natural resources.
- Many developing countries have had substantial periods of economic growth. The miracle of the Asian Tigers may be tarnished in view of financial and political events since the late 1990s; nevertheless, the economic growth in these countries was often referred to as an "economic miracle." In 2000, Singapore's GDP per capita was US$27,690, compared to US$36,200 in the United States, illustrating the levels that some developing countries have reached.[5] These growth rates, in economic terms, suggest the potential for the developing countries as a whole.
- Many developing countries have relatively warm climates that are attractive to the growing, aging population of the developed world. These so called "baby boomers" from the developed countries have substantial wealth and may see the countries with warm climates as a place to enjoy retirement.

The conclusion that emanates from these facts is that the developing world offers substantial possibilities. The developing world may well be the engine of economic growth for the entire world in coming decades. In order to achieve this potential, however, this part of the world needs to grow economically. The following parts discuss definitions of development, characteristics of developing countries, and the management implications of these characteristics.

Definitions of development

Defining where, or what, the developing world is, is problematic. The United Nations says: "The term *developing countries* includes low- and middle-income economies and thus may include economies in transition from central planning, as a matter of convenience. The term *advanced countries* may be used as a matter of convenience to denote the high-income countries."[6]

Definitions of *development* are sensitive because the concept of development is value-laden. Different groups interpret the word differently at different times. Sometimes being classified as *developing* is advantageous for a country, when, for example, it wants to receive development aid or other donor assistance. At other times a country may want to think of itself as developed, for example, when it wants to attract foreign investment and high-technology firms. The United States Council for International Business used the following definitions,[7] which are helpful in understanding the most commonly accepted distinctions between developed and developing countries:

- *Developed countries*: Industrialized countries as distinguished from developing countries or Less Developed Countries (LDCs). Generally, this term is understood to refer to the 24 members of the Organization for Economic Cooperation and Development (OECD)[8] and in some cases, the industrialized countries of Eastern Europe.
- *Developing countries*: This term is used most commonly at the United Nations to describe a broad range of countries including those with both high and low per capita national incomes and those that depend heavily on the sale of primary commodities. These countries usually lack an advanced industrial infrastructure as well as advanced educational, health, communications, and transportation facilities.

This lack of precise definition is further complicated by the myriad of additional terms used in conjunction with or as substitutes for the term *development*. Some examples:

- *Under-developed and LDCs*: Poorer, developing countries were often called *under-developed* some fifty years ago. This terminology has been described as a carryover or colonial condescension, and was changed to *Less Developed Countries (LDCs)* in order to be less demeaning. This term has also been considered negative, and is seldom now used for the developing countries as a group. The term LDC now describes the *Least Developed Countries*, the poorest nations in the world, which receive particular development attention from the United Nations.[9] In 2001 there were 48 LDCs, using this definition.
- *Third World*: The Third World designation for developing countries was used in contrast to the First World, OECD countries, and the Second World, communist countries. The Third World encompassed the countries that were not aligned with either the First or Second Worlds. Since the collapse of the Soviet Union, this terminology is less frequently used, but *Third World* is still in common usage, usually referring to the poorer countries of the world.
- *North/South*: The majority of the richer countries are north of the majority of the poorer countries. The *North/South* distinction began through an attempt to be neutral and the *North/South* terms are used by many development organizations in the

context of a North–South divide. The North is seen as the "haves" and the South seen as the "have-nots."

◆ *Transitional* or *industrializing*: Recently, as some countries have embraced new economic forms, they have been considered as becoming developed or industrialized. The countries of the former Soviet bloc are often described as *transitional economies*, and countries with substantial industrial bases, such as South Korea, Taiwan, and Brazil, are often described as *industrializing* or *Newly Industrialized Countries (NICs)*. These countries are also described as *Emerging Markets* to indicate the substantial markets that they represent.

The varying terminology stems from attempts to wrestle with several concerns. There are clear differences among countries in terms of their economic resources and level of industrialization. The United Nations and various development organizations, as well as the general population, want to recognize these differences. Much as with the term "development" itself, words used to recognize the differences in development levels are inevitably value-laden. Newly devised terms carry with them the promise of value-neutrality; as this neutrality fades and embedded connotations take over, new terms arise. For example, "LDC" was used in the 1950s to describe countries as "less developed." Eventually this term was thought to be as demeaning as "under-developed," so "developing countries" became its more acceptable replacement. *Developing* versus *developed*, however, suggests that one set of countries has reached a desired level of economic achievement to which the other set should aspire. The North/South terminology sought to differentiate without judging, but this approach did not succeed either. In effect, the rich and powerful "North" was usually depicted in a negative light as exploiting the poor and powerless "South," both with mutual antagonisms.

The terrorist attacks of September 11, 2001 have made people everywhere more conscious of the way words can have different meanings to different people. Hence, sensitivity in the use of language is often important when people relate to others of different backgrounds. As recent events have made clear, "jihad" does not mean the same thing to all Muslims, and it is often interpreted differently by non-Muslims. "Crusade" is used commonly in English to mean any concerted and continuing effort, but to Middle Easterners it clearly refers to the Christian Holy Wars against the Arab world. The development terminology is not an exception. Managers should be aware of the diverse terminology used to describe countries that fall into different economic classifications and be conscious of the various implications these terms may carry.

The issue of describing differences without making judgments is likely to continue, and this chapter will not resolve it. This chapter will use the term "developing" for those countries that are its particular focus. The term "developed world" will be used to refer to the OECD countries and the rest of Western Europe, and the term "developing world" will refer to the rest of the world. The major distinctions between *developed* and *developing* are that the developed world countries, on average, have a higher per capita income than the developing world, and rank higher on the United Nations World Development Index. What these distinctions mean for managers is that the business environment can be substantially different in the two regions. The differences provide opportunities and challenges, both of which need to be understood. In the following discussion, these differences are explored.

The next sections provide an overview of some of the main characteristics that differentiate the developing countries from the more developed ones. Several of these characteristics will be examined in greater depth in subsequent chapters.

CHARACTERISTICS OF DEVELOPING COUNTRIES

As defined, the developing world encompasses a large and diverse group of countries. Clearly, it is difficult to talk of shared characteristics among such a heterogeneous group. It includes the very small island states of the Caribbean and Pacific islands and the extremely large subcontinents of China and India. It includes a variety of political forms – communist states, kingdoms of various kinds, and democracies. It includes all ethnic groups, all races, and all religions. The discussion of shared characteristics should not be interpreted as suggesting that the countries will be alike. Each country or region has its own unique mix of characteristics which make it special; nevertheless, an understanding of the shared characteristics can assist in building an understanding of management in the group of countries we call the developing world.

There are two important measures that underlie the following discussion, per capita GDP and the World Bank Development Index. The real GDP is the total domestic economic production, adjusted for local purchasing power. The per capita GDP is total production divided by the total population. The second measure, the World Bank Development Index, is a measure that incorporates factors other than economic production, such as health and education, to assess the broader quality of life in various countries. There is a high correlation between per capita GDP and the Development Index. All of the countries that have high per capita GDP rank high on the Development Index. In fact, the OECD countries plus Iceland are ranked as the top 15 countries. There are, however, a number of countries which rank high on the Development Index that are not high in terms of per capita GDP: in 1999, the following countries were considered high in terms of the development index – Antigua and Barbuda, Argentina, the Bahamas, Bahrain, Barbados, Brunei, the Czech Republic, Chile, Costa Rica, Cyprus, Greece, Hong Kong, South Korea, Kuwait, Luxembourg, Malta, Poland, Qatar, Singapore, Slovakia, Slovenia, the United Arab Emirates, and Uruguay.[10]

There is, thus, a substantial group of developing countries that have relatively high World Bank Development Index scores and lower per capita GDP. This indicates significant development that is not purely economic. These countries have done well in terms of providing a high quality of life for citizens, an achievement which underscores the need to understand both the similarities and differences among developing countries.

Economic characteristics

The developing world is characterized by fewer economic resources than the developed world. More simply, the developing countries are poorer than the developed. The consequences of poverty are clear:

- People are concerned with basic needs, or, in the less poor of these countries, with achieving economic stability.

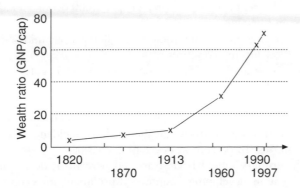

FIGURE 20.1 Ratio of GNP per capita for the 20 richest to 20 poorest countries

- Infrastructure is limited. Roads, railways, ports, and other physical facilities are non-existent in some locations and only adequate in the less poor countries.
- Social services are limited. Education, health, and other social services are non-existent in some locations and only adequate in the less poor countries.
- Resources are scarce, and projects need to be clearly justified to warrant governmental or non-governmental support.

In spite of the relatively high rating for some countries on the World Bank Development Index, the economic disparity between the developed and developing countries is startling in many ways, as the following statistics illustrate:

- The richest 20 percent of the world have 86 percent of the world's GDP, the middle 60 percent have 13 percent, and the poorest 20 percent have only 1 percent.
- GNP (Gross National Product, including cross-border transactions) per capita in the developed world is $22,785 compared to $5,725 in the developing world.

Of even greater concern is the growing disparity between the rich and poor countries. Comparisons of per capita GNP for the top and bottom 20 percent of all countries over the past almost two centuries show a dramatic increase in wealth disparities. In 1820 the ratio was 3:1, in 1870 it was 7:1, in 1913, 11:1, in 1960, 30:1, in 1990, 60:1, and in 1997, 74:1. There is no question that the rich have been growing richer, and the poor have not been catching up, as figure 20.1 illustrates. This disparity is important from a management perspective, and managers in the developing countries feel disadvantaged by this disparity.

The lack of economic resources in the developing countries means that there are few resources for government expenditure on infrastructure.

Some examples illustrate the differentials in these factors between the developed and developing countries:

- High-income countries consume 5,783 kilowatt hours of electricity per capita; middle-income countries consume 1,585; and low-income countries consume 188.
- High-income countries have 92 percent of their roads paved; middle-income countries have 51 percent paved; and low-income countries have 19 percent paved.

- High-income countries have 286 newspapers per 1,000 people; middle-income countries have 75; and low-income countries have 13.
- High-income countries have 1,300 radios per 1,000 people; middle-income countries have 383; and low-income countries have 147.
- High-income countries have 269 personal computers per 1,000 people; middle-income countries have 32; and low-income countries have 4.
- Developed countries have 253 doctors per 100,000 people; developing countries have 76. Tuberculosis rates are 15 percent in developed countries, 79 percent in developing countries. Low birth-weight babies have incidence rates of 6 percent in developed countries, 18 percent in developing countries.
- Enrollment in primary school is close to 100 percent in developed countries and about 86 percent in developing countries. Enrollment in secondary school is 96 percent in developed countries and 60 percent in developing countries.

These comparisons illustrate the dimensions of the gap between the rich and poor countries. Richer countries spend more on infrastructure, both physical and intellectual. The consequence is that developing countries lack roads, railways, and ports, and their people have limited training; and medical care is often limited, as is access to information.

Access to information through the Internet is often identified as contributing positively to development, and providing a means to overcome some of the economic constraints. The Internet can potentially provide everything from basic schooling to contact with the best medical authorities and research scientists. There is little question that the Internet may provide substantial benefits for the poorer countries, but, as Bill Gates has noted, Internet access is not helpful when you have no water or electricity. In 2000 the richest 20 percent of the world accounted for 93.3 percent of Internet users. While that imbalance continues, one cannot think of the Internet as a tool for development. The development of wireless communication technology may provide increased opportunities for the developing world, and some developing countries are doing well in terms of technology[11] – the Republic of Korea and Singapore are included as leaders in the 2001 Human Development Report. Potential leaders include the Czech Republic, Hungary, Slovenia, Hong Kong, Bulgaria, Poland, Malaysia, Croatia, Mexico, Cyprus, Argentina, Romania, Costa Rica, and Chile – suggesting potential for the developing world. Interestingly, low-technology products also provide opportunities. Wind-up radios have given low-cost, easy access to information and news media in parts of Africa that had no such access previously.

Initially, the economic characteristics identified paint a negative picture of poor countries. A moment's thought, however, leads to an opposite conclusion: these countries need so much that there is an almost limitless market for all kinds of products and services. One is reminded of the anecdote of two shoe salesmen going to Africa in the 1950s. One returned, saying there was no market because the people did not wear shoes. The other returned, saying the market was huge because the people did not *have* shoes. The outcome of the story? The second salesman was from the Bata Shoe Organisation, a Canadian company founded by a Czech family that had emigrated to Canada, and Bata became so dominant in the footwear market in Africa that the word *bata* is used for *shoe* in both East and West Africa.

From the perspective of indigenous companies, the vast regions that constitute the developing countries comprise enormous diversity. Indigenous businesses realize that they can find markets in developed countries as well as in other developing ones. In the developing world, indigenous and foreign companies are likely to be most successful when they work together. Market access strategies often include cooperation between foreign and local firms through strategic alliances, joint ventures, manufacturing licenses, and so on. This cooperation suggests that understanding and being able to work effectively with the other is especially important.

Developing countries have been encouraged to move toward freer trade, and many have done so, in the context of freer trade leading to improved economic conditions. This move is likely to be beneficial, but it is hampered by the developed countries retaining protectionist policies in the very industries where the developing world might compete effectively. The United States' introduction of increased agricultural subsidies in 2002 led many developing countries to question their own trade liberalization moves.

Demographic characteristics

There are several important demographic differences between the developed and the developing countries. These include population growth, population dispersion, age distribution, literacy and numeracy levels, and gender roles.

Population growth

At 2 percent, population growth rates were substantially higher in the developing world than in the developed, at 0.6 percent for the period 1975–7. This is also evident in fertility rates in the developing world, which are at 5 conceptions per woman as compared to 1.9 in the developed world. These differences are expected to continue. Combined with the increasing income disparity previously outlined, this means a growing proportion of the world will be poor, and a smaller percentage of the world population will control an increasingly greater share of the resources and wealth. This situation does not sound like one that is sustainable, and managers need to be aware of the tensions that are created by such a situation. At the same time, the developing world's positive attributes of a large potential market and workforce are increasing as their populations grow.

Population dispersion

The world as a whole is becoming more urban. About 50 percent of the world's population lives in cities, but the developing world is still substantially more rural than the developed world. In 1997, 78 percent of the developed world lived in cities compared to only 38 percent of the developing world. Sub-Saharan Africa, East Asia, and South Africa were still relatively rural, but the rates of urbanization were highest in these regions. In developing countries, the cities are seen as the places where opportunities exist, and major movements of people from the rural areas to the urban often results in cities that are overcrowded and under-serviced, with a substantial number of people living in very poor circumstances.

Age distribution

The average age of populations in developed countries is increasing while that in the developing countries is declining. In 1995 the over-65 population in developed countries was about 15 percent compared to 5 percent in developing countries. This gap was predicted to widen to 18 percent in developed countries by 2015, while remaining at a constant 5 percent in developing countries. Developing countries thus have an increasing abundance of younger, less experienced workers. If education and training are available for these workers, they could provide the base for a productive workforce.

Literacy and numeracy

Literacy and numeracy rates are higher in the developed countries. There are developing countries with good educational systems, and there is concern about the deterioration of education in North America and Europe. Nevertheless, on average, people in the developed world have access to better education, which results in functional literacy and numeracy as the norm. This is not the case in the developing world. The lack of literacy and numeracy in the workforce has major implications for the type of work that can be done, the use of technology, the testing and training that is needed, the need for supervision, and the opportunities for advancement.

> A US company with a subsidiary in a small island state hired a local manager to run the subsidiary. The local manager came well recommended by local contacts, was intelligent, well spoken, and related well to the local workers. She was interviewed by a representative from headquarters and seemed to be an ideal choice for the position. Initially, operations went well, but it soon became clear that there was a problem, as major discrepancies surfaced in terms of inventory levels and accuracy counts of parts shipped. The underlying problem was finally uncovered. The manager could not do the basic arithmetic of adding or subtracting, and operating the subsidiary relied on these skills. No one had thought to ask about these skills because they were simply assumed.

Gender roles

Gender role distinctions are more pronounced in developing countries. Laws discriminate against women in terms of landownership, family inheritance, education, and a variety of other factors. Women often do much of the work within the family, and receive little, if any, compensation for their home labor. Where there are minimum wage regulations, these may favor men. The United Nations computes a gender-related development index that incorporates male/female differences in life expectancy, education, literacy, and GDP per capita. Countries that score high on the overall development index also score high on the gender development index. The richer and more developed countries thus appear to provide more equal opportunities for women than do the poorer, developing countries. These differences in how women are viewed and treated can cause difficulties. For example:

- ◆ Where women are in a subordinate position, it is often impossible to make full use of their expertise and experience. Managers from developed countries may have problems implementing the equal opportunity policies that they feel are appropriate, and people in these countries may be offended by such policies.

◆ Male managers from these developing countries may have difficulty interacting with women counterparts from developed countries and may feel compromised, both religiously and socially, by such interactions.
◆ Women from developed countries working in countries where women are treated differentially may face barriers to effective performance.

Although there is still substantial discrimination in favor of men, particularly in the business and professional world, the role of women is changing in many developing countries. Women are playing an increasingly active role in business. These women are often especially committed, hardworking, and innovative. They can be seen to provide an additional benefit for those who do business in these countries. An example of successful women in developing countries is offered by the Grameen Bank in Pakistan, which has made a series of small loans to women to support their developing businesses. The Grameen Bank has found that their small businesswomen clients are successful and meticulous about repaying their loans.

Cultural characteristics

Hofstede's work on culture was discussed in Part I. Interestingly, some of Hofstede's dimensions of culture seem to differ depending on the level of development. The developing countries, for the most part, are low on individualism and high on power distance (see figures 20.2–20.5). This means:

◆ *Individualism*: The richer, more developed countries view the individual as the more appropriate focus of attention, while the poorer, less developed countries view the group as the appropriate focus.
◆ *Power distance*: The richer, more developed countries see equality as a desirable goal and minimize power differentials, while the poorer, less developed countries accept differences in power as appropriate.

These cultural variations between the two sets of countries are certain to affect management practices and to result in difficulties when managers from one set interact with personnel from the other. Hofstede discusses development assistance:

◆ With individualism, "donors will want to serve certain categories, like the urban poor or the small farmers," while "leaders in the receiving countries may, for example, want to repay their own village or tribe for its sacrifices in providing them with an education and enabling them to get into their present power position."
◆ With power distance, "donors' representatives try to promote equality and democratic processes at the receiving end" and "tend to be disturbed that they cannot avoid powerful local leaders who want to use at least part of the aid to maintain or increase existing inequalities."[12]

Similar reactions are likely in the approaches to management in the two sets of countries. Hofstede notes that there is no clear distinction between the sets of countries in terms of his uncertainty avoidance and masculinity indices. In general, however, the developing countries tend to be somewhat higher on uncertainty avoidance, and the developed countries somewhat higher on masculinity. Higher uncertainty avoidance indicates a

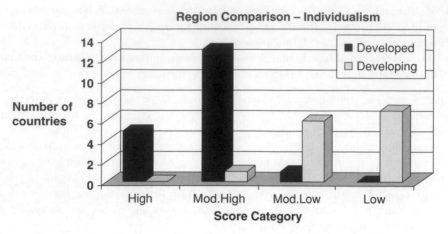

FIGURE 20.2 Region comparison: Individualism

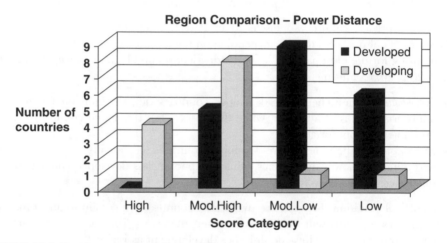

FIGURE 20.3 Region comparison: Power distance

preference for situations that are well defined and clear, with risk aversion, and possibly with relatively low entrepreneurial capacity. Higher masculinity indicates a competitive approach with a preference for tangible rewards. Figures 20.2–20.5 illustrate the cultural profiles of developed and developing countries. Using data from Hofstede's study, countries were classified as High, Moderately High, Moderately Low, or Low on the four cultural value dimensions of Individualism, Power Distance, Uncertainty Avoidance, and Masculinity. The developed and developing countries were compared on each of these value dimensions.

Other cultural characteristics that have sometimes been identified as distinguishing developed countries from the developing ones are need for achievement and locus of control. Some developing countries have been described as having a relatively low need for achievement. This characteristic is perhaps attributable to the limited economic

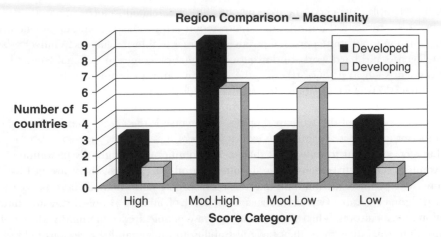

FIGURE 20.4 Region comparison: Masculinity

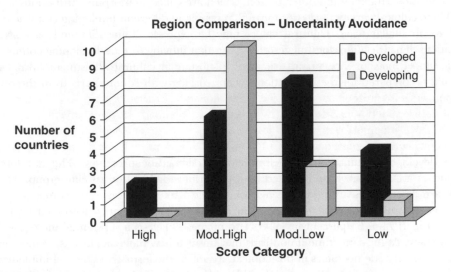

FIGURE 20.5 Region comparison: Uncertainty avoidance

base in these countries, which means that other needs are paramount. A low need for achievement has, like high uncertainty avoidance, been associated with limited entrepreneurial activity.[13] The author's experience suggests that developing countries may be more likely to exhibit an external locus of control than an internal one. This means that in those countries people are more likely to attribute what happens to external forces, perhaps the gods, luck, or their ancestors, rather than to their own actions. For example, in the Caribbean dialect, if someone is late for the bus they say "De bus lef' me." If they drop a glass, they say, "De glass mash." When someone reported on a woman falling at work she said, "De groun' slip from under she." These examples indicate a high degree of external attribution.

In the examples just cited, the external attribution is related to locus of control. It may also be an example of the fundamental attribution error. This perceptual bias describes our inclination to attribute personal positive outcomes to internal factors in ourselves such as intelligence and hard work, and negative personal outcomes to external factors in the environment such as a lousy teacher, the economy, and government rules. Conversely, when others do well we attribute the positive outcome to external factors, and when they do poorly we attribute the negative outcome to internal factors in them.[14] Note, however, that in the example of the woman slipping, the reverse is the case – that is, the negative outcome for another is attributed to external factors.

Managers will want to remember that such attributions are culturally conditioned and will want to avoid attribution errors. In intercultural interactions, there are at least two reasons why people's attributions may be more problematic than if these people were from the same culture. One is the increased level of anxiety people bring to communication across cultures. The second is that because people are less familiar with the other culture than with their own, they have less ability to understand the reasons behind the other's attributions.[15] The goal would be an ability to make attributions which are the same as those made by the other person, which are called isomorphic attributions.

These cultural variations do not mean that people in different developing countries will behave in similar ways. Cultural values may be expressed quite differently in various locations. The variation does suggest, however, that moving from a developing country to a developed one, or vice versa, will involve substantial cultural adjustment. Managers should be prepared for these variations when working with counterparts from the other region.

Political characteristics

The developed countries have well-developed democratic processes. The developing countries are more likely to be ruled by a powerful individual or an elite group. Those that are democracies are relatively new ones. The United Nations reports that the percentage "of some form" of democracy at country-level governance increased from 28 percent in 1974 to 61 percent in 1998. This increase suggests a substantial move toward democracy. At the same time it confirms that this is a new movement; thus, many countries classified as democracies in this context are still in the formative stages of implementing democratic principles. Prior to World War II, most poorer countries were colonies of the richer countries. In the 30 years after the war, most of these countries became independent.

Democracy emphasizes individualism and equality, a low power distance in Hofstede's terminology. "One person one vote" exemplifies these values. Non-democratic states clearly do not subscribe to these values. In such states, usually power is vested in a few, powerful people who consider those belonging to their in-group as particularly deserving. New democracies may nominally subscribe to democratic values, but these values have seldom become an ingrained part of the society. These political values show up in a "rule of law" in developed countries and a "rule of man" in many developing countries. A rule of law suggests that there should be a clear statement of what is right or wrong and that it should be applied equally to all people. A rule of man suggests that what is right or wrong may depend on the situation, and each situation should be interpreted by those in positions of power. Some societies believe that rules apply the same way to all people, others, that rules change depending on circumstances.

Democracy, although it often means regular changes in government, implies an order to the change in government. When elections will take place, who can be elected, and what the platforms are for those vying to be elected are clearly set out. Newly formed democracies aspire to the same ideals but are often not able to implement them effectively. Thus changes of government may combine democratic ideals with those in positions of power seeking to retain their power by any means, or people demonstrating en masse to change governments before the appointed time. Non-democracies are stable because the people in power are expected to remain for the long term and their views are known; however, those in power can be overthrown, and power positions can change suddenly and unexpectedly.

Political realities are reflected in business and management in a number of ways. Businesses must function in the context of the political environment, so managers learn to deal with their own particular political environment. In contrast, learning to deal with a foreign government that behaves in unaccustomed and often unexpected ways can be quite difficult.

In the developed world, there is a substantial separation between government and business, and, by and large, there is support for free markets and free enterprise. In the developing world, there is generally a closer link between government and business, and this link is considered appropriate. Issues of conflict of interest are not seen as a concern, and business people may continue to run their businesses while serving in top government posts as Minister of Trade or Finance, for example. In many developing countries, the state is also seen as the agent of economic change, and state planning is believed to be essential for the economy as well as for a fair distribution of resources. The state is paramount in centrally planned, communist countries, such as the People's Republic of China and Cuba, but even where developing countries have free-market economies, they are more likely to look to the state to play an important role in regulating the free market system. For example, in the kingdoms of the Middle East – Bahrain, Kuwait, Oman, Qatar, Saudi Arabia, the United Arab Emirates – the rulers still rule, and therefore have a substantial influence on how business is carried out; at the same time foreign investment can be welcomed, and some – Saudi Arabia, for example – have laws to protect these investments.[16]

There is an interesting link between economic freedom and income levels as well. The Fraser Institute describes economic freedom as encompassing personal choice, voluntary exchange, freedom to compete, protection of person and property – and "institutions and policies as consistent with economic freedom when they provide an infrastructure for voluntary exchange, and protect individuals and their property from aggressors seeking to use violence, coercion and fraud to seize things that do not belong to them"[17] (this description includes much of what we associate with democracy). The Institute reports that countries in the top quintile of economic freedom have a per capita gross national income on average of US$23,450, those in the next quintile drop to US$12,390, then US$6,235, US$4,365, and US$2,556 for the lowest quintile. Clearly, as incomes increase, countries are more likely to embrace ideas of economic freedom.[18]

An understanding of variations in political structure and government attitudes toward businesses is an important component of doing business successfully. "At home," because the structure and attitudes are well known, there is usually little explicit concern with political risk. Internationally, this changes because the structures and attitudes are not well known. Managers need to assess and manage country risk in an explicit way. This is especially the case when managers from the developed world are doing business with the developing world, or vice versa. A Canadian consultant tells the following story about a project in the People's Republic of China:

> The Canadian consultant met with a group of Chinese managers from the Chinese auto-
> motive parts industry. The Chinese asked what they needed to do to sell their products in
> Canada. The consultant responded that the requirements were the right product, consistent
> high quality, at a competitive price, with reliable, on-time delivery. The consultant expected
> the Chinese managers to accept this as a challenge, but something they could address.
> Instead, the Chinese expressed surprise. "*Why?*" they asked. It became clear, with further
> discussion, that, because the consultant's client was the Canadian government, and the
> consultant was accompanied by the Canadian Trade Commissioner, the Chinese managers
> had assumed that the Canadian government could simply require Canadian auto companies
> to buy their Chinese parts. The consultant's assumption was that these business arrange-
> ments were made on a company-to-company basis; the Chinese managers' assumption was
> that these would be government-to-government arrangements. These different assumptions
> about the political environment were based on the different structures and attitudes to which
> each party was accustomed in their respective home locations.[19]

Corruption

There are other characteristics that may differentiate the developed and developing countries. For example, developing countries are believed to be generally more corrupt than
developed countries. That is, there is more need for unreported payments and gifts in
business dealings. These payments may be to civil servants, government officials, or other
businesses. Transparency International's Corruption Index of 38 countries (reported in
The Economist)[20] lists the bottom 17 as developing countries, and the top 17 as either
developed or well on their way to being developed, such as Singapore, Hong Kong,
Chile, Taiwan, and Hungary. There is evidence that links corruption and development
quite closely. The 2001 World Development Report[21] argues that corruption has large
costs for development and that there is strong evidence that higher levels of corruption
are associated with lower rates of growth and lower per capita incomes. *The Economist*[22]
illustrates the impact of corruption on foreign direct investment (FDI) by correlating FDI
inflows with perceptions of corruption, and finds a clear link – countries considered more
corrupt receive much smaller amounts of FDI.

Some countries and companies have established rules to eliminate corruption. The
United States Foreign Corrupt Practices Act makes any payments by US companies (other than small facilitation payments) to foreign officials or political candidates
illegal; the United Kingdom has enacted legislation extending its anti-bribery laws
to cover British nationals and companies abroad. Many multinational companies
have "no bribery" policies and codes of ethics that include statements about corrupt
practices.

The situation faced by managers in foreign countries where bribery is commonplace is
not always straightforward. For example:

- In India, a bribe may be expected to get your goods through customs or to be allowed to register at a hotel, and managers may have little choice. In Nigeria (rated as the most corrupt country by Transparency International) bribery is taken for granted, and managers may find themselves receiving gifts that they are unsure if they should accept.
- In the People's Republic of China, corruption is dealt with harshly, but gifts among associates are expected, and the difference between a gift and a bribe is not always clear.

A manager of a Canadian company, with a subsidiary in Mexico, illustrated the difficulty of dealing with corruption in the following story. The Canadian CEO of the Mexican subsidiary went to a party one night. Unfortunately he stayed out too late and had rather too much to drink. On his way home he was arrested and put in jail in Mexico City. The company had a strict "no bribe" clause in its code of ethics and the Mexican police would not release the Canadian unless they received an appropriate sum of money. The solution was to hire a Mexican attorney to make the payment. The managers could claim they had not contravened the code – they had simply paid the attorney. The attorney was happy to receive his fee that also allowed him to pay the bribe to the police.

The foregoing story illustrates the ease with which rules can be contravened. While there are laws and codes of ethics, it remains relatively simple for companies to participate in corrupt activities. The Economist[23] suggests that the incidence of bribery may be growing, and notes that in Uganda bribery is estimated to increase companies' costs by 8 percent.

By and large, the developed world seeks more policing of corruption, and the developing world is more likely to be the locale for corruption. A characteristic like corruption is less clear-cut than those previously discussed, however. One can argue that businesspeople from developed countries contribute to the existence of corruption as much as do their counterparts in the developing world.

SUMMARY

This introductory discussion has focused on differences between the developed and developing countries that are well established and documented. The other chapters in this part will explore how the differences identified here impact on a variety of management practices.

The discussion here has illustrated that there are some clear distinctions between those countries that we have defined as developed and those defined as developing. The primary distinction is that the developed countries are richer, and have higher per capita incomes than the developing ones. Many other distinctions flow from this basic fact. While the distinctions allow a discussion of developed versus developing countries, we should not forget that the developing world, itself, is certainly not homogeneous. In fact it is very diverse, and managers will find many and substantial differences among countries described as developing. China and India, for example, both very large and populous, have completely different languages, religions, politics, social structures, and so on. Singapore and Jamaica, both small islands, are equally different.

Those in the developed world often think of the developing world in negative terms. While poverty and illness are facets of the developing world, there is much more of importance. The developing world provides many opportunities for international businesses. This 80 percent of the world is potentially a very large market and source of resources, it can provide new products and services, and it has a young labor force. If significant increases in income among the majority of the world's population that lives in the developing world can be achieved, the developing world can be the engine of world economic growth. This chapter, and those that follow in this part, will give managers, both from developed and developing countries, a good foundation for doing business together.

NOTES

1 Hamlin, S. (2002), WOW! What is this?, *New York Times*, May 1.

2 Thomas, A. (1996), A call for research in forgotten locations, in B. J. Punnett & O. Shenkar (eds.), *Handbook for International Management Research*, Cambridge, MA: Blackwell, pp. 485–506.

3 Baruch, Y. (2001), Global or North American? A geographical based comparative analysis of publications in top management journals, *International Journal of Cross Cultural Management* 1(1), 109–126, p. 116.

4 The Top 15 countries in the 2001 report were – from No. 1 to No. 15 – Norway, Australia, Canada, Sweden, Belgium, the United States, Iceland, the Netherlands, Japan, Finland, Switzerland, Luxembourg, France, the United Kingdom, and Denmark. The bottom 15 countries were – from the bottom up – Sierra Leone, Niger, Burundi, Burkina Faso, Ethiopia, Mozambique, Guinea-Bissau, Chad, Central African Republic, Mali, Rwanda, Malawi, Guinea, Gambia, and Eritrea. United Nations Development Programme (2001), *Human Development Report*, Oxford: Oxford University Press.

5 United Nations Development Programme (2000), *Human Development Report*, Oxford: Oxford University Press.

6 United Nations (2000), *Entering the 21st Century. World Development Report*, Oxford: Oxford University Press, emphasis added.

7 United States Council for International Business (1985), *Corporate Handbook to International Economic Organizations and Terms*, New York: USCIB.

8 In 1999 the Organization for Economic Cooperation and Development (OECD) comprised Australia, Belgium, Canada, Denmark, Finland, France, Germany, Ireland, Israel, Italy, Japan, the Netherlands, New Zealand, Norway, Portugal, Spain, Sweden, the United Kingdom, and the United States.

9 http://www.unctad.org/en/subsites/ldcs/aboutldc.htm, 4 April 2001 *About LDCs*.

10 These countries may change from year to year. Note, for example, that Argentina was No. 34 in the 2001 report, but has very likely slipped with its currency and economic problems of 2002. Unless otherwise noted, statistics on the World Development Index are from United Nations Development Programme (1999), *Human Development Report*, Oxford: Oxford University Press.

11 Human Development Report 2001 – www.undp.org/hdr2001

12 G. Hofstede (1991), *Cultures and Organizations: Software of the Mind*, London: McGraw-Hill, p. 216.

13 McClelland, D. C., & Winter, D. G. (1969), *Motivating Economic Achievement*, New York: The Free Press.

14 Berry, J. W., Poortinga, Y. H., Segall, M. H., & Dasen, P. R. (1996), *Cross-cultural Psychology*, Cambridge: Cambridge University Press, p. 301.

15 Brislin, R. (2000), *Understanding Culture's Influence on Behavior*, 2nd edn., Forth Worth, TX: Harcourt College Publishers, p. 46.
16 Time travelers, *The Economist*, March 23–29, 2002, p. 12.
17 Gwartney, J., & Lawson, R. (2002) *Economic Freedom of the World – 2002 Annual Report*, Vancouver, BC: Fraser Institute, p. 5.
18 *Ibid.*, p. 20.
19 Personal communication with Donald M. Wood, CMC.
20 *The Economist*, Sept. 16–22, 2001, p. 126.
21 United Nations (2001), *World Development Report*, Oxford: Oxford University Press.
22 Bribery and business, *The Economist*, March 2–8, 2002, p. 64.
23 *Ibid.*, pp. 63–65.

21

Leadership and Teamwork in the Developing Country Context

Zeynep Aycan

As we have seen in earlier sections, effective leadership and teamwork are the keys to organizational success in developed countries. Thus, they are the focus of this chapter. The criteria for leadership and teamwork, as well as the determinants of their effectiveness, are culturally determined. A leadership approach or a teamwork practice that may yield excellent results with employees in one particular cultural context may create resentment and demotivation among them in another. This chapter reviews the sociocultural context for leadership and teamwork in developing countries and then presents research-based evidence of developing-country leadership profiles. The discussion then moves to the practice of leadership and motivation. A section follows on teamwork and communication, with a focus on the barriers to effective teamwork and suggested ways to overcome them. The chapter closes with a look at the challenges and opportunities that await global leaders who function successfully in developing countries.

To comprehend and appreciate organizational dynamics in any country is difficult without an understanding of the culture. Building on the discussion of the developing world in the previous chapter, the first section of this chapter discusses the sociocultural context in developing countries.

THE SOCIOCULTURAL CONTEXT

The sociocultural environment consists of prevailing shared values, norms, assumptions, belief systems, and behavioral patterns in a society or a cultural group.[1] The economic and political environment, as well as historical events, shape culture. Although a description of the interactions among various forces that influence culture is beyond the scope of this present work, research suggests that the similar cultural characteristics which may be observed within the group of developing countries seem to be attributable to their similar historical backgrounds (autocratic rule, colonialism), subsistence systems (reliance on agriculture), political environments (volatility and instability, improper law and enforcement system), economic conditions (resource scarcity, insufficient technological infrastructure), and demographic makeup (young workforce, unequal opportunity to access high-quality education).[2] The following brief summary of the research on cultural characteristics of developing countries is based on findings of large-scale cross-cultural research by scholars in the field.[3]

Developing countries represent almost 80 percent of the world population. With such a large and diverse group of countries, to arrive at a unified portrayal of cultural characteristics to represent the entire group is almost impossible. There are three caveats to remember in interpreting these findings. First, there may be significant differences across individual developing countries. Therefore, to put a country into one distinct category, such as individualistic versus collectivistic, would be inaccurate. We know from research that many of the developing countries are collectivistic, but not to the same extent and not in every social context. Second, there are individual, subcultural, and organizational differences within developing countries. These differences may be based on the individual's education, socioeconomic status, or age, the individual's region, or their ethnicity, among other attributes. For example, values, beliefs, and behaviors of a highly educated Indian manager working in a subsidiary of a multinational firm in India would be surprisingly similar to the values of a US manager, compared to an Indian manager with a low educational background working in a family-owned firm. Subcultural variations exist in every country, but the magnitude of such differences seems to be much higher in developing countries compared to the developed ones.[4] Third, there are seemingly conflicting value orientations that coexist at the individual level in developing countries that may confuse global managers.[5] For example, one may observe modesty and status-consciousness in an individual at the same time. Such paradoxical dualities will be highlighted in this discussion whenever possible. Given these caveats, the following observations are meant as guidelines, subject to confirmation through careful observations, not as a set of rules.

Relationship orientation

One of the most salient cultural characteristics in developing countries is the importance of relationships and the networking that sustains them. Interdependence in a trusting relationship serves a critical role to reduce uncertainties and to get the maximum benefit where resources are scarce. Harmony within the group is preserved at all costs. Relationships and networks supersede rules and procedures in every aspect of social, political, and economic life. The rules, seen to be universalistic by many in the developed world, are known but not applied for everyone under every circumstance. Relationship-based organizational practices such as staffing, rewarding, performance evaluations, and promotions may give rise to favoritism and nepotism among the in-group members, and to discrimination, alienation, and withdrawal among the out-group members. Family and relatives are natural in-group members. In-group membership is also extended to those from the same ethnic, religious, or caste group, as well as to close friends. Getting in or getting out of the in-group is difficult. Loyalty is the glue that keeps the in-group intact and is the second most important determinant of membership status; acceptance to and dismissal from the in-group depend on the level of loyalty.

Family orientation

Family is very important in every society's livelihood. In developing countries, however, family, both nuclear and extended, is the primary focus in people's lives. Work and family spheres are closely interrelated. Work is perceived as a duty done in service of the family. An achievement at work is not as much valued as a means to increase one's sense of personal accomplishment as it is valued as a means of satisfying family needs and increasing family status in society. Also, family ethos is created in the organizational context. First of all, organizations are expected to take care of their workers as well as the workers' families. Some organizations institutionalize such practices; they offer health and educational services for employees' spouses and children, contribute to their housing and heating costs, and provide them with financial assistance when needed. Moreover, employees feel entitled to absent themselves from work for family-related reasons. Work always comes next to family in importance, and there is nothing more natural than this. Second, the subordinate–superior relationship resembles that between parent and child. Superiors treat their employees as if they were their children, a common practice referred to as *paternalism.*

Performance orientation

Developing country members do not attach a high value to job performance and its outcomes. In human resource management practices such as staffing and performance evaluation, in-group favoritism plays a more important role than job-related competencies. The criteria used for selection and performance evaluation include harmony in interpersonal relations, as well as loyalty and obedience toward superiors. In fact, performance evaluations serve to perpetuate the power structure and instill loyalty.[6] Because employment contracts are emotional and psychological rather than transactional, meeting contractual obligations does not fully represent good performance. Getting along is more important than getting ahead.[7] In fact, those who get ahead and stand out in their group inculcate jealousy and disturb group harmony. The paradox is that those who are bright and have the potential to excel in their careers are almost afraid of performing well because of such cultural barriers. Also, low performers are tolerated on the basis of compassion,[8] and intention is weighted more than the actual outcomes achieved.[9]

Control orientation

Individuals have a low sense of control and self-efficacy due partly to turbulence, instability and unpredictability in social, political and economic life, and partly to collective responsibility sharing, authoritarianism, and paternalism in cultural life. Feelings of helplessness and fatalism are common cultural traits.[10] People who have low self-efficacy have a tendency to attribute causes to external reasons. Sometimes this external attribution may be used as a way to avoid responsibility for making long-term plans, meeting deadlines and setting goals. Because interdependence is fostered as a cultural value, self-reliance has a negative connotation, as it is deserting the group.[11] Owing to low self-efficacy belief, individuals refrain from being proactive and taking initiative, which may increase risks and uncertainty in the environment. The *status quo* is not challenged and mediocrity is readily accepted as destiny. Thus, there is resistance to change.

Communication pattern

The pattern of communication in organizations is indirect, non-assertive, non-confrontational, and usually downward. Such patterns are problematic in performance evaluations because superiors, subordinates, and peers avoid giving negative feedback to one another. Negative feedback is viewed as destructive criticism rather than as constructive comment that could lead to further improvement. Because personal and work lives are intertwined, negative feedback is also misconstrued as an attack on the person rather than as an observation on behavior.[12] Presentation of self, which results in the way a person is perceived by others, is extremely important. Negative feedback has the potential to tarnish reputation and honor in the eyes of others. It also implies losing face to the employer and the supervisor, to whom the person feels indebted and loyal. Moreover, due to low self-efficacy and high fatalism, people are reluctant to accept responsibility and blame for mistakes. In a highly personalized work relationship, negative feedback is also considered harmful to group integrity and harmony. Usually, negative feedback is given in an indirect and subtle manner, with the involvement of a third party. In a high power-distance cultural context, subordinates refrain from giving performance feedback to their superiors. Finally, in developing countries, there is strong preference for face-to-face communication rather than communication through technology. Also, the context determines the way in which information is coded and understood. As such, there is much room for a subjective interpretation of both the intent and the content of the message.

Authority orientation

Respect, loyalty, and deference toward those with authority are among the most salient cultural characteristics in developing countries. People respect authority rather than rules. Obedience to authority is a prescribed norm in some religions and belief systems such as Islam and Confucian ideology. Authority is rarely challenged or questioned. The person holding the power and authority is trusted for his/her knowledge, expertise, and achievements. S/he is entitled to have certain privileges that others don't have. Many examples of the paradoxical dualities discussed above are found in the superior–subordinate relationship. First, there is high respect but also high affection toward the superior. As such, there are elements of both love and fear in this relationship. Being an in-group member, the person of higher status is considered as "one of us," but being a person with higher status, s/he is "unlike us." Superiors have close relationships with their subordinates and are involved in all aspects of their lives, but this closeness does not translate to an informal, friendship relationship. Instead, the subordinate–superior relationship is formal and distant. Granell describes this relationship in his work on using culture to support managing in Venezuela: "In Venezuela, you cannot be distant if you are the boss, you cannot sit in an office like an executive . . . you have to be out there with them so that they feel you are their equal whilst, at the same time, making them recognize that you are the boss and know more than they do."[13]

Leadership and motivation

The sociocultural context has a great impact on leadership and motivational practices. A review of the cross-cultural literature on leadership and motivation in the developing country context concurs that prevalent leadership traits and behaviors reflect the cultural characteristics outlined in the previous section. That is, the most salient leadership practices involve personalized relationships with subordinates and the exercise of power and authority. However, research also reveals that there is a significant gap between the "actual" and the "ideal" leadership characteristics.[14] Here is a review of leadership style in the developing nation context compared to research observations on leadership style and motivational practices.

Relationship orientation in leadership

One of the most striking characteristics of leaders in developing country organizations is that they place great importance on establishing close interpersonal relationships with subordinates as well as with people in higher authority. Subordinates expect personalized relationships, protection, close guidance, and supervision.[15] Leaders are willing to assume responsibility for their followers,[16] and in return, leaders seek the followers' loyalty. The interaction between leaders and followers resembles the parent–child relationship in traditional cultures. This prevalent leadership style is referred to as *paternalism*.[17] It is one of the most salient leadership characteristics of Pacific Asian, Middle-Eastern, and Latin American cultures. Paternalism is built upon the traditional value of familism, with a strong emphasis on patriarchal, patrilocal, and patrilineal relationships within the family unit.[18] Over time, family-based paternalistic relationships developed beyond family boundaries, and vertical relationships in the family were extended to those based on seniority and gender in the workplace and social life.[19]

The paternalistic relationship is hierarchical: the superior assumes the role of a father who protects and provides for the subordinate, whereas the subordinate voluntarily submits to the superior, showing loyalty and deference. The leader is assumed to "know better" for the subordinates. As such, he guides the subordinate in every aspect of his/her life. The paternalistic leader gives advice (often times unsolicited) and guides employees in personal, professional (career planning on their behalf), and family-related matters (marriage counseling, dispute resolution between husband and wife); shows concern for the well-being of the subordinate as well as his/her family; attends congratulatory and condolence ceremonies of employees as well as their immediate family members (such as weddings and funerals); provides financial assistance to employees when in need (donations or loans) for expenses such as housing, health care, and children's education expenses; allows them to attend to personal or family-related problems by letting them leave early or take a day off; acts as a mediator in interpersonal conflicts among employees, and even talks to the disputed party on behalf of the other (without his knowledge or consent) to resolve the conflict.

Employee loyalty and deference is manifested in various forms, such as engaging in extra-role behavior or working unpaid overtime upon the request of the supervisor; not quitting the job, even if one receives a much better job offer, because of loyalty; following the paternalistic superior to another organization if s/he quits the company; not questioning or disagreeing with the superior in decisions regarding the company or the employee (performance evaluations, career planning); doing personal favors for the superior when needed (helping him during the construction of his house); putting extra effort into the job and working hard, so as not to lose face to the superior.

> When something goes wrong or when only a part of the project is completed, our Western partners leave the next day. But we cannot do it. We lose face to our company if something goes wrong. We cannot leave until we make sure that everything is fine. Our superiors trust us. How can we possibly fail them?
>
>   – A Kazak employee working in an American plant in Kazakhstan

Paternalism is a leadership style that is strongly criticized in the Western industrialized countries. Involvement in personal life is perceived as intrusive and invasive of an employee's privacy. Close guidance and supervision go against the Western cultural tradition that supports autonomy, self-reliance, and self-determination. Assumed superiority of the leader is also challenged on the grounds of egalitarianism. Moreover, the emotional bonding is considered unprofessional in a business relationship. What Western scholars and business people fail to understand, however, is that there is a reciprocal consent for this relationship. In fact, employees feel resentment and rejection if their managers leave them to make important decisions by themselves and are not involved in their personal lives.

> Things got tough around here after the American expatriate boss has arrived. He seems that he has no time for us. Can you imagine, he never asks about our families or our health – unless it interferes with our work efficiency. He, on the other hand, never mentions about his wife or family. Life is just work for him, and we pity him for this. . . . He also does not care about our careers. When we ask for his advice, he says that *we* are the best judges for our own lives. How can we know better than him what is good for us? Apparently, he does not take any interest in our future in this plant.[20]
>
>   – A Mexican worker's letter to his brother

> I told you; I knew that there was something wrong in the office. My supervisor did not hug and kiss me yesterday morning!
>
>   – A clerk working in a Turkish state library

However, the dark side of paternalism is that it may create differential treatment among workers.[21] Research attributes this effect to the increasing size of the organization as well as to the employer's liking of some members better than others:

> The differential love and care [of the paternal boss] are generally reciprocated by similar feelings and acts. The loved and cared ones get increasingly close to the father (the paternal figure) while others are distanced. . . . The leader indeed starts believing that so-and-so is really bright and dynamic and therefore, in good faith, tends to extend favors to him.[22]

In such cases, paternalism paves the way to nepotism and favoritism. The ones who are not loved and cared for may be deprived of some privileges. That is why paternalism is sometimes referred to as "discrimination without the expression of hostility."[23] It also elevates sibling-like rivalry and jealousy among employees.

The importance of relations goes beyond organizational boundaries. Leaders are also expected to establish good interpersonal relations with people in higher authority in government, supporting institutions, and negotiation parties.[24] In order to protect the institution and draw political, technical, and financial support, leaders invest a substantial amount of time and effort in such networking. Thus networking and diplomacy are among the common characteristics of effective leaders in developing countries.

Power orientation in leadership

In developing countries, that leaders desire to exercise power is another salient leadership characteristic.[25] This desire to exercise power may often result in an authoritative style, a high level of status consciousness and the use of status and power for personal benefit, a centralized decision-making process which results in unilateral decision making and little commitment to the preparation of subordinates for decision making, and a consultative approach. That leaders wish to maintain good interpersonal relations with the subordinates on the one hand, and act in an authoritative way on the other, is one of the paradoxical dualities that is difficult to comprehend. A paternalistic leader is someone "nurturant, caring, dependable, sacrificing and yet demanding, authoritative, and a strict disciplinarian."[26] The Western management literature addresses this paradox by describing paternalism as "benevolent dictatorship."[27] In the family context, too, in developing countries the father is caring, but at the same time authoritative. An authoritative attitude on the part of the leader involves discipline and control for the benefit of the subordinate.

However, that leaders use their status and power for personal benefit is also very common. For instance, high-level managers clearly favor their in-group members in personnel decisions such as staffing. In some extreme cases, one can find many workers with the same family name in the organization. However, such practices, which are at the root of corruption, are severely criticized at the normative level in developing countries. For example, Mohammed, the Prophet of Islam, says "When a person assumes authority over people and promotes one of them because of personal preferences, God will curse him forever."[28] "There is nothing wrong in the top officials' favoring their relatives. If your relatives and caste-fellows do not benefit from the authority you possess, what use are you to your society?"[29] "The deleterious effects of tradition are compounded by the practice of appointing a family member as head of the organization without any regard to the individual's competence, so creating a unique management style derisively referred to as 'management by chromosomes.'"[30]

Leaders are highly status-conscious. They may resist change so as not to lose power or relinquish authority. They want to remain in power at all cost to maintain their and their families' status in society. Despite close and good interpersonal relationships with workers, they demand formality and respect. Workers are strongly discouraged to bypass authority: "Promotions are valued not for a better career but to get a better match for a daughter, or for the pride it would bring to their family."[31]

Usually the decision-making process found in the developing-country context is centralized, and the decisions are made unilaterally. This process reflects power inequality and results partly because the leaders do not want to relinquish power by being participative. Subordinates also expect the leader to be decisive, not only because they trust his wisdom, knowledge, and competencies, but also because they are afraid of taking the risk and responsibility of involvement in the decision-making process. "No one wants to say, 'Boss, are you sure that's the way you want to do it?' They don't want to help you make decisions; they want to agree if you have an opinion. It is harder to find leaders with risk-taking attitudes in Mexico."[32]

Leaders do not invest effort to prepare subordinates for participative decision making, because they assume that employees lack confidence, competence, and willingness to exercise autonomy and accept responsibility for problem-solving.[33] The image of a strong leader is someone who knows it all and who is a hero and a savior. A leader who goes along with employees' suggestions is perceived as weak and incompetent.

Although leaders are not participative, they are consultative. In fact, consultation is encouraged by, for example, the Quran, which attests reward for consultation. But because it also states "Obey God . . . and those charged with authority among you (4:59)," there is great tension between the consultative approach on one hand, and the authoritative approach on the other.[34] Consultation is usually done to show that employee opinions are valued. Employees expect the leader to seek their opinion but make the final decision unilaterally.

> You see this pen? Suppose that my manager decided to buy it. He comes to us and asks whether or not he should buy it. Does he not know what he should do? Of course, he does. He made up his mind even before coming to us. But, he shows courtesy by taking our opinion. That is what makes him a great guy!
> – A human resource manager, large manufacturing company, eastern Turkey

Preferred leadership characteristics and motivational practices

Robert J. House and 170 local investigators completed major cross-cultural research on leadership and organizational effectiveness. A total of 62 countries representing all continents participated in this major undertaking, the GLOBE project (Global Leadership and Organizational Behavior Effectiveness). According to the preliminary findings,[35] the most preferred leadership characteristics in all countries, developing and developed alike, involve charisma, participation, and team integration. In fact, all these leadership qualities are important and relevant particularly for developing countries.

Charismatic leadership, which is also referred to as transformational leadership, has been investigated for the last 25 years in the Western management literature.[36] The most important characteristics of charismatic/transformational leaders include their emphasis on change and transformation through a strong vision and sense of mission for the organization, intellectual stimulation (helping followers to recognize problems and solutions), individualized consideration (giving followers the support, attention, and encouragement needed to perform well), and inspirational motivation (communicating the importance of the organization's mission and relying on symbols to focus their efforts).

According to the Conger–Kanungo Model of Charismatic Leadership,[37] there are three critical stages in leadership. First, the leader should evaluate the present *status quo* by assessing environmental resources and follower needs. Second, the leader formulates and articulates the organizational goals. Finally, the leader determines the means to achieve the goals. Kanungo and Mendonca[38] assert that charismatic leadership is particularly relevant to and effective in the developing country context, which, as explained in the introductory chapter, is characterized by high complexity and uncertainty, instability and low predictability, and low employee self-efficacy. Kanungo and Mendonca outlined charismatic leadership behavior for developing countries (see table 21.1). In this framework, charismatic leaders are encouraged to use the existing cultural characteristics to motivate employees (loyalty, the family metaphor, respect and support for their superiors),

TABLE 21.1 Charismatic leadership behavior for developing countries

Step 1: Assess the environment:
◆ Identify factors that facilitate or hinder achievement of organizational goals
◆ Assess minimum conditions needed for implementing short- and long-term goals
◆ Determine key stakeholders and nature of transactions

Step 2: Visioning and responding to the environment:
◆ Establish dominant goal and direct efforts to achieve it
◆ Move from pilot testing to implementation on a larger scale
◆ Mobilize demand
◆ Develop support network

Step 3: Means to achieve:
◆ Establish affective reciprocity relationship
◆ Be confident in follower's ability for task accomplishment
◆ Nurture follower self-efficacy through coaching, modeling, encouraging, and rewarding
◆ Idealize organizational and work values
◆ Discourage manipulative ingratiation relationships
◆ Avoid lording behavior and "pulling rank"
◆ Avoid negativism
◆ Avoid favoritism
◆ Promote performance-based reward system
◆ Promote loyalty to organization and work values rather than loyalty to people in position power
◆ Recognize dependence of subordinates for developing task competence versus dependence for material gain. Be supportive of subordinates in the former case
◆ Use a family metaphor for organizations
◆ Be fair and firm to all members
◆ Be open, available, and accessible
◆ Be sociable and collegial to members (use existing rites and rituals as occasions for relating to members)
◆ Show constant concern for improving quality of life of members as one would do for own self
◆ Groom second line in command
◆ Show respect and support for others' position and authority
◆ Promote information sharing, participation, and communication

Source: Kanungo & Mendonca (1996).

while removing cultural barriers that prevent effective functioning (dependency-proneness and a sense of helplessness, favoritism, manipulative ingratiation).

Employees in developing countries, especially the young and well-educated generation, seek more participation in the decision-making process, especially with issues that concern them. The Nurturant-Task (NT) Leadership Model proposed by Sinha[39] increases employee participation by combining performance orientation with paternalism. An NT leader "cares for his subordinates, shows affection, takes personal interest in their well being, and above all is committed to their growth."[40] The difference between paternalistic and NT leadership is that the paternalistic leader's nurturance is contingent upon loyalty, whereas the NT leader's nurturance and care are contingent upon the subordinate's task accomplishment. As such, the NT leader is more performance-oriented than the paternalistic leader. In Sinha's model, the nature of the subordinate–superior relationship changes over time. Initially, the subordinate relies heavily on the superior for guidance. As s/he gains more experience, knowledge and skills about the job, s/he develops self-confidence and needs less direction and guidance. At this point, the leader grants more autonomy and responsibility while maintaining the supporting and nurturing relationship with the subordinate with constant encouragement. When the subordinate's level of preparedness increases (less preference for dependency and personalized relationship with the superior; more acceptance of his/her own status as competent and knowledgeable), the superior involves him/her fully in the decision-making process. The process gradually progresses from a strongly NT style to a fully participative one through an intermediary stage of a mixture of NT and participation. Similar to the charismatic approach, the process is empowering for the subordinate, which is particularly important in developing countries.

An ideal leader is also a team integrator, who can facilitate equal participation and effective communication among members. As will be discussed in detail in the next section, effective teamwork may be difficult in developing countries. Leaders who are able to overcome the cultural barriers to motivate and mobilize employees to do teamwork are considered to be highly effective.

In summary, the ideal leader profile in developing countries is:

- transformational and empowering
- participative but also decisive
- trustworthy: knowledgeable, skillful, and administratively competent
- nurturing/paternalistic and also performance-oriented
- fair and just, especially in interpersonal relationships
- diplomatic
- status-conscious but at the same time modest and humble
- competent as a team integrator.

Research has also suggested motivational techniques that have a high level of effectiveness in the developing world. They include:

- increasing the feeling of security (job security as well as feeling of belonging and acceptance)
- providing opportunities for personal and professional development
- recognizing the individual performance of subordinates, preferably not publicly
- showing interest and care for the well-being of employees and their families
- listening to and understanding employee concerns and suggestions
- being fair and just, not discriminating between in-group and out-group members
- reinforcing the feeling of loyalty, affection and respect for the superior.

Personal bonds with the superior determine whether or not workers come to work every day and are willing to do overtime or work industriously.[41]

Given the importance of teams and team integration to leadership in the developing world, an understanding of the importance of the sociocultural context in their integration is critical. The next section discusses some of the potential barriers to teamwork and communication in the developing world and offers recommendations for overcoming them.

BARRIERS TO TEAMWORK AND COMMUNICATION

> People like to work with others . . . you find that there are few who stay by themselves in the office . . . they are always with someone else . . . that does not mean, though, that they are working as a team.
>
> – German expatriate working in Ghana

Some of the sociocultural characteristics of developing countries may not be conducive to effective teamwork. Relationship-orientation may be perceived as an asset for teamwork, but the nature of relationships and in-group dynamics may hinder team effectiveness.

There are five main barriers to teamwork effectiveness.

1 Team formation and member composition

In most of the organizations, team members are appointed on the basis of their task-related knowledge and competencies. However, because of the strong in-group and out-group differentiation in developing countries, it is difficult to persuade people to work with those who are perceived to be out-group members. In fact, if given the chance to self-select the team members, workers will form teams on the basis of friendship relationships. Interpersonal harmony in teams weighs more than task accomplishment. As such, team members find it very difficult to work with someone whom they don't know or don't like. Members who have the potential to disturb in-group harmony are not wanted, no matter how competent they may be.

> In her first year of teaching back at home, a US-educated Turkish professor randomly assigned senior students into teams for their final class projects by drawing a lottery. This was a common practice back in the United States. To her, it was an excellent opportunity for students to practice and learn how to work with different people in real life. Soon after, a student came to her office in tears saying: "Professor, you put me in the same team with someone who I have not been talking to since we were 8 years old. Under the circumstances, I have to drop the course." The professor was in shock. Which was worst? Was it that the student blamed the teacher for this sheer coincidence, or that the student was not talking to someone for more than ten years, or that she dropped the course because of this?

2 Team cohesion

Teamwork requires egalitarian relationships and cohesiveness. Some status-conscious members may be reluctant to cooperate or share information with others in order to maintain their powerful position in the team. This hurts team cohesiveness and also delays task completion. "There is a real fear about someone else taking over your job. . . .

These feelings result in the control and retention of information . . . people get hold of information hoping that this makes them indispensable."[42]

Also, in-group rivalry may occur to get the praise and recognition of the superior. To the other extreme, excessive team cohesiveness may result in groupthink because some members may be reluctant to voice their disagreements so as not to risk their positions on the team.

3 Performance feedback

Team members who do not perform at the expected level rarely receive negative feedback from others. If a member receives negative feedback, s/he takes it personally and takes offense. Criticisms that are delivered publicly or that represent a group's opinion are especially hurtful to the critiqued member's public image and honor. The member who receives such feedback may leave the group immediately and may even try to sabotage the group process. It is not appropriate or common for team members to give performance feedback to one another in an open manner. It is also not appropriate to report the low-performing team member to higher management. Such an act of whistle-blowing is considered unethical and immoral. Therefore, oftentimes the low-performing members hide in the group and go unnoticed.

4 Division of responsibility

Social loafing is more likely to occur on teams where there are no consequences to low performance, as explained above. Team members feel compelled to protect one another from the reprimands of management. Reliance on "backing up" among team members increases social loafing. Another factor that increases social loafing is the members' need for clear role differentiation and task assignments. Lack of clarity in task assignments may sometimes be used as an excuse not to take on extra responsibility.

> This is a story of "everybody", "somebody", "anybody" and "nobody" working in a Zimbabwean firm: There was some very important work to be done and everybody was sure that somebody would do it. Anybody could have done it but nobody did it. People were very angry because it was everybody's job. Everybody thought that anybody could have done it, but nobody realized that somebody wasn't doing it. The story ends with everybody blaming someone when nobody did what anybody could have done.[43]

5 Evaluation apprehension

Self-presentation is an important concern for people in developing countries. Team members may hesitate to participate in group discussions because of concern for how they are perceived and evaluated by others. Others' perceptions and evaluations are important because they determine whether or not the group accepts or rejects the individual. Evaluation apprehension exists especially when a member has to present a counter-argument or bring a new perspective to the group's attention. Evaluation apprehension is a serious barrier to innovation and creativity in teams.

SUGGESTIONS

In order to improve teamwork and communication effectiveness in developing countries, the following suggestions may be useful.

- Teamwork effectiveness is enhanced if there is a leader who is skillful in both maintaining good interpersonal relations and setting high performance standards. Leaderless or autonomous groups are less likely to succeed in a developing country context.
- Leaders must be sensitive to feelings of insecurity among members. Leaders have to spend considerable time and effort to inculcate feelings of acceptance and indispensability among team members to minimize in-group rivalry and increase group cohesiveness.
- In order to decrease uncertainties and social loafing, individual roles and responsibilities should be clearly stated. In addition, team goals have to be well defined and articulated clearly by the management.
- Members will benefit greatly from training in effective teamwork, where they will acquire knowledge and skills about performance management and communication in teamwork.
- Before starting to work together, the team should establish norms on how to handle difficult team members as well as on the ground rules in meetings. Once the group sets these norms jointly and agrees upon the repercussions for violating them, team members who receive negative performance feedback are less likely to take it personally and withdraw from the group.
- In forming the team, members' compatibility in terms of interpersonal relations should be given special attention. That is not to say that only close friends should work in teams, but it should be remembered that interpersonal conflicts do interfere with effective teamwork functioning.
- Social activities that will improve interpersonal relationships among team members should be organized to increase cohesiveness. People need time to get to know one another before working together.
- Team members' performance evaluations should not be done individually. However, poor performers should be monitored through either periodical and anonymous peer evaluations or careful observation during group meetings. The manager or the team leader should give the negative feedback in a private meeting. Team success should be rewarded as a group.

CONCLUSION: GLOBAL LEADERSHIP CHALLENGES AND OPPORTUNITIES

A developing country may be defined as one in which too many opportunities go unexploited, undeveloped, unrealized. And the entrepreneurial manager seeks out, exploits, and develops these opportunities.[44]

Indeed, the cultural context in developing countries may present too many opportunities for global leaders. Workforce characteristics that have great potential to enhance organizational performance, if utilized effectively, include loyalty, trust, and affection for the leader; harmonious interpersonal relationships; desire to learn and motivation to develop; self-sacrifice for the well-being of the "in-group"; and flexibility. On the other hand, the global leader will be challenged to gain acceptance as an in-group member, motivate employees for higher performance, improve communication effectiveness, overcome the sense of insecurity, helplessness and dependency proneness, and administer participative decision-making. For Westerners, turning barriers into opportunities is a journey that takes time, patience, and courage. To many, however, this journey has been immensely rewarding spiritually and professionally.

NOTES

1 Hofstede (1980).
2 Abdalla & Al-Homoud (2001); Adler & Boyacigiller (1995); Austin (1990); Hickson & Pugh (1995); Hofstede (1980); Jaeger & Kanungo (1990).
3 Hofstede (1980), Sagiv & Schwartz (2000), Trompenaars (1998), and House et al. (1999), as well as the work of others including Triandis (1994), Hall & Hall (1995), Ronen & Shenkar (1985), Glenn & Glenn (1981), Jaeger & Kanungo (1990), Sinha (1995), Kao, Sinha, & Wilpert (1999), Puffer (1996), Hickson (1997), Aycan & Kanungo (2001), Adler (1997), Lane, DiStefano, & Maznevski (1997), and Thomas (2002).
4 Neghandi (1983).
5 E.g., Sinha & Kanungo (1997).
6 Sinha (1995).
7 Abdalla & Al-Homoud (2001).
8 *Ibid.*
9 Ali (1999).
10 Aycan et al. (2000).
11 Abdalla & Al-Homoud (2001).
12 Kanungo & Mendonca (1996).
13 Granell (1997), p. 37.
14 House et al. (1999).
15 Kanungo (1990); Sinha (1990).
16 Abdalla & Al-Homoud (2001); Puffer (1996).
17 Aycan (in press).
18 Kim (1994).
19 Kim (1994); Redding & Hsiao (1995).
20 Modified from Kras (1989).
21 Sinha (1995).
22 *Ibid.*, p. 78.
23 Jackman (1994, p. 10).
24 Hardy (1990); Miles & Snow (1978).
25 Puffer (1996).
26 Sinha (1990), p. 68.
27 Northouse (1997), p. 39.
28 Quoted in Abdalla & Al-Homoud (2001).
29 Gupta (1999), p. 108.
30 Mendonca & Kanungo (1990), p. 237.
31 Kalra (1981).

32 Stephens & Greer (1997, p. 110).
33 Kanungo & Mendonca (1996).
34 Ali (1999).
35 Hartog et al. (1999).
36 E.g., Bass (1985); House (1977); Shamir, House, & Arthur (1993); Yukl (1998).
37 Conger & Kanungo (1998).
38 Kanungo & Mendonca (1996).
39 Sinha (1980).
40 Sinha (1980), p. 55.
41 de Forest (1996), p. 293.
42 Granell (1997), p. 21.
43 Modified from Granell (1997), p. 36.
44 Mendoza (1997), p. 71.

References

Abdalla, I. A., & Al-Homoud, M. A. (2001). Exploring the implicit leadership theory in the Arabian Gulf States. *Applied Psychology: An International Review*, 50(4), 506–531.

Adler, N. J. (1997). *Organizational Behavior*. Cincinnati, OH: South-Western College Publishing.

Adler, N. J., & Boyacigiller, N. (1995). Going beyond traditional HRM scholarship, in R. N. Kanungo (ed.), *Employee Management in Developing Countries*. Greenwich, CT: JAI Press, pp. 1–13.

Ali, A. J. (1999). The evolution of work ethic and management thought: An Islamic view. In H. S. R. Kao, D. Sinha, & B. Wilpert (eds.), *Management and Cultural Values: The Indigenization of Organizations in Asia*. New Delhi: Sage, pp. 139–151.

Austin, J. E. (1990). *Managing in Developing Countries: Strategic Analysis and Operating Techniques*. New York: The Free Press.

Aycan, Z. (in press). Paternalism: Towards conceptual refinement and operationalization, in K. S. Yang, K. K. Hwang, & U. Kim (eds.), *Scientific Advances in Indigenous Psychologies: Empirical, Philosophical, and Cultural Contributions*. London: Sage.

Aycan, Z., & Kanungo, R. N. (2001). Cross-cultural industrial and organizational psychology: A critical appraisal of the field and future directions. In N. Anderson, D. S. Ones, H. Kepir-Sinangil, & C. Viswesvaran (eds.), *International Handbook of Work and Organizational Psychology*. London: Sage, pp. 385–408.

Aycan, Z., Kanungo, R. N., Mendonca, M., Yu, K., Deller, J., Stahl, G., & Khursid, A. (2000). Impact of culture on human resource management practices: A ten country comparison. *Applied Psychology: An International Review*, 49(1), 192–220.

Bass, B. M. (1985). *Leadership and Performance beyond Expectations*. New York: The Free Press.

Conger, J. A., & Kanungo, R. N. (1998). *Charismatic Leadership in Organizations*. Thousand Oaks, CA: Sage.

de Forest, M. E. (1996). Thinking of a plant in Mexico?, in S. M. Puffer (ed.), *Management Across Cultures*. Cambridge, MA: Blackwell, pp. 289–300.

Glenn, E. S., & Glenn, C. G. (1981). *Man and Mankind: Conflict and Communication between Cultures*. Norwood, NJ: Ablex.

Granell, E. (1997). *Managing Culture for Success: Challenges and Opportunities in Venezuela*. Caracas: Refolit.

Gupta, R. K. (1999). The truly familial work organization: Extending the organizational boundary to include employees' families in the Indian context. In H. S. R. Kao, D. Sinha, & B. Wilpert (eds.), *Management and Cultural Values: The Indigenization of Organizations in Asia*. New Delhi: Sage, pp. 102–120.

Hall, E. T., & Hall, M. R. (1995). *Understanding Cultural Differences.* Yarmount, ME: Intercultural Press.

Hardy, C. (1990). Leadership and strategy making for institution building and innovation: The case of a Brazilian university, in A. M. Jaeger & R. N. Kanungo (eds.), *Management in Developing Countries.* London: Routledge, pp. 83–100.

Hartog, D. N., House, R. J., Hanges, P. J., et al. (1999). Culture-specific and cross-culturally generalizable implicit leadership theories: Are attributes of charismatic/transformational leadership universally endorsed? *Leadership Quarterly,* 10(2), 219–256.

Hickson, D. J. (ed.) (1997) *Exploring Management Across the World.* London: Penguin.

Hickson, D. J., & Pugh, D. S. (1995). *Management Worldwide: The Impact of Societal Culture on Organizations around the Globe.* London: Penguin.

Hofstede, G. (1980). *Culture's Consequences: International Differences in Work-related Values.* Beverly Hills: Sage.

House, R. J. (1977). A 1976 theory of charismatic leadership. In J. G. Hunt & L. L. Lawson (eds.), *Leadership: The Cutting Edge.* Carbondale: Southern Illinois University Press, pp. 189–207.

House, R. J., et al. (1999). Cultural influences on leadership and organizations. *Global Leadership,* 1, 171–233.

Jackman, M. R. (1994). *The Velvet Glove: Paternalism and Conflict in Gender, Class, and Race Relations.* Los Angeles: University of California Press.

Jaeger, A. Am, & Kanungo, R. N. (eds.) (1990). *Management in Developing Countries.* London: Routledge.

Kalra, S. K. (1981). Family life of high achievers – A study of business organization. *Indian Journal of Social Work,* 42(3), 252–263.

Kanungo, R. N. (1990). Work alienation in developing countries: Western models and Eastern realities. In A. M. Jaeger & R. N. Kanungo (eds.), *Management in Developing Countries.* London: Routledge, pp. 193–208.

Kanungo, R. N., & Mendonca, M. (1996). Cultural contingencies and leadership in developing countries. *Sociology of Organizations,* 14, 263–295.

Kao, H. S. R., Sinha, D., & Wilpert, B. (1999). *Management and Cultural Values: The Indigenization of Organizations in Asia.* New Delhi: Sage.

Kim, U. M. (1994). Significance of paternalism and communalism in the occupational welfare system of Korean firms. In U. Kim, H. C. Triandis, C. Kagitcibasi, S. Choi, & G. Yoon (eds.), *Individualism and Collectivism: Theory, Method and Applications.* Beverly Hills: Sage , pp. 251–266.

Kras, E. S. (1989). A letter from Mr. Gonzalez. In H. W. Lane, J. J. DiStefano, & M. L. Maznevski (1997). *International Management Behavior.* Cambridge, MA: Blackwell, pp. 158–161.

Lane, H. W., DiStefano, J. J., & Maznevski, M. L. (1997). *International Management Behavior.* Cambridge, MA: Blackwell.

Mendonca, M., & Kanungo, R. N. (1990). Performance management in developing countries. In A. M. Jaeger & R. N. Kanungo (eds.), *Management in Developing Countries.* London: Routledge, pp. 223–251.

Mendoza, G. A. (1997). The transferability of Western management concepts and programs: An Asian perspective. In S. Lawrence, J. Coleman, & J. Black (eds.), *Education and Training for Public Sector Management in Developing Countries.* New York: Rockefeller Foundation, pp. 122–146.

Miles, R., & Snow, C. (1978). *Organizational Strategy, Structure, and Process.* New York: McGraw-Hill.

Negandhi, A. R. (1983). Management in the Third World. *Asian Pacific Journal of Management,* 1(1), 15–25.

Northouse, P. G. (1997). *Leadership: Theory and Practice.* Thousand Oaks: Sage.

Puffer, S. M. (1996). Understanding the Bear: A portrait of Russian business leaders, in S. M. Puffer (ed.), *Management across Cultures.* Cambridge, MA: Blackwell, pp. 300–322.

Redding, S. G., & Hsiao, M. (1995). An empirical study of overseas Chinese managerial ideology. *International Journal of Psychology,* 25, 629–641.

Ronen, S., & Shenkar, O. (1985). Clustering countries on attitudinal dimensions: A review and synthesis. *Academy of Management Review*, 10(3), 435–455.

Sagiv, L., & Schwartz, S. H. (2000). Value priorities and subjective well-being: Direct relations and congruity effects. *European Journal of Social Psychology*, 30(2), 177–198.

Shamir, B., House, R. J., & Arthur, M. B. (1993). The motivational effects of charismatic leadership: A self-concept based theory. *Organization Science*, 4(4), 577–594.

Sinha, J. B. P. (1980). *The Nurturant Task Leader*. New Delhi: Concept Publishing House.

Sinha, J. B. P. (1990). *Work Culture in the Indian Context*. New Delhi: Sage.

Sinha, J. B. P. (1995). *The Cultural Context of Leadership and Power*. New Delhi: Sage.

Sinha, J. B. P., & Kanungo, R. N. (1997). Context sensitivity and balancing in Indian organizational behaviour. *International Journal of Psychology*, 32(3), 93–105.

Stephens, G. K., & Greer, C. R. (1997). Doing business in Mexico: Understanding cultural differences, in H. W. Lane, J. J. DiStefano, & M. L. Maznevski (eds.), *International Management Behavior*. Cambridge, MA: Blackwell, pp. 107–124.

Thomas, D. C. (2002). *Essentials of International Management: A Cross-Cultural Perspective*. London: Sage.

Triandis, H. C. (1994). Cross-cultural industrial and organizational psychology, in H. C. Triandis, M. D. Dunnette, & L. M. Hough (eds.), *Handbook of Industrial and Organizational Psychology*, 2nd ed. Palo Alto, CA: Consulting Pychologists Press, vol. 4, pp. 103–172.

Trompenaars, F. (1998). *Riding the Waves of Culture: Understanding Cultural Diversity in Global Business*. NewYork: McGraw-Hill.

Yukl, G. (1998). *Leadership in Organizations*. Englewood Cliffs, NJ: Prentice-Hall.

22

Gaining Legitimacy: Management's Challenge in Developing and Transitioning Economies

Daniel J. McCarthy and Sheila M. Puffer

The initial chapter in this part of the book provided an introduction to the developing world and described the context of opportunities and challenges in which executives need to view strategic initiatives as they engage in business and make investments in transitioning and developing economies. These strategic initiatives include decisions about products, marketing, sourcing, operations, and technology, as well as to the implementation of these decisions. This chapter, as well as this part of the book, emphasizes the importance of foreign managers becoming informed about the country-specific context as they frame and implement the strategic decisions involved in entering transitioning economies and operating businesses there. The chapter is intended to help managers from developed countries think about these decisions more fully in order to make them as effectively as possible. To achieve this objective we will explore brief examples of strategic initiatives undertaken by four firms from developed countries as they committed to a sustained presence in transitioning economies: GlaxoSmithKline, General Motors, Nypro, Inc., and Lucent Technologies.

The key premise of the chapter is that in order for managers from developed economies to succeed in transitioning economies, they and their firms must gain legitimacy. As will be seen in the examples, they accomplish this by making decisions that benefit host countries as well as their own companies. This mutuality requires thinking and acting in a socially responsible manner, which demonstrates respect for universal principles of ethical behavior as well as respect for the generally accepted cultural norms and laws of the host nation. Profitable operations are an objective, but to accomplish more than short-term profits, firms must develop long-term relationships within the developing country. The building of such relationships requires a legitimacy or acceptance of a firm's right to operate that can be gained most readily when the host country also benefits. From the developed-country managers' point of view, host-countries are best seen as presenting opportunities for more complete business development as well as providing markets, sources of labor, and other resources. Developing countries can be sources of interesting and creative products, talented employees, and skillful managers with considerable value to foreign companies.

The chapter thus is aimed at managers who intend to enter and operate in transitioning economies with a long-term view and who have a willingness to share positive outcomes with the host country. Such an approach excludes those looking primarily for short-term returns through deal-making and other transactions that exploit the host country. Transitioning countries can be a target for such a short-term approach because of their higher risks and relatively low levels of economic freedom, which require higher returns. Transitioning economies tend to rank low on indices such as the Index of Economic Freedom[1] and are inherently far less stable on various political, economic, and social dimensions than the economies of developed countries.

The failure by companies from developed countries to be socially responsible when doing business in other developing countries has caused many to question their actions, and has formed the critical basis for claims against the legitimacy of globalization. These claims, made by people concerned with social justice, have led to demonstrations around the world protesting the failures of globalization and castigating institutions such as the World Trade Organization, the International Monetary Fund, and the World Bank. Without ethically based, socially responsible strategic initiatives, businesses and institutions from developed countries are likely to find more such negative responses to their forays into transitional economies. Although companies may gain short-term profits, without a socially responsible approach, their long-term prospects may well be dashed by a continuing backlash from groups both in developed and developing countries.

How Strategic Initiatives in Transitioning Economies are Different

By their very nature, transitioning economies have higher levels of uncertainty in many areas, including the economic, political, and socio-cultural environments. These countries are generally in a state of flux. Their economic system and conditions, political system and influences, and socio-cultural norms and guidelines for behavior may be undergoing substantial change which in some cases may lead to social unrest and violence. Additionally, the ethical guidelines for doing business may be changing. Such conditions are accompanied by high levels of uncertainty in the legal system, particularly in the enforcement of laws in the areas of property ownership and property rights, taxation, labor laws, the business permits process, and government-required reports. In such situations, the government usually is more deeply involved in decisions affecting foreign businesses than would be the case in developed countries. These high levels of uncertainty and change often put foreign firms at substantial risk of threats to their business; such threats include total confiscation of assets and the forced closing of the business.

The examples presented in the chapter illustrate how four companies from developed nations succeeded, navigating their way through difficult circumstances. Aspects of their strategic initiatives will be framed within the economic, cultural, demographic, and political conditions discussed in the opening chapter of this part. The initiatives will then be analyzed and their insights reviewed.[2]

Strategic consideration of entry and operating decisions in transitioning countries

In general terms, the more the investment by a firm and the higher the degree of participation by nationals in ownership and key decision-making, the greater the potential is for benefits to the transitioning country. Some options, such as exporting, involve little in the way of direct operations in the country and involve no direct sharing of ownership with nationals. Some companies, after exporting for a period, decide to establish sales and service center subsidiaries in transitioning countries. A sales office involves more direct participation in the country than does exporting, yet it does little to increase the business impact in the host country, with little investment in plant, processes, or people. Franchising, licensing, and contracting products or processes are other methods of entry that can develop local investors and entrepreneurs, although they do not directly share ownership in the basic product or process.

Investing in plants, forming well-conceived joint ventures, and sourcing from local companies may involve substantial investment in facilities and people, and the sharing of ownership with transitioning-country nationals. Companies that evolve to this stage, investing either on their own or in joint ventures with country nationals, have the potential to add more value to the transitioning country. Nevertheless, unless the foreign firms are involved enough to be assured that plants are being operated in socially responsible and ethical ways, there remains potential for various abuses, among them child labor and exploitive wages.

Direct foreign investment in the form of plants and subsidiaries is often considered a primary way to produce gains for the host country, yet contracting arrangements can also produce significant benefits. A foreign company might establish its own software development subsidiary in a transitioning economy such as India, or contract its software development needs to Indian-owned companies. In both cases, the benefits of building intellectual capital in the country will be realized, as will the foreign firm's business needs.

In transitioning countries, foreign companies should act in socially responsible ways, even if the host country has a tradition of child labor, long work hours, and substandard working conditions. Local traditions and norms may differ, yet firms have a responsibility to maintain standards that respect human dignity and basic needs. These standards are based on the universal ethical principles that are fundamental to human existence: human rights, respect for human dignity, and good citizenship. Even if the foreign companies are not directly involved in ownership of plants or their supply chains, they should ensure that they could stand behind the standards their suppliers employ. One way to do this is to ensure that both local standards and more widely shared standards of human dignity are met. Firms should refuse to do business with those who do not adhere to such standards. For some companies, this may mean establishing their own plants and developing the infrastructure to supply the materials needed in those operations.

In addition to entry and operations, a foreign firm must make other strategic decisions, such as what products or services should be sold within the country and how they should be marketed. Advertising, other forms of promotion, and distribution should be conducted with sensitivity to the local culture.

For example, with regard to product selection, some products might be needed within the country, while some, such as cigarettes, might be considered harmful, and others, such as hamburgers in some parts of India, culturally inappropriate because Hindus regard the cow as sacred. Other products might be outmoded versions of domestic products with limited utility or perhaps excess inventories, such as computers with software that is no longer supported or serviced. Rather than take such mercenary and culturally insensitive approaches, companies can meet the demands of transitioning and developing economies "by creatively developing innovative products and services, and developing the distinctive operating practices necessitated by Third World business environments."[3] The key to socially responsible operations in transitioning economies is to reconcile these distinctive operating practices, such as human resources policies, with the operating standards established by the company for all of its operations. Companies that hire and develop nationals as managers for their businesses also are likely to be viewed as legitimate members of the country's business sector. As the examples in this chapter illustrate, such approaches can be profitable and create long-term viability for the company in the transitioning economy.

Unfortunately, in some transitioning economies, the benefits of foreign investment accrue to members of various elites, such as unelected rulers and their families, other public officials, and their favored business associates rather than to the country as a whole. In such countries, managers from developed countries must act with the highest ethical business practices to avoid being compromised by such people and systems. Laws such as the US Foreign Corrupt Practices Act, which is also the basis for new legislation within the European Union as well as in Japan, can be useful in justifying ethical behavior and decisions.

Responsible management in transitioning countries

What constitutes generally accepted ethical business behavior is quite well understood by managers from most developed countries. Much of this understanding goes to universal ethical principles: human rights, respect for human dignity, and good citizenship.

In addition to these universal principles are local ethical norms established and accepted within various communities or groups in a country. The business community is one such group, and specific ethical guidelines stem from group-specific experiences.[4] In Russia, for example, when laws are considered senseless and contradict each other or prevent the reasonable functioning of business, even though ignoring them may be illegal, most Russian business people would not consider this to be unethical.[5]

Because of such culturally specific approaches, what constitutes ethical behavior and social responsibility can often be confusing to the outsider, particularly in transitioning economies. The laws in these countries are typically in flux, there is often a poor legal infrastructure, and enforcement is generally nonexistent. In addition, the cultural norms may also be in flux. When dealing with situations which seem to be dictated by local ethical principles, foreign managers will usually be well advised to follow the local approach if it represents widely held local views, and if it does not conflict with universal ethical norms, such as not endangering human life[6]. However, managers from developed countries also must be guided by home-country legal requirements. For example, Americans are subject to the US Foreign Corrupt Practices Act.

Managers from developed countries will likely apply the universal ethical principles described above, but such managers must also be guided by the country-specific norms and practices. These local practices will often be influenced by the economic, demographic, political and cultural characteristics, as emphasized in the previous chapter in this part.

Corporate examples

Examples of strategic decisions made by managers from developed-country firms as they entered and operated in transitioning economies portray the positive aspects of socially responsible behavior in those regions. Each example will be followed by a review of the insights gained from an analysis of the situation. Four global companies, one with its headquarters in the United Kingdom and three in the United States, all leaders in their industries, will be featured. In contrast to the following chapter, which focuses on one region, Africa, this chapter looks at five regions: Latin America, Africa, Russia, China, and India.

The analysis of the strategic decisions will focus on the choice of market entry and operating decisions, as well as the processes needed to successfully implement such decisions. Key processes include building legitimacy, reputation, and social capital. Legitimacy commonly refers to the right to exist and perform an activity in a certain way.[7] Reputation in the context of this chapter is the perception of Western firms by host countries. Social capital consists of the actual and potential resources managers and companies gain from knowing others, being part of a social network, or having a good reputation within a network.[8] Additional processes include networking, relationship building, and fair and open negotiations. Other processes crucial for companies in transitioning economies include organizational learning and innovation, the building of intellectual capital, the establishment of control and coordination, boundary spanning within and across organizations, and identifying and combining partners' core competencies.

GLAXOSMITHKLINE'S HEALTH-CARE INVOLVEMENT IN EMERGING ECONOMIES

GlaxoSmithKline's strategic initiatives in Latin America and Africa

GlaxoSmithKline (GSK) of the United Kingdom is a major global healthcare company focused on the creation, discovery, development, manufacturing, and marketing of pharmaceutical products. With sales in 2000 of $27.5 billion and a net profit of $7 billion, GSK holds almost 7 percent of the $317 billion worldwide pharmaceutical market, making it the world leader in market share within the pharmaceutical industry.[9] As the result of the 2000 merger of Glaxo Wellcome and SmithKlineBeecham, GSK is also one of the world's most valuable companies, ranking fifteenth in market value in mid-2001, and second among pharmaceuticals.[10]

The company has over 100,000 employees worldwide, with operations in 70 countries, including 108 manufacturing sites in 41 countries. It coordinates activities through its global enterprise systems and software. GSK spends about $4 billion on research and development annually, and employs 16,000 people in R&D at 24 locations in 7 countries. The company produces and distributes tens of thousands of sizes and packaging varieties of its 1,000 basic products, and introduces 2,000 new varieties each year. The company's products are sold in 140 countries, encompassing virtually all the nations of the developed and developing world. The company's mission is "to improve the quality of human life by enabling people to do more, feel better and live longer."[11]

GSK employs nearly 8,000 people in Latin America and 4,500 in Africa–Middle East. Company sales in 2000 in Latin America were around $1.1 billion and over $830 million in Africa–Middle East. GSK has operations in 14 Latin American countries, including 4 production facilities, and in 6 Africa–Middle East countries, including 2 production facilities. In addition to operations in these transitioning economies, GSK also operates extensively within developing countries of the Asia-Pacific region and in Central and Eastern Europe. However, the company conducts no R&D within developing countries.

GlaxoSmithKline is a leader in recognizing the pharmaceutical industry's social responsibilities. In many countries GSK faces serious threats of restrictions from competitive pressures and government regulations: drug approvals, price controls, generic substitutes. GSK recognizes the additional risks inherent in conducting business in transitioning countries, such as nationalization and/or expropriation of property, capital regulation, unfavorable currency fluctuations, and the absence of effective patent protection. The firm realizes that responsible corporate behavior is in the company's self-interest as well as in the interests of the citizens of the transitional economies in which it operates.

In this highly regulated industry, pharmaceutical companies such as GSK are often targets of governments and international groups who criticize their high profit levels relative to most other industries. These groups often see pharmaceutical company profits as excessive, given that the primary focus of their activities is to improve human health. A counterargument is that to develop products that improve health, such profit levels are necessary to fund the extraordinarily high levels of R&D and the related long product development cycles, including FDA approvals. One observer exemplified this viewpoint: "Indeed, industry execs argue that if prices were squeezed, the world can forget about new and better drugs."[12] As GSK's CEO, Jean-Pierre Garnier, explained: "The problem is that without profit there will be no new drugs. We have to be very responsible."[13] If GSK is to live up to its mission and gain legitimacy around the world, it must pay particular attention to the needs of the poorer, transitioning nations.

GSK is in a position to do just that as the leader in four major therapeutic areas – anti-infective drugs, drugs for the central nervous system, and respiratory and gastro-intestinal/metabolic drugs, as well as vaccines. This portfolio positions the company to help alleviate healthcare problems particular to developing nations. In fact, GSK has committed to eliminating life-threatening diseases in the developing world, and leads the industry in tropical disease R&D, including establishing a multidisciplinary team in 1994 to identify and develop drugs for diseases endemic in the tropics. This includes a vaccine program for the developing world to help eradicate HIV, malaria, tuberculosis, hepatitis E, and dengue fever. GSK continues to develop drugs for other diseases, including hepatitis A and B and polio. Many of the company's efforts are directed toward helping children in developing countries. Its Scott's Emulsion, a cod liver oil supplement to support healthy growth in children and help ward off infections, is widely distributed, particularly in Latin America, Africa, and Asia. Additionally, GSK developed a personal hygiene and sanitation education program for children aged 6 to 13, with the goal of reducing diarrhea-related disease caused by poor hygiene habits. This program has been piloted in several African and Latin American countries.

GSK's stance on generic drugs: Another example of responsible behavior

In 2001 the World Trade Organization decided to authorize some countries to manufacture inexpensive generic drugs in times of medical need. GSK stated that it did not regard these authorizations as deterrents to its expansion in such countries, but that it closely reviewed methods of operations and developed strategies to respond to changing economic and political conditions. Thus, the firm recognizes that to continue its global growth it must expand its activities in transitioning economies, and do so responsibly, while taking into account the risks involved.

Additionally, GSK has a 20-year history of offering substantial discounts on medicines to governments and other public health agencies in developing countries. GSK's CEO recently observed that in transitioning countries,

> [we] have already discounted the drugs by 90 percent on what we charge in the U.S. or in Europe but we can go even further if the demand for the product increases because we would have economies of scale and we are committed to passing on the extra savings to the people who are buying the drugs and need them badly. . . . We are selling them at cost, but somebody has to pay for R&D and that's why we charge higher prices in Europe and the U.S. In a sense we are asking the rich countries to pay for R&D and we are providing drugs basically at the lowest possible cost to the least developed nations.[14]

GSK is building social capital using a wide range of global community partnerships with governments and many public and private organizations. These programs blend traditional philanthropy with major partnership commitments to public health for the developing world. For instance, GSK's malaria initiative is encompassed in a focused program, called the president's millennium vaccine initiative, that includes pediatric clinical trials of a new vaccine conducted in the Gambia, Africa, in partnership with the Walter Reed Army Institute and the London-based Medical Research Council. In its role as a partner with the World Health Organization and a cross-section of public and private organizations committed to eliminating lymphatic filariasis (elephantiasis), GSK has pledged $1 billion over 20 years. Additionally, GSK donated more than 34 million treatments of its antiparasitic drug to more than 20 developing countries in 2000, as part of the 5 billion doses it has committed to donate.

A positive development for GSK in 2001 was the South African government's agreement to comply with the international Trade-Related Intellectual Property Rights Agreement on patent protection, which affords protection to a company's intellectual property, as well as to consult with the pharmaceutical industry on associated regulations. According to GSK's Garnier: "The South African Government's willingness to respect intellectual property rights and to consult creates the basis for a new spirit of co-operation. This must provide encouragement to the industry to invest in future research and development of new medicines including those for diseases of the developing world."[15]

The company also demonstrates responsibility in its strategic initiatives as they relate to the environment, to health and safety, and to human resources policies. For instance, GSK has established global standards and guidelines for action, and is in the process of seeking company-wide ISO 14001 certification in recognition of its approach to the environment. A department is dedicated to enforcing these standards around the world, including in the operations of its suppliers. GSK also conducts audits in countries in which it operates and rewards business units that achieve excellence in these areas. GSK's executive and leadership development program identifies and prepares management talent around the world to manage its future growth. Company compensation and benefit packages are enlightened, competitive, and tailored to local markets. Leadership decisions are also tailored to local markets, with area nationals heading operations in Latin America and the Middle East–North Africa.

Such a record of decisions is not only evidence of responsible business behavior, but should also in the long run enhance GSK's legitimacy and build its social capital in these regions. As the economies of these developing nations improve, they will become more attractive markets for GSK because of such responsible strategic initiatives. Thus, the company is behaving responsibly, but also with enlightened self-interest.

Lessons from GlaxoSmithKline in Latin America and Africa

GlaxoSmithKline demonstrates well the types of strategic initiatives that are likely to be rewarded with corporate legitimacy in developing nations. The company has utilized its core competencies in product decisions, focusing major efforts on disease categories in which it has built reputation and capabilities. GSK has dedicated substantial R&D and introduced numerous innovative products to treat diseases that are particularly prevalent in tropical climates, where many developing nations are located.

GSK has used marketing techniques to identify target groups such as children and women, and disease categories that constitute major needs in transitioning economies. The company has invested heavily in strategically located plants and distribution systems within developing regions including Latin America and Africa, in addition to providing employment for thousands of local citizens in these regions. GSK clearly has formulated its initiatives in developing nations, paying close attention to their specific economic, political, cultural, and demographic characteristics and needs.

It is socially responsible and ethical for companies in healthcare industries to follow such strategic initiatives, since their products affect health and possibly life, and are subject to constant scrutiny by governments, other regulatory bodies, and public opinion. Because of the nature of their business, they must build social capital, as GSK appears to have been doing in Latin America and Africa. GSK's long-term approach to business and record of responsible decisions creates local legitimacy that provides an important counterbalance to the criticism that companies such as GSK receive. GSK's strategic decisions show that social responsibility is indeed good business and demonstrate enlightened self-interest. GSK appears to have built an ability to balance its own needs with those of the developing nations where it operates.

To accomplish this, the company has employed nationals to run the businesses in areas such as Latin America and Africa. Their understanding of the economic, political, and cultural situations of the regions should help the company better adapt to these conditions. Nationals bring an ability to enhance organizational learning about these regions, as well as to engage in social networking and boundary spanning within their regions and with other GSK business units. They also understand effective approaches to leadership and teamwork in their country. The company coordinates and controls activities with a sophisticated information system that allows units of its vast global network to communicate. Its approach to environmental issues, as well as health and safety, in these regions appears to be similar to its activities in developed countries. Such sensitivity in its strategic decisions in developing regions is likely to result in a positive reputation and increased social capital for GSK.

The UK firm has invested in major partnership efforts to activities aimed at improving the health and quality of life for inhabitants of developing nations. Its partners include numerous governments, governmental agencies, world health organizations, and private businesses. Its initiatives are directly appropriate to the needs of people in developing nations such as Latin America and Africa. Its approach is long term and widespread in these countries, seeking to solve endemic healthcare problems there. GSK devotes enormous efforts and substantial resources to these partnerships, and shares jointly in decisions about how the ventures' resources should be allocated. The company recognizes that its efforts directly benefit developing nations and their people, and the company as well. Developing nations are seen by GSK as major markets, with enormous needs at present, but even more importantly, as markets which will carry into the future as their health and living standards improve.

GENERAL MOTORS AND AvtoVAZ: JOINT MANUFACTURING IN RUSSIA

General Motors' strategic initiatives in Russia

General Motors (GM), the world's largest vehicle manufacturer, designs and manufactures cars and trucks worldwide. The company had sales in 2000 of over $180 billion and profits of $5 billion. Employing 363,000 people around the world, GM operates in more than two dozen developing countries in Africa and the Middle East, Latin America, Asia-Pacific, and Eastern Europe.

GM was determined to enter the Russian car market because it perceived an exceptional opportunity for growth in that country, with its projected demand for 1.4 million automobiles in 2002, at a time when most of Europe had a slowing demand for cars. The company included Russia among the eight nations expected to account for two-thirds of global growth in car sales in the first decade of the new century. Given the economic situation, as well as its sales experience in the USSR dating back to the 1970s, GM was willing to take chances. In 1996, the company entered a joint venture with the Russian Republic of Tatarstan to assemble its Chevy Blazer sport utility vehicles; in 1999 this operation switched to the limited assembly of GM's Opel Vectra.

By 2002, GM expected to be producing the Niva sport utility vehicle, in a $332 million joint venture signed in 2000 with the former state-owned Russian automobile company AvtoVAZ and the European Bank for Reconstruction and Development (EBRD). Each of the automakers obtained 41.5 percent ownership, with the EBRD holding the remaining 17 percent. GM invested $100 million in building a plant on AvtoVAZ's site in Togliatti, Russia, and established an arm of its worldwide purchasing staff operations in Moscow. The AvtoVAZ contribution consisted of design and engineering capabilities and additional facilities. The EBRD contributed financing and its expertise developed in its participation in many investment projects in Russia. The venture had the objective of producing 75,000 vehicles annually by 2004.

GM was willing to incur substantial risk in this joint venture that produced cars engineered and designed by its Russian partner, a company that, earlier in the decade, had
been plagued by gross inefficiency and corruption. In addition, the country itself had
undergone tremendous economic, political, and social strains during its transition to a
market economy, underway since the late 1980s. By 2002, however, AvtoVAZ was Russia's leading automaker, with a 68-percent market share in Russia, as well as a 34-percent
share in Central and Eastern Europe. The company was also predicted in 2001 to
become one of the "big three" Russian automakers in an industry consolidation in which
the top firms would become global competitors, especially in price-sensitive markets.[16]
Other positive factors for GM were the government's tax reforms and foreign investment
incentives, and its development plan to make Russia globally competitive in automotive
standards and worldwide sales volume.

Regarding the strategic benefits of sourcing parts from Russian suppliers, in addition to
the government's strict local-content requirements on foreign manufacturers in Russia,
one analyst noted: "Global players like Ford and GM like to stay with their traditional
suppliers wherever they go, but if the production volume is too low, suppliers need to look
to opportunities in technology transfer to Russian suppliers, where the volume in production is."[17]

GM's decisions required a high level of trust on the part of GM executives, especially David Herman, vice-president for Russia and the Commonwealth of Independent
States (CIS), comprising the 12 republics of the former Soviet Union. According to
Herman: "This investment is part of our long-term business strategy for the Russian
market. GM is taking an intelligent, reasoned approach to a market with a huge potential by building on the proven engineering expertise of AvtoVAZ."[18] Herman, the former
head of GM's Opel division in Germany, had planned initially to assemble Opels
in Russia with large subassemblies exported from Europe. Herman's experience in the
USSR dated back to 1976, when he was GM's manager of sales development for the
country.

Herman negotiated for two years to reach a settlement in 2000 that both sides felt
could work.[19] He had to convince both his Russian counterparts and his superiors within
GM that this unconventional strategy of utilizing Russian design and engineering, as well
as Russian suppliers, could be effective. In contrast, most other automobile companies
from Europe and North America relied on a more traditional approach, using Western-
engineered and designed models, assembling them in Russia, using historically reliable
suppliers. GM also agreed to develop other compact models with AvtoVAZ that would
bear the Chevy name.

GM's strategy was expected to result in a vehicle priced at around $7,500, realistic
in a country where 95 percent of vehicles sold for less than $10,000. The Chevy would
be price competitive with most domestic Russian vehicles and cheaper than any
North American or European car in the Russian market, and competitive with most
domestic Russian vehicles. With production of the first vehicles scheduled for 2002, GM
had a prime opportunity to crack one of the world's largest growth markets for autos.
For its part, AvtoVAZ would have proven its ability to design, engineer, and produce
a high-quality automobile. What AvtoVAZ had to give up in the process was exclusive ownership of their new vehicle, called the Niva, to the joint venture. But unable
to finance its production, the Russian company too had to take less than it wanted in its

negotiations with GM. Each side had to give up some of what it would have liked, and GM gave up substantial control over design, engineering, and parts procurement.

Lessons from General Motors and AvtoVAZ in Russia

David Herman, GM vice-president for Russia and the CIS, recognized the give-and-take required in his Russian joint venture. He recognized the risks involved for both GM and AvtoVAZ. He understood the situation of his Russian counterparts, who felt they were giving up control over their newly designed vehicle and the related profit potential, as well as the profit and business objectives of his own organization. Each party had to take risks and give up some objectives, including compromising on the mix of core competencies that would be drawn from each partner. Yet both parties realized that this was a reasonable route to a satisfactory resolution.

The essence of GM's strategic decision was to forge an entry strategy with a Russian joint-venture partner, capitalizing on the core competencies of both parties. The Western managers, particularly David Herman, with his long experience in the USSR, realized that mutual trust and honest negotiation were fundamental to the long-run success of such a joint undertaking. He and the AvtoVAZ managers were able to develop mutual trust and respect, which allowed them to forge a mutually satisfactory partnership. As in many transitioning economies, the Russian nationals regarded trust as a fundamental underpinning of a successful partnership. Herman understood this and was guided by this reality; still, it took two years of negotiation following several years of relationship building to gain the trust of his Russian counterparts. In the long run, GM stands to establish itself as a leader in one of the world's largest potential automobile markets and in doing so, to also gain legitimacy and social capital in that crucial market.

AvtoVAZ as a company was resuscitated, its engineering and development competencies were tapped, and its intellectual capital was enhanced in the process. Additionally, Russian workers found a new employment opportunity, and the country itself gained an important addition to its industrial base. These benefits to the country were important in a transition economy such as Russia because of the country's desperate economic situation, including a disintegrated industrial infrastructure, outmoded and inefficient plants, and ineffective management structure. In short, the GM–AvtoVAZ joint venture had the potential for positive outcomes for all parties, owing primarily to the socially responsible way in which GM approached the negotiations. This mutually advantageous approach pursued by GM managers, in the process of negotiations, illustrates socially responsible behavior on the part of managers who had come to understand and respect the economic, social, cultural, and political situation of Russia, and considered these factors in their market-entry decision.

Nypro, Inc. in China: Joint Ventures and Contract Manufacturing

During the past several years, Nypro, Inc., a leading US plastic injection molding and contract manufacturing company, has established itself in Shenzhen, Tianjin, Pan Yu, and Suzhou, China. Its 5 plants continue its 25-year commitment to a global company strategy. Following this approach, which led to opening 27 plants in 12 countries, by 2001, the Massachusetts-based firm had 16 consecutive years of record growth and profitability. In 2001, the company reported worldwide sales of $495 million. This constituted the company's share of sales from all plants around the world, which totaled $682 million, including joint-venture partners' share of $187 million. Nypro's net profit that year was $32 million, a 25 percent increase from the previous year. In addition to its China operations, Nypro opened facilities in 5 other transitional countries in 2001 – India, Russia, Hungary, and two Latin American countries, Mexico and the Dominican Republic. A notable feature of Nypro's strategy has been its commitment to joint ventures, both foreign and domestic. As often as possible, these ventures are structured on a 50–50 ownership basis with local partners, and it is they who manage the operations of the joint venture.

In entering developing nations, the private company's president and owner, Gordon Lankton, has strived to treat his partners in the same fashion as he does those in the United States and in other developed countries. Within existing local laws, he attempts to share equal ownership in the joint ventures, and prefers local management of the joint venture's operations. Nypro provides the expertise required to have world-class operations in these transitional environments, as it does in developed countries. For instance, its Chinese operations use the latest robotic technology in molding and assembly operations, and the Suzhou operation has a large, new, and sterile clean-room facility. These world-class technologies are the same as the company has in its operations in the developed countries of North America, Europe, and Asia. Similarly, the company is committed to protecting the environment, as evidenced by its ISO 14000 designation, which it is seeking for its Chinese operations also.

In addition to the learning and knowledge sharing that occurs from using the most advanced technologies available, the host developing countries have the opportunity for knowledge sharing and learning through other processes and techniques. The board of directors of each joint venture is composed of Nypro employees from various parts of the world including the host countries. Such inclusion facilitates interaction and shared learning among Nypro managers and employees, including those of the developing countries. The company's educational program, Nypro Institute, offers courses on the Web to employees around the world.

Nypro's approach to operations and partners in developing countries is the result of the values, attitudes, and experiences of Gordon Lankton, its long-term president, CEO, and primary owner. Lankton began traveling extensively in his youth and has never stopped. He went to Japan while a young man, assimilated the culture, and made many valued friends with whom he later established joint ventures as they opened businesses in the United States. Lankton's relationship-building and boundary-spanning activities thus have often preceded the establishment of Nypro's joint ventures, and also occur continuously as Lankton travels to company sites, customers, and suppliers around the world.

These activities also help build Nypro's legitimacy, reputation, and social capital. Finally, Lankton's personal involvement with joint-venture partners and their boards of directors facilitates effective control of global operations. Using innovative technology, such as local area networks, wide area networks, and electronic data-interchange systems, Nypro ensures that all locations can communicate seamlessly, allowing coordination of regional and worldwide efforts and a continuous overview by Nypro's headquarters. His sense of sharing and fairness in negotiations is manifested in his decision to establish an Employee Stock Ownership Plan (ESOP) that resulted in the ownership of Nypro by its employees. He also seeks fairness in working with Nypro's joint ventures, advocating equal 50–50 ownership positions for Nypro and its partners. Finally, he seeks fairness by encouraging his joint-venture partners to share benefits from operations with their employees, just as he does. Thus, Nypro gains legitimacy in transitioning economies by demonstrating the company's social responsibility through advocating fair treatment of employees in all locations around the world.

Lessons from Nypro's approach to joint-venture partnerships

Lankton's social responsibility is evident in Nypro's strategy for global expansion. He ensures that he enters all countries with local joint-venture partners in order for Nypro to be able to operate with sensitivity to prevailing political and cultural conditions. He has operated with socially responsible business practices by respecting legitimate local cultural norms and values, and ensuring that nationals head the operations in each country. Such practices have resulted in substantial economic development, particularly within transitioning economies. Nypro has experienced extraordinary success by following its customers around the world to both developing and developed countries.

At the same time, his joint-venture partners in developing countries have shared in the development and ownership of substantial businesses. Lankton's strategy is to equip operations in transitional economies with the same innovative, state-of-the art technologies, machinery, and processes the operations would use in developed countries. Nypro has provided access to all of its core competencies, and coupled them with those of its local partners, particularly their knowledge of local laws, social norms, and other requirements, such as dealing with national and local governments. These benefits are at the national level, too, especially with regard to Nypro's investments and the knowledge and experience that the company has been willing to share.

Nypro's experience shows that operating in transitioning countries with sensitivity to their needs builds a legitimacy that can produce exceptionally positive business results.

LUCENT TECHNOLOGIES IN INDIA: TECHNOLOGY SHARING AND DEVELOPMENT

Lucent's strategic initiatives in India

Lucent Technologies of the United States, with $21 billion in revenues in 2001, is one of the world's leading communications companies. Its business focus is the design and delivery of systems software, silicon, and services for communications networks operated by service providers and other enterprises. Bell Labs, its R&D arm, is the world's largest R&D organization dedicated to communications, with approximately 30,000 employees in 30 countries. In spite of its prominent history and position as a leading telecommunications company, Lucent in recent years has experienced hard times and intense competition, resulting in substantial downsizing, cost reduction, and employee layoffs. Concurrently, the company has realized that its future depends heavily on its success outside the United States, and particularly in transitioning economies, where the growth rates for telecommunications infrastructure are predicted to be substantial. Lucent has recognized India's distinctive competence in telecommunications technology and software development, and its reservoir of talented and technically skilled human resources. This has led the company to concentrate on India as a burgeoning market and as a major source of the company's R&D and product innovation.

Lucent's Bell Labs has offices in New Delhi, Bangalore, Bombay, Hyderabad, Kerala, Chandigarh, Jaipur, and Pune. The opening of the Hyderabad facility in 2000 was expected to double the company's R&D capability in India. Lucent directly employs more than 700 people, including 500 software engineers, in the company's 12 global business units represented in India. The company's joint ventures employ an additional 600 employees. Lucent's major manufacturing operation in Pune, supported by its own R&D lab, is the regional manufacturing base for highly advanced interconnect systems requirements for India, Asia-Pacific, Europe, and the Middle East. The company's power systems division set up its first design center in Bangalore to carry out power-system development activities for large computers and telecommunications equipment. Its microelectronics group also created a development center in Bangalore to carry out core R&D for microelectronics in the areas of digital signaling processing tools and applications. Additionally, the company's state-of-the-art switching factory in Bangalore received the prestigious Approved Inspection Scheme from the Indian Department of Telecommunications that allows it to conduct its own quality inspections on equipment it produces.

Rather than take a short-term approach in India, Lucent has committed to a long-term involvement there. In 2000, Lucent was already the leader in the Indian telecommunications marketplace when it appointed Indian nationals to head both Lucent Technologies India and Bell Labs India.

Lucent's operations in India serve as an example of how good strategic business decisions can include social responsibility. The company entered India, with its one billion citizens, in search of a major growth market for its broad line of telecommunications products. Lucent realized that this vast nation was on the verge of the communications age. Company officials realized that, to become the leading provider of telecommunications equipment in that country, they had to establish legitimacy and reputation, and that taking a long-term approach was crucial. They met with India's prime minister and leaders of various regions to discuss the country's goals in areas where Lucent could play an important role. This constituted social networking at the highest levels to develop trust and understanding with host-country officials and build social capital for Lucent.

In discussions with India's Prime Minister in 2001, the Bell Labs president explored steps to strengthen India's position as an information technology (IT) superpower with the Indian government's support. The prime minister stated that "India needs to bring communications to the full population by creating a future-proof low cost network architecture," including shared services for villages. He also noted that "India should leverage its existing infrastructure and phenomenal skill base" of about 280,000 citizens working in the software and services sector, which is the world's second largest IT workforce.[20]

In such meetings, Lucent company executives were making clear statements that they understood that their success in India would be tied to and shared with the goals of the Indian government. Lucent's business in India would be fostered by its involvement in implementing the government's telecommunications growth plans. Bell Labs in India will function as a development site for Lucent's globally distributed products. With this approach, the company has built legitimacy and helped to ensure a long-term presence in an attractive growth market.

India has become a major hub for R&D activities for Lucent. Its labs in Bangalore and Hyderabad offer key support to Lucent technologies around the world. At the opening of the Hyderabad facility, the region's chief minister stated: "I desire and hope that Bell Labs would develop solutions specially relevant to India's needs, in particular, to improve our rural connectivity and reliability so that it would be used for the benefit of all sections of people in every field of human and economic interest."[21] The Bell Labs India president was honored in 2000 by the Indian government for outstanding contributions to the country.

Lucent India has developed an extensive network of business partners anchored by its BusinessPartner Advantage Program that offers a comprehensive accreditation process for market-channel partners to become trained, tested, and certified experts across Lucent's broad range of business solutions. Thus the company engages in partnerships and helps to develop the capabilities of those partners. The company's recognition of the need for mutual advantage is captured in the words of the president and CEO of Lucent Technologies India: "We recognize the important role of our partners in helping us gain a stronger hold in the Indian marketplace. We succeed if our partners succeed."[22] On the same occasion, the managing director of Convergent Communications India, a key market-channel partner, noted that the company gains "access to a unique combination of world-class technology, global services, and a legacy of innovation. This relationship will help us further our position in the India networking market."

Through its partnerships, Lucent has penetrated much of the vast Indian subcontinent. Among its major alliances are those with Tata Teleservices Ltd. for the state of Andhra Pradesh, with a contract value of over $31 million. Another, valued at more than $154 million over 5 years, is with Shyam Telelink Ltd., in the state of Rajasthan, to build a communications network covering 85 percent of the state's 52 million people in 22 key cities, as well as many remote villages. An especially large partnership, valued at $175 million, is with Hughes Tele.com (India) Ltd., to build the country's first truly broadband telephone network in the states of Maharashtra and Goa. These partnerships are indicative of the business development opportunities for Lucent, as well as the benefits to their Indian partners, and to the Indian citizens in these states. India benefits from the technological developments, communications networks, and social benefits that come with these technological advances supported by Lucent's involvement.

In addition to its business involvement, Lucent has introduced social programs in India, including the Global Science Scholars Program, whose objective is to encourage the world's youth to follow careers in communications technology. This program rewards outstanding students in math and science, including engineering students. The company has also initiated the India R&D Bell Labs Scholarship Program, aimed specifically at promoting careers in telecommunications software. It includes an employment offer from Lucent upon graduation. In addition, the Lucent Technologies Foundation established a fund to help more than 4,000 young people across India. This foundation has financed the education of homeless youths in several major cities.

Lessons from Lucent in India

Lucent committed to a mutually beneficial approach to business in India. Because the company became involved in large-scale contracts and other opportunities, India's communications infrastructure was developed. Communication was established among many of the country's regions, including remote villages, some receiving such services for the first time.

Other advantages to the country were the creation of 500 sophisticated technological jobs in the telecommunications and software sector, among its 700 positions. Additionally, the country, and Lucent, benefited from selecting Indian nationals to run Lucent Technologies India Ltd and Bell Labs India. Lucent recognized the unique capabilities and technical talent that were a key core competency of the country, and committed to building its operations around them. Additionally, the country gained access to much of Lucent's leading technology and the company was depending on Bell Labs India to extend the limits of its technology. India also began serving as a base for exporting products throughout the Asia-Pacific region. Thus, both Lucent and India itself benefited from extensive mutual sharing of intellectual capital and other knowledge.

Through such enlightened strategic decisions, Lucent succeeded in becoming the telecommunications equipment leader in India. Another decision crucial to Lucent's success in India is the use of joint ventures with Indian partners who had knowledge of how to function in the country's vast territory and diverse regions, a critical competency. They were key to accessing markets and establishing distribution channels within those markets. Negotiations often had to be carried out with regional officials to establish infrastructure within their boundaries, and Indian partners were crucial to winning contracts. To be successful in this environment, Lucent had to negotiate successfully with numerous joint-venture partners, and then participate with them in negotiations with customers. Their success in doing so helped to create the social capital, legitimacy, and reputation that Lucent has come to enjoy in the country.

In establishing itself as a responsible corporate citizen in India, Lucent fostered and contributed to many social initiatives, some of which were related to its business, such as the development of the country's technological talent through scholarship and employment programs. Other efforts were aimed at more general social service initiatives. Thus, in addition to becoming the market leader in the telecommunications equipment sector in India, Lucent consistently demonstrated its intention to be a responsible partner in the country's development. Leveraging this learning into other transitional economies is an additional benefit to Lucent of its Indian involvement.

CONCLUSION

Foreign firms in such unpredictable environments as transitional economies should be aware that socially responsible actions can in the long run bring mutual benefits to these firms and host nations. Such action requires thinking and acting in ways that demonstrate respect for universal principles of ethical behavior as well as respect for the generally accepted cultural norms and laws of the host nation. Foreign firms can gain legitimacy and reputation, while host countries benefit from economic and social development.

In this chapter we have discussed examples of strategic initiatives undertaken by four firms from developed countries as they pursued long-term commitments in different transitioning economies: GlaxoSmithKline, General Motors, Nypro Inc., and Lucent Technologies. GlaxoSmithKline, for instance, expanded worldwide sales to become the pharmaceutical industry market leader, and in the process contributed substantially to improving the health of people in Latin America, the Middle East, and Africa. General Motors solidified its position in Russia, one of the fastest-growing automobile markets in the world, while the host country gained thousands of jobs through domestic production of Russian-designed vehicles. Nypro, Inc., enhanced its reputation as the highest quality, as well as the fastest growing, plastic injection molding company in the world, while bringing its cutting-edge technology and cooperative management approach to China. Lucent Technologies gained many first-mover advantages in the burgeoning high-technology industry in India, and at the same time provided both advanced technology to India and employment for skilled local professionals and executives.

Although such positive behavior may not prevent problems for Western firms, it does contribute to a positive reputation in their home country and within the global business community. Since the September 11, 2001 terrorist attacks on the World Trade Center and the Pentagon, the basic tenets of corporate social responsibility have been discussed broadly within the context of globalization. One source urged "a new social responsibility amendment to the U.S. Constitution that would make a corporation's ability to operate in the U.S. dependent on its ability to prove a history of social responsibility both in the U.S. and around the world."[23] Although developed nations will not likely initiate such a dramatic response, this view underscores the new scrutiny that corporations will likely face. It seems reasonable to predict that, in the context of profit objectives, corporations will be expected to exhibit high levels of social responsibility around the world, and their actions in developing nations will be subject to increasingly closer scrutiny.

Managers from developed-country firms must understand the risk, uncertainty, and environmental forces inherent in transitioning economies. The management philosopher Charles Handy captures the importance of such understanding. He believes that business needs a "license to operate from its surrounding society, but that informal license can be given only by the members of the society affected by the business. . . . The first step . . . is to ask the people what the company needs to do to earn that license."[24] Even when thoroughly prepared to enter a transitioning economy, however, managers from developed countries must always be ready for changes and surprises, because these economies, at their current stage, are typically in a state of flux.

NOTES

1 O'Driscoll, Holmes, & O'Grady (2002).
2 Works examining strategic initiatives in transitioning economies include those by Katsioloudes (2001); Legewie & Meyer-Ohle (2000); Levy-Livermore (1998); Lloyd & Xiao-Guang (2001); Mirza & Wee (2000); Peng (1999); Puffer, McCarthy, & Naumov (2000); Rich (2001); & Sears & Tamulionyte-Lentz (2001).

3 Govindarajan & Trimble (2002), p. 31.
4 Donaldson & Dunfee (1997).
5 Puffer & McCarthy (1995); Puffer & McCarthy (1997).
6 Donaldson & Dunfee (1997).
7 Suchman (1995).
8 Nahapiet & Ghoshal (1998).
9 Anonymous, AIDS and the profit factor, CNN.com Europe, June 7, 2001, /www.europe.cnn.com/
10 BusinessWeek Global 1000 (2001).
11 /www.gsk.com/
12 Carey & Barrett (2001).
13 Anonymous (2001a).
14 *Ibid.*
15 GlaxoSmithKline website, April 19, 2001.
16 Kamins (2001).
17 Cited in *ibid.*
18 General Motors website, Investor News, February 27, 2001.
19 White (2001).
20 Bell Labs President discusses with prime minister of India steps to further India as an IT superpower, website, February 6, 2001.
21 Chief Minister of Andhra Pradesh, Chandrababu Naidu, and president of Bell Labs, Arun Netravali, inaugurate Bell Labs Center at Hyderabad, India, website, February 9, 2001.
22 Lucent Technologies appoints Convergent Communications as business partner in India, website, June 21, 2001.
23 Editors, the (2002), p. 20.
24 *Ibid.*, p. 32.

BIBLIOGRAPHY

Ahlstrom, D., & Bruton, G. D. (2001). Learning from successful local private firms in China: Establishing legitimacy. *Academy of Management Executive*, 15(4), 72–83.

Anonymous (2001a). AIDS and the profit factor, CNN.com Europe, June 7, www.europe.cnn.com

Anonymous (2001b). The stars of Europe – Value creators: Jean-Pierre Garnier. *BusinessWeek*, June 11, www.businessweek.com

BusinessWeek Global 1000 (2001). *BusinessWeek*, July 9, 75–90.

Carey, J., & Barrett, A. (2001). Drug prices: What's fair? How can we encourage research and still keep prices within reach for Cipro and beyond? *BusinessWeek*, December 10, 60–70.

Donaldson, T., & Dunfee, T. W. (1997). Toward a unified conception of business ethics: Integrative social contracts theory. *Academy of Management Review*, 19, 252.

Dutrenit, G. (2000). *Learning and Knowledge Management in the Firm: From Knowledge Accumulation to Strategic Capabilities*. Cheltenham: Edward Elgar.

Editors, the (2002). Below the bottom line. *Across the Board*. January–February, 20–32.

General Motors, Inc. website, www.gm.com

GlaxoSmithKline plc website, www.gsk.com

Govindarajan, V., & Trimble, C. (2002). Below the bottom line: Private investment is not enough. *Across the Board*, January–February, 30–31.

Handy, C. (2002). Below the bottom line: Creating wealth is not enough. *Across the Board*. January–February, 30–31.

Kamins, J. (2001). Key investments invigorate Russian auto sector. *Bisnis Bulletin*. US Department of Commerce, August/September, 1, 6.

Katsioloudes, M. I. (2001). *Global Strategic Planning: Cultural Perspectives for Profit and Non-Profit Organizations*. Oxford: Butterworth-Heinemann.

Legewie, J., & Meyer-Ohle, H. (eds.) (2000). *Corporate Strategies for South East Asia After the Crisis*. Basingstoke: Palgrave.

Levy-Livermore. A. (ed.) (1998). *Handbook on the Globalization of the World Economy*. Cheltenham: Edward Elgar.

Lloyd, P., & Xiao-Guang, Z. (2001). *China in the Global Economy*. Cheltenham: Edward Elgar.

Lucent Technologies website, www.lucent.com

McCarthy, D. J., & Bhardwaj, G. (1997). Nypro, Inc.: Strategy for globalization. *Case Research Journal*, 17(1&2), 49–70.

Mirza, H., & Wee, K. H. (eds.) (2000). *Transnational Corporate Strategies*. Cheltenham: Edward Elgar.

Nahapiet, J., & Ghoshal, S. (1998). Social capital, intellectual capital, and the organizational advantage. *Academy of Management Review*, 23, 242–266.

Nypro, Inc. website, www.nypro.com

O'Driscoll, G. P., Jr., Holmes, K. R., & O'Grady, M. A. (eds.) (2002). *2002 Index of Economic Freedom*. Washington, DC: The Heritage Foundation.

Peng, M. W. (1999). *Business Strategies in Transition Economies*. Thousand Oaks, CA: Sage.

Puffer, S. M., & McCarthy, D. J. (1995). Finding the common ground in Russian and American business ethics. *California Management Review*, 37(2), 29–46.

Puffer, S. M., & McCarthy, D. J. (1997). Business ethics in a transforming economy: Applying the integrative social contracts theory to Russia. *University of Pennsylvania Journal of International Economic Law*, 18(4), 1281–1304.

Puffer, S. M., McCarthy, D. J., & Naumov, A. I. (2000). *The Russian Capitalist Experiment: From State-Owned Enterprises to Entrepreneurships*. Cheltenham: Edward Elgar.

Rich, P. G. (2001). *The Future for Latin America in the Global Economy*. Basingstoke: Palgrave.

Rifkin, J. (2002). Below the bottom line: Re-globalization from the bottom up. 2002. *Across the Board*. January–February, 29.

Sears, W., & Tamulionyte-Lentz, A. (2001) *Succeeding in Business in Central and Eastern Europe*. Oxford: Butterworth-Heinemann.

Suchman, M. C. (1995). Managing legitimacy: Strategic and institutional approaches. *Academy of Management Review*, 20, 571–610.

White, G. L. (2001). How the Chevy name landed on SUV using Russian technology: To crack market, GM trusts former Soviet auto maker that has a troubled past. *Wall Street Journal*, February 20, 1, A8.

23

Management in Action in Developing Countries

Terence Jackson

Developing countries present managers with many contradictions and complexities, as addressed in previous chapters in this part. This chapter explores the types of competencies that managers require in order to manage effectively in this developing-country context. The challenge is to describe a complex process that goes far beyond the development of a list of competencies that can be identified among potential expatriate managers or for which potential managers can be trained. It involves skills that support managing a diverse workforce, including both the dynamics of multiculturalism and the issues that stem from an awareness of self and one's own culture, and an awareness of what ways self and culture may influence the management of people. This challenge also has to address ways to manage the interests of a number of different stakeholders: local and expatriate managers, often under-skilled employees, shareholders and the local community, and government and business interests. It also includes skills needed to address workforce issues related to HIV and AIDS. Finally, this challenge includes the description of the skills needed to motivate a workforce and manage in a local developing country context that is affected by global competition.

How to manage in developing countries is an issue that is gaining importance, largely because huge markets have been opening to the West in developing countries. This change stems from the break-up of the former Soviet Union; the opening up of the People's Republic of China to East–West joint ventures; the end of apartheid in South Africa, a change which had domino effects throughout sub-Saharan Africa; and the economic liberalization process in India since the 1980s. These movements have provided openings for business development within these regions and led to opportunities for Western management theories to be tried out, adapted, reconciled to local practice, and in some cases, even imposed on non-Western organizations. At a basic level, Western managers in the developing world would do well to remember that they are in situations that may have different logics, priorities, and patterns of behavior from those cultures within which Western management theories were developed.

The management skills required for effective management in a developing country context may be broken out into five core management competency areas:

Competency 1: Managing the dynamics of diversity

Understanding the social environment in order to manage its diversity is a key requirement for managing in the developing world. This understanding involves the social environment, oneself, and one's culture, and how self and culture impact one's own management style.

Competency 2: Managing complexity

An understanding of the many operating constraints in the developing world is critical. Developing ways to manage them so that they are at least neutralized and, at best, the source of strength, is a necessity.

Competency 3: Accommodating multiple stakeholders

This process includes recognizing a wide range of interests, both within the organization and in the larger social environment.

Competency 4: Motivating the workforce

This skill involves obtaining commitment, motivation, and participation. Reconciling conflicts between work and home/community life is a key aspect of motivation in many developing environments.

Competency 5: Assessing appropriate management approaches

This skill involves the assessment of appropriate management techniques in different sociocultural contexts.

Each country that may be placed under the heading *developing* is unique. Yet many of the factors that relate to global management competencies in the context of developing, emerging, or transitional countries can be discussed by an initial focus on South Africa within the context of sub-Saharan Africa, and then connected to other emerging countries and regions. South Africa contains all the factors discussed in the description of the competencies above, to the extreme. If managers can get it right in South Africa, managers can get it right in most emerging countries across the globe.

The weight of these five competency areas will vary by country. For example, although the Czech Republic is not a multi-ethnic society, managers are increasingly having to manage across cultures within international joint ventures,[1] and having to assess the appropriateness of Western management techniques (American, German) to the sociocultural environment. Hence German–Czech interaction may be an issue in Volkswagen–Skoda, a German–Czech joint venture. Yet the degree of complexity encountered there will differ dramatically from that found in the workplace in a society such as South Africa.

In South Africa, as in many emerging countries, Western and non-Western cultures have for many years existed side by side, perhaps not too happily, with the enforced policy of separate ethnic development warping the relationship. The end of the Cold War and the collapse of the communist system may well have undercut the ideological platform of the African National Congress and the contra-ideology of the National Party.[2] This led to the broad common acceptance of the central role of the market in future South African economic development, which paved the way for agreement on the end of the old regime. With the ending of apartheid, the situation has been left, perhaps as it always was, with a multicultural, polyglot society with 11 official languages. In South Africa the Western manager will find overwhelming complexity, deep historical antagonisms, and profound differences between rich and poor. As in the former Soviet countries,

China, and other emerging countries around the world, managers in organizations in South Africa are grappling with the problems of managing change and developing people within an economy in transition. They are also faced with issues of multiculturalism, in common with other African countries and those in other regions. India, for example, has a range of multicultural complexities, including 18 official languages.

COMPETENCY 1: MANAGING THE DYNAMICS OF DIVERSITY

Diversity management in the South African context involves a complex notion of diversity: a legacy of colonialism, under-skilled workers, demographics, and AIDS all contribute to a management situation rife with contradictions. Management approaches that can deal with these contradictions and can thrive under adverse conditions are the foundation of this competency area. Multicultural management skills and knowledge of one's own cultural patterns and how they affect management style are core aspects of an ability to manage diversity. The key management challenge has to address the integration of the dispossessed, which, in South Africa, is the majority.

Overcoming the legacy

African countries were economically structured as primary producers under colonial administration, as were many of the former Soviet republics, and today export concentration ratios reflect this. In most countries over 75 percent of export earnings are accounted for by one or several primary products from agriculture or extraction.[3] Although export-based, in 1986 the continent's share of world exports was only 3 percent. At the same time 3.5 percent of world imports went to Africa.[4] Although South Africa today has far lower export-concentration ratios, its original economic development was based on extraction and agriculture aimed at an export rather than a domestic market. This focus on export-led production resulted in no development of a consumer-based economy and led to the underdevelopment of processing and service industries and the skills associated with these sectors. In South Africa the distinction between labor, which was predominantly for mining and other heavy industry, and a much smaller population base for consumer products, was formalized by apartheid along racial lines. The movement of labor was heavily controlled through a migratory system. Homelands were created and black Africans were excluded from white urban areas.

While other African countries could simply be described as "poor," the situation in South Africa is more complex than this, and full of contradictions. The GNP per capita of US$2,470 places it in the upper middle-income group of semi-industrialized economies, yet it performs more in line with the typical lower middle-income countries if one considers its social indicators. Health performance is worse than some low-income countries such as Sri Lanka and China. It has the lowest life expectancy (62 years) of the upper middle-income countries, and a quality of life index of only 66.[5] With a population exceeding 39 million at the 1991 census (75.5 percent black, 13.1 percent white, 8.6 percent mixed races, and 2.5 percent Asian), 29 percent are unemployed, with informal estimates as high as 50 percent,[6] and an estimated 8.3 million adults are illiterate.[7]

Eskom, the biggest provider of electricity in southern Africa and a state-owned company, has been a major player in the new South Africa's Reconstruction and Development Programme, providing basic amenities to the majority of the population, and assisting in the uplifting of previously disadvantaged communities. A main thrust of this program has been to positively discriminate toward the previously disadvantaged in terms of job and development opportunities within companies such as Eskom.

Underskilled workers

The concept of affirmative action in South Africa is quite different from that in the United States. Providing opportunities and equity for minority groups is the main concern in the United States. In South Africa, blacks comprise the majority of the population. The modern South African economy will not be viable without the upskilling and inclusion of this majority. Separate educational systems established under apartheid, with an under-resourcing of education for this majority of the population,[8] ensured the under-education and under-skilling of people who are now ill equipped for jobs in a highly competitive global marketplace. This under-skilling reflects the situation in many African countries and, indeed, in other emerging regions. Even countries such as the Czech Republic, with a fine educational tradition, has found itself ill equipped with the expertise needed in a modern global economy.[9] In South Africa, by 2005 there is expected to be a shortage of 920,000 skilled workers and a surplus of 11.5 million unskilled or semi-skilled workers.[10] The details of the need to upskill are addressed under Competency 3: Accommodating stakeholders.

Demographics and AIDS

Demographic constraints in South Africa include not only a growing population but, contained within this, a high dependency ratio, a youthful age structure, and a continuing high rate of urbanization.[11] The high incidence of AIDS in South Africa, as in other African countries, could be a contributing factor to the high dependency ratio of the population. For example, although the figures for cases of HIV and AIDS are hotly contested in South Africa, the Stellenbosch University Bureau for Economic Research projects that the labor force will shrink by 21 percent by 2015 because of AIDS, and that real GDP will be 1.5 percent lower by 2010 than it would be without AIDS, and is predicted to be 5.7 percent lower by 2015.[12]

African countries are dealing with the HIV/AIDS problem differently. In interviews in Zimbabwe in 1998, personnel managers reported that they had stopped investing in training. "What's the point?" asked one insurance company manager. "When you spend money on training somebody, he then dies." Companies in Botswana appear to be testing people for HIV before they will employ them, and some companies also appear to be doing that in Kenya. A medical office from one company reported that this would be part of the routine medical examination for a person before he was formally taken on.

Multiculturalism

Because of the multicultural nature of South African society and corporations, South African management seems highly placed within the global management community to take a lead in developing innovative ways to manage multiculturalism. By the very nature of the ethnic composition of African countries generally, the growing stress on regional cooperation among African countries and the intercultural influences of post-colonial, Western, Eastern, and African influences, effective management in Africa is premised on effective cross-cultural management.

Approaches to cross-cultural management can be categorized into maximalist and minimalist.[13] Maximalist approaches are content-focused and involve providing descriptions of different cultures. Much of this work is typically built on Hofstede's[14] work of distinguishing country cultural groups by reference to broad value orientations. For example, research[15] in South Africa indicates that black managers are more collectivist than white managers who are more individualistic; white managers show a higher intolerance for uncertainty than black managers; white and black managers show no significant differences in power distance; black managers measure higher than white managers on humane orientation (that is, the degree to which a society encourages and rewards fairness, altruism, generosity, and kindness, as opposed to aggressiveness and hostile actions); white managers measure higher than black managers on assertiveness and gender egalitarianism (masculinity as opposed to femininity); white managers score higher on performance orientation than black managers (the extent to which society encourages and rewards achievement and excellence). Many scholars support this type of model.[16] They conclude that one of the main purposes of management development in South Africa should be to enable management to be more sensitive to an African and Africanized workforce, and to move toward Afrocentric approaches to training and development, that is, moving corporations toward a more African-based value system.

Perhaps one of the major problems with the maximalist approach to understanding cultures is that concepts such as those developed by Hofstede may describe national culture in a very general way, but they do not provide enough detail and sensitivity to describe the many different cultures represented in South African society and, indeed, the numerous cultures within sub-Saharan Africa, and in other regions such as the Indian subcontinent. They also do not provide the means for describing the manifestations of those cultures in corporate life. For example, there has been much debate around the concept of collectivism: that it is target-specific and that its influence on corporate life may vary considerably among countries,[17] let alone within culturally heterogeneous countries such as South Africa. More specific information is needed on the way people feel about their own culture, and on the way they feel about others' cultures.

Another criticism of the maximalist approach is based on the assertion that it creates stereotypes. Because these stereotypes are value-laden, they have serious implications for how individuals and groups perceive themselves and how they are perceived by others. They therefore may acquire a self-fulfilling nature. Previously these led to perceptions about the inferiority of black cultures from both blacks and whites. One researcher in particular, Human, argues for a minimalist position, which "takes an interactional approach to culture and argues that culture constitutes a subconscious part of a person's identity as a communicator and is therefore constructed to a large extent by the perception of the other party in the interaction."[18]

One conclusion that may be drawn from this discussion is that in order to manage effectively across cultures, an awareness of the kind of stereotypes that one is working with is necessary. In this perspective, multiculturalism is a positive attribute whereby different stakeholders from different cultural perspectives can make a variety of contributions. Their input is not simply desirable; it is necessary to economic and social prosperity.

A starting point is for individuals to develop a high awareness of their own cultural background, its values, and the contribution that these values, perceptions, and expectations can make to the organization.

Awareness of one's own cultural values

In a multicultural context, the lack of understanding and articulation of the nature and influence of one's culture may be a serious stumbling block to building synergies from cultural diversity. Yet research suggests that this is not enough. A clear understanding of the way power relations impact the stereotyping of groups and the perceptions of individuals, including the expectation one has of such individuals, is necessary. One researcher active in this area describes the managing diversity skills training program that she has been involved in with companies in South Africa. The program is designed first to make managers aware of the negative impact of the maintenance of inaccurate stereotypes and resulting expectations, based on power relations that are transmitted through ideas relating to culture. Secondly, it attempts to make managers understand themselves. Thirdly, it attempts to provide the communication skills that are needed to minimize the impact of negative stereotypes and expectation, and to reinforce the process by which more accurate, and presumably more positive, stereotypes may occur. This is all dependent on a high level of awareness of one's own and others' cultures, and the perceptions and expectations that have occurred as a result of the legacies of the past. Applied to other parts of Africa, such an approach may involve grappling with many of the legacies of colonialism and their impact on cultural perceptions and stereotypes.

Work on the relation of African culture to management is quite recent, such as that of Lovemore Mbigi in South Africa.[19] Other African countries may be lagging behind in this articulation. White managers in South Africa may yet be lacking in confidence to clearly articulate the relation of their culture to management in the wake of apartheid, or simply blocked by their assumption of the universality of management principles[20] through an education heavily influenced by American/Western traditions. The articulation of the interaction between indigenous and Western cultures has progressed in India through the work of T. V. Rao, and through the development of the field of human resources in India, which has led to attempts to combine the humanism of indigenous approaches with the instrumentalism of Western approaches.[21]

COMPETENCY 2: MANAGING COMPLEXITY

It is easy for managers to enumerate the constraints and threats of operating in South Africa, in sub-Saharan Africa as a whole, and in other developing countries. Foremost may be the socioeconomic threats to stability, employment, and profitability. These may also include the problems of successfully completing the transition away from authoritarian rule toward a robust democracy with inherited economic problems, as well as high inequalities of wealth, ethnic rivalry, and levels of violence. These issues have echoes as far away as the former Soviet countries. Such domestic issues are further complicated by the competitive forces related to globalization.

Ethnic constraints are inherent within South Africa's highly fragmented society and moves toward redistribution through affirmative action, and the implication of discrimination against those not covered by affirmative action may harbor further threats,[22] many of them of concern for other African countries as well. Yet an organization's ability to be able to turn these constraints around into opportunities may make the difference between a maladaptive management system and a highly adaptive system.

One of the greatest challenges today in South Africa, as in so many other African countries, is how to reconcile both the need to grow people within the wider society, and for corporations to contribute to that through employment equity and development opportunities within the organization, and the need to be globally competitive and to develop a profit focus. Following the end of apartheid and sanctions, South Africa has been launched into a competitive global marketplace whose overriding trend goes to radical change by downsizing and delayering in order to make the organization more competitively meaner and leaner.[23] As in many sub-Saharan African countries, these changes in South Africa follow the adoption of World Bank- and International Monetary Fund-led structural adjustment programs. As a result, companies in South Africa are becoming increasingly results-focused, and along with that, have shareholder value as their main strategic driver.

It may be that a globally competitive position is untenable in Africa and that the prevailing global logic of downsizing and delayering does not hold true with the presence of such an underdeveloped skills base as is found in South Africa. There is a pressing need for organizations to be a means to develop people for the future.[24]

Yet there is a need for a company such as Eskom to be globally competitive. This need introduces a major contradiction which firms in many developing and emerging economies face: how can the company be mean, lean, and competitive, and at the same time, employ under-skilled and under-educated people in order to develop them and contribute to the uplifting of the community?

Japanese managers in an automobile manufacturer in Johannesburg appear positioned to cope with many of these complex issues. They talked about Afro-pessimism and the "bad-neighbor" syndrome, referring to the political and economic problems of their neighbor Zimbabwe, and the extent to which its problems could spill over to South Africa. This is said in the context of growing interest by Japan in South Africa as a main trading partner within the African continent. Japanese direct investment in South Africa is now valued in excess of US$500 million.[25] The *Sunday Times* (Johannesburg) reported that Trade and Industry Minister Alec Erwin announced the Japanese commitment of a multi-billion-rand private-sector investment in the automotive, chemical, and metal industries. This was at a time of a significant trade mission to Japan led by President Mbeke, who reported an "inspiring mood" in the Japanese business community toward the South African economy. The *Sunday Times* also reported that teams from both countries would work together to flesh out practical projects, and that this would see the rapid expansion of Japanese investment in South Africa. Perhaps more importantly, this direct investment initiative was seen as a staging point for investment into sub-Saharan Africa as a whole.

South African companies, in common with companies in many countries that had protected economies and that maintained high levels of staff, such as China, India, and countries of the former Soviet bloc, were faced with global competition as soon as their economies were liberalized. Companies started to radically downsize – "right-size" is the polite term in South Africa – as was the global trend throughout the 1990s. This was also driven by International Monetary Fund and World Bank conditions for lending: that recipient countries introduce structural adjustment programs which included radically liberalizing the economy, opening up for imports, eliminating tariff and other restrictions, and floating the currency. Very few countries in the developing and emerging regions escaped these measures, including most of the African countries[26] and those of the former Soviet bloc.[27]

The former East Germany, under reunification, had to radically reduce the number of staff in its formerly state-owned industries. This created widespread job losses, while discipline improved among those left in jobs, and general efficiency increased. However, there was also large-scale investment by the government to redress social inequalities arising through such trends as higher unemployment.[28] This investment has created a social safety net, which often has not been possible in other former Soviet countries, and certainly not in African countries.

Organizations do thrive and prosper under adverse conditions. Despite the huge problems faced by Kenyan companies – negative economic growth and poor infrastructure, including telecommunications, problems of personal security, and high unemployment – managers interviewed in Citibank in Nairobi consistently pointed to the huge potential the country has to offer, particularly in terms of its human resources. One manager's view reflects this optimism: "The country has so much to offer in terms of business, and has very hardworking people. . . . There is a growth hungry culture among the organization's workers. . . . Employees are challenged to produce and are promoted and rewarded for their contribution to company growth."

A critical awareness of operating constraints is a starting point for managers, both local and expatriate, in emerging countries. However, a key competence, perhaps a prerequisite competence for a management team, is to know how to turn political, economic, legislative, social, and cultural constraints within a complex operating environment into opportunities. This was essential for the management at Eskom in the latter half of the 1990s. The company approached this through a strong commitment to the development of its people, not least because of the recognized need for an educated workforce to operate and maintain its sophisticated technology, and for appropriate management to take it into the future. Its management development focus was therefore on basic education, opportunity, and the ability to manage change. Affirmative action was seen as central, with an objective of at least 50 percent of managerial and supervisory staff to be black South Africans by 2000. This stood at only 6.1 percent in 1994.[29] The company was also involved in a number of community projects, and played an important part in the government's Reconstruction and Development Programme initiatives, such as electrification.

Eskom also developed a policy to enable its employees to own their own homes. The company already owned some 14,500 employee houses. With this stock, and the conversion of its single-gender hostels to married accommodation, it encouraged workers to bring their families to live permanently with them. All employees received a housing allowance based on their salary band. The company also ran its own medical scheme with 28,540 members and over 43,000 dependants subsidized within it. Management–union relations were built by encouraging more participative management: establishing forums at a number of levels from the strategic level through to business unit forums, and work-team sessions where issues were addressed locally. Joint task forces were established to look at issues such as Eskom's long-term viability as a top performing utility; trade union involvement in decision making; business training and development of shop stewards; trade union representation on the Electricity Council; education, training, and development; optimal sharing of information and financial disclosure; and workers' accommodation.

Eskom's investment in education and training is substantial, with an emphasis on technical skills. It is also aiming to employ 370 black trainees on bursaries (scholarships) each year, although this does not exclude other trainees on these schemes. In addition, Eskom invests significantly to minimize illiteracy among the estimated 11,000 employees without basic education.[30]

The ability to draw opportunities from such conditions also involves the capability to include within strategic objectives the multiple interests of a wider stakeholder base. To a certain extent, Eskom has been able to do this. This brings us to the third competency area: the willingness and ability to incorporate the interests of multiple stakeholders, including employees and their representatives, managers, community, government, suppliers, and customers into the organization's strategic objectives; and not merely the interests of its shareholders.

COMPETENCY 3: ACCOMMODATING THE INTERESTS OF MULTIPLE STAKEHOLDERS

South African managers in the late 1990s indicated that their organizations had a low priority toward employees, managers, and the local community as stakeholders. They reported that their organizations saw quality and growth as important key success factors, while they saw job satisfaction and success of affirmative action as having low importance as success factors.

For organizations in Africa and beyond to be effective by all other measures apart from profit and financial efficiency, they have to reflect the multiple interests of a broader base of stakeholders and incorporate these interests within the strategic objectives of the organization. With a broader understanding of the stakeholders, managers have broader goals and can interpret more widely the ways in which constraints may be turned into opportunities. In the same study, managers were asked to indicate the level of importance given by their organizations to various stakeholders, defined as "those who have an interest in the organization." Managers indicated customers first, shareholders second, and government third. Of least importance as stakeholders at the bottom of the pile were suppliers, employees, managers, and the local community. This would seem to indicate that managers see their organization's focus as more toward their business, rather than toward their employees, managers, and local community. These results also support a view of the strong influence of government on organizations within South Africa, a situation that is reflected in other emerging and transitional economies.

The largest group of stakeholders in South Africa, workers and potential workers, are severely under-skilled. The modern South African economy will not be viable without their upskilling and inclusion. Separate educational systems established under apartheid, with an under-resourcing of education for this majority of the population,[31] ensured the under-education and under-skilling of people who are now ill equipped for jobs in a highly competitive global marketplace. This under-skilling reflects the situation in many African countries and, indeed, other emerging regions. Even countries such as the Czech Republic, with a fine educational tradition, have found itself ill equipped with the expertise needed in a modern global economy.[32] In South Africa, by 2005 there is expected to be a shortage of 920,000 skilled workers and a surplus of 11.5 million unskilled or semi-skilled workers.[33]

In the manufacturing industry in South Africa, which now accounts for 23.5 percent of GDP, productivity, which is a function of skills, technology, capital, and labor, has been slow to grow. It edged forward 0.4 percent in the 1970s and 0.5 percent in the 1980s. This reflects the poor education provision under apartheid for the black population. The 1994 World Competitive Report, covering 42 country economies, ranked South Africa 35 out of 42. The "people dimension" of this assessment covered public expenditure on education, pupil–teacher ratios, company investment in training, economic, and computer literacy, and the availability and quality of human resources. This portion of the assessment ranked South Africa number 42.[34]

To address the up-skilling issues in South Africa, the government has initiated a series of progressive employment equity laws. The irony is that, initially, the employment of affirmative action employees may actually contribute to an under-skilling of the workforce[35] through the replacement of skilled white workers by under-educated and under-skilled black workers. Yet one black manager interviewed in Cape Town disputed this: "White managers were previously employed and promoted simply because they were white, not because they had the necessary competencies."

Despite the difficulties of under-skilling, private-sector organizations in South Africa spend only an estimated 2 percent of their payroll per year on education and training, compared with 6–8 percent in the leading industrial nations.[36] There are also lower levels of tertiary education in technical and scientific subjects than in other developing countries. This is likely to affect the skills pool.

Colgate-Palmolive operates a subsidiary of the American company in South Africa and offers an example of a perhaps well-intentioned yet misdirected approach to stakeholder accommodation.[37] Many American companies have developed social responsibility programs in South Africa under the guidelines of the Sullivan Code, under which Colgate-Palmolive has achieved "an outstanding Category 1 rating."[38] Its contributions have been to fund various educational projects at schools and universities (equipment, electricity, burglar-proofing of premises, supplements for teacher upgrades, outreach programs, student bursaries, provision of career advice); and community projects (water purification and sanitation, funds for centers for the aged, road races, drug rehabilitation, mental illness, AIDS). The list is long, and includes a number of health and dental projects. The code requires that the company direct 12 percent of its salary budget to such projects.

With annual revenues of $100 million and a workforce of 600 employees, the company set up the $3-million Colgate-Palmolive Foundation. The management and allocation of funding to projects was the responsibility of the company-appointed management rather than of representatives of the various stakeholder communities that stood to benefit from these projects. One stakeholder group, the trade union, has criticized the company for not involving them. Other criticism suggests that sometimes, in the area of dental care, for example, projects were funded out of enlightened self-interest (as part of marketing its own products) rather than out of altruism or a sense of what may be required to contribute to the development of people within the community.

Many companies like Colgate-Palmolive have been radically downsizing and operating with a minimum of staff. While Eskom, for example, has also been downsizing, it has attempted to balance the needs of developing people and thereby contribute to the community, rather than simply donate to worthy causes.

In contrast to Colgate-Palmolive, the management at Eskom has made serious attempts to involve multiple stakeholders through forums and task forces to address issues within the organization and the community. This approach enabled Eskom to make use of opportunities within the country to succeed as a strong, viable company. Today, this is reflected in their brand positioning. In a recent survey conducted by the *Sunday Times*,[39] Eskom came second only to Coca-Cola in brand recognition. The accompanying article went on to explain that "in rural areas . . . Eskom has contributed to improving lives. . . . This could explain its high position. . . . For rural people, having . . . electricity for the first time is a thing to be hugely grateful for."

It may be that other companies, such as Colgate-Palmolive, have not got the stakeholder relationships right. Not including the different stakeholder groups in the decision-making process in emerging and developing countries can be problematic. In order to incorporate the interests of multiple stakeholders, it would seem logical that organizations must have effective means to give voice to those interests, and incorporate them within the dialogue of the organization, its strategy, objectives, policies, and practices.

COMPETENCY 4: MOTIVATING THE WORKFORCE: ENCOURAGING PARTICIPATION

Within the complex arena a developing context provides, the manager who is committed to broaden the stakeholder base, to develop real and effective internal means for incorporating the perceptions, expectations, strengths, and interests of these different cultural and gender group stakeholders into the decision-making process, and to manage change requires a critical competency. Active participation is the key to this competency.

Studies of South African organizations, along with studies in other developing countries, suggest that management in developing countries is conservative and traditional. Based on a legacy of racial discrimination, organizations in South Africa have adversarial employee relations and often have discriminatory employment practices.[40] Dominant management styles tend to be autocratic.[41] South African organizations are generally over-managed and under-led. Survey research reveals that management styles are often seen as rigid, bureaucratic, directive, and task-oriented, and sometimes decision-making is over-centralized; and leadership aspects such as direction, vision, and effectiveness are often seen as lacking.[42]

This certainly reflects the perceptions of other studies within the developing world where management is seen as fatalistic, resistant to change, reactive, short-term, authoritarian, risk-reducing, context-dependent, and as basing decisions on relationship criteria rather than universalistic criteria.[43] With the influence of democratic processes from Western approaches to management and from indigenous approaches, organizations in Africa and the developing world generally may be looking toward more involvement of their people in decision processes. Recent research has found elements of consultative management within organizations seen as hierarchical, centralized, and fairly rule-bound, with no evidence of participative management.

It does appear that although participative management is not found, it is being talked about in South African organizations, and this may be the case in other emerging countries. Often downsizing and delayering lead to empowerment of managers and staff at lower levels of the organization than was previously required.[44] This may well lead to the impression of participative management. Yet because of the diversity of interests in South African organizations, as in many African countries, participative management may only arise through the active empowerment of all such interest groups. With more than 79 percent of the management population white, and over 78 percent of all managers being male,[45] full participation in decision-making of all members of the stakeholder populations of organizations may be some way off. For example, while managers in South Africa would report one view of the level or participation in decision-making, the subordinate groups of managers would tell a different story. Black managers in South Africa would give an account of failure to bring in other groups. Junior black African managers in Kenya would describe the autocratic/paternalistic attitudes of their senior Asian managers.

AECI Explosives Ltd. is a joint venture between ICI plc (United Kingdom) and AECI Ltd (South Africa), with ICI holding a 51 percent interest. The joint venture company is incorporated within ICI's explosives division, and the chairman is based in London. It is a leader in explosives products (detonators, packaged explosives, bulk explosives, initiating systems, and ammonium nitrate) within the continent of Africa, and its main customer is the mining, quarrying, and construction industry. Its major business objectives are the market-driven innovation of products, winning in quality growth markets worldwide, inspiration and reward of talented people, exemplary performance in health and safety, responsible care for the environment, and pursuit of operational excellence.

Its people-policy objectives include providing a safe working environment, ensuring equality of opportunity, providing attractive compensation packages, emphasizing training and development, developing an atmosphere of trust and mutual respect, encouraging innovation, fostering open communication, implementing management processes to support these policies, and conforming with the relevant laws.

However, the company was seen to be rule-driven, with formal written instructions at all levels: company directives, company standards, departmental procedural instructions, job descriptions, quality plans, operating instructions, and test methods. The company had embarked on an internal literacy project with a target of full literacy by 2005. However, a very clear policy on affirmative action had not been formulated. There also was little or no involvement in community or social obligation projects, although an environmental remedial project was underway where land that the company had contaminated was being cleared up.

The company still had vestiges of high power distance and hierarchy and mistrust from the past. With dated, labor-intensive technologies and increased competition, there was a need to reduce waste and increase efficiency. This involved further downsizing, but it was also hoped that this would lead to a flattening of hierarchy, and a move toward more participation in decision-making. In the meantime this was creating uncertainty in job security, which contributed to lower productivity.[46]

Although companies like AECI Explosives in South Africa are attempting to introduce participatory approaches, the vestiges of colonialism often mean major attitude transformations are necessary within developing countries. If such transformations are not successful, lip service to participatory management may be the result. Then, too, Western participatory approaches may not be appropriate. Empowerment may be seen as a means to get a manager to take on more responsibility with fewer resources and for the same money in a period of organizational downsizing.

As in the case of South Africa, the concept of empowerment must also stretch out to the community. Institutions alien to African communities were developed during the colonial period, and the legacy of this approach remains today.[47] In African societies, as in many communalistic societies, the barriers between community life and organizational life must be broken down in order to provide a context for commitment and motivation of the workforce. This may go hand in hand with bringing in a form of participation that involves stakeholder interests from the community as well as from within the corporation. Managers must be able to obtain commitment and motivation by developing understanding of the relationship between community/family life and work life, and the way this relationship is differently perceived by people with different cultural perspectives.

One basic approach to the community/family life and work life relationship is to recognize and then reconcile the potential conflicts between work and home/community life. The recognition of these potential conflicts is critical to an understanding of motivation and commitment in the organization. A number of African managers have reported that going to work in the morning means stepping outside of their culture. When they go home at night, they step back into their culture. African employees in sub-Saharan African countries have an instrumental view of their work organization; that is, they work in order to earn money to pay for what they and often their extended family need.[48] There is an indication of lack of commitment to the organization by employees.

Corporations in Japan have been successful in harnessing the wider societal collectivism to corporate life, in order to foster commitment by employees in a reciprocal relationship with the corporation. Corporations in most other collectivistic societies have failed to do this, mostly because of the legacies of colonial institutions and their failure to integrate with their host societies. In a recent study, managers from a predominantly black sample were asked to rank order their important life aspects.[49] "Giving plenty of time to my family" was ranked number one. "Making work central in my life" was number two. "Being actively involved in the community" was ranked third. "Pursuing my religion" was ranked fourth, and "pursuing my leisure activities" was ranked last. This seems to indicate a primacy of family life in one's total life, rather than an alienation from the workplace. That work life and community life were ranked second and third indicates the importance of these aspects, without indicating how well integrated these aspects are.

An organizational climate survey of 200 employees in three organizations in South Africa indicates that there is generally higher satisfaction with working conditions, job content, and job security, yet lower satisfaction with appraisal systems, recognition of employee worth, union–management relations, among other factors, and the extent to which employees feel involved in matters that affect them. These results may well indicate the extent to which employees in South Africa feel separated from decision-making, although there is no indication of a low level of disengagement from the corporation.

COMPETENCY 5: ASSESSING APPROPRIATE MANAGEMENT APPROACHES

The way a corporation pays attention to employee commitment and motivation through integrating the links between corporation and community, the bringing in of different stakeholder interests, and the regard for its people, is driven by its management systems, that is, its principles, policies, and practices. In South Africa, as in other African countries, these systems are culturally influenced through a combination of post-colonial, Western, perhaps Eastern, and African inputs. The management of these inputs in hybrid systems of management that are likely to be adaptive, rather than maladaptive, to their African context may depend to a large extent on managers' abilities to recognize and articulate these cultural influences. This area constitutes the fifth competency area: the need to maintain a high level of awareness of the contributing factors to the way the organization is managed through principles, policies, and practices, and their appropriateness to the sociocultural contexts within which the organization operates.

There is an apparent antithesis between Western and non-Western ideas of organization and management, between an idea of people as a resource (human resource management) and people with a value in themselves (*Ubuntu*, from a Xhosa proverb *Ubuntu ungamntu ngabanye abantu*, "people are people through other people").[50] It may be possible to reconcile this antithesis, but it would seem logical that before this can happen, managers should be aware of these different perspectives. In a recent study with a predominantly black management sample, managers saw themselves as generally oriented toward the view of an intrinsic value of people for themselves rather than as a means to an end of the organization. The consensus was that people should be valued in their own right, they should be consulted, and they should be treated fairly and ethically in an organization that is not merely concerned with short-term results and making profits or gaining results above all else. Whilst the study indicated that organizations are making strides to address the developmental aspects of people, there still seems to be a gap between humanistic and developmental intentions of organizations and their somewhat instrumental orientation. Organizations are often seen as hierarchical, authoritarian and rule-bound, and are perceived as trying to move toward a results focus as well as toward the development of participation. This indicates a move from postcolonial influences toward Western influences and is reflected in a number of other studies.

It may also be that there is still a low articulation of an African indigenous approach, and very little evidence that, for example, *ubuntu* principles are being applied. This may be in part due to a lack of articulation about these different influences, as a result of a lack of conscious management of multiculturalism not only at the macrolevel of management systems, but also at the level of managing a culturally diverse workforce with different expectations about the way people should be managed. Managers need to consciously manage the dynamics of multiculturalism in order to develop strengths and synergies from these, including the management of equal opportunities of individuals from different ethnic and gender groups to influence the direction of the organization.

TABLE 23.1 Breakwater survey results, 2000

Racial grouping	Worker population (%)	Manager population (%)
African	49.2	9.52
Indian	5.63	5.53
Colored	14.42	5.31
White	30.76	79.64
Female	27.93	21.34
Male	72.07	78.66

The management of multiculturalism can be undertaken from a number of perspectives. In South Africa, as in most African countries, this would involve not only managing differences in culture and gender from the point of view of understanding different cultures. It would also involve managing the power relations that are bound up with the relationships among people of different cultures.[51] A huge distortion in the relative power of different cultural groups exists as a result of apartheid in South Africa. In other African countries with large white settler populations, such as Zimbabwe, such distortions also still exist. In most other African countries dominant and subordinate cultural groups can be identified, either at country or corporate level. Again, this is reflected in many other developing countries around the globe. The central Asian states, such as Kazakstan, have large Russian settler populations that have been dominant within their industrial economies.

In South Africa, managing such relationships involves compliance to employment equity legislation in order to redress the imbalances between dominant and disadvantaged groups both at corporate and country level, as well as consciously managing the process in the workplace. Recent figures from the Breakwater Monitor[52] which monitors employment equity in South Africa through some 200 voluntarily participating organizations, indicates that there still appears to be considerable room for further redressing the power balances in corporations among the racial groupings in South Africa (see table 23.1).

With these imbalances in South Africa, which are historically derived and still prevalent, it is difficult for corporations to argue that simply complying with the legislation is sufficient. Proactive management across cultures would seem necessary in order to redress some of the power imbalances by building awareness and also the development of general cross-cultural competences.

Although training courses in intercultural management and awareness sessions address issues of interaction, they may add very little directly to addressing issues arising from power imbalance within corporations that are culturally related. Nor do they address imbalances within the total stakeholder population. Just looking at this statistically, the racial split in the population of the Breakwater Monitor is fairly representative of the economically active population according to the 1999 Household Survey, although it overrepresents whites, and underrepresents African females. The number of Africans outside the economically active population indicates a disparity in power relations among the racial groups in the total stakeholder community. This situation would be repeated among developing countries as different as India and Kazakhstan.

CONCLUSION

Developing competencies in order to manage the complexities and contradictions of developing countries is not a matter of producing a neat list of attributes. Areas of competencies must be identified, discussed, and developed by the management group in their organizations, so that they address both the specific global influences on managing and the specific indigenous influences.

Developing these competencies as part of a global management mindset is important for two reasons: they are needed in the developing world; and their acquisition makes possible that the Western manager on a developing world assignment may be able to learn about managing complexity from developing country colleagues. Although the developing–developed world paradigm suggests that the developing world must move more toward the developed world, that managers in Africa, South Asia, Central Asia, Latin America, and even East and Central Europe must learn from Western managers, experienced international managers know that this is not the case. This mindset is prevalent in the developed world and also in the developing world.[53] Despite the Western world's belief that the 80 percent of the globe comprising the developing world has nothing to offer the developed world, think of the challenges developing country managers must face. Managers have to address the intricacies of multi-ethnic interaction in the workplace; they have to address serious, widespread skills deficits; they have to deal with the demographic impacts of issues such as AIDS/HIV; they have to negotiate the interests of numerous stakeholders; they have to balance the instrumental approaches of the West with the humanistic instincts of communal life; they have to reconcile postcolonial, Western, and indigenous systems of thought and organization within their daily working lives. The global management community can learn much from developing country managers.

Some would argue that management development in South Africa still reflects strategies used by the European colonial powers, and has been dominated by rationalism, individualism, and autocracy.[54] They further argue that Western approaches have a high degree of legitimacy, while African co-operative and communal philosophies are ignored. This has the effect of predominantly white managers pushing a largely Third World workforce to accept First World productivity standards and value systems. They suggest that this is why efforts to modernize, which include merit pay systems and formal grievance procedures, have largely failed. They ignore local cultural values. These researchers urge South Africa to develop its own unique approach that builds in the context and indigenous philosophies and values. This would include values of personal trust as a moral base rather than the "cold" approaches to eliminating unfairness, interdependence, emphasizing cooperative relations and wealth being best achieved through a pragmatic but humanistic approach to business, and spiritualism, combining celebration and ceremonies with leadership that provides moral guidance.

A number of organizations in South Africa have taken up management development processes that incorporate the values of *ubuntu*,[55] yet this may be far from widespread. A number of companies in India have taken up the hybrid Human

Resources Development approach of T. V. Rao in an attempt to integrate a results focus and an indigenous values focus. The hegemony of Western management principles, bound up with the type of power relations discussed above, may take time to supersede. The development of adaptive hybrid management systems in South Africa, Africa, India, and other emerging regions, through concerted efforts that reflect the five competency areas, may be the way forward.

NOTES

1 See Cyr, D. J., & Schneider, S. C. (1994), Creating a learning organization through HRM: a German–Czech joint venture, INSEAD case collection, in G. Oddou and M. Mendenhall (eds.) (1998), *Cases in International Organizational Behaviour*, Malden, MA: Blackwell, pp. 197–210; and Gutmann, B. (1995), Tandem training: The Volkswagen–Skoda approach to know-how transfer, *Journal of European Industrial Training*, 19(4), 21–4.

2 Munslow, B., & FitzGerald, P. (1995), The reconstruction and development programme, in P. FitzGerald, A. McLennan, & B. Munslow (eds.), *Managing Sustainable Development in South Africa*, Cape Town: Oxford University Press, pp. 41–62.

3 Derived from UN Expert Group figures, 1982–6: Barratt Brown, M. (1995), *Africa's Choices: After Thirty Years of the World Bank*, London: Penguin.

4 Ibru, O. M. (1997), The development of international business in Africa (1947–1997), *International Executive*, 39(2), 117–33.

5 Luiz, J. M. (1996), The socio-economic restructuring of a post-apartheid South Africa, *International Journal of Social Economics*, 23(10/11), 137–49.

6 Suzman, M. (1996), Africa's lion cub learns to roar, *Asian Business*, June.

7 Hofmeyr, K., Templer, A., & Beaty, D. (1994), South Africa: Researching contrasts and contradictions in a context of change, *International Studies of Management and Organization*, 24(1–2), 190–208.

8 Jackson, T. (1999), Managing change in South Africa: Developing people and organizations, *International Journal of Human Resource Management*, 10(2), 306–326.

9 Koubek, J., & Brewster, C. (1995), Human resource management in turbulent times: HRM in the Czech Republic, *International Journal of Human Resource Management*, 6(2), pp. 223–47.

10 Mills, G., Beeg, A., & Van Nieuwkerk, A. (1995), *South Africa in the Global Economy*, Johannesburg: South African Institute of International Affairs.

11 Luiz (1996).

12 *Sunday Times Business Times* (Johannesburg), October 7, 2001, p. 6.

13 Human, L. (1996), Managing workforce diversity: A critique and example from Southern Africa, *International Journal of Manpower*, 17(4/5), 46–64.

14 Hofstede, G. (1980a), *Culture's Consequences: International Differences in Work-Related Values*, Beverly Hills, CA: Sage.

15 Booysen, L. (2001), Cultural influences among white and black managers in South Africa, *Management Today, Yearbook 2001*, 32–35.

16 McFarlin, D., Coster, E. A., & Mogale-Pretorius, C. (1999), South African management development in the twenty-first century: Moving towards an Africanized model. *Journal of Management Development*, 18(1), 63–78.

17 Hui, C. H. (1990), Work attitudes, leadership styles, and managerial behaviour in different cultures, in R. W. Brislin, *Applied Cross-Cultural Psychology*, Newbury Park, CA: Sage.

18 Human (1996), p. 51.

19 Mbigi, L. (1997), *Ubuntu: The African Dream in Management*, Randburg, South Africa: Knowledge Resources; Mbigi, L., & Maree, J. (1995), *Ubuntu: The Spirit of African Transformational Management*, Randburg, South Africa: Knowledge Resources.

20 See, for example, Hofstede, G. (1980b), Motivation, leadership and organization: Do American theories apply abroad?, *Organizational Dynamics*, Summer, 42–63.

21 Rao, T. V. (1996), *Human Resource Development: Experiences, Intervention, Strategies*, New Delhi: Sage.

22 Luiz (1996).

23 Beaty, D. T. (1998), Colgate Palmolive in post-apartheid South Africa, reprinted in G. Oddou & M. Mendenhall, *Cases in International Organizational Behavior*, Malden, MA: Blackwell, p. 136.

24 See Cameron, K. S. (1994), Strategies for successful downsizing, *Human Resource Management*, 33(2), 89–211; and, Freeman, S. J. (1994), Organizational downsizing as convergence or reorientation: implications for human resource management, *Human Resource Management*, 33(2), 213–238.

25 *Sunday Times Business Times* (Johannesburg), October 7, 2001.

26 Barratt Brown, M. (1995), *Africa's Choices: After Thirty Years of the World Bank*, London: Penguin.

27 Glenny, M. (1993), *The Rebirth of History: Eastern European in the Age of Democracy*, London: Penguin.

28 See Blum, K. (1994), Managing people in Germany, in Garrison, T., & Rees, D., *Managing People across Europe*, Oxford: Butterworth-Heinemann, pp. 40–62; and Lawrence, P. (1994), German management: at the interface between Eastern and Western Europe, in R. Calori & P. De Woot (eds.), *A European Management Model: Beyond Diversity*, London: Prentice Hall, pp. 133–64.

29 *Personnel Management* (London), December 1994.

30 Jackson (1999).

31 *Ibid.*

32 Koubek & Brewster (1995).

33 Mills, Beeg, & Van Nieuwkerk (1995).

34 Watson, C. (1996), Directions for HR directors, *People Dynamics* (South Africa), 14(1), 19–25.

35 Bowmaker-Falconer, A., Horwitz, F., Jain, H., & Tagger, S. (1998), Employment equality programmes in South Africa, *Industrial Relations Journal*, 29(3), 222–233.

36 Horwitz, F. M., Bowmaker-Falconer, A., & Searll, P. (1996), Human resources development and managing diversity in South Africa, *International Journal of Manpower*, 17(4/5), 134–151.

37 Beaty (1998).

38 *Ibid.*, p. 136.

39 *Sunday Times* (Johannesburg), October 7, Special Supplement, p. 1.

40 Roodt, A. (1997), In search of a South African corporate culture, *Management Today*, 13(2), 14–16.

41 Viljoen, J. (1987), Corporate culture: the perceptions of personnel managers in South Africa, *South African Journal of Business Management*, 18(4), 235–42.

42 Hofmeyr, K. (1998), South African managers need to be more positive, *People Dynamic*, 16(10), 16–20.

43 Kanungo, R. N., & Jaeger, A. M. (1990), Introduction: The need for indigenous management in developing countries, in A. M. Jaeger & R. N. Kanungo (eds.), *Management in Developing Countries*, London: Routledge, pp. 1–23.

44 See Cameron (1994); Freeman (1994).

45 Breakwater Monitor (2000), Breakwater Monitor Report 2000/1, Cape Town: University of Cape Town Graduate School of Management.

46 Jackson (1999).

47 Dia, M. (1996), *Africa's Management in the 1990s and Beyond*, Washington, DC: World Bank.

48 Blunt, P., & Jones, M. L. (1992), *Managing Organizations in Africa*, Berlin: Walter de Gruyter.

49 Jackson (1999).
50 Hofmeyr (1998).
51 Human (1996).
52 Breakwater Monitor (2000).
53 See Jackson, T. (2002), *International HRM: A Cross-cultural Perspective*, London: Sage, where this argument is further developed.
54 McFarlin et al. (1999).
55 Swartz, E., & Davies, R. (1997), Ubuntu: the spirit of African transformational management – A review, *Leadership and Organization Development Journal*, 18(6), 260–94.

Index